THE IMPACT OF RAILWAYS ON VICTORIAN CITIES

STUDIES IN SOCIAL HISTORY

edited by

HAROLD PERKIN

Professor of Social History, University of Lancaster

A catologue of books available in the
Studies in Social History and new books
in preparation for the Library will be
found at the end of this volume

THE IMPACT
OF RAILWAYS ON
VICTORIAN CITIES

by
John R. Kellett

Senior Lecturer in Economic History
University of Glasgow

LONDON: Routledge & Kegan Paul
TORONTO: University of Toronto Press
1969

*First published 1969
in Great Britain by
Routledge & Kegan Paul Limited
and in Canada by
University of Toronto Press
Printed in Great Britain
by C. Tinling & Co. Ltd
Liverpool, London and Prescot*
*RKP SBN 7100 6315 6
UTP SBN 8020 1584*

to Margery Abrahams

Contents

Part Three: The Impact of Railways on Victorian Cities

Plates

In the text

Sketch maps to show the built-up area, 1840 and 1900, with location of the principal stations in order of authorisation.

Preface

It has long been clear on the other side of the Atlantic that the motor-vehicle is an instrument which will prise apart the compact European city. Since the *Buchanan Report* the minds of policy-makers in this country have also been exercised to analyse and evaluate the city as Europeans have experienced it. There is detailed professional discussion of the mechanisms of zoning, ring-roads, pedestrian precincts, and mono-rails by which vestiges of 'the human scale' are to be preserved in the reconstructed cities of the late twentieth century for people to walk about and look at; rather as the parks, museums and art-galleries of the Victorian city were preserved as shrines to the aristocratic values the Victorians had themselves overthrown.

Some town planners, architects and academics, who had recognized the problem a long time before the *Buchanan Report* made it a public issue, had already despaired of the possibility of incorporating a rational transport system within the fabric of a nineteenth century city. Instead they have suggested variously, new towns—sweepingly modern in lay-out but still recognisably towns; or linear cities—in which the spinal function of urban transport was formally recognised, indeed exaggerated. Perhaps in this ferment of ideas and formulae it is time to look dispassionately at a chapter in urban morphology which is closed—that of the steam age and the Victorian city.

The impact of the last revolutionary mode of transport upon British cities was complete before Victoria's death, indeed, it was almost complete by 1880, as the material gathered below suggests; and the horse omnibuses and tram cars acted, even from mid-century, as a strong secondary influence. Yet it was the influence of the railways, more than any other single agency, which gave the Victorian city its compact shape, which influenced the topography and character of its central and inner districts, the disposition of its dilapidated and waste areas, and of its suburbs, the direction and character of its growth; and which probably acted as the most potent new factor upon the urban land market in the nineteenth century.

The first chapter, therefore, sets out the list of questions prompted by the railways' arrival in the major British cities, and indicates the extent to which existing historical source material will yield answers.

Subsequent chapters, in Part One, consider the processes by which the decisions re-shaping nineteenth century cities were arrived at; looking, in turn, through the eyes of the central government, the railway companies and the municipal corporations. Part Two gives detailed *Case Histories* of the five cities chosen for study. Since they are the five largest cities in Britain, and muster over 20 % of the national population, there can surely be no quarrel with the sample chosen. And, in any case, the research materials and techniques used can readily be employed for other cities to modify the impressions gained from the present study. Those readers who, for reasons of local interest, wish to turn to the *Case History* of their own city should perhaps glance at the Birmingham chapter first, where they will find introductory generalisations in each section, and bibliographical footnotes which have not been repeated.

I should like to thank the University Court of the University of Glasgow for kindly granting a period of sabbatical leave, which served greatly to expedite the completion of the final stages of research and writing, the Carnegie Trust for the Universities of Scotland for their generous grant to meet the costs incurred in travel and research, and Professor S. G. Checkland for his encouragement and practical help at every stage from the book's inception.

In the course of my enquiries I have incurred lasting obligations to the staffs of the repositories visited. Above all to Mr. Maurice Bond's able and patient staff at the House of Lords' Record Office, and to the Assistant Clerk of the Records, Mr. H. S. Cobb, who placed his wide-ranging knowledge unreservedly at my disposal. I should also like to place on record my thanks to the staffs of the British Museum, the County Record Offices at London and Preston, and of the civic reference libraries: the Mitchell Library, Glasgow, a ready source of information, often at the shortest notice; the Central Library, St. Peter's Square, Manchester, where an excellent local history collection, and helpful advice, enabled every moment of my stay to be put to the maximum use; the Picton Library, Liverpool and the Central Library, Birmingham, where the staffs gave unstinted help both during my visits and in correspondence. The British Transport Commission's Historical Records sections, both at Paddington and Edinburgh, gave my enquiries a reception which combined enthusiasm for their subject with an extraordinary grasp of detail.

At Glasgow University Library the staff also merit the warmest commendation, particularly (if it is not invidious to mention individuals) Miss Jack, the Supervisor of the Parliamentary Papers collection. I am also greatly obliged to Professor Miller, and the members of the Geography Department (Miss Robertson and Miss Brass), who gave me cartographical assistance, to Mr. W. Forsyth who undertook the planimetric measurements used in chapter 10, and to Miss Ross, Miss

Moir and Miss Marlow for the typing and re-typing involved. To my editor, Professor H. J. Perkin, must go a tribute for the ideal blend of expedition and courtesy he has shown throughout. I should also like to thank the editors of the *Economic History Review* and the *Journal of Transport History* for permission to reproduce passages from articles which I published in 1964.

It is obvious that—however much original material one may consult —it is necessary to lean heavily upon the published work of one's academic colleagues, and of many other writers, in attempting to cover so large a theme; and I hope that these debts have been fully acknowledged in the proper places. My own interest in the matters discussed below has also been sustained and encouraged by many meetings and personal conversations, both with present and past members of my own Department, and with colleagues in the Urban History group of the Economic History Society. Since their names appear elsewhere, in the text and index, it is not necessary to enumerate them all, but merely to express my pleasure at finding that I share an interest in the history of British cities with so many whom I hold in high regard.

Finally, and at a personal level, my warmest thanks must go to the lady to whom this book is dedicated, and to my wife's mother and uncle, whose hospitality made possible, over many summers, the extended research necessary; to my parents in Yorkshire, to my good friends in Manchester, Liverpool and London, and to my wife, to Penny and to Jonathan for the countless ways in which they have helped.

A Note on Abbreviations

Railway Companies

THE question of abbreviating the descriptions of the large number of railway companies which inevitably recur in the text has been solved by compromise. Nothing could be more rational, in theory, than reducing them all to strings of initials; nothing more exasperating to the reader in practice. Initials have therefore been used only where the company concerned has recently been mentioned in the text.

Printed Papers

The printed papers, often referred to ambiguously as 'Parliamentary Papers', in fact comprise two complete and separate series, one published for the Lords and the other for the Commons. Both contain material from each other's proceedings which it was thought of interest to reproduce. These have been distinguished by the prefix H.C. or H.L. Where the officially re-numbered manuscript pagination has been employed the form becomes simply *e.g.* H.C., 1905, XXX, 560. Sometimes, however, unofficially bound collections—by Local Libraries, Chambers of Commerce, Railway Solicitors etc.—may have been more convenient to use. In these cases the printed page numbers of the individual Command Paper or House Paper have been employed. On this basis the same page number quoted in the example above would become H.C., 1905 (Cd 2597), 16. This difficulty does not usually arise where the questions have been officially numbered, and so, wherever possible, the question numbers have been used.

Manuscript Sources

Since the MS. notes of Select Committee proceedings can only be consulted at the House of Lords Record Office the designation HLRO precedes such material. Once again the HLRO papers include both Lords' and Commons' Select Committee Minutes (distinguished by the prefixes H.L. and H.C.), and it is important to note that the pagination starts afresh each day of the committee's proceedings. Where it has seemed of interest, the name of the witness giving evidence has been enclosed in brackets after the day and page number.

Sometimes several references to the same Minutes have been necessary, sandwiched between footnotes containing entirely different material. In these cases the original reference has been slightly telescoped so that *e.g.* HLRO, Min., H.C., 1846, 25 June, pp. 220–3, S.C. on Birmingham Wolverhampton and Dudley Railway, would, if repeated later in the same chapter, become HLRO, Min., (B.W. & D.), 25 June, pp. 220–3. Where one footnote immediately follows another, referring to the same committee's proceedings, the convention *loc. cit.* has been used if the page reference is to the same day's proceedings, *ibid.* if the page reference is to a different day's proceedings of the same committee.

List of Abbreviations

BM	British Museum
BRL	Birmingham Reference Library
BTHR	British Transport Historical Records
GRL	Glasgow Reference Library
HLRO	House of Lords Record Office
LRL	Liverpool Reference Library
LRO	Lancashire (County) Record Office
MRL	Manchester Reference Library
P & S	Plans and Sections
B. Ref.	Books of Reference
Min.	Select Committee Minutes
Ec.H.R.	Economic History Review
JTH.	Journal of Transport History

A Note on the Maps

THE illustrations which follow are intended to act as diagrammatic keys to the location of the principal stations, and the extent of the built-up area at the beginning and end of Victoria's reign. For convenience of reference they are placed together at the beginning of Chapter I.

Other, smaller, diagrams accompany each of the *Case Histories*, on which all buildings, except the railway stations, have been removed, to show the underlying pattern of land titles. The station reference numbers in these landownership diagrams correspond to those in the introductory maps.

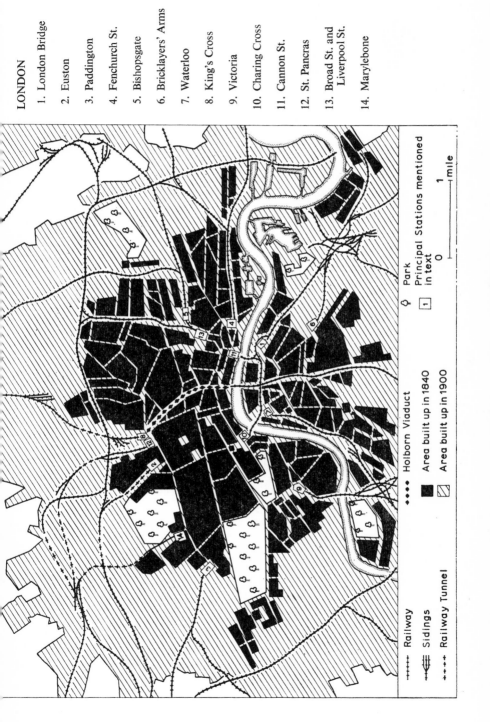

LONDON

1. London Bridge
2. Euston
3. Paddington
4. Fenchurch St.
5. Bishopsgate
6. Bricklayers' Arms
7. Waterloo
8. King's Cross
9. Victoria
10. Charing Cross
11. Cannon St.
12. St. Pancras
13. Broad St. and Liverpool St.
14. Marylebone

···· Railway

⟨⟨⟨ Sidings

···· Railway Tunnel

••••• Holborn Viaduct

⬛ Area built up in 1840

▨ Area built up in 1900

♧ Park

⬚1 Principal Stations mentioned in text

0   1 mile
├────┴────┤

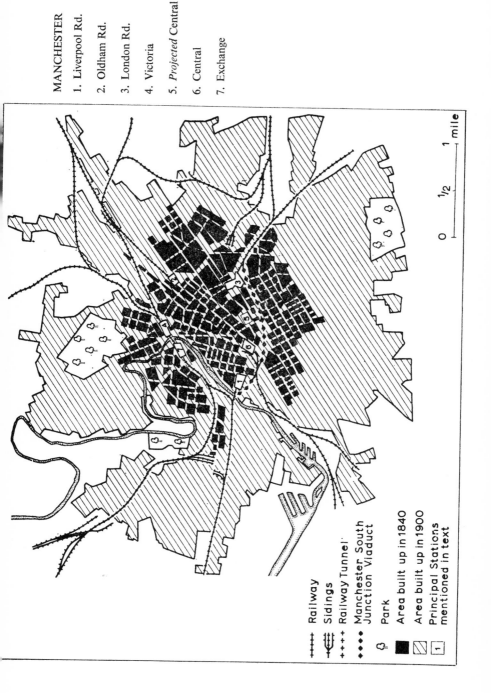

MANCHESTER

1. Liverpool Rd.
2. Oldham Rd.
3. London Rd.
4. Victoria
5. *Projected* Central
6. Central
7. Exchange

Railway
Sidings
Railway Tunnel
Manchester South
Junction Viaduct
Park
Area built up in 1840
Area built up in 1900
Principal Stations
mentioned in text

0   1/2   1 mile

BIRMINGHAM

1. Curzon St.

2. New St.

3. Snow Hill

Railway
Sidings
Railway Tunnel
Duddeston Viaduct

Park
Area built up in 1840
Area built up in 1900
Principal Stations
mentioned in text

0   1
└─┴─┘
mile

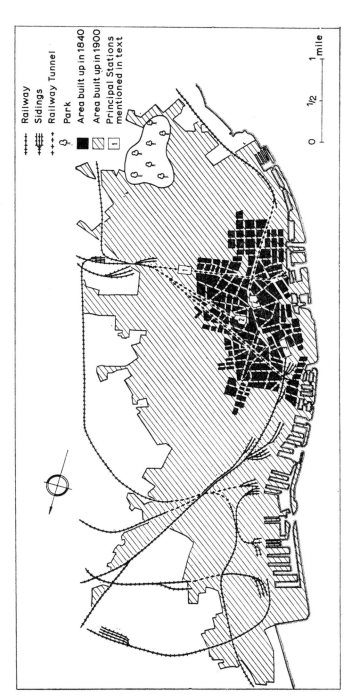

LIVERPOOL

1. Crown St.   2. Lime St.   3. Exchange   4. Central

Legend:

- Railway
- Sidings
- Railway Tunnel
- Park
- Area built up in 1840
- Area built up in 1900
- Principal Stations mentioned in text

0   ½   1 mile

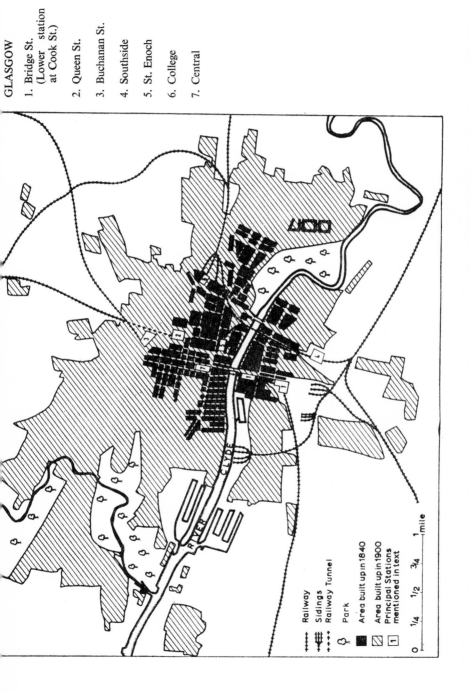

GLASGOW

1. Bridge St.
   (Lower station
   at Cook St.)
2. Queen St.
3. Buchanan St.
4. Southside
5. St. Enoch
6. College
7. Central

Railway
Sidings
Railway Tunnel

Park

Area built up in 1840
Area built up in 1900
Principal Stations
mentioned in text

RIVER CLYDE

0   1/4   1/2   3/4   1 mile

I

Introduction and summary

1. *Introduction*

ONE of the main problems confronting urban historians in Britain at the present moment is that of discovering ways in which valid comparisons can be made between the major British cities of the nineteenth century without denying or reducing their highly individual character. Their economic bases are similar only by coincidence and in limited measure; often they are totally dissimilar.[1] Their forms of enterprise, the response of their business communities and the policies of their civic administrations vary widely. Comparisons which do not take account of these divergences can easily be misleading. Yet though the local histories of Liverpool, Manchester, Birmingham and Glasgow each have their unique flavour the urban historian cannot be content to treat them individually, in isolation. They, and other British cities, did not live in separate worlds in the nineteenth century, but were all subjected to certain common economic events.

One such major incident in the life of all British cities between 1830 and 1900 was the impact of railways upon the urban fabric and economy. By tracing the varying responses of British cities to this event comparisons can be made which often illuminate the subsequent form and direction of urban growth in individual cases, and yet which bring out the common, overriding influences to which all major cities were subjected. After all, a distinguishing feature of the revolutionary new mode of transport was that, unlike the profitable Victorian omnibus and carting businesses, it did not perform its service within the existing framework of social overhead capital.[2] It had to provide a completely new transport network within each town and new generating points for traffic.

[1] Asa Briggs, *Victorian Cities* (1963), 32, 46–54.
[2] T. C. Barker and Michael Robbins, *A History of London Transport* (1963), 241–4.

In the course of this transformation of urban traffic the railways made a massive and tangible impact upon the fabric of each major British city. By 1890 the principal railway companies had expended over £100,000,000, more than one-eighth of all railway capital, on the provision of terminals, had bought thousands of acres of central land, and undertaken the direct work of urban demolition and reconstruction on a large scale. In most cities they had become the owners of up to eight or ten *per cent* of central land, and indirectly influenced the functions of up to twenty *per cent*.[3] The plans of British towns no matter how individual and diverse before 1830, are uniformly super-inscribed within a generation by the gigantic geometrical brush-strokes of the engineers' curving approach lines and cut-offs, and franked with the same bulky and intrusive termini, sidings and marshalling-yards. Even in the most cursory map analysis these block-like specialised areas, and the rivers of steel flowing between them, stand out by their scale and artificiality, and by the durable, inconvertible nature of their function. In an environment where so much development was small-scale and left to piece-meal speculation, the railway builders and the great estate developers were by far the most important individual figures. Fowler, the Stephensons, Vignoles, Hawkshaw, Sacré, were the conscious moulders of Victorian cities.

2. *Delimitation of subject*

Before proceeding further with a study of the effects of railway building upon Victorian cities it is necessary to delimit the practical scope such an enquiry can encompass. It does not seem wise or practicable, for example, to attempt to calculate the indirect effects of railways upon cities. Yet this is not to deny their importance. In each town, large or small, the economic base was affected by the fuller pursuit of specialisation which the cheap transport linkages made possible: and since the logistic problems of supplying towns with food, building materials, fuel, raw materials and labour were solved, a rapid rate of urban growth could be maintained, in spite of the new dimensions of mid-century towns. There were accentuated problems of administration and public health in the 1840's and 1850's, but no signs of the slackening rate of physical growth some had predicted.[4]

This profound indirect influence upon the internal functions and the overall size of towns must be conceded: but insoluble difficulties arise when we try to demonstrate it specifically. It is one thing to follow a narrative of the opening of a certain terminus by a story of rapid growth of population and output, illustrated statistically, and to assume

[3] *Infra* Chap. 10, sec. 2.
[4] A. F. Weber, *The Growth of Cities* (Cornell, 1963), 49 *et seq.*

tacitly that the one partially results from the other. It is quite another task to distinguish the components of growth which are due to the railways from those which are due to independent factors.

One way this difficulty may be tackled is to select special examples of towns like Crewe, Swindon, Wolverton or Redhill, all of them railway creations, with railway companies providing 25–30% of total employment, dominating both manufacturing and service industry, closely engaged in housing, and even taking over the 'management' of the town.[5] These railway towns are interesting and impressive examples if one wishes to make out an extreme case for the impact of railways upon urban development. In each town the influence of the railway is so magnified that the need to isolate it from other factors hardly arises, unless one seeks to explain the later progress of economic diversification.[6] But such company towns are by no means as common in Britain as their counterparts in the United States; and though of great analytical interest, they are of questionable value as a general guide.

Another approach would be to select for study the second flight railway towns—those more representative towns which had a firm and independent economic base of their own but gained abnormally, for some reason or other, from their railway linkage. Examples of this type are Middlesbrough and Barrow, where raw materials were unlocked by unusually early and effective railway enterprise, or Carlisle and Derby, where certain route advantages, which already gave a marked nodality, were further confirmed by the railway's arrival.[7] Such towns would be arguably more representative than Crewe or Swindon, and it would be possible with them to put forward a strong case for the railways as the predominant growth factor.

It is far more difficult, however, to isolate and assign a measurable component for growth if we select our cities with reference simply to their size and importance and not with a view to illustrating the effects of railways. How much did the five principal British cities owe to the railways? London, Birmingham, Manchester, Glasgow and Liverpool could hardly be described as creations of the railway. Indeed, one

[5] W. H. Chaloner, *Social and Economic Development of Crewe, 1780–1923* (Manchester, 1950), 40–66. P. Richards, 'The influence of the Railways on the Growth of Wolverton', *Records of Buckinghamshire*, XVII (1962), 115–26. E. F. Carter, *The Story of Redhill as a Railway Centre* (Redhill, 1954). D. E. C. Eversley, 'The Great Western Railway Works, Swindon', *A History of Wiltshire*, IV (V. C. H., 1959), 207–19. B. J. Turton, 'The Railway Town; a Problem in Industrial Planning', *Town Planning Review*, XXXII (1961–2), 97–115.

[6] D. E. C. Eversley, 'The Great Western Railway and the Swindon Works in the Great Depression', *University of Birmingham Historical Journal*, V (1957).

[7] S. Pollard and J. D. Marshall, 'The Furness Railway and the Growth of Barrow', JTH, I (1953), 109–26. Asa Briggs, 'Middlesborough: the Growth of a New Community', *Victorian Cities* (1963), 247–82. J. D. Standen, *The Social, Economic and Political Development of Derby, 1835–88* (Leeds M.A. thesis, 1958).

manifest characteristic of the early railway age in this country was that, at the time the railway arrived, the major British towns were already further committed to machine production than most of their European or Transatlantic counterparts.

Yet if we examine, not the incalculable indirect effects of the nineteenth-century railways but, more modestly, their specific impact on the major British cities there remains much that is amenable to study. What decided the location of railway facilities and the timing of their provision in a town? Who owned the land on which the railways were built, what did it cost and why did those costs rise steeply? Is any pattern discernible in the process of land acquisition on which urban railway building depended? How critical was the particular stage of rivalry or monopoly prevailing between railway companies serving a town? What direct influence did railway building have upon the old central core of a city? To what extent did the railways on the one hand, demolish, on the other, preserve but dilapidate the existing urban fabric? Was any attempt made to understand the indirect social costs and benefits which urban railway building incurred? Was the railway's role in stimulating suburban extension as important as is usually assumed; and how, precisely, did the provision of services by profit-making companies link up with the promotion of suburban building? Evidence exists to suggest answers to all these questions.

3. *Early problems of railway access*

The initial phase of railway development in most towns in the 1830's was characterised by good opportunities for approach and terminus building not fully utilised because of unduly low capitalisation for the task in hand, this lack of means being accompanied by a corresponding lack of influence in dealing with proprietors.[8] The chief commercial need at this time was, above all, to get a portion of the line into operation as quickly as possible and to see some return for the heavy initial expenses on Parliamentary charges, rolling stock and permanent way. The typical stations of this period were all, as the accompanying maps show, on the outskirts of the then built-up areas.[9] The main consideration in their siting was to achieve the cheapest and simplest approach and terminus, with the minimum disturbance of property, even if (as in three of these cases) this involved a final stretch of line served by a tunnel and stationary cable engine. Usually the last part of the approach

[8] It was not until the second railway boom in the 1840's that there was comment upon 'the greatly increased favour and support which, as compared with the projects of former years, these undertakings now receive from the owners of Landed Property in the districts through which they pass'. H.C., 1844, XI, 5.

[9] See captions to Figs. 1–5. The stations are numbered chronologically in order of authorisation.

line ran through open land leased out in small market-gardens or through slum terrace and cellar dwellings leased in batches of eight or ten to middlemen, but, in each case, conveniently owned by a few larger landowners whose goodwill had been secured. The termini themselves were mere departure sheds with clumsy roofing covering only the track and leaving the passenger platform exposed. Even at the finest and most spectacular of the London termini, Euston's splendid arch led only to the ramshackle collection of one-storey brick ticket offices which so much engaged Pugin's scorn.[10]

Yet despite their anxiety to avoid adding to the total cost of their projects by disproportionate expenses entering the city, the railway companies of the mid-1830's immediately encountered the shock of urban land prices. 'I think I may safely say that in our London termini there is nothing extravagant and nothing done for display,' claimed William Reed, Secretary of the London and Southampton Railway Company, 'but yet it has cost us a great deal more money than we had calculated for the whole of our stations.'[11]

At this early stage the expense was principally experienced by the companies operating from London. John Moxon, Chairman of the London and Croydon Railway, spoke for all the London companies. 'Every railway we apprehend in its first mile costs more than in any other part of the line, but ours is peculiarly so.'[12] It was this burden, and not, as so often repeated, the ransom payments to country landowners, which brought the London and Birmingham company back to Parliament to secure permission to raise more capital in 1839. 'The very principal excess', said Robert Stephenson, 'or at least a large part of the excess, arose entirely from the stations on the line.'[13] The Secretary, Richard Creed, supported him. 'There is one expense no engineer could estimate, the expense of stations, and there we have arrived at a most fearful excess.'[14] The extension of the London and Birmingham from Camden Town to Euston alone, little more than a mile, cost £380,000 and had to be supported by a special toll above the statutory fares.[15]

The London and Birmingham Company's credit was sufficient and

[10] 'This piece of Brobdingnagian fantasy must have cost the company a sum which would have built a first rate station.' Christian Barman, *An Introduction to Railway Architecture* (1950), 16.

[11] H.L., 1839, XXIII, 61.

[12] *Ibid.* 161.

[13] *Ibid.* 351.

[14] HLRO, Min., H.C., 1839, 20 March, p. 113, S.C. on London and Birmingham Railway.

[15] H.C., 1839 (442) XIII, QQ. 102, 776. By the end of 1838 land and compensation costs had exceeded the original estimates by 115%, works, track and station costs by 85%. H. Pollins, 'A Note on Railway Constructional Costs, 1825–1850', *Economica*, 19(1952), 404.

management good enough to survive this miscalculation, but another railway, the Eastern Counties, must remain a classic example of a railway which totally miscarried through failure to estimate urban property values realistically. Henry Bosanquet, their Chairman, disclosed to the Commons' Select Committee that over three times the total sum estimated for land purchase had already been expended and the line had not yet been half laid down, to Colchester instead of Great Yarmouth as planned.[16] This was, in fact, as far as the Eastern Counties company, as originally constituted, ever got. The section from Mile End to Bishopsgate Street had proved too much for their resources.

Yet the obvious solution to these difficulties, the sharing of terminal approaches and facilities, could not be made workable without a measure of goodwill which the competitive nature of company promotion precluded. In London the Great Western and the London and Birmingham companies wisely decided not to share Euston as had originally been planned: the long and bitter rivalry between the companies and their technical disagreements over gauges would have led to scenes of unimaginable friction and confusion.[17] But the four south-eastern railway companies which did share London Bridge station found it quite impossible to agree on the terms of joint-ownership. The Commons' Committee which brought the four chairmen together finally despaired of compromise and recommended Lewis Cubitt's plan for one of the earliest 'secessionist' stations, Bricklayers' Arms (No. 6 on London map).[18]

In Liverpool and Birmingham the problem of shared stations had not yet arisen. In Glasgow the Glasgow, Paisley, Kilmarnock and Ayr, and Glasgow, Paisley and Greenock companies, and in Manchester the Liverpool and Manchester and the Grand Junction companies, shared stations harmoniously, but only because the companies themselves had a system of overlapping directorates: at the latter terminus the companies soon followed their surrender of operational autonomy by actual amalgamation into the London and North Western group.[19] By the end of the thirties there were already indications that sharing of termini by genuinely independent companies would raise endless difficulties. 'Joint Stations', a witness said to the 1852 Parliamentary Committee, 'have been a more fruitful source of quarrels, litigation, Chancery proceedings and disagreements than almost anything else connected with the railway system.'[20] Appreciation of this point is of

[16] H.L., 1839, XXIII, 189–92 (Bosanquet). £200,000 had been estimated for land, £650,000 had already been paid.

[17] Ibid. 352 (Robert Stephenson).

[18] Ibid. 261 (Cubitt).

[19] Ibid. 234 (Moxon). For the amalgamations see Case Histories, infra.

[20] H.C., 1852–3, XXXVIII, 137 (Huish). There were also, he alleged, ten times the volume of complaints from the public at joint stations.

critical importance in understanding the network of urban railways and termini.

The attitude of the railway companies towards terminal facilities and the land-acquisition problems they encountered during this early phase of their development can be shown in more detail by a brief examination of the siting of two of the important new Manchester stations; the Manchester and Leeds Company's at Hunt's Bank (Victoria, 1839, No. 4 on map) and the Manchester, Sheffield and Lincolnshire Company's at Store Street (London Road, 1837, No. 3 on map). The property designated by Charles Vignoles for the site of the M.S. & L's terminus was occupied by a smithy yard, small factory and a group of houses, loosely arranged with a good deal of waste space and all owned by a Joseph Dyer.[21] The remaining 100 or so properties through which the approach line passed consisted of occupied cellars and houses, bakehouses, a coachmaker's works and stables, wheelwright's shop and houses building. A mere 200 yards and £40,000 was enough to clear the built-up area to the fields beyond; though as the Manchester Commissioner of Police, Mr. George Hall, stressed, the delay, even of a year, would 'cause the land in the neighbourhood to be raised in nominal if not real value by this proposal.'[22] In the previous six months more building than he had ever seen in that area had been commenced. In his opinion it was a deliberate attempt to enhance the value of the land by opportune speculation; but it could also be interpretated as the first signs of the genuine functional competition for land in the area adjacent to the city centre. The Committee, in fact, asked Mr. Hall directly whether he did not regard the building of houses as of equal importance to the railways' proposed use of the land. 'Buildings are necessary of course,' he replied, 'but at least they are erecting; but the Railway is also a very important accommodation for Manchester.'[23]

In George Stephenson's evidence for the Hunt's Bank extension the same resistance to the railway's intrusion arose over issues of cost and space. He was persistently attacked in the Parliamentary Committee for his extravagant claims for land and his disturbing vagueness about the uses for which it would be needed. He came before the committee without a detailed plan for the terminal, explaining bluntly 'I do not like to lay out a Depot in the beginning.'[24] Instead he preferred to lay out the space for which compulsory purchase orders had been granted

[21] HLRO, P & S, B.Ref., 1837, Sheffield, Ashton-under-Lyne and Manchester Railway. Properties 1 to 25. The site was shared with the Manchester and Cheshire Junction Railway, H.L., 1836, XXXIII, 321–2.

[22] *Ibid.* 436.

[23] *Loc. cit.* The properties were probably those belonging to John Satterthwaite, who is shown as owning 18 unfinished and 5 empty houses.

[24] HLRO, Min., H.C., 1837, 17 March, p. 22, S.C. on Manchester and Leeds Railway.

'with reference not to the present traffic, but to the possible or probable increase of it.'[25] The Liverpool and Manchester Company, for which he was engineer, had failed to do this at both ends of their line 'for want of capital', and were now trying to increase their depots 'by giving extraordinary prices' for small plots at the Manchester end (No. 1 on map) and 'by constructing a new entrance at Liverpool' (No. 2 on map).[26]

The provision for future growth at the new Hunt's Bank terminal which seemed, no doubt, eminently reasonable to George Stephenson, was represented to the Committee in quite a different light by counsel for the landowners. 'Do you think you are justified in calling upon Parliament to oblige men of property to part with their land without first having determined how far it is necessary that the power should be extended?'[27] In fact, it had been largely to avoid these troubles with existing landowners that the Hunt's Bank site had been chosen, because, although the approach to it ran through some 250 shops, cottages and cellar-dwellings a large parcel of them were owned by one proprietor, the Earl of Derby; and another titled proprietor, Lord Ducie, owned most of the land adjacent to the proposed terminal.[28] The necessary property transactions involved were kept to a minimum by the route chosen.

The scuffle for railway access to Britain's major cities in the 1830's had already disclosed three features of considerable significance for future urban development. In the first place all railway promoters had grossly underestimated the expenses involved and so their schemes often fell short, or remained modest and peripheral. The opportunity was lost for a direct penetration to the central areas at a time when the operation could have been carried out painlessly. Within a decade the original stations on the outskirts were encrusted, like flies in amber, by the rapid extension of building. The approach routes became longer, more expensive and more limited in choice. At the same time difficulties in station sharing had arisen which ensured that future terminal projects would be put forward which made sense in the railway boardrooms but not in terms of urban transport economics. Finally, the intrusive land acquisition and change of use the approach lines and termini required had already encountered a resistance compounded of inertia and financial opportunism. This was reflected twice; once in the delays and costs of securing the bill, and again in the 'extraordinary prices' which had to be offered.

Already, by the 1830's, the railway companies had begun to seek a

[25] Loc. cit. p. 9.
[26] Loc. cit. pp. 9, 17, 18, 22, 24, 28, 29.
[27] Loc. cit. p. 13, George Stephenson questioned by Mr. Hildyard Q.C.
[28] HLRO, P & S, B.Ref., 1839, Manchester and Leeds Railway.

way to avoid this resistance and delay by laying out routes through the areas where they had managed to find groups of substantial proprietors. These formed a species of fissure in the complex pattern of ownership in Britain's great cities along which the railways could chisel their way to the fringe of the town centre. These 'fissures' frequently provide, both in the 1830's and later, the specific explanation for route and site choices within the very broad limits suggested by geographical and engineering factors.[29]

Yet in spite of the unexpected costs of the 1830's the returns to early establishment or improvement of terminals were very great both in terms of traffic and profits. The one mile Hunt's Bank extension and Victoria Station of 1839, instanced above, was constructed for £475,000, equal to $2\frac{1}{2}\%$ off the Manchester and Leeds company's 8.8% annual distributed profit for one year; a small price to pay for an investment which would assure the company's long-term prospects and establish a firm and permanent foothold in Manchester.[30] In the amalgamation phase of the following decade it was noticeable that the partner which always came out on good terms was 'the Company which works the main Trunk line and possesses the principal terminal Stations.'[31] It is also clear from the confidential figures published by accident in the Second Report of the Select Committee on Railway Acts, that the profits of most railway companies between 1837 and 1846 were more than sufficient to have digested a larger expenditure on provisions in cities.[32]

4. *Terminals in the 1840's*

By the 1840's the modest nature of the railways' installations was becoming apparent, as the profit-making and traffic-generating potential of steam transport unfolded in each great city. 'The possession of good railway communications', the Board of Trade's 1845 report on railway schemes in Lancashire concluded, 'has now become almost as much a matter of necessity as the adoption of the most improved machinery to enable a manufacturing community to contend on equal terms with its rivals and to maintain its footing.'[33] In Manchester, where fluctuations of taste had always made time most important in the staple industry, 'the reduction in the period for the return of orders

---

[29] By 1845 locomotives were sufficiently powerful to ascend gradients of 1 in 42 leaving urban terminals in Glasgow, London and Manchester, H.L., 1845, XXXIX, 40.

[30] HLRO, Min., H.C., 1837, 16 March, p. 4, S.C. on Manchester and Leeds Railway. P & S, 1839, M. & L. Rly.

[31] H.L., 1845, XXXIX, 35.

[32] H.C., 1846 (687) XIV, 5 *et seq.*

[33] H.L., 1845, XXXIX, 238.

and the shortening of the process of textile manufacture itself' which early railways brought, led to rapid expansion of employment, saving of capital and even, it was claimed, improvements in machinery.[34]

In Birmingham it seemed equally urgent to improve facilities for different reasons. 'Economy of transit should be carried to the greatest possible extent, *more particularly in a district so far inland*', the city magistrates stated.[35] Similar evidence is available for Glasgow where the need to compete on equal terms with Manchester and Liverpool is stressed. The competitive inter-city advantages brought by good terminal facilities were sufficiently clear by the mid-1840's to quieten criticism and unlock funds for the assault upon the central areas of each city.

In London, in 1846, no fewer than 19 projects for urban railways were put forward, involving so great a change in land use that the Select Committees considering each bill on its individual merits were reinforced by a Royal Commission to consider the general effects of railway schemes upon 'the thoroughfares of the metropolis and the property and comfort of its inhabitants.'[36] In Liverpool, likewise, the urgent need for 'extending station accommodation and giving increased facilities for ingress and egress', and the immense expense of achieving it, was made the main argument for justifying the 'union of capital' of the three companies terminating there, and the formation in 1846 of the L. & N.W., the largest railway in Britain, with a capital of over £17 millions.[37]

With the huge combined capitals amalgamation provided, and the flood of new investment during 'railway mania', the railway companies had ample means to command space even in the bidding against well-established commercial land users. The central business districts, where high rents and land values had always kept a species of monopoly, found themselves unable to exclude the railways by the customary sanction of offering central business district land prices. Nearly 1,000 acres of land had been authorised 'to be taken for Warehouses, Stations etc,' by various acts in the 1830's. Most of this had been taken up by the mid-1840's and stations built which cost, on the average, three times as much per route mile as their European equivalents in 1844.[38] The railways' land hunger added considerably to this in the next five years. By 1849 the 26 largest railway companies had laid out £19,240,000 on land purchase, the relative costs of this land varying in relation to constructional costs from 64% for the mostly urban Manchester

[34] *Ibid.* 237.
[35] HLRO, Min., H.C., 1846, 24 June, pp. 3–4, S.C. on Birmingham, Wolverhampton and Dudley Railway.
[36] H.C., 1846 (719) XVII, 21.
[37] H.L., 1845, XXXIX, 267. Report on the proposed L. & N.W. amalgamation by the Board of Trade (unfavourable).
[38] H.C., 1844, XI, 610–30.

South Junction railway, to a mere 15% for a line which was rural or had running powers into urban termini like the Eastern Union company.[39] In general, land costs ran at about a quarter of the amounts expended upon the actual construction of railways, and were half as large again as the cost of rolling stock, engines and plant.

As a broad item of national rail costs during the constructional phase, the expenditure on land was more considerable than has recently been suggested. Of course, it is possible by citing spectacular individual examples of 'blackmail' land prices to give an exaggerated impression of the burden laid upon railway finance by land purchase; and the statements of an earlier generation of railway historians have been subjected to sceptical analysis by Harold Pollins. The danger now appears to be that of over-correction, for there are good reasons—given in detail elsewhere—for believing that average land costs during the period 1825–50 did not come to 13·9% as Pollins has argued, but to over 16·5% of aggregate expenditure.[40] In relation to the very large amounts of capital deployed this proportion represents a considerable expenditure, perhaps the greatest single influence of the period upon the national land market; and nowhere were higher prices paid than in the strategically placed approaches to Victorian urban terminals.

The particular need experienced by the major railway companies in the mid-1840's was for improved and more central stations for passengers, who still provided 61% of overall revenues.[41] The rapid growth in volume of local, short-distance traffic, also placed the 'annexe' stations, a mile or more from the centre, at a further discount. An irresistible solution to these traffic problems in the forties was to convert the old terminals to goods depots and to extend the lines further into the core of the city to new passenger stations. As the cities extended outwards (and for many of them the 1840's was the fastest decade of their growth), so the railways penetrated further into their central business districts. The practice was widespread (see maps) and quite deliberate, as Robert Stephenson testified: the extension from Curzon Street to New Street in Birmingham was exactly modelled on the advance from Camden Town to Euston at the southern end of the London–Birmingham line.[42]

---

[39] The M.S.J. costs for land and property came to £200,000, the cost of actual construction £313,000; for the Eastern Union the figures were £172,000 and £1,158,000. This compares only land costs and construction costs. For a fuller break-down of the figures, including Parliamentary expenses, Law charges, Engineers' charges and Plant see App. 1.

[40] See App. 1 *infra*.

[41] H.C., 1852–3, XXXVIII, 299 (Simmons). By 1853 the proportion of revenue earned by passenger traffic had declined to 53%.

[42] HLRO, Min., H.C., 1846, 12 June, p. 63, S.C. on London and Birmingham Railway (Birmingham Extension).

Of the five major cities, Birmingham came out of this phase of central terminus building most transformed, with two new central stations forming landmarks within which the shopping and business area tended to be confined. Robert Stephenson's New Street station (No. 2 on Birmingham map) had the advantage of being an extension by a well-established company and of 'removing a certain class of the inhabitants living just behind the principal and best streets', by its chosen route through the slums and brothels behind Navigation Street.[43] The contribution to social costs, which railway demolition in this area constituted, secured the approval of the Birmingham Commissioners, who were already considering building a commodious new road out to the old Curzon Street station. 'I need scarcely ask you', counsel for the Bill remarked, rhetorically 'whether having been prepared to make that sacrifice of the Town's funds to achieve that object you would think it a very desirable thing to have the Station brought into the Town?'[44] The properties on the terminal site were mostly owned by small, non-resident proprietors in batches of two to eight, but municipal goodwill, compulsory purchase orders and tempting cash offers broke up this maze of titles.

Brunel's rival central station at Snow Hill (No. 3 on map) was also carried through, if not with the entire favour of the Birmingham Commissioners, at least with the militant partisanship of a faction of them, together with the M.P. for Birmingham, Richard Spooner. They pointed to the limitations of New Street, a passenger station only, very convenient for the carriage traffic from the middle-class Edgbaston area, but not able to cope with the small masters, bringing in their manufactures 'on their backs and in carts to the neighbourhood of Snow Hill.'[45] Above all, a second station, of equal dimensions, and linked with the G.W.R., would 'free Birmingham from the thraldom of the network which the London and Birmingham railway propose to throw over it.'[46]

Brunel and MacLean had the slight advantage of dealing with only one owner, William Inge, whose workshops, houses and yards, and five or six warehouses, covered the terminal site: but their mile-long approach routes by tunnel and viaduct affected nearly 1800 properties.[47]

In the other major cities in the 1840's the transformation was less complete. In Glasgow, though there were several schemes for river

[43] *Ibid.* 11 June, pp. 58–9 (James, late Mayor).

[44] *Loc. cit.* pp. 6–7, counsel addressing Daniel Malins, High Bailiff.

[45] HLRO, Min., H.C., 1846, 25 June, pp. 220–3, S.C. on Birmingham, Wolverhampton and Dudley Railway.

[46] *Ibid.* 22 June, p. 26.

[47] HLRO, P & S, 1846, Birmingham and Oxford Junction Railway (Birmingham Extension Railway). HLRO, P & S, 1846, Birmingham, Wolverhampton and Dudley Railway.

crossings and ambitious central stations, none matured. In Manchester the only new station was a minor one, though the existing termini were enlarged and a unique new link railway was set in hand, Joseph Locke's Manchester South Junction Railway, entirely urban, crossing 30 streets on its 1½ mile viaduct. In London, where the Royal Commission's intervention has been noted, three ambitious schemes for central termini fell under the veto on central building, but at Waterloo and King's Cross (Nos. 7 & 8 on London map) two important fringe additions were sanctioned and an inner ring railway commenced. In Liverpool a second entry to the central business district was effected, from the North at Exchange Station (No. 3 on Liverpool map), and Lime Street station was greatly enlarged; the extension at Lime Street by Joseph Locke being achieved by the stroke of a pen transferring 260 properties belonging to the Mayor and Burgesses to the existing station site, in marked contrast to Thomson & Hawkshaw's task, ploughing laboriously and expensively through 500 multiply-owned properties to reach the Exchange site.[48]

It is clear that in all of these central schemes a critical new factor in the 1840's was the approbation, or, at any rate, the friendly neutrality of the new local authorities. Schemes which were insufficiently canvassed fell through, whatever their merits and whatever the resources of the company. The choice of routes through cities and the dimensions of the terminal sites were subjected to a new influence; the corporate ownership of land (as in Liverpool), or corporate views on desirable areas for demolition (as in Manchester, Birmingham and Glasgow).

The costs of effecting these inroads into the central business district, although they had not grown as rapidly as the railway companies' resources, nevertheless increased beyond all reasonable anticipation. Instead of the £135,000 (Lime Street, Liverpool, 1832) or £475,000 (Victoria, Manchester, 1839) of a decade earlier, £1,000,000 was needed for the new Snow Hill Station at Birmingham (1846); and increases in other towns were of a similar order.[49] Some small part of this increase came from the more substantial nature of the termini. Dobson, Wyatt, Hardwick and Cubitt began to lay out permanent station buildings in

[48] Fuller information and references to all the schemes mentioned in this paragraph may be found in the *Case Histories*.

[49] The figures quoted are engineers' official estimates contained in the relevant Plans and Sections. These cover the buildings, land purchase and immediate approach route, but, of course, were frequently exceeded by considerable margins in practice. Unfortunately it is not possible to produce a comprehensive list of estimated urban costs because in many other cases the engineer's estimates cover the whole railway without differentiating terminal expenses; e.g. Vignole's estimate for London Road station, Manchester, includes forty miles of track. The deposit of overlapping plans for shared stations further complicates the problem of assessing terminal costs. See *infra* Chap. 3, sec. 4.

the late 1840's in a style and with materials more fitting to those wealthy and massive additions to the Victorian city centre.[50] But most of the expense arose from the rapid inflation of site prices which the railways had themselves precipitated.

5. *Railway contractors and property owners in the 1860's*

The railway companies' purchase of a sizeable percentage of the central business districts left a mark not merely on the Victorian townscape, but also on the companies themselves, and affected the timing and character of their last major assault on the fabric of British cities, in the 1860's. The profits, even of the largest companies, tended to sag for a time where an ambitious programme of terminus building had been undertaken. George Carr Glyn, the Chairman of the L. & N.W., who had stressed the cardinal importance of securing bills 'for the improve-ment of our stations in Manchester, Birmingham, London and Liver-pool' at the 1st General Meeting in 1846, had the mournful task of reporting the halving of dividends over the next seven years. 'In seeking to find the reasons for this remarkable decline of dividend' writes the L. & N.W.'s historian, 'we must attribute it partly to the large capital expenditure on more or less unproductive improvements.'[51]

A result of the increased cost of sites in the larger cities in the 1840's was that the projecting of such schemes tended to become a separate speculation, almost the monopoly preserve of a few great contractors and engineers. John Hawkshaw and John Fowler were two ex-engineers who, by dint of their expertise and their ability to act as intermediaries between the railway companies and the large contractors, were able to turn entrepreneur and amass great personal fortunes during this phase of city railway building. Hawkshaw and Fowler between them accounted for the building of Charing Cross, Cannon Street and Victoria stations in London, (Nos. 10, 11 & 9 on London map), Central station, Liver-pool (No. 4) and St. Enoch's and Central stations, Glasgow (Nos. 5 and 7). In each case a separate company was floated to build the terminus and few miles of necessary approaches. Work was carried out on credit, and share capital for these specialised terminus companies was sometimes advanced (in return for monopoly privileges) by Waring Brothers, Betts and Peto, the great contractors, who had by now developed a vested interest in demolishing and remaking cities. In these ways risk capital was concentrated by those most directly concerned with urban railway building in the 1860's, and sufficient leverage

[50] Christian Barman, *An Introduction to Railway Architecture* (1950), *passim.* Carrol L. V. Meek, *The Railway Station: an Architectural History* (1957).
[51] W. L. Steel, *The History of the London and North Western Railway* (1914), 148, 151–2.

obtained for the increasingly difficult task of breaking into the cities' inner districts.[52]

Even so a great deal of ingenuity was needed to find the fissures in the ownership pattern along which approach routes could be made. Fortunately, for the projectors of the 1860's, a few large individual titles to land still existed. The Marquis of Westminster owned the greater part of the property along the route of the Victoria Station and Pimlico Railway Company. The decision to cross the Thames by striking westward from London Bridge (No. 1) and setting up the Charing Cross and Cannon Street termini was also influenced by the location of large block holdings. The Archbishop of Canterbury's and the Right Rev. Lord Bishop of Winchester's vast slum holdings in Southwark and Lambeth alone made it possible to contemplate driving a surface railway two miles across south London. In Manchester and in Glasgow the last large central holdings in personal ownership were tempted onto the market by railway prices in the 1860's.[53]

Increasingly, however, the railways came to rely for urban land upon corporate bodies, the Hungerford Market Co. and the Drapers' Company, St. Thomas's Hospital and Emanuel College, which owned the terminal sites of Charing Cross, Cannon Street and Holborn Viaduct stations respectively in London; the municipal corporations in Liverpool and Glasgow for the new central sites there; the Grosvenor and the Rochdale canal companies, on whose basins Victoria Station, London, and the projected M.S. & L. Central Station in Manchester (No. 5 on map) were laid out. The 1860's, however, was the last decade in which such large units of ownership could readily be found: afterwards the most important developments in urban railways were underground.

6. *Effects on the central and inner districts*

The opening of stations in the central business districts of the provincial cities, and on the immediate periphery of the central area in London, produced both a redistribution of land uses and a re-alignment and stimulation of internal traffic routes. The Select Committee on Railways had already spoken, in 1844, of 'the control which Railway Companies possess by means of their Station-yards over the traffic of the neighbouring districts.'[54] The professional carrying companies redistributing railway loads by horse waggon, Pickfords, Kenworthy's and Baches found themselves, like many passenger cab drivers, engaged in the

---

[52] *Infra* Chap. 3, sec. 3.

[53] Detailed source references for the statements made in this and the next paragraph may be seen in sections 1 and 3 of the *Case Histories*.

[54] H.C., 1844, XI, 32.

1840's in endless squabbles concerning access and facilities; and litigation continued even after it had been recommended that 'reasonable preference may be given to favoured agents, but vehicles tendering themselves to take up or set down Passengers, Luggage and Parcels ought not to be excluded.'[55] Inter-station traffic came to form up to half the livelihood of some cab owners and influenced the framework of central horse omnibus routes. Where river bridges interposed between stations and the business areas, as at Jamaica Street, Glasgow, or at London Bridge, the traffic-generating power of the new termini was vividly underlined.[56]

More slowly, a realignment of land uses around the central termini and along their access routes took place. The early misgivings of insurance companies, three-quarters of which increased their rates for sites adjacent to the railways in the 1840's, were soon overcome, and the new transport medium's capacity to attract some expanding land uses and to repel others was given free rein.[57] Attracted to the termini were retail shopkeepers and transit warehouses; repelled were residential and, on the whole, business users. Business users and specialised warehouses built, like those in Manchester, for sale and exhibition rather than mere storage, preferred to keep a reasonable distance between themselves and the railway. Those heavy industries whose bulk requirements called for special rail facilities tended to falter at the central land prices and seek riverside or suburban accommodation.[58]

This gradual redistribution of uses was sometimes given specific lines of demarcation by a massive new feature of the urban scene in the 1840's, the railway viaduct, striding past working class houses at rooftop level, 'pinning down' areas socially and intersecting them physically. Occasionally these great stone viaducts were constructed to secure the right elevation for crossing a river or for entering a terminal site, but usually their main purpose was to avoid street closures, and it was this feature which gave them their extremely widespread use. Each major town has its lengthy stretches of elevated track, but perhaps the most striking example to take would be that of the Manchester South Junction.

The M.S.J. had been conceived of by Joseph Locke as 'a species of bridge' to provide a cross-town communication, and there could be no doubt of the need it satisfied in the transport network.[59] By the 1860's it was so crowded with east/west traffic that an hour's wait on

[55] *Ibid.* 33.
[56] *Infra* Chap. 10, sec. 4a.
[57] H.L., 1847–8, XLVII, 419–421.
[58] *Infra* Chap. 10, sec. 4b, Chap. 11, sec. 2.
[59] HLRO, Min., H.C., 1866, 9 May, p. 17, S.C. on Manchester Sheffield and Lincolnshire (Central Station and Lines).

its arches was not unusual.[60] But the effects on the area it crossed were dilapidating in the extreme. Those arches which were let were used for 'smithies, marine stores, stables, mortar mills, the storage of old tubs, casks and lumber, and other low class trades.'[61] The condition of the unlet arches was even more notorious. According to the city surveyor, speaking in 1866, 'No improvement has taken place in that district in the proximity of the viaduct. We have still the low class of property which was there years ago when the viaduct was built.' Other parts of Manchester had increased in value by 75% in the 20 years after the M.S.J. had been formed, he estimated, but values had remained static around the viaduct.[62]

In other cities where the line was not elevated, but passed at ground level through the property enclaves where streets had not been laid out, the effect was hardly less marked. Since the Parliamentary 'limits of deviation' made a generous allowance for railway needs, the companies often found themselves with a belt of superfluous land for disposal, usually to non-residential users. This helped them to recoup some of their expenditure, but increased the barrier effects of such routes. Segregation 'on the wrong side of the tracks' could have a disastrous effect upon the development value of vacant land. By mid-century smaller Parliamentary bills already show 'shadow areas' being created by the criss-crossing of supplementary lines driven relatively cheaply through a wilderness of so-called 'gardens', middens, claypits, 'scavengers yards with old boilers thereon.'[63] Within two decades the outward growth of building had made these disused areas potentially valuable central land, but the maze of tracks now prevented the land's development. The completion of urban link railways and cut-offs, which continued during the 'Great Depression' of the 1870's, came to cover scores of acres of east and north Liverpool, east Birmingham, south Manchester, Glasgow and London with a tangle of interconnecting lines and sidings, crystallising these areas' dereliction.[64]

7. Inter-city comparisons

A lengthy sequel to the work of the first 30 years of urban railway building could be written. Continued inter-company rivalry and the endless possibilities for friction which shared stations involved led to a few more large 'secessionist' stations later in the century, of which

[60] *Ibid.* 9 May, p. 28.
[61] HLRO, Min., H.L., 1866, 12 July, p. 8, S.C. on Manchester, Sheffield and Lincoln-shire (Central Station and Lines).
[62] *Loc. cit.* pp. 6, 7 (Lynde).
[63] HLRO, P & S, 1846, Manchester South Junction and Altrincham Railway (Branch in Salford to join the Manchester, Bolton and Bury Railway).
[64] *Infra* Chap. 10, sec. 2, Chap. 11, sec. 1.

the most important were Central, Glasgow (No. 7 on map), built for tactical reasons by the Caledonian Railway Company, and Exchange, Manchester (No. 7 on map), built end-on to Victoria. Some stations were substantially enlarged and their approaches broadened between 1870 and 1900 to cater for the doubling of traffic over those thirty years. The territorial expansion of goods accommodation, moreover, grew more quickly and in a more direct relationship to the increase of traffic than did the passenger stations in the last decades of the century, and this was reflected in the expanding yards and sidings along Thames, Mersey and Clydeside. Again it was only in the last two decades that, with the slow growth of cheap ticket commuter traffic, the railway companies began to make a marked impression, in London, at any rate, upon the Victorian suburbs, influencing their social composition and their direction and rates of growth in a way which is only now receiving attention from economic historians.[65]

Yet, on the whole, the main physical impact of railways upon the heart of the Victorian city and upon the urban property market was over by the end of the 1860's. The claims to land staked during the previous thirty years were sufficient, and the facilities established sufficiently flexible, with improved traffic control, to cater for the transport needs of the rest of the century without further re-shaping of the central areas.

Comparison between the emergent railway systems of each of the five cities brings out marked local differences in provisions. Liverpool was the nearest to a monopoly town, held in the grip of the L. & N.W. almost completely until the mid-1860's, when the M. S. & L. and the Cheshire Lines Committee introduced a competitive element. But even after this, formal complaints of relatively high mileage rates, inferior services and terminal charges 50% higher than anywhere else except London were lodged by the Chamber of Commerce in 1867, and reiterated in a memorandum to Mr. Gladstone in 1872.[66]

In Manchester, by contrast, the picture is one of the most extreme competition, with the L. & N.W., Midland, G.N., Lancashire and Yorkshire and M. S. & L. railways forming shifting temporary alliances, building stations of tactical necessity, introducing projects whose main purpose was to block attempts to improve services by rivals, making no attempt to co-ordinate timetables, and even (some alleged) arranging them to clash deliberately. 'The jealousies of the companies have prevented that convenience . . .,' stated Mr. Thomas Bazeley in evidence before the Commons' Committee of 1852/53, 'I am strongly

---

[65] For a full discussion of this subject see *infra* Chap. 11, sec. 3, and Chap. 12.
[66] H.C., 1867, XXXVIII, Pt. 2, App. K, Memorial by Henry Grainger, Liverpool Chamber of Commerce, to T. Milner Gibson, M.P., President of the Board of Trade. H.C., 1872, XIII, Memorial to Mr. Gladstone, 11 March.

of the opinion there ought to be a controlling power.' This from the Chairman of the Manchester Chamber of Commerce.[67]

In Birmingham, although the early days of shared stations produced similar scenes, including a classic pushing match between the locomotives of rival companies at the opening of New Street Station, these early excesses soon abated to leave Birmingham the best provided town.[68] The provision of the principal stations and through routes was carried through early, on paper by 1847, in iron and masonry by the early 1850's, and despite minor criticisms, its central stations catered for half a century's traffic growth. Certainly there are no signs that inadequacies in her railway linkages held back Birmingham's development in the later nineteenth century, quite the reverse. A balance of genuine competition between the L. & N.W. and G.W., perhaps arising partly from the incompatibility of gauges, provided all the advantages claimed universally for the *laissez-faire* system. Even Birmingham was not without its follies: the famous Duddeston viaduct (see map) setting off on towering arches across the city to nowhere, never completed but still standing, without a rail laid, a monument to the tactical needs of a passing phase of railway competition.

In Glasgow a more substantial monument was left in the form of St. Enoch's Station, built by the G. & S.W. and its satellite Union company in a vain attempt to exclude the Caledonian Railway Company. In Glasgow the disposition of competitive forces was so equal and the deadlock between them so bitter as to lead to the frustration of all comprehensive projects in the 1840's and to needless reduplication later.

In London the formation of main line termini and urban link railways fell into a special category for two reasons: it was by far the largest city and tended to magnify external diseconomies intolerably; it was also the seat of the national government and came more particularly under the oversight of central authority. Since it was also the focus for nearly all the great railway companies it was subjected even more directly than Manchester to the disruptive force of *laissez-faire* competition. Schemes put forward in the one year 1863 proposed to raise £33 million, lay out 174 miles of track in the Metropolitan area, build four new bridges across the Thames and schedule one quarter of all lands and buildings in the City of London for compulsory purchase and demolition. Parliament could not stand back idly whilst London and Westminster were torn to pieces by competing companies and so in the 1860's, as in the 1840's, fresh parameters for future urban railways were imposed.[69]

[67] H.C., 1852–3, XXXVIII, 228–9.
[68] A full description of this, as of the other issues mentioned for each city will be found in the Case Histories *infra*.
[69] *Infra*. Chap. 2, sec. 3 and 4.

The individual and distinctive nature of the impact of railways upon each of the five major British cities cannot be glossed over, but at the same time certain overriding similarities can be discerned in the problems faced and in the general effects upon the fabric of each city. It would be equally foolish either to underestimate the former or to overlook the latter.

Differences in the competitive postures of the companies exploiting each city and in the amount of surveillance exercised by local and central authorities left their mark, quite literally, upon the development of each city. But this diversity should not obscure the many common features: the similar effects upon the central business districts and their traffic, the demolition of certain areas of low quality housing in each city and the perpetuation of others, the similar problems of securing land title along the access routes and the similar effects upon the urban land market. Here are topics which draw the study of British cities closer together and afford an extensive field for urban comparisons.

Part One

'Natural Growth' In Urban Railways

II

◇◇

Did the Victorians count social costs?

◇◇

1. *Introduction*

T HE study of Victorian railways begins with a paradox. On the one hand the choices of particular railway routes and sites and of particular operational policies were made privately and according to the ordinary calculations of profitability on investment which prevail in a *laissez-faire* economy. The railway companies were business enterprises floated with private capital, and in the long run their success and survival depended upon the return they were able to give their shareholders. The paramount consideration, therefore, in the minds of the projectors and managers of Britain's nineteenth-century railway system when making decisions was a simple one: what balance could be expected between the direct private costs and private benefits of the investment?

Of course, the procedures for weighing the possible gains which alternative decisions might bring were far from simple. It was not merely a question of maximising immediate profit upon all parts of a railway as soon as it was built. Investments which would bring a doubtful, low or long-term return had to be undertaken to strengthen a company's future growth prospects; other funds had to be deliberately wasted upon 'blocking schemes' which preempted the development of important strategic areas, or upon the purchase of complementary but over-valued rail networks or urban terminus companies. Yet although formal decisions reached are recorded in the railway Board Minutes, our insight into the exact nature of the calculations which led to these decisions must continue, in most cases, to be founded upon deduction, because of their extremely confidential nature and the empirical and unsystematic way in which the calculations were made. The Victorian railway entrepreneur was guided by experience and commonsense, raised to a very high order, not by systems analysis.

25

Somewhere in the calculations, however, the indirect social losses and gains caused by railway decisions entered into consideration, even from the earliest days. This chapter attempts to analyse the changing emphasis consciously given to social costs through the nineteenth century by the railway companies and by those whom they had to consult to gain the necessary authorisation for their schemes. Yet whatever the changing weights given to indirect social costs and benefits, the search for orthodox direct monetary return on investment remained the essential feature of Victorian railway enterprise. The writings of such influential contemporaries as Herbert Spencer, Charles Dickens and the magazines *Punch*, the *Edinburgh Review* and *Fortnightly Review* cast the railways in the role of a mindless juggernaut, grinding private rights into the ground in the blind quest for profit.[1] Nowhere did this picture seem more appropriate than in the Victorian city, for it was against an urban background that the chain of indirect social costs could be seen most clearly and dramatically.

On the other hand, and here is the paradox, although British railway companies existed and operated within the normal business rules of price and profit, they were, from the beginning, granted two unusual public privileges; corporate form and the power to acquire property by compulsory purchase. The first privilege, granted by the Private Act of Parliament incorporating each railway company, exempted it from the ban upon raising capital from more than six people which had been imposed after the fraudulent company flotations associated with the 'South Sea Bubble' in 1720. As far as English manufacturing industry was concerned this prohibition remained in force until the 1860's.[2] Such a privilege immediately removed railways from the world of private partnership firms and family businesses, typical of the industrial sector in early Victorian Britain, and put them amongst the small number of concerns which had been allowed the unusual concession of joint-stock incorporation by Private Act, or Letters Patent. Nearly all of these exceptions to the 'Bubble Act' were in the field of public utilities, paving and improvement projects, canal and turnpike companies, a few Fire and Marine Insurance companies, the West India and London Dock companies and so on; all large-scale undertakings, quite beyond the means of half a dozen private individuals, and all enterprises which, it could be argued, were in the public interest.[3] The basis of their founda-

---

[1] H. Spencer, *Railway Morals and Railway Policy* (1855), C. Dickens ed., *Household Words*.

[2] H. A. Shannon, 'The Coming of General Limited Liability', *Economic History* II (1931), 267–91. In Scotland co-partneries and unincorporated companies had a different legal standing. R. H. Campbell, 'The Law and the Joint Stock Company in Scotland', *Studies in Scottish Business History* (ed. P. L. Payne, 1967), 148.

[3] B. C. Hunt, *The Development of the Business Corporation in England, 1800–1867* (Cambridge, 1936) 46–52.

tion was that they would provide services and benefits which would accrue not merely to their shareholders but would spread outwards through whole regions.

Added to this was the second privilege, of purchasing, by the compulsory procedures described elsewhere, any property which lay on their chosen line, within a generous band on either side, called the 'Limits of Deviation'. This statutory power, to which even the greatest landowners had to bow once the Private Bill had been passed, placed the railways in a position of even greater privilege than those companies which had, on account of their supposed public merit, been allowed wide powers to borrow or raise capital.

So here were two points for contact between the private commercial criteria upon which the railways operated and their involuntary social aspect; and they provided the main themes of Parliamentary legislation and enquiry in the 1830's and 1840's. Respect for property, after all, was one of the cardinal features of early Victorian society, and here was one field in which the interests of a certain section of the public were guarded with the greatest vigilance. Newspapers and Journals, M.P.s, and counsel watched this aspect of the 'public interest' very closely during the first generation of railway building. 'Novel and extraordinary powers have been given to the projectors of railroads', complained the *Morning Herald* in 1834. 'In besieged towns, or in conflagrations, demolitions have been sanctioned, but they should not be for private profit.'[4] The question which was raised was not merely one of damage but one of principle, and the type of property to be taken by compulsory powers was irrelevant, as counsel for the landowners argued, on more than one occasion. Mr. Talbot Q.C., put the matter most clearly to Serjeant Wrangham, counsel for the abortive Manchester and Southampton Railway, on 20 August 1846. 'If there were not a shade of residential injury from one end of the line to the other, and if I represented only so many lots of potato-ground, I am entitled to call upon my learned friend to make out, affirmatively, his right to violate the common law of the land; which common law says with respect to the land, as to the house, of an Englishman, it is not compulsorily to be taken from him, except upon the clearest proof of the greatest and most undeniable public necessity.'[5] Eighteen years later his words were re-echoed by *The Economist*, speaking (as the *Morning Herald* had in 1834) of schemes for scheduling land in central London. The power to take land

[4] Quoted in Thomas Hammond, *A few Cursory Remarks on Railways, showing their Beneficial Tendency* (1835), MRL, Tracts on Railways, P1163. Hammond disagreed, and asserted his conviction that 'the railway might extinguish one of the vilest nuisances in London—the ill-ventilated *culs de sac* and dens of wretchedness in the vicinity of Shoe Lane and Saffron Hill.' *Ibid.* 9.

[5] From one of the rare summing-up speeches of counsel, MRL, Tracts on Railways, 1396 h 17, 1846–55.

by compulsory procedures, it argued, could only be justified 'by public necessity as essentially national as an efficient iron-clad fleet.'[6]

In response to pressures such as these all property owners were, under Parliamentary procedure given *locus standi* to object to schemes which touched their interests directly. Standing Orders already evolved from experience with turnpikes, canals and street improvements immediately applied to railway bills, ensuring, by means of *Books of Reference, Lists of Consents and Dissents*, that no Bills involving property could be rushed through, undermining owners' rights to oppose by keeping them in ignorance.[7] Of course, the whole scale of property acquisition changed so radically as increasingly far-ranging and numerous railway schemes were authorised in the 1830's and 1840's that these defences of the public interest required substantial buttressing, by the Lords' Select Committee on Compensation to the Owners of Real Property, which considered financial losses caused by the severance of property and injury to residences in 1845, and by the Lands Clauses and Railways Clauses Consolidation Acts, which clarified common law procedures for compensation, in the same year.[8] According to these procedures any member of the public whose property was scheduled for purchase, either in whole or in part, was entitled to oppose the Bill, or to use the threat of opposition to force the railway projectors to settle with him. The use made of this right tended to vary according to the size and value of the property holding, as John Clutton, land agent and solicitor to the South Eastern Railway Company, made clear in his evidence:[9]

'It is only Parties who have some influence in opposing railway companies that are settled with before the passing of the Bill.'

'Some means of giving you trouble in the Committee?—Yes. With small proprietors, and I would class with them all the middle men, the costs of a petition to Parliament are so heavy that they are afraid of it.'

If this led to the exaction of inflated prices, such as those encountered by the Eastern Counties railway company, which 'paid more smartly than any other company for land', the Lords' Committee concluded that the additional charge was a legitimate price for the property owners to exact.[10] 'In the case of the Railways, though the public may be considered ultimately the gainers, the immediate motive to their construction is the Interest of the Speculators, who have no Right to complain of being obliged to purchase at a somewhat higher Rate, the Means of carrying on their Speculation.'[11]

[6] *The Economist*, 13 February 1864, 198.

[7] H. S. Cobb, 'Sources for Economic History amongst the Parliamentary Records in the House of Lords Record Office', *Ec.HR*, XIX (1966), 161–2.

[8] H. C., 1845 (420) X. 8 Vic. c. 18, and 8 Vic. c. 20.

[9] H. C., 1845 (220) X, 29 May, QQ. 140–1.

[10] *Loc. cit*. QQ. 50, 77.

[11] *Ibid*. Report.

The other main public consideration which preoccupied the legislature was that of providing reasonable information to prevent repetition of the large scale swindling which had accompanied public forms of enterprise on previous occasions. After all, the railway shareholders (or 'proprietors' as they were called in the thirties and forties) *were* members of the public, entitled to protection. At first, in the early thirties, the investors were principally local businessmen, Quaker financiers, country solicitors, and a hard core of Lancashire speculators known as 'the Liverpool Party', who invested not merely in railways in Lancashire but also in East Anglia and from London to Southampton.[12] They were a relatively small group of men used to putting their money out at risk, and they were capable of taking care of themselves without any protective surveillance from the State.

In the investment booms of 1837 and 1846, however, the whole character of the investing class changed. An entirely new range of small shareholders pressed forward to offer their savings, or even the working capital from their businesses. In the words of James Morrison, M.P., one of the most effective early critics of railway speculation, 'There is not a nook or cranny throughout the land into which it has not found an entrance. Allured by the prospect of immense gains and rapid fortunes, all classes have rushed eagerly into railroad speculation. The manufacturers and traders starve their businesses that they might buy shares.'[13] Because of the relatively high unit cost of early railway shares, it can be assumed that the majority, if not all of this numerous group were from the middle class, were politically enfranchised, and therefore proportionately influential in making their disappointment felt when they saw their investments more than halved in value in 1846 and 1847.[14] Their resentment was increased by the knowledge that a great part of their loss could be assigned not to legitimate business miscalculations but to the sharp practices listed by Lewin, Francis and others—misleading prospectuses, payments of dividends out of capital, rigged Board Meetings, accounts 'audited by daring amateurs'.[15] Perhaps the fault lay ultimately, as *The Economist* suggested, with the 'undue desire for wealth which pervades the middle classes—the classes which have taken a lead in forming and managing the railways. We are individually

[12] H. G. Lewin, *Early British Railways, 1801–1844* (1925), 71. J. H. Clapham, *Economic History of Modern Britain* (2nd edit 1930), I, 386–7. R. C. O. Matthews, *A Study in Trade-Cycle History: Economic Fluctuations in Great Britain, 1833–42* (1954), 110.

[13] James Morrison, *The Influence of English Railway Legislation on Trade and Industry* (1848), 5.

[14] C. N. Ward Perkins, 'The Commercial Crisis of 1947', *Readings in Business Cycles and National Income* (ed. A. H. Hansen and R. V. Clemence, 1853), 12–16.

[15] H. G. Lewin, *The Railway Mania and its aftermath, 1845–1852* (1936); J. Francis, *History of the English Railway* (1851). The phrase quoted is from John Hollingshead, *Ways of Life* (1861), 243.

and collectively too much in a hurry to get rich. We would rather get it honestly if we can, but we must get it somehow or other.'[16] Yet the game of charlatans and dupes had undoubtedly been made easier by the apparent security with which Parliamentary sanction appeared to invest each scheme. 'It was specially sanctioned too by Parliament' complained *The Economist*, 'and spoken of with much honour by the highest men in the land. When men of that class took up the project the bulk of the community thought themselves perfectly safe.'[17]

From 1836 onwards, therefore, Standing Orders began to lay down rules to protect the general investing public. The engineering difficulties, the number of passengers and income expected, the estimates of cost, were all subjected to closer scrutiny, by the first twenty Standing Orders for railway bills, to make sure that the line had at least a reasonable prospect of success; and it was not unknown for some of the less well presented schemes to fail at the Standing Orders stage, without even reaching a Select Committee.[18] Of course, ways round the Standing Orders could be found by ingenious and experienced council. The line had to be plausible rather than viable, and so further attention was given by a series of Railway Acts Enactments Committees in the late forties to attempt to plug these loopholes, and ensure that railways to which Parliament gave countenance were respectable, at least at their inception.[19]

One might say, then, that the Government was aware, at an early date, of the interests of the two sections of the public whose property and purses were most directly affected; the owners of land scheduled for purchase and the gullible small investors. Arrangements to scrutinise railway schemes, by means of Standing Orders and, for a time, reports by the Board of Trade, would not merely safeguard the interests of property owners and investors, but would also, it was believed, benefit the general public indirectly by eliminating extravagant schemes. 'It must be assumed', ran one such report, in 1847, that the public are directly or indirectly affected by any loss incurred by an unnecessary expenditure either of labour or material.'[20] But such a general concern

---

[16] *The Economist*, 1854, 1149.

[17] *Ibid.* 1849, 1185.

[18] O.C. Williams, *The Historical Development of Private Bill Procedure and Standing Orders in the House of Commons* (1948), I, 61–3. Williams gives 1836 as the key year, in which 57 railway bills accumulated, and M.P.s were asked to authorise second readings without adequate information.

[19] H.C., 1846 (687) XIV, S.C. on Railway Acts and Enactments. H.C., 1847–8, XVI, S.C. on Railway Bills.

[20] H.C., 1847 (461), Report of Commissioners on Railways on the Merits of two Competing Railways between Harwich and the Metropolis, 3 June, p. 2.

for the public interest is a far cry from the systematic calculation of social costs and benefits.

In the 1830's and 1840's the difficulty of extending the range of calculation further was accentuated by the novel and widespread nature of the repercussions set up by railway building. Like many other great innovatory forces it destroyed as well as created capital. If social costs were to be measured, what compensation should be offered, for example, to the innkeeper 'measuring the time he must go into the Gazette', with his 'empty yard, deserted rooms, pining chambermaids and misanthropic ostlers'?[21] And if the innkeeper was entitled to consideration, what about the coach-owner or the Turnpike Trustees, who likewise were called upon to pay part of the cost of the railway programme? Even an econometrician equipped with twentieth-century statistics would find it difficult to trace and measure the ripples which spread outwards through the economy.

As far as the direct competitors were concerned—the Turnpike Trustees and Canal Companies—the possible injury and financial loss they might suffer was acknowledged by allowing them *locus standi* to oppose any railway bill.[22] Moreover, as the railway network grew there were few routes which were not contested between rival simultaneous schemes, or by companies already established. These were also given the right to object, and draw attention to the possible social costs the proposed schemes might incur; and, in fact, the greatest opposition to each railway bill came from other railway companies. It was fondly hoped that just as the public interest would be assured by competitive management of fares and services, so the wider interest of the public affected by railway promotion and construction would be guarded by the Private Bill procedure.

The Speaker's Counsel, Mr. Rickards, summed up the position very clearly for the House of Commons' Committee on Procedure. 'It is only through the medium of opponents, according to the mode in which private legislation is carried on, that the public are heard at all against the Bills. . . . The preamble states, in every Bill, that it is expedient for the public interest that such and such works should be done; the opponents controvert this, and they put themselves in the shoes of the public and allege all the public objections they can.'[23] The rival companies left no stone unturned to have any new Bill which seemed to threaten their interests thrown out. 'The most plausible and forceful means they can devise for doing that is to take up the cause of the public, and they do that.'

This procedure meant, however, that the raising of public issues

[21] Charles Knight, *London* (1841), 313.
[22] O. C. Williams, *op. cit.* II, p. IX.
[23] H.C., 1865 (393), QQ. 1052-3.

depended upon the fluke of opposition.[24] No one took up the public cause from public motives alone, and if they did they would only have *locus standi* if they were affected directly themselves. Even the Chambers of Commerce had to wage a long campaign into the 1880's before they were allowed the right to any hearing: and whilst Municipal Corporations could be heard, it was only with reference to their corporate property, and not as general defenders of the public interest; although the right to appear before the Select Committee did give their counsel opportunity to raise wider issues.[25]

Such fortuitous representation of the public interest may at first sight seem to be far removed from the detailed statistical calculations of the secondary costs and indirect benefits of particular schemes recently carried out by C. D. Foster, M. E. Beesley, and others.[26] But it can be shown that as the wide urban repercussions of railway investment became apparent, there were increasing attempts, particularly in London, where the incidental social costs of railway building were early and hypertrophied, to accumulate the evidence necessary to understand and measure such indirect gains and losses as, for example, the influence of urban rail schemes upon street improvement plans, upon the speed and congestion of road traffic, upon the amount and cost of carting within a city, upon the health and living conditions of the poorer classes, and upon the siting of new residential housing.

The techniques used for measurements were rudimentary, and the final weighting was a qualitative rather than a quantitative assessment, but they provide the key to the enormously important decisions taken concerning metropolitan thoroughfares, improvements and property, and explain the exclusion of railways from central London. To this extent they meet R. N. McKean's definition of a cost benefit study as 'policy-oriented economic analysis'. 'Typically their preparation is an extremely complicated and time-consuming task,' writes McKean, 'though sometimes it should be mentioned, extremely valuable analyses consist of simple, back-of-the-envelope-calculations.'[27] This was the

[24] O. C. Williams, *op. cit.* I, 218–21.

[25] The right to appear without proof that they were aggrieved was granted to Chambers of Commerce by the Railway and Canal Traffic Act, 1888, 51 & 2 Vic. c.25, sec. 7. For a sample of the campaign see Birmingham Chamber of Commerce Papers (BRL L62.52), Letter from C. of Commerce to Pres. of Bd. of Trade (i.e. Joseph Chamberlain), 23 October 1880. Their hearing, and that of municipal corporations, took place before the Railway Commissioners and not the Parliamentary Select Committees, unless their property was affected. W. Hodges, *Law of Railways* (1888), I, 433–4.

[26] C. D. Foster and M. E. Beesley, 'Estimating the Social Benefit of Constructing an underground Railway in London', *Journal of the Royal Statistical Society*, 126 (1963,) 46–78. Nathaniel Lichfield, 'Cost-Benefit Analysis in Plan Evaluation', *Town Planning Review* XXXV (1964), 159–69.

[27] Roland N. McKean, 'Cost Benefit Analysis and British Defence Expenditure', *Scottish Journal of Political Economy*, X (1963), 20.

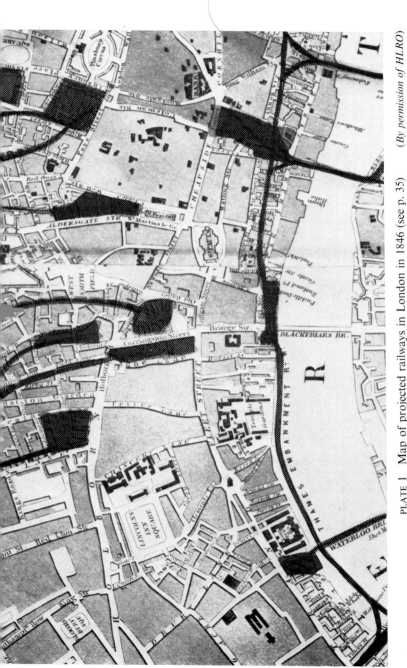

PLATE 1 Map of projected railways in London in 1846 (see p. 35)   (By permission of HLRO)

PLATE 2   A Metropolitan line Workmen's Train (see p. 98)

type of calculation initially laid before the policy makers by James Pennethorne, Charles Pearson, J. H. Stevens, J. W. Bazalgette, and others.

2. *Criteria used for early improvement schemes*

Although it was the impact of railways which forced the first serious essays at calculating the indirect benefits and costs of schemes involving large changes in urban land use, tentative enquiries which pointed the way had been conducted as early as the mid-thirties by a series of Select Committees of the House of Commons on Metropolitan Improvements.[28] Their remit was a general one, to consider all schemes for improving the access and increasing the amenity of London, Southwark and Westminster. No fewer than 15 fine new streets were proposed to them, and are shown in their plans: from Oxford Street to St. Giles, from the Bank and Newgate Street to the G.P.O., and etc. Their attention was also directed particularly by the Commons' resolution which appointed them, to the problem of purchasing the Waterloo and Southwark bridges from their proprietors and throwing them open free of toll. All the schemes were praiseworthy, and it soon became evident that the major questions to be solved were—How was the money to be raised and who would principally benefit from the improvements? Schemes for a lottery were considered and dismissed, and the increase of the Coal Tax, levied by the Corporation of London upon coal imported by sea, was hit upon as the best method of finance. The coal tax only cost £250 per year to collect, and an increase of 6d per ton would bring in the annual amount necessary to service a loan for £1,500,000 to cover the cost of the proposed improvements.[29]

The second problem facing the committee was that of deciding whether those paying the tax increase would all benefit equally from the improvement. The suggestion that coal merchants might absorb the 6d a ton out of their profits, (that they could easily absorb 2s 6d if necessary), was emphatically rejected by William Horne, Secretary and Treasurer to their Society.[30] Why should the Coal Merchants as a class pay for London's improvement? The tax would be handed on. Since the average member of the labouring classes used two tons of coal per year he would be indirectly taxed at 1s per year.[31] For those using the Southwark and Waterloo Bridges, the saving on toll at 1d per foot-passenger would repay their tax in a couple of weeks. But large numbers

[28] H.C., 1836 (517) XX, S.C. on Metropolis Improvements. Other enquiries and reports followed; 1837–8 (418, 661) XVI, 1839 (136) XIII, 1840 (410, 485) XII, and a further six reports in 1844–6.
[29] H.C., 1836 (517) XX, Q.80.
[30] *Ibid*. Report, pp. III, IV.
[31] *Ibid*. Q.274.

lived in areas where it was unlikely that they would make even twelve crossings, and there was evidence, moreover, that the numbers who would *directly* benefit were very small, simply because they already avoided the toll by using the public Westminster and Blackfriars bridges. The receipts at Waterloo Bridge were a disappointing 1% on the £1,000,000 capital expended—£12,500 a year less expenses. Most of the daily traffic consisted of women crossing over between 5 and 7 a.m. carrying 8 or 10 baskets of dinners; not a single stage or omnibus used Waterloo bridge.[32] The primary beneficiaries would be those who *would* find it convenient to use the bridge if the toll were removed. 'It would be not only a benefit in point of convenience but a real benefit to the poorer and labouring classes?—Yes, it would be a saving either of time or money, which would be the same thing.'[33] In the estimation of Mr. William Routh, a member of the Corporation, the bridge and street improvements together would cut down some journeys from 60 minutes to 25 minutes.[34] Others pointed also to the very considerable benefit which would be felt, probably a 30% increase in value, by the proprietors of houses on the Waterloo Bridge road.[35]

Already, by 1836, one can see the stirrings of awareness that schemes of improvement might yield their greatest benefit indirectly; and although there was nothing approaching a systematic study of costs and benefits, such statistics as were presented in evidence received a weight in the Report which was out of proportion to their simple character. By the time the Royal Commission on the Improvement of the Metropolis presented its Report, in 1842, the great indirect benefits of improved or newly-opened lines of communication were readily admitted.[36]

'This description of improvement is, perhaps, at the same time the most useful and the most difficult. It necessarily involves the invasion of private rights, and often, to a great extent, of private comforts, by the compulsory acquisition of property for which the pecuniary indemnities may not always be an adequate compensation. It also unavoidably requires some outlay of the public money. But recent experience has fully demonstrated how extensive have been the advantages of such changes to the community in general, and how much exceeding the sacrifices made to obtain them.'

'To such a city as London, with its immense wealth, its commercial circulation, its retail traffic, its mechanical industry, and its manufactures, far surpassing in these particulars every other capital in Europe, all such increased facilities for social and commercial intercourse must be matter of interest and advantage to every portion of its dense and varied population.'

[32] *Ibid.* QQ. 443–86.
[33] *Ibid.* Q.136.
[34] *Ibid.* QQ. 132–3.
[35] *Ibid.* Q.516. Similar calculations were carried out later in the nineteenth century when road tolls were removed. Mark Searle, *Turnpikes and Toll Bars* (n.d.), II, 685.
[36] H.C., 1844 (15) XV, R.C. on Metropolis Improvements, Report, p. IV.

It is evident, in fact, from the early Victorian scrutinies of Improvement Schemes, that whilst substantial agreement on policy could be reached without too great a difficulty, the implementing of schemes whose social benefit was beyond dispute tended to flag for want of a strong incentive towards their completion, such as that which the price and profit mechanism provided for the railways' schemes of urban reconstruction and demolition. Whatever the criticisms one might make of them, the urban railway projects had, in comparison with municipal improvement schemes, the pre-eminent merit of prompt execution. They were impelled by one of the most powerful driving forces in early Victorian society—the prospect of personal gain, which animated engineers, counsel, directors, landowners and constructors. If this urgency could be tempered with a sense of duty, the railway companies, it became clear in the 1840's, could carry out large works of public merit with far more speed and address than any existing local authorities or public bodies.

3. *Analysing costs and benefits in the 1840's*

The opportunity to harness the energy of railway schemes to social purposes came as early as 1846 in London where, at the height of railway mania, no fewer than nineteen urban lines and termini were projected; and if sanctioned they would, as the map (Plate 1) shows, have completely altered the topography and character of west and central London, of Southwark and Lambeth. London was the seat of Government and, as the largest city in the Western world, demonstrated on a magnified scale the social consequences of railways in great towns. Not even the most *laissez-faire* of administrations could sit back and allow the wholesale demolition and severance of urban property and the intersection of crowded thoroughfares which the schemes, if authorised piecemeal, would involve. The Metropolis would literally have been cut to pieces.

So the Select Committee procedure, by which each bill was considered separately on its own merits, was on this occasion reinforced by a Royal Commission with powers to invite evidence from a wide range of public bodies which normally would have had no *locus standi*; the Corporation of London, certain Parish bodies, the Official Referees of Metropolitan Buildings, the Surveyor of Pavements and Sewers, the Commissioners of Her Majesty's Woods and Forests, the Improvement Committee, and various independent valuers and would-be planners.[37] Also called before the Commission were the urban carriers and omnibus operators, and the railway projectors, with their retinue of traffic managers, solicitors, engineers and land-agents. But though the voice of self-

[37] H.C., 1846, XVII, R.C. on Metropolis Railway Termini.

interest was as articulate and trumpet-tongued as ever, there were, at least, other dissenting voices to be heard for the first time.

'It appears to me too much to be borne with' said one witness, to whom the Commissioners paid particular attention, 'that lines coming only eight or nine miles are to cut up the suburbs and the town by their separate rails and termini, and have liberty to take down property; in fact to advance their own prospects of benefit, and annoy the public beyond their value. It strikes me we have been a little railway mad, as if everything was to give way to railways: there is an immense mass of the public to be considered, hundreds and thousands, who have nothing to do with railways, and never will have; they want to get about, and are entitled to that consideration which is necessary for an increasing population.'[38]

The witness who made these remarks was an independent valuer and surveyor, Mr. J. W. Higgins, whose views and recommendations can be seen almost exactly reflected in the Report the Commissioners finally agreed upon. He was speaking to them on the subject of *The Sacrifice of Property*, the second of the Commission's heads of consideration, and a subject upon which evidence was also heard from William Hosking, one of the official Referees of Metropolitan Buildings, James Pennethorne, architect to H. M. Woods and Forests (a body which dealt with urban affairs in spite of its bucolic title), and Charles Pearson, solicitor to the Corporation of London. These men, in particular, presented more detailed evidence on urban affairs than had ever been submitted previously to a policy-making body.

The exact effects of demolition and rebuilding upon the rents of neighbouring areas, were subjected to crude measurement. 'I have in my hand a report made to me', stated Pearson, 'by a gentleman appointed for the purpose, who has visited all the neighbourhoods where these improvements have taken place. He has gone from street to street, and from house to house, to ascertain what effect has been produced upon the condition of the poor by these improvements. He finds the rents of the wretched hovels of the poor increased 10, 15, 20 and 25 per cent in all the surrounding districts where these improvements have taken place, and that the weekly rents of their rooms have generally increased also.'[39]

The returns of these particulars were available for the Commissioners to study, as was the detailed transcript of evidence by William Hosking upon the comparative effects of railways in cuttings or on viaducts upon the value of adjacent property.[40] James Pennethorne and William Higgins also examined in detail the evidence relating to two of the social

[38] *Ibid.* Q.2200.
[39] *Ibid.* Q.2351.
[40] *Ibid.* QQ.2621–33.

benefits most frequently claimed on behalf of the railways, *viz.*, that they let in light and air by providing open spaces and air courses through densely crowded and noisome areas of working class housing, and that they improved the drainage.[41]

Higgins also raised the question of the loss of custom which extensive demolition involved for small traders on the fringe of the area marked for purchase, 'especially trades of a sound character, and rooted as it were, to a spot, no reasonable compensation does pay them. Many, in a small way, waste the few pounds or hundreds they receive. With regard to parties on the opposite side of the street, or in the neighbourhood, whose property is not touched, they do not get paid, and their trade is damaged to a great extent by sweeping away their customers.'[42]

Other evidence was led, particularly by Pearson, which raised the most important social question of all. What happened to the poor who were displaced by railway rebuilding? 'A poor man is chained to the spot; he has not the leisure to walk, and he has not the money to ride. They are crowded together still more, they are pressed together more densely in a similar description of houses to those which they formerly inhabited', Pearson concluded, after an extremely lengthy examination.[43] Higgins had even gone to the lengths of conducting, somewhat amateurishly, an enquiry of his own to discover what happened to those who were displaced.[44] Higgins' and Pearson's evidence was supported by the Rev. T. Gibson, incumbent of St. Matthew, Bethnal Green, who gave detailed particulars about the streets to which the refugees from East End railway schemes had moved.[45]

In addition to drawing this large issue to the attention of the Commissioners, witnesses also put forward for consideration, at various times, the side effects of vibration, particularly upon the watchmakers and other craft trades in the land traversed by the Eastern Counties railway; the effects of tunnelling upon houses; of smoke, sparks and noise; of the loss of intercommunication caused by embanked or viaduct railways 'enclosing the area as it were with a brick wall'; and the effects of the railways' arrival in an area upon the parish rates.[46]

Another major topic opened for discussion was that of the comparative social merits of the alternative courses of building a railway or of building a road through a slum area. The main advocate for road improvements was James Pennethorne who was called back to elaborate

[41] *Ibid.* QQ.708–30 (Pennethorne), QQ.2187–93 (Higgins).
[42] *Ibid.* Q.2185.
[43] *Ibid.* Q.2355. Pearson was recalled to give evidence a second time and answered over a hundred questions, sometimes at great length. The answer to Q.2355 runs to 1500 words, for example.
[44] *Ibid.* QQ. 2207–18.
[45] *Ibid.* QQ.957–67.
[46] *Ibid.* QQ.803; 1218–26;818–19; 2807–10 and App. 1, p. 249 *et seq.*; 3029, 3100.

his views. In particular, he was asked to be specific about the contribution to public improvements which might reasonably be expected of the railway companies. 'If they consider it for their advantage to have good access and good streets to their termini it must be to their advantage to contribute towards making them.' A levy of £2,000,000 should, therefore, be made, Pennethorne asserted; but he stumbled over the difficult question of how much each individual railway company should be required to contribute to make up this sum. 'I have not considered the subject, nor are there any data upon which I could form an opinion. It would be necessary to have exactly where the termini are to be, what traffic there would be likely to be, and how far they are likely to be benefited by the new streets formed.'[47] Nevertheless, in spite of these practical difficulties, the idea of combining terminus building with street improvement had a strong appeal; and railway projectors were obviously aware of the weight attached to it by the Commissioners. 'There is scarcely one amongst the schemes which we have before us of which the Promoters have not expressed their intention to combine, more or less with their own works and at their own expense, the improvement of existing or the formation of new thoroughfares for the benefit of the public.'[48]

Indeed there can be no doubt, in view of the mass of evidence heard by the Commissioners upon the head of *The Sacrifice of Property* alone, that the range of topics raised in the course of their enquiry was wide enough to delineate clearly the nature of the choice before them. On the one hand, if they allowed the wholesale invasion of Central London presently intended they would 'fill in an area already crowded beyond endurance'; on the other, if they left the termini too far out they would block up the thoroughfares with 'leviathan waggons and vans sometimes creeping about the streets, having a few articles at the bottoms of the waggons with their names "carriers by railway" displayed upon the vehicle, as if by way of advertisement; at other times . . . with loads overhanging on each side the foot-pavement of the narrow streets and lanes through which they pass.'[49]

The other three heads of consideration for the Commissioners, *As to the convenience and benefit of the Public, As to the Interruption of important Thoroughfares,* and *As to interference with Plans of Improvement already suggested,* enlarged the consideration of social costs still further. On the last mentioned—the effect of the railways upon further improvement—the evidence of Pennethorne, Richard Jones, of the Improvement Committee, and Richard Kelsey, the Surveyor of Pavements and Sewers, convinced the Commissioners of the serious impedi-

[47] *Ibid.* QQ.731–49, 3047–72. Quotations are from Q.3366 and Q.3372.
[48] *Ibid.* Report, p. 7.
[49] *Ibid.* Q.2192 (Higgins); App. 23, p. 283 (Pearson).

ment to improvement already given by the Blackwall and the Eastern Counties railways, and of the likelihood that the railway projects under consideration would cause 'the intersection of any future thoroughfare, East and West, which may be opened to the north of Holborn, and the want of which, as an accommodation to the traffic of the Metropolis, is sensibly felt.'[50]

In the course of examination upon this and the other two heads of enquiry a great deal of new statistical information was presented relating to the relative direct and indirect costs of urban railway schemes. What, for example, would be their effect upon surface traffic? Upon the answer to that question might turn the whole issue of social benefits; and detailed statements were made by W. J. Chaplin, B. W. Horne, Joseph Baxendale and Joseph Hayward, to supplement the data from official sources. Of course Chaplin and Horne, and Pickfords (represented by Baxendale and Hayward), as the largest carriers in the country, might be expected to show a strong bias against railway intrusion, but this does not appear to have been their attitude for two reasons. First, Chaplin was also Chairman of the London and South Western railway company, and Baxendale Chairman of the South Eastern; Benjamin Horne was likewise a large shareholder in several railway companies and claimed, in so many words, that this offset his partiality as a manager in the carrying trade.[51] In the second place they seemed to entertain genuine misgivings as to the possible effects upon traffic circulation of the projected central termini, and to be anxious to accumulate and lay before the Commissioners data bearing upon the subject.

The key to their anxiety can be seen in Joseph Hayward's answer to the question. 'Would the loss of time by the obstruction of the streets be perhaps quite equivalent to the expected gain from bringing the station so far into the metropolis?—It would be more. Our average time of waiting at all the stations except the Great Western (where it is longer) and the London and Birmingham (where we have our own warehouse and work as we like) is two hours; now we can hire a horse and cart at 1s 3d per hour, that is equal to travelling two miles, so that we might as well have the station two miles further off.'[52] Far more to the point would be to cut down the two hours queuing of waggons at the existing termini instead of further congesting the streets by debouching additional traffic into the centre from the projected new stations. 'The Railway Companies generally were too diffident in providing accommodation at their stations,' claimed Baxendale. 'The limited space in

[50] Ibid. QQ.705–34 (Pennethorne); 1202–5 (Jones); 2247–82 (Kelsey); Report, p. 9.
[51] Ibid. QQ.1541–52 (Chaplin), QQ.542–600 (Baxendale), QQ.441–6 (Horne).
[52] Ibid. Q.1411.

which the stations are confined will put an extinguisher upon them altogether.'[53]

A great deal of further evidence, running to many pages, was delivered on the subject of alternative costs and overall journey times by rail and road, both for goods and for passengers. Horne, in particular, presented extremely exact information, specially gathered over a period of a month, to show the direction and numbers of cab and omnibus passengers. From this it was possible to deduce the relative expenditure of time and money which passenger journeys currently involved, and *would* involve if the London and Birmingham terminus were carried down to the proposed site at Farringdon Street.[54] Because of the difficulty of evaluating the time saved—a problem which contemporary writers on cost-benefit analysis have described as 'the hardest nut to crack'—the commonsense assumption was made that delays and uncertainties in cross-town travel caused, for the business classes, appointment books which erred on the side of conservatism, and cut down their total number of business engagements per day, by causing them to assume that all essential engagements would be subjected to the maximum delay.[55] The effect was viewed not in terms of individual time lost, but in terms of marginal transactions forgone.

Horne also furnished the Commissioners with the numbers of interstation passengers by omnibus and by cab, and raised the public question of the traffic congestion caused by the alternative modes of transport, using the modern criterion of assessing the road space occupied. Since cabs took, on the average, a load of one and a half passengers, eight, or even ten, would be needed to carry the number which could leave by one omnibus. The omnibus traffic into the City and West End from Nine Elms and Paddington was large, from Euston much smaller, from London Bridge almost non-existent; those who did not walk from the more central stations preferring to cab it and pay a shilling instead of the 6d omnibus fare, 'so that as they are distributed these passengers occupy more space.'[56] In other words, there was a marginal distance for termini beyond which omnibus feeder services became much more greatly patronised.

Horne's interest in this matter, as an omnibus proprietor, was fairly transparent, but the point he had raised remained a valid one, and was taken further still by Richard Kelsey, Surveyor of Pavements to the City of London. Was it in the public interest, given the extremely crowded conditions prevailing in Cheapside, Cornhill, Ludgate Hill,

[53] *Ibid.* Q.546.
[54] *Ibid.* QQ.501–5.
[55] *Ibid.* Q.1541; A. R. Prest and R. Turvey, 'Cost-Benefit Analysis; a Survey', *Economic Journal*, LXXV (1965), 683–735.
[56] H.C., 1846, XVII, QQ.494–8.

Fleet Street and Charing Cross, that people should move by omnibus, or occupy eight times as much road space by resorting to cabs and private carriages? Then again, as Richard Jones of the Improvement Committee pointed out, when some of the thoroughfares required only a little extra traffic to flow into them at an awkward spot to cause a complete choke or stoppage, was it wise to give railway companies the power to opt for mere fragments of street widening, and spaces for cabstands on their private ground, as their sole contribution to easing the traffic problem they created? Was it desirable, moreover, asked William Hosking, that London's thoroughfares should be abandoned to the through traffic generated by stations situated in the heart of the town and accessible only by its leading streets? Apart from the unnecessary crowding and uncertainty in the timing of journeys this caused, the streets' trading and shopping functions would be impaired if they were 'inconveniently and unnecessarily used for the purposes of the railways, independently of their more proper uses.'[57]

In spite of the wide range, the conscientious detail and the unexpectedly modern nature of many of the topics drawn to the Commissioners' attention, it cannot be denied that these early attempts to measure social costs and benefits were extremely tentative. There were obvious gaps in the information in two major respects, without which properly calculated decisions were impossible. Neither the Commissioners nor their witnesses were properly informed about the volume and speed of the traffic flow, or the saving or loss of time which alternative schemes might involve; and this was one of the gaps in knowledge which later inquiries attempted to fill. Nor were they supplied by the railway companies with the essential figures for the costs and volumes of passenger traffic which the projected extensions into London would involve.

As a result it was possible for Mr. Arthur Wightman, traffic superintendent of the Blackwall Railway, to rebut Pennethorne's evidence concerning the expensive extension through the densely populated area around Fenchurch Street. 'It is possible', Pennethorne had alleged, 'that if the Blackwall Railway Company instead of going to the expense of extending their railway across the City, had only brought up the property and formed a new street to their terminus in the Minories it might have paid them better.' By analogy, he suggested, the same argument applied to the Eastern Counties' projected advance to Finsbury Square.[58] In answer, Wightman disclosed that the cost of the extension had been, in fact, £250,000 for the 400 yards encroachment through the densely built East End, and for the new station site. To offset this cost, however, passenger traffic had increased by 50% in three years. Fares had not

[57] *Ibid.* QQ.2260–1, 2277 (Kelsey); QQ.1157–66 (Jones); QQ.2603–6 (Hosking).
[58] *Ibid.* Q.764.

been changed, so what had produced the rapid growth of traffic was 'the great advantage of fast and rapid transit' as near the centre of London as possible. In the opinion of the railway company, 'the whole of that increase is attributed to the extension.' William Tite, the engineer, who had valued the Blackwall railway added his support. 'The whole cost a million, and it was better to spend the million to run to Fenchurch Street, than to spend £750,000 and stop at the Minories. I am sure that neither the Directors nor any one else ever regretted it.' [59]

Tite and Wightman might possibly have been right. Without the relevant figures it was rather difficult to argue with them. The solution to the problem adopted by the Commissioners is described in their *Report*.

'It must be observed, however, that *Traffic Tables*, the usual data by which the demand for railway accommodation, and the convenience which it will bestow upon the public, are estimated, have throughout our investigation been very imperfectly furnished to us. We do not mention this as a matter of reproach to the promoters of the schemes which have been brought under our consideration, for it is manifestly impossible to calculate the direction and extent of the traffic which takes place to and from the different parts of London and its suburbs, with the accuracy which is expected in dealing with ordinary lines of railway; but because the want of such evidence has compelled us to found our conclusions rather upon the judgment of persons of experience and upon our own observation, than upon numerical returns.

'We have not considered it necessary to determine whether the expense which will be incurred by the companies in carrying their lines far into the town is likely to be compensated to them by increased profits, although we see great reason for doubting it.'

In spite of the reluctance or inability of the railway companies to present them with a break-down of traffic figures the Commissioners felt able to conclude that 'the advantage to the public of such accommodation as would be afforded to them by bringing the railway stations further into the City appear to us exaggerated.'[60]

This unfavourable ruling on the first head of consideration, *As to the convenience and benefit of the Public*, was a foretaste of the decisions on later counts. On the second head, *As to the sacrifice of Property*, they found it difficult, in view of the evidence of appreciation of rents and central land values, to reach an unfavourable conclusion. 'Although in most cases injurious, it is not necessarily and invariably so'. On the third

---

[59] *Ibid.* Q.1123 (Wightman); QQ.387–8 (Tite). George Hudson showed a similar attitude towards the projected Eastern Counties extension. 'In a question of this kind a couple of hundred thousand pounds never weigh against what we consider a good and convenient access; it is spread over capital of a very large amount.' Q.2684.

[60] *Ibid.* Report, pp. 5, 7.

head, *As to the Interruption of important Thoroughfares*, the Commissioners did not find that the enlargements proposed, 'and general accommodation which they offer to the public is, in any case, commensurate with the inconvenience which might be expected to result from the extension of their scheme'. On the fourth heading, *As to interference with plans of Improvement already suggested*, they concluded, 'Whether the course which railways might take in passing through the Town would be fatal to the future carrying out of any improvement, would at present depend mainly upon the pleasure and convenience of the respective companies. But this is a state of things which cannot, we humbly submit, in safety continue.'[61]

However fragmentary and inadequate the data, therefore, the final result of the Commissioners' deliberation upon the evidence on social costs presented to them by spokesmen of the public, and after the production 'of such Books, Documents, Papers and Returns, as have appeared to us calculated to assist our researches', represented a complete rout for the railway interest. Of the 19 schemes 17 were rejected and only conditional assent given to the other two, both of them extensions south of the river. 'Under no circumstances', concluded the Commission, 'should the thoroughfares of the metropolis and the property and comforts of its inhabitants be surrendered to separate schemes brought forward at different times and without reference to each other.'[62]

These conditions were later eroded in the 1850's and early 1860's, and substantial exceptions were made to the *veto* imposed by Lord Canning and the other Commissioners; but although the later railway encroachments were extensive, the first battle for London in 1846 had not been an illusory victory. Sweeping though the changes finally appear by the late sixties, they were still not as drastic as those projected for the one year 1846, when the schemes, in the words of one of the witnesses, 'appear to require as much space as almost to take the whole City. . . . If you took a sponge and sponged out the whole of the City, leaving St. Paul's standing in the midst, I think you would have accommodation for carrying on your traffic.'[63]

Almost two decades were gained, in fact, and although it is easy to telescope mid-nineteenth century dates mentally, the seventeen years between 1846 and 1863, when the next great railway intrusions were scheduled, gave the legislature and newly formed public bodies the opportunity to begin to come to grips with a phenomenon which produced so many novel and unanticipated effects.

---

[61] *Ibid.* Report, pp. 7–9.
[62] *Ibid.* Report, p. 21.
[63] *Ibid.* Q.589.

4. *Further data in the 1850's*

Because it was both unusually early and showed a remarkable and detailed concern for the public interest, the *Evidence* and *Report* of the Royal Commission of 1846 has been described in some detail. Clearly, it would be impossible, for reasons of space, to give an equally full account of each further step towards evolving techniques for understanding the complex economic and social issues which railway communication raised in Victorian London. But there would certainly be no shortage of material with which to illustrate similar studies for 1854–5, 1863, 1864, 1872, 1884, 1895, and 1902. Each decade after 1846 brought the problems of analysing and weighing the problems of railway costs and benefits before a new Select Committee or Royal Commission; and with each decade the techniques of measurement became less primitive and inaccurate.

The evidence of Charles Pearson, of John Pennethorne (now surveyor for the new Board of Works), of Joseph Paxton, and of J. H. Stevens (the surveyor for the Western Division of the City) laid before the Commons' Select Committee on Metropolitan Communications of 1854–5 a new range of subject matter, substantially filling out the data presented earlier and raising a number of secondary benefits and costs for consideration.[64]

Amongst these was the particularised discussion of savings improved urban rail facilities might bring to the different consumer markets in London, from perishable foodstuffs to coal, and to London manufacturers by reducing trans-shipment of goods during the actual process of manufacture; the propriety of throwing all the cost of an improved communications network upon the present generation, and the means by which the costs could be postponed or amortised; the question of whether capital expenditure might be reduced by combining public improvements 'such as economising the waste spaces of the river, or opening new streets through poor neighbourhoods' with newly sanctioned urban railways; the exact percentages purely commercial undertakings might be expected to return on capital, compared with the percentage return on a semi-public scheme (like Paxton's project for a £34,000,000 government-sponsored 'Girdle Railway and Boulevard'), or the percentage loss on capital a strictly public improvement like New Cannon Street had incurred.[65]

The far greater sophistication and accuracy of the techniques of measurement is apparent, even in the space of eight years. Pearson had appointed traffic-takers 'at all the principal entrances to the city of

[64] H.C., 1854–5, X, S.C. on Metropolitan Communications.

[65] *Ibid.* QQ.1231–51 (Stevens); QQ.1442–78 (Pennethorne); Report, p. IV; QQ.61–4 (Tite), 1029–32 (Gisborne), 762–93 (Paxton), 502–5 (Hall).

London, to take their station from eight o'clock in the morning till eight o'clock at night. I had relays of them, so as to assure myself of tolerable accuracy.' The estimates were supplemented and cross-checked by statistics from the railway companies, worked out from the tickets sold and therefore 'not so reliable as the others, which are an actual enumeration'; by returns from the omnibus and cab proprietors; and by the Excise licences for omnibuses and carriages.[66] George Parrott, who was co-operating with Pearson on what was to become the Metropolitan Railway, London's first underground railway, also carried out a separate series of calculations concentrating on the Oxford Street/ Holborn and Piccadilly/Strand routes.[67]

With these painstakingly gathered figures it was possible to piece together, for the first time, a rough picture of London's traffic flows and the elements which made them up. 'The inference which I desire to draw' said Pearson, after presenting his statistics, 'is that the overcrowding of the City is caused, first by the natural increase of the population and area of the surrounding district; secondly, by the influx of provincial passengers by the great railways north of London, and the obstruction experienced in the streets by omnibuses and cabs coming from their distant stations, to bring the provincial travellers to and from the heart of the City. I next point to the vast increase of what I may term the migratory population, the population of the City who now oscillate between the country and the City, who leave the City of London every afternoon and return to it every morning.'[68]

Each of these elements was then analysed in detail. The first point was supported by simple figures for the relative crowding in the inner and outer wards of the city based upon the ratio of inhabited houses to population; figures which were cross-checked both by a report from Mr. Simon, Officer of Health, and by separate calculations 'made by Mr. Stevens without any communication with me'. To illustrate his third point the comparative numbers arriving by train, steam boat and omnibus or (still the majority) on foot were produced.[69]

Estimated number of Persons and Vehicles going into and out of the City daily, counting them all both ways

Estimated number of persons brought into and taken out of the City daily by omnibuses (counting both ways) ..	88,000
Estimated number of omnibus journeys	7,400
Estimated number of persons by steamers	30,000
Estimated number to and from the Fenchurch-street and the London Bridge Railway stations	54,000

[66] *Ibid.* QQ.1340–4.
[67] *Ibid.* QQ.965–8.
[68] *Ibid.* Q.1345.
[69] *Ibid.* QQ.1345–8; App. pp. 215–6, Tables II and IV.

Estimated number of vehicles of all descriptions, except omnibuses	52,000
Estimated number of foot passengers into and out of the City daily, omitting foot passengers from railways and steam-boats	400,000
Estimated number to and from the distant Metropolitan stations, Paddington, Euston and King's Cross	8,440

Although these figures take no account of loading factors or speed, they give us our first rough picture of internal traffic for any city and may be used as the basis for further calculations.[70] Further perspective to the search for understanding internal traffic flows was also given by the first rudimentary attempts to list and classify the types of building which generated traffic.

Pearson's remaining point was supported by evidence dividing the railway traffic into three classes, according to the frequency of their journeys and the relative amount of crowding of the streets each group occasioned; viz, 'Family' or 'Trade' 'Yearly', or 'Monthly', and 'Residential' or 'Weekly'. The daily commuter does not yet figure in the calculations, but the family traffic coming to London from the provinces, or going to Brighton or the Continent for a month 'with the valets and the ladies' maids, and all portmanteaus and band-boxes and the bonnet-boxes' should, he argued, be assigned an importance out of proportion to their relatively small numbers. In Pearson's view each family created more confusion and interruption in the stations and streets than '50 or 100 merchants or bankers, or persons coming for the purpose of trade, from Liverpool, or Manchester or Birmingham . . . with a return ticket, or perhaps spending the night, and bringing a carpet bag, as it may be.'[71]

Pearson's detailed traffic observations constitute one important essay to improve the techniques of understanding urban problems. Perhaps even more in advance of their time for the mid-1850's were the specific calculations of one category of indirect costs and benefits suggested by J. H. Stevens: the financing of street improvements by loans 'extending over a period of 40 years, on the security of the rateable difference between the present annual value of the property to be purchased for the improvements, and the additional value such property will derive from its proximity to the new streets and railway.'[72] In other words, one side of the equation, the direct cost of schemes, would have been calculated on a more reasonable basis than the railway companies' simple rule of thumb. Instead of merely accepting the contractors' estimate of probable

[70] Eg. T. C. Barker and Michael Robbins, op. cit. 58 (footnote), where T. C. Barker uses Pearson's figures to deduce that probably 6,000 to 10,000 daily commuters were using the London stations. See infra Chap. 3, sec. 5, Chap. 11, sec. 3.
[71] Ibid. Q.1348.
[72] Ibid. Q.1202. Stevens assigns the idea to Pearson.

costs, the accuracy of which affected only the railway company and the contractor, the neighbourhood costs should be estimated in the following way. Set on one side would be the total rental of the built-up area before improvement and railway clearance, compared with the amount realised for ground rents sacrificed for lands 'thrown into streets', and, of course, the cost of acquiring and clearing the ground. On the other side of the equation would be increased rentals realised after improvement and railway clearance, together with the large, but incommensurable, sanitary gains from clearing the area.

Although giving clear money values to the calculation of benefits, Stevens' scheme was impractical for administrative reasons, and would, in any case, fall into the category of 'double-counting'. 'We have to eliminate the purely transfer or distributional items from a cost-benefit evaluation,' enjoin Prest and Turvey, 'we are concerned with the value of the increment of output arising from a given investment, and not with the increment in value of existing assets.' By this criterion a net rise in rents or land values would simply be 'a reflection of the benefits of more journeys being undertaken than before'.[73] One might also add that assigning the whole of a given increase in rents or values in adjoining areas to the spillover of the improvement itself is an extremely dubious calculation, especially if carried out over an extensive span of time, and that it raises knotty topographical problems in defining the areas, or frontages, to be included in the equation.

Although it may be criticised upon these, and other grounds, Stevens' proposals can at least be taken as evidence of the desire to quantify the data laid before the Select Committee. Indeed, without further elaboration, it is clear that the Select Committee of 1854–5 was considerably better informed than any previous body of enquiry. There was talk of consciously 'developing a new and more convenient traffic'; and in cross-questioning the phrase 'taking it as a question of time and money' is used, with the implicit assumption, found in modern cost-benefit studies, that time is valuable and would be employed profitably if saved.[74] There is also a dawning awareness that 'the causes of the overcrowding of the habitations of the poor by night, and of the street by day, are the same, and the cure must be the same', and a practical grasp of the expediency of carrying out simultaneous schemes of improvement and of private profit-making railway enterprise.[75]

As one looks through the great bulk of evidence and statistical appendices, the same questions which arose with the Royal Commission of 1846 inevitably recur. What were the fruits of this increased

[73] A. R. Prest and R. Turvey, *loc. cit.* 688.
[74] H.C., 1854–5, X, QQ.1220–1. The idea of 'diminishing the great pressure from traffic' and redistributing it is taken further in H.L., 1859, VIII, 77.
[75] *Ibid.* Q.1345, Report, p. IV.

understanding of the complex influences at work, in terms of policy; and how effectively were measures of restraint and control implemented? Once again, the direct results of the Select Committee of 1854–5 have tended to be underestimated. The Metropolitan Railway and the Thames Embankment were both foreshadowed in the *Report*, and both were based upon recognition of the principle that railways in towns should make a contribution to public amenity and not merely intrude at will. The construction of co-ordinated arterial routes and removal of road tolls were other issues indirectly connected with the railways and raised by the Select Committee; it also begged 'earnestly to impress upon the House the extreme importance of practical steps being at once taken by authorities, properly constituted and armed with full powers and means' to control the problems it had described. The establishment of the Metropolitan Board of Works was 'warmly welcomed' as a step in the direction of controlling or restraining the great commercial forces of urban reconstruction.[76]

However, we are concerned at the moment, not primarily to assess the outcome of the Select Committee in terms of effective policy, but to ask whether the Victorians were conscious of the larger urban repercussions of railway building, and to see what progress is perceptible in the techniques of social accounting evolved for assessing the new problems with which the Victorians were faced. And there is an unequivocal change, by the mid-fifties, in the type and volume of information available for policy-makers, in London at any rate, to use as the basis for disinterested public evaluation of the schemes placed before them. This, perhaps, is as much as one can reasonably expect to demonstrate, for even nowadays the most adequate and detailed statistical analysis tends to become only one of several factors moulding final decisions.

The essence of a 'planning balance sheet', according to a recent writer on the subject, is to aid rational choice by rendering 'systematically, in descriptive and tabular form' a set of social accounts, so that the costs and benefits accruing indirectly can be seen, measured in money or physical terms as far as possible, or otherwise noted as intangible and merely listed, with their suggested weight. Its object is to 'clarify the issues and so reduce to a minimum the area of value judgement, opinion and prejudice, over which so much of the debate rages', and to enable 'endless and meandering discussion, disputation and negotiation to be cut down.'[77]

The data laid before Parliamentary Committees by the mid-1850's was already beginning to go some way towards this objective. Before the 1850's, the only people who really knew exactly what was going on,

[76] *Ibid.* Report, pp. IV, V, VI.
[77] Nathaniel Lichfield, *loc. cit.* 168.

were the railway solicitors and engineers; and they were not concerned with the social side-effects of their schemes. They had no time, in the press of rapidly-moving events, to take a detailed interest in the social ramifications of their action, nor were they held accountable for them. Although the railways arrived with the impact of a minor earthquake, their constructors were able, when pressed for details of their schemes' consequences, to reply tersely, in the words of one engineer, 'I am giving you the conviction of men's minds who are spending their own money.'[78]

Such brevity was clearly unacceptable to the 1854 Committee, and in the 1860's there is a general trend for those professionally concerned to take greater cognizance of the social effects of their projects. Edward Watkin or William Birt represent the second generation of railway managers to whom it came naturally to speak of social consequences; though it remains an open question (discussed elsewhere) as to how much of this was lip-service and how much a genuine change of spirit.

5. *The Metropolitan crisis in the 1860's*

Succeeding enquiries brought further refinements of technique. The House of Lords' Select Committee on Metropolitan Communications heard evidence, reproduced in their *Third Report* of 1863, from new spokesmen of the public interest: J. W. Bazalgette, Engineer to the new Metropolitan Board of Works (which had been granted special *locus standi* to appear by means of designated witnesses); Colonel Yolland, Inspector in the Railway Department of the Board of Trade, (appearing at the request of James Booth, Secretary to the Board); and W. Haywood, Surveyor to the Corporation of London. Witnesses were also called who represented a wide range of opinion amongst contemporary railway engineers and managers: G. P. Bidder of the Great Eastern, a strong advocate of elevated, as opposed to underground, urban railways, and desperately concerned to gain more central access into the City for his company; Frederick Slight of the London, Brighton and South Coast and Cornelius Eborall of the South Eastern railway companies, who both reflected, for similar reasons, the conservative railway point of view; and John Hawkshaw and John Fowler, whose key roles in the construction of central termini have already been noted. The evidence heard from these and other witnesses was voluminous and searching in the extreme; and it is difficult to believe that the public

[78] H.C., 1846, XVII, Q.438 (Tite). This attitude was sympathetically reflected by writers in the 1840's. 'Let those who advance their money be the best judges of that question.' *The Economist*, 6 July 1844, 962. 'Could there be any other country in the world where it is so hard to obtain leave to spend one's money.' Charles Knight, *op. cit.* 310.

interest was not thoroughly aired, either by design or by accident, during the arguments and counter-arguments of the different railway interests.

One of the shortcomings of earlier evidence concerning the indirect social costs caused by congestion of the streets had been lack of information on traffic speeds. William Haywood now attempted to put this right by the use of police returns, and by carrying out experimental timed journeys, with an assistant, on the omnibuses and four-wheeled carriages on various routes through the City. The mean of from 35 to 69 observations on different routes gave 3·28 mph to 4·55 mph.[79] His conclusion, however, was that, although some of the underground or link railways under discussion might ease this flow, and the projected Central Station might worsen it, equally marked effects in the saving of the public's time might be achieved more simply, 'If powers were given to determine the course which public vehicles might take', and if the omnibus proprietors' extraordinary freedom from observing fixed stopping places or timetables, or consulting about routes, were curbed.[80]

Apart from questions of traffic speed, another new public issue raised before this Committee concerned the comfort and convenience of urban travellers. Already mentioned earlier by Joseph Paxton, who had hoped in 1854 to make London travel 'pleasant', the point was taken much further in 1863 when the comparative merits of underground and elevated travel, from the public's point of view, were argued by G. P. Bidder and John Parson. The subway saved in the cost of land and reduced 'public disfigurement'; it could also be more easily combined, by the new 'cut-and-cover' method, with street improvement. The elevated railway did not interfere with the network of gravity-fed sewers or cause damage by vibration, and gave a cleaner, better lit and ventilated ride with easier station access.[81] Bidder even went so far as to assign a quantitative figure to the difference between the two modes, though he spoke with commercial, rather than cost-benefit considerations in mind. 'The Metropolitan has been a great commercial success undoubtedly but, in my view, in spite of its being underground. If the Metropolitan had been on a viaduct, as far as my opinion goes, it would be worth a million more money than it is.'[82]

Another technical alternative considered, not merely in terms of profitability, but of its possible public amenity, was the pneumatically operated railway, to which were ascribed many of the merits actually possessed by the electric trains of thirty years later. Here again a ruling

[79] H.C., 1863, VIII, QQ.1226–8.

[80] As a result of the S.C.'s recommendations the City authorities were empowered in 1863 to regulate omnibus operation, but did not even insist upon the picking up and setting down of passengers on the left-hand side of the road until 1867. T. C. Barker and Michael Robbins, *op. cit.* 243.

[81] H.C., 1863, VIII, QQ.778–800, 963–5, 1025.

[82] *Ibid.* Q.623.

of permanent importance was given by the Committee; for just as the underground was preferred, on balance, because it could 'be combined with the contemporaneous construction of new streets', so the pneumatic railway was forbidden on the grounds that it was not desirable that experiments should be carried out on important Metropolitan routes.[83]

A further practical point affecting the public interest was raised by John Thwaites, of the Metropolitan Board of Works. He and other public engineers had had only three weeks to study the submitted plans of new railways through London, and to make their tracings. 'Besides which, we do not know whether they propose to pass an important street by a graceful curve or whether they propose to erect those hideous girders we now find everywhere crossing our streets. We do not know the span, nor do we know the headway. Many of the schemes before Parliament are perfectly silent upon these important points.'[84] The reticence of railway projectors upon such technical points did not, however, prevent J. W. Bazalgette, from submitting a detailed statement, covering four pages, of the damage to public works the schemes could involve.[85]

The outcome, in terms of policy recommendations, of the 1863 Committee, and of the 1864 Joint Committee of Lords and Commons which considered the same issues, was again a noteworthy victory for the public interest. 1863 was the peak year of Britain's third and last railway boom of mania proportions, and the 13 bills referred to the Committee on Metropolitan Communications proposed to schedule property along 174 miles of Metropolitan routes and demolish a quarter of the City of London.[86] The ordinary Private Bill Committees could not be expected to cope with this onslaught, and the standard procedure of considering each bill separately on its individual merits would clearly have broken down in the face of such a complex and overlapping series of simultaneous projects. 'A protracted and costly Parliamentary struggle between the promoters of the rival projects must therefore be looked for, if this is to be permitted', concluded the 1863 Committee. 'Nor can any confidence be felt that such a contest would lead to a satisfactory result; not one of the projects brought before Parliament might prove to be in all respects a good one, and yet the Committees of the two Houses to which they would be submitted would possess no power of making changes of importance in the schemes which they

[83] H.L., 1864 (87), Joint S.C. on Metropolitan railway schemes, Report, p. 2.
[84] H.C., 1863, VIII, Q.1056.
[85] H.C., 1864 (59), Report of the Engineer of the Metropolitan Bd. of Wks in return to H. of C. Order 8 February 1864, 13–17.
[86] 'London is to be burrowed through and through like a rabbit-warren', wrote a resident who had contributed 5% of the rental value of his house towards a campaign fund to oppose the railways. Quoted in T. C. Barker and Michael Robbins, *op. cit.* 148.

were asked to sanction but would only have the chance of passing or rejecting them.' The resulting rivalry could not be tolerated 'in the constricted interior of the metropolis.'[87]

Ten of the thirteen bills, including most of the larger and more elaborate ones were, therefore, rejected. In deciding upon this, it was explained, 'The Committee have been strongly influenced by the consideration of the great public inconvenience and pecuniary loss to the inhabitants.' On the other hand, a link underground railway in continuation of the Metropolitan Railway was sanctioned, because by providing a substitute for cab and omnibus traffic it might relieve the streets and so perform a public service. To guard against this leading to an unduly profitable monopoly for the Metropolitan, it was suggested that half of any dividends over 8% should be paid to the Metropolitan Board of Works for public uses; although this recommendation was both extremely difficult to enforce and, as it turned out, quite unnecessary.[88]

The only major new intrusion into the central area permitted was that from the east by the Great Eastern's Liverpool Street extension, and this was only allowed upon condition that clauses were included in the Act compelling the company to run cheap workmen's trains daily.[89] This was the first major attempt to force a commercial company to offset the social costs incident to an urban terminal scheme by providing, as Pearson had advocated in 1846, a bulk service at low margins of profit per unit; a significant new development, and one which had far-reaching effects upon the growth of later nineteenth-century working-class suburbs to the east and north-east of London.

6. *Major topics raised in the later nineteenth century*

By the mid-sixties the basic techniques of measurement on which informed decisions concerning the public interest could be made were already well developed. The final assessment was still a qualitative weighing of the factors rather than a quantitative and systematic calculation of costs and benefits, but though less exhaustive and thorough, it served the same purposes as a modern cost benefit study. It enabled choices to be made between different proposals involving

[87] H. C., 1863, VIII, Report, pp. XII, XIII. The contrary view had been put to them most forcibly by John Hawkshaw. 'It is difficult to get parties to believe in schemes which are laid down by committees. If it be attempted to stereotype them and say these are to be the railways for London I think it would be a mistake.' *Ibid.* QQ.1109, 1092.

[88] H.C., 1864 (87), Report, p. 2. H.C., 1863, VIII, Report, pp. IV, XIV.

[89] Great Eastern (Metropolitan Station) Railway Act, 1864, 27 & 8 Vic. c. 313, sec. 80. The earliest insertion of special 'workmen's' clauses took place in 1861 in the North London (City Branch) and the Metropolitan (27 & 8 Vic. c. 233) Acts.

investments which were large and indivisible. It provided a valuable means for marshalling issues, enumerating affected parties, and indicating who might suffer and who might gain. After all, the claims for statistical accuracy made by modern exponents of cost-benefit analysis are disarmingly modest. 'Judgment plays such an important role in the estimation of benefit-cost ratios', concluded a recent survey, 'that little significance can be attached to the precise numerical results obtained.'[90] It is clear that the ultimate value of modern cost-benefit studies—the rejection of inferior projects, 'promoted for empire-building or pork-barrel reasons'—may also be realised by non-statistical consideration of the benefits and costs. This is particularly the case if consideration of non-statistical material, for all its shortcomings, has genuinely *preceded* and illuminated the political decisions, rather than *vice versa*.

In the later nineteenth century further enquiries added to the accumulated information already available to policy-makers. The Royal Commission of 1867 heard evidence on urban railways from Edwin Chadwick and Rowland Hill, both well known for their public services in a wider context. Its appendices and text include the first information upon the relationship between urban railway costs and their terminal charges, upon the seasonal patterns of passenger demand, upon the railway companies' excursion and cheap fare policies, upon the frequency and cost of suburban services, and other topics which can more properly be discussed elsewhere.

From their evidence, however, and that of William Galt, emerged the first indications of a new public concern—railway pricing policy. After all, as the urban surface railway networks began to assume a definitive and final shape, it was natural that discussion should turn from securing the public interest during construction to securing it during operation. The same major issue was brought into still clearer focus in the evidence placed before the Select Committee of 1872 by Captain Tyler and T. H. Farrer, Permanent Secretary to the Board of Trade. What should be the policy pursued over urban and suburban fares, and what surcharge could reasonably be levied on goods to defray the expense of urban terminals? These two topics dominated legislation, railway law cases and local Chamber of Commerce proceedings in the 1870's and 80's.

They raised again, in slightly differing form, questions of social accounting. Given the fact that the social costs incidental to urban railway construction had been, or were, in large measure, being paid, the scale of benefits depended largely upon the facilities for residential escape, and for the cheap supply of goods and foodstuffs, which the railways could now offer in return. The extent of these benefits depended, in turn, upon the railways fares policy, which now became one of the two major social issues in the field of communications in the last

[90] A. R. Prest and R. Turvey, *loc. cit.* 728, 731.

quarter of the century. To put it in cost-benefit analysis terms, 'distributional constraints' now came to figure more largely in the process of decision-making. Maximising the net gain, or minimising the net loss, to particular groups whose economic welfare was of increasing political significance in the closing decades of the century became a major issue; and this issue was seen to be inextricably entangled with railway pricing policy.

The other major topic, which had already been prematurely and ineffectually ventilated in the 1850's and 1860's, was the effect of railway demolition upon working-class housing. As already mentioned above, the effects upon residential densities had received attention as early as 1846. By 1853 a committee had met, under the chairmanship of Lord Shaftesbury, to consider 'whether those houses can be taken without occasioning any pecuniary or other injury to such persons (of the labouring class), and without being likely to occasion any overcrowding of any other dwellings.'[91] From 1853 onwards the 'Shaftesbury Standing Order' (S.O. 191), required the preparation of a statement as to how many working men were likely to be evicted by each urban railway scheme; and these 'Demolition Statements' have already formed the basis for a pioneer study by H. J. Dyos which will be familiar to readers of the *Journal of Transport History*.[92]

The shortcomings of the 'Demolition Statement' procedure as a formal safeguard of the public interest was apparent to all by the early 1880's, and was subjected to critical comment, both in the Select Committee on Artizans' and Labourers' Dwellings *Report* of 1882, and in the evidence laid before the Royal Commission on the Housing of the Working Classes of 1884–5. Detailed and specific evidence by Miss Octavia Hill, H. G. Calcraft (Assistant Secretary to the Board of Trade), Joseph Chamberlain and the Rev. William Denton set forth clearly the relevant information concerning rents, fares and land prices upon which policy conclusions could be based.[93] At the same time, their evidence emphasised the link between the problems of re-housing the urban working class and of providing cheap bulk transport. They were not alternative, so much as complementary methods of tackling one of the most pressing urban problems of the late nineteenth century.

Steps were taken, on the first count, to tighten up Standing Orders.

---

[91] *H. of L. Journals*, LXXXV (1853), 140. The committee at first recommended that if more than 30 houses be taken in one parish 'adequate provision be made by the undertakers within three years and within a convenient distance', but this crucial phrase was dropped in the Standing Order. Fuller history of the S.O. is given in O. C. Williams, *op. cit.* II, 65 *et. seq.*

[92] H. J. Dyos, 'Workmen's Fares in South London, 1860–1914', 'Railways and Housing in Victorian London', 'Some Social Costs of Railway building in London', *JTH*, I (1953), 3–19, II (1955), 11–21, 90–100, III (1957), 23–30 respectively.

[93] H.C., 1884–5, XXX, QQ.8841–9112, 9991–10138, 12426–12522, 10667–10737.

The local re-housing by the railway companies of those displaced by their schemes was recommended, clearance was to be gradual, re-housing to proceed simultaneously, and the local authorities to ensure that notice to quit was not served subsequently on those re-housed.[94] On the whole these new provisions were of limited effect. If one compares the short formal statement of the numbers displaced which accompanied the schemes of the late fifties or sixties, with the voluminous and detailed plans, showing the position of working-class houses scheduled in 1892 for the Manchester, Sheffield and Lincolnshire Railway's extension to Marylebone, and 'stating the number of persons residing therein, so far as can be ascertained by house-to-house enquiry', it is possible to see how much less casual the approach to social costs had become.[95] But this did not prevent marked delays in rehousing during the Marylebone scheme, leading to a further overspill into the adjacent slum area of Lisson Grove; and the difficulty of securing that the same tenants were readmitted to the new upgraded accommodation was virtually insoluble.[96] Nevertheless the approach to demolition in the nineties was much more solicitous for the public interest.

However, the building of Marylebone Station was the last and only major terminal scheme to be carried through in London after 1884. The new provisions to reduce 'systematic evasion' and 'gross inaccuracy of returns' by bodies demolishing residential housing unfortunately fell most heavily not upon the railway companies, whose major constructional phase was over by the 1880's, but upon the Metropolitan Board of Works, demolishing for street improvements, and upon bodies proceeding under the Torrens (1868) and Cross (1875) slum clearance acts.

On the complementary problem of supplying suburban transport which was cheap, ran at convenient times, and in adequate quantities, policy recommendations were still less effective. The 1882 Artizans' and Labourers' Dwellings Committee was directly responsible for the passing of the 1883 Cheap Trains Act; but this measure was itself of debatable practical influence. However, the point which is germane here is that, after the Cheap Trains Act of 1883, at least there was a systematic attempt to collect statistics; and the direction in which the statistics pointed, as they accumulated over the next two decades, was towards the principle of a publicly controlled and operated network of local rail and street tramways. The data which was gathered enabled the

[94] S.O. 184.

[95] HLRO, P & S, Demolition Statement, 1892, Manchester, Sheffield and Lincolnshire Railway (Extension to London).

[96] Many of the inhabitants of Lisson Grove were already refugees from an earlier demolition, when New Oxford Street was cut through St. Giles, Charles Booth, *Life and Labour of the People of London* (1892), I, 289. Also H. J. Dyos, *JTH*, II (1955), 19.

Board of Trade, the new London County Council and the public pressure groups (The National Association for the Extension of Workmen's Trains, and the London Reform Union), to conduct a campaign which came to a successful conclusion in the Select Committee on Workmen's Trains, 1903–5, and the Royal Commission on London Traffic, 1903–5.

One has only to contrast the many volumes of detailed statistical evidence available to these early twentieth-century policy-making bodies with the hearsay, the private impressions and personal opinions of sixty years earlier, to see the progress made towards listing exhaustively for consideration the wider social costs which might be incurred, and the wider social benefits which might accrue, from an efficient network of urban rail transport. There is a heading, in the Royal Commission's *Report* of 1905, for example, which lays down the following principle for assessing the *Characteristics and Functions of Urban Railways*. 'It is necessary at the outset to form a clear conception of the function of railways' states the *Report*, 'as part of the general scheme for locomotion and transport in London.'[97] It goes on to distinguish between the types of railway accommodation required for trunk, suburban, urban and merchandise traffic, and in every point of its analysis the implicit assumption is made that the primary consideration which it is proper to set before Parliament is that of the public interest. The basic yardstick applied is not profitability but functional adequacy. How can the 'imperfect and disjointed' organic system of railways serving a great city like London, be adapted to changing public requirements? This is the question the Commission sets before itself and the vocabulary, concepts, and terms of reference it uses are already those of the modern planner.

'The occupation of any location must be regarded as a permanent assignment to the railway, and, both for physical and financial reasons, any substantial interference with it in future is impossible. Hence it is essential that the railway system, as a whole, should be supervised, in its growth and development, on definite, consistent and carefully-formed principles, directed towards the achievement of a clearly conceived result.'[98]

The same criteria and the same mode of thought can be seen in the *Draft Reports* of the Select Committee on Workmen's Trains, in 1905. Though not as compendious as those of the Royal Commission on London Traffic, which ran to eight volumes, its statistics were sufficiently elaborate to enable the fixing of suggested fares. Details of working class budgets, rent differentials between suburban and central areas, and valuation of the time spent in travelling, indicated a figure of 2d per day

[97] H.C., 1905, XXX, 605–11.
[98] *Ibid.* 605.

as the marginal fare if the working classes were to become daily consumers of railway services. In putting this figure to the railway companies the *Draft Report* observed, 'In the case of London, and probably also in other towns, a workman has some inducement to live in the outlying districts, from the fact that he can obtain housing accommodation at a lower rent. This difference in rent counterbalances the amount paid in railway fares provided the latter are low. The time spent in travelling to and fro each day has also to be taken into account as well as the fact that the workman cannot obtain his meals at home.'[99]

In other words, not merely was the pattern of railway services to be judged by functional rather than financial criteria, but some, at any rate, of the fares were to be fixed by marginal social cost pricing.

7. *Conclusions*

In London the counting of the social costs incidental to urban railway building began surprisingly early, in the mid-forties of the century, and the methods used were refined and extended in the fifties and sixties. Of course, the presence of well-digested studies did not necessarily lead to immediate and single-minded action in the mid-nineteenth century any more than in the days of the *Buchanan Report*; but the fact that such conscientious investigations were carried out and given a hearing should correct the widely-held impression that the Victorians were entirely careless of the effects of the great works of urban reconstruction they were executing.

Whilst it cannot be argued that the evidence presented satisfies the exacting statistical standards of modern studies, it does fulfil several of the major requirements of cost-benefit analysis. The proposed schemes or groups of schemes were fully defined, together with some possible alternatives, within the limits imposed by the Parliamentary time-table; even though the time taken for deliberation was shorter, and the decisions at least as binding, as in present-day enquiries. Approximate estimates for costs were given, and attempts made, from the mid-1850's, to value the different benefits from the proposed schemes by methods appropriate to their nature. In the Bidder-Parson debate on elevated railways, in the studies of the comparative returns on public and private investments, and in discussion on the influence which railway projects might have upon the speed and costs of street traffic, there can be discerned the first efforts to decide which courses would yield the most widely spread social benefits. Likewise, the consideration, under separate headings, of evidence concerning the railways' demolition or depreciation of adjacent property, their interruption of street communications or public works, and their blocking of future improvement

[99] H.C., 1905, VIII, 511.

plans, represents the first attempt to distinguish benefits and costs which were real, and not cancelled out by corresponding gains or losses to other sections of the community omitted from the accounting.

Indeed the later studies—such as the *Memorandum* submitted to the Royal Commission of 1903–5, by Sir John Wolfe-Barry and R. C. H. Davidson, upon the monetary value of the time lost to persons and vehicles through defective communications—begin, in some respects, to resemble sketches of modern statistical analyses. Wolfe-Barry eliminated those engaged in domestic occupations, and those not likely to be affected by the time spent travelling, from the 1901 *Census* occupational categories for the London area, assigned a daily wage based upon Charles Booth's calculations to the remaining proportion, and assumed the earning capacity to be spread over an eight hour day. On this basis, an extra quarter of an hour spent travelling would equal three *per cent* of the total, i.e. time worth £5,000,000 *per annum.* to the employers. 'The whole of the time estimated as lost is treated as having the money value of the various classes of persons employed. . . . Thus the money taken from the ratepayers to pay for such improvements may be justified and more than justified by the value to them of the extra travelling facilities gained.'[100]

Though these types of enquiry were far from being exhaustive or systematic, one must not overlook the fact that they were original essays in an entirely new field of public administration. On the other hand, Victorian enquiries fell short of modern analysis in several important ways. No attempt was made to exclude benefits which would emerge in any case, even if the investment under consideration were not executed. There was a tendency at first to accept uncritically even the most partisan claims for indirect benefit—for example over the good effects allegedly created by railway employment. But from the 1860's onwards, attempts to assess the costs as well as the benefits became increasingly searching.

In summary, one might say that, apart from the leeway allowed in the selection of witnesses, the evidence presented to Parliament on the occasions described above at least escaped the charge, sometimes levelled at cost-benefit studies, of being commissioned to justify rather than to influence political decisions; and that, in addition, it went a considerable way towards identifying a wide range of costs and benefits which ought to be taken into account, and deciding what political and administrative constraints applied. On the other hand the major tasks of measurement were only sporadically and partially accomplished; and consequently there was a general tendency to undervalue the social importance of time-saving.

However incomplete, by modern standards, the material gathered for the 'planning balance sheets', of the 1840's and 1860's, or however in-

[100] H.C. 1906, XLVI, 675–7.

adequate the manner of its presentation may seem to be, there can be no doubt as to the importance of the decisions which emerged. Not merely was the topography of London's West End and City profoundly influenced by the *veto* on central schemes but, in the opinion of the Royal Commission on London Traffic of 1905, 'the whole course of railway construction around London was influenced by the policy adopted in excluding railways from the central area.'[101]

Between 1864 and 1905 the search for positive standards for the development of future urban and suburban rail services was gradual and laggardly in relation to the marked social, political and demographic changes of those four decades. The principal emphasis of social accounting, one might argue, was a negative one during these years. This was certainly the view expressed by Sir Benjamin Baker, in an outburst to the Joint Committee on Electric and Cable Railways (1892), which is worth quoting in full.

'I thought it would be not at all unnatural that the Committee would wish to know how it is that for 25 years past nothing whatever has been done in the heart of London to meet the growing necessities of the City traffic. Nothing whatever has been done for 25 years; that I think I can offer an explanation presently, whilst at the same time New York, which followed the lead of London some years afterwards, has not stood still as London has done, but has gone ahead, and has got 40 miles of urban railway now; so that a New York business man can travel almost anywhere at ten miles an hour, whereas a man in London has to travel six miles an hour. In the last 30 years the whole of that map has been scored with proposals of lines for promoters, many of them following very nearly the same routes as the present lines, and you can hardly draw a red line on which some line has not been deposited; and yet not a single one of them has been carried out. And the reason is this: That in the first instance, when Sir John Fowler was promoting the original Underground railway, he got the cordial co-operation of all the public bodies. Since then, the public bodies have not assisted in the same way as they did originally, but they have too much sought the advice of professional advisers, and when, of course anyone consults an engineer, he thinks he must get something always for his client; and the result is that when the Bills leave the Committee, they are so often loaded with onerous clauses that you cannot raise the money.'[102]

Baker's comments were shrewd, and by no means untypical of the point of view held by many late Victorian railway promoters and managers. To them it seemed that in the last decades of the nineteenth century far too much concern for public costs and benefits was shown by too many local and central bodies.

[101] H.C., 1905, XXX, 611.
[102] H.C., 1892, XII, 132.

III

~~~~~~

Railway profits and the Victorian city

~~~~~~

1. *Introduction*

T HE various public enquiries studied in the last chapter, however dissimilar their subject matter, shared one common feature. They were all
conducted against a metropolitan background, and a substantial proportion of the problems raised were discussed in an exclusively urban
context. Consequently the connection between the content of the
Reports and *Evidence* alluded to, and the subject matter of urban
history was sufficiently clear to need no underlining.

This is not the case when we turn to examine Victorian railway
development through the eyes of the railway entrepreneurs. To them
the impact of their railways upon urban affairs was of distinctly peripheral importance compared with the general, day-to-day business
tasks of raising capital and organising a profitable and competitive
service. The great bulk of railway records, whether *Accounts and
Statements* for public consumption or internal *Minutes* and *Special
Reports*, show little or no grasp of the immense influence for good or
ill their business schemes exercised upon the towns which were the
scene of their operations. There was not any attempt to break down
traffic figures or divide costs and charges in such a way that the direct
impression a company made upon a particular town could be distinguished. The business statistics upon which operational decisions
were based remained undifferentiated, overall figures. The total numbers carried, the fares paid, the changing proportion of receipts between
goods and passengers, and the changing proportion of the passenger
classes; these were all dutifully reported, together with the overall
working expenditure.[1] These statistics, all produced by the companies

[1] H.C., 1890, LXV, 680–1 gives the working expenditure, receipts, etc. for each
year from 1860–89. *Railway Returns* and *Abstracts* provide other figures, used for
tables in B. R. Mitchell and Phyllis Deane, *Abstract of British Historical Statistics*
(Cambridge, 1962), 225–7. The limitations of the information given are discussed in
W. M. Acworth and G. Paish, 'British Railways, their Accounts and Statistics',
Journal of the Royal Statistical Society, LXXV (1912), 687–730.

to the order of Parliament or the Board of Trade, are extremely interesting in themselves and reliable indicators of general growth; but they are of distinctly limited use for analytical purposes. Indeed the railway companies found it to their advantage, W. Burdett-Coutts M.P., Chairman of the Railway Shareholders' Committee, alleged, deliberately to suppress the publication of figures which were 'too illuminating'. 'We turned to the reports of the companies for information and could make nothing of them', he told the Departmental Committee on Railway Accounts and Statistical Returns, in 1910. Even at this date the statistics available to a shareholders' committee did not enable a breakdown to be made on the earnings from ordinary passenger traffic and cheap ticket traffic, or—'a still more serious omission'—the average distances travelled. 'In fact we could discover nothing about the passenger traffic which would assist us in ascertaining whether or not the railway companies had performed more work for the money they received from passengers to account for the proportionately greater increase of expenditure than of gross earnings.'[2] Evidence placed before this committee of the Board of Trade by the Traffic and General Managers of the L. & N.W., North Eastern, Great Central and Great Northern railway companies, did little to suggest that the managers of these companies were themselves better informed; and the same impression, of decisions taken upon very limited and general statistics, is confirmed in George Findlay, General Manager of the London and North-Western railway company, *The Working and Management of an English Railway*, 1891.[3]

Since the statistics collected were inadequate, even for the examination of major topics of contemporary concern, such as changes in operating efficiency or returns on capital, it is not surprising that they should be of still more limited value for the urban historian. The questions to which one would really like to know the answers were considered either too troublesome or of insufficient immediate interest for constant numerical measurement. Where did the passengers get on and off, and how far did they travel? What traffic used the suburban stations and how did it vary over a given time span? How much was actually spent, by stages, upon acquiring the land, building, reconstructing and running each of the great urban terminals and goods yards? What traffic did each deal with and what relationship did the

---

[2] H.C., 1910 (Cd 5052), 320–1.

[3] George Findlay, *The Working and Management of an English Railway* (1891), 244–57. W. R. Lawson, *British Railways: a Financial and Commercial Survey* (1913), repeats the charges of 'foolish expenditure' and 'useless statistics' . . . 'A loss distributed amongst many being too often regarded as in effect no loss at all', 19–22. Still more serious was the allegation by Burdett-Coutts that 'the resources of these great companies, both as to funds and staff, can be, and will be utilised by the boards against shareholders who ask for such information.' H.C., 1910 (Cd 5052), 327.

traffic bear to the costs which had been incurred in siting, constructing and operating it? What was the pattern of traffic in and around the major cities at different seasons of the year and at different times of day? Except in a handful of cases mentioned later, the material upon which answers to these questions could be based was simply not collected. Indeed, even in the late 1950's, one of Dr. Beeching's complaints about railway costing was that it was 'global' in character. All moneys for one region were put into a bag, so to speak, from which certain traditional disbursements were made, and the resultant surplus or deficit was left on general account.[4]

The only exceptions to this rule came into three categories. There were the individual analyses made, usually for submission to Select Committees or Royal Commissions; like those of 1867, 1872, 1881 and 1884/5, which were each supplied with tit-bits of specific information by the railway managers. There were a few individual reports, like that of the General Manager of the G.W. railway to his Board when it required 'some information on the progress of the Suburban passenger traffic' in February 1869. There were the far more detailed breakdowns of traffic dealt with at each station and goods depot on the G.W. and G.E. railways compiled after 1903.

Future research may, one hopes, uncover further internal evidence of systematic and continuous analysis by the railway companies of the factors which they encountered in their urban operations. But there seems little doubt that a great deal of the necessary operational data was never accumulated, because of the great railway managers' ability or imagined ability to 'play it by ear', using their long and detailed first-hand experience of the growing railway system's notorious failures and successes, rather than preliminary traffic studies and costing breakdowns, to guide their decisions.

The usual method of making decisions which concerned investment in new urban sites or services was empirical and opportunistic rather than rational. The managerial approach can be glimpsed in some of the topics raised in the *Special Report* of 1869 mentioned earlier. Although the Great Western railway had put up money for the Metropolitan line and negotiated for access to the new Victoria station ten years earlier, the *Special Report* still finds it necessary to pose the belated questions, How can the Victoria Station and line best be utilised? and, What number of trains should be run over the Metropolitan railway under the agreement with that company? Some of the problems facing the G.W. company arose from technical and operational difficulties in

---

[4] *The Reshaping of British Railways* (H.M.S.O., 1963), I, 5. On early traffic analyses in the 1840's and 1850's see BTHR LNW 1/716 and T. R. Gourvish, *British Railway Management in the Nineteenth Century, with Special Reference to the Career of Captain Mark Huish (1808–67)*, (London Ph.D. thesis, 1967).

underground, joint station and broad gauge working, some from railway politics; but none of them was unforeseeable.[5]

It may seem reasonable that such detailed and practical considerations might well have preceded the large investment decisions concerning the Metropolitan line and Victoria station, but this, in fact, was typical of the railway companies' mode of procedure. The territorial claims were staked upon general grounds; the detailed traffic consequences were faced later. If they led to embarrassment then the authorised work could be slowed down to a crawl, a Bill allowing further extension of time could be procured, and the landowners, Chambers of Commerce and general public kept in suspense for a decade or more.

A similar approach is revealed, in the *Special Report*, towards the development of suburban traffic. The large traffic from Windsor and Ealing takes the General Manager of the G.W. by surprise, so he opens stations at Hayes and Acton, which produce only forty or fifty passengers a day, 'nothing like the amount of traffic which was anticipated.' In spite of this he affirms to the Board 'It will be desirable to afford further accommodation from time to time for the suburban traffic with a view to inducing City people to live down the Great Western line, as frequent service of trains upon the Southern lines and now upon the Midland and Great Northern afford considerable advantages to passengers living on those lines.'[6]

The decision, in other words, is based simply upon observation of a competitor's success under dissimilar circumstances of landownership, income and employment patterns, in a different area. There is no attempt to assess the attitudes of landowners on the Great Western's route, survey the possible market for season tickets, define, even approximately, who the 'city people' were likely to be, how frequently and how far they would travel, and whether they would find accommodation at the rents they could afford, or to take into account the fact that the southern and south-eastern commuters arrived at terminals on the fringe of the City, not at a remote West End station. Not surprisingly the Great Western's schemes for developing suburban traffic in the sixties miscarried and managerial interest waned.[7] By the end of the century, when a new campaign was begun, the Great Western,

---

[5] BTHR, General Manager's Report, 4 February 1869, GW 18/6. For the clash between the Metropolitan and Great Western railways see T. C. Barker and Michael Robbins, *op. cit.* 122–6.

[6] BTHR GW 18/6.

[7] Another possible interpretation, reading between the lines of the Report, is that Grierson was satisfied to run a traffic limited in numbers. The Great Western suburban services (defined by Grierson as stations to Wycombe and Reading) carried 800,000 passengers in 1867 for receipts of £100,000, i.e. an average fare of 2s 6d per ticket; by comparison the Metropolitan (Hammersmith branch) averaged 3d per ticket.

together with the L. & N.W. and the Midland, had earned the reputation of being the most indifferent and exclusive of London-based railway companies in the provision of suburban services.[8]

The social and urban consequences of railway building, it will be suggested in the *Case Histories* which follow, were, in a majority of cases, precipitated inadvertently by the railway entrepreneurs. It was not that their actions were hasty and ill-considered, though some decisions fell into this category. It was rather that their horizon was contained by the ephemeral and rapidly changing business situation in which they found themselves; and that the need for circumspection and calculation was reduced by the character of Parliamentary procedure, and by the increasingly monopolistic nature of railway operations. Once Parliamentary authorisation had been given to take the land for a certain urban site, or once a rival, however small, had established a claim to certain routes or terminals, a new balance was struck between the competing companies which only amalgamation, a Bill conceding running powers over the rival line, or the construction of duplicate facilities could redress. If it were determined, on general strategic grounds, that it was desirable to gain a stronger foothold in a town, all that remained was to pay whatever current price was necessary. In the course of this reasoning it was not unusual for a railway manager to find himself in the position of a man at an auction who found afterwards that he had bid far too much. The Liverpool Street terminal, at £2,000,000 'when it was first built was looked upon by everyone' writes Acworth 'as a white elephant of the very largest size.'[9] But having got it, it was necessary to charge for it upon every branch of traffic. In William Birt's words, 'There it is, and it must be paid for.'[10]

To a greater or lesser extent all the other railway companies found themselves, at different times and in different cities, in situations where the only course of action seemed to be to pay first and to meet the cost afterwards. Indeed it is an open question whether the financial burden their urban land acquisition laid upon them was disproportionately heavy, even for their vast resources.

Before touching upon this important question, however, it would be best, in the interest of clarity, to take in sequence the other main topics of urban significance in which the investment decisions, or operational practices, of the railway companies, whether inadvertant or no, left a mark on Britain's major cities. These can be discussed under four main

[8] In the years just before the First World War the G.W. launched a 'Homes for All' campaign to provide services, information and a 'Residential Guide and Property Register' for those who could afford to buy houses 'in Chalfont country or Beechy Bucks'. BRL. L47.37.

[9] W. M. Acworth, *The Railways of England* (1900), 410.

[10] H.C., 1884–5, XXX, Q.10197.

PLATE 3　Estate development in south central Manchester, 1794 (see p. 154)

PLATE 4   The London, Chatham and Dover railway
company's viaduct across central London (see p. 281)

headings; the first connected with the constructional phase of urban railway building, the second with the organisation and control of urban projects, the third concerned with the effects of construction, the fourth with operational policy. Associated with these is the still larger issue of the railway's relationship to the urban and suburban market for land: a topic in which, more than in any other, the railways are seen as a product as well as a cause of wider social and economic changes. Discussion of this, though relevant to the issues treated below, is postponed to a later chapter.

2. The constructional phase

There were several ways in which the competitive spirit could manifest itself during the first quarter century of urban railway building. One was by price competition, reducing fares and paring profit margins to a minimum; and as the trunk railway system neared completion, in the early eighteen fifties, such contests reached a climax. In 1854 the Edinburgh and Glasgow and the Caledonian railway companies, competing for inter-urban traffic, reduced the fares to 6d. third class for a journey (by the Caledonian route between Edinburgh and Glasgow) of 57 miles. The contest lasted until July 1856, when the two companies made a joint purse agreement, argued to an incredible two points of decimals; 30·64% to the Edinburgh-Glasgow, 69·36% to the Caledonian.[11] From October 1857 to the end of 1858 a most intense price competition raged between the London and North Western railway and its new rival in the northern cities, the Manchester, Sheffield and Lincolnshire, during which the fare from Liverpool to London was brought down to 5s return. 'Then we came to our senses', said Sir Edward Watkin, General Manager of the M.S. & L.[12] Similar examples can be multiplied for cut-throat competition between the South Eastern and the London, Brighton and South Coast railway companies, or the London and North Western, the Midland and the Great Northern companies, during which fares fell to ¼d per mile first class, ⅓d per mile second class.[13] 'Larger and larger advertisements are issued,' the *Illustrated London News* remarked, 'and larger placards; "sandwiches" perambulate the streets in various directions; and individual touters, armed with piles of small bundles, pester and bespatter the passengers with their recommendation and announcements.'[14]

Such fierce price competition in regular services and in excursions brought nothing but benefit to the poorer classes in the great cities,

[11] BTHR RAC(S) 1/73, July 1856.
[12] BTHR PYB 1/128, p. 6.
[13] H.C., 1867, XXXVIII, Q.7362.
[14] *Illustrated London News*, 23 February 1856.

and the fifties was the decade in which occasional railway travel became part of the life of the humbler artisan and factory worker. From the companies' point of view, however, although traffic increased by up to 40%, with a corresponding strain upon terminal facilities, the margins of profit fell, in some cases very markedly.[15] 'Coming to their senses' involved principally the signing of legally binding private agreements to divide traffic and share receipts, accompanied by the tacit and simultaneous raising of fares. In many cases the agreements were binding for periods of up to twenty-one years.

These agreements to moderate the extremes of price competition did not lead to the immediate and complete suppression of rivalry, so much as to its diversion into new channels. Of particular moment for the urban history of the five great towns of Victorian Britain was the tendency for the expression of rivalry to shift to competition over urban sites and facilities.

Looking back in 1872 over the previous decade, James Allport, General Manager of the Midland railway, described the course of events as follows:

Counsel (alluding to the close similarity between fares on the L. & N.W. and Midland lines)

'Is it not the fact that in places where two great companies compete, there is almost always an agreement as to what shall be the charges made to the public?—That is true, but still you will always find that the competition is very keen. *I do not mean competition by charge but competition by accommodation*, and you will find that the public are generally very much better accommodated.'

'In keeping up competition you want to lower the rates to the public?—Not lowering the rates; I think the rates are low enough now speaking generally.'

'Then all you must compete for is not to lower the rates for the advantage of the public, but for the purpose of keeping up the present high rates and putting them in another pocket?—I do not say that at all; I say that the rates are not high by any means; I say that the present rates are very much below the (statutory) maximum, and although it may not be a competition of rates it is a competition of accommodation.'[16]

Later in his evidence Allport went on to make it clear that a feature of this competition for accommodation tacitly accepted by the railway managers was that it could be carried on even during the period of a Traffic Agreement between two companies.[17] The period of truce could be used for strengthening and reinforcing a company's territorial grasp on a major city, and at least two of the major urban terminal schemes of the 1860's were conceived in these terms. Like the L. & N.W. and

[15] H.C., 1867, XXXVIII, Q.7372, Tables 4, 5 and 6.
[16] H.C., 1872, XIII, QQ.428, 457–8. My italics.
[17] *Ibid.* QQ. 506–7.

the Midland railway companies, the Glasgow and South Western and the Caledonian, or the London, Chatham and Dover and the South Eastern companies, went through the phase of rivalry which Allport had described: the signing of a truce and traffic sharing agreement, followed or accompanied by an intensified rivalry over urban accommodation.[18] The continued vigilance of the signatories to the truces is shown by the tone of the communications between them, which read like diplomatic notes between sovereign powers. 'If either endeavours to shut out the other from what should be neutral ground', the Caledonian Committee of Management determined, 'or monopolise the whole trade of the District, it is evident that *peace* is impractical.'[19] Or— to take an example of the language used by two rival southern companies later in the century—the L.C. & D. speaks of 'unwarrantable acts of aggression', and the need for 'the principle of absolute neutrality and forbearance from all encroachments by one company upon the other', whilst the Chairman of the South Eastern denies the intention 'to carry the sword into a neighbouring country', and speaks of the desire 'to live peaceably and harmoniously with their neighbours.'[20] It is clear, without multiplying examples, that the language of diplomacy and military strategy came naturally to the minds of railway company managers; for the *détente*, the *fait accompli*, the treaty, alliances, truces, territorial boundaries were the terms in which railway managers thought of their vocation. Consequently when a particularly violent phase of price and traffic rivalry had pared away all profit, competition tended to be diverted into other channels rather than suppressed.

Competition over terminal sites and routes had also been a feature of the earlier railway booms, in 1837 and 1847. George Carr Glyn, Chairman of the L. & N.W. had admitted, in 1848, that the principle of competition had 'forced upon us the necessity of defending our own property, by compelling us to undertake schemes which, I take upon myself to say, on behalf of the Board, would otherwise never have entered into our imaginations.'[21] As the competition over fares was curbed, however, and as the absolute volumes of passenger traffic doubled, in the 1850's, the emphasis shifted to even more intense competition over terminal facilities. Only in the 1870's did it move back to a contest over speed, improved rolling stock and service.[22]

[18] John R. Kellett, 'Glasgow's Railways, 1830–80', *Ec.HR*, XVII (1964), 365. P. S. Bagwell, 'The Rivalry and Working Union of the South Eastern and the London, Chatham and Dover Railways', *JTH*, II (1955), 68.

[19] BTHR CAL 1/7, 26 February 1847, p. 556.

[20] P. S. Bagwell, *loc. cit.* 68, 74.

[21] Speech to shareholders, 18 February 1848, quoted in Samuel Salt, *Railway Commercial Information* (1850), 86.

[22] W. Ashworth, *An Economic History of England, 1870–1939* (1960), 120–3. O. S. Nock, *British Steam Railways* (1961), 131–60. Jack Simmons, *The Railways of Britain* (1961), 24–6, 114–7, 144.

What this meant to Victorian cities can best be particularised in detail, but it would be a reasonable generalisation at this point to say that those eligible areas of the older city centre which had escaped the railway companies' attention in the forties, especially those covered with cheap lower-class housing, held in large, easily-acquired units, were now torn down. In his study of *Demolition Statements* for London H. J. Dyos comments upon the comparatively short period during which the most intense activity was concentrated: 37,000 displacements of working-class inhabitants between 1859 and 1867, out of the (recorded) total of 76,000 between 1853 and 1901.[23] A brief glance, in turn, at the parenthood of some of the schemes put forward in Glasgow, London, Manchester, Liverpool and Birmingham in the early sixties, may serve to illustrate the competition over accommodation to which Allport referred.

In Glasgow the first central terminal for trunk routes from the south, St. Enoch Station, and the first crossing of the river Clyde, was deliberately devised during a period of truce between the main rivals for trunk traffic, the Glasgow and South Western and the Caledonian railway companies. The avowed intention of the terminal was to give the G. & S.W. company competitive advantages when the twenty-one year Agreement it had signed in 1853 with the Caledonian expired.[24]

In London, apart from the extensive river crossings carried through, and the Great Eastern's metropolitan extension, the Midland railway company also forced its way, at great expense, to a separate station of its own at the Euston road. Half the Somers Town slums were demolished to make way, at St. Pancras, for a large passenger and goods station linked by tunnels to the new Metropolitan underground. The underlying idea at St. Pancras, as at the other termini of the sixties, was to stake a claim on future traffic by establishing an advantage in terminal facilities. As a contemporary periodical pointed out, 'The Metropolitan tunnel to bring passengers from Manchester directly to Moorgate . . . or by Metropolitan Extension to Victoria Station at Pimlico will probably give the Midland company an advantage over the chief competitor, the L. & N.W. railway.'[25] South of the river the London companies likewise spent enormous sums, not on improving their rolling stock, which was 'filthy and poverty stricken', but on cutting into the central district and establishing new stations at Victoria, Charing Cross and Cannon Street.[26]

In Manchester the feud between the M.S. & L. and the L. & N.W. had reached the stage of open warfare at the London Road station

[23] H. J. Dyos, JTH, II (1955), 14.
[24] *Infra* Chap. 8, sec. 2.
[25] *Illustrated London News*, 15 February 1868.
[26] C. Hamilton Ellis, *British Railway History* (1954 & 9) I, 244.

by 1857, when the L. & N.W.'s directors formally returned their 17 ivory free passes.[27] The division and rebuilding of London Road station, and the proposal of drastic new schemes for a large new Central station in 1866 and 1872 were the results of this acute rivalry, and involved large encroachments on central property. In Liverpool also, the cutting of a new Central station, product of the L. & N.W. and Cheshire Lines Committee's rivalry, dates to the same period; and in Birmingham extensive reconstruction, doubling the size of New Street and bringing the Midland railway into the city centre, carved out a further fifteen acres for exclusively railway uses.[28]

In short, the outcome of the railway companies' shadow-boxing over fares, combined with their real competition over sites, facilities and territory, was a renewed and determined invasion of the central core of the Victorian city in the 1860's. Even though the most ambitious plans for urban through-railways were abandoned, in Liverpool because of the expense, in Manchester because of Corporation opposition, in London because of Parliamentary disapproval, the transformation of central land uses reached its peak in the decade of the 1860's. In this decade, more than any other, the railway engineers and managers, by their decisions, remoulded the fabric and accelerated functional changes in the central districts of the major Victorian cities. Indeed it is arguable that no other group of men exercised, to the same extent, such a conscious power to alter cities in the nineteenth century. Certainly the essays at urban renewal by municipal authorities, under the series of Cross and Torrens Acts and Amendments, appear by comparison small in scale and dilatory in action.[29] Even the cutting of boulevards by Joseph Chamberlain in Birmingham and by the Metropolitan Board of Works in London, or the razing of the older parts of Glasgow by the Improvement Trust—all impressive and difficult achievements— did not require such extensive uprooting of homes and businesses, or demolition of property, as the railway operations of the sixties.[30]

One can only speculate about the possible scope for alternative or different decisions which might have existed. As already suggested, it appears likely that full information on the larger effects, or even the direct impact, of railway schemes was not taken into consideration at board-room level. Land agents and solicitors working for the com-

---

[27] Which had permitted them to travel *gratis* over the M.S. & L. railway. G. Dow, *Great Central* (1959), I, 180.

[28] *Infra* Chap. 5, 6 and 7, sec. 2 and 3.

[29] 31 & 2 Vic. c. 130, Torrens Act, 1868; amended by 42 & 3 Vic. c. 64, and 45 & 6 Vic. c. 54. 38 & 9 Vic. c. 36. Cross Act, 1875; amended by 42 & 3 Vic. c. 63, and 45 & 6 Vic. c. 54.

[30] Asa Briggs, *op. cit.* 228–40. C. M. Allan, 'The Genesis of British Urban Development with special reference to Glasgow', *Ec.HR*, XVIII (1965), 599–613. P. J. Edwards, *History of Street Improvements, 1855–97* (1898).

panies had a much clearer and more detailed picture, usually of a small component part of each scheme, but they were acting as servants executing a policy already decided upon; and it is clear, from the few records of Land Purchase committees which have survived, that they were working under extreme pressure, with advisory powers which were limited to practical details.[31]

To a certain extent the railway managers themselves were not entirely free agents. Their policies concerning railway construction, fares and services could not be chosen purely at will. Certain general demand forces at work in the mid-nineteenth century played an obvious part in inclining the railway companies towards a major reconstruction of the central urban area. The high costs of unloading and trans-shipment compared with the low marginal costs of operation can be seen working persistently towards an urban railway system with central, linked sites. The steady increase in volume of short-distance passenger traffic likewise increased the competitive pressure upon railway companies to secure more central sites.

There were also strong public demands for local expenditure on enlarged central accommodation. Manchester 'had been almost insulted by the way in which the inhabitants had been treated by the railway companies'; and by their failure to provide an inch more space, the *Manchester Guardian* reported in 1860.[32] In Liverpool the complaint in 1856 was that 'Goods are still tumbled about from railway to cart, from cart to quay, exposed to dirt, rain and pillage. . . . Passengers still depend on the crowded and tedious omnibus. . . . Why have public men turned away, apparently startled, from schemes affording complete internal communication?'[33] In Glasgow central railway accommodation was 'so inadequate and defective as to endanger life and limb', and inspired letters from the Town Clerk to the Home Secretary, and the Board of Trade.[34]

There were, then, both long-term economic reasons and strong local pressures for concentrating upon terminal facilities in the sixties. The railway managers acceded to them, though the total burden of fixed investment this might finally involve was not carefully considered. By comparison, there were also strong and persistent public pressures towards a policy of cheap fares—fares which were not lowered artificially and temporarily, from expediency, as in the mid-fifties—but were

---

[31] BTHR MSJ 1/1–1/13. Minutes of the Manchester South Junction Lands and Compensation Committee.

[32] *Manchester Guardian*, 17 February 1860.

[33] *Transactions of the Liverpool Polytechnic Society* (1856) 205, 212. LRL H 680.6 POL.

[34] MS correspondence between the Town Clerk, the North British railway company, the Board of Trade and the Home Secretary, September 1873–October 1876. GRL D 397154.

lowered as part of a coherent and sustained attempt to increase traffic. As early as 1844 *The Economist* had sounded the call it was to repeat, at intervals, throughout the next two decades.

'Far be it from us to insinuate that it is the duty of a railway company to sacrifice its interests and profits for the purpose of inducing a great locomotion amongst the people . . . but railway companies have hitherto committed the common fault, which has been apparent in every pursuit in this country in its infancy—that of looking chiefly for support to the higher and wealthy middle classes; whereas experience has proved that in every pursuit, even in literature, that the policy is most profitable which embraces the wants and patronage of the great masses of the working population, whose united incomes are infinitely greater than those of any other class. Some years ago dealers all flocked towards Bond Street, Piccadilly and the neighbourhood of wealthy and aristocratic dwellings—splendid hotels were built only in the precincts of our best squares, or in the wealthiest parts of the city; but in modern times the united earnings of the operative classes have raised up perfect palaces for the sale of drapery and groceries, as well as gin and beer, and the supply of all their other wants, in the leading thoroughfares, through all the manufacturing parts of the metropolis, and in every manufacturing town and village throughout the country. Ingenuity and art have been in a peculiar way, both amongst our manufacturers and dealers, engaged of late years in ministering to, and catering for, the wants of this new and important class' . . . 'The time we have no doubt will come when railway companies will discover this new secret in trade, and, when they do, we feel assured their practice of it will prove peculiarly successful.'[35]

The 'ready money of the million' was the formula for success held out to the railway managers by *The Economist*. In an article entitled 'Why do Railways succeed mechanically and fail commercially?', eleven years later, *The Economist* was still repeating its message. 'Railways cannot succeed commercially by studying the interests of a small class. They must carry the great multitude and the commodities they use.'[36] By 1865, tired of the deaf ear the companies had turned to its advice, *The Economist* had concluded, 'The Government, if they owned the railways, might give the working classes their share in the benefits of quick locomotion, though they will never get it from others.'[37]

A really cheap fare policy might possibly, as some claimed, have been comparable in effect to customs reform or postal reform; but the pressures for it, unlike those for expanded terminal facilities, were *not* heeded.[38] Yet, viewing the huge, indivisible and permanent capital

---

[35] *The Economist*, 20 July 1844, 1011.
[36] *Ibid.* 22 September 1855, 1038.
[37] *Ibid.* 7 January 1865, 2.
[38] H.C. 1867, XXXVIII, Report, p. CVII, comments on evidence by Rowland Hill. Hill had expressed the same views more than twenty years earlier, *Railway Reform* (1844), 97. MRL, Political Tracts, P 3411.

expenditure involved by the wholesale intrusion into city centres, one cannot help wondering, whether even the goal of railway profits might not have been better served by a tacit agreement to place terminals in areas not quite so central and to concentrate upon a marked and progressive reduction of overall fares and transport charges.

3. *The organisation and control of urban projects*

To understand further why the railway companies assumed their expensive and self-appointed task of remoulding the city centres in the eighteen sixties, it is necessary to examine the organisation of urban railway building, the changes in railway financing, and the rise of the contractor and the consultant or independent railway engineer. They represented a new constructional industry and a new professional vested interest which had grown up, step by step with the growth of the railway system itself, in the eighteen thirties and forties.

The scale and specialised techniques of railway building had rapidly ensured that, though there was still a small place for local firms in the execution of railway works, the great constructor, handling large numbers of men and great quantities of equipment, soon came to take the greater share of contract work.[39] Thomas Brassey, Morton Peto and Edward Betts, Lucas and Waring Brothers, Charles Fox, James Falshaw, John Kelk and others emerged as the leading entrepreneurs in a field where energy and the willingness to take risks were at an unusual premium. They were a small body of men, often acting in combination with each other—their names can be seen in changing associations on the *Printed Specifications and Tenders*—and had begun to hold quarterly meetings as early as 1839. By 1848 *Herapath's Railway Magazine* was complaining of the lack of competition in tendering, and the growing practice of tendering for the whole line.[40] The contractors had also begun, even in the 1840's, to accept payment for their work, not in cash, but in shares or in mortgage bonds; thus, as it were, *volunteering* their own working capital and their credit towards railway promotion.

All the elements for a powerful lobby, whose prime interest lay in works of demolition and construction, had assembled by the mid-forties. Not merely were the contractors an able and closely knit group, whose increasingly large capitals were committed to railway promotion, but regiments of solicitors, counsel, and land and law agents, all stood to gain from the promotion of further schemes; and, like the contrac-

[39] Terry Coleman, *The Railway Navvies* (1965), 51–63.
[40] *Railway Times*, 6 April 1839, 295; *Herapath's Railway Magazine*, 4 November 1848, 1161. Both references, and examples of payment by mortgage bond are from Harold Pollins, 'Railway Contractors and the Finance of Railway Development in Britain', *JTH*, III (1957), 46.

tors, they were able to direct very large sums, of their own and of their clients' money, into whatever promising project could be launched. Many, like William Burchell, John Lingard, or John Fleming, were not merely large subscribers but sat on the Board as directors of the companies.[41] These men had nothing to gain from cheap fares for a lower social class, except where opportunities for adroit land speculation presented themselves. On the other hand, a great deal of lucrative employment could stem from a well contested Parliamentary Bill with a complex network of urban properties on the schedule. 'There were,' a contemporary wrote of the Brighton line, 'about twenty counsel engaged, headed by six King's Serjeants and King's Counsel; there was a regiment of twenty eminent solicitors, each flanked by a brigade of parliamentary agents and a whole army of surveyors and engineers.'[42] The legal expenses for this bill came to £100,000; and, in fact, if one works out the legal charges, not merely at the Parliamentary stage but also (and this is sometimes left out of consideration) at the land requisition and purchase stage, the legal profession's income from the immense capital outlay on railways may have come to between five and seven *per cent* of the total.[43]

The engineers and surveyors added to the strength of the railway promotion lobby. They did not have large permanent staffs, labour forces and expensive capital equipment to keep fully employed, like the contractors, nor did they have sums to advance to originate new projects comparable to those in the hands of contractors and solicitors, but their careers were even more directly and personally engaged. Some of them received enormous fees, like John Fowler, who received over £300,000 for two urban projects (the Metropolitan and the District lines). 'Taking it any way you like,' Edward Watkin wrote to him, when he was called in to put the Metropolitan's affairs on a sound financial footing, '. . . time, speciality, risk, quantity, value or all combined, you have set an example of charges which seems to me to have largely aided in the demoralisation of professional men of all sorts who have lived upon the suffering shareholders for the past ten years.'[44]

[41] These were solicitors who actually sat on the Boards of the Metropolitan, Manchester, Sheffield and Lincolnshire, and Edinburgh and Glasgow railways respectively, and also handled their legal affairs. On other occasions, though not invited to join the Board, solicitors handling land purchase were large shareholders, and their names can be found in the Subscription Contracts.

[42] *Railway Reform* (1844), 68. MRL, Political Tracts, P 3411.

[43] Law charges and Parliamentary expenses 1825–50 came to 5.1% of total expenditure, or £5,940,000 (See Appendix 1.) Other conveyance and law charges were concealed under the heading of Land and Property, and are occasionally specified. At a reasonable minimum these further charges came to £1,250,000 or just over 1% of total expenditure in 1850 for the 26 companies examined.

[44] T. C. Barker and Michael Robbins, *op. cit.* 94.

There was no danger that this group of professional men would lack a voice in Parliament. The 'Railway interest' was variously estimated at different times to number between 50 and 150 M.P.s.[45] Some had already become directors before they moved into public life; others had become M.P.s first and received the invitations to the railway boardroom afterwards. 'We have friends in the House who are willing to join us,' was the argument the Chairman of the L. & N.W. company used for increasing the number of directors from eighteen to twenty-four.[46] Altogether they formed a very powerful group whose interests were best served, not by internal changes of policy on fares, but by new construction. A contemporary commented as early as 1846 upon the way the elements of this group had already come together. 'Many of the railway companies would be better satisfied to have no more termini in the metropolis, provided all others could be kept out. I do not know that this applies generally, neither do I think it would be the same with surveyors and lawyers, engineers and architects; they would wish very much to have these stations carried out.'[47]

After 1850, during the cautious years which followed the collapse of railway share prices in 1847, the influence of the contractors increased still further. The general public showed a marked reluctance to invest again on the same scale in the risk-bearing Ordinary shares, which carried voting control, but instead inclined strongly towards Debenture and Preference stocks, shares which carried a safer, fixed yield. By the end of the sixties Ordinary shares made up less than half the total capital of all railway companies; fifty-seven per cent was in Loans, Guaranteed and Preference stock and Debentures.[48] This was symptomatic of the new financial situation in which railway companies found themselves in the 1850's and 1860's; a situation which created an unusual opportunity for the contractor. 'For most companies after 1850,' writes Harold Pollins, 'it was singularly difficult to raise capital. It is

---

[45] P. S. Bagwell, 'The Railway Interest: its Organisation and Influence', JTH, VII (1965), 65–86, gives a table derived from W. O. Aydelotte showing, annually, the number of members of both houses holding railway directorships, reaching its peak of 215 in 1867. On the other hand, members might also have other interests, and in the mid-1860's 436 members with landed and 545 with industrial, mercantile and financial interests could be counted. J. A. Thomas, *The House of Commons, 1832–1901, A Study of its economic and functional character* (Cardiff, 1939), 4–7.

[46] *Reasons in favour of a Direct Line of Railroad from London to Manchester* (1846), 15.

[47] H.C., 1846, XVII, Q.600.

[48] H.C., 1872, XIII, Appendix N, p.88. The preferential issues, on which money could often be raised even by companies paying little or no dividend upon their ordinary shares, totalled 7% Guaranteed, 23% Preference, 10% Debenture stocks, and 17% loans at this time.

difficult to find examples of new companies obtaining their funds entirely from the public.'[49]

As Pollins points out, the railway companies of the late fifties and early sixties had to compete for investment funds with domestic industry, to which limited liability was being extended, and with foreign railway schemes. 'You will find that capital is going out to India, and all over the world seeking for employment in railways', the Chairman of the L. & N.W. complained in 1863, 'What is the state of things in England? There is not one of the great companies in this country who can raise sixpence without preference or guaranteed shares. There are no proprietors willing to come forward to make a railway. They are made by contractors, engineers, and speculators, who live on the fears of the companies.'[50]

Their principal fear in the 1860's was that of being left out in the cold with inferior access and facilities at the great cities where the busiest lines terminated. Consequently the same pattern is repeated in each. In Manchester and Birmingham existing large companies executed large extensions. In Liverpool, Glasgow and London the schemes were originated by the contractors and engineers themselves, usually with the assistance of finance companies. 'Certain "Finance Companies", were formed', the Chairman of Committees in the House of Lords asserted in 1864, 'for the avowed purpose of providing the capital which would enable contractors to carry out their schemes' ... 'Last year all the schemes which were brought before Parliament by Bills more or less looked to these finance companies for assistance.'[51]

T. C. Barker's and Harold Pollins's researches have shown specific links between Edward Betts and the promotion of the West End and Crystal Palace Railway (in which he was the largest shareholder); Charles Fox, Morton Peto and Edward Betts and the London, Chatham and Dover Railway; John Kelk and the Metropolitan extensions to Moorgate and Farringdon Street; Peto, Betts, Kelk and Waring Brothers and the Metropolitan District line.[52] To these can be added the combined activities of the consulting engineers and contractors at other terminals, John Fowler and John Kelk at Victoria; John Fowler,

[49] Harold Pollins, JTH, III (1957), 44.

[50] *Ibid.* 44.

[51] *Ibid.* 106. Other finance houses already well established also lent heavily to contractors. The most notable example is the house of Overend, Gurney and Co. which crashed in May 1866, and brought down the firm of Peto and Betts. Joseph Firbank, another contractor, who was building the South London line just after the Overend, Gurney collapse, continued to accept payment in stock which fell for a time to 38% of its face value—a gesture of confidence greatly appreciated by Samuel Laing, the line's sponsor. F. McDermott, *The Life and Work of Joseph Firbank* (1887), 41–2.

[52] Harold Pollins, JTH, III (1957), 48. T. C. Barker and Michael Robbins, *op. cit.* 126, 151, 142.

Brassey, Peto, Betts, Kelk and Waring Brothers at Glasgow, St. Enoch; John Fowler and Waring Brothers at Liverpool, Central.[53] With each terminus the procedure adopted was the same; a nominally independent company was floated, with a huge and valuable urban site and a few miles of track, which drew a substantial amount of its capital from those directly concerned with the construction. In some other cases, as with John Hawkshaw, Samuel Smiles and the South Eastern Railway Company at Charing Cross and Cannon Street, the schemes clearly formed part of a large parent company's plans from their inception.[54] Even here, however, they owed something to the persuasiveness of the consulting engineer, and the contractor's willingness to accept shares for payment, and fell into a different category from the straightforward company-promoted St. Pancras or Liverpool Street schemes. It may well be, as Pollins suggests, that 'not only did the contractors build new lines but they probably stimulated older companies to build in order to protect their territories . . . to take up new schemes for self-preservation, as well as for meeting the demand of traffic.'[55]

In other cases contractors and solicitors were not merely the originators of the terminal schemes, but went beyond the bounds of what might be termed *bona fide* speculations by specialised investors, and crossed into the territory of fraud. Both the St. Enoch, Glasgow, and the Central, Liverpool, fell into this category.

The St. Enoch station, together with the seven miles of urban branch lines, cost the City of Glasgow Union Railway Company some £2,000,000. The raising of such a sum taxed the contractors' ingenuity to the utmost and led to accusations of financial irregularity.

The Union's *Subscription Contract* had undoubtedly been spurious and in exposing it the Caledonian company's counsel revealed that there were important influences bearing upon policy of which the public were unaware. The Union engineer James Ferrie Blair was questioned intensively about who was actually 'to provide the sinews of war'.

Mr. Mundell (counsel for the Caledonian Railway Company): 'Who was to pay you then if Parliament was not to grant this Bill?'

Mr. Blair: 'Well I have never thought of that matter.'

Mr. Mundell: 'That is one of the very first things that I should think of myself and I should have thought you would have been equally provident.'[56]

The full story, extracted item by item, was that Blair, after conducting

[53] According to Mark Fladgate, solicitor to the Victoria Station and Pimlico Railway company, Kelk was a shareholder to the extent of £100,000. BTHR PYB 1/107, 21 March 1860, S.C. on London, Brighton, and South Coast and Vic. Stn. and Pim. Rly. companies. See *infra* for Fowler at Glasgow, St. Enoch and Liverpool, Central.

[54] Edwin Course, *London Railways* (1962), 45–54.

[55] Harold Pollins, *JTH*, III, (1957), 45.

[56] HLRO, Min., H.C., 1864, 13 May, pp. 260–6.

'independent surveys' and receiving encouragement but no promise of capital from certain quarters, had been introduced by his friend and fellow-engineer John Fowler to Sir Morton Peto. Peto, Thomas Brassey and others, offered to put up the necessary capital to get the venture under way, some £400,000, on condition that they were made contractors for the scheme with a guaranteed 10 *per cent* profit on their work; and an extraordinary contract to this effect was produced by order of the Commons' Committee.[57] The other subscribers of capital were the Glasgow and South-Western and Edinburgh-Glasgow railway companies subscribing corporately and not in the individual names of their directors. Only £47,000, about 6 *per cent* of the total, was to be raised from the public as 'new capital'.

The Commons' Committee, confronted by these facts, decided that 'the mode in which it was proposed to raise the capital for this Bill was not such as ought to allow the Bill to be passed.'[58] After a week's adjournment, however, the Union Company was able to come forward with what appeared a more satisfactory subscription contract and the bill was proved.[59]

In Liverpool, John Fowler again, this time in conjunction with the engineer Walter Brydone, with the solicitor John Towers Smith, and the contractors Waring Brothers, laid out a series of short lines to give urban access from the south to the centre of Liverpool: the Garston and Liverpool, the Liverpool Central Station and Railway, and the Birkenhead and Liverpool lines. This series of acts, obtained between 1861 and 1865, gave a new route, obviously tailor-made for sale to the Manchester, Sheffield and Lincolnshire railway; and in due course the schemes were taken over by that company, on the special condition that the same engineers, solicitors and contractors were retained.[60] The nominal directors of the original terminal company, Mr. Birkett, Mr. Reeves and Colonel Parke, at first represented to be substantial local shareholders, turned out not to have invested a penny of their own money in the scheme.[61]

Mr. Aspinall, counsel for the L. & N.W. whose long and profitable monopoly of the Liverpool traffic was being brought to an end, went to some lengths to bring out the curious nature of the arrangement. He insisted that a *Speaker's Warrant* be issued to compel Colonel Parke to attend. He lived, not at Liverpool, but High Wycombe, and, when he finally appeared, confessed that the enterprise had, in fact, been

[57] See App. 2.
[58] HLRO, Min., H.C., 1864, 26 May, p. 1.
[59] *Ibid.* 1 June, p. 1.
[60] G. Dow, *Great Central* (1962), II, 132.
[61] HLRO, Min., H.C., 1865, 15 May, QQ.1–55, S.C. on Birkenhead and Liverpool Railway. The solicitors and engineer operated 'in exactly the same mode in respect to the Liverpool Central Station Railway', Q.297.

proposed to him by the solicitor for the Bill, J. T. Smith. Where had the money he invested come from? Mr. Smith lent it to him 'having previously obtained it elsewhere.' 'Is this it', asked Mr. Aspinall sarcastically, when J. T. Smith had been called, 'that you, being solicitor for the directors, have lent the money to yourself as solicitor for the borrowers, upon the understanding that you as solicitor to the lenders are to look after it and see that it does not get into the control of the borrowers?'[62]

Colonel Parke and the others were, in fact, men of straw, employed by the solicitors for the Bill, and lent money raised upon the contractors', solicitors' and engineers' credit. To add to the piquancy of the situation the *Plan and Section* and *Books of Reference* reveal that one hundred and seventy of the properties now purchased for the central site had already been bought up earlier by Thomas Brassey.[63]

It is clear, in fact, that the promotion of urban schemes, though partly a response to traffic demands, was also given a particular impetus by contractors, engineers and solicitors, all directly interested parties, and likely to profit from the stirring up of the larger established companies' dormant rivalries and anxieties. Indeed the process did not escape the notice of contemporaries, though the law of libel compelled them to keep to generalities. *The Economist* wrote in 1854, as these schemes gathered momentum, 'The engineers have a common interest with the lawyers; they work together, and there has grown up between them a well-organised system of co-operation, rendered more efficient by the wealth and influence which both have each year accumulated. To promote their ends, influential solicitors place their nominees on the board of directors, and engineers of lines as shareholders propose extensions which they will have to execute. With these two contractors, now men of vast wealth, co-operate, and by their united influence lines are fostered into being which it is known from the beginning will not pay.'[64] Again, in January 1865, 'We have now made ninety-nine hundredths of the railways we ought to make but still the "engineers' and lawyers' railway projects" go on.'[65] By 1872, when Captain Tyler, of the Board of Trade, presented his report to the Joint Select Committee on Railway Companies Amalgamations, it seemed a matter for impartial historical record that the major companies 'damaged themselves, not

[62] *Ibid.* QQ.83, 111, 126.
[63] HLRO, P & S, B.Ref., 1861–2, Manchester, Sheffield and Lincolnshire Railway (Liverpool Central Station Railway). Thomas Brassey was acting as a trustee under Joseph Locke's will. He and Locke had been close friends and rented, at one time, a joint shooting in Dumfriesshire. Arthur Helps, *Life and Labours of Mr. Brassey, 1805–1870* (1872), 294.
[64] *The Economist*, 21 October 1854, 1148.
[65] *Ibid.* 14 January 1865, 36. *The Economist* later estimated that two-thirds of the capital authorised in the years 1864–6 was for 'contractors' lines', *Ibid.* 9 March 1867, 31, and H. Pollins, *loc. cit.* 103.

only by direct expenditure before Parliament, and for extensions, branches and block lines, but also by too eagerly grasping at quasi-independent lines, constructed for the purpose by ingenious promoters.'[66] Indeed, but for the forty two warrants of abandonment which were granted after the general panic of 1865, there would have been even more plausible urban extensions looking for a permanent owner.

4. The effects of construction

The commercial performance of railway companies is a complex product of many factors, and it would be naïve to expect the annual tables of dividends in *Bradshaw's Shareholder's Guide* to yield a direct reflection of the heavy burdens put upon railways by their large urban land purchases in the 1840's and 1860's.[67] The fluctuating market values of stocks, the numerous exchanges, conversions and issues of scrip would ensure that any percentage dividend series which was not repeatedly corrected and qualified would be an unreal guide.[68] A direct correlation between urban railway investment and dividends cannot be shown statistically.

Nevertheless the huge sums involved, particularly in the 1860's, cannot easily be set aside; £2,000,000 for one scheme at Glasgow, £1,000,000 at Liverpool, £4,000,000 for the four miles of extensions at Charing Cross and Cannon Street, £2,000,000 at Liverpool Street.[69] Each of these sums represents between $\frac{1}{8}$% and $\frac{1}{2}$% of the entire annual national income in the mid-sixties; or translated into modern terms, they were equivalent investment efforts to raising between £40,000,000 and £160,000,000 for each project.[70]

Moreover, it is conspicuous that those companies which plunged most deeply into urban terminal schemes were also amongst the least successful from the shareholders' point of view. The Great Eastern and the London, Chatham and Dover were brought to Chancery; the South Eastern railway company's dividend performance for the rest of the century after its Charing Cross scheme was disappointing.[71] The

[66] H.C., 1872, XIII, Appendix N, p. 92.

[67] *Bradshaw's Shareholders' Guide*, published 1853–62, merged into the *Railway Manual, Shareholders' Guide and Official Directory* after 1863.

[68] Michael Robbins, *The Railway Age* (1962), 114.

[69] The references for these estimates may be found *infra* in the *Case Histories*.

[70] B. R. Mitchell and Phyllis Deane, *Abstract of British Historical Statistics* (1962), 367. Phyllis Deane, 'Contemporary estimates of the National Income in the second half of the nineteenth century', *Ec.HR*, IX (1956–7), 451–61.

[71] C. F. Dendy Marshall, *A History of the Southern Railway* (1963), II, 342–3. The L.C. & D. railway company was unable to pay its creditors, stated the six-monthly report, because of the unexpected delays and cost of the Metropolitan extension and the City and Victoria Station works. For the L.B. and S.C. see Bradshaw's *Railway Manual etc.* (1889) 91–2.

Metropolitan Railway, which had been held up as the shining example of a profitable urban line, only managed to pay its 5% dividends by skilful management of surplus lands; and the District only paid 2% to 2½%.[72] By comparison, the London General Omnibus Company's horse-drawn vehicles earned a steady 10% to 12½% for their proprietors. The contrast is so marked as to lead T. C. Barker, in *A History of London Transport*, to speculate, 'It is tempting to argue that the railways bestowed the largest social benefit upon London by enabling it to grow outwards, yet derived the smallest economic reward.'[73] Excessive investment in urban works is one of the factors which explain this disparity in dividend earning capacity.

In the North, the railway company which played the most active part in carving out new termini for itself in Manchester and Liverpool— the Manchester, Sheffield and Lincolnshire—paid such poor dividends that the shareholders ironically suggested that the company's initials stood for Money, Sunk and Lost. Even the 3% which it achieved once or twice in the 1880's vanished when the company decided upon the grandiose scheme of another new urban terminal, in London (at Marylebone in the nineties). The 'Great Central' railway (as the M.S. & L. was now officially named) never paid any dividends at all on its Ordinary shares; 'Gone Completely' was the nickname given by the shareholders.[74]

There remain the major railway companies, the L. & N.W., the G.W. and the Midland, all returning dividends of five to six *per cent* regularly in the second half of the nineteenth century. On the face of it very satisfactory results, but in each case the General Managers felt that an excessive amount of their total capital had been expended upon terminals. 'I asked our engineer to try and make a calculation of what the cost of the stations and sidings on the Great Western was,' James Grierson, General Manager of the G.W. testified in 1867. He found that of the £45,000,000 capital, £6,500,000 had been spent on the terminals and sidings. William Cawkwell, General Manager of the L. & N.W. estimated that out of his company's capital of £44,000,000, £8,000,000 had been spent on stations, the greater part of it before 1849 when sites were cheaper. James Allport, of the Midland, reported 'as nearly as we can get it, out of a total capital of £20,900,000 we have spent on our stations £4,250,000.'[75] He later corrected his statement,

---

[72] From 1863–8 the Metropolitan railway was able to pay 7% on its ordinary shares, and its financial success was, in fact, one of the proximate causes of the 1863 railway boom. Then its dividends fell dramatically. The London General Omnibus Company reached its high dividends in the 1880's. T. C. Barker and Michael Robbins, *op. cit.* 151, 159, 175, 252.

[73] *Ibid.* 272.

[74] Jack Simmons, *op. cit.* 29. Michael Robbins, *op. cit.* 114.

[75] H.C., 1867, XXXVIII, QQ.13495, 11562–8, 13724–31.

saying that he had left out the new work on the London approaches (St. Pancras and Somers Town) for which another three or four million should be added. 'In our case one fifth of our capital has been spent on terminals'.—'You have probably not expended much more upon stations than other companies have in proportion to the wants of your line?—'No'. If expressed as a levy, in round figures, it would amount to about 2s 3d per ton at each end, or 4s 6d per journey. 'I mention those figures' Allport added 'to show the injustice that would be committed upon railway companies if they were prohibited from making a charge for terminal expenses.'[76]

On average the three largest companies had expended $17\frac{1}{2}\%$ of their capital upon their terminals and sidings. If reproduced by other companies, this would mean that something like £85—£90 millions had been expended on urban facilities out of the total of £500 millions of national railway capital invested. 'The interest on the cost of these premises', John Hawkshaw pleaded in his evidence, 'is surely a legitimate terminal charge.'[77]

Here, then, was a possible solution to the heavy financial burden the railway companies' urban land acquisition had laid upon even the largest of them. It could hardly be met by increasing the general level of fares, many of which were limited by statute and were already far too high in the opinion of many traders, businessmen and railway reformers; but a supplementary charge could be made for terminal facilities. 'The terminal expense not only includes the labour that is employed in loading and unloading', James Allport claimed in 1872, 'but the necessary adjuncts to enable that loading and unloading to be done. You must have, for instance, a shed and land; you must have lights, and you must pay taxes and gas, and, I think, *a fair interest upon the outlay upon the station*; and I think that all those items should be taken into account in fixing what the terminals should be.'[78] During the 1860's and 1870's the major railway companies, operating through agreed Clearing House 'terminal charges', attempted in this way to pass off onto the public a supplement, over and above their rate per mile, to recoup the heavy expenditure on urban stations and yards.

In a sense they were perfectly justified; at any rate, in part of their claim. For the railway companies had always differed from canals in operating not merely as toll companies, charging so much per mile for the use of their permanent way; but, unlike the canal companies, they had become, almost immediately, the sole carriers over their own

[76] *Ibid.* QQ.13728–9, 13725.
[77] *Ibid.* Q.14470. U.K. paid-up railway capital in 1867 was £502,262,887. H.C. Sessional Papers, 1890, LXV, p. 680. For Great Britain alone it was £464,900,000. B. R. Mitchell and Phyllis Deane, *op. cit.* 225.
[78] H.C., 1872, XIII, Q.4430. My Italics.

routes.[79] In most towns they arranged collection, but even when goods were carted independently to their termini for shipment, the reception, storage and loading was in company hands. What this meant in practical terms can be seen from a comparison of two of the Great Western railway's termini at Birmingham: Snow Hill, an exclusively passenger station, with receipts (in 1902) of £162,400 and a staff of 193 employees; and Hockley Goods terminus, with receipts of £225,670 and a staff of 1,000.[80] At the passenger stations the customers, so to speak, loaded and unloaded themselves, and the argument for a surcharge was weak. Cornelius Eborall, General Manager of the South Eastern railway company was, not surprisingly, one of those who felt, in 1867, that a terminal charge should be made even for passengers; but the Secretary of the Railway Clearing House made it clear, in 1872, that the general consensus of opinion was to disallow terminal charges on passenger traffic.[81] However the terminal freight supplements were 'blanket charges', not published or defined beforehand, and used for general railway purposes after collection. So long as the money to pay for the urban sites came in from somewhere, the exact source of the levy was immaterial.

In raising again the distinction between tolls and carriage, and in making an unspecified addition for 'terminal charges', the railway companies aroused suspicion and ill-will concerning preferential rates and their carriage monopoly, and laid themselves open to endless litigation. Actions were brought, in turn, before the Railway Commissioners, the Court of Queen's Bench and the House of Lords, against the Midland, the M.S. & L., the L. & N.W., the G.N., the G.E., the Lancashire and Yorkshire, the London, Chatham and Dover, the London, Brighton and South Coast railways.[82] Decisions in these cases did little to clarify and a great deal to complicate the issue.

At first, as in *J. & F. Howard v. the Midland Railway Company* the ruling was given that 'station expenses do not form an element of definite extra charge'; and although there was general agreement that 'a reasonable charge should be made for accommodation offered and services rendered' the Royal Commission of 1867 commented unfavourably upon the interpretation set upon this by railway companies, 'as authorising them to make additional charges for the expense of *construct-*

---

[79] W. Hodges, *Law of Railways* (1888), I, 440, 543–4. Canal companies were not allowed to enter into working and traffic agreements or act as carriers until 1845. *Correspondence between the Board of Trade and T. Grahame Esq.* (1852), 5–6. B.M. 8235 c. 42.

[80] BTHR GW 4/281 pp. 13, 14.

[81] H.C. 1867, XXXVIII, Q.16, 136 (Eborall). H.C., 1872, XIII, QQ.5564–5 (P. W. Dawson, Secy. to Clearing House).

[82] H.L., 1884–5, XII, 555–7.

ing sidings as well as of working them.'[83] In the cases of *Gidlow v the Lancashire and Yorkshire Railway Company* and *Berry v the London, Chatham and Dover Railway Company* further attempts to clarify terms also led to decisions against the railway companies. In the Gidlow case it was ruled that giving the use of premises was not the same thing as performing a service, and the power to charge for a service did not include the power 'to demand a sum in the nature of rent or interest upon the outlay for structures.'[84] In the Berry case, Counsel for the L.C. & D. pleaded that the L.C. & D. (Metropolitan Extensions) Act of 1861 'was passed on the supposition that the Company had such a power to charge for station expenses as they claim to have; for otherwise the large outlay involved would not, they say, have been undertaken.'[85] In support, J. S. Forbes, the General Manager of the L.C. & D., produced one of the earliest detailed break-downs of terminal costing. The Blackfriars Goods station (at which the excessive charge complained of had taken place) had cost £600,000, of which £475,000 was spent on the part appropriated to goods traffic. Wages, maintenance, lighting and rates came to £25,388—this part of the cost was conceded—but a sum almost as large, £23,759, was claimed as interest on the capital outlay. The total of £49,147 was divided by the tonnage in and out (213,211 tons), giving a justifiable surcharge of 4 shillings and 7·32 pence per ton. Judgment was given against the L.C. & D.[86]

In the course of this lawsuit the further question arose as to what service charge was allowable for different classes of goods and merchandise. In the Berry case it was hops, in Gidlow's coal, in others straw, cement and builders' materials. Surely different service charges should be allowable for different classes of goods? And so a further round began of complex litigation before the law courts, and attempts at classification in the Clearing House.

Finally the whole legal position regarding terminal charges, built up by precedent in the 1870's, was thrown back into the melting pot, in 1885, by the most notorious of all the decisions on this subject, that of *Hall & Co. v. the London, Brighton and South Coast Railway*. Using a clause which occurs in the Acts of every other railway company in the Kingdom, the L.B. & S.C. railway claimed for station accommodation and the use of sidings, as well as for 'weighing, checking, clerkage, watching and labelling.'[87] The Railway Commissioners had held all these to be incidental to conveyance; 'in no part of this clause is it

---

[83] W. M. Acworth, *The Railways and the Traders* (1891), 304.
[84] H.L., 1884–5, XII. 568.
[85] *Ibid*. 568.
[86] *Ibid*. 567.
[87] *The Economist*, 11 July 1885, 839. The clause was section 80 of 16 and 17 Vic. c. 218.

possible to find any sanction for charging for general station accommodation—or for the value of the station itself.'[88] Mr. Justice Wills, in the Court of Queen's Bench, decided that 'to give a man a roof over his head is as much performing him a service as giving him a dinner', and reversed the decision.[89] 'We can only hope' wrote *The Economist*, 'that an appeal may be possible, and that the Railway Commissioners interpreted the law more truly than the judges.'[90]

The issue of 'terminal charges' was also aired for twenty years before the general public, particularly by the Liverpool traders and Chamber of Commerce, and in Parliament, before the Royal Commission of 1867 and the Select Committees of 1872, 1881 and 1882. At the end of this protracted and extremely bitter controversy, although terminal charges were still legal, and still imperfectly defined, the important concession was gained that terminal charges should be fixed and published.[91]

One might wonder why the railway companies objected so strongly to the public knowing before they paid what part of the charge was mileage rate and what proportion the terminal charge. There were three main reasons. First was the sheer problem of accounting. 'I have no means of judging how far the Clearing House terminal charges may be taken as representing the actual cost and the interest of capital involved at stations,' G. P. Bidder, a director of the Great Eastern admitted in 1867. James Allport took the same line in his evidence to the Joint Select Committee in 1872. 'You do not make an arithmetical calculation, so much for carriage and so much for terminal?—Never. As I understand, you have no actual register or record of how any of those charges are divided into terminal charges and other charges?— No.' 'It could be done, but it would cause an immense amount of calculation', Allport objected. 'It would involve calculation at every station in the kingdom, and those terminals would vary from time to time. . . . Perhaps you have bought land originally at £1,000 an acre; you increase your station at a cost, perhaps, of £2,000 or £3,000 an acre, and that alters the cost of the terminals.'[92]

[88] H.L., 1884–5, XII, 571.

[89] W. M. Acworth, *The Railways and the Traders* (1891), 308–9.

[90] *The Economist*, 4 July, 1885, 813. The Court of Appeal, however, had no jurisdiction against this judgment and Hall's case came to establish an important precedent to which railway companies could appeal to support charges for station accommodation, the use of sidings, weighing, checking etc. W. Hodges, *op. cit.* I, 562.

[91] By the Regulation of Railways Act, 1868, 31 and 2, Vic. c. 119, section 17, and the Regulation of Railways Act, 1873, 36 and 7 Vic. c. 48, sections 14 and 15, companies were compelled to keep rate-books at all stations and mineral sidings, and on application by interested parties the Railway and Canal Commissioners could require a statement distinguishing conveyance and terminal charges.

[92] H.C., 1867, XXXVIII, Q.17177 (Bidder). H.C., 1872, XIII, QQ.4416–35 (Allport).

The sort of difficulty to which the publication of detailed figures would lead can be seen in the trial costings which George Findlay, General Manager of the L. & N.W., submitted to the Select Committee of 1881, separating his company's service charges from its interest on capital expenditure:—

Cost per ton of	London	Manchester	Birmingham	Liverpool
working goods	2s 11·08d	1s 8·47d	1s 5d	1s 7·7d
Interest on stations at 4%	4s 3d	2s 4d	1s 9d	2s 3d

Nearly 60% of the total consisted of what amounted to a rent charge on the expensively acquired urban terminals.[93] If this were made public, and the exact amount of mileage and terminal charges attached to each individual station, there would be grave implications. As W. M. Acworth, spokesman of the railway interest, wrote in *The Railways and the Traders*, 1891, such specific location of charges 'would render it impossible to bring in bricks or carry out street refuse over railways which have cost hundreds of thousands of pounds per mile.'[94]

In other words, if the real direct costs incurred by urban railway building were worked out properly and attached to the specific lines and stations concerned, bulky, low-value goods would virtually be excluded from many stations in the major Victorian cities. The interest, for example, on the Huskisson goods station, built on the dockside at Liverpool at a cost of £712,527 by the Cheshire Lines Committee, would come to 3s10½d on every ton which entered. 'In any town above 50,000 or 60,000 inhabitants' Charles Scotter, Goods Manager of the M.S. & L. asserted, 'the terminals allowed by the Clearing House are totally inadequate to cover the actual expense involved.'[95]

Finally, as Allport explained, the statement of separate terminal charges for different stations within one town would have the serious objection to it that 'you would have all the goods sent by the traders to that station where the rate was lowest.'[96] Faced with the prospect of paying real direct costs many of the dealers would choose to consign their goods to an outlying station (say Edgehill, instead of Huskisson at Liverpool) and to arrange cartage.

When they came to count the cost, then, the companies themselves were disturbed at the amounts they had bid to gain central access to Britain's major cities, and made every attempt to pass the charge on to the public by a concealed levy. But the fact remains that the pro-

[93] H.C., 1881, XIII, 682. Table submitted to illustrate Q.14117.
[94] W. M. Acworth, *op. cit.* 32.
[95] H.C., 1881, XIII, QQ.14951–3.
[96] H.C., 1872, XIII, Q.4424.

portionate capitals which they, compared with other land users, had been able to deploy in the 1840's and 1860's, and the exact timing and nature of their intrusion into the growing cities, enabled them to establish title to urban land on a scale not paralleled even by the wealthiest industrial or commercial users. By a unique blend of private enterprise and statutory powers they were given licence to engross thousands of properties into their hands in the central areas of the major British cities during a critical period of their growth. These property titles constitute the most formidable of urban obstacles. They are not movable, except by expensive and devious procedures, and city growth tends to be carried out, even today, piecemeal, by renewal or functional rearrangement within the lines dictated by the underlying pattern of property titles.

5. Operational policy

The implications for the Victorian city of the railway company policies discussed under the last three headings were fairly well-defined. The decision to concentrate upon territorial competition for accommodation, and the changed methods of financing and promoting urban schemes, invisibly affected the scale, quantity, and even choice of site, of railway building operations in most mid-Victorian cities. When the bill was presented for the expensive purchase of five to nine per cent of central land, the railway companies reacted by levying 'terminal charges', and adopting a much less light-hearted approach towards urban land acquisition. From the mid-sixties onwards most schemes were completions or extensions of sites already chosen; and between 1870 and the end of the century far more interest was shown than had been evident in the previous thirty years in the more efficient working and control of traffic. Though the telegraph had been available from the 1840's, it was not until 1875 that it was interlocked with the operation of signals,—significantly by the L.C. & D. railway at Brixton junction in south London. [97] Between 1870 and 1900 more than one site doubled, or even trebled, its passenger handling capacity with only a 40% extension of territory.[98]

This more economical use of space by the railway companies is one operational change in the later nineteenth century which has obvious connotations for the changing land-use patterns of the growing cities. It is much more difficult to pin-point equally narrowly any other aspects of railway operational policy which had specifically urban repercussions. Yet perhaps of even greater influence was the policy adopted by railway

[97] Michael Robbins, op. cit. 101.
[98] Clapham Junction, for example, where 225 trains per day had been handled on a 15 acre site in 1857 was coping with 724 on a 21 acre site thirty years later. F. McDermott, op. cit. 132.

companies concerning passenger fares and the development of new suburban services. Upon the fares policy depended the numbers and the social class of those who travelled regularly, and upon the distribution of cheap and frequent services depended, to a certain extent, the direction of growth in the outer suburbs.

The typical changes in the social composition of the suburbs and of the inner zones, and the part railways may be considered to have played as a separate factor in the topographical extension of Britain's major cities, are discussed elsewhere. In this chapter we are concerned primarily to view the matter through the eyes of the railway managers. What was their attitude towards cheap fares and the extension of suburban travel? Was the tidal movement of people in and out of the city centres, which became such a prominent feature of late Victorian city life, viewed with enthusiasm?

Captain H. W. Tyler, one of the Board of Trade's inspectors, looking back in retrospect over forty years of railway operation in 1872, expressed reservations on the subject. 'The oft-repeated dictum that the real interests of the public and of the railway companies are identical is only true to a limited extent. It is quite true that by improving and cheapening facilities for intercourse and conveyance the companies frequently increase their business; but a maximum of profit *at the most paying rates and fares* is or ought in the interests of their shareholders to be their chief aim. . . . The object of company management is within certain limits and under certain circumstances to keep the charges at the figures which yield the highest dividends.'[99] If any dictum did apply, it was not the one alleging identity of interest between the public and the companies but, as Tyler suggested later in his report, the dictum that the object of company management had been 'to obtain a maximum of profit out of a minimum of services.'[100]

The creation of substantial new traffic by the lowering of fares, whether carried out as a steady and coherent policy, or as a measure of competitive expediency, could cause a reduction of dividends. Railways did not operate, like textiles or iron works, in such a way that they benefited from economies of scale as they increased their output. They were selling a service which tended to be used most unevenly by seasons and by times of day; beyond a certain point larger traffic spelt a diminishing, rather than an increasing utilisation of their total plant and staff, and an increase in their working expenses and in the administrative tasks of organisation.

If only the new traffic created were constant and sustained, and were evenly spread over their network, and arrived at the prepared points in the hoped-for amounts, then something like the economies of a

[99] H.C., 1872, XIII, Appendix N., p. 94.
[100] *Ibid.* p. 96.

production line in a factory would have been possible. In that case the railway companies' reluctance to expand traffic permanently by drastic price cuts would not have been so pronounced. Demand, however, had shown itself to be a very inconstant and capricious factor. It was not that the companies grossly underestimated the capacity of lower fares to generate additional traffic; they had already had unpleasant experience of what this might mean during the price wars of the 1850's. Apart from overstraining terminal facilities, price reductions on particular trains tended to drain traffic from other parts of the system; they gave rise to acute problems in assembling the rolling stock needed for the enlarged trains in the right places at the right times; and they detracted from both the service and the takings on ordinary trains.

These were the practical objections raised by railway managers, and the only effective answer they could see to the difficulties was the excursion train. This, particularly if it were assembled, carried a good load, waited till evening, and returned the same day, could make available to the public startling reductions of fares, and still show a profit comparable to the satisfactory levels, achieved far more easily and regularly, on the ordinary traffic. Even so, it was open to two fundamental objections. In the first place it was even more intensely intermittent and irregular than ordinary passenger demand, although this itself was highly seasonal, as may be seen from the accompanying graph.[101] The Great Western railway, for example, ran a large number of excursions, but though the response at Whitsuntide and Easter was excellent, 'towards the close of the season our trains ran comparatively empty.'[102]

'Why is that?' Lord Stanley asked James Grierson, Traffic Manager of the G.W.,—'Because you cannot induce the working classes to travel above a certain extent. They will spend a certain amount of money in pleasure, but they have little or no occasion to travel on business; and they spend their money generally at certain fixed times— at Whitsuntide or Easter, or other holidays throughout the year. If we charged them very much less than the ordinary excursion fare it would scarcely induce them to travel more frequently. . . . I do not mean to say that they would travel at only two periods of the year. All railway companies give them excursion trains throughout the whole season; but as a rule, we find that the excursion trains towards the end of the season hardly pay.'[103]

[101] Founded on H.C., 1867, XXXVIII, Appendix CD., p.225. Total receipts from passengers varied seasonably between February and August (it will be observed) in the ratio of 180:390. Some individual termini showed even greater fluctuations. Appendix CF, p.229 gives the passengers booking out of Paddington, which show a sevenfold increase between February and the first week in June.

[102] *Ibid.* Q.13293.

[103] *Ibid.* QQ.13294–5.

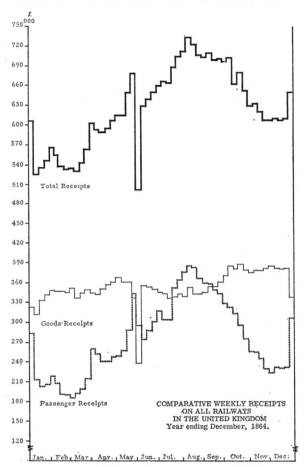

COMPARATIVE WEEKLY RECEIPTS
ON ALL RAILWAYS
IN THE UNITED KINGDOM
Year ending December, 1864.

The other objection, which applied not merely to excursion trains but even to attaching third class carriages to ordinary trains, was voiced particularly by the companies serving the northern cities. James Smithells, Traffic Manager of the Lancashire and Yorkshire railway summed up the railway managers' attitude in 1866 in his reply to the question 'Would it not be advantage to the public to attach third-class carriages to all trains?' 'I should scarcely call it an advantage. Our district is full of men who have risen by their own industry and energy, but their economy is such, although they occupy a respectable position in life, that if third-class carriages were put on with every train they would avail themselves of them. I think that many persons who take advantage

89

of third-class trains ought not to do it, and it would be a boon to the public in that respect.' 'When you say they ought not to take advantage of the third-class trains, is it not a mere matter of choice with a man whether he will submit to rougher company and more imperfect accommodation?—Yes; but still we think that when a man has amassed a fortune it is natural to expect that he would travel either second or first class.'[104] A similar note, part indignation and anxiety, part humbug, was struck by other managers. Six county families with their servants had come up on the excursion trains in 1862; a Glasgow Baillie, more mindful of his pocket than his status, made a regular practice of travelling third class; the improvement of second-class carriages was 'a sheer gift' to those who had previously been prepared to travel first.[105]

Complaints of this sort were symptomatic of the railway companies' preoccupation with 'the most paying rates and fares.' These were not to be found on the worn, dusty, draughty, bare, wooden trucks of the third-class, 'in winter an ice-refrigerator, in summer an oven of baked varnish', but in the padded saloon coaches of the first-class, with their 'sandwich boxes, wine flasks, fur rugs, scotch shawls and languid Corinthian passengers.'[106] The third-class trains had to be run, of course, under Gladstone's Act of 1844; and tax concessions allowed on fares below 1d per mile offered additional inducements. Yet the basic proposition put forward by William Galt remained unchallenged: 'If we carry 100 passengers at the highest paying price the railway will pay 5%; if we carry 200 passengers at a much lower rate it will be $4\frac{1}{4}$%; if we carry 300 passengers at a still greater reduction in fares it will pay $3\frac{1}{2}$%.'[107] Between 1850 and 1870, there was a marked increase in the numbers of all passengers, and particularly of third-class passengers; the numbers carried per year and the gross receipts in each class went up from:—

1st class. 7·1 million (£1·8 million) to 27·0 mill. (£3·3 mill).
2nd class. 22·8 million (£2·4 million) to 66·7 mill. (£4·3 mill).
3rd class. 28·5 million (£1·6 million) to 194·8 mill. (£6·1 mill).

The increase in the proportionate share of the third-class, the increase in total volumes, and the relative cheapening of first-class fares, stand out from these figures.[108] What is also apparent, however, is that to increase receipts by £1·5 millions it was necessary to carry 20 million more first-class passengers: to increase receipts by £4·5 millions in the third-class category 166 million extra passengers had to be carried. Admittedly the costs of working first-class services were higher, but not

104 *Ibid.* Q.12996–7.
105 *Ibid.* QQ.13298, 12879.
106 John Hollinghead, *Odd Journeys In and Out of London*, (1860), 66.
107 H.C., 1867, XXXVIII, Q.8509.
108 H.C., 1872, XIII, Appendix M, p. 85.

in the same proportions; and the short average distance and critical volumes of the third-class traffic presented problems which did not occur with the first-class services.[109] This is one of the basic reasons why there was no response in the middle of the nineteenth century to Charles Pearson's suggestion of a commuter's suburb for 'the superior order of the mechanical poor', or James Hole's 'model villages to relieve the crowded seats of population'; and why, in the later nineteenth century, the provision of cheap suburban services was incomplete and laggardly.[110]

Other reasons were given at the time, to excuse the railway companies' reluctance to take *The Economist's* advice and 'carry the multitude and the commodities they use.' The working classes had not time to travel, Daniel Gooch, of the G.W. alleged, with some justification.[111] The offering of low fares was 'an inducement for a great many people to take advantage of them and take long journeys which they can badly afford to do,' in William Cawkwell's opinion, 'the labouring classes spend a great deal of money in that way sometimes which would be better spent at home.'[112] Cawkwell's concern for the domestic expenditure of the mid-Victorian working class echoes the Duke of Wellington's anxiety that the railways might act 'as a premium to the lower orders to go uselessly wandering about the country.'

The Gooch-Cawkwell arguments, that the working classes had not the time and could not properly afford the money to travel extensively, and that therefore no regular provision in the form of low fares need be made, obviously lost their force in the last quarter of the century. In the 1870's hours of work fell from the feverish levels of early Victorian times. 'A fifty-four hour week was as typical of the fourth quarter of the nineteenth century', wrote Clapham, 'as the sixty-three hour week was of the first and second.'[113] The Bank Holidays Act of 1871 acted as a relief valve for the urban population, and brought new annual peaks of popular traffic to the railway. The Saturday afternoon off, considered by visitors from abroad so remarkable as to be dubbed '*la semaine anglaise*', dates from the same period; and most of the football clubs and many music halls originated during the new leisure of the 1870's and 1880's.[114] Real wages also rose by a third in the last quarter of the century from standards of living which were already

---

[109] The L. & N.W. found that, even in 1871, 47% of its net profits were achieved on the 1st class services, although this fell to 8% by 1888. George Findlay, *op. cit.* 254.

[110] James Hole, *The Homes of the Working Class* (1866), 63.

[111] James Hole, *National Railways* (1893), 151.

[112] H.C., 1867, XXXVIII, Q.11619.

[113] J. H. Clapham, *An Economic History of Modern Britain* (1932), II, 449.

[114] J. A. R. Pimlott, *The Englishman's Holiday: a Social History* (1947), 141–170.

beginning for most people to show less precarious margins above subsistence.[115]

Under the circumstances railway passenger travel continued to rise; rather more than doubling between 1870 and 1890, whereas it had trebled between 1850 and 1870. Moreover the third-class carriages and service were at last upgraded, and the gross receipts from this source trebled, to £18.2 million, whilst the receipts for first-class actually declined (particularly in the 1880's) from £3.3 to £2.6 million.[116] It is noticeable, however, that the increase in receipts from third-class fares kept pace with the increase in numbers. In a period when most prices were falling markedly, there were no substantial reductions in railway fares. The patterns of demand still remained highly seasonal, and linked with the spending of leisure, rather than with cheap and regular daily travel to and from work.

Between 1870 and 1890 the national increase in passenger journeys only raised the annual average from 14 to 24 journeys per head *per annum*. Even if all these journeys are assumed to be work journeys (which certainly was not the case), and are concentrated upon the head of each household, the figure still comes to only 60 to 100 journeys per year, or one return trip per week. In the London area the average was somewhat higher, but even if we take the detailed figures for those arriving by local trains for 1901 handed in by the L.C.C.'s Statistical Officer, they only come to 36·8 journeys per head per year, or a return trip every four or five days, if concentrated upon the head of the household.[117]

Annual takings for season tickets trebled, to £2 million, and many companies, by 1890, showed signs of overcoming their reluctance to issue season tickets in the third-class category; but the sums involved, at typical season-ticket rates, only represent perhaps 100,000 to 150,000 regular commuters spread through the whole country. The long-term contract tickets the companies were prepared to offer, if used for a return journey every day, were in some cases actually cheaper than workmen's daily tickets; but the necessity for advance, lump sum, payment ensured that these commuters were confined to the middle-classes.

In spite of the impressive total numbers of passengers conveyed *per*

[115] G. H. Wood, 'Real Wages and the Standard of Comfort since 1850', *Journal of the Royal Statistical Society*, LXXII (1909), Table 2.

[116] The improvement in third class standards was very slow. Charles E. Lee, *Passenger Class Distinctions* (1946), 68. Receipts 1870–90 from James Hole, *National Railways* (1893), 149.

[117] Population of Great Britain/passengers carried annually; 1870 26,072,000/ 322,200,000, 1890 33,029,000/796,300,000. B. R. Mitchell and Phyllis Deane, *op. cit.* 8, 225–6. The estimate of 36·8 journeys per head per year is from H.C., 1905 (Cd 2597), 8, 26.

annum, railway travel remained too expensive to be part of the daily life of the urban working class, even in the late 1890's. There were some exceptions to this rule. In the services to the north-eastern and some of the southern suburbs of London the railways can be seen developing a unique urban role of moving the working class from their homes to their daily work; but even here the provision of services was reluctant, and a survey carried out in 1897 by the L.C.C. suggested that only half the possible cheap-fare demand was satisfied.[118] On the southern routes 74% of the passenger travel was still on ordinary, not on cheap-fare tickets at the end of the century; on the northern routes the percentage was nearly 80, on the western 65, and even on the eastern 54.[119]

Railway services for cheap daily travel were also provided, but on a still more limited scale, in the four major provincial cities. In the Glasgow area the daily traffic flows differed radically from those in Liverpool, Manchester, Birmingham and London, i.e. they flowed *outwards* from the crowded central zones of the city to work destinations down-river, or to Newton, Coatbridge, Paisley and Hamilton, reversing flow back into Glasgow in the evenings. The Caledonian railway was most active in the provision of cheap services, running 130 trains, with eight thousand passengers paying between twopence and sevenpence per day. The North British railway company put on workmen's services to the special station at Singer's of Clydebank, and carried a further three thousand per day at cheap rates to Coatbridge, Airdrie and Dumbarton. The Glasgow and South Western company also offered concessionary early morning fares for services to Govan, Springburn, Neilston, and to Renfrew and Paisley; the two latter services, at 2d return for eight to ten miles, offering the nearest approach outside London to the Great Eastern railway company's charges.[120]

In Liverpool, in the 1890's, the numbers of workmen who travelled regularly on cheap tickets was exceedingly small, less than five hundred a day on the L. & N.W. On the Lancashire and Yorkshire line, although the traffic into Liverpool Exchange station was heavy, it was all at full fare, 'ordinary trains being ample for all requirements'. Marsh Lane and Kirkdale were the only local stations from which workmen's tickets (at 2½d or 3d) were issued in significant numbers, but even here the daily tickets were measured in dozens rather than hundreds; and for the entire Liverpool and West Lancashire district the L. & Y. railway company issued only 400,000 cheap tickets in the year 1898, or about six or seven hundred passengers per day. The Cheshire Lines Committee, the third major railway serving Liverpool, added only a

[118] H. J. Dyos, JTH, I (1953), 12.
[119] H.C., 1906, XLI, App. 6, p. 170.
[120] H.C., 1900 (187), 305–8, 321–31, 309.

further three hundred cheap-ticket travellers per day; and at 1d per mile return, its fares were not outstandingly low, even on the special tickets.[121]

In Birmingham the L. & N.W. carried approximately a thousand cheap-tickets holders per day, the Midland under a hundred, and the Great Western a further four hundred per day, although Great Western policy was directed rather to the development of contract tickets for the middle class.[122] In Manchester, L. & N.W. traffic, which was not so much suburban as inter-urban in nature, brought in some two thousand five hundred passengers a day on cheap, early morning tickets, from Bolton, Macclesfield, Stockport and Rochdale. The Lancashire and Yorkshire railway brought in three thousand three hundred a day, on 1½d to 4d tickets, from Miles Platting, Crumpsall, Pendleton, Heaton Park and Failsworth; the Great Central two thousand from the Gorton and Oldham line, the Midland under a hundred a day from Stockport at a single fare for the double journey.[123]

Even the largest provincial workmen's traffic at the end of the century however, at Manchester or Glasgow, is unlikely to have greatly exceeded fifteen to twenty thousand per day: a relatively small number for cities with populations between three-quarters of a million and a million, and not enough to ease substantially the residential problems in the decaying inner zones during the period up to the Great War. Cheap travel for the poorer classes in city and suburbs remained an opportunity lost to horse-drawn omnibuses and tramcars. The shooting-out of a working-class suburb served by rail remained a curiosity in the provinces, and was not as common as might reasonably have been expected even in the Metropolis.

To this extent the effect of the railway companies' policy was a negative one; the pressure of population in the inner regions of the compact Victorian city was not relieved. Clerks and tradesmen moved out of town, and commuted daily by train in numbers which were relatively small in all cities except London, where a case can, perhaps, be made out for the precocious development of 'railway suburbs'. But even there two passengers travelled by horse-tram or omnibus for every one who used urban railways; although the effect of the early morning arrivals was magnified to spectacular proportions by the rush-hour bottlenecks at stations like London Bridge or Liverpool Street. The great bulk of those engaged in casual and day labour in the markets, the docks, in small workshops, or street trading, still lived within walking distance of their work, and, if transport were required, used the

---

[121] *Ibid.* 181 (L. & N.W.), 52 (L. & Y.), 113, 117, (Marsh Lane and Kirkdale), 123 (the 400,000 tickets), 6–8 (C.L.C.).

[122] *Ibid.* 181 (L. & N.W.), 247 (Midland), 45 (G.W.).

[123] *Ibid.* 181 (L. & N.W.), 55–97 (L. & Y.) 20 (G.C.), 248 (Midland).

cheap-fare tram far more commonly than the cheap-fare train ticket.[124] With their free passes, railwaymen themselves were the most footloose of the working class, showing a predilection for the extreme outer suburbs which excited Charles Booth's attention in his *Survey*.[125] Otherwise life in the outer 'railway' suburbs was for the relatively well-to-do; or, paradoxically, for the unemployable flotsam of urban life who had no work-journeys to consider.

For most of the inhabitants of the major Victorian cities the railway journey was a rarity; the daily journey to work quite outside their experience. 'It is only the man whose position is assured', Charles Booth wrote, in the 1890's, 'who can treat railway or tram fares as a regular item of his daily budget.'[126] In London itself at the turn of the century there cannot have been, on the most generous estimate, more than 250,000 commuters by rail out of a population touching six and a half million.

Once again, justifications for the fares policy were found, though the ground had to be shifted, in the closing decades of the century. The most persuasive, perhaps, were the arguments advanced by W. M. Acworth. Cheap fares, he wrote in the *Quarterly Review* of 1892, would go in part to subsidise employers as a rate in aid of wages. 'An American artisan considers that his wages should be sufficient to cover the cost of everything that is implied in decent living.'[127] Why should a British artisan be encouraged to expect a disguised subsidy in the form of non-profit making services by commercial railway companies? Cheap fares would also go in part (and here Acworth raised a large question, discussed elsewhere) to yield an additional rent to suburban landlords, in whose profits the railway company would have no share.

The railway managers themselves, though they applauded such rationalisations of their complaints, and even quoted them *verbatim*, were chiefly concerned with the practical, day-to-day, difficulties of operation which cheap or workmen's fares would cause at the urban termini and their approaches. The doubling of urban tracks and tunnels would add to the heavy terminal expenses of which they had been complaining since the sixties. The Great Northern railway, for example,

---

[124] H.C., 1905, XXX, 570. 611 million journeys *per annum* were made by tram and omnibus (of which 341 million were by tram) compared with 236 million journeys by local train services.

[125] 'Nor is the system of free passes or reduced fares an unimportant item in the net advantages, enabling the men to avail themselves of the cheaper rents obtainable in the outer circle. This they have not been slow to do, no less than 81½% of the men living in the outer ring of the metropolis.' Charles Booth, *op. cit.* IX (1892), 349.

[126] Charles Booth, *op. cit.* I (1892), 263.

[127] Quoted in James Hole, *National Railways* (1893), 175. Hole's own reply was 'The question cannot wait for the conversion of the capitalist to proper views on wages'.

was obliged to spend over £1,000,000 upon suburban widening, including the tripling of the Copenhagen tunnel bottleneck just outside their station at King's Cross, in the attempt to rid themselves of what their historian C. H. Grinling called 'the suburban incubus'.[128] Grinling also entered the lists on this issue in 1903 with the publication of *British Railways as Business Enterprises*. 'Far be it from me to argue', he wrote, 'that the working class should not be given all possible facilities to live in the suburbs, but these facilities ought not to be expected by law from commercial companies to their own loss. This is brigandage in the form of legislation.'[129]

The London, Brighton and South Coast railway, to take one more example, had spent £2,000,000 on widening at Victoria station and objected to the swamping of their new facilities by extra trains run under the Cheap Trains Act. 'It will turn Victoria into an Elysium for workmen and a Hades for the rest of the community', William Forbes, the General Manager, complained.[130]

Forbes was one of the few General Managers prepared to condescend to details about the profit margins on his different services; Birt of the Great Eastern, for example, merely stated they were so nicely adjusted as to 'about pay the cost, as nearly as possible.'[131] The L.B. & S.C. railway was carrying, by 1904, some 8·7 million cheap ticket passengers —about 15,000 a day—on trains yielding receipts of 3s 1¼d per ton mile. Ordinary traffic yielded 5s 4¾d per ton mile, and the average running expenses were 3s 6½d; so, for what it is worth, Forbes claimed his cheap services, to bring in artisans and salesmen from New Cross, Honor Oak, Brockley and Bermondsey, were run at a direct loss.[132] Whether or not the figures can be accepted as accurate, there can be no doubt about Forbes' anxiety not to have his profitable traffic, to Holmswood, Ockley and other stops, twenty miles out in Surrey, choked off by the suburban workmen's trains. 'If we are supposed to put on another twenty or so workmen's trains between 8 and 9 a.m., we simply should not be able to accommodate anyone living 20 miles down the line.'[133]

It is clear, without multiplying examples, that workmen's traffic caused a large number of practical difficulties. It frequently required double running (i.e. journeys with the train empty in one direction), particularly for the very early morning service. Loading was also extremely irregular, since everyone wished to catch the last train to

---

[128] C. H. Grinling, *The History of the Great Northern Railway, 1845–1902* (1903) 300–2, 354–6, 376.

[129] C. H. Grinling, 'British Railways as Business Enterprises', *British Industries* (1903, ed. W. J. Ashley), 163.

[130] H.C., 1904 (305) VII, QQ.898–9, 907.

[131] H.C., 1884–5, XXX, Q.10223.

[132] H.C., 1904 (305) VII, QQ.860–70.

[133] *Ibid.* Q.901.

work and the first back. The result was that instead of running a series of 600 passenger trains, on which a profit could be shown, the last trains in and the first out were overloaded by up to 100%, and the other trains made their scheduled journeys half empty.[134]

Perhaps the most frequently voiced objections, however, concerned the passengers themselves, objections which were not always consistent. On the one hand, reviving earlier complaints, it was objected that people who had no right to use the trains took advantage of the cheap fares. Clerks and salesmen who, supposedly, could afford to pay more, used some of the lines, particularly in south London; on the north-eastern routes some of the trains carried (it was claimed) up to 75% of shopkeepers coming in at 6 a.m. to Covent Garden and other markets.[135] The hours which were originally supposed to ensure against the intrusion of those whom the cheap services were not intended to serve were obviously not enough. The Deputy General Manager of one railway company reported indignantly seeing a party of revellers in full evening dress using the early morning train. Yet there were only two prosecutions in twenty years for travelling on a workman's ticket without being an 'artisan, mechanic and daily labourer male or female'; though informal methods of discouragement were occasionally used.[136]

The complexities of the English class system ensured that variable charges based upon social status would be unworkable. How could the railway companies possibly carry in their workmen's trains, as was at one time suggested, 'apprentices, shop and warehouse assistants, builders' foremen, barmaids, barmen, cabdrivers, charwomen, checkers, corn-samplers, commissionaires, coachmen, costermongers, errandboys, lift boys, postmen, pageboys, poulterers, signwriters, sorters & etc.', whilst refusing 'clerks, collectors, typists, copyists, draughtsmen, recruiting sergeants, canvassers and telephone agents'? So the trains remained open to all willing to travel at that hour and under those conditions.[137]

The second vein of complaint concerned those undoubtedly *bona fide* members of the working class who did use the service. Their clothes were dirty, 'and without saying anything in the least degree offensive to the men, the condition in which they are after a day's work at bricklaying, or other work, is such that it disturbs the coats, at all events, if it does not ruffle the tempers of other passengers.'[138] The 'other

---

[134] H.C., 1905 (270) VIII, QQ.130–56. H.C., 1904 (305), VII, QQ. 422–43.

[135] H.C., 1884–5, XXX, QQ.10102, 10178–80; H.C., 1894 (C7542), 8–9, on the evidence of 'an intelligent fellow sent by Mr. Birt'. They returned by ordinary fare trains back to the suburbs after 9 a.m.

[136] H.C., 1904 (305) VII, QQ. 18, 65. The L.C. & D. carried out the prosecutions, the S.E. was known for its brusque methods of discouragement.

[137] H.C., 1905 (270) VIII, Draft Report, p. XVIII.

[138] H.C., 1894 (C 7542), 6.

passengers', about whom Henry Oakley, of the Great Northern, was expressing concern, were the better paying ticket holders who encountered the workmen on their way back, either in the train or on the platform. 'Of an afternoon when our city trains are going out between 5 and 6 o'clock', explained William Birt of the Great Eastern, 'they run out of the suburban side of the station at the rate of sixteen in the hour filled with well-to-do city men and their wives and daughters; and it is not an agreeable thing for them to hobnob with these working men, excellent men perhaps in their walk of life, but the language which they naturally use is very offensive to most people. Again, they have a rough, boisterous way about them; it is difficult perhaps to say that it is wrong; it is natural with them, but still it is very annoying indeed to a very large section of our passengers.'[139]

Apart from using language the workmen spat on the floors, smoked offensive pipes, cooked herrings in the waiting rooms if they were left open, cut off the leather window straps and stole them, and, if they arrived too early for work, hung about the station killing time, 'with evil consequences' for some of the young female workers.[140] They had a way of 'taking a train over' even if it was not full, and some of the trains on the Tilbury or Great Eastern lines, were so crowded that, as a witness told the members of the Select Committee on Workmens Train, 'you would have my utmost sympathy if you tried to travel down by one of their trains this evening. You would have an experience that would astound you.'[141] They also took advantage of the ensuing rush, getting on and off the trains, to evade payment, or even (the 'final insult' complained the Caledonian railway company's General Manager) handed in tram tickets.[142]

The railway companies' experience of cheap travel, when it came, was not a pleasant one, as may be judged from the managers' remarks. But perhaps they could have overcome their disapproval if the fares had been enough to show a profit.[143] The expensive terminal provisions, together with the operational difficulties already mentioned, made it difficult to cater for cheap travellers. Myles Fenton, General Manager of the South Eastern railway company, expressed this view very strongly

[139] H.C., 1884–5, XXX, Q.10207.

[140] H.C. 1905 (270) VIII, QQ.76–8; 1884–5, XXX, Q.10279; 1905 (270), Report, p. XVII.

[141] BTHR MT2/57 (Workmen's Trains Reports 1883–1905), p.11; H.C., 1904 (305) VII, Q.769.

[142] H.C., 1905 (270) VIII, Q.188.

[143] Their profits on the morning journey were marginal, but may have been higher on the return journey. H.C., 1906, XLI, Appendix 77, p. 761. The point was that the profits did not come easily. 'The working men in the East end look at a halfpenny before they spend it. A halfpenny a day to them is a consideration.' H.C., 1894 (C 7542), p .24 (Birt).

to the Board of Trade and the L.C.C. in June 1893. The South Eastern's stations (at Cannon Street and Charing Cross) had been built at a cost of over £4,000,000. 'These are circumstances which ought to be carefully considered when you are fixing what is the value and what is the worth of the accommodation that you get for workmen.'[144] Other companies also agreed that very low fares were ruled out by high terminal costs, and either did not allow them (like the North Eastern Railway Company) or did so under duress (like the Great Eastern). 'The Great Eastern might just as well have thrown their £2 million of money into the Thames,' the L.C.C. were told, 'because they cannot under the present state of things hope to get a penny return on it.'[145]

One possible way out, which the Great Eastern directors had 'seriously under consideration' was to reserve the expensive inner stations for those who paid enough to meet their real costs, and to 'turn the workmen's trains out of the main line onto some cattlepen siding at Bishopsgate', where a large platform would be set aside, particularly for the return journey.[146] To entertain this suggestion was, surely, to admit that the central sites which had been acquired were too expensive for the traffic which Victorian cities most needed in the last decades of the century.[147]

The same *impasse* reached by 1900 over the provision of cheap urban housing for the working class, was also reached at the same time over the provision of mass railway travel for the working class; and in each case the principle of subsidy was foreshadowed in the years before the Great War. To the Victorian railway manager such a principle could not be contemplated. 'We have the two sides of the question to consider,' said Myles Fenton, 'not only the poor workmen, but the poor shareholder as well.'[148]

[144] *Ibid.* p. 24 (Fenton).
[145] H.C., 1905 (270) VIII, Q.289 (N.E.); 1894 (C 7542), p. 15 (G.E.).
[146] H.C., 1884–5, XXX, QQ.10210–2, 10365–70.
[147] 'You do not keep the trains in London until the evening?—The land upon which our Liverpool Street station stands cost a million and a quarter of money; so that you will see that land can never be provided in the City of London for the standing of trains.' H.C., 1884–5, XXX, Q.10231.
[148] H.C., 1894 (C 7542), p. 16.

IV

Municipal authority and the railway
companies

1. *The machinery for railway regulation*

THE Metropolitan area provided examples of the indirect effects of urban
railway building which were as extreme as any in Victorian Britain: the
benefits were of unusual importance for a town which had already
reached such huge proportions by 1830; the costs were rendered more
formidable because of the number and concentration of railway schemes
in the metropolis.

Although its problems may have been unusual, however, London
was the seat of government, and fell under the surveillance of the
supreme legislative body. Three Royal Commissions and several Select
and Joint Select Committees of both Houses analysed the problems of
Metropolitan railways in careful detail, and their *Reports* (to the extent
to which they were adopted by Parliament) had immediate and un-
questioned force. The large issues involved were not left to the control
of the Corporation of London, or the various statutory and parochial
bodies. If they had been, the railway map of the central London area
would undoubtedly have been very different from the one familiar to
us today. Not until the establishment of the more effective government
of the London County Council in the 1880's would local authorities
in the London area have been able to meet the great railway companies
on equal terms.

None of the major provincial cities was treated in a similar manner.
In the period from 1830 to 1900 not one Select or Joint Select Committee sat to consider their problems, and only one Royal Commission,
that on Railway Communication in Glasgow, in 1846.[1] Otherwise the
development of provincial Victorian railways was left almost entirely
to the piecemeal procedures of parliamentary Private Bill Committees,
before which the only municipal corporation, of the four cities selected

[1] H.L., 1847, XL, Report, pp. 361–6.

for study, with *locus standi* to appear was the Corporation of Glasgow. This was one of the special privileges of Royal Burghs under Scottish law. 'Supposing Glasgow were not in Scotland, then they would not have the right of appearing', Mr. Venables, Q.C., counsel for the Caledonian railway argued, deviously, in 1873. 'Railway companies understand railway traffic and railway access, and all the conditions of this question infinitely better than the corporations. Nor has it ever been, as far as I know, claimed by any corporation in this kingdom that it should dictate these matters to us. When the railways came into Liverpool the stations and the lines there were arranged by the various companies; the corporation appearing for the protection of the streets and of any property which it might have which was affected by them. With regard to the railways that have been made into London, no public or municipal body has affected to dictate where they should come.'[2]

Municipal corporations, in other words, were not bodies empowered to tell the railway companies how and where access routes and termini were to be sited; nor were they qualified to suggest what fares should be charged or which routes should be chosen for developing traffic. They had only the same rights to appear as other property owners, when municipal property or streets were affected.

As the complex network of municipally-owned water, gas and sewage pipes began to spread further along the beds of the urban thoroughfares with each decade, the municipalities tended to be brought in on an increasing scale. By trial and error the corporations learned to protect their specific interests until, by the mid-sixties, it was only necessary to instruct that 'the usual clauses for the protection of the corporation be added.'[3] However, there is a marked difference between taking action with such a limited and defensive scope and appearing, by right, as official spokesmen of the wider public interest; and the English municipal corporations were at no time invested with such a right.

Nor, indeed, is it likely, even if they had had the right that they

[2] The summing-up speeches by counsel—often more illuminating, and certainly more concise than the Evidence—have not been preserved, unfortunately, amongst the official Parliamentary records. They may occasionally be found, however, amongst local collections, solicitors' papers, and Select Committee proceedings deposited by the companies concerned. This speech is in BTHR PYB 1/579, 27 May 1873, pp. 5–6.

[3] Many examples of these routine considerations could be quoted from each of the five cities. The Liverpool Borough Engineer was the only one (as far as written records go) to inform his council of the practical points he looked for in a Railway Bill. (1) No street closures. (2) Bridges to be provided for *projected* streets. (3) Footpaths not to be included in Limits of Deviation. (4) Parapets by railway to be high enough. (5) Stations to be set back 10 ft. (6) No level crossings. (7) Lighting of bridges. (8) Tunnels not to affect thoroughfares. (9) New sewers. (10) Corporation to be re-imbursed for altering street levels. LRL, Corporation Minutes, 1865–6, p. 664.

would, in the first decades of railway building, have been able to afford the time or the money to scrutinise railway bills, or the legal and technical officers to carry out the burden of additional work any attempt to control railways would have involved. The records of the municipal corporations in the early railway age show a preoccupation, first with administrative and procedural matters, next with the pressing problems of policing and sanitation. Accommodation, the building of the borough court house, jail, and town hall, the methods of appointment of officers, salaries and fees, the procedure between council, committees and subcommittees, the admission of strangers to meetings, the inspection of markets, slaughterhouses and nuisances, the report of the Watch committee, the disposal of sewage, and, later, the problems of housing and water supply: these were the day-to-day concerns of the municipal authorities, and they kept the corporations' time and energies fully extended without the voluntary addition of gratuitous new duties.[4]

At first, it must be remembered, the municipal corporations established by the Municipal Corporations Reform Act of 1835, did not directly have many powers conferred upon them. They provided, rather, the *nuclei* of effective local governing bodies, and could apply for the transfer of the powers of *ad hoc* local commissions to them; they could also, with one eye on the expense, apply for new powers.[5] Nor could they even claim, with electorates limited, in the 1830's, to between five and ten thousand ratepayers, or 2% to 5% of their total populations, that they enjoyed a popular mandate.[6]

It took several decades for their powers and franchises to mature, and this was the very period of the first waves of railway incursions upon their cities. Only in the railway boom of the sixties were the provincial municipal corporations powerful enough to defeat or deter the railway projectors. Before that their limited powers, their preoccupation with pressing administrative and sanitary problems, together with the possibilities for 'influence', ensured that the railway companies could safely ignore or manipulate municipal action. So, for

---

[4] MRL, Index to Minutes of Council, 23 October 1838–31 October 1900; Council Proceedings, 1838–42, 1842–4. LRL, Liverpool Council Books, XVII, XVIII.

[5] K. B. Smellie, *A Hundred Years of English Government* (1937), 130. E. P. Hennock, 'Finance and Politics in Urban Local Government in England, 1835–1900', *The Historical Journal*, VI (1963), 214–7. B. Keith Lucas, 'Some influences affecting the development of Sanitary Legislation in England', *Ec.HR.*, VI (1953–4), 295.

[6]

	Municipal Electorate	Parliamentary Electorate	Population
Birmingham (1838)	5,025	7,309	180,000
Liverpool (1835)	5,838	11,283	185,000
Manchester (1838)	9,118	11,185	200,000

Sheena Simon, *A Century of City Government 1838–1938* (1938) 429.

the first decades of the railway age, the only curbs to railway enterprise in the provinces were not local, but were imposed by the central government through its Select Committee procedure and (for one brief but noteworthy session in 1845) through the specially formed Railway Department of the Board of Trade.

The Select Committees suffered from three disadvantages which considerably reduced in practice their theoretically absolute powers. First, they dealt specifically and piecemeal with individual projects which had been put before them by railway promoters: they could reject the preamble to the draft bill, turning down the scheme in principle; they could insist on clauses being added or changed. However, they could not themselves take any initiative in suggesting an alternative, or (if two schemes were being considered) a compromise. All they could do was to send the promoters back to think again. Second, the committees of both Houses were made up of members who were 'interested', in both senses of the word. It seemed most natural that, when lengthy and often boring proceedings required time and attention, the work should be delegated to members who, even if they knew little, were at least concerned with the issues discussed. This was the traditional way the House had organised its business, and, not to mince words, it was one of the reasons for taking up a political career. Not until 1858 did the Commons pass the resolution 'It is contrary to the usage and derogatory to the dignity of this House that any of its members should bring forward, promote or advocate in this House any proceedings or measure in which he may have acted or been concerned for or in consideration of any pecuniary fee or reward.' Even this resolution, partly instigated by the growth of the Parliamentary railway interest, left a good deal of scope for influence in a more general sense. For although a Commons' rule that Members should not vote on questions in which they had a direct pecuniary interest had been in operation, according to Erskine May, from as early as 1811, it was established in 1859 that interested Members could still continue to propose motions and amendments on any question, so that the practical effect of the 1858 resolution was greatly diminished.[7] It was still possible for an M.P.'s speech to be described in the 1880's as 'the cry

---

[7] H.C., 1863, VIII, Report, P.XII. 'The Committees of the two Houses to which they would be submitted would possess no power of making changes of importance in the schemes which they were asked to sanction, but would only have the choice of passing or rejecting them'. Even if a Select Committee scheme were proposed, the further problem of finance would arise. 'It is difficult to get parties to believe in schemes which are laid down by a Committee'. *Ibid.* Q.1109 (Hawkshaw). For the Commons' resolution of 1858 see *Commons' Journal*, vol. 113, 247–8, 361. For the Commons' action, 1811 and 1859 see Erskine May, *Treatise on the law, privileges, proceedings and usage of Parliament* (17th ed., 1964), 435–40.

of the distressed railway director'.[8] In Committee the railway directors sat at both sides of the table; the Railway Surcharges Committee, for example, included amongst its nine members, seven directors connected with thirty five companies, according to Samuel Laing.[9] On the floor and in the lobbies of both houses there were many members, particularly before the electoral reforms of 1867 and 1884, whose known 'constituency' was one or other of the larger railway companies. It was even ironically suggested that the new era in Parliament should be marked by discontinuing formal civilian attire and 'the new force suitably organised, with their proper uniforms, ticketed and labelled in an appropriate fashion.'[10]

The third main disadvantage of the Select Committee procedure, and one which Parliament constantly sought to put right, was its 'amateur' quality. Although the same names recur, and some members earned a reputation as chairmen of railway committees, the personnel shifted and changed constantly. No continuity of approach, no building up of experience was possible. This was the defect which, more than any other, enraged *The Economist*:

'The more this subject is investigated, the more it will be found that the defects of the system and the huge abuses to which private interests are exposed, originate in the expensiveness and unfitness of the tribunal to which such business is referred. Could the imagination create anything worse? Five gentlemen are chosen who have been elected to the House of Commons for reasons altogether different from any that can possibly be suggested as connected with the duties of a Committee upon a private bill:—one, perhaps, because he is in favour of the ballot; another, because he agrees with Mr. Spooner about Maynooth; a third, because he favours the Birmingham passion for paper money; a fourth, because, having just returned from India or Australia, with his pocket full of gold, he was willing to pay for a hot contest; and a fifth is put in the chair, because he is a respectable, though very slow, if not stupid country gentleman, of whom all you can say is, that he is far above doing any wrong, if he knows it:—and then, perhaps, the Committee is what is called "fairly appointed" from both sides of the House—that is, half Tory and half Liberal, in other words, composed of members who, as a matter of practice, if not of principle, are apt to be found consistently opposed to each other, no matter what the subject. These five gentlemen find themselves placed round a horse-shoe table; for the first time in their lives called upon to examine witnesses, to weigh evidence, to hear of curves and inclines, and to listen to technical language as intelligible to them as Chinese, and to suffer under the excruciating agony of counsel trained for years in the

[8] BTHR LNW 4/150. The cry of distress was from Col. Mellor, M.P. for Radcliffe, who represented the Metropolitan railway company.
[9] Samuel Laing, 'Our Railway System', *Fortnightly Review* (April 1886), quoted in James Hole, *National Railways* (1893), 61.
[10] *Reasons in Favour of a Direct Line of Railroad from London to Manchester* (1846), 15.

rt of puzzling and mystifying committees so composed. There are no such
elpless victims in the world as these five men. What between astute inquiries,
vitnesses, and sharp legal advocates, who apply argument, threat, persuasion,
nd cajolery with the utmost skill, what chance has such a Committee? And
et it is to the decisions of this tribunal, with "the room cleared", made in
rivate, and though after discussions, yet with no reasons given, that the
ravest questions are finally decided affecting the interests of thousands. How
ontrary is this to all English notions of determining contested rights and
ealing with property.'[11]

One outstanding attempt to avoid this amateurishness, and to subject
egional groups of railway schemes to a body of professional men who
vould not be 'helpless victims', occurred in 1844, with the formation of
he short-lived Railway Department of the Board of Trade.[12] Springing
rom a recommendation of the Select Committee on Railways, *Fifth
Report*, in 1844, and from an initiative by Gladstone, the department or
•oard consisted of an enlarged staff of Board of Trade officers; Captains
)'Brien and Coddington, Major-General Pasley, Samuel Laing and
i. R. Porter, all treated as colleagues and equals, and allowed a vote
nder the chairmanship of Lord Dalhousie.[13] The following session,
845, brought before them a record number of bills, part of the cres-
endo of legislation leading to 'railway mania', and there exists a
emarkable volume in which all the competing schemes for each district
n 1845 are held under close and professional scrutiny.[14] The main
•rinciples upon which they based their examination of schemes and of
•roposed amalgamations were, in their own words, 'to secure the best
•ermanent lines of railway communication for the Country at large
nd for the wants of the District', to ensure that no 'inferior or un-
iecessarily circuitous routes' were constructed, and to prevent 'several
apitals being expended performing the business which could have been
qually well, or perhaps even better, performed by one.'[15]

The reports of 1845 were remarkable for their clarity, wide grasp and
horoughness, but were discontinued after only one session, and the
lepartment disbanded, putting an end at once to any attempt at
ureaucratic supervision over provincial railway schemes. The experi-
nent was abruptly terminated for two main reasons. The Railway
)epartment gave the main parties a hearing, but not in open court,
ind published their decisions before they published their reasons. Since
ı favourable report might possibly send up railway company shares by,
n one estimation, £20 per share, there was immediately a clamour by

[11] *The Economist*, 17 July, 1858, 783.
[12] Henry Parris, *Government and the Railways* (1965), 61–102.
[13] H.C., 1872, XIII, QQ.7297–300 (T. H. Farrer).
[14] H.L., 1845, XXXIX.
[15] *Ibid.* 33–4. They advertised the five criteria by which lines would be judged in
The Economist, 30 November 1844, 1478.

disappointed parties.[16] 'Amongst other things,' T. H. Farrer, Permanent Secretary of the Board of Trade said later, in 1872, 'serious imputations were made against members of the Board.'[17]

The other, and more inescapable reason for the short life of the Railway Department, was that it ran counter to the exclusive and absolute power of the Commons. In most cases the Board and the particular Select Committees considering each project agreed, but on several important bills they did not.[18] What was to happen then? Peel, then Prime Minister, made it clear that the Government intended the reports only to be advisory and not to encroach in any way upon Parliamentary power. He then followed up his words by himself voting in favour of the Select Committee *Report* on the Oxford, Worcester and Wolverhampton Bill, which reversed the Railway Department's decision. Dalhousie wrote to Peel expressing his mortification at action which could only 'overturn the authority . . . of the Railway Department and throw discredit on the officer who conducts it.'[19] Peel wrote a reply, on 22 June 1845, standing his ground upon the authority of Parliament, but regretting 'the unanimous decision of a Committee which had most zealously discharged its duty, being overruled by members, few of whom had read a word of the evidence, many of whom were brought together by dint of private canvass, and were prepared to vote on other considerations than those of the merits of the questions.' The whole affair was, in Peel's words, 'the results of active canvass by powerful companies.'[20]

Dalhousie suggested the Railway Department *Reports* should be discontinued; the following month the board was broken up by the transfer and resignation of Laing, Porter and Pasley, and the reports from that period were confined, in T. H. Farrer's words, 'to points of much smaller importance.' For twenty years the reports continued, so much 'waste paper', in Farrer's opinion, until 1866.[21] This was the end of an experiment which was described as 'a vigorous attempt to guide the practice of Parliament', but which, like the contemporary Board of Health, ran ahead of its time.[22] Nothing of its kind was attempted again, and the Board of Trade confined itself thereafter to recommendations on brakes and signals. Occasionally the chairman of a Select Committee would ask the Board of Trade for technical en-

[16] Henry Parris, *op. cit.* 82.
[17] H.C., 1872, XIII, Q.7241.
[18] On 23 occasions, out of 245 schemes, the S.C.'s decisions were at variance with the Board's reports. H.L., 1845, XXXIX, 19 et. seq. (Return of 18 July).
[19] Henry Parris, *op. cit.* 85.
[20] *Ibid.* 86.
[21] H.C., 1872, XIII, QQ.7241–5. Farrer's remark about 'waste paper' referred to the Board's activities after 1845, and not to its operations August 1844–July 1845.
[22] *Ibid.* Q.7241.

lightenment upon some point of railway legislation which had come before him, and this would be 'willingly given', either in open committee, or as *amicus curiae* to the chairman behind the backs of the parties involved.[23] When it was suggested, in 1872, that the Board of Trade might have *locus standi* on behalf of the public to give evidence in cases where the public were not otherwise represented, the suggestion was rejected by the Board of Trade. 'I doubt very much whether it would be desirable for a Minister of the Crown to appear in one of those arenas; it would at once be alleged that he was taking a part with one of two private interests; it is the most difficult thing in the world to separate public and private interests in these matters.'[24]

2. *The influence of railway companies upon municipal authorities*

In view of the railway interest's capacity to raise obstacles to effective action even in Parliament, the extent of their influence over the narrow-franchise 'infant' corporations comes as no surprise. By its nature, of course, 'undue influence' is not amenable to the techniques of the historian studying surviving written sources. From the evidence which remains, however, it is reasonable to suggest that it comprised three different species. First, personal bribery; the buying of an opinion or a vote by the offer, either of money (usually in the form of shares at par), or of status and power (usually by directorships, sometimes, as it were, postdated). Other methods of assuring a favourable opinion were by the granting of contract work or by generous purchases of property. Although written evidence of these types of transaction is most difficult to trace, some examples have survived from each major city, and they may well have been as widespread as some contemporary writers suggested. There is a vein of cynicism which runs through private papers on the subject which was restrained in public utterance by fear of libel action.

The second way in which the railway interest influenced local politics was probably more important, but even harder to assess; the possibility of bias arising from the overlapping personnel of local corporations and of the great railway companies. For instance, the list of those who attended and chaired the shareholders' protest meetings in 1849 in Manchester, Birmingham and Liverpool to demand the reduction of local rates on railway property, reads like a council meeting; and, indeed, the Manchester meeting was actually held in the Council Chamber.[25] There were many who, like James Bancroft, could doff their

[23] *Ibid.* Q.7261–2.   [24] *Ibid.* Q.7263.
[25] *Public Meeting of Railway Shareholders*, (1849), Clarendon Rooms, Liverpool, 16 April 1849, Mr. Bramley-Moore in the chair, the Earl of Sefton present. *Rating of Railways—a Public Meeting at Manchester* (1849), Council Chamber, Manchester 19 March 1849, Henry Houldsworth in the chair. *Rating of Railways; a Public Meeting* (1849), 8 March 1849, Birmingham, Samuel Thornton, mayor, in the chair.

aldermanic hats for the railway director's topper, and speaking within the council, say they had authority to undertake or guarantee certain courses of action by their railway company; though few could go as far as he did in appending his signature to both sides of a document of agreement, once in his capacity as a railway director and once as an alderman.[26]

It is difficult to know exactly what score to set by this overlapping of personnel. In one sense it was quite unexceptionable and, indeed, inevitable that the railway interest should be strongly represented amongst the civic patriciate. Mayors and aldermen, bailiffs and street commissioners tended to be chosen from amongst the entrepreneurs in locally important manufactures and trades, and no one saw any objection to this practice. Where else would councillors be recruited if not from the ranks of the locally influential and successful? To admit railway directors to the council chamber seemed a natural extension of the usual methods of selection to which the limited municipal franchise conduced; and it was even arguable that the foreknowledge and inside experience they brought might benefit the municipality in its corporate action. One can only judge them, if at all, by their behaviour on those occasions when their civic and personal interests divided, and such test cases are recorded below.

The third type of influence was probably the commonest of all, and was not merely harmless but in many cases beneficial to the public; the overlapping of *corporate* interests between the railway companies and the municipal corporations. This was seen particularly in the demolition of poorer residential districts, where the railways could quite sincerely be represented as doing part of the municipality's job of slum clearance. In the middle years of the century, in fact, the 'ventilation' of the city, by cutting swathes through the foetid and overcrowded slums, was taken as being a sufficient service in itself.[27] Later, as awareness grew of the further internal problems of redistribution and overcrowding which demolition caused, there was increasing pressure upon the railway companies to rehouse (or cheaply transport) the dispossessed.[28] Yet although the railway companies undoubtedly used every device to evade responsibility for rehousing, it should be pointed out that even in Glasgow and London, where the most determined efforts were made by local authorities to re-accommodate those

[26] MRL, Council Proceedings, 1861–3, p. 73.
[27] John R. Kellett, *Ec.HR*, XVII (1964), 362–3.
[28] LRL, Corporation Minutes, 1864–5, 7 December 1864, p. 36. 'The Finance Committee is instructed to afford every possible facility for the erection of Model Cottages . . . and also to use their best exertions with the owners of land in the vicinity of the Boro., and with the Railway Companies having stations in the town for the erection of suburban dwellings for the above classes and conveying workmen by Railway to and from their work at cheap prices.'

affected by urban clearances, the task of providing acceptably cheap *central* housing defeated both the L.C.C. and the City Improvement Trust. In Manchester and Liverpool municipal efforts were confined, in the nineteenth century, to a few token schemes; and in Birmingham demolition was accompanied by changes of land use rather than by schemes for municipal rehousing.[29]

Here, and in such smaller matters as re-aligning streets, bridges and drainage systems, is one field in which the railway companies could be said to have bought approval for particular schemes by offering the corporations a *quid pro quo*. In like manner, the influence and goodwill of local statutory bodies could be secured; that of the Mersey Dock and Harbour Board by offering to run the public telegraph *gratis* through the Mersey railway tunnel (at the moment when the Board was contemplating an overhead wire system of great expense and dubious practicability); that of the Clyde Trustees by selling to them some spare ground for making docks at a bargain price.[30]

Each of these different types of influence can be illustrated. Often they worked in combination, but there was a tendency for the type favoured to shift from the more obvious forms of personal bribery to the corporate *solatium* in the last third of the century. Perhaps the clearest way to show the complexity of railway influence at work would be to take, in turn, examples from each of the major cities chosen for study.

Manchester, amongst the larger provincial cities, provided a theatre for the most extravagant and many-sided railway rivalries, and, perhaps for this reason, furnishes us with one of the best examples of influence at work. The first substantial bites out of the town, at Liverpool Road, London Road and Oldham Road stations had all, in fact, preceded the establishment of a reformed Municipal Corporation; and the extension across town to join the Liverpool and Manchester to the Manchester and Leeds railways, and to form a station at Hunt's Bank, was authorised in 1839, in the first year of the municipal corporation's existence. The exact stages by which the decision was made concerning the siting of the link-line and the Hunt's Bank (Victoria) station are described

---

[29] It is worth underlining the point that the corporations were defeated by the same rising land values and cumbersome purchase procedures which so much embarrassed the railway companies. 'With the amount at its disposal', wrote Joseph Chamberlain, 'the Birmingham Corporation might have dealt with 2 or 3 areas as large as that selected, if they could have been secured against the exorbitant valuations of arbitrators and juries, and the extravagant expenses allowed in connection with them.' *Fortnightly Review*, new series XXXIV (1883), 772. The Manchester Officer of Health, commenting upon Chamberlain's speech, reported in the *Manchester Guardian*, added his own emphatic endorsement. Report, M.O.H. 1884, MRL 614.0942 M4.

[30] HLRO, Min. H.C., 1865, 12 May, QQ.143, 225. H.C., 1846 (212) XII, QQ.42–3, 212–35.

elsewhere; but it may be noted here that the corporation was not consulted, or expected to express an opinion, at any stage.[31]

Although the corporation did not, in fact, set up a Parliamentary Sub-Committee to scrutinise (and, if necessary, oppose) bills affecting the town until 1863, its General Purposes Committee did receive advance information about the next major project, the trans-urban Manchester South Junction railway, in 1846, and were satisfied with the result of their negotiations.

'Your Committee deem it only due to the companies concerned to say that they exhibited every disposition to satisfy your Committee, and to submit to all reasonable stipulations, and your Committee anticipate with confidence, that when the railways referred to are constructed, the inhabitants generally will be satisfied with the mode in which the works will be carried through the town, and with the additional facilities for communicating with different parts of the borough which have been secured.' Although they were later disappointed by the outcome, it did seem at the time that the municipal authorities had secured 'an equivalent for the disadvantages which almost necessarily result from the passage of a railway through a town.'[32]

By the early 1860's, however, the drawbacks of the M.S.J. viaduct, and of the joint working at London Road and Victoria stations, were apparent to the corporation. In February 1860 a public meeting of protest was called, followed by lengthy and heated correspondence in the *Manchester Guardian*. Alderman Bancroft had proposed, in his capacity as L. & N.W. director, that London Road station should, with the corporation's permission, be advanced to Piccadilly, and took offence at remarks which the ex-mayor William Neild had made about the L. & N.W. 'With regard to the remarks of Alderman Neild upon the Board of Directors, he would answer that in point of intelligence, experience, probity of character and every necessary quality the board would not fear comparison. There was no love of diplomacy, nor was there any such spirit of jobbery as that to which Alderman Neild had referred.'[33]

The Town Clerk had also attended the public meeting and received other representations, which he summarised in a five-page internal report to the corporation on 28 June 1861. The council took note of the discontent expressed at the public meeting and expressed their

[31] *Infra* Chap. 6, sec. 3. The first book of Council Proceedings, 1838–42, contains no mention of railways, and the second, 1842–4, only passing references concerning established lines. Only in 1845 was the General Purposes Committee 'empowered, if they think it desirable, to petition . . . against the proposed North Connection Railway.'
[32] Council Proceedings, 28 January 1846, p. 57. The clauses they secured were 8 and 9 Vic. c. 111, sec. 43–63 inclusive.
[33] *Manchester Guardian*, 17 February 1860.

confidence that the L. & N.W. and the L. & Y. railway companies would now take action.[34] This confidence was based upon an agreement which had been drawn up between the corporation and L. & N.W. for the extension of the London Road station, permitting the building of extensive and enormously wide bridges, to pass a whole stream of traffic over the streets leading to Piccadilly, and guaranteeing road alterations at the company's expense.[35] This document was signed by Alderman Bancroft on behalf of the L. & N.W. railway company.

In April of the following year, 1862, the railway companies announced that, though they had carried out the first part of the scheme giving extra land around their station, 'having made a careful estimate of the expenditure which would be involved in bringing their station forward to Lees St., they had come to the conclusion that they would not be justified in incurring the large expenditure required to complete the scheme', and had abandoned all idea of applying for Parliamentary powers.[36] The Corporation's General Purpose Committee intimated that it was 'much surprised as well as disappointed.' The L. & N.W. offered to pay £5,000 fine for not continuing with the scheme, but the Committee regarded the agreement as unconditional and stressed their view in several interviews with representatives of the company. 'It was', they pointed out, 'in consideration of their obtaining from the railway companies an undertaking to carry out that great and much-required improvement (the widening of Piccadilly) that the Corporation agreed upon such reasonable terms to sanction interference with the streets on the southern side of Ducie Street.'[37] The matter came to a vote on a motion that the corporation should take counsel's opinion upon compelling the companies to adhere to their agreement. The motion was defeated by 33 votes to 14; a result which can be interpreted either as a victory for the L. & N.W. interest or, more plausibly, as commonsense reluctance to engage in litigation with so powerful an opponent.[38]

At the other station, Victoria, the battle between the two railways concerned (in this case the L. & N.W. and the Lancashire and Yorkshire companies) spread out from the station precincts into the road approaches, where, standing upon its rights as land owner, the L. & Y. company resisted all attempts by the L. & N.W. to make a joint carriageway. The Town Clerk, attempting to mediate, found himself interviewing on the one hand the L. & N.W.'s representatives, Alderman

---

[34] Council Proceedings, 3 July 1861, p. 181. Report (dated 28 June) presented.
[35] Council Proceedings, 5 February 1862, pp. 70–2. Terms had been agreed in 1861, were revised on 17 April 1862.
[36] *Ibid.* p. 75.
[37] *Ibid.* pp. 76–7.
[38] *Ibid.* p. 80.

Bancroft and Mr. Tootal, and on the other the L. & Y's chairman, Mr. George Wilson, who had been secretary of the Borough Reform Association during the struggle for the incorporation of the town, had been offered the post of first treasurer to the newly-formed borough corporation, and was also an ex-councillor and chairman of the Anti-Corn Law League.[39]

'Bitterly disappointed' over Victoria, and let down over London Road, the corporation next turned to the M.S. & L., which was attempting to secure a new foothold in the city.[40] The General Purposes Committee held interviews with the chairman and engineer of the M.S. & L. and agreed, in 1865, to the proposal of a new connection between Manchester and Liverpool, the Old Trafford–Garston line, to break the 'divided monopoly' enjoyed by the L. & N.W. and the L. & Y.[41] What they did not evidently realise was that the Manchester, Sheffield and Lincolnshire railway company had no intention of stopping in the outskirts of Manchester, but planned a huge railway, raised for 3 miles on a viaduct, crossing Deansgate, Oxford Street and Piccadilly on arches, with a new central station, costing between one and a half and two millions. This scheme, though it was the obvious and logical counterpart to the extension of the railway from Garston into the city centre of Liverpool at the other end of the line, was deliberately concealed, not merely from the corporation, but from Parliament. 'I should be very sorry to say', Mr. Vernon Harcourt remarked to the Commons' Select Committee, 'that my old friends and clients, the Sheffield Company, ever intentionally misrepresented to Parliament the condition of things. We are in days when piecemeal legislation is not approved of.' Nevertheless he must take strong exception to the fact that, after coming forward with a scheme costing £750,000, which they had represented as complete in itself, in the previous session, they were now saying another £2,000,000 was necessary. 'Sir, if that is the way in which Parliament is to be dealt with, then your control over the expenditure of capital on this matter is illusory and must be defeated—the whole theory of the estimates, and the whole theory of the allowance of expenditure by railway companies, becomes a mockery, a delusion and a snare.'[42]

The Manchester Town Clerk, Joseph Heron, also testified that at the time the Corporation had given its 'hearty support' to the line from

[39] Council Proceedings, 2 March 1864, p. 291. 7 September 1864, pp. 292–4. Norman McCord, 'George Wilson: a great Manchester man', *The Manchester Review*, VII (1956), 432.
[40] Council Proceedings, 5 April 1865, p. 102.
[41] *Ibid.* 5 April 1865, p.101. Meeting with Watkin and Sacré.
[42] BTHR PYB 1/383, 17 May 1866, p. 3. Copy of Commons' S.C. on M.S. & L. (Central Station and Lines), Bill, 1866, belonging to J. R. Lingard, solicitor, and including counsel's speeches.

Old Trafford to Liverpool they had not known another station and viaduct was contemplated; and that the M.S. & L. had deliberately put down a bill outlining a modest butt-end terminal near Victoria 'to mislead the Corporation.'[43] As a result, he had gone down with a corporation delegation to London to see 'a most important gentleman connected with the company', who had offered to meet any financial demand within reason. Heron had turned the scheme down unconditionally. 'Then, I presume, that it is really war to the knife', the gentleman (Watkin?) had concluded. 'I said "war to the knife, certainly, if you attempt to go beyond Oxford Street".'[44]

When the bill came up for a hearing before the Select Committee in 1866, however, representatives from the corporation attended to give evidence both for and against it. Mr. Robert Falkner, a Manchester businessman, asked to comment upon this strange state of affairs let slip the expression, 'They are a very squeezable kind of body, there are some here to give evidence in favour of the Bill.'[45] Mr. Denison, Q.C., counsel for the M.S. & L., pounced upon the phrase, and used it during his interrogation of Joseph Heron. 'He said that the Corporation were a very squeezable kind of body; they are only convertible in their views, not squeezable, you think?'[46] The Town Clerk admitted that the two gentlemen who had come to speak in favour of the bill, Councillors John Marshall, an auctioneer, of Hulme Ward, and William Booth, a warehouseman, represented 75,000 inhabitants, but on the other hand six councillors who had been approached had stayed away. 'I am quite sure that if they could have been persuaded to come up here and give evidence, they would have been, from what I know of the influence used to bring up the two gentlemen.'[47]

During the Whitsun recess, which interrupted the Parliamentary Committee's sittings, a corporation Committee for General Purposes and for Urgent and Special Business was hurriedly called in Manchester at the request of Messrs Marshall and Booth, who had raced back to move an amendment reversing the corporation's motion to oppose the M.S. & L. The amendment was thrown out by 22 votes to 6, the Town Clerk reported, when the Select Committee resumed its sittings. 'The small number dissenting', Heron remarked, 'is a matter of some surprise, I think, to those who know the ramifications of railway companies.' Mr. Burke, Denison's junior, did not let the innuendo pass unchallenged. 'Were any of these gentlemen who voted for it (the resolution to oppose the M.S. & L.) North Western shareholders?—I really have not the

[43] *Ibid.* QQ.2996–3003.
[44] *Ibid.* Q.3004.
[45] *Ibid.* Q.329.
[46] *Ibid.* Q.3066.
[47] *Ibid.* QQ.619–54, 3068–9.

slightest idea. Will you undertake to say that they are not?—No; I have no knowledge about it.'[48]

Denison himself concentrated especially, in his summing up, upon the hostile evidence offered by Messrs. Fowler, Barber and Bancroft. Mr. Robinson Fowler, a stipendiary magistrate, had given evidence upon the danger of accidents caused by the sudden transition to darkness and noise in the tunnels formed by the bridges near Victoria station. 'Having one nuisance I would do as much as I could to prevent the second.' 'We are pleased,' Denison remarked sarcastically, 'that Mr. Fowler, struck with artistic objection at having to drive under the bridge at Piccadilly, has been brought up to the less murky atmosphere of London, where that petition was signed on Derby Day.'[49] Mr. Robert Barber, High Sheriff of Cheshire, who had objected to the scheme as 'cutting up the town very much,' was given similar shrift. 'You bought land under an idea that the railway would come?—It was represented to me by an agency that the railway would improve it.'[50] Unfortunately, he had bought the wrong land for the M.S. & L. scheme, which only planned a through-route raised on a viaduct.

James Bancroft, no longer an alderman, had also given evidence before the Select Committee roundly condemning the scheme. 'It would disfigure the only part of Manchester worth notice.'[51] Though taciturn and wary, he was forced by Denison into making some revealing and damaging admissions: 'I believe it is the practice of the London and North Western company to divide their direction into various committees who look after the interests of various districts?—Yes. Is it part of your province and speciality to look after the Manchester district?—Amongst others.'[52]

In spite of all the weight of evidence against the scheme, the Commons authorised it; and only after the same evidence had been repeated and expanded in the Lords was the preamble rejected. The M.S. & L. withdrew, and did not return for six years; and then with a much more modest scheme (the present Manchester Central) in conjunction with the Midland and Great Northern railways.[53]

The rejection of the M.S. & L. bill in 1866 has been described in some detail because, apart from the scheme's intrinsic interest—it was the largest railway scheme ever proposed in Manchester and would

[48] *Ibid.* QQ.2983, 3370–81.
[49] *Ibid.* Q.3367 (Fowler). 29 May, p. 19 (Denison).
[50] *Ibid.* Q.2549.
[51] HLRO, Min., H.C., 1866, 15 May, pp. 167–8, S.C. on M.S. & L. (Central Station and Lines).
[52] BTHR PYB 1/383, QQ.2043–4.
[53] *Infra.* Chap. 6, sec. 3.

have greatly altered the central district—the veil of official discretion which usually covered the informal operations of railway influence was lifted for a moment. The episode also reveals the not insubstantial weight given to the opinion of corporate bodies. It was, finally, the corporation's determined (if not unanimous) opposition which frustrated the scheme. It also reveals the range of personal susceptibility to influence amongst those concerned with local government. At one extreme, the town clerk, a professional servant of the corporation, tried to steer an impartial course through a long and complex series of events. In the centre, the great local figures, like Henry Houldsworth, who when put to the test were inclined to recall that the railways were one of their interests which required, if not an open vote, at least a discreet absence or abstention. At the other extreme were councillors Marshall and Booth and Alderman Bancroft, men whose views were as predictable as those of the paid advocates who argued the bill before the Select Committees, and for the same reasons.

In Glasgow, in the same decade, a similar struggle was taking place over the Union Railway Company bill (1864), which authorised the first river crossing and central station. Once again, to condense a long story, the same general features can be discerned. Playing the role of railway spokesmen, for their different reasons, were the Lord Provosts, Peter Clouston, James Lumsden and James Campbell. Clouston, an insurance broker, and Provost from 1861 to 1863, took the unusual step of appearing as 'the chief witness' on behalf of the Union company, even though the corporation had declared its opposition 'on all scores'.[54] The drift of his argument was that the demolition of the slum Wynds by the Union company would be of such merit in 'opening up' the city, as to override all other objections.[55] This sanitary argument was a strong one, and may well have been advanced sincerely by Clouston; but his behaviour nine years later, when he appeared again before a Select Committee, does little to suggest this. He was by now a director of the Union Railway Company, and explained their demolition plans in a manner which was so evasive that the chairman intervened. 'We have had that expression several times—"reconstitute" the area—what is the meaning of it?—The reconstitution, as I understand it, means, first of all that all these places should be cleared out, and after that the space should either be used for railway purposes or for building purposes, whichever is most suitable and required.'[56] The building would not include rehousing the large number—six thousand according to the official return under Standing Order 191, twenty thousand according

[54] HLRO, Min., H.C., 1864, 12 May, p. 45, S.C. on Union Railway.
[55] Loc. cit. p.33.
[56] BTHR PYB 1/579, 17 May 1873, Q.81.

to unofficial estimates—who had been rooted out by the scheme. 'I do not think there is a great desire to make houses for the poor in that locality very much,' Peter Clouston observed.[57]

James Lumsden, Lord Provost from 1866 to 1869, also agreed that no obligation fell on the railway companies to re-house. 'There may be exceptional cases, but I think upon the whole they have been driven out into healthier parts'; an extraordinary observation from an official of a corporation which within the next decade was confronted by a problem of housing densities unequalled in Britain.[58] In 1870, upon leaving the corporation, Lumsden became chairman of the Glasgow and South Western Railway Company, co-sponsor of the St. Enoch terminal scheme. Lumsden's motives and conduct during this period were subjected to critical examination by Mr. Denison Q.C. 'Mr. Lumsden comes here under the garment or garb (I was going to say under the disguise—but I will not say so) of his three years' patriotism, as Provost of Glasgow, to talk of public interests.'[59] Yet he had, whilst he was on the Parliamentary Bills Committee of the Corporation of Glasgow, suggested a scheme to the Caledonian Company that they should merge with his own company, the Glasgow and South Western; a scheme which, whatever its merits to the two companies concerned, would certainly be ruled to be against the interest of the general public. 'I asked him whether he did not feel that it was his duty to tell the Committee of the Town Council, on which he was specially appointed to look after Parliamentary Bills, something of this curious scheme? No it was not. Well, of course, he has his own view of duty; but I thought he was put upon that Commitee for the purpose of looking after the interests of the City of Glasgow.' Instead, Denison put it to Lumsden, 'You have three years' patriotism and then you relapse into railroadism?—Yes.'[60]

James Campbell, a warehouseman and another ex-provost, gave evidence criticising the existing goods station arrangements which the proposed College or High Street terminal would augment. Part of the proposed scheme involved the removal of the University of Glasgow from its old site in the High Street to a new West-end location at Gilmorehill, where the land was owned by the Gilmorehill Land Company, chairman and chief shareholder the same James Campbell. Other lands either purchased or affected by the railway schemes

[57] *Ibid.* 13 May, 1873, Q.13.
[58] *Ibid.* 14 May, QQ.736–7.
[59] *Railway Pamphlet*, B.M. 8235 bbbI (2), pp. 20–1.
[60] *Ibid.* p. 19. Although Lumsden was made chairman of the G. & S.W. company in 1870, the year after he retired as Lord Provost, this could hardly be called a 'relapse' since he had already been made a director of the G. & S.W. in 1849. *Memoirs and Portraits of 100 Glasgow Men* (Glasgow 1886) II, 183.

belonged to James Lumsden and Andrew Orr, another ex-provost.[61]

It is possible, of course, that these men found it easy in their minds to distinguish always the single-minded and impartial conduct of municipal objectives from the pursuit of their private interests, or that they genuinely believed the two coincided, and that what was good for the Glasgow and South Western Railway Company was good for Glasgow. Whatever their motivation may have been, their resulting actions and public statements fitted the railway companies' intentions perfectly, and the railway companies were not ungrateful.

The Lord Provosts were not the only influential local people to throw in their weight with the Union Company. Charles and John Tennant, Walter MacFarlane, William Stirling, and other local businessmen were prepared to lend their names, but not their money, and to act as a 'front' for the contractors Betts, Brassey, and Peto, who really stood behind the scheme.[62] One can readily appreciate that the prospect of improved transport facilities, particularly those connected with the new College Goods station, might in itself be enough to persuade local businessmen—especially if like the Tennants they were concerned with the heavy chemical industry—to practise a little harmless deceit on the public. Less easy to fit into this category was the man whose name headed the list of promoters, the local M.P., Walter Buchanan. Though he was named as a director in the prospectus, counsel for the Caledonian Railway Company alleged he had taken no shares and preferred another scheme.[63] To rebut this the Union company, ten days later, produced Buchanan to testify to the Select Committee that he had authorised his name to be used, to give the impression of respectability and local participation, but only after receiving 'a guarantee from the promoters that he should be held harmless if he lent his name for the scheme.'[64]

A rider should be added to these observations. The picture in Glasgow was, in fact, a great deal more complicated than this simple example may suggest. As in Manchester, the Council was the arena for combat between several companies, all of whom had their spokesmen in local government; and it, also, went through an internal constitutional crisis, 'the little Whitsuntide Revolution', as counsel called it.'[65] This crisis was precipitated by the action of Messrs. Muir and Craig, who called a public meeting to propose that an alternative North British railway extension scheme in George Square should be preferred,

---

[61] HLRO, Min., H.C., 1864, 12 May p. 107. *Infra* Chapter 8, sections 1 and 3 (Lumsden and Orr). Andrew Orr was Provost 1854–7, Chairman of the G. & S.W. 1849–70; Peter Clouston was Provost 1860–3, Chairman 1879–83; James Lumsden was Provost 1863–6, Chairman 1870–9.

[62] *Ibid.* 12 May, pp. 56–9.

[63] *Ibid.* 13 May, p. 269.

[64] *Ibid.* 23 May, p. 243.

[65] *Ibid.* 23 May, p. 207.

and by Councillor Dreghorn, chairman of the Parliamentary Bills Committee of the Corporation, which voted by 6 to 3 to disaffirm the action of the Lord Provost and of the delegation accompanying him to Westminster, and asked for delay whilst the Caledonian counter-proposal was considered.[66] So the Lord Provost, John Blackie, found his authority questioned from two sides, by a committee of the corporation, and by a public meeting, one inspired by the Caledonian, the other by the North British railway companies; and had to choose to ignore the former action as unconstitutional, and to ride out the latter.

Blackie himself was possibly the most active and public spirited of all Glasgow's nineteenth century Lord Provosts. He had no connections of any sort with the railway interest, and from his record with the City Improvement Trust alone, it is clear that he had the general interests of the inhabitants of central Glasgow very much at heart. Yet he fell victim to one of the more complicated forms of influence referred to earlier, and accepted what one might call a 'corporate bribe', in the form of a detailed ten-page safeguard by the Union company to the corporation, and the purchase from the corporation for £42,000 of derelict property for which the corporation had just paid £19,675.[67]

Although, by this deal, Blackie made a double profit for the rate-payers—the derelict and insanitary houses were removed by the railway company and twice the amount originally expended was made available for the purchase of similar slum properties out of the line of railway advance—it might be argued that, by failing to oppose the preamble of the Union bill, he compromised over some of the larger issues. Certainly it was suggested, in so many words, that the corporation had been 'bought off by some adventurous gentlemen, strangers, contractors and others.'[68]

As far as the compromise was concerned it might well have been felt that some sort of settlement was inevitable sooner or later with one of the three great companies poised to invade the central district, unless the corporation was to be kept indefinitely, year after year, to the expense of scrutinising bills, petitioning Parliament and employing counsel. Yet, although the St. Enoch station project was a large one, and although undertakings were given that it would be open to all comers, in fact the Caledonian rejected all the terms offered for admission by its entrenched rivals as 'paying for the whip with which they meant to scourge us', and kept up constant pressure for an equally large station of its own, reduplicating the St. Enoch facilities.[69] By

[66] *Ibid.* 23 May, pp. 10–26, 141–8, 152.
[67] *Ibid.* 23 May, pp. 91–100.
[68] *Ibid.* 12 May, pp. 46–8, BTHR PYB 1/579, 6 May 1873, p. 5.
[69] HLRO, Min., H.C., 1873, 6 May, pp. 63–5, S.C. on Caledonian Railway Glasgow Central Station.

1873, the corporation was reduced to petitioning 'to be protected from the great expense they are yearly put to in protecting the interests of the city against schemes promoted by the different companies in antagonism to each other, for their own purposes rather than that of affording and completing that accommodation which the public interests require.'[70]

The case of the Union railway station at St. Enoch's in Glasgow illustrates the wide variety of weapons in the railway companies' armoury. Pressure could be applied by the threat of tiresome and expensive litigation, by 'corporate bribery', by the offer of directorships, of legal and surveying retainers, of contract work, or of shares under guaranteed terms.

The same influences can be seen at work in Liverpool. Unlike the other municipal authorities, Liverpool corporation had retained a grip on the common lands, and was one of the largest landowners in the borough. As described below in the *Case Histories*, the railway companies found themselves, from the building of Lime Street station onwards, concerned with the corporation as a direct vendor; a relationship which helped to smooth over many differences which might otherwise have arisen. Mr. Richard Earle, agent for the Stanley family, spoke his mind on the matter when he was approached by the corporation Finance Committee over the purchase of land for a borough gaol. He did not feel that he would be performing his duty as agent to the Earl of Derby if he did not protest at the corporation selling land to the railway companies with one hand and buying it from the Derby estate with the other. 'It certainly was never any intention to sell either to the county for the Lunatic Asylum, or to the Corporation for the Gaol, any portion of this land which could be required by the Railways, because they are obviously better paymasters than either one or the other.'

'I merely allude to this to insist that Lord Derby and not the Corporation is entitled to the enhanced price obtainable from the Railways.'[71]

The connection over land dealings was even closer than Earle suggested, for apart from the corporate interest, there were two strong personal ties of interest between the members of the corporation and the railways. The first of these went back to the earliest of all urban railway projects, the abortive Liverpool and Manchester scheme of 1824. On 2 June 1824 the council had instructed Charles Lawrence, the mayor, to communicate with Mr. Moss, the chairman of the projected railway. By the beginning of the following year Moss had demoted himself to Deputy Chairman, and the chair of the Liverpool

[70] *Ibid.* 7 May, p.19.
[71] Finance Committee, Vol. 12, p. 464, 27 August 1847.

and Manchester was occupied by Charles Lawrence.[72] Later Moss became chairman of the associated Grand Junction railway, on whose board sat as director Mr. G. M. Lawrence. G. M. Lawrence was also chairman of the Finance Committee of the corporation, a division of loyalty to which the *Liverpool Mercury* strongly objected.[73] Another member of the Finance Committee, which handled both property sales and parliamentary bills, was John Shaw Leigh, who became mayor in 1841 and was himself one of the largest landowners in Liverpool, selling land to the Liverpool and Bury railway to the reputed sum of £250,000.[74]

In Birmingham, not to labour the point, the same divided councils and overlapping of personal and municipal interest can be seen. P. H. and Frederick Muntz, for example, were general merchants who had become magistrate and member of parliament respectively for Birmingham; both became shareholders, and Frederick a director, in the Snow Hill station company, and gave evidence extolling the scheme to the Parliamentary Select Committee.[75] Richard Spooner, M.P., who gave evidence hostile to the Snow Hill project was a director in the London and Birmingham railway's New Street scheme; Samuel Beale, an ex-commissioner and mayor, who also gave hostile evidence, was a director in the Midland railway, which intended to 'follow in on the London and Birmingham lines.'[76] Piggott Smith, the Surveyor to the Birmingham Street Commissioners and later to the corporation, was offered a lucrative job by the London and Birmingham railway solicitors which he felt he should decline in case it might appear to influence his professional opinion.[77] William Matthews, a Birmingham magistrate and entrepreneur in the iron and coal trade, who forcefully supported the Great Western interest, both before the Broad Gauge Committee of 1845 and before the Snow Hill committee, was paid for his services by a Deputy-Chairmanship in one G.W. subsidiary and the award of 300 free shares in another.[78]

[72] James Touzeau, *The Rise and Progress of Liverpool 1551–1835* (Liverpool, 1910), II, 817–8, 858. A majority of the council itself had also accepted shares at a premium, T. Baines, *A History of the Commerce and Town of Liverpool* (1852), 609.

[73] *Liverpool Mercury*, 9 January 1846. Earlier the Finance Committee, in addition to land sales had been given brief to watch over Parliamentary Bills. Council Books, Vol. 17, p.423, 16 November 1836.

[74] J. A. Picton, *Memorials of Liverpool* (1875), II, 47.

[75] HLRO, Min., H.C., 1846, 23 June, p. 95, 24 June, pp. 259–66, S.C. on Birmingham. Wolverhampton and Dudley Railway.

[76] *Ibid.* 25 June, pp. 302–5; HLRO, Min., H.C., 1846, 12 June, p. 32–3. S.C. on London and Birmingham Railway (Birmingham Extension).

[77] *Ibid.* (L. & B. Ext), 11 June, pp. 127–8.

[78] *Ibid.* (B.W. & D.), 24 June, pp. 94–8. For the Broad Gauge Committee see E. T. MacDermot, *History of the Great Western Railway* (ed. C. R. Clinker, 1964), I, 115.

'In gratitude perhaps?', counsel suggested. 'I do not call it their gratitude.' 'Well perhaps it was put in the shape of some reward for benefits to come? —I do not think they would have ventured to put it in that shape to me. If so I should have denounced them in the most emphatic terms. I do not think they would have ventured to do so.'[79]

Apart from these considerations, he and another local businessman, who gave favourable evidence, were also tendering to supply material for part of the projected works; circumstances which, taken in conjunction, would appear to detract considerably from the impartiality of his evidence.[80]

The examples cited above for Manchester, Glasgow, Liverpool and Birmingham give a cumulative impression of railway influence in municipal affairs which cannot be ignored. During the period when railway companies were most active in transforming the central districts, up to the mid-1860's, no corporation could stand undivided and uninfluenced by the various forms of persuasion available to their gigantic clients. In the later decades of the century the corporations began to demonstrate a more independent spirit, to impose more stringent conditions, and to strike harder bargains with railway companies requiring access, but by this time the basic outlines of urban railway development had already been sketched in.

In fairness to the great cities involved it should be added that the instances cited could probably be paralleled in any sizeable town in Britain. In London, for example, although the corporation's powers to interfere with railway plans were limited, both by its own refusal to extend its administrative boundaries and by the direct interest shown by Parliament in metropolitan affairs, such schemes as did fall within the purview of the city corporation provoked a response compounded of similar elements to those in the provincial cities. London was the seat of the legal profession, and centre of banking and financial interests, both of which were closely engaged in railway promotion; and although the officers of local government continued to be drawn from the Livery Companies and Gilds, the City Companies themselves, in their capacity as great landowners, must have been amongst the largest corporate beneficiaries of the whole railway movement, and cannot have been totally detached in their selection of policies. They also set one of the few recorded examples of defiance to a Royal Commission's powers of enquiry in nineteenth-century constitutional history, by refusing to lay their affairs open to public examination in the 1880's.[81]

[79] *Ibid.* (B.W. & D.), 24 June, pp. 100–1.
[80] *Loc. cit.* pp. 104–5.
[81] H.C., 1884, XXXIX.

Moreover it is clear that a spirit of condemnation is quite irrelevant to the simple statements of fact made above. Because of the wide ramifications of railway activity it was probably more difficult to separate private and public considerations over railway issues than in any other business field. Yet unless the whole system of amateur, elective, local government were replaced by professional administration, the problems to which this gave rise could not have been avoided. It may give a scrap of comfort to moralists, that the full-time professional servants of local government, the municipal architects, surveyors and engineers, the clerks and legal officers were, on the whole, admirably public spirited and impartial, often in the face of considerable temptations and pressures.

Part Two

Case Histories

V

◇◇

Birmingham

◇◇

1. *The property ownership pattern*

IT is one of the recurring themes of this book that the underlying pattern formed by units of land ownership is one of the critical factors in explaining the routes cut through Victorian cities by the railway builders, and the choice of site for the termini and yards. One might legitimately go further to say that the ground plan formed by property titles can serve as the key to explaining the whole course of development of certain types of urban area, and the emergence of characteristic residential and industrial zones in each city. For example, the establishment of successful, high-class residential areas like Belgravia in London, Kelvinside in Glasgow or Edgbaston in Birmingham depended upon the ownership of very large units and the pursuance of a policy of lease or sale under restrictive covenants forbidding the introduction of non-residential land uses or unduly crowded house building. In other areas like Saltley in east Birmingham, Somers Town and Camden Town in north London, or Tradeston in south Glasgow the land-owners might hold equally large units, but for reasons best known to themselves, they were prepared to break up their estates and allow mixed industrial and residential uses.

In other cases, indeed more commonly, the title to urban land was highly fragmented. Except for public houses and the larger factories, the owner-occupied property was relatively unusual. More frequently urban land consisted of houses, yards and gardens which were owned in groups of eight to twelve by members of the lower-middle class, retired tradesmen or their widows, or by executors and charitable trustees. Sometimes they were held, in much larger units of fifty or more properties, by ex-landed gentry, whose manors had been partially covered by the extension of building on the periphery of each great town; sometimes the larger units or groups had been assembled to-

125

gether in the space of a decade or two by solicitors, land valuers and larger builders. In the latter case, although the estates could be run as *bona-fide* ventures in residential housing, it would be naïve to exclude the possibility that these owners had an eye to the strategic positioning of their houses on the fringe or possible route of urban railways. Some of those who had accumulated, not inherited their land (like John Chesshire in Birmingham or J. S. Leigh in Liverpool) operated as agents or land auctioneers, and must have had a very shrewd idea of the possible windfall increases in capital value timely purchases in particular areas might bring.[1]

The size and disposition of this patchwork of urban land titles was of crucial importance for any great new force impingeing upon land use. For the railways, in particular, the prospect of dealing with a few owners offered a simplicity and speed which alone made it possible to carry through large schemes within reasonable margins of time and cost. It was well worth paying through the nose to conclude such a series of deals privately, and to disarm the opposition which every landowner was entitled to offer by petition and counsel before the Parliamentary Committees if his purse was large enough and his nerve cool enough. Reaching a settlement with the larger urban landowners had the further advantage of avoiding the endless reduplication of legal and survey charges connected with small cases, the endless delays which arbitration procedure presented, and the high awards sympathetic juries tended to give.[2]

Yet in spite of the importance of a comprehensive knowledge of property titles as a sound basis for all urban history, no research work has yet been done to piece together maps of the comparative ownership patterns in our major cities. No doubt this is partly due to the extreme difficulty of assembling the necessary information. Property transactions are, after all, a type of confidential business transaction, and often an extremely profitable one. Even twentieth-century administrators have been known to lose themselves in the maze of legal and informal relationships which connect the ground owner, occupier, tenant and sub-tenant. The task, therefore, cannot be undertaken lightly. Yet even a tentative and sketchy map is better than none, and might provide the basis for further, more detailed and accurate work. It is in this spirit that the ownership maps which follow for Birmingham and the other cities are presented.

---

[1] Chesshire was a land valuer and auctioneer in Birmingham, owning land, in conjunction with others, on the route of the Birmingham West Suburban railway, and also selling railway surplus lands by auction, BRL 427290. For J. S. Leigh see *infra* Chap. 7, sec. 1.

[2] For an outline of the compulsory purchase procedure which railway companies had to follow see App. 3.

The documents available for constructing a land ownership map for Birmingham consist of *Estate Maps*, of varying dates throughout the nineteenth century, to be found amongst the deposited Collections of Solicitors' Papers, *Tithe Maps* for the Parishes of St. Martin, St. Thomas and All Saints in 1847, *Enclosure Awards* for Saltley and

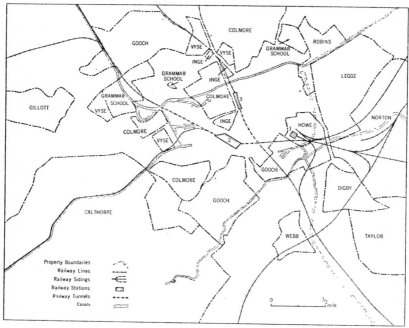

Property ownership and railways in Birmingham.

Washwood districts in east Birmingham, *Plans of the Manors* of Duddeston, Netchells, Bordesley, Aston, Saltley and Little Bromwich, showing field owners, and the invaluable railway companies' *Plans and Sections* and *Books of Reference* deposited at Westminster and with the local County Clerk. The material from these sources has been summarised in the map above.[3]

[3] The Birmingham Reference Library has a large number of Plans and Sections etc. of local interest conveniently assembled under the heading 'Birmingham Railways'. An unusually large number of estate family and solicitors' papers have also been deposited, including the Lee Crowder, the Jewel, Baillie, the Harward and Evers, the Gooch, and the Colmore papers, W. Powell and H. M. Cashmore, *Catalogue of the Birmingham Collection* (Birmingham, 1918), and its supplement (1918–31), list miscellaneous topographical material. Pigott Smith's survey of property boundaries 1824–5, and the *Birmingham Weekly Post*, Freeholders' Map, 6 June 1891 contain further useful information.

In the central area, that covered roughly by late eighteenth-century Birmingham, ownership is so fragmented that it is difficult to generalise, though detailed information on the land acquired by each railway scheme is available from the *Plans and Sections* and *Books of Reference*. The 'New Town', which was developing in western Birmingham (as in so many other great cities) in the later part of the eighteenth century, was the first urban area to extend over the lands of really large proprietors—the Colmore family.[4] 'The place was possessed by a tenant as a farm', commented the contemporary William Hutton, 'but Birmingham, a speedy traveller, marched over the premises and covered them with 1200 houses on building leases.'[5] The Colmores held some 66 acres, divided into no fewer than thirty-five estates with values ranging from £2,000 to £12,000 in the mid-1820's.[6] The largest of these were the Bell's Barn and Birmingham Heath estates.[7] They, with the other properties, were held from 1807 to 1837 by the last direct representative of the family, Miss Caroline Colmore.[8] Afterwards they were administered by her trustees, and then by Frind Cregoe, Esq., a friend of Miss Colmore, who changed his name by deed-poll to Frind Cregoe Colmore upon inheriting the estates. The Colmores were by far the largest central landowners, and it was with them and their agent, Digby Latimer, that the railway companies and the Corporation Public Works Committee had to deal. Miss Colmore and Frind Cregoe were both absentee landlords, non-resident in Birmingham, leaving their estates in the hands of professional agents, men who, one may presume, were well capable of weighing the railway companies' attractive money offers against the possible damage the lines might cause by severance and dilapidation of the estate properties.

In the event, as will be seen from the map, the major railway companies' lines to the north-west from New Street and Snow Hill both discreetly skirted the Colmore's valuable New Hall estate. The Snow Hill line ran on a viaduct close to Livery Street through land covered with low-grade cottage property owned by William Inge and leased to a group of middlemen (and women); then crossed through only one block of Colmore property before passing through further properties belonging to William Inge and to the Reverend Samuel Martin, and

[4] M. J. Wise, 'The changing regional pattern', *Birmingham and its Regional Setting* (British Association, 1950), 175-7, Map Fig. 39.

[5] William Hutton, *A History of Birmingham* (ed. James Guest, Birmingham, 1835), 26.

[6] Tithe Map and Apportionment of Rent Charges, St. Martin's Parish, 1847. Plans of the Colmore Estates, 1788-1920.

[7] Plans of Bell's Barn Estate 1793-1875, Plans of Birmingham Heath Estate 1801-35, BRL 411566.

[8] Particulars and valuation of Miss Caroline Colmore's estate, 1826, BRL 414908.

into the countryside.[9] Digby Latimer did not oppose the railway bill either by petition or counsel. The New Street line by tunnelling to the north-west likewise affected only the fringe of the Colmore properties, and though the name of Digby Latimer is to be found on a number of the properties listed in the *Books of Reference*, far larger quantities of land were supplied to the railway by the Governors of the Free Grammar School, the Trustees of Lench's Charity, Sir Thomas Sherlock Gooch and two members of the Gough family.[10]

Indeed from the point of view of the railway companies responsible not merely for the northern exits but for the southern approaches to New Street and Snow Hill, Sir Thomas Gooch was by far the most important landowner in Birmingham, holding some 250 properties, let out in groups of a dozen or so to non-resident lessees, along the chosen railway routes.[11] Gooch was a substantial squire owning 146 acres of land on the fringes of Birmingham at the time the railways arrived, some of it arable and pasture, some already laid out for building or built upon; and five railway companies had to come to terms with him and his son Sir Alfred S. Gooch. He was also, like the Colmores, non-resident and already an elderly man in the 1840's, dying at his home at Benacre Hall, in Suffolk, at the age of 85 in 1851. The price paid for his land was obviously sufficient to disarm opposition, for when he sent his agent, the Birmingham solicitor Mr. George Whately, to appear before the New Street Parliamentary Committee, the evidence submitted was very favourable to the scheme.[12]

The other principal landowners with whom the railway companies requiring access to Birmingham had to deal fell into two groups. The remaining large titled owners, holding ex-manorial lands in the suburbs of the city, and the Corporate bodies, holding both suburban and central properties.

The chief of the corporate bodies in Birmingham were Lench's Charity, which had moderate sized holdings, and the Free Grammar

[9] HLRO, P & S, B.Ref., 1846, Birmingham, Wolverhampton and Dudley Railway. Properties 140–279 (Inge), 280–9 (Latimer).

[10] HLRO, P & S, B.Ref., 1846, London and Birmingham Railway (Birmingham Extension). B.Ref., 1846, Birmingham, Wolverhampton and Stour Valley Railway, Properties 34–8 (Latimer), BRL 317206.

[11] 250 properties on the routes of the Birmingham Extension railway cited in the preceding footnote and on the southern approach to Snow Hill. HLRO, P & S, B.Ref., 1846, Birmingham and Oxford Junction Railway (Birmingham Extension). Properties 724–920. The land had originally been purchased by a member of the family who was Bishop of London, but his objection to building had been set aside in 1766, William Hutton, *op. cit.* 79.

[12] Whately claimed that Gooch owned 'perhaps one half' of the land needed. HLRO, Min., H.C., 1846, 12 June, p. 16. S.C. on London & Birmingham Railway (Birmingham Extension). Whately appears again in *Railway Times* XI (1848), 18 March.

School, which had seen its extensive fields on the outskirts of the old town rapidly and densely covered with houses.[13] From the railway companies' point of view these corporate bodies in Birmingham, as elsewhere, offered attractive market opportunities. Taking, as they did, an impersonal view of their property and disposing of it in relatively large units, they were infinitely preferable to the small, obstinate proprietor, armed with arbitration and jury procedures. Although they often took a highly competitive view of the value of their property, especially that which chanced to lie in the path of a railway company, they did not usually put forward the startlingly inflated claims of the small owner. Moreover in the case of Lench's Charity and the Free Grammar School their governing bodies were conscious that some of the urban lands they owned were far from creditable, or were submerged in districts which were seedy and disreputable in the extreme. Consequently once their price had been met they were prepared, like the Reverend Charles Lee, Head of the Free Grammar School, to appear before the Parliamentary Select Committee and admit that the removal of these houses would be a great benefit to the town.[14]

Of even greater importance to the railway companies was the existence of the second type of corporate body holding central properties —the canal companies. The first of these in importance was the Birmingham (more correctly the Birmingham and Wolverhampton) Canal Company, which had secured a perpetual lease on six acres of central land, just east of Paradise and Navigation Streets, from Sir Thomas Gooch.[15] The Birmingham Canal Company, in fact, owned no less than 98 acres (53 comprising a reservoir) in the central and northwestern Birmingham district, adding a further cogent reason to that of suppressing price competition for the railway companies to acquire an interest in it.[16]

Advantageous though it was to deal with a handful of large proprietors wherever possible, the properties of the canal companies were even more of a boon. They did not merely dispose of large amounts of land, but this was situated in valuable central sites, or commanded strategic routes into the cities. To schedule them for compulsory purchase in the *Plans and Sections* was out of the question, since, like the railways themselves, they had been given power to acquire their land by statutory authority, and it was manifestly absurd for Parliament to take away by compulsion what it had previously sanctioned in

[13] A. Musgrove, *The History of Lench's Trust, Birmingham, 1525–1925* (Birmingham, 1926).
[14] *Ibid.*, (L. & B. Ext.), 11 June, p. 85. The Free Grammar School received £39,000 for its property. J. MacMillan, *Newspaper Cuttings on Birmingham Railways* (n.d.), BRL 147.31.
[15] At £47 *per annum. A Pictorial Guide to Birmingham* (1849), 159, BM 1303 a 35.
[16] Tithe Map, St. Martin's Parish, 1847.

the public interest. In the early stages, therefore, canal companies were treated with formal respect before the Select Committee. Their land was crossed no more than was necessary; deviations and expensive accommodation works being conceded to disarm opposition.

However, as the railway companies grew in scale and capital, there was nothing to prevent the outright private purchase of the canals, by means of share exchange, or the leasing of the canal for a term of years. Even after the Government, alarmed by the prospect of monopoly, had forbidden railway companies to acquire any more canals a loophole was still left; canals could be acquired by another canal company, and that canal company might already be a client of one of the larger railway companies.[17] In Birmingham, it is clear that attempts to prevent take-over by the railway companies were ineffectual. By 1870 a special committee of the Birmingham Chamber of Commerce, set up to study the subject, had concluded, 'The Birmingham Canal Company is just another name for the London and North-western Railway!'[18]

The foundations of a close financial understanding had been laid in the earliest years between the Birmingham and Wolverhampton Canal Company and the Stour Valley Railway, whose line, as it cleared the built-up area, ran parallel to the canal, and very close to it, for a good part of its route to the north-west.[19] This doubling up of the canal and railway routes—so frequently repeated in Britain's industrial zones—was not primarily caused by technical reasons; though the canals, with their cautious avoidance of gradients, did choose routes which George Stephenson felt would often serve as a model to the railways. But a more important consideration was that of land ownership. This can be seen in Manchester, London, and Glasgow, where the routes or the terminal sites of the older transport network became more and more tempting as the railways' land hunger grew, and the value of urban land rose.

In Birmingham the tendency to superimpose railway routes upon the old canal pattern, and to absorb the central canal warehousing and wharfage area is equally marked. James Allport, General Manager of the Midland Railway, was perfectly frank as to his reasons for buying up the Worcester and Birmingham Canal Company. 'We propose to convert the large surplus property which they have in Birmingham for the purposes of a Goods Station; that is the chief object we have.'[20] The Worcester and Birmingham canal also provided a similar south western exit to that provided in the north-west by the Birmingham and

---

[17] The Leeds and Liverpool canal's boats, horses and carrying establishment was bought up (and tolls trebled) in 1851 by the use of this fiction. BM 8235 c 42.
[18] Chamber of Commerce Reports, 13 July 1870, p. 9. BRL L62.52.
[19] G. Auden, *Birmingham*. (British Association, 1913), 437.
[20] H.C., 1872, XII, Q.640.

Wolverhampton canal; and, as can be seen from the map, the Birmingham and West Suburban Railway was constructed along its banks, following closely every curve, not for technical reasons, but primarily to avoid the complexity of arbitration procedures with a large number of owners.[21]

The last group of proprietors whose disposition influenced the plans of the railway companies were the ex-manorial suburban squires, particularly Heneage Legge, Earl Howe, and the representatives of the Gough and Adderley families—Lord Calthorpe and Lord Norton. The Goughs had owned extensive lands one and a half miles to the south and south-west of the centre of Birmingham since 1717, when Sir Richard Gough bought the manor of Edgbaston, and by the time the major railways were projected a large and exclusive villa estate had been established, sufficiently new and remarkable to excite questions from the Select Committee when Mr. Piggott Smith, surveyor to the Birmingham Commissioners, gave his evidence.[22] 'I believe there is almost a new town in the lower part of the map called Edgbaston?—Yes, it is the residence of the more respectable members of society—the principal merchants and manufacturers—occupied by villas with several acres, not densely built upon.'[23] This was the way the Goughs intended to keep it—at a discreet carriage distance; and even after the Birmingham and West Suburban Railway had secured a route through their estate, by following the Worcester Canal, the first station out from Birmingham was at Selly Oak, to the south of their property. Apart from the small sales of some of the central properties, which they also owned, the only transaction the Goughs had with the railways was in 1890, to oppose the Birmingham, Kidderminster and Stoke branch line.

The other group of gentry, owning east Birmingham, formed a very striking contrast to the Goughs. Heneage Legge and Charles Bowyer Adderley had been the chief beneficiaries of an Enclosure Award carried through as late as 1817, which had handed over to them 20 and 30 acres, respectively, in Saltley and Washwood.[24] A third large proprietor, Earl Howe, owned land described as 'small gardens', just to the north and south of Curzon Street.[25] Soon his lands had disappeared

[21] Apart from the Worcester Canal company Thomas Catell was the largest owner. Birm. W. Suburban Rly, P & S, Session 1871 BRL VI.

[22] Allan E. Everitt, 'Our Neighbourhood', *Trans. Birm. and Midland Instit., Arch section* (1880), 2.

[23] *Ibid.* (L. & B. Ext.), 11 June, pp. 121–2. The map referred to was a dubious one produced by the Society for the Diffusion of Useful Knowledge and 'put up in the Committee room merely to look pretty'. (*Ibid.* 12 June, p. 26). It is probably the same reproduced as BRL 369796.

[24] BRL Inclosure Award, Saltley and Washwood, 1817.

[25] Beillie, Knott, Beillie, *Map of Birmingham 1824–5* (1828), BRL Jewel, Baillie collection 116–17.

entirely beneath the formidable maze of tracks constituting the Vauxhall and Curzon Street goods stations. The Adderleys' lands were too extensive to be swallowed whole, but the conveyance of large tracts are recorded, between 1838 and 1878, in the *Catalogue of the Norton Papers*.[26] When these land sales began the population numbered a mere 400, and most of these had just moved in to find employment at the railway carriage works; by the time the inevitable Boundary Question arose (in 1888, in the case of Birmingham and Saltley) the population had reached over 8,000, 'a compact district with a growing population, clearly divided from the borough of Birmingham', as the Chairman of the Saltley Local Board pointed out, 'by the Midland Railway, the river and the canal.'[27]

By the end of the century in fact, the complaint, ironically enough, was that, far from improving communications, the invasion of the Adderley Estates by the railways had cut Saltley off from Birmingham, both physically, by its sidings, link lines, bridges and cut-offs, and also practically, as a result of the railway fares and service policy. 'Neither of the two railways which serve the district has yet realised the possi- bilities of a liberal arrangement of trains' wrote the *Birmingham Daily Mail* in 1903. 'What Saltley needs now to push it along the path of progress is a more adequate means of vehicular commun- ication with the city. When the up-to-date electric cars go skimming across the railway bridge every few minutes out to Washwood Heath, Saltley will run, so to speak, where it has hitherto been walking.'[28]

A more extreme contrast to that of Edgbaston could hardly be found by the end of the century, as a consequence of the wholesale intrusion of railway yards and associated trades into east Birmingham. Of course, the pressures and inducements offered by the land-hungry railway companies, from the days of the Grand Junction and London and Birmingham companies onwards, were so great in this area that it is difficult to see how any estate policy could have retained the ideal of homogeneous residential zoning. But the result of the uncontrolled mixing of residential and industrial land uses which resulted was that housing became merely a means for the small speculative builder to fill in the interstices between the railway lines. Such new housing as had been constructed, on the fringe of the Curzon Street cattle market and goods yard, in the triangle formed between the New Street and Snow Hill lines and the Duddeston viaduct, was singled out for condemnation

[26] BRL Lf 70.18.
[27] James Adderley, *Sixty Years of Saltley Parish* (Birmingham, 1911). C. Hough- ton, *A Short History of the Boundary Question* (Birmingham, 1888), 6, 10.
[28] *Birmingham Daily Mail*, 1 October 1903.

by the Artizans' Dwellings Inquiry of 1884 as being the worst extreme of jerry-building in Birmingham.[29]

Lord Norton, once again, was an absentee landlord, living at Ham House, a deeply religious man, passionately interested in the High Church controversy of the late nineteenth century. He gave Adderley Park to the public, the first of a series of benefactions, and generously endowed a training college; but the twelve-acre park and college shared the manorial lands with over thirty acres of sidings and approach lines, with Brown Marshall's, the Metropolitan Carriage Works, and those other common features of mixed industrial zoning, a sewage farm and gas works.[30] On his visit to the district, to open the training college, Lord Norton was moved to utter a public prayer, which his biographer faithfully records. 'Oh God,' said Lord Norton, 'Bless what we are doing for Saltley.'[31] To which the Midland, and the London and North Western railway companies no doubt added their amen.

2. Conditions of competition between railway companies

It has already been argued earlier that a knowledge of the competitive stances adopted by the railway companies concerned with gaining access to Britain's major cities can serve as a key to the explanation of the urban railway network. The site, route and timing of these intrusions into the established pattern of land uses cannot be explained retrospectively by reference to the map. The urban railway networks do not merely fail to make sense nowadays; they never did make complete sense, but were products of expediency and compromise. Shifting and ephemeral rivalries and alliances between companies throw light upon many of the decisions which seem later to be so immutable; tactical blocking manoeuvres and acts of commercial pique help to explain many of the surviving quirks and follies of urban railways.

In Birmingham the case is relatively simple, certainly by comparison with the other provincial cities or with London: and, indeed, as is suggested in Section 4 below, the pattern of railway accommodation which emerged was correspondingly durable and well conceived. The protagonists were few and the position between them not as fluid as in the other cities, where the battles between rival companies continued into the 1870's and 1880's.

The two main companies serving Birmingham, the L. & N.W. and the G.W. had built their redoubts (at New Street and Snow Hill) by the early 1850's. The L. & N.W. was Britain's largest railway amalgama-

---

[29] *Report of Committee of Inquiry into Artizans' Dwellings*, 3 June 1884, pp. 48–52. Bad ventilation and construction. BRL 155942.

[30] *The Heart of Industrial England* (Birmingham, 1891), 39.

[31] W. Childe-Pemberton, *The Life of Lord Norton* (1909), 132.

tion, whose strength arose from the spinal trunk route its constituent companies had pioneered between the four largest English cities.[32] The Liverpool and Manchester railway, between the two cities of those names; the Grand Junction, running from the point half-way between the Liverpool-Manchester axis (at Newton-le-Willows) to Birmingham; and the London to Birmingham railway: these were the three companies which joined together in 1846 to form the L. & N.W. amalgamation, and to them Birmingham represented a vital point half way up the spine. The Great Western was the second largest railway company in Britain, also branching out from London, but in the only other main direction for trunk routes, towards Bristol and the West Country.[33] The whole posture of the G.W. and the L. & N.W. towards each other was one of independence and suspicion, flaring up, at the points where they converged, to one of open hostility; an attitude which, in fact, can still be seen reflected in the pages of their standard histories. To E. T. MacDermot, historian of the G.W. Railway, Captain Huish, General Manager of the L. & N.W. appears as a model of vindictiveness and duplicity; a coldly calculating villain who might, one feels, have been drawn, complete with his name, from Victorian melodrama. To W. L. Steel, historian of the L. & N.W., Huish was 'one of the most able of railway administrators and diplomatists who ever lived.'[34]

The only major working arrangement over urban railways ever suggested between the G.W. and L. & N.W. companies was the short-lived scheme for sharing Euston station.[35] Usually they found themselves on opposite sides of the table at the Parliamentary Select Committees, or waiting in turn in the anterooms of Corporation chambers. Over no issue was their rivalry more vehement than over the Broad Gauge question, and after this had apparently been decided in favour of the narrow gauge companies in 1846 it came as an unpleasant shock to find, with the passing of the Birmingham and Oxford Junction Bill, that the break in gauge was not to be made at Bristol or Gloucester

[32] In addition to the three major companies there were 15 smaller companies which had been absorbed at the time of the L. & N.W.'s formation in 1846. The genealogy is traced in a table in G. Ottley, *A Bibliography of British Railway History* (1965), App. IIIb, and the history of the component companies traced in entries on pp. 377–94. The best history of the L. & N.W. is W. L. Steel, *The History of the London and North Western Railway* (1914).

[33] Ottley, *op. cit.* App. IIIa (genealogy), pp. 358–70 (bibliography). Standard history E. T. MacDermot, *History of the Great Western Railway* (1927, 31); for the period 1833–63 C. R. Clinker has produced a revised ed. of MacDermot.

[34] W. L. Steel, *op. cit.* 179. E. T. MacDermot, *op. cit. passim*; 'politely menacing, a display of bad temper, questionable action, bullying, spiteful attempt, unscrupulous efforts, a reputation for finding pretexts to avoid agreements which had become inconvenient.' On Huish's retirement MacDermot relents sufficiently to describe him as 'the old warrior'.

[35] E. T. MacDermot, *op. cit.* (ed. C. R. Clinker, 1964), I, 22–4.

but at Birmingham.[36] Not that the Great Western broad gauge express route to London was able to hold out a very serious threat to the more direct L. & N.W. route; but the Great Western commanded a considerable area of its own, and the mere possibility of price and traffic competition was enough to curb any inclinations the L. & N.W. might have had to exercise arbitrary monopoly powers.[37] Witnesses before the Snow Hill Select Committee stressed the need for a second completely independent access to Birmingham. 'The London and Birmingham Company have not the confidence of the commercial people at Birmingham . . . they are the worst managers for the public in England but not for themselves, they are too selfish.'[38] A businessmen's memorial, asking for night trains, which had been sponsored by Mr. Chance, the local entrepreneur in glass making, was ignored until the Bill for the G.W.'s satellite, the Birmingham and Oxford Junction railway, was passed; then hurried provisions were made and the fares reduced by 30%, even before competition materialised.[39]

The third major company serving Birmingham, the Midland railway, adopted a policy of friendly alliance with the L. & N.W.[40] Indeed since it depended upon the L. & N.W. for access, both in east Birmingham and later, in the 1870's, for a share of central access at the rebuilt New Street station, it could hardly do otherwise. On the other hand, when the Midland Railway Company fell under the energetic guidance of James Allport, although the *entente* was maintained in Birmingham, his abolition of the second class, improvement of third-class accommodation and all-round reduction of fares in 1875 gave English railways their most important competitive jolt since the short-lived wildcat price battle of the early 1850's. The Midland's role in Birmingham, therefore, was that of the joker in the pack, upsetting the game of routine competition to which the L. & N.W. and G.W. had settled down by the late 1860's.

All this, as will be seen by comparison with other major cities, led to a provision of service, accommodation and fares which followed demand reasonably sensitively, and with a time-lag which was unexceptionable. There was anxiety about the rate-fixing for iron and other goods in the Midland region, but little or no dissatisfaction with the central passenger and goods service for Birmingham.[41] Indeed, the Corporation went so far, in July 1866, as to describe Birmingham as

[36] *Ibid.* I, 126–8.
[37] *Ibid.* I, 230.
[38] HLRO, Min., (B.W. & D.), 23 June, pp. 17–23, 25 June, p. 254.
[39] *Ibid.* 24 June, pp. 252–4.
[40] Ottley, *op. cit.* App. IIIc (genealogy), pp. 410–2 (bibliography). Standard histories F. S. Williams, *The Midland Railway, its Rise and Progress* (1876–88), E. G. Barnes, *The Rise of the Midland Railway, 1844–1874* (1966).
[41] S. Timmins, *The Resources, Products and Industries of Birmingham* (1866), 74.

'first class station on the L. & N.W., the G.W. and the Midland railways.'[42] Admittedly this expression of opinion was intended not so much to congratulate the companies as to strengthen the Corporation's argument against the establishment of a District Will office at Lichfield; but it stands in marked contrast to the official complaints made in the same decade in Glasgow, Liverpool and Manchester. The chief complaints that were made by the Corporation and contemporary press in the later years of Victoria's reign were, in fact, concerned with a much more general failure of the railway companies, not confined to Birmingham: their reluctance to provide comprehensive and cheap suburban facilities in anticipation of demand.

3. *The development of railway facilities: a chronological sketch*

The fortunate balance of forces which prevailed in Birmingham was not established until 1851; up to that time the situation was extremely fluid and unstable. On the map the railway facilities of the late thirties and early forties show a deceptive simplicity; there was only one station site at Curzon Street, a terminal driven like a broad wedge into the outskirts of east Birmingham. To this eastern terminal site came not merely the south-eastern approach lines from London, and the north-eastern lines from Derby—following obvious and direct routes—but also the north-western approach lines from Crewe, and the south-western lines from Gloucester; the last two approach routes curving round in complete half circles to make this eastern entry. The Birmingham and Gloucester, and Birmingham and Derby lines (which later merged into the Midland railway) were both allowed, under running powers secured in their Bills, to run into the London and Birmingham's passenger station at Curzon Street. In the cause of independence, however, the Birmingham and Derby Railway Company opened a separate low-level station built upon low-lying ground a little further out, at Lawley Street, from which each carriage had to be lifted on to the London and Birmingham tracks.[43] The Grand Junction Railway (from Crewe) also built its own stations, first a temporary one at Vauxhall; then, when the twenty-eight arch Lawley Street viaduct had been built, it opened its own separate station facing Curzon Street.[44]

So there were really four separate stations all blanketed under one name, involving complications in levels and running arrangements which caused no little confusion in the minds both of the Parliamentary Committee and of the directors of the newly formed Midland Railway

[42] BRL, Council Proceedings, 1 July 1866, p. 223.
[43] C. E. Stretton, *The Railways of Birmingham* (1897), 10 February 1842. HLRO, Min., (L. & B. Ext.), 12 June, pp. 56–61.
[44] W. L. Steel, *op. cit.* 90–1.

Company.[45] Soon afterwards a fourth company, the Manchester and Birmingham, was also granted running powers, although in fact it came no nearer Birmingham than Crewe, whence it followed the Grand Junction's rails to the Curzon Street terminus.

By the mid-1840's, therefore, there were three pressing reasons why the existing facilities should be by-passed and radical new accommodation provided. The first, which has already been mentioned, was the large number of companies jamming themselves into the city's only point of access. To a certain extent this difficulty might have been eliminated by amalgamation. The sharing of stations sometimes led to the creation of such groups. But the formation of these alliances was not as inevitable as retrospective histories make it appear. In Birmingham, for example, in the year before the L. & N.W. merger, relations between the Grand Junction and London and Birmingham companies were extremely strained, and an amalgamation was even discussed for a time between the Grand Junction and the Great Western Railway; which would not merely have brought the Great Western into Curzon Street, but also have led to the building of broad gauge lines to Liverpool and Manchester.[46]

The second reason was simply that the traffic itself had expanded beyond the capacity of Curzon Street, even under unified control. The point was underlined by counsel's questioning of a city magistrate, Mr. Charles Shaw, before the Parliamentary Committee on Snow Hill station.

Mr. Shaw: 'Fifteen years has created a great change in the wants and requirements of the town. We were very well satisfied then if we could get a railway brought into the town at all.'

Chairman: 'At that time I believe it was invariably the practice for most railways to stop outside the town?—It was.'

'That was done in almost every town in England?—Yes, and more especially in the town of Liverpool.'

Mr. Richards (counsel for the bill): 'Are you aware that the business of railways has been so much increased beyond what was expected that the space which was formerly deemed sufficient for a station in a populous town has since been found to be quite insufficient?—Yes, there is no doubt of that. The people at Birmingham now have more work than they know what to do with in their present station.'[47]

The third reason for by-passing Curzon Street, and it was this which helped to persuade members of the Select Committee to sanction the railways' encroachment, armed with powers of compulsory purchase,

[45] HLRO, Min., L. & B. Ext., 12 June, pp. 39, 70. Samuel Beale, ex-mayor, was the Midland director whose notions were corrected by Robert Stephenson.

[46] E. T. MacDermot, *op. cit.* I, 127.

[47] HLRO, Min., (B.W. & D.), 25 June, pp. 237–43.

upon central properties, was the inconvenience of the existing road approaches within the town itself.[48] The streets were narrow and incorrectly aligned to handle the increasing cab and omnibus traffic to and from the station. Since the omnibuses, which had started operating in Birmingham in 1834, were conveying 30,000 people per week across the town by 1846, congestion was rapidly building up in the central business district.[49] Moreover, to reach the Bull Ring, High Street or New Street from the railway station either meant a lengthy drive round two sides of a triangle, or a difficult journey through tiny back streets and alleys, which were often blocked.[50] The whole approach was not worthy of a major city, and the Birmingham Commissioners, in fact, had carefully considered the idea of cutting a fine new approach to Curzon Street at their own expense. The route, which is shown in a map prepared by Charles Edge in 1838, would have cut diagonally across existing streets and houses from the junction of High and New Streets to the entrance of the London and Birmingham Railway at Canal Street; a route, in fact, parallel and slightly to the north of the railway route later adopted to New Street station.[51] Mr. Daniel Malins, the High Bailiff of the Borough, and Mr. Pigott Smith, Surveyor to the Birmingham Commissioners, both gave evidence to Parliament on the new and commodious street which had been in contemplation by the Street Commissioners to improve railway access to the town.[52]

They do not say what happened to the scheme, but it is reasonable to guess that it was shelved when the Commissioners realised the immense cost and complication of a half mile cut through urban property. There was also a good deal of opposition from interested property owners on the route, witnessed by the interesting pamphlet *Observations on the Projected Improvements of the Town in reference to the Railways*.[53] The best retail grocery in town would be annihilated, the Court of Requests would have to be rebuilt, an important wholesale establishment destroyed, and many of the smaller publicans, all mentioned affectionately by name, would suffer by the change. Yet the distance to the station would still remain too great and the large flow of street traffic generated would ruin the amenity of the neighbourhood. 'Commonsense,' the anonymous pamphleteer makes these points as he conducts the reader on an imaginary stroll down the new boulevard

[48] *Ibid.* 24 June, p. 316.
[49] *Ibid.* 25 June, p. 223.
[50] Apart from the cab-fare of 1s, E. C. & W. Osborne, *Grand Junction Railway Guide* (1838). Later in the nineteenth century Curzon Street was used for meat, fish, fruit and vegetables, and for excursion trains during the busiest part of the year.
[51] Charles Edge, *Plan of an Intended New Street*, (1838), BRL 260988, cf. HLRO, P & S (L. & B. Ext.), 1846.
[52] HLRO, Min., (L. & B. Ext.), 11 June, pp. 6–7, 142.
[53] 'Commonsense', *op. cit.* (Birmingham, 1838), BRL 72264.

(pointing out *en route* the damage and severance caused) by pretending that the reader has begun to flag after a hundred yards or two. 'I hope you are not tired. Keep up your spirits my dear sir. We will sit and rest ourselves a little while on the steps of St. Martin's Churchyard and watch (in mental anticipation) the different vehicles as they pass us from the Railways.' On this occasion, at any rate, sentiment and economics coincided, and the railway boulevard remained a plan only.

However, the need to provide more central access had been freely admitted by the mid-1840's, when funds on a sufficiently large scale to tackle the problem became available. Yet the question still remained open as to where the site or sites should be, and which of the companies uneasily sharing the Curzon Street group of stations should be allowed priority to exploit the new route and premises. It was of vital importance to the main protagonists involved to secure independent access of their own and, if possible, to subvert rival schemes; and they were prepared to go to any lengths to achieve this.

As far as the selection of sites was concerned there was little to choose between the two proposals. The proposed Navigation Street (later called New Street) station was within a hundred yards of Birmingham's best hotel, the Royal; it was near the Post Office, banks, professional quarters, old coach offices and within a few paces of the principal markets.[54] The Parliamentary Select Committee, quite reasonably, was convinced by the evidence of Mr. Daniel Malins, the High Bailiff, and Mr. James James, late Mayor and Chairman of the Paving and Parliamentary Committee appointed by the Commissioners. 'The line adopts the best possible route to avoid injury to property . . . I do not think you could have a station more centrally situated without destroying very valuable property. It is the most convenient, with the least interruption of the property of the town.'[55]

Still another important point in its favour was that the property which it did erase was 'a collection of streets and houses that it would be advantageous to Birmingham altogether to get rid of, both physically and morally.'[56] There was no objection to stopping up the Froggeries, Peck Lane and Little Colmore Street, which were all either *cul-de-sacs* or alleys along which it was not wise to venture, packed with brothels and thieves' nests, breeding grounds for typhoid, cholera and crime. J. T. Bunce, historian of Birmingham Corporation, recalled in a newspaper article in 1899 the grim scene sixty years earlier at the Froggeries, and at the Inkleys and the Gullett, adjacent areas which were forbidden ground to a middle-class boy, and contrasted it with the bright and

---

[54] HLRO, Min., (L. & B. Ext.), 11 June, pp. 9–16.
[55] *Ibid.* 11 June, pp. 38, 52.
[56] *Ibid.* 11 June, p. 18.

amusing scene of the open third-class trucks and stage-coach shaped first-class carriages arriving at Vauxhall.[57]

The performance of this public service, the removal of seven acres of the slums 'just behind the principal and best streets', exempted the bold New Street scheme from criticism, but cost the London and Birmingham railway £350,000, for an extension of seven-eighths of a mile. Trustees for Lench's Charity and the Free Grammar School, and Sir T. S. Gooch, had large unified holdings on the approach route, but the station site itself was covered with small property units; and the expense which fragmented ownership involved was increased by the multiple tenancies, up to 22 occupants per property.[58]

Theoretically, of course, the owners could simply evict their tenants, but in practice the railway companies had to move very carefully. A legal case surviving amongst the Lee, Crowder papers shows why caution was necessary. In the case of *Charles Burkinshaw versus the Birmingham and Oxford Junction Railway Company*, the plaintiff owned three dwelling houses and shops on the route chosen for the southern approach to Snow Hill, and instructed his solicitors, Lee, Pinson and Bent to settle for no less than £4,500. On 26 January 1847, the agent for the railway company, Mr. Hornblower, alarmed by the possibility of the work being held up, called and told three tenants, Messrs. Rogers, Waring and Carter, that they must get out by March. Two left at once, one claiming the refund of large sums laid out in repairs; the third stayed but 'paid no rent after the Railway interference.' Judgment and costs of £141 were obtained.[59] To avoid the expense and delay of such litigation a simpler procedure was to offer a premium for persuading each tenant to leave voluntarily. However, though expensive in the short run, the London and Birmingham's action in choosing the New Street site turned out to be extremely judicious and far-sighted. For apart from the merits of the site itself, there remained, to the south-west, a further seven or eight acres of scandalously dilapidated housing which constituted a natural area for expansion when the L. & N.W. and Midland railways were ready to take their next bite out of the central district.

The merits of the Snow Hill site were argued equally forcefully. Snow Hill was higher in the town and more conveniently placed for the manufactories and warehouses in the north of the central Birmingham district. Several witnesses gave evidence testifying to the projected station's easy access to the warehouses which the small hardware

---

[57] *Birmingham Weekly Post*, 25 March 1899.

[58] HLRO, P & S, B.Ref. (L. & B. Ext.), 1846. Also includes the estimate of costs by Robert Stephenson and William Barker.

[59] BRL, Lee, Crowder papers, 241. The small sums of 2s 6d or a guinea compensation sometimes quoted were for 'weekly tenants'.

dealer or manufacturer would visit. In addition Snow Hill was wider than the widest part of New Street, which at its narrowest point was only 13 yards wide, and had recently required the stationing of two policemen to prevent accidents.[60]

For their part counsel representing the L. & N.W. Railway did their best to sabotage the bill. Under re-examination one of the favourable witnesses, Mr. Samuel Thornley, had to admit that he was selling property to one of the companies planning to build the Snow Hill station; another, the Birmingham magistrate Mr. William Matthews, that he had received a gift of shares in an associated railway company and had been allowed to tender for the works.[61] Perhaps the most damaging evidence of all was the opinion expressed by the L. & N.W. engineer, Robert Stephenson, that Snow Hill and New Street were incompatible; an opinion which took some erasing from the minds of the Committee.[62] Once their minds had been set at rest upon this point, however, objections to Snow Hill were removed and both central sites were sanctioned in August 1846.[63]

The question of sites was settled, but the issue of control and operation was still a matter for contention. The already delicate relationship between the railways sharing the east Birmingham terminals was further complicated by the appearance of four new companies, all with claims to the new central stations. For the next five years Birmingham was the scene of a struggle for control as obstructive and turbulent as those enacted over longer periods in the other major cities. The situation can briefly be summarised as follows. At Snow Hill Parliamentary authorisation had been given to a newly formed company, the Birmingham, Wolverhampton and Dudley Railway, to build a line from the northwest to the Snow Hill site, and to another recently formed company, the Birmingham and Oxford Junction Railway, to build a line from the south-east. At Snow Hill both shared equal and overlapping rights, so the obvious step, proposed at the first general meeting of each company, was for the two railways to amalgamate, and then to sell or lease their amalgamated lines to the Great Western railway company. These resolutions were carried, and a deputation from both companies met the Great Western directors, who agreed to buy the two undertakings on the basis of an offer of £30 5s 0d for each £20 share, a very handsome profit to show in so short a time on the combined capitals of £1,700,000.[64]

However, this was not the end of the matter, for George Carr Glyn,

---

[60] HLRO, Min. (B.W. & D.), 24 June, pp. 240–3, 25 June, pp. 221, 269.

[61] *Ibid.* 25 June, p. 281 (Thornley). He owned a printing office, bakehouse, warehouse, eight houses and shops, and leased others in the area.

[62] *Ibid.* 23 June, pp. 77, 79, 90.

[63] 9 & 10 Vic., 315 and 359.

[64] E. T. MacDermot, *op. cit.* I, 129.

the Chairman of the newly formed L. & N.W. Railway Company, with his fellow directors, and the General Manager, Captain Huish, set about buying up the Birmingham and Oxford Junction shares to obtain a controlling interest in the company, repudiate the deal with the Great Western, and deny it access to Birmingham. By offering large premiums they were able to secure 80% of the shares, divide them into lots of ten—the minimum size for a vote—and distribute them amongst the directors, solicitors, clerks and even the engineers and porters of the L. & N.W. These new shareholders arrived at Curzon Street station by special train from Euston on 13 March 1847, attended the Extraordinary General Meeting and elected six new directors from their own ranks. The old directors, having taken counsel, refused to retire, and remained in *de facto* control whilst the argument was taken to Chancery, and by special petition, to the House of Lords. The following January the last appeals were thrown out by the Lord Chancellor, and the two companies permitted to carry out their agreements with the Great Western Railway.[65] One tangible monument of this struggle was left behind, however, in the form of Duddeston Viaduct, an urban branch 50 chains in length, carried on 58 brick arches, which the Great Western railway company was compelled to build in accordance with a clause inserted in the Birmingham and Oxford Junction bill. It could hardly be called a branch line, since no rails were ever laid and no connection made at the Northern end; yet it was a small price to pay for securing a central station at Snow Hill.[66]

The other two new companies which appeared on the scene had the power to run into New Street station. One, the Birmingham, Wolverhampton and Stour Valley Railway, was obviously a speculative terminal company, floated in the same spirit as the Birmingham, Wolverhampton and Dudley, and the Birmingham and Oxford Junction railways. Like them it intended to sell at a premium the authority to traverse Birmingham's suburbs which Parliament had granted. The second company, the Shrewsbury and Birmingham, was somewhat grandiloquently named for a line which only ran from Shrewsbury to the outskirts of Wolverhampton, where its act allowed running powers over the Birmingham, Wolverhampton and Stour Valley Railway. When the Shrewsbury company signed a traffic agreement with Charles Saunders, the General Manager of the Great Western, however, and proposed to exercise its running powers into New Street station, the small company assumed a tactical importance out of proportion to its size.

[65] *Ibid.* I, 130–3.
[66] *Ibid.* I, 140, G. A. Sekon, 'Birmingham's never-used railway viaduct', *Railway and Travel Monthly* (March 1920). C. E. Stretton, *The Railways of Birmingham* (1897), *idem. A History of the L. & N.W. Railway* (Leeds, 1902).

Once the Board of Trade inspectors had reported the line to be satisfactory the Shrewsbury company announced it would run a train into New Street on 1 December 1851. Since the Stour Valley railway's lines finished at the northern entrance to the station, the L. & N.W., which had built the southern approaches and the station itself, determined to resist the use of their terminal by an ally of the Great Western.[67] Stern written exchanges having failed, they sent an engine, driven by the Stour Valley's engineer, Mr. Baker, and loaded with solicitors and officials, to intercept and check the Birmingham and Shrewsbury's inaugural train. The Birmingham crowds and local newspaper reporters enjoyed a field day as the Shrewsbury train approached, with its whistle sounding shrilly, and attempted to push the L. & N.W. engine backwards into the station.[68] The symbolic nature of the encounter did not escape the *Wolverhampton Herald* reporter. 'The two engines standing opposite each other in the closest proximity with the steam power of their gigantic bodies issuing from the various safety valves in voluminous quantities with a hissing noise presented an exciting spectacle, representing the antagonism of their respective proprietors.'[69]

The attempt to force an entry by steam power failed and the directors and solicitors adjourned to the magistrate's court at the Town Hall, from which the argument proceeded to the Board of Trade, and finally the Court of Chancery. It was three years before toll arrangements were agreed under which the Birmingham and Shrewsbury's trains were allowed to enter New Street.

This was the fitting climax to the battle between the L. & N.W. and G.W. railways, however. Once each had established clear rights to its own station the tacit apportionment of their shares of Birmingham's traffic soon followed, together with an uneasy agreement on equal rates and traffic divisions in 1857.[70] The later expansion of station accommodation fitted into this pattern.

4. *Summary and general considerations*

In many respects Birmingham provides a text-book model for the impact of railways upon a great city. Its termini are central and provide underground through-transport beneath the city centre. The cross-town link railways, which caused such expense to shareholders and dis-

---

[67] E. T. MacDermot, *op. cit.* I, 188–93.

[68] 4,000 to 5,000 people watched the scene. J. F. Nicol, the secretary of the Shrewsbury company, was on the train's footplate. A second line of L. & N.W. defence was to take up the track behind their locomotive. C. E. Stretton, *The Birmingham, Wolverhampton and Stour Valley Railway* (1886).

[69] E. T. MacDermot, *op. cit.* I, 194.

[70] *Ibid.* I, 219.

satisfaction to travellers in other cities in the 1860's and 1870's, were not necessary in Birmingham because large and early decisions were taken. Birmingham also emerged with the nearest approach in any of the major cities to a single Grand Central Station, when New Street was enlarged to fifteen acres in the early 1880's.[71]

Moreover, with certain exceptions which will be noted, the decisions on the siting and routes of Birmingham's railways and termini in the mid-nineteenth century seem to have been taken, by the various interests concerned, in a manner which was not merely timely and rational, but was also peculiarly single-minded. Birmingham is free of the huge number of confusing alternatives which one finds canvassed in the local press of most of the other cities, and submitted, at great expense, to Parliamentary Select Committees.

It would be possible, for example, if one assembled evidence from the *Plans and Sections* and *Books of Reference* submitted to Parliament in support of those schemes which fell through, to draw up a hypothetical picture of urban railways which would have been substantially different in Glasgow, Manchester and Liverpool, and virtually unrecognisable in London. Not so with Birmingham, where the path of railway construction is not littered with second-thoughts and might-have-beens. The only substantial scheme which was proposed but fell through was for a central station at Broad Street, mid-way between those actually built and to the west of them; and the reason why this scheme aborted was simply that in 1831 it was too grandiose and premature. As Mr. Charles Shaw, one of the projectors, explained, 'That was always a favourite scheme of mine as being more central, but railway profits had not then developed themselves and this would have cost more capital than we dare undertake to raise.'[72]

The only considerable after-thought, or later modification of the urban railway pattern in Birmingham, was in the opening of a further small depot at Moor Street, at the end of the century. This addition was not compelled either by the failure of existing working arrangements between companies, or because of the conspicuous overloading of existing facilities. It came into being largely because the disposal of a substantial central area covered by the old Police Station and Public Offices presented an unusual opportunity in the urban land market, which a small company, the Birmingham, North Warwick-

---

[71] By Additional Powers Bills, in 1881 and '82, the Midland railway company took in 756 further properties. Vyse's trustees and Thomas Catell's executors held parcels of up to 50, but mostly ownership was fragmented. The chief point of significance was that, at this relatively late date, the railway companies had learned to purchase in advance. At least 90 properties had been brought up beforehand, in three main blocks, by the Midland company. BRL, P & S, Midland Railway, 1881–2.

[72] HLRO, Min. (B.W. & D.), 25 June, pp. 233, 245, 249.

shire and Stratford upon Avon Railway, was launched to exploit.[73] For the rest, Birmingham's facilities retained substantially the form in which they had been delineated by the late 1840's. Goods yards and sidings were considerably enlarged, tracks and tunnels broadened, and both New Street and Snow Hill stations extensively rebuilt, but there was no need to erase or re-draw the essential outlines laid down as early as 1846. Even the increment of suburban traffic, associated with the opening of the Harborne, Birmingham and Henley in Arden, and Birmingham West Suburban railways, in the 1860's and 1870's, was contained within the original framework without great difficulty, by the construction of link lines. Apart from the Moor Street terminal station which, as just mentioned, was opened in the last decade of the century 'to cope with the growing short distance traffic', the only other station envisaged was that of the Birmingham and West Suburban Railway at Granville Street (or Old Wharf) immediately to the west of New Street Station; and since this small company was, from the start, proposed as a toll railway, it is difficult to avoid the belief that it was established, like so many other small urban lines, with the express intention of attracting a wealthy patron from the larger companies.[74] Certainly this was the course events took. Within six years the West Suburban's parliamentary authorisation to purchase the lands of the Worcester Canal Company (which formed their approach route), had been acquired by the Midland Railway, and a new tunnel projected from the Old Wharf at Suffolk Street, to join the main line tunnel to the north-west of New Street Station. This measure, together with the doubling of New Street Station's size, enabled the only other projected central terminal to be eliminated and another new line to be woven into the pattern established earlier.[75]

In no other major city was so simple and definitive a plan laid down so early; and yet the accommodation provided was sufficiently flexible to stand until the end of the century with only minor modifications. It presents an altogether unusual picture amongst the major Victorian cities.

Why should Birmingham have experienced relatively little difficulty in coming to terms with the railways? Any explanation of this phenomenon would need to take into account four major factors. In the first place, the provision of railway facilities in any city can only be explained

[73] Apart from the Mayor, Aldermen and Citizens, Lench's Charity, Thomas Catell's Trustees, King Edward VI's School, Sir Alfred Gooch and the Ecclesiastical Commissioners were the principal owners. BRL, B.Ref., B.N.W. & S. upon A. Railway, 1893. The G.W. absorbed it in 1908. *Great Western Railway Magazine*, May/June 1916.

[74] R. P. Mears, 'Snow Hill Station', *G.W.R. Magazine*, August 1911.

[75] BRL, P & S, B.Ref., B.W. Suburban Railway, (Sessions 1871, 1873), Midland Railway New Works (Session 1876).

by examining the relative conditions of competition prevailing at the time between those companies which originated the urban railway schemes. In Birmingham's case the postures of the rival companies engaged were such as to produce a working compromise at a very early stage, as explained above in Section 2. Secondly, such a durable plan might survive because it was well conceived and rational, and contained within itself, partly by design, partly by accident, the potentiality for continuous growth and evolution matching that of the city. To a certain extent this was the case, as Section 3 above attempts to explain and illustrate. Thirdly, the comparative absence of difficulties in Birmingham might be due to favourable physical and geographical factors, which made railway access unusually simple. And, indeed, the conformation of the central Birmingham area is such that the Snow Hill lines could approach the terminus on a viaduct and leave it through a tunnel without encountering any gradients which were insuperable, even in the early days of steam power. The New Street lines also run through tunnels into a species of natural bowl, or amphitheatre; so that both the two main railways take their course naturally underground through the city centre in the best approved modern manner.[76] Moreover these underground cross-urban routes were selected as early as 1846, so that the exorbitantly expensive task of taking the steam railways underground, encountered later in the century in Liverpool and London, did not present itself in Birmingham.

Finally one must consider the possibility which exists, in theory at any rate, that the urban railway pattern might owe its longevity and stability to a relatively slow local growth in trade, industry and population, and to retarded traffic demands in the area it served. This, clearly, was not true of Birmingham and the Midland industrial zone except in the following special sense. The region centred on Birmingham undoubtedly enjoyed a rate of growth which was both firmly based, and sustained without flagging into the twentieth century, because it was admirably diversified. The security which industrial diversification gave to the region was one of the boasts of the Birmingham merchant. 'Look here,' one said to John Pendleton in 1896, 'if the shipping trade isn't good, Liverpool's all awry; if there's a dispute in the cotton trade, Manchester suffers keenly; but nothing upsets us. You see, we've all sorts of trades, from guns to pens and buttons.'[77] These varied products of the small craft workshops, which were still typical of Birmingham in 1900, formed a compact and valuable merchandise traffic little subject to seasonal fluctuation, and relatively immune to the cyclical depressions of the last quarter of the century. The raw materials and finished

[76] August Lösch, *The Economics of Location* (Yale, 1954), 443.
[77] John Pendleton, *Our Railways: their Origin, Development, Incident and Romance* (1896), I, 240.

products of local and regional industry were enough to occupy the great goods yards at Curzon and Lawley Streets fully, but they did not pose as acute a traffic problem as those encountered in northern cities, which dealt with a highly irregular traffic in relatively bulky raw materials and finished goods, and which also had to cater for the problems of warehousing and trans-shipment which maritime commerce involved. Large though the Birmingham goods yards were, they occupied at the end of the century only about two-thirds of the space which had to be made available elsewhere; some 390 acres, as opposed to between 590 and 680 acres at Glasgow, Liverpool and Manchester.[78] Birmingham did not have the problems of a terminal and trans-shipment point, but was able to choose which items of the through traffic would terminate in the city's yards, and which would be channelled to the four hundred or so private industrial sidings which existed in the Birmingham, Darlaston, Tipton region.[79] As a manufacturer of valuable and imperishable small wares Birmingham did not have a warehousing problem comparable to that of Manchester. Nor did Birmingham experience the acute problems which irregular daily traffic brought to a trading city like Liverpool, where 60% of each day's railway goods traffic arrived between 3 p.m. and 7 p.m.[80] In the evidence on Terminal Charges in the 1860's and 1870's, the problem towns most often quoted were Liverpool and London; the former as an example of the miles of wasteful sidings which had to be provided to meet an irregular peak traffic, the latter because the extraordinary land values prevailing made any sort of central goods accommodation extremely expensive. Birmingham does not receive a single mention in the lengthy evidence put forward by Cawkwell, Grierson and Allport on behalf of their companies, the L. & N.W., the G.W., and the Midland, presumably because its problems were considered relatively tractable.

This characteristic feature in the city's economic base may help to explain the relative ease with which the growing *goods* traffic was accommodated without undue consumption of urban space or intrusion into the central district, but it does not explain why there was no counterpart in Birmingham to the expensive and belated reorganisation of suburban passenger accommodation in late nineteenth-century London.

The main explanation of this is to be sought in the policies of the railway companies. For reasons discussed elsewhere the three major companies possessing access to Birmingham failed to exploit the potentialities of the region for mass suburban travel. Instead they cut

[78] *Infra* Ch. 10, sec. 2.
[79] P. L. Clark, *Studies in the Railway Geography of the Birmingham Region* (Birmingham B.A. thesis, 1951), 54.
[80] H.C., 1867, XXXVIII, Q.12954.

the traffic to suit the system by means of a high fares policy, by their reluctance to issue third class season tickets, and by their point-blank refusal to put on Workmens' Trains. Their existing passenger facilities, therefore, were sufficient, with a little stretching, to serve the restricted function deliberately chosen for them.[81] The attempt to capture local residential traffic, typified by the G.W. Railway's 'Homes for All in Rural Birmingham' campaign, in the years before the Great War, was left too late, and restricted in its appeal to the middle classes. As a consequence many of the small branch stations opened in the period between 1890 and 1914 had only a short life before closure in the 1920's and 1930's. The problem of the urban commuter was not solved by the railway network in Birmingham, but by other means.

Railway services in the four other great cities shared this shortcoming to differing degrees. Birmingham's increase in passenger traffic was not of a lesser order than theirs, yet it was handled by the simple extension of existing facilities over a seventy year period, in a way which was not paralleled elsewhere. None of the other major cities studied was able to secure so large and so central a site for a through-railway terminal, at such an early date and reasonable cost, or operate it with so little friction between companies afterwards. In Birmingham there was an equipoise in the competitive interests, combined with peculiarly favourable features in the land-ownership and land use pattern in the central district, which made it possible not merely to secure at New Street an unequalled site, but to expand it progressively, and with public approval, into one of the largest passenger stations in Britain.

[81] *Infra* Ch. 11, sec. 3.

VI

◇◇

Manchester

◇◇

1. *The property ownership pattern*

MANCHESTER is particularly fortunate in possessing an outstanding series of maps and estate plans. The reason may partly be the accident of their survival; but it is also possible that as one of the most extraordinary towns in late eighteenth-century Europe—the first fully-developed example of the new type of town associated with the Industrial Revolution—Manchester received unusually close attention and study. Certainly Laurent, the continental map-maker, considered it worth his time to pay an extended visit to record the city. Excellent though his map is, however, it is surpassed by the detailed cartography of William Green: and indeed, a whole series of maps of unusual quality, by local map-makers like Richard Thornton, Joseph Adshead and Richard Bastow, extends through the nineteenth century.[1]

From these maps, and from estate plans, it is possible to piece together a picture of Manchester during the railway age, broken into highly fragmented units of ownership in the central area, but ringed by a dozen or so large estates, which lay in the route of the city's outward expansion, and of its railway approaches. The evidence, which is represented in the diagrammatic map opposite, does not include those great landlords like Sir Humphrey and Sir Thomas de Trafford or the Earl of Stamford, whose holdings, though extensive, were situated a little further from the centre. Nor does it include the large suburban holdings of families familiar in Manchester's history, the Chethams,

---

[1] C. Laurent, *Topographical Plan of Manchester and Salford* (1793), W. Green, *Plan of Manchester and Salford* (1794). Though early, both show the property boundaries and 'allotments of Land proposed to be built on' in great detail. R. Thornton, *Banck's and Co.'s Plan of Manchester and Salford and their environs* (1832), J. Adshead, *Twenty-four Illustrated Maps of the Township of Manchester* (1851). The still more remarkable map by Bastow (1881) was not published, but prepared for the Corporation's internal use. See *infra* Chap. 11, sec. 1.

the Assheton-Bennetts or the Andrews.[2] Indeed the coverage chosen cannot do justice to the true size of the Mosley, Derby and Egerton/ Bridgewater holdings, which extended far off to the east, north and south-west.

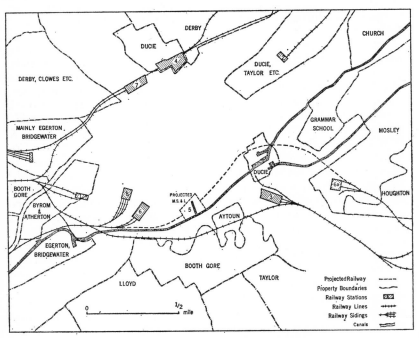

Property ownership and railways in Manchester.

The Earl of Derby, in fact, owned 68,000 acres of land with annual rents of £160,000 in the early 1880's, apart from 900 acres of land leased for building purposes, on which the annual value was not returned, and was the greatest landowner in Lancashire.[3] It was with him that the Manchester and Leeds railway company had to negotiate concerning the route for the first major through-station; and the perseverance with which the extension across north Manchester recommended by Thomas Gooch, the Manchester and Leeds company's consulting engineer, was carried through, in spite of the deliberate policy of temporising pursued by the other partner to the linkage, and in spite of two well supported alternative schemes, was partly due to the speed and simplicity of the property transactions involved. The

[2] *A History of the County of Lancashire*, IV (V.C.H., 1911) 237–337.
[3] J. Bateman, *Great Landowners of Great Britain* (1883), 127.

whole extension line from the earlier terminus at Oldham Road lay on property owned by the Earl of Derby, whose name recurs two hundred and fifty times in the *Books of Reference*. Somewhat ironically, in view of the Stanley family's later pronouncements upon the subject of slums and railway demolition, the properties swept away were 'cottages with outbuildings' and 'cellar dwellings' of the meanest quality.[4] Robert Slatter, and later Richard Earle, Lord Derby's agents, became adept at dealing with railway companies, which were now placed at the head of the list of clients for the Stanley family's extensive urban lands.

The principal customers for Derby's lands were the London and North Western and the Lancashire and Yorkshire railway companies; the most important area for the land dealings was north Liverpool. However, the Derby Papers, at the Lancashire County Records Office, also reveal close contact between Henry Booth, Secretary of the L. & N.W., and the Earl's agents in north Manchester and in Salford.[5] Co-operation is requested by the secretary of the railway company in removing small cottagers who are interrupting operations in Salford.[6] The possibility of combining street frontages of cheaper residential accommodation with sale of the land behind them for sidings is pointed out. Constant assurances are given that 'railway companies always pay a good price for what they buy.'[7] Perhaps the tone of the transactions may be caught in a short extract from Henry Booth's letter to Richard Earle in 1847 concerning land at Ordsall Lane, in Salford.

'We have no right, and do not wish to criticise the price which you name for the land in question at Orsal Lane (*sic*) but we do look at the large sum we should have to pay for a plot of ground on which to put aside some empty wagons. Our Board do not meet on Tuesdays but I will venture to give 16s per yard for the whole plot; and if you take into consideration the large *proportion* of backland for any ordinary purpose of sale—a kind of Terra incognita. When you have built a row of cottages in front, I trust you will consider the arrangement I now propose as fair to both sides.'[8] For his part the Earl of Derby left his agents in no doubt that although they could stand off to bring the railway companies to advantageous terms, they should not allow their reservations on particular points to be mistaken for root and branch opposition to the schemes proposed. 'I do not wish, if we can avoid it,' he wrote to Earle, 'to get into a Parliamentary conflict with so powerful a body as the North Western company.'[9] Such mutual respect enabled

[4] HLRO, P & S, B.Ref., 1839, Manchester and Leeds Railway.
[5] LRO DDK 683/1/1 *et seq.*
[6] *Loc. cit.* 683/1/4.
[7] *Loc. cit.* 683/1/24.
[8] *Loc. cit.* 683/1/25.
[9] *Loc. cit.* 683/1/28.

the speedy transaction of business, and may partly explain the success with which the Victoria station approaches were carried half-way across Manchester whilst the companies based at Liverpool Road and London Road stations were still debating the route a link line should take.

This impression is strengthened by two other features of the land ownership pattern in Manchester. First, the site to which the Manchester and Leeds company was able to advance so expeditiously through Derby's lands was itself also owned by one landlord, the Earl of Ducie (No. 4 on sketch map).[10] He had already indicated in the mid-1820's his willingness to develop his estates on the east bank of the Irwell, immediately north of the Collegiate Church (later Cathedral), by laying it out in building lots, and attempting to improve its poor road communications.[11] Naturally the railway company had to pay generously for the site of their station at Hunt's Bank (Victoria), and the price they offered took into account the embryonic development value of Ducie's estate. But in return for this the Manchester and Leeds railway company gained the inestimable advantage of negotiating with two landlords only for the greater part of their route; with the added bonus thrown in, when later extensions to the station became necessary, that there was plenty of spare land adjacent to their terminus still left in Lord Ducie's hands, and that they would, therefore, only have Ducie's agent to deal with for further land acquisitions.

The second feature is the contrast between land dealings on the northern link route, and the south junction line. The Manchester South Junction Lands and Compensation Committee's minutes show the laborious bargaining required to cope with the land on the route of their trans-urban viaduct. Two solicitors were appointed to work full time on the project, one to the east and one to the west of the small Oxford Road station, and were kept under such pressure that the health of the older partner broke down.[12] Apart from this, Mr. Baker (the engineer-in-chief) his four assistants, and the individual members of the committee, were given unusual powers to negotiate directly with proprietors.[13] Yet, in spite of this, the works took seven years to complete; and although, in 1842, the two schemes had been canvassed as rival and contemporary projects, the Hunt's Bank extension opened on 1 January 1844, the Manchester South Junction not until 1 April 1849.[14]

[10] J. Bateman, *op. cit.* 140; HLRO, P & S, (M. & L. Ext.), 1839.

[11] *Plan of Land in Strangeways belonging to Lord Ducie to be sold in lots for building upon* (1823), MRL. John Reilly, *History of Manchester* (Manchester, 1865), 346.

[12] BTHR MSJ 1/13.

[13] BTHR MSJ 1/1.

[14] 'A History of Manchester Railways', *Manchester City News, Notes and Queries Supplement* (1881–2), 16, 23.

The two most influential proprietors with whom the M.S.J. Lands committee had to negotiate were Sir Thomas de Trafford and Lord Francis Egerton. Though awkward about accommodation works, de Trafford was content to allow the scheme to go through unopposed. Egerton, because of his family connections with the Bridgewater canal, showed greater reluctance, and was only persuaded to support the scheme by the offer of a large number of shares in the company. Since the M.S.J. company was a shadow company, with shares owned by the two railway companies effecting the junction, Egerton was thereby placed in an unusually favoured position, as the only member of the public allowed to hold direct shares.[15] After this inducement had been offered he agreed to take charge of the Bill in Parliament.

The other major proprietors along the southern route were the Croft Dickenson family, who had bought Garrat Hall and estate from Roger Aytoun, after he had squandered his patrimony; and Sir Booth Gore, who owned an estate on the south bank of the River Medlock, at Chorlton Hall.[16] Sir Booth Gore did not take kindly to the idea of a viaduct railway severing his estate from the centre of Manchester. Unlike Lord Ducie, whose intentions to develop his land at Hunt's Bank had got no further than a few market gardens and two dye works, Sir Booth Gore had laid out his estate with a Grosvenor Street, Grosvenor Square, Russell and Bedford and Clarendon Streets. Admittedly the buildings which had been erected by 1846 did not live up to the aristocratic promise of the street names, but the area might have shared more readily in the appreciation of central land values if the Manchester South Junction viaduct had not interrupted communications with the central district, and drawn a wall of ramshackle housing, mills, and timber yards, between Gore's lands and the central district.[17]

The railways produced an even more immediate and dilapidating effect upon Manchester's new West End, laid out by Mr. Henry Atherton, and afterwards by his widow Mrs. Ann Atherton and Miss Eleanora Byrom (see sketch map). There, a mere four hundred yards to the west of Deansgate, an estate was laid out with covenants against manufactures or trades, 'in an eligible situation . . . with proper streets and approaches.' 'It is obvious,' they petitioned, 'that the inconvenience and danger which will of necessity arise from the passing of locomotive engines, in addition to the great and offensive nuisance attending the use of them, and more particularly where many of the engines are collected together at the depot, will not only cause great alarm to the inhabitants, but will also materially injure, if not wholly destroy their comforts, and actually compel them to desert their residences. The

[15] He later re-sold them to the M.S. & L., *ibid*. 23.

[16] V.C.H., *op. cit*. IV, 253.

[17] J. Adshead, *op. cit*. Sheets 4–8.

building of houses of the description of those already erected must necessarily be stopped; and if other inferior houses are built, they must alter the whole character of the neighbourhood, and materially injure the value of those already erected.'[18]

The tone of Atherton and Byrom's petition was no doubt influenced by the extreme novelty of railways at the time—it dates back to the abortive Liverpool and Manchester Bill of 1825—but the cutting of the Liverpool Road terminus through their estate eleven years later did produce precisely the effects they had forecast. It is difficult, of course, to imagine high-class residential housing surviving for any length of time against the encroachments likely on an estate with such a central location; but it was by no means uncommon for buildings which had been laid out spaciously for expensive housing to convert admirably to professional and business uses, and form a natural annexe for the central business district. Instead, the establishment of the Liverpool Road terminus, and the cushion of mean housing which surrounded it, tended to provide a westward barrier to the expansion of the business district.

To the east of the city centre the principal estates were held by the Mosley family, Sir Henry Houghton, Lord Ducie and various trustees, of which the most important were Manchester Church and the Grammar School. As already mentioned, the London Road terminus in east Manchester was cut with little trouble, entering Manchester from a direction in which very little building had been carried out in 1836, when the bill was authorised. Rapid building of a speculative nature followed, mostly over the lands of small owners or lessees, like Thomas Tipping, whose proprietorships have been handed down to an undistinguished immortality in the current street names.[19] A larger parcel of land in Ancoats remained in the hands of the Mosley family until the late 1860's, when the Midland railway company negotiated with them to buy an extensive area adjacent to Ancoats Hall for their goods terminus. Thereafter, although describing themselves as the Mosleys of Ancoats and Rolleston, they ceased residence, and their sombre mansion was used for business offices by the Midland railway company.[20]

Apart from the individual landowners and trustees mentioned, several canal companies also commanded important approach routes and central sites; but although the same considerations applied as those mentioned in Birmingham's case, the influence of the previous locations selected by canal companies was of a lesser importance.

---

[18] *Case of Mrs. Ann Atherton and Miss Eleanora Byrom, petitioners against the Bill* (1825), MRL.

[19] Tipping owned fields, in 1794, to the south and east of the future London Road terminus. W. Green, *op. cit.* The Mosley's estates are shown in Hillkirk, *Map of the Estates of the Mosley family 1805–8*, MRL ff 912.4273.

[20] James Croston, *County Families of Lancashire and Cheshire* (1887), 341, 345.

Nevertheless, the large basins and extensive storage yards for timber, flagstones and coal, shown so clearly on Adshead's map of 1851, persuaded the railway companies to acquire the Rochdale, Ashton and finally the Bridgewater canals.

The Ashton canal, of little importance apart from its useful site, was leased in perpetuity by the Manchester, Sheffield and Lincolnshire railway company in 1858 for a sum of £12,363 *per annum*.[21] For the larger premises of the Rochdale canal the M.S. & L. had to share a joint twenty-one year lease with the Lancashire and Yorkshire and the L. & N.W. railway companies.[22] The Rochdale canal also possessed a junction canal which ran across Manchester to connect with Bridgewater's canal; though since it was largely built over, its value as a cleared route was negligible. However, there were occasional loading and storage points where the canal ceased to be subterranean, and it was, in fact, one of these basins which the M.S. & L. railway company chose for its projected Central station of 1866 (No. 5 on sketch map).

The only through-route of any significance taken over from the canals was the suburban branch of the Manchester South Junction company's line, which followed the banks of the Bridgewater canal to Altrincham; though subsequent services in mid-century were not designed to encourage the flow of large commuter traffic along that route.

The general impression gained from a study of the land-ownership patterns in Manchester, and their influence upon the railway companies' land acquisitions is, once more, that large unified holdings afforded an opportunity for expeditious and convenient building operations in which legal charges and delays could be kept down to a minimum. This factor was particularly important in the early stages of a scheme's inception. 'In such a neighbourhood as Manchester,' James Hayward, a Parliamentary agent, told Sir James Graham, 'the moment you get up a scheme there are half a dozen others started of the same description and it becomes quite a scramble. . . . In that scramble would there not be a competition of ingenuity and intellect?—Certainly.'[23] In such a delicate and competitive situation, where speed of operation was at a premium, the goodwill of larger landowners, or the good fortune to select a route with the minimum number of claimants, was enough to swing the balance in favour of one scheme rather than another. Similar considerations also applied, though with diminished force, even after the routes and sites had been chosen, though by this stage circumstances were often quite outside the railway companies' control. As they

[21] H.C., 1872, XIII, App. I, pp. 236–7.
[22] *Ibid.* 21 years from 1 September 1855.
[23] H.C., 1836, XXI, QQ.641–2.

committed themselves to choices of site, so the companies reduced their future room to manoeuvre in the course of bargaining.

To take two contrasted examples: extensions to the Oldham Road station (No. 2 on sketch map) planned by John Hawkshaw in 1845 could count upon dealings with only two proprietors for the whole range of housing scheduled for purchase. Mary and Sarah Taylor owned, as direct proprietors (without intervening lessees), a hundred cottages, houses, rag shops, smiths', coopers' and wheelwrights' workshops; even a public house and police lock-up.[24] By comparison, when Hawkshaw planned extensions to the Victoria station, sixteen years later, in 1861, the position was very different. His line (fore-shadowing the secessionist Exchange station) was constructed across the Salford side of the Irwell, through the gap shown in the diagram-matic map between Lord Ducie's, and Lord Derby's, the Reverend John Clowes' and others' property further west. Its purpose was deliberately to reduplicate the L. & N.W. line and give the Lancashire and Yorkshire railway a technical advantage in the increasingly bitter struggle between themselves and the L. & N.W. at Victoria station. This rivalry was no secret to members of the public; indeed they had been the principal sufferers from it and had complained openly. When Hawkshaw came to construct his 940-yard viaduct, therefore, he found his path barred by fragmented multiple ownership. Yet, only a little time before, most of the land had belonged to Lord Ducie and the Reverend John Clowes (whose families had held the land earlier, when it was devoted to agricultural or market garden uses). Although there can be no clear proof in the matter, it is difficult to avoid drawing the inference that many of the resident lessees who seized the opportunity to purchase their holdings, and many of the completely new buyers who arrived in the district, had an eye to railway extensions from the station on the other side of the river. It is certainly noticeable amongst the holders of land on this route, and on the site of the future Exchange station, that there was an unusual proportion of solicitors and trustees under wills, holding blocks of ten or twenty dwellings; and Captain J. W. Fox and Sarah Holland, though they might possibly have been intending merely to provide a nest-egg for retirement by purchasing a group of thirty houses for rent, may also have been directed to this particular, rather unpromising, residential area by a process of choice which was more venturesome or better informed than usual.[25]

Of course the landowners, though placed in an extremely strong

[24] HLRO, P & S, B.Ref., 1846, Manchester and Leeds Railway (Station Extensions). Pt. 2. The property was described in Committee as 'the disgraceful and dilapidated land belonging to the late Henry Taylor.' Min., H.C., 1846, 29 June, p. 14.
[25] HLRO, P & S, B.Ref., 1861, Lancs and Yorks Railway (New line from Salford to Victoria Station).

position by the Parliamentary Private Bill and the Lands Clauses procedure (as explained elsewhere), had to be careful not to overplay their hand. On the whole trustees, under wills, and for charitable or corporate bodies, were reasonable clients to the railway companies, and were content with a generous return to investment, counting it a success if they obtained, over a decade or two of investment, a sum equal to twice or three times the property's value for non-railway uses. In view of the steady and general rise of values in and around all the major cities this was perhaps a reasonable return.[26] The railway companies encountered far more rapacious claims from the small owner, who was quite capable of asking twenty times the railway company's valuation.

It is difficult to apply similar standards of measurement to the larger hereditary landowners, for several reasons. The landowners' parcels of land were frequently so large, and had either been held in the family for so long, had been acquired *gratis* under Enclosure Bill procedures, or had been purchased under such vastly different circumstances—how does one assess the £9,000 paid for the Hall and forty three acres of Hulme manor in 1764?—that it is difficult to say whether the enormous sums which were paid over to the great landlords should be viewed as reasonable returns on investment, or as aristocratic extortion.[27]

One thing which can be said with reasonable assurance, however, is that the rule not to overplay one's hand applied even to them. Lord Derby's caution in this particular has already been noted. Mr. Wilbraham Egerton, of Tatton Park, another very large landowner, provides an excellent example of the type of proprietor who, although in an extremely strong position initially, over-reached himself; not by seeking to strike too hard a bargain financially, but by intervening publicly to influence decisions which were essentially political in nature. Egerton abandoned the guise of neutrality which those vendors of land who were most successful usually maintained, no matter how much they might privately favour particular schemes, and declared overtly his root and branch opposition to one of two rival schemes.

The schemes were both similar in general conception; attempts, in 1835, to provide a direct southern route from Manchester to replace

[26] H. Baker, 'On the Growth of the Commercial Centre of Manchester, Movement of Population, and Pressure of Habitation 1861–71', *Trans. Manch. Stat. Soc.* (1868–72) 93–4, gives thirty to forty *per cent* as an average increase in values per decade. The prices per sq. yd. of central business district land in Piccadilly or John Dalton, Cross or King Streets rather more than doubled per decade.

[27] Herbert Clegg, 'The Third Duke of Bridgewater's canal works in Manchester', *Trans of Lancs. and Chesh. Antiq. Soc.* LXV (1955), 96–7. MRL, *Plan of Estates in Holm Moss side and Charlton Row belonging to George Lloyd* (1760), *Plan of Land in Township of Hulme to be sold in Lots for building upon by Thomas Hill* (1836), show the formation and break up of Lloyd's large estate.

the roundabout Grand Junction route. The Manchester and Cheshire Junction scheme, sponsored by the wealthy Manchester merchants Robert Barbour, John Brooks, Joshua Westhead, Thomas Ashton, John Chippendale, and others, was the less ambitious of the two schemes, planning to cross over easy country to Crewe.[28] There the engineer Rastrick planned to join the Grand Junction, after cutting fifteen miles off the journey from the south, at the expense of building only thirty miles of track. The Manchester South Union scheme, with George Stephenson for engineer, planned a much more elaborate and difficult route cutting out the Grand Junction line altogether.[29] Both schemes required to pass through Wilbraham Egerton's land, and he frankly espoused the cause of the South Union, in a most open and partisan manner.

His opposition was not without its effect, for the Manchester and Cheshire Junction, which was the more obvious and less controversial scheme, was rejected as a result of his counsel's vigorous opposition; but on the other hand, the South Union Bill was also thrown out, and the two schemes were merged with a third, the Manchester and Birmingham Direct, the following year (1836). The compromise line (including the remarkable trans-urban viaduct a hundred and ten feet high at Stockport) was then put in hand, and a site cleared at Manchester. The more ambitious southern tail to the scheme was abandoned during the 1837 depression. But over the next eight years, at intervals, traces of the original (South Union) idea of a more direct line through the Midlands can be detected in route choice, and in the engineering and boardroom personnel, of the Stafford and Rugby railway company and the Trent Valley railway company.[30]

Wilbraham Egerton's opposition to the Manchester and Cheshire Junction Bill has been referred to in some detail because it brought into the open an important point of principle concerning the relationship between landowners and railway companies which has a far wider application than the context of suburban Manchester in which it originates. It was one thing for a proprietor to hold out for generous compensation from any and all comers; quite another to take it upon himself to decide between the merits of rival schemes. This was a point seized upon eloquently by Mr. Serjeant Merewether in his summing-up speech before the Lords' Committee:

'If Mr. Egerton came before your Lordships to protect the residence of himself upon the estate he had received from his ancestors, and begging you

---

[28] £488,900 out of the total of £654,000 initial capital was subscribed by (282) Manchester men, MRL F 625 M7.

[29] 'A History of Manchester Railways', *Manchester City News* (1881–2) 7.

[30] *Ibid.* 8–21. Henry Tootal of the M.S.U. was on the Board of both later companies.

not to let parties interfere with his residence, he would be in a strong position before your Lordships.

'My learned friend, Mr. Wrangham, who appeared for Mr. Egerton, has relieved me of all possibility of doubt or difficulty upon this part of the case. For my learned friend came forward and avowed, openly and distinctly, "It is not so much Mr. Egerton's private rights I am considering, but Mr. Egerton has pledged himself to the people of Stockport to support the other line that will go through that place".

'I state this thus distinctly, because I combat it as an objection not competent for a landed proprietor to take—I say he has not a legitimate right to urge such a ground before your Lordships, because it is nothing more or less than making an individual whose property happens to be interposed in the way of a great work of this description, the arbitrator upon this matter, and taking away from the Legislature the power of deciding upon it.'[31]

Although, in fact, successful in dragging down for one session a railway scheme which crossed his land, Egerton gained little credit or profit from the action. He finally had to accept a compromise line which differed substantially from the one for which he had originally expressed a preference, and his land was tied up, his attention engaged, and considerable legal expenses incurred over the following decade. Perhaps it was this type of episode which James Croston had partly in mind when he referred, in his *County Families of Lancashire and Cheshire* (1887), to the Egerton family as 'seldom profiting by the varying vicissitudes which enabled many of its neighbours to enrich themselves.'[32]

2. *Conditions of competition between railway companies*

In no city was the competition for railway access more bitter and protracted than in Manchester. The numbers of companies involved reached nine—a figure exceeded only in London; and the quarrels over right of way and site facilities were carried on with unremitting vehemence, not for fifteen or twenty years, as in Birmingham, but for half a century. The outcome of this highly competitive and long-sustained struggle can be seen in the proliferation of stations and the complexity of sharing arrangements.

To condense the story in as brief a compass as possible: the protagonists, in order of appearance, were the Liverpool and Manchester, the Grand Junction, the London and Birmingham railways, which operated (the two latter under toll charges) from Liverpool Road station (No. 1 on map); the Manchester and Leeds, which operated

[31] MRL, *Tracts on Railways*, 385 81 M1, contains Merewether's speech to the Lords' S.C., 22 July 1836. Quotation is from pp. 9–10.
[32] James Croston, *op. cit.* 216.

from Oldham Road, and later from Hunt's Bank (or Victoria) station (Nos. 2 and 4 on map); the Manchester and Bolton, which, after operating from a temporary station at New Bailey Street in Salford, joined with the Manchester and Leeds to use Victoria; the Manchester and Birmingham railway, which built the Store Street (or London Road) station (No. 3 on map), together with the Sheffield, Ashton-under-Lyne and Manchester railway, which ran, on payment of a toll, into the Manchester and Birmingham terminus; and the later arrivals on the scene, the Midland, and the Great Northern railways, whose foothold was never very strong, but who joined with the Sheffield and Manchester railway to form a consortium, the Cheshire Lines Committee, to build the Central station (No. 6 on map).[33] To complicate matters further, not merely were the station names changed, from Store Street, to London Road, to Piccadilly, etc., but the companies changed their names, from the Sheffield, Ashton-under-Lyne and Manchester railway, to the Manchester, Sheffield and Lincolnshire, to the Great Central, etc., and they also formed changing groups and alliances. 'These things are constantly shifting,' stated Seymour Clarke in 1860, 'like moves on a chessboard.'[34] It is perhaps significant that Clarke was giving evidence to a Select Committee on problems raised by station-sharing in London, which had naturally turned to London Road station, Manchester, as a conspicuous example of what to avoid.

The most important permanent grouping of companies to emerge in Manchester was the amalgamation, in 1846, of the three companies operating from Liverpool Road, into the London and North Western railway company, and (here was where the principal friction originated) the absorption of the Manchester and Birmingham railway into the L. & N.W. company. This gave the L. & N.W. control of both Liverpool Road and London Road stations, and provided a renewed incentive to press on with the difficult Manchester South Junction viaduct scheme. The Manchester, Sheffield and Lincolnshire railway company, which, because of the engineering difficulties and unexpected expenses of its line, had been glad to share the Manchester and Birmingham station at London Road on any terms, now found itself sharing instead

---

[33] This section is largely based upon primary official sources, but also draws upon the standard railway histories by Steel, Dow, Grinling and Williams, and on the anonymous but detailed and authentic account in the *Manchester City News* (1881–2) already cited. M. D. Greville and G. O. Holt, 'Railway Development in Manchester', *Railway Magazine*, 103 (1957); 613–20, 720–6, 764–9 provides a painstaking collation of material of local relevance from the Railway Journals, and there is also a well-illustrated survey based on secondary sources by J. A. Patmore, 'The Railway Network of the Manchester Conurbation', *Transactions and Papers*, Instit. of Brit. Geog., 34 (1964), 159–73.

[34] BTHR PYB 1/107, p. 151.

with the newly-formed L. & N.W.[35] This confronted the M.S. & L. with a situation very different from the one it had originally envisaged. Relations between the two companies 'ceased to be the good things they had been'; and the L. & N.W. used its control of staffing to put every possible pressure upon its small but determined rival.[36] Signs were painted out, notices torn down, members of the public misdirected, or even taken into custody for using the wrong platforms or tickets, timber trains were left in front of the M.S. & L. expresses, ticket clerks forcibly ejected through the booking office windows, a pitched battle took place for physical possession of a shed claimed as their property by the M.S. & L.[37] In the late 1850's London Road, Manchester, provided an extreme example of the ill-feeling, litigation and public inconvenience station-sharing at its worst could involve.

Scenes which were similar in kind, if not degree, also characterised the shared station in north central Manchester. Here again, the emergence of the powerful L. & N.W. amalgamation presented to the company with whom they shared new conditions charged with possibilities for friction. Since, at the Hunt's Bank (Victoria) station, shared facilities were combined with through-working, disharmony between the companies might easily lead to danger as well as inconvenience. The Town Clerk in a report to the Corporation in 1861 spoke of 'not only frequent delay, but constant and serious danger to the lives and limbs of passengers'; and, a few years later, Edward Watkin expressed the opinion that 'Victoria station, Manchester, is the most dangerous station in England for passengers.'[38]

The Manchester and Leeds railway company, by whose initiative the Hunt's Bank site had been secured, and the Victoria station built, had faced the Liverpool and Manchester company on terms of near equality in the years between 1839 and 1842, when the agreement to share had originally been made. Indeed—if one can for a moment completely erase the knowledge of what was to happen between 1842 and 1847—nothing could have seemed more reasonable and beneficial at the time than an amalgamation between the Manchester and Leeds and the Liverpool and Manchester companies. After both had been enlarged by amalgamation with other companies, however, the possi-

[35] During the difficulties with the Woodhead Tunnel 'the Manchester and Sheffield line people would have been prepared to give away their holdings to escape liability for further calls'. *Manchester City News* (1881–2), 15. They agreed to pay interest charges and a toll per passenger.

[36] BTHR PYB 1/107, p. 151.

[37] George Dow, *The First Railway between Manchester and Sheffield* (1945), 41. *Idem, Great Central*, 1 (1959), 187–91.

[38] Council Proceedings, 1859–61, p. 181; HLRO, Min., H.C., 1866, 9 May, pp. 24–5, S.C. on M.S. & L. (Central Station and Lines).

bility of unified control at Victoria receded indefinitely. At one stage, in 1871, amalgamation was, in fact, discussed between the large L. & N.W. and the Lancashire and Yorkshire railway companies; but the discussions were abandoned as politically unrealistic, in face of the strong protest which such a near-monopoly provoked. It was possible, of course, to conclude traffic-sharing agreements privately between two companies without seeking an Amalgamation Bill in Parliament; but, as already pointed out elsewhere, the drawing up of traffic-sharing and joint purse agreements often tended to intensify and focus rivalry upon facilities and accommodation.

For four decades, therefore, the leading decisions on the siting, enlargement and working of Manchester's railway termini were coloured, in the north by the rivalry between the L. & N.W. and Lancashire and Yorkshire companies, in the south by the M.S. & L. railway company's attempts to free itself from the severe limitations which station-sharing with a large and hostile company imposed. The later arrivals on the scene can be fitted into this competitive framework. The Midland and the Great Northern both gained access as allies of the M.S. & L. railway company, called in to redress the balance against the L. & N.W. In 1861 the Midland secured running powers into the M.S. & L.'s portion of London Road station, worsening the congestion there. The arrangement was one of convenience, as part of 'Mr. Allport's plan to break out to the coast'; and although it was cemented by a committee (Cheshire Lines Committee) set up to handle various joint projects for the break out to the coast further west, it remained as uncertain as most alliances between autonomous companies.[39] In 1875, although still allies and co-members of the Cheshire Lines Committee, the M.S. & L. gave the Midland three years' notice to leave the London Road premises.[40]

A more permanent acquisition by the Midland company, however, was at Ancoats, where authorisation was obtained in 1865 to build a substantial goods depot (No. 6a on sketch map). The Corporation at first lodged a petition against the project, but withdrew it after generous terms had been proposed at a meeting between the Mayor, Town Clerk and Surveyor, and Allport, Hutchinson and Crossley.[41]

The Great Northern railway company was the third member of the C.L.C., and it was in this capacity that it gained access to Manchester; first as joint contributor to the Central station (sanctioned 1872, opened 1880), then as the last substantial depot builder, constructing a large goods station adjacent to the Central, in the 1890's.[42]

[39] *Manchester City News* (1881–2), 28.
[40] G. Dow, *Great Central*, II (1962), 139.
[41] Council Proceedings, 1863–5, pp. 98–9, 5 April 1865.
[42] J. A. Patmore, *loc. cit.* 170.

3. *The development of railway facilities: a chronological sketch*

Only the earliest termini escaped the influence of the intense and protracted rivalry described above. Naturally the Liverpool Road station (No. 1 on sketch map) was free of such influences, since it constituted the eastern terminus of the unique Liverpool and Manchester railway, the pioneer of all major inter-city lines. The considerations which received most weight in determining the size and location of this early terminus were mostly operational, or connected with land ownership patterns. The need to prove the technical and commercial feasibility of rail transport in the shortest possible time led, at both ends of the line, to skimping over terminal facilities. A temporary station with makeshift accommodation, particularly for warehousing and storage, and for locomotive repair and servicing, was pressed into use. It was not quite as badly situated as the early Liverpool terminal, in George Stephenson's opinion, but in the other respects just mentioned, it was even more inadequate.[43]

Land lay near to hand for station extensions. A dye works, which had stood on the Byrom/Atherton property between Water Street and the river Irwell, was secured as the site for an improved passenger station by the company's surveyor John Dixon, and the erection of a commodious arrival station announced in the company's six-monthly report for June, 1836. On the Salford side of the Irwell, in the Bridgewater and Booth Gore lands, a five-acre field, and other miscellaneous parcels of land, were added, for the supplementary purposes—repair, storage, marshalling—which had been underestimated.[44] At this early stage the securing of land was easy, although relatively high prices immediately marked the railway's arrival in the land market. Yet the land was still undeveloped, or even open agricultural land; and though the selling price appreciated greatly, the sums involved constituted no burden upon the changed use to which the land was now converted. The Lands Clauses Act, ordering and consolidating purchase procedures had not yet been passed, and land acquisition followed experimental and rule-of-thumb methods. A director of the company, for example, bought land, in anticipation of future plans, from Miss Byrom for 8d per square yard, and sold it to his company for 10s per square yard; and his exploit was openly reported to a Parliamentary Committee.[45] Such overt speculation would later have been frowned upon.

George Stephenson's second terminus, for the Manchester and Leeds

---

[43] HLRO, Min., H.C., 1837, 17 March, pp. 27–8, S.C. on Manchester and Leeds Railway. Stephenson, of course, was the engineer to both the Leeds and Manchester and the Manchester and Liverpool lines.

[44] *Loc. cit.* pp. 31–4. *Six-monthly Report*, Liverpool and Manchester Railway, 27 July 1836.

[45] HLRO, Min., (M. & L.), 17 March, p. 36.

line at Oldham Road (No. 2) on sketch map) was also sanctioned in 1836 in the same pragmatic spirit. The Parliamentary *Plans and Sections* themselves were missing when the Select Committee began its enquiry. They had been drawn up unsatisfactorily, it was explained, and the plan drawings had been observed not to correspond to the sectional side-view drawings.[46] Nevertheless, even without this evidence, which would have later been considered essential for any legislation, the Bill was heard and approved, with virtually no discussion of the terminal.[47] Such lax procedures and faulty presentation would later have caused any railway Bill to be thrown out on Standing Orders, before reaching the Committee stage.

A relaxed and liberal spirit also attended J. U. Rastrick's and Charles Vignoles' proposals for a south-eastern approach at Store Street (No. 3 on sketch map). Rastrick, the Engineer for the Manchester and Cheshire Junction (later Manchester and Birmingham) railway company, gave evidence, framed in the most general terms, concerning the convenience of the site, its accessibility to the hotels, business places and canals, and its superiority to the projected rival (Manchester South Union) station at Oxford Road.[48] Letters from the Liverpool and Manchester company offering a junction with their new Water Street (Liverpool Road) station, from the Sheffield, Ashton-under-Lyne and Manchester company offering to share the Store Street site, and from the Manchester and Leeds company offering a viaduct or tunnel link from Oldham Road station, were all freely mentioned and laid before the Committee in July 1836, in a manner which seems almost ingenuous, and in marked contrast to the guarded, or even misleading, information on their future prospects and intentions which the Manchester-based companies circulated twenty years later.[49]

The land to be acquired presented no financial or procedural obstacles. John Lowe and John Ashworth, the company's surveyors and valuers, listed the landowners, and the estimated sums for purchase; a mere £54,000, £49,000-worth of it belonging to landowners who had given their assent, and £38,000 covering both the cost of the old inn and market at London Road and the land purchase for 13 miles of the approach to the city, 'liberally and fully'.[50] The supplementary Bill brought forward in the following year, to provide additional space at London Road for the Sheffield company, was also characterised by similar ease and cheapness of access.[51]

[46] HLRO, Min., H.C., 1836, 4 March, pp. 1–3.
[47] *Ibid.* 2 May, pp. 57–60, 171 *et seq.*
[48] H.L., 1836, XXXIII, 18 July, pp. 321–2.
[49] *Loc. cit.* pp. 323–6.
[50] *Ibid.* 20 July, p. 423, 21 July, p. 438.
[51] HLRO, Min., H.L., 1837, 18 April, p. 35 (Vignoles).

Yet already, even in the late 1830's, the fierce competition, which was to dominate railway history in Manchester, was beginning to manifest itself in the rival link-line proposals described below; and for the next four decades hardly a scheme was put forward which did not play some part in the 'chessboard moves' of which the Great Northern railway company's manager had spoken. Most urgent and persistent of the impulses given to urban railway construction in Manchester, and most far-reaching in its effects, was the struggle between the Manchester, Sheffield and Lincolnshire railway company and the L. & N.W. amalgamation.

The M.S. & L.'s perseverance in seeking improved station facilities in the 1850's and 1860's was enhanced and sustained by several factors. Although relatively small, compared with the L. & N.W., the M.S. & L. had as chairman Edward Watkin, a man of unusual tenacity and drive. Their search for independent stations was also encouraged by the sponsorship and credit the great contractors were prepared to extend—even to the point of promoting their own station company to take the M.S. & L. into Liverpool. Moreover, as the strategy of the M.S. & L.'s territorial plans unfolded, the room for compromise and manoeuvre disappeared. The M.S. & L. was the most important company (excepting only the Great Western) to rely upon east-west traffic. It invested heavily at Grimsby and Hull, and by its running arrangements with the Midland and Great Eastern, had 2,000 rail miles converging from the east on Manchester. In the west it had gained access to Liverpool, and only a gap of twenty-five miles prevented completion of an east to west coast railway.[52] The M.S. & L. company, therefore, found itself in a position where, regardless of the immediate interests of its shareholders, it was compelled to pursue, at unrealistic cost, a militant and persistent policy in Manchester.

The L. & N.W. attempted to anticipate the M.S. & L.'s schemes by proposing, in the early 1860's, that the approach lines running into London Road station from Ardwick should be doubled, and the station itself rebuilt as a 'side-by-side, rather than a joint station', to accommodate the rival companies more harmoniously. The M.S. & L. readily agreed to find the half a million needed to carry out this expensive alteration.[53] But if the L. & N.W. had hoped to frustrate the M.S. & L.'s future intentions, or reduce them in scale, by committing both companies to an immediate and heavy expenditure, the tactic misfired. The M.S. & L., in addition to finding the money for this extensive alteration, agitated for the doubling of the M.S.J. viaduct, and for the

[52] HLRO, Min., H.L., 1865, 30 June, pp. 15–17 (Watkin), S.C. on M.S. & L. Railway Extensions.
[53] HLRO, Min., H.C., 1866, 9 May, pp. 19–23 (Watkin), S.C. on M.S. & L. Central Station and Lines.

building of a further, large, straight-through station. 'The other thing which I particularly want to lay stress upon which we want,' Watkin stated, 'is to abolish the system of having butt-end stations.'[54] Cawkwell and Moon, the General Manager and Chairman of the L. & N.W. company, were prepared to make concessions, even, reluctantly, upon the doubling of the M.S.J. line; but Watkin still persisted with his ambitious trans-urban viaduct and Central station project, using every subterfuge and form of pressure to overcome opposition.[55]

The argument against the M.S. & L. Central station project was extremely thoroughly presented by no fewer than six Q.C.'s, led by Mr. Vernon Harcourt, whose own conduct of the case may be judged from his summing up on 18 May 1866. Reference had been made to the fact that he himself had, in previous years, been retained to advocate railway schemes by the very company he was now opposing. It was true, he admitted, that the M.S. & L. company was amongst his oldest and most valued clients.

'My only satisfaction is that, if, in the evidence I have been able to lay before you, or by any observation I have been able to address to you, I should have in any way contributed to the defeat of this favourite scheme of theirs, I should have rendered them far greater services as an opponent than ever I have been able to render them when acting on their side.'[56]

Despite this ingenious peroration, the Commons' Select Committee approved the Bill; but in the Lords' Committee a month later, although the evidence presented was similar, the atmosphere had changed. Mr. Denison, Q.C., counsel for the M.S. & L., wound up their case halfheartedly, as if he already knew the outcome of the Committee's recommendations; and his faltering presentation was still further weakened, in his closing sentences, by a request for a year's suspension of the scheme so that it could be brought forward again in modified form.[57] It is not difficult to speculate as to what those modifications would have been. Further discussions would have taken place with the Town Clerk and Council, together with further efforts to influence voting indirectly. After these further discussions had taken place a curtailed version of the M.S. & L. Central scheme might have been submitted in the following session.

The land available for the proposed station site, although immensely expensive, did present the last, rapidly-fading opportunity for a large scale intrusion into the central business district. The approach from the west, between the Manchester South Junction railway and the Rochdale canal, ran mostly through small parcels of cottages with

[54] *Loc. cit.* p.29.
[55] *Ibid.* 17 May, p. 37 (Cawkwell).
[56] BTHR PYB 1/383, 18 May, p. 10.
[57] BTHR PYB 1/384, 16 July, p. 34.

yards and outbuildings, owned in groups of seven or eight by individual proprietors, quite a few of them trustees under wills, and through fifty or so cottages, coalyards, sheds and wharves owned by the Rochdale canal. £163,800 was the estimated cost of land purchase; an approximately equal amount, £162,350, was to be expended on the railway, of which £135,000 was upon the $1\frac{3}{4}$ mile viaduct. This section, Railway No. 1, would have taken the M.S. & L. to its chosen site between Oxford, David, Portland and Hunt streets.[58] There the Rochdale canal basin (under lease to the M.S. & L.) and a forge and timber yard belonging to David Bellhouse's Trustees formed the nucleus of a potential site. John Collier Harter, owner of forty shops, houses and pubs, and the Manchester Real Property Company, owners of a shooting gallery, a circus ground (let to Sangers') and some shops, were also willing to sell, and, indeed, presently expecting offers from business users for their small enclave. The fifth and last owner of ground for the potential station site was a corporate body, the Booth Charities. They did not reply to the railway company's invitation to treat for the sale of their property.

The estimated cost of these central properties, ripe as they were for re-development, was an intimidating £617,000, to which a further £150,000 would have to be added for the station building itself and £14 000 for the $\frac{1}{8}$ mile of viaduct and rails. Altogether, with 10% for contingencies, nearly £800,000.[59] The two miles of trans-urban viaduct, which was to leave the north-eastern end of this straight-through station and curve across over Piccadilly to join the Midland line near Ancoats goods station, was scheduled at a further £445,000; only a tenth of which sum was to be expended on the railway, the rest on constructing the viaduct and on land purchase, including a hundred and twenty further properties from the Booth Charities.[60] There can be little doubt that these estimates would, in practice, have been exceeded; and no doubt whatsoever that the return, under Standing Order 191, of 1275 people of the labouring classes to be evicted, was a gross understatement. As an urban railway it stood, amongst Victorian projects, second only to the great operations at Charing Cross and Cannon Street, Liverpool Street and St. Pancras.

Apart from the objections raised to it on public and municipal grounds (already described elsewhere), a further extremely damaging objection to the scheme had, in fact, been directed against the putative ability of such a small company to carry out so ambitious a scheme. Mr. Hope Scott, Q.C., summing up for the L. & N.W., against the Bill

---

[58] HLRO, P & S, B.Ref., 1866, M.S. & L. Central Station and Lines. Pt. 2, Railway No. 1, Estimate by Sacré.
[59] *Loc. cit*. Railway No. 2.
[60] *Loc. cit*. Railway No. 3.

before the Lords' Committee, had spoken of 'a vicious practice of poor companies or no companies coming to Parliament for powers relying on the speculative chance of other companies having the money to execute the works.'[61] Mr. Vernon Harcourt spoke in similar vein before the Commons' Committee. Had the Midland or Great Northern companies, whose shares stood at, or above, par, come forward and associated themselves with such a scheme, Harcourt argued, it would at least have had a semblance of plausibility. Instead, the company taking the initiative in this large urban scheme was the M.S. & L., whose shares stood at 60. 'If Mr. Watkin can get a million and a half in the City of London he is a more fortunate man than most of us.' The shadowy moral support offered by the Midland was brushed aside. 'The Midland is too old a monkey to put their fingers into schemes of this description—and therefore if the M.S. & L. company will raise two million pounds of money towards it, they are very willing to send Mr. Allport here to give evidence in favour of the scheme, but they take care Mr. Allport shall not have authority to pledge them in spending one single sixpence in favour of it.'[62]

The obvious remedy to these criticisms was to draw back for a few years, ask Charles Sacré to devise a more modest scheme, and call upon the Midland and the Great Northern companies to associate themselves openly and unequivocally as allies in the new project. The compromise Central station, sanctioned in 1872, and also designed by Charles Sacré, but this time for the Cheshire Lines Committee, was no more than a logical sequel to the struggle just described.

It was very much less ambitious, however, and very much better prepared. Approaching from the west along a route parallel to the M.S.J., through Sir Humphrey de Trafford's and the Devisees of the late Duke of Bridgewater's lands, it turned northwards soon after crossing Deansgate. There was evidence of advance purchase of property; eleven cottages and a twine warehouse, to the east of Deansgate, already being in the hands of Edward Ross, agent to the C.L.C.

Two substantial landowners provided the approach route from Deansgate to Great Bridgewater Street: Sir George Philips, who owned a site given over to fringe industrial uses—a sawmill and yard, a packing case maker's shop, a lime and cement store, drysaltery, oil and paint warehouses; Mrs. Isabella Bowers, a clergyman's widow, owned the remaining parcel of a hundred and sixty properties, mostly cottages and dwelling houses, leased out in groups of six—and it is observable that the C.L.C. had already take up the lease on some of these batches—together with various shops, beerhouses and four Temperance Halls. Although the approach was simple, the two hundred degraded dwellings,

[61] BHTR PYB 1/384, 16 July, p. 1.
[62] BTHR PYB 1/383, 17 May, pp. 9–10.

cellars and yards which covered the Windmill Street site itself were owned by eight landlords, usually administering their properties directly without the intermediacy of lessees. The total estimated expenditure for land came to £278,000—little more than a quarter of the earlier scheme's land costs—with a further £100,000 for the station, £90,000 for the viaduct and £10,000 for the permanent way.[63]

Since the friction between the L. & N.W. and the M.S. & L. railway companies began in 1846, and Central station was not fully opened to traffic until 1880, a whole generation passed in the quest for a stable definition of spheres of influence; and during this period both the planning of routes and termini and the working arrangements in south Manchester were dominated by the competitive postures taken up by the companies concerned.

A similar, and equally protracted struggle, this time between the L. & N.W. and the Lancashire and Yorkshire railway companies, affected the northern termini in Manchester from 1842 to 1884. The Hunt's Bank (Victoria) station had, from its very inception, been unpopular with the Liverpool and Manchester railway company. No one could deny the urgent need to form some linkage, in the early 1840's, between the three quite separate stations at Liverpool, Oldham and London roads (Nos. 1, 2 and 3 on sketch map). From the Liverpool and Manchester railway company's point of view, however, it would have been very much better to form the linkage by lines between Oldham Road and London Road, and between London Road and Liverpool Road stations. In this way the Manchester and Leeds (later Lancashire and Yorkshire) company would be diverted inconveniently around the east of Manchester, instead of gaining a well placed new station, and direct trunk route access to the Liverpool traffic. The fact that the projected Oldham Road to London Road link would have necessitated a 1,160 yard tunnel, the trans-shipment of goods by crane between the stations to be built at two levels at London Road, and would be virtually useless to the Manchester and Leeds company as a through route, either to the south, or (when the South Viaduct scheme was completed) to the west, gave the tunnel project positive merit in the eyes of the Liverpool and Manchester directors.[64]

Naturally Henry Houldsworth and the board of the Manchester and Leeds company could not be expected to concur with these views, and they pressed forward energetically with a counter-scheme of their own— the Hunt's Bank station and link-line. They were assisted, as already explained, by favourable land ownership features, and pursued their project with the utmost determination. If the Liverpool and Manchester

---

[63] HLRO, P & S, B.Ref., 1872, C.L.C., Manchester Central, Railway No. 1. Properties nos. 60–98 (Philips), 100–260 (Bowers).
[64] *Manchester City News* (1881–2), 14.

company should refuse to meet them at Hunt's Bank, they threatened, then an alliance would be formed with the Old River company, the Irwell/Mersey navigation would be enlarged and improved, and goods for Liverpool trans-shipped to the wharves and barges at Hunt's Bank.[65] It must remain a matter of some doubt as to whether the Manchester and Leeds company would ever have carried out its plans for this extraordinary composite traffic, by rail and canal, but the threat was enough to achieve the required result.[66] The long-delayed link line, one mile long, on arches through Salford, from the entrance to Liverpool Road station to Hunt's Bank (Nos. 1 and 4 on sketch map) was put in hand by the Liverpool and Manchester in May 1842.

Victoria station, Hunt's Bank, opened on 1 January 1844, though for a time the largest in the kingdom, provided a theatre for unseemly and bitter arguments between the rival companies sharing the site. Enlarging the facilities in 1864 eased some of the problems which arose, but only at the cost of raising further acrimonious debate on the division of costs and of rights to use the newly created space. 'A little more concession and a little more friendly conference between the two companies', the L. & N.W. traffic superintendent wrote later, 'could have produced—so I have often thought—a far more successful joint station.'[67] Instead, after almost forty years of ill-feeling, the principle of sharing was abandoned, and Exchange station (No. 7 on sketch map) was built by the L. & N.W. in the 1880's as an annexe, adjacent to Victoria station.

4. *Summary and general considerations*

The sustained competition in Manchester was a measure of the particular importance of the new medium of transport to a great textile city placed, as Leon Faucher put it, in 1844, 'like a diligent spider . . . in the centre of the web.' The distances which separated Manchester from the specialised manufacturing villages and towns which surrounded her were not too short for effective and profitable railway service, nor so great that the linkage became cumbersome and expensive. A pair of circles drawn at intervals of ten and thirty miles from Manchester would include most of the satellite manufacturing and processing centres, 'formerly villages, but now towns, which serve as outposts to the great centre of industry.'

[65] *Six-Monthly Report*, Liverpool and Manchester Railway, 26 January 1842. MRL *Miscellaneous Tracts* P2896.

[66] *Special Meeting of the Manchester and Leeds Railway Company*, 23 December 1841, MRL 625 M12. The holders of (it was claimed) $\frac{7}{8}$ of the stock agreed to tranship to barges.

[67] George P. Neele, *Railway Reminiscences* (1904), 296.

'The Leeds railway', Faucher's description continued, 'connects Manchester with Oldham, which contains 60,000 inhabitants; also with Bury, Rochdale and Halifax, each of which numbers from 24,000 to 26,000 souls; the Bolton railway connects it with Bolton, Preston and Chorley, which together have more than a hundred factories and 114,000 inhabitants. On the Sheffield line a few minutes suffice to reach the establishments of Stalybridge, Ashton, Dukinfield and Hyde, peopled by more than 80,000 inhabitants; the Birmingham line incorporates with it, so to speak, the 50,000 inhabitants of Stockport; and that of Liverpool connects it with Wigan and Warrington. Thus we have 15 or 16 sets of industry forming this great constellation. . . . Execution is almost as quick as thought.'[68]

Railways effectively created in Lancashire, even within two decades, a system of cities which was dominated operationally by Manchester. Faucher, the percipient foreign visitor, may have left us the best early description of the system's function, but his analysis is amply supported by contemporary evidence of the most varied nature—Board of Trade reports, Guide Books, Railway Prospectuses. The *Preston Chronicle* described rapturously the extraordinary speed with which the thirty-mile Preston linkage worked as early as 1839. Brokers despatched the cotton yarn from Manchester at 3 a.m., arriving (the newspaper stated precisely) at 9.08 a.m., being converted to cloth by 11.30 a.m., sent back as shirting material on the 4.20 p.m. train, arriving at 7 p.m. and being put on sale the next morning—'the very millenium of railway velocity.'[69] The broadside *Reasons in Favour of a Direct Line of Railroad from London to MANCHESTER* (1846) spoke of Manchester's special claim to speedy rail communication since 'the productions of its looms and mills form indisputably the largest and most important branch of our national industry', and also stressed the unexpected importance to industry itself of the rapid flow of passenger traffic, small masters, and salesmen by train, causing 'changes in all departments of trade far beyond the contemplation and conception of those who originated these schemes.'[70]

Such arguments, though used with special reference to Manchester, could be asserted to have wide and general application to all five of the cities chosen for study. But there were differences of degree; and Manchester found itself in a position which was in some respects unusual. Neither Liverpool, Glasgow nor London employed its rail linkages in quite the same way—virtually as production lines in a system of industrially inter-related cities; although to say this is not to argue that the indirect benefits the former cities received from mineral,

[68] Leon Faucher, *Manchester in 1844* (1844), 15.
[69] *Manchester as it is* (Manchester, 1839), 171.
[70] *Reasons in favour etc.* (1846), 1–5.

foodstuff and commercial connections were of a lesser order of importance.

Birmingham was more akin to Manchester in the functional role it fulfilled for a hinterland of smaller manufacturing towns; but its staple manufactures were neither so perishable, so bulky to store, nor so subject to the whims of season and fashion. In Manchester, the Board of Trade reported, the effect of the railways had been to break down, even by 1845, the old system of manufacturing and of forwarding large quantities of goods 'in anticipation of the probable demand of particular seasons and markets.' Instead there was a considerable saving of capital tied up in stocks, and a reduction to reasonable physical compass of the urban space demanded by the warehousing associated with an annual output of a million yards of material and a hundred and forty million lb. of twist and yarn. Also, and equally important, there was a reduction in 'the risk of fluctuation and loss arising from miscalculations as to the probable nature and extent of demand in distant markets. Even with a view to following the fluctuations of trade and fashion in foreign markets, it often becomes exceedingly important to hasten, by even a day, the execution of an order.'[71]

The dependence of Manchester upon a ring of specialised towns admirably situated for a fixed route transport system to operate most efficiently, and the peculiar force, in Manchester's staple industry, of the inventory factors mentioned in the Board of Trade report, help to explain why the city became an arena for sharp contest between so many railway companies. They also help to explain the Corporation's attitude towards the railway companies.

At first the Corporation could not have been more complaisant. Its Improvement Committee reported, on 22 September 1845, that the land required to improve the approach to London Road station had been purchased and laid to the street, adding, almost gratefully, 'The Manchester and Birmingham Railway company have agreed to pay half the cost of this improvement.' The Corporation, of course, paid the other half.[72] At the other end of the town a mere intimation from the Engineer of the Manchester and Leeds railway company, on 21 June 1846, that the land bounded by the Irk might be required for railway purposes, and requesting the re-direction of an intended new road, was enough to cause the Corporation to 'examine the locality and alter the plans'; and subsequently to arrange to sweep away the old Apple market, and straighten or eliminate several small streets, to secure a more commodious approach to the station.[73] The Committee for General Purposes, having considered a letter from the Lancashire

[71] H.L., 1845, XXXIX, 235–41.
[72] Council Proceedings, 1844–6, p. 203.
[73] Ibid. 21 January 1846, pp. 41–2.

and Yorkshire railway company on 1 December 1847 recommended that all clocks under the control of the Corporation, and that of the church wardens, should be adjusted by the necessary nine minutes, to conform with railway time; a symbolic act of homage by a mercantile and industrial community to the new masters of its traffic.[74]

By the end of the following decade the Corporation's courtship of the railway companies was over. The Corporation itself had been split, and unscrupulously manipulated, and the poor amenities, together with the 'insufficient and unnecessarily expensive' services had led to 'a sense of bitter disappointment.'[75] Thereafter, the Corporation adopted a far more suspicious and legalistic attitude towards the private companies providing the city's rail transport—as its dealings with the C.L.C. and Great Northern railway companies in the later nineteenth century testify.[76]

The declension of the Corporation's willingness to co-operate freely, and to make concessions to encourage railway enterprise in Manchester, was paralleled by a similar deterioration in the general public's view of rail services. By the late 1850's, complaints about the existing services, and suggestions as to likely sites for new and improved stations, had become a regular pastime of the *Manchester Guardian's* correspondence columns: a new terminus should be sited at Stevenson Square, or at Granby Row Fields, or at Charles Street and Brook Street, or between Oxford Road and Garrat Road; alternatively (it was suggested) there was no real need for any further building, 'by a little cordial co-operation on the part of the two companies whose trains come into London Road station all the difficulties of deficient accommodation might be removed . . . Ardwick could become the second Camden Town.'[77]

Some of the letters written during the 'pick a station' correspondence were obviously inspired either by the railway or landed interests concerned, but some reflected a genuine concern on the part of disinterested citizens and tradespeople that Manchester should be better served than it was in the mêlée of excessive competition.

[74] Council Proceedings, 1846–8, 1 December 1847.
[75] Council Proceedings, 1863–5, 5 April 1865, p. 102.
[76] Council Proceedings, 1874–5, 3 March 1875, p. 203; 1897–8, 5 January 1898, pp. 402–5.
[77] *Manchester Guardian*, 20, 27 February, 4 March 1860.

VII

◇◇

Liverpool

◇◇

1. *The property ownership pattern*

LIKE most large provincial cities Liverpool at the beginning of the nineteenth century had a central district honeycombed with individual property titles, usually to relatively small parcels of land, established by enterprising commoners during the period of rapid commercial growth in the late eighteenth century. The names of these individual proprietors and lessees can be compared on Charles Eyes' detailed *Plan of the Town and Township of Liverpool* (1796), and Jonathan Bennison's *Plan of the Town and Port of Liverpool* (1835 and 1841). Such ownership of urban sites was either a symptom or a cause of acceptance into one of the social 'sets', in the days of the closed municipal franchise. 'All tradesmen and shopkeepers, and everything retail, were carefully excluded' wrote a contemporary. Patronage lay in the hands of 'the fashionable set, the wealthy and commercial set and the Corporation set'—the Hollingsheads, Drinkwaters, Harpers, Cases, Aspinalls, Clarkes and Branckers—and the association between freehold and franchise closed the circle of ownership and of political and social status.[1]

The surrounding outer townships, or suburban areas, of Everton, Kirkdale, West Derby and Toxteth, however, formed a ring of large estates, which were retained in even fewer hands than usual. Essentially there were only three great landowners: the Stanley and Molyneux families, Earls of Derby and of Sefton respectively, who had long-standing territorial connections with the Tower and the Castle of Liverpool; and the Corporation of Liverpool which had succeeded, to an unusual degree amongst the corporations of the five major cities, in retaining land in common ownership, and in acquiring large additional areas by purchase.[2]

[1] James Aspinall, *Liverpool by an Old Stager* (Liverpool, 1852). BM 10359 aa 78.

[2] George Chandler, *Liverpool* (1957). Henry T. Hough, 'The Liverpool Corporate Estate', *Town Planning Review*, XXI (1950), 237–52.

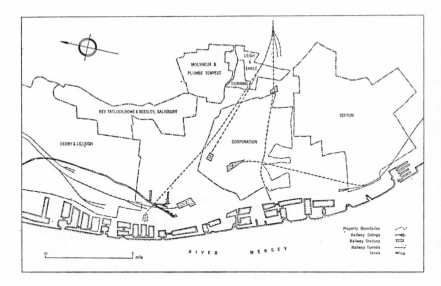

Property ownership and railways in Liverpool.

The oldest portions, fifty acres in Saltonsmoor, in north Liverpool, had largely been alienated by the early nineteenth century; but, more than making up for this, the Corporation acquired, during the seventeenth century, a 1,000 years' lease on waste lands south of the Pool. In 1777 the Council also purchased the reversion of this lease for £2,250; an extraordinary municipal bargain, which gave them full possession of all the lands south of the Pool, including the whole central area of Lime Street, William Brown Street and London Road, as far east as Crown Street, and as far south as Parliament Street.[3] This area is indicated on the sketch map above as a solid block, but there were in fact quite large gaps, particularly just north of centre, where land had been disposed of for private development, or for a cemetery, an asylum, a workhouse, and other sombre functions of the early nineteenth-century city. Nevertheless the Corporation retained possession of an unexampled proportion of the central lands into which building was extending most rapidly in the late eighteenth century and early nineteenth century.

Beyond it, to the north, the greater part of the parish of Kirkdale was owned by the Earl of Derby, or by his agents and solicitors, John Leigh and John Shaw Leigh. The Leighs also held land strategically placed by the entrance to the Edgehill tunnel, in the Lovat,

[3] Henry T. Hough, *loc. cit.* 240–2.

176

Troughton, Cardwell Street districts.[4] Richard Earle, another of Derby's agents also owned land in this area; and he and the Leighs accumulated considerable fortunes both as *rentiers* of residential cottage property, and from sales to the railway companies. Part of their land acquisitions had sprung from their connection with the Derby family, but large areas of John Leigh's estates were the result of speculation on credit. He was noted as an extensive and tireless purchaser of land, far beyond his resources. J. A. Picton, himself a land valuer later in the nineteenth century, commented upon the, as it seemed, excessive land purchases in north and east Liverpool to which John Leigh committed himself.[5] Although at times hard pressed by the interest burden upon his loan he continued with his purchases; the Golden Lion at the top of Dale Street (later sold to the Royal Bank), the Old Hall and Sandhills estates.[6] The latter estate he converted immediately from pasture to brickfields—a common practice in rapidly growing cities at the turn of the eighteenth century—and lowered their level by seven or eight feet. These routine procedures for developing land on the fringe of a city were revolutionised by the arrival of the railways in north Liverpool in the 1840's. Land which had been bought at £200 or £300 per acre now sold at £2 or £3 per square yard. As J. A. Picton reflected, 'That he had a keen foresight beyond most of his contemporaries into the coming greatness of Liverpool there can be no doubt, but the actuality far exceeded his most sanguine anticipations. The railway demands formed an element altogether outside of his calculations, however shrewd.'[7]

His son, John Shaw Leigh, who became mayor of Liverpool in 1841, reaped the benefit of the opportune investment John Leigh had carried out. A portion of the northern estate was sold to the Liverpool, Ormskirk and Preston railway company for a reputed £250,000 in 1846.[8] Apart from this direct gain, the railway approach converted what had been market gardens, brickyards or cottage properties into valuable sites for warehousing, further sidings, and for conveniently situated and easily rented houses; and, according to J. A. Picton, 'enhanced materially the value of the other portions which have since come into the market for commercial purposes, extensions of the railways and general use, opening a mine of wealth to the fortunate proprietor.' John Shaw Leigh, in fact, was one of the first landlords to sweep away the erratic system of leasing property by 'lives' and years, which had

---

[4] Jonathan Bennison, *Plan of the Town and Port of Liverpool* (1835). This map shows property boundaries on the outskirts of Liverpool; the 1841 edition merely shows the central portion.

[5] J. A. Picton, *Memorials of Liverpool*, (1873), II, 190.

[6] *Liverpool Mercury*, 11 January 1866. *Daily Post and Mercury*, 21 December 1910.

[7] J. A. Picton, *op. cit.* II, 54.

[8] HLRO, Min., H.C., 1846, 30 June, p. 7, S.C. on Liverpool and Bury Railway.

obtained in Liverpool, and to standardise seventy-five year leases; a measure also adopted by the Marquis of Salisbury, the Earls of Derby and Sefton, and the Corporation.[9] In 1843, Leigh had the old mansion at Sandhills taken down, and Victoria and Sandhills roads cut through the area; on the remaining portion, though somewhat intersected by the cutting of main roads and railway lines, the Errington, Grundy, Holmes Street areas were laid out.[10]

Similarly to the east, near the Edgehill railway terminus, the site was bordered by another John Shaw Leigh property; the seventy-five or so houses known as Spekefield Cottages.[11] The Leighs, in fact, carried a flair for the timely and well-sited purchases of property to a remarkably high degree. And although, no doubt, their dealings with the railway companies on behalf of the great landowners they represented gave them both an unusual measure of inside information and a degree of monopoly control as vendors of land, the skill with which they made capital from these assets in the early railway age is unusual. The Duke of Norfolk's agent, Michael Ellis, and the Duke of Bridgewater's, James Loch, were also able to turn their stewardships to advantage; a railway directorship in one case, a seat in Parliament in the other.[12] Yet it would be difficult to find agents whose land speculation equalled the scope and opportunism of the Leighs.

The ability of their agents, Robert Slatter, John Leigh and Richard Earle, and the sheer breadth of acreage belonging to the Stanleys in Liverpool's environs, brought the Earls of Derby recurrent increments of wealth over the half century after the railways' arrival. The Stanleys of Knowsley, who had merely been prosperous provincial aristocrats, qualified, by 1865, for inclusion in Sanford and Townsend's *The Great Governing Families of England*. 'The growth of Liverpool and the cotton trade has poured wealth into their coffers', the authors comment; and without in any way minimising the importance of their growing agricultural rent roll, or their increasing income from urban residential property, it is worth underlining the large part in their fortunes which land-sales to railway companies played.[13] They were of particular significance in that, without making sizeable inroads into the total estates, they allowed vast occasional lump sums to be on call, and thereby went some way towards solving the problems of liquidity which

[9] *A System for the Better Management and Improvement of Landed Estates* (Liverpool, 1844), 8.
[10] J. A. Picton, *op. cit.* II, 467.
[11] J. A. Picton, *op. cit.* (1875 ed.) II, 441.
[12] BTHR PYB 1/90, Commons' S.C. on M.S. & L. and G.N. Railways, 1858, 13 April. David Spring, *The English Landed Estate in the Nineteenth Century, its Administration* (1963), 89–94.
[13] J. L. Sanford and Meredith Townsend, *The Great Governing Families of England* (Edinburgh, 1865) I, 111.

often harassed even the greatest landed families. For although their annual rent rolls were very impressive, quite frequently marriage settlements, family portions and annuities, debt charges, and the overheads of maintaining several large households in appropriate style, ran away with the greater part of the day-to-day revenues.[14] Against this background the opportunity to realise appreciable sums for mere chips of the estate—parcels measured not in acres but in square yards—was especially welcome.

Unfortunately the Derby Papers which survive, at Knowsley and the Lancashire County Record Office, do not give a full picture of the increments from land sales to railway companies. Most of the very substantial earlier sales in the 1840's are missing, but even if one looks only at the smaller sales for 'widenings' and 'easements' of existing termini and approach lines, for the later period 1864–1892, the Derbys' recorded conveyances total £483,408.[15] Their dealings brought them into contact with the London and North Western, the Lancashire and Yorkshire, the Midland, the Manchester, Sheffield and Lincolnshire railway companies and the Cheshire Lines Committee, in addition to several smaller concerns such as the Liverpool and Bury, and the Preston and Wyre railway companies. This list is probably incomplete, and refers only to the Kirkdale, Walton and Bootle districts, nor within the dates specified does it include the purchase price of the Regent Road goods station; so the £483,408 is clearly an understatement, even of the partial coverage afforded by the records.

Some idea of the general order of magnitude by which the value of their estates appreciated when the railways entered the land market may perhaps be glimpsed by comparing the prices Robert Slatter received on the Derby's behalf in the late 1820's, which ran to 9d or 1s per square yard for township properties, to the 40s or 50s per square yard received for comparable properties a half century later.[16] Land sales were only the most direct and obvious way in which the railway's arrival could be turned to account by the owners of urban property. The substantial enhancement in capital value of the other advantageously sited, perhaps adjacent, property which was retained frequently formed another major consideration; and there were still further incidental benefits, the nature of which is revealed in the correspondence between another great Liverpool landowning family and their agents.

The family was that of Molyneux, Earls of Sefton, and the estate—

---

[14] Rent rolls of £43,000 and £163,000 for Sefton and Derby in the 1880's, excluding 'building land in and close to Liverpool', or 'leased for building'. J. Bateman, *Great Landowners of Great Britain* (1883), 127, 401.

[15] Stuart A. Moore, *A Calendar of the Muniments of the Earl of Derby* (1894). The references are too lengthy to list, but mostly occur amongst the Deeds and Conveyances calendared as Nos. 650–63, 674–6, 691–4.

[16] LRO Derby 683/1/1.

which forms the subject of an interesting correspondence worth pausing to study in detail—was their park at Croxteth, situated to the north-east of Liverpool (a little too far out to be shown on the sketch map) on the route fiercely contested in 1845/6.

The steward, R. Ledger, was the first to draw the Earl of Sefton's attention to the matter in a letter of 12 October 1844. 'If your Lordship has had the Liverpool papers of this week you will see in the present mania for Railways that, in addition to the one from Preston to Liverpool via Ormskirk, another is started to be called the Bolton, Wigan and Liverpool, which . . . proposes to pass through the Township of Bootle, Walton, Knowsley and consequently very proximate to Croxteth——An advertisement states that all the shares are allotted in the Liverpool and Preston line.'[17] This was the beginning of a complicated three-cornered rivalry between the two companies mentioned by Ledger, and a third, the Liverpool and Bury railway company; a contest which soon surpassed the steward's experience and competence. He was left dealing with tithes, rent arrears and potato blight, whilst the task of advising his master on railway affairs passed into other more capable hands. In particular C. P. Grenfell now came forward as the Earl's adviser and negotiator with the Liverpool, Bolton and Wigan railway company. 'I have told the Director and their Lawyer,' he wrote to the Earl of Sefton on 7 January 1845, 'that I consider it arranged that you are to have the option of demanding at Par 200 shares in the railway at any time within twelve months of the passing of the Act,' and such an agreement had been drawn up by solicitors. 'The advantage of this arrangement', he went on to explain, 'will be that without any advance of funds you can insist upon the profit upon 200 shares whenever you please, and I have no hesitation in saying that I believe you would put £40,000 in your pocket at the very least.'[18]

The Earl of Sefton obviously agreed to this proposal, for Grenfell's letters to him take on a more familiar and urgent tone. On 13 January 1845 a letter instructs him in the basic advantages of 'our Project' (as the scheme is now called) 'which is the only safety valve for the public against the combination of the Liverpool and Manchester and the Water, now wholly monopolised by Egerton, and secures to the County a North Entrance to Liverpool which is much wanted.' 'Put your shoulder to the wheel, combine with Brook and Willis,' urges a letter of 18 January, 'You cannot lose and may gain very largely.' Later letters urge Sefton to play a more active part in the promotion of the railway. The arguments he is to use are rehearsed again, and no fewer than eight 'lines we are interested in' are set down for his information. 'There's a pretty list . . . Our own stands on its own merits but the

[17] LRO Molyneux Papers DDM 6/123.
[18] *Ibid.* DDM 6/1.

development of its success will be much aided by the other fine schemes.'[19] He is exhorted to use his utmost influence in and out of Parliament. 'Our opponents,' writes Grenfell 'are powerful and active ... We must exert all our energies to induce members of Parliament to attend and give us support on the *2nd Reading* of the Bill. That will be the true war, and that sly fellow Locke, as Lord Francis and the Duke of Sutherland's agent, will do his utmost to throw it out.' Sefton should write at once to his influential friends, 'and let me know who they are, that I may whip them up against the day of struggle.' If Sefton uses his influence and the line succeeds, 'I have no doubt whatever that before 12 months are over you will clear your Belgrave Square house and something to spare.' 'I think you might insist upon having a director or two or your own,' he adds, 'if you think of retaining a large interest in the concern.'[20] Possible objections to the Liverpool, Bolton and Wigan railway from the Earl of Derby were overcome. 'I saw Stanley yesterday with our Wigan friends. His objections were all or nearly so removed as to his Bootle property, and Stewart (presumably one of the partners from Messrs. Foster and Stewart, the solicitors employed by the Molyneux family) is with him now to explain further.'

The turning point came on 24 February 1845, when the Railway Department of the Board of Trade reported in favour of the scheme. 'Never was such astonishment than that produced upon the conflicting Parties by the decision of the Board of Trade,' wrote Grenfell jubilantly. 'We have done it so quietly that everybody was astonished.' 'In both your interests and my own,' he concluded, 'I have become a director ... The best is you do not advance a shilling ... I have had to stump up £2,000.'[21] This correspondence, which could no doubt be paralleled by similar exchanges between other great landowners and their agents, illustrates both the considerable advantages to railway companies of the active support of landowners during projects' formative phases, and the not inconsiderable benefits, apart from land sales, which accrued to the landowners from railway company promotion.

In fact, to conclude the narrative of this particular incident, the Earl of Sefton stood to make yet further gains from other changes in the fortunes of the competing companies. In spite of the jubilant tone of Grenfell's final letter, the issue was not settled by the Board of Trade's decision. The Liverpool, Ormskirk and Preston line (which had bought J. S. Leigh's land), and the Liverpool and Bury company, still pressed for the reading of their bills in the following session; and Ledger, the steward, reported Grenfell's disappointment with a certain lugubrious

[19] *Ibid.* DDM 6/8.

[20] *Ibid.* DDM 6/5 and 6.

[21] *Ibid.* DDM 6/9 and 10. The Board of Trade Report mentioned is in H.L., 1845, XXXIX, 240–1.

satisfaction in a letter on 4 April 1845, to inform the Earl of Sefton that a Mr. Heron, Secretary to the Liverpool, Bolton and Wigan railway company, had visited him with a petition in favour of the line 'and was desirous that your Lordship's tenants on the line should sign it, as, he states, Mr. Grenfell promised they should do, and I gave him such authority, as I have to that effect.'[22]

The two rival railway bills came up before Select Committee in June and August of the following year, 1846, and as the dates drew nearer they became both more anxious to compromise with each other and to reach an accommodation with Sefton. The Liverpool, Ormskirk and Preston company's solicitor, Joshua Lloyd, opened a correspondence in June, 1846, 'to commence with your Lordship as a landowner and ask whether there are any arrangements which you would wish considered and concluded so that the Company may have your Lordship's assent to the measure.' Instructions by Sefton to Eden and Stanistreet, solicitors, to oppose the Liverpool, Ormskirk and Preston Bill brought a frantic reply from Lloyd. 'I have received a note from Messrs. Eden and Stanistreet stating that they are instructed to oppose the Bill in its future progress, and I am perhaps taking a liberty in addressing your Lordship after the receipt of their note, but my first communication was made and your Lordship's reply received before I had heard from Messrs. Eden and Stanistreet. If your Lordship will please direct those gentlemen to negotiate an arrangement I can say that my clients are prepared to meet the question most liberally.'[23] The date of Lloyd's letter was 3 July 1846, and on 7 August the Liverpool, Ormskirk and Preston Bill was due to go before the House of Lords' Committee. Evidently the settlement was sufficiently liberal, for three days later Lloyd wrote that he was coming to Liverpool and regarded the matter as settled. A sum was deposited at Sefton's account in Heywood's Bank, London, and in due course, when the rival lines had merged into the East Lancashire railway company, the agreement was confirmed.[24]

The critical balance and timing of Parliamentary Bills clearly played an important part in dictating the terms of this settlement. From the railway company's point of view one more opponent, especially if he were represented by able counsel, might have tipped the scales; with the result that all the sums already expended on surveys and legal expenses might be wasted, and the scheme irrevocably miscarry. To contemplate returning, with renewed expenses, in the following session would have deterred even a large company, with revenues flowing in from the routes it had already opened to traffic. It would clearly have

[22] LRO Molyneux Papers DDM 6/126.
[23] *Ibid.* DDM 6/314 and 5.
[24] *Ibid.* DDM 6/316–9.

been fatal to a small company, like the Liverpool, Ormskirk and Preston, which had no rails laid, only existed on paper, and drew its most likely prospect of profit, or recoupment of the money already invested, from its promotional value. If the Bill failed, it was not merely the scale of future business that was at stake, but the whole corporate existence of the railway company.

The panic which prompted Lloyd's extraordinary letter in July 1846, virtually offering Sefton a blank cheque, must also be considered, not merely against the background of the imminent Lords' Committee, but also the more general alarm of 'railway mania'. Railway share prices had already dipped in October 1845, even for the large companies; and July 1846 was the last peak before the disastrous two-year slide which brought even Great Western or Midland £100 share quotations down from 150 to 80 in the exchanges.[25] Under the circumstances a strategically placed and influential landowner could hardly fail to command settlement on his own terms; and it should not escape notice that this settlement in 1846 was made with companies which were rivals to the one in which Sefton and Grenfell had been concerned the year before. Whichever company succeeded, tribute was forthcoming to landowners upon whose estates the railways were, in Lloyd's words, 'unavoidably thrown'. Few *rural* landowners commanded tracts of land so enormous that they could not be skirted if necessary. But in the outskirts of Britain's great cities the landowner was presented with unusual economic opportunities, as the route choices narrowed in focus, and as land which had been given a predicative 'development value' by the presence of occasional houses, or extant plans for building, came under discussion.

On a smaller scale the same opportunities also presented themselves to the lesser urban landowners; and though, by their nature, the cases tended to be less well documented, some detailed examples in this category are cited elsewhere.[26] Beneficiaries of this smaller sort included Colonel Plumbe-Tempest, some of whose properties are indicated on the sketch map, and whose name also appears in the *Books of Reference* for the Exchange station line.[27]

Most of the medium-sized property holders, however, lay out of the general route of railway approaches, and were only affected marginally.

[25] C. N. Ward Perkins, 'The Commercial Crisis of 1847', *Readings in the Business Cycles and National Income* (ed. A. H. Hansen and R. V. Clemence, 1953), 19.

[26] *Infra*, Ch. 8, sec. 1, and John R. Kellett, 'Urban and Transport History from Legal Records: An Example from Glasgow Solicitors' Papers', *JTH*, VI (1964), 222–40.

[27] HLRO, P & S, B.Ref., 1846, Liverpool and Bury Railway (Plan for extension to Tithebarn Street and Liverpool Docks).

The considerable urban estates of Robert Durning and Thomas Molyneux fell into this category; as did those of the Reverend H. Tatlock, a clergyman *rentier* with unusually large holdings, not merely in the area of present-day Tatlock Street, but also further east, in the area shown on the sketch map.

The owners who lay directly on the routes of the Exchange and Central approach lines (Nos. 3 and 4 on sketch map) were mostly landowners with more modest holdings. Frequently resident themselves, they held title to relatively small batches of properties—a minimum of two, and a maximum of seventeen.[28] Some idea of their leverage over the railway companies can be gained from solicitors' papers surviving for the Cheshire Lines Committee's operations in 1870. A sample of these suggests that the amounts awarded by jury trial or arbitration procedure came to between two and three times the amount offered by the C.L.C.'s solicitors. For half-a-dozen cases selected at random £5,680 was the amount offered, £13,310 the amount awarded; sums which approximate to the amounts offered and awarded elsewhere in the same decade. Of course the original offers made by the railway company for these smaller properties on their route were intended partly as bargaining figures; and there was evidently a tendency—at least in the eyes of the arbitrators—for the smaller encroachments upon property to be accorded a derisory sum in compensation. Alexander Matheson, a portion of whose property was scheduled under the C.L.C. Liverpool Central Station Acts of 1864 and 1866 was offered a mere £50, claimed £1,869, and was awarded £710; James Jeffery was offered £10, claimed £1,036, and was awarded £600; John Jackson and Zacharias Sillar, who had been offered £100 each, were awarded £2,900 and £3,300.[29]

The larger claims were treated more carefully, however, and were subjected to independent valuation by up to six experienced valuers. The estimates they gave, though sometimes discreetly toned down by the railway company, bore a relationship to accepted values which could be made to stand up in court. A margin of 30–50% over the stated offers was contemplated, but the actual awards, which came to a half, or two-thirds of the asking price, were usually between 100% and 200% above valuation.

The inflation of values which arose for the small properties through which the railway companies sometimes had to plough to reach the central district in the 1860's can, perhaps, best be illustrated by taking one specific example in detail. Thus, for instance, a stable and two small buildings off Ranelagh Street in Liverpool, with a rental of £114 *per*

[28] *Ibid.* and HLRO, P & S, B.Ref., 1862, M.S. & L. Railway (Liverpool Central Station Railway).
[29] LRO Deeds QDD, December 1869–November 1870.

annum, were valued in 1867 by J. A. Picton on behalf of the Cheshire Lines Committee at £5 per square yard, or £2,320. When £80 had been added for old materials and 10% for forced sale, the total recommended came to £2,640. It was 'a good place for workshops but not well adapted to general business' he declared; and the proposal to erect a showroom there was absurd. James Holme, another reputable valuer, took a lower view of the property. Even at 20 years' purchase it would only raise, after deduction for necessary repairs, £2,184. Moving half way between that figure and the more generous estimate of £5 per square yard which Picton had suggested, and adding 10% for forced sale, gave a total of £2,477. Two other, less well-known valuers recommended similar offers.[30] The owner claimed £14 per square yard or £7,145: to put it in James Holme's terms, '60 years' purchase'; a sum difficult to justify upon any reasonable grounds.[31]

The course of arbitration, and the size of the final award corresponded quite closely to the typical pattern suggested above. The award was £5,800, or about two-thirds of the asking price, twice the valuation, and representing nearly £12 per square yard.[32] A rather unusual note was struck, however, by the exchange of letters between the spokesmen of the railway company and of the late owner, Mrs. Fairclough, commenting upon the case publicly in the pages of the *Daily Courier*. This correspondence helps to throw light upon how it could come about that reputable professional valuers employed by both parties were prepared to stand up in court and make firm valuations which conflicted so violently. Nearly always there was some point of interpretation and opinion which could be seized upon, usually connected with the potential or development value of the site in question. There was no need to read more into this than a genuine disagreement of opinion, combined perhaps with a legitimate determination to get the best for one's client. It was most unworthy, one of the pseudonymous correspondents wrote indignantly, to make of this an occasion for ascribing lack of professional competence to those who 'viewed the property . . . in justice to their employers.'

In the Fairclough case the point of disagreement was whether her premises should be valued as old houses on a side street, or as a site 'forming a valuable adjunct to Ranelagh Street', ideally placed for potential extensions by shopkeepers. 'Such practical men as Messrs. Picton, Holme and Co. are not slow to discover the fact that the mere taking down of a party wall, or the opening up of a wide arch or doorway in a wall, very frequently develops in an astounding manner the value of land near a main thoroughfare for business purposes. Why,

[30] *Daily Post*, 5 September 1867. LRL.
[31] *Daily Courier*, 25 September 1867.
[32] *Daily Courier*, 17 October 1867. LRL Town Clerk's Newscuttings, II, 176.

then, it may be asked, did they purposely shut their eyes to the fact that this land was precisely in this position?'[33]

The arbiters took the view in this case, as in most of the others, that it was no more than reasonable to expect the railway companies to pay a sum in anticipation of the possible development value of a site which was being handed over reluctantly. This development value, moreover, could be influenced even by something as easily accomplished as the taking down of a party wall. In fact the railway companies were asked to pay, not for what the property was currently worth, but for what it might be worth in ten years' time under favourable circumstances. If a sympathetic local jury were empanelled the award might be still more generous. The result of the tendency to over-value smaller properties, illustrated in the example just quoted, together with the delays and legal complications of dealing with a multiplicity of small parcels of land, was the same in Liverpool as in Birmingham or Manchester. Railway companies were inclined, still more strongly, to choose, for preference, areas where they could deal with one large proprietor.

Apart from J. S. Leigh and the Sefton and Derby families, the only other proprietor on a similar scale was the Corporation; and two of the large central terminals were located upon the inexpensive sites which the Corporation made available. That at Lime Street (No. 2 on map) was built very early (in 1832), and upon largely open ground used as a cattle market.[34] One might, therefore, expect it to avoid heavy costs for these reasons; but even the extensive additions made by Joseph Locke to George Stephenson's original station, in 1847, allowed only £70,000 in its estimates for the 263 adjacent properties scheduled, all of which belonged to the Mayor and Burgesses.[35]

The Central Station (No. 4 on map) planned by the Manchester, Sheffield and Lincolnshire Company, and executed by the Cheshire Lines Committee (in a similar manner to that already described for Manchester Central), was also influenced in its site location by the presence of a substantial block of Corporation property. On the original site, at the corner of Bold Street and Ranelagh Street, the Corporation owned sixty houses and shops, and the Rotunda gymnasium.[36] A disreputable arcade, a 'mart for second hand furniture and resort for improper characters', made up the remaining space for the

[33] *Daily Courier*, 28 September 1867. LRL Town Clerk's Newscuttings, II, 160–1.

[34] HLRO, P & S, B.Ref., 1832, Liverpool and Manchester Railway (Branch from West Derby to Lime Street).

[35] HLRO, P & S, B.Ref., 1847, L. & N.W. Railway (Lime Street Station).

[36] HLRO, P & S, B.Ref., 1862, M.S. & L. Railway (Liverpool Central Station Railway). Corporation properties form the triangle just north of the line's termination at Ranelagh Street. The row of houses along the track itself, and in Cropper Street belonged to Thomas Brassey (q.v.).

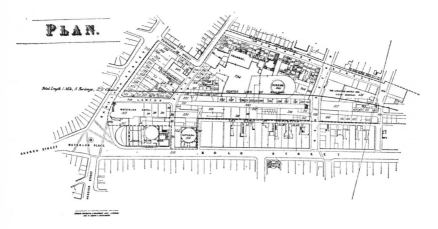

Liverpool Central Station, 1862.

M.S. & L.'s first purchases, scheduled in 1862.[37] Later additions, by the C.L.C., relied upon a further block of fifty Corporation properties at Cropper Street, scheduled in November 1871, and upon eighty more miscellaneous properties—bricklayers' yards, stables, shops, houses and outbuildings—also belonging to the Corporation, and scheduled in November 1873.[38]

The railway companies' reliance upon the Corporation, and upon Derby and Sefton, for substantial units of land was all the more pronounced because of the relative absence of charities and private corporate bodies upon the railway routes in Liverpool. At no time in their dealings were the railway companies able to acquire large blocks from a hospital, an almshouse, a well endowed Grammar School or College, a City Guild or Company, or a board of charitable trustees. In Glasgow, Manchester, Birmingham and London, such corporate bodies were an important source of land for railway schemes.

Similarly, there was no counterpart in Liverpool to the important role in landownership patterns played in all four of the other cities by canal companies. In Liverpool the principal canals gained access to the Mersey upstream, and their wharfage mingled with the riverside dock installations. A notable exception to this rule was the Leeds and Liverpool canal, which (as the sketch map shows) had been devised by Brindley to make a direct and easy approach from the north to within half-a-mile of the central area. This route was, in fact, George Stephen-

[37] J. A. Picton, *Memorials of Liverpool* (1873 edn.), II, 231.
[38] HLRO, P & S, B.Ref., 1872, C.L.C., and 1874, C.L.C. (North Liverpool Extension to Ranelagh St.).

son's first choice for the line of the Liverpool and Manchester railway in 1824, before the Earl of Derby had come to accept railways.[39] It was also the route chosen, in 1846, by the competing schemes searching for a northern entrance to Liverpool. Yet although their extensive operations in north Liverpool caused the C.L.C., the L. & N.W., and the Lancashire and Yorkshire railway companies, to bridge and traverse the Leeds and Liverpool canal repeatedly, and to schedule, or purchase by agreement, a good part of its bankside space, the canal was not directly used as a route for a main line approach, nor was the terminal basin filled in for a station. Part of the western basins, between the Exchange Station line and Howard Street (see sketch map), was taken over by the Lancashire and Yorkshire railway for extra goods space. But in the Plumbe-Tempest lands at Tithebarn Street, the L. & Y. already had a terminal site which brought passengers three or four hundred yards nearer the central business district. So the main basins of the canal, off Vauxhall Road and Leeds Street, remained undisturbed. Indeed, although the Lancashire and Yorkshire and the L. & N.W. railway companies took steps to secure joint control over this important route, by acquiring an annual lease, the Leeds and Liverpool continued to operate as a canal, conveying 2,100,000 tons of goods in 1868; a mere 100,000 tons decline on the traffic figures of thirty years earlier.[40]

2. *Conditions of competition between railway companies*

From the opening of the Liverpool and Manchester railway, on 17 September 1830, until the middle of the 1870's, railway traffic in Liverpool experienced conditions of competition quite unlike those in any of Britain's four other major cities. Whereas a lively contest to extend facilities, and to open new and independent routes of access, took place during the late 1830's and mid-1840's in the other cities, Liverpool was subject to a régime of virtual monopoly.

For sixteen years Liverpool's traffic remained entirely in the control of the Liverpool and Manchester railway company, and that of its partner, the Grand Junction. Although seven years junior, the Grand Junction route was longer (from Warrington to Birmingham), the company was more heavily capitalised, and its commercial performance was equally successful. After an initial struggle with Birmingham promoters its management fell into the hands of the Liverpool party, and both in the board-room and in share-holding there was a close identity of interest between the two concerns. Operationally the Grand Junction relied upon the toll-route over the Liverpool and Manchester's rails for access to Liverpool, and felt sufficiently confident to establish

[39] T. Baines, *Liverpool in 1859* (1859), 70–1.
[40] H.C., 1872, XIII, App. T.

its first locomotive works at Edge Hill, on land which could only be reached by the toll-route. It was also rumoured that many of the older company's major shareholders had transferred their interests to the Grand Junction after granting it a cheap toll rate.[41]

In effect, therefore, the two companies were one, long before their formal amalgamation in July 1845. The only attempt to infringe their monopoly produced by the 1837 railway boom was a plan, not very seriously intended, to run ferry-boats from Liverpool to Chester, to link with the services of the newly promoted Chester and Crewe railway company, whose Bill passed through Parliament on 30 June, 1837. This threat was easily countered by the Grand Junction's purchase of the small Chester and Crewe company before it came into operation.

Even the railway boom of 1846, which produced an embarrassment of schemes in London and Glasgow, and finely-balanced projects of genuinely competitive authorship in Manchester and Birmingham, only gave rise to a faint echo of railway mania in Liverpool. The northern approaches to the city were the scene of a fierce, but short-lived, contest between a number of small promotional companies, the Liverpool, Ormskirk and Preston, the Liverpool and Bury, and the Liverpool, Bolton and Wigan railway companies, to whose fortunes reference has already been made in the preceding section. All these client companies were absorbed within five years, by larger partners in a complicated series of amalgamations. The Liverpool, Ormskirk and Preston first negotiated with John Shaw Leigh for the necessary land for its approaches to a station near the Borough Gaol, at Great Howard Street. These powers were taken over by the Liverpool and Bury railway company, which also secured Parliamentary permission to extend the line to Tithebarn Street. The Liverpool and Bury company was then absorbed, in 1846, by the Manchester and Leeds railway company; itself a partner to the merger known as the Lancashire and Yorkshire railway company in the following year. To add to the complication, two lesser companies also gained access to the new northern station (No. 3 on map); one, the East Lancashire, with equal powers, and the consequent friction which station-sharing on these terms usually involved; the other, the small Liverpool, Crosby and Southport company, enjoying only running powers under payment of toll charges.[43]

At the end of all this, however, although an important, independently owned, and well situated new station had been added to the Liverpool townscape, conditions of competition had hardly changed at all. The Lancashire and Yorkshire company operating from Exchange Station,

[41] M. D. Greville and G. O. Holt, 'Railway Development in Liverpool', *Railway Magazine*, 105 (1959), 78.
[42] *Ibid.* 79.
[43] *Ibid.* 82–4.

and the London and North Western group of companies, operating from Lime Street, were unequally matched in Liverpool, and performed services which were complementary rather than competitive. Until the goods stations at North Docks and Sandhills were opened the L. & Y. had no goods facilities to compete with the L. & N.W.'s stations in the central dock area, at Wapping and at Waterloo (at the western ends of the two tunnels shown on the sketch map). Nor was the main direction of the flow of goods and of passengers competitive. Though it was possible to travel from Manchester to Liverpool over the L. & Y.'s tracks, the route was devious, and took an hour and a half to the one hour of the L. & N.W.'s direct route. For passengers and for goods the L. & N.W. continued to dominate the main national traffic and trunk routes.

An analysis of the traffic in and out of Liverpool carried by the L. & N.W., prepared by their Goods Manager, Braithwaite Poole, in 1851, shows that far and away the greater proportion went to, or was received from Manchester—125,000 tons in the year. Birmingham and the Staffordshire district accounted for 26,000 and 30,000 tons each; Sheffield and London 29,000 and 27,000 tons per year. Cotton (88,000 tons), Packed Goods (96,000 tons), Bales and Cases (73,000 tons), Raw Materials (45,000 tons), Grain (41,000 tons), Timber (39,000 tons), Iron (32,000 tons) and Hardware (18,000 tons), were the principal items in the two-way traffic. Coal was conspicuous by its absence.[44] The coal fields to the east and north of Liverpool were largely catered for by the tributary railways which ran into the Lancashire and Yorkshire system. These collieries, together with the West Riding urban centres, and the smaller Lancashire manufacturing towns, formed the main originating points of the L. & Y. traffic.

To both systems Liverpool was a terminus. However, since their routes were oriented to the north-east, and to the east and south-east respectively, dealings between the two were not as competitive as in other theatres. By 1852, in fact, the Select Committee of the House of Commons' *4th Report* had singled out the companies serving Liverpool for particular comment: 'The Liverpool and Manchester, the Lancashire and Yorkshire railway via Bolton, Bury and Wigan, the East Lancashire railway, the Bridgewater canal and the Old River Trust all have a common understanding.'[45] Indeed the first and principal business of the Chamber of Commerce, founded in Liverpool in 1851, was to commence agitation upon this very question. Both as the first President of the Chamber of Commerce, and later as M.P., T. B. Horsfall urged

[44] T. Baines, *History of the Commerce and Town of Liverpool* (1852), 828.

[45] Reference to H.C., 1852–3 (310) XXXVIII, quoted, significantly, by the Special Committee on Railway Amalgamation set up by Liverpool Corporation. LRL, Corporation Minutes, 1871–2, p. 667.

better and more competitive services: 'The carriage question is one of the most vital and important on which our attention has been engaged; and while we do not disguise the nature and magnitude of the opposition . . . we shall continue our most zealous exertions to secure success.'[46]

The situation was rendered all the more serious for Liverpool and profitable for the L. & N.W. company by the fact that much of the traffic took the form of transit trade, was growing very rapidly, and by the 1850's appeared to many to be constricted both by the scale of charges and the inadequate facilities provided. Debate on the subject became so heated at one of the meetings of the Liverpool Polytechnic Society in 1853 that the discussion had to be cut short to allow tempers to cool. Braithwaite Poole, after speaking of the growth of railway traffic, had alluded to the lack of facilities at the docksides, and the congestion caused by the 4,000 carts occupying waterfront space.[47] To this Bramley-Moore, Chairman of the Dock Committee, replied in caustic terms. Liverpool was the father of the railway, its Corporation had contributed liberally towards the facade of Lime Street station, but every shipowner and broker had a right to complain of the facilities provided by the railway companies: 'And if the London and North Western railway company, of which Mr. Poole is head of the goods department, will carry goods from Manchester to Liverpool at the same mileage rate as they charge from Manchester to London, they will afford practical proof of their desire to increase and enlarge the commercial facilities of Liverpool.'[48] Called upon to reply, Braithwaite Poole, rather indiscreetly, brought the L. & N.W.'s profits into the discussion. Taking into account the terminal expenses his company cleared only three times as much, he revealed, on goods going from Manchester to London as from Manchester to Liverpool. Braithwaite Poole was, diplomatically, absent from the next meeting, a month later, in February 1853; much to the disappointment of Bramley-Moore, whose 'chief object was to listen to Mr. Braithwaite Poole who was to floor him altogether.'[49] The following month, in March, Braithwaite Poole attended for the discussion of another paper on the same subject, but made it clear that when he expressed his views he did so 'as a rate-payer', and not as Traffic Manager of the L. & N.W. railway company. No further public revelations of the L. & N.W.'s thinking on profit margins and terminal facilities were forthcoming.

The monopoly which had seemed irksome in the 1850's seemed intolerable by the following decade. Although there were signs that a new spirit would presently be introduced, as the Manchester, Sheffield

[46] W. A. Gibson Martin, *A Century of Liverpool's Commerce* (1950), 15.
[47] *Transactions of the Liverpool Polytechnic Society*, 31 January 1853, 29–30.
[48] *Ibid.* 32.
[49] *Ibid.* 28 February 1853, 38.

and Lincolnshire company's planned invasion drew near, all that had actually happened in the late 1850's, despite bitter complaints, had been that the shared monopoly had been slightly tightened by the merger of the Lancashire and Yorkshire and East Lancashire railway companies in 1859. In addition to this, the further growth of imports placed a growing strain upon such facilities as the L. & N.W. continued to provide. Imports of corn increased by 50% in the first six years of the 1860's, to become Liverpool's largest single item. John Patterson, the Liverpool Corn Dealers' spokesman, gave copious evidence to a Royal Commission of 1867, upon the restrictions felt by Liverpool merchants.[50] 'The injury which such excessive charges inflict is not confined to any one branch of trade,' Henry Grainger, of the Liverpool Chamber of Commerce added, 'but is felt with peculiar severity by all who deal in goods of which the value is small in proportion to the weight.' 'The extra charges are so imposed,' he continued, 'as to force the traffic out of its natural channels, and enable the Companies to offer a bounty to divert it into the channels through which it would not otherwise flow. The fact is that the traffic to and from Liverpool frequently overtaxes the means provided for its accommodation, *and the Companies, instead of affording increased traffic, endeavour to divert the traffic by exacting excessive rates.*'[51]

Early in the 1870's the whole matter came to a head with the rumour of an Amalgamation Bill, to combine the Lancashire and Yorkshire and the London and North Western railway companies. This would have made Liverpool unique amongst great cities in being served by only one company. A special committee of the Town Council was set up to examine the proposed merger in 1871; and on 26 January 1872, its chairman, W. B. Forwood, laid a detailed forty page *Report* before the Council. By manipulating terminal charges, and using the leeway which the very liberal maximum rates granted by their statutes allowed, railway companies were free, the *Report* concluded, to 'turn the stream of traffic over such portions of their system as they may elect.' By this means 'the Directors would control the trade of large and important districts through which the lines pass, and would be able to further or retard the prosperity of any particular district or town on their system, to the injury or advantage of others, as the interests of their shareholders would seem to indicate.'[52] In August 1872 W. B. Forwood appeared before a Parliamentary Joint Select Committee, to give evidence in the same vein on the railway rates and provisions—'a grievance for upwards of twenty years.'[53]

[50] H.C., 1867, XXXVIII, Q.222 and App. C.
[51] *Ibid.* App. K. My italics.
[52] LRL, Corporation Minutes, 1871–2, p. 700.
[53] H.C., 1872, XIII, Q.974.

Although the grievance over rates was not entirely removed, accommodation and facilities in Liverpool did get their largest competitive jolt since 1830, when the Brunswick, Central Station, and Huskisson Goods terminal schemes were carried through, by gradual stages, between 1864 and 1880. Once again, as in Manchester, the initiator of change was the Manchester, Sheffield and Lincolnshire railway company under Edward Watkin, with assistance from the Great Northern railway company, and later still from the Midland company; the three operating after 1866 through the agency of the jointly controlled Cheshire Lines Committee. Although these were companies prepared to spend heavily to establish themselves in Liverpool as their western terminal, and to introduce the nearest approach to competitive services between major companies which Liverpool had experienced, the process of forcing an entry into a great city where rivals were already well entrenched was an extremely costly and slow process. The problems encountered in acquiring the land for new station sites are described in Section 3, *infra*, but here it might be relevant to trace briefly the stages by which independent access routes were secured.

In 1861 a small line, four miles in length, was authorised from Garston, south of Liverpool, to a station at Parliament Street (some half-way along the tunnel section leading to No. 4 on the sketch map).[54] In the event, Walter Mar Brydone's more modest approach was adopted, to run to Brunswick passenger and goods station, whence an omnibus service ran to the city centre. Brydone was engineer to the Great Northern railway, which had previously relied entirely upon what Watkin called 'an unhappy alliance' with the L. & N.W. to gain access to Liverpool.[55] Indeed, for a time, although they now had an independent terminal, the Great Northern and the M.S. & L. still relied upon running powers over the London and North Western rails from Manchester to the southern end of their short line at Garston. Then, in July, 1865, the M S & L.'s Liverpool Extension Act was obtained, and the building commenced of a twenty-four mile link between Manchester and Garston, to allow for the development of traffic in a manner not possible whilst the L. & N.W. controlled the permanent way, and to provide a third independent route between Liverpool and Manchester.

Naturally the scheme was opposed vigorously by the L. & N.W. and the Lancashire and Yorkshire railway companies. James Smithells, the L. & Y.'s Traffic Manager, protested, 'If the district between Liverpool and Manchester were filled with lines it would not remove the difficulty we now suffer at Liverpool as regards stations.' 'Is the

[54] At Garston the site of an old tide-mill had been used as a station. J. A. Picton, *op. cit.* (1875 edn.) II, 463.

[55] HLRO, Min., H.L., 1865, 30 June, p. 14, M.S. & L. (Railway Extensions).

difficulty of the Liverpool traffic a station difficulty or a difficulty occasioned through the want of line?—It is entirely a station difficulty.'[56] The Lancashire and Yorkshire, however, experienced some difficulty in arguing consistently here, since they and the L. & N.W. had already opposed, in the previous session, the projected extension of the Garston/ Brunswick line through to the new Central Station, at Ranelagh Street (No. 4 on map); and a mere catalogue of their own proposed spending upon extensions of space at Exchange, Great Howard Street, Sandhills, and Bootle goods and timber sidings, though impressive, was not enough to convince the Select Committee that the station space they intended to make available would be adequate.[57] Edward Watkin's arguments carried more authority. Trade in Liverpool should not, in his opinion, be judged by the current levels to which the American Civil War, and consequent 'cotton famine' had reduced it. 'It is almost an axiom in Liverpool that the trade doubles itself every fifteen years. . . . When this war is fairly over more facilities will be desperately needed.'[58]

The completion of the new Liverpool to Manchester route, and the cutting of the expensive Central Station took a long time. It was not until 1874 that the first C.L.C. expresses were put into service; sixteen per day, and with cushioned seats, even in the third-class compartments. In 1876 hourly expresses covered the 34 miles from Manchester in 45 minutes, and the second and third-class return tickets were reduced from 6s 9d to 6s, and from 5s 3d to 4s 6d, to the *Manchester Guardian*'s satisfaction. The L. & N.W. and the L. & Y. responded by bringing down both their times and their prices to meet those of the C.L.C.[59]

Unfortunately, although the 1870's saw a new spirit of competition in passenger services, the arrival of the C.L.C. did not make the difference which had been hoped for in the carriage of goods. Indeed, when they took into account the heavy expenses of their Huskisson goods station in north Liverpool, and the further expense of building a loop line around the eastern fringe of Liverpool to gain access to Huskisson, the C.L.C. had even more cause than their entrenched rivals to cling to supplementary terminal charges. Huskisson goods station was not opened until 1880, the Central Station until 1874, and the expensive and belated character of their intrusion, together with the quasi-monopolistic nature of the situation in which they now found themselves as newcomers, appear to have made the C.L.C. willing, as far as goods traffic was concerned, to accept the L. & N.W.'s lead on charges and facilities. When further complaints and representations

[56] *Ibid.* 1 July, p. 283.
[57] *Ibid.* 1 July, pp. 278–82, 284–92 (Smithells); 3 July, pp. 274–7 (Cawkwell).
[58] *Ibid.* 30 June, pp. 25–6.
[59] R. P. Griffiths, *The Cheshire Line Railway* (1947), 8–9. The expresses left Manchester from a temporary station behind the Free Trade Hall until Manchester Central station was fully opened in 1880.

from steamship owners, the corn, timber, sugar and cotton merchants' associations, the dock board, and City Council reached their height, in March 1881, at the special meeting called between the Liverpool merchants and the railway companies, it was noteworthy that, although the Chairmen of the Midland, the M.S. & L. and Great Northern railway companies were all present, all remarks were directed to Richard Moon of the L. & N.W. and he replied on behalf of all the railway companies.[60]

Forwood, now Mayor, spoke at length and eloquently, upon the subject of terminal charges, railway ports and the general effect of the railway monopoly upon Liverpool as a great entrepôt. 'While we prosper, we do not prosper to the full extent we have a right to expect, and it is the action of the Railway Companies which deprives us of that benefit. . . . You hold in your hands the very arteries through which the life blood of the city pulsates, and just as in proportion as your grip is tightened or relaxed, so will our trade diminish, remain stagnant, or grow with great and abundant activity.'[61] In the course of the 1870's, Forwood continued, Liverpool's share of the total British grain trade had fallen from 28% to 21%, partly because of preferential rates given by the railway companies to parts where they themselves owned docks: Fleetwood, Barrow, Holyhead, Goole, Garston and Avonmouth. The burden of heavy terminal charges was not excused, as the railway managers alleged, by the vast cost of their stations in Liverpool. 'I would remind you,' Forwood pointed out, 'that the Legislature has always said that the cost of stations was an incident of carriage and not a terminal expense; and terminal expenses have been limited over and over again in Acts of Parliament to the mere labour of loading and unloading the waggons and covering the same.'[62]

Moon rejected all these arguments, pointing once more to the railway companies' need to recoup their heavy investment, and the impossibility of making concessions without running into protest from all other towns in the fares table. Possibly, he concluded, the House of Commons' Committee which was due to consider the question shortly, might take a different view; a sop which provoked the sharp reply from Forwood that the Commons' Committee would have had a greater amount of confidence attached to it if it had not been so largely composed of Railway Directors.[63] LIVERPOOL SNUBBED, ran the headline in the March 1881 editions of the Liverpool *Liberal Review*, a penny weekly. 'The deputation have come home sadder and wiser men.' Their

[60] *Railway Rates and Railway Administration as affecting the Trade of Liverpool* (Liverpool, 1881).
[61] *Ibid.* 13–14.
[63] *Ibid.* 9.
[63] *Ibid.* 32, 39.

visit 'in the hope of finding the Railway Ogre in a propitious mood' had been a waste of money.[64] The newspaper was also dissatisfied with the performance put up a little later, before the Commons' Select Committee in June 1881, by Forwood, John Williamson and E. K. Muspratt. 'What then is the reason that with so strong a case Liverpool has made so poor a show before the Railway Charges Select Committee?', the *Liberal Review* asked. 'Is it that the railway interest itself is so strong in the Dock Board, City Council, and other public bodies that, by working the oracles the secrets of which are so well known to our local social aristocracy, the local committee entrusted with the matter has been induced greatly to drop it?'[65]

Such personal charges seem unfair, taking into account the comprehensive and forceful nature of Forwood's evidence; and they are in any case irrelevant. Far more was required than arguments or personal influence to move the railway companies from their chosen policy. A more effective lever was the threat to use alternative means of transport; and it is ironical that, just as carts had been used in pre-railway days to break the canal monopoly, so in 1881 large carters began to offer to undercut the railways by 25% for horse-drawn loads with a guaranteed minimum of 1,000 tons or more per week, and to give comparable delivery times, for the complete journey, with trans-shipments, from Liverpool dockside to Manchester warehouse.[66]

However, although such an offer showed enterprise on the part of individual local carters, it was not practicable on a sufficiently large scale to disturb the railway managers. But the projected Ship Canal, in spite of all its initial difficulties, produced an immediate change of mood far more effectively than Forwood's representations. In October 1885, charges for leading classes of freight were reduced by 10%, and terminal charges were modified. 'These important changes,' wrote *The Economist*, 'are regarded as an answer to the projected Manchester Ship Canal, and if so the difference between competition rates and the monopoly rates which usually exist is very distinctly shown. . . . But— the great policy of the railways has been to concede nothing except when practically forced to do so.'[67]

3. *The development of railway facilities; a chronological sketch*

In Liverpool, as in Manchester, the earliest terminals, both for passengers and goods, were those associated with the pioneer Lvierpool

[64] *Liberal Review*, 12 March 1881.
[65] *Ibid.* 4 June 1881.
[66] *Railway Rates etc.* (1881), 7. The hypothetical rate offered was 8/- per ton, as against 11/6d by rail.
[67] *The Economist*, 31 October 1885, 1321.

and Manchester railway. In both cities the facilities required were grossly underestimated, but the extension of accommodation was further complicated at Liverpool by technical difficulties arising from the direct eastern approach which had been forced upon George Stephenson. Taken in conjunction with the geographical characteristics of east Liverpool, and the small reserves of power initially possessed by the early locomotives, the result was a strange and inconvenient series of tunnels, stationary engines and rope or cable linkages. Even the short run from Edge Hill to the first passenger station at Crown Street (No. 1 on map), was worked by ropes, as was the longer run to the goods sidings alongside the Mersey at Wapping.

The meagre and disorganised facilities at Crown Street, and its distance from the city centre led to immediate complaints. Angry correspondents writing to the *Liverpool Mercury* spoke of the 'sea of mud and filth in Crown Street, from Oxford Street to the Railway Station', and of the 'posse of individuals calling themselves porters, obnoxious in their eagerness to possess the luggage.'[68] The railway company itself laid on a service of short-stagecoaches to take first-class passengers to Dale Street, where the company's offices, and nine of the principal hotels, were situated; but the delay and expense of this terminal service gave cause for dissatisfaction within the first year.[69] 'The experience of twelve months', the Chairman, Charles Lawrence, reported on 28 September 1831, 'has exhibited the inconvenience and very serious disadvantages of the Railway for Passengers terminating a mile and a half from the centre of business. The delay of 30 minutes in accomplishing the first mile and a half of the journey, and the necessity of resorting to the very imperfect and expensive accommodation of the Omnibuses, have proved the extreme importance of bringing the Railway Carriages to the centre of the Town.'[70]

This was the first emergence of the principle which was to guide other railway companies' urban policies, here and elsewhere, as they prospered. According to the Liverpool and Manchester Directors' calculations the capital charge of constructing a further cable-operated tunnel from Edge Hill to a new site at Lime Street would cost no more to service per year than the omnibuses; i.e. the interest on the £100,000 estimated cost of making the tunnel was set against the £4,000 or £5,000 per year which the omnibus service under contract was costing. Later estimates, laid officially before Parliament in 1832, gave the cost of the tunnel and Lime Street site as £135,000, and this was handsomely exceeded [71] But one could still say that such calculations of the relative

---

[68] *Liverpool Mercury*, 8 and 17 January 1834.

[69] M. D. Greville and G. O. Holt, 'Railway Development in Liverpool', *Railway Magazine* 105 (1959), 77. *The Stranger's Pocket Guide to Liverpool* (Liverpool, 1842)

[70] *Six-monthly Report*, 28 September 1831.

[71] *Six-monthly Report*, 27 July 1836.

costs of omnibus feeder services and railway extensions made good sense in the 1830's; although this was hardly true in the 1840's or 1860's, when so many of the extension lines into the central districts of Britain's cities were executed.

Lawrence had been 'happy to add that the project is approved by the Mayor and Common Council'; and the *Minutes* of the Corporation Finance Committee, together with the *Plans* and *Books of Reference* of the 1832 Bill, tell the rest of the story.[72] The Corporation owned nearly all the 250 properties scheduled, mostly cottages, shops and stables on lease (120 of them to one landlord, Benjamin Branfield); a smithy, a joiner's yard, store yards for timber and coal, the usual 'rope-walk' which open spaces in maritime cities attracted, and a cattle-market, occupied the actual site designated for the terminus itself. Apart from a few sharp words exchanged between the Corporation's Finance Committee and the Liverpool and Manchester company's solicitors, Messrs. Clay and Swift, in February 1832, when the railway company attempted to escape from the condition that the station 'be appropriated to passengers only', the construction of Liverpool's second major station went ahead smoothly and rapidly. One or two complaints, of a trivial nature, found their way into the pages of the *Liverpool Mercury* from the inhabitants of the smarter area around Abercromby Square when the blasting started; 'the glassware on the table and the furniture throughout the room was most sensibly affected', and the residents would 'look for redress to the authors of this annoyance if there is anything like equity in English law.'[73] A letter, a week later from the company, apologised for the 'temporary inconvenience'. By 1836, passengers were 'gliding through the lurid and spectral glare' of the tunnel to Lime Street; descending by gravity, and being hauled back by rope and stationary engine.[74] And this, until the years of railway mania, in the 1840's, remained the sum total of Liverpool's railway provision for passenger trains.

There were rumours that the northern approach line originally projected by Stephenson was to be revived; and a lively correspondence on the subject took place as early as September 1833. To some contributors the projected link seemed to be 'fooling away the capital of the country', the projector to be 'a hungry engineer in want of a job who thinks Lancashire people have lost their wits.' 'I do not recollect any project', wrote one correspondent, 'which seemed to hold out so meagre a prospect of remuneration . . . and I know something of the

[72] HLRO, P & S, B.Ref., 1832, Liverpool and Manchester Railway, LRL Finance Committee 7 September 1831, p. 158, 24 February 1832, p. 222, 2 March 1832, p. 229.
[73] *Liverpool Mercury*, 21 February 1834.
[74] *The Stranger's Pocket Guide* (Liverpool, 1842).

cost of these undertakings.'[75] To others it seemed that north Liverpool, with its brickyards and dilapidated cottages, interspersed with 'disagreeable manufactories, chemical works, oil mills, soda manufactories, charcoal works and etc. with their chimneys and corresponding effluvia' was a neighbourhood which admitted of great improvement.[76] 'Owners of land at the north end of the town,' wrote 'Investigator', 'may readily subscribe for 20, 50 or 100 shares each, not with the view of the benefit they may derive from the undertaking as a railway, but from a shrewd calculation of the advantages that may result from an increase in the value of their property in land and houses by its formation.'[77] It was worth dropping 20% on 50 shares, 'Investigator' pointed out, if it encouraged a project which enabled one to clear £3,000 or £4,000 on property sales. However, the project remained no more than a rumour for twelve years; though it is interesting to see how early and accurately future developments were forecast. The pages of the *Liverpool Mercury* also predicted, in 1833, a communication between the north and south ends of the town via the dock quays—a project which recurred in various forms throughout the next half century—and predicted, in 1834, a station at Ranelagh Street on the site of Mayor Staniforth's mansion—the location adopted by the C.L.C. thirty years later.[78]

In 1845 the group of promotional schemes which were later to merge into the Lancashire and Yorkshire railway company, in the way already described earlier, began to cut their approaches from the north. The Corporation was not directly affected by this new move. Its Finance Committee directed the Surveyor, on 8 August 1845, to give facilities for the Liverpool and Bury company to inspect land and property, but only a mere four hundred pounds-worth of property was made over as a result of the inspection.[79] The northern companies relied far more upon the Earls of Sefton's and of Derby's, Sir Thomas Hesketh's and Lord Skelmersdale's lands on the initial run-in, and upon those of John Shaw Leigh in the more immediate station approaches.[80] The site itself, covering the ground where Plumbe, Lumber and Brixteth Streets met Tithebarn Street, was mostly occupied by poor quality cottages and dwelling houses, together with a couple of pubs. The largest parcel, of 45 properties, was owned by Colonel John Plumbe-Tempest, and Trustees owned a further 20, but mostly the ownership was extremely fragmented; twenty-five proprietors having

[75] *Liverpool Mercury*, 27 September 1833, 19 December 1834.
[76] *Ibid*. 15 August 1834.
[77] *Ibid*. 19 August 1834.
[78] *Ibid*. 6 June 1834. J. A. Picton, *op. cit.* (1875) II, 205–6.
[79] LRL Finance Committee Minutes, 8 August 1845, p. 139, 30 April, 1847, p. 414.
[80] HLRO, Min., H.L., 1846, 7 August, pp. 29–41.

title to the remaining 175 houses and pieces of land scheduled. The half-mile approach route on a viaduct likewise passed through scores of tightly-packed slum houses, mostly owned in batches of half a dozen, frequently by women. Under the circumstances it is not surprising that James Thomson's estimate for the extension line from Great Howard Street to Tithebarn Street came to £297,000 for half a mile.[81]

The Corporation kept watch on these developments, although its Parliamentary Sub-Committee only reported verbally, and no separate book was kept for their reflections until 1866.[82] However, it was much more closely affected, as proprietor, by the L. & N.W. extensions carried out at Lime Street and at Wapping stations, in 1845–8; and by their construction of a new tunnel down to a more northerly goods terminus (the Waterloo station), which was situated very close to the northern companies' projected Great Howard Street station, but between it and the dockside.[83] In all these sites the Corporation had an interest. At Waterloo 18,000 square yards were made over to the L. & N.W. for £82,071, something like £4 10s 0d per square yard; whilst to replace the Borough Gaol—which was scheduled for demolition—the Finance Committee was instructed to buy replacement land further out, in Walton, at £225 per acre, or 1s per square yard.[84] At Lime Street, Joseph Locke's extensions to the station likewise fell on adjacent land owned wholly by the Mayor and Burgesses; over 260 small properties being transferred to the L. & N.W. railway company.

By the early 1850's therefore the situation in Liverpool was one which a contemporary described, not unfairly, as 'an entangled web'. The railway facilities so far provided were all terminal, or 'butt-end' in character. There was no through station, nor any cross-town communication. 'We now vainly regret,' said John Grantham in his paper to the Liverpool Polytechnic Society in 1856, 'that some master mind had not been employed, with a cooler judgment and a more impartial hand'; shortcomings which he now proposed to remedy with a comprehensive and interesting plan of his own.[85] The managers of the major railway companies, however, chose to treat Mr. Grantham's paper as a contribution in similar vein to the one he had read to the Polytechnic Society in 1844 on 'Land Sailing Machines'.[86] And there was, indeed,

[81] HLRO, P & S, B.Ref., 1846, Liverpool and Bury Railway. The Gt. Howard St. station, originally intended for the terminus, was reclassified to goods.

[82] LRL Finance Committee Minutes, 3 January 1845, p. 34, 2 May 1845, p.88, 2 January 1846, p. 206.

[83] LRL Council Books, 29 October 1845, p. 43. The site may be seen on the sketch map.

[84] LRL Finance Committee Minutes, 27 August 1847, p. 464.

[85] J. Grantham, 'Railways within the Borough of Liverpool', *Trans. of Liv. Poly. Soc.* (1856), 204.

[86] *Ibid.* (1844), 38.

something of the visionary and crank about Grantham's Central Station and High-Level through-communication; though one might well have said the same thing about Charles Pearson's similar proposals in London. Whereas Pearson's scheme was realised, in modified form, in the late 1850's and early 1860's, Grantham's remained a curiosity; unless one ascribes to it the inspiration for the small-scale elevated railway opened in Liverpool in 1893.[87]

In the 1860's the chief interest in the development of Liverpool's urban railways lay in the gradual approach of independent companies from the south. At the time Grantham wrote, 1856, they were already visible 'wending their way into the town . . . but unwilling even to enter the suburbs, and terminating about 5 miles from the exchange—the directors probably waiting the turn of events to enable them to complete their work, not a little deterred from their undertaking by uncertainty as to the best way of entering the town, and the enormous expenses it will involve.'[88] The companies concerned, the Great Northern and the Manchester, Sheffield and Lincolnshire railway companies, were indeed concerned with the tactics and (as well they might be) with the expense of making a new breach in the built-up area, but they were not deterred. Stimulated, in the ways described elsewhere, by the intervention of John Fowler and Waring Bros., and by the formation of the C.L.C. alliance, the original plan for a modest station at Brunswick Dock and connecting omnibus service to James Street, was replaced, even before the Brunswick station was opened in 1864, by a far more ambitious scheme to drive a mile and a half nearer the city centre.[89]

The first version of the Liverpool Central Station and Railway scheme was submitted as early as the 1861–2 session by W. M. Brydone, with an estimated expenditure of £400,000. In 1864 the plan and estimate were revised by Brydone and Fowler, an Act secured, and work begun upon the tunnel and new terminal at Ranelagh Street.[90] As already mentioned, the site itself was owned partly by the Corporation, partly by Thomas Brassey; but on the approach route over 460 parcels of property were affected, including 135 houses officially designated as 'occupied by the labouring classes' under Standing Order 191.[91] Almost all of these were owned in small batches; and one can well understand James Allport's exasperation when he came to report the final cost in 1874: 'in round figures, £6,000,000' for the whole Central Station project.[92]

[87] C. E. Box, *The Liverpool Overhead Railway 1893–1956* (1959), 15.
[88] J. Grantham, *loc. cit.* 206.
[89] M. D. Greville and G. O. Holt, *loc. cit.* 198.
[90] 27 and 8 Vic., c. 215; 29 and 30 Vic., c. 294; 30 and 31 Vic., c. 207.
[91] HLRO, Demolition Statement, 1864, Liverpool Central Station Railway.
[92] HLRO, Min., H.C., 1874, 28 April, pp. 3–4.

Even so, the link between north and south, which Grantham had urged, had not been achieved. Several bills were deposited in the 1870's with the further object in view of getting *through* Liverpool. 'I think Mr. Fowler has had one or two schemes, and other engineers have projected schemes, and the West Lancashire Company have been twice to Parliament.'[93] The C.L.C. had been prepared to share the £1,500,000 or so of additional expenses to be incurred for a subterranean through-route by the West Lancashire company, but the Commons' committee, dissatisfied both with the effect further tunnelling might have in the central districts, and with the shaky finances of the West Lancashire company, threw the Bill out in 1872.[94] Since the C.L.C. had already bought extensive lands for a new goods station in north Liverpool at Huskisson, the only alternative presented when the through-railway finally miscarried was to begin construction of a peripheral scheme, the North Liverpool Extension railway, in 1874.[95]

There were, in fact, further objections to tunnelling for main-line trains through city centres, apart from those of expense and public inconvenience. Although the approach to the C.L.C. Central Station at Ranelagh Street (No. 4 on map) had been made with steam working in mind, and designed in short, ventilated sections, the result was only a marginal improvement on the cable working still used, until 1870 at Lime Street, 1895 and 1896 on the Waterloo and Wapping goods tunnels.[96] Obviously ventilation was even more critical on the underground steam sections intended for passenger traffic. And, indeed, the Mersey Railway Company's plan to make itself an attractive promotional line for C.L.C. purchase, by forming an underground linkage between the new C.L.C. Central Station and Birkenhead, succumbed to these technical difficulties. To cope with the smoke produced by locomotives toiling up gradients of 1 in 27 the company installed huge steam-driven fans which, in the words of M. D. Greville and G. O. Holt, 'not only expelled the fumes but absorbed the profits of the undertaking.'[97]

4. *Summary and general considerations*

It will be clear from what has already been said under other headings that Liverpool was, to an unusual extent amongst Britain's major cities, held in the monopolistic, or quasi-monopolistic, grip of a few large railway companies. The question still remains as to why such a

[93] *Loc. cit.* p. 13.
[94] R. P. Griffiths, *op. cit.* 12.
[95] HLRO, Min., H.C., 1874, 29 April, pp. 5–9 (Underdown).
[96] M. D. Greville and G. O. Holt, *loc. cit.* 268–69.
[97] *Ibid.* 270.

wealthy and successful maritime city, handling almost half of Britain's exports by the mid-nineteenth century, should fail to secure better and more competitive railway provisions. Partly it was due to accidents in the timing and promotion of schemes: the firm hold established in the first fifteen years by the alliance between the Grand Junction and Liverpool and Manchester railway companies; the unequal and complementary nature of the Lancashire and Yorkshire company's services; and the belated and expensive nature of the C.L.C.'s intrusion in the 1860's and 1870's. One might almost say that the moment the projected alliance between the Great Western railway company and the Grand Junction railway company fell through, in 1846, and the broad-gauge Great Western was banished to the Birkenhead side of the Mersey, the chances of keen competition were reduced.

Another ground of explanation would be concerned with the particular position Liverpool occupied in the railway network. Its traffic tended to be terminal in nature. As Wilfred Smith has already stressed, Liverpool was mainly a trans-shipment point from land to sea, and not primarily a link in land communications; and this discontinuity may help to explain the relative absence of trunk route rivalries.[98] There is, however, a third reason for Liverpool's failure to escape from the trammels of monopoly; less obvious but no less important than those already mentioned. Liverpool's prosperity at the beginning of the nineteenth century already depended to a marked degree upon the successful establishment of one form of monopoly—its docks—and to maintain a closed dock policy whilst throwing the interior rail linkage open to wholesale competition was to pull in two different directions. The railway monopoly was, in a sense, no more than a reflection of the restrictive dock policies which were pursued, certainly until 1857, and arguably until the 1880's.

The Mayor, W. B. Forwood, summed up Liverpool's position at the railway rates meeting, on 8 March 1881, in the following words.

'We are not a manufacturing town, or a town having any mineral resources. Our prosperity is entirely dependent upon our close proximity to the great manufacturing centres of Lancashire, Yorkshire, Staffordshire and Shropshire.

'Liverpool is simply a vast entrepôt, depending for her prosperity entirely upon her facilities and the cheapness of her communication with the interior.'[99]

Such a prosperity may, in fact, be far more firmly based than appears at first glance; but there is little doubt that to contemporaries there seemed to be something circumstantial and insecure about so rapid a

[98] W. Smith, *Merseyside: A Scientific Survey* (British Assoc., 1953), 189. J. A. Patmore, 'The Railway Network of Merseyside', *Transactions and Papers*, Instit. of Brit. Geog., 29 (1961), 231 *et seq.*

[99] *Railway Rates etc.* (1881), 5–6.

growth unsupported by directly productive industry. Fewer than five *per cent* of Liverpool's population in mid-century were engaged in industry, and this was reflected in the city's social structure.[100] Instead of a lower class composed of factory workers, and a civic governing group drawn from the ranks of the manufacturers (as in the industrial towns), the working class in Liverpool consisted largely of seamen or of unskilled and casually employed dock labourers, and the wealthy civic élite consisted primarily of merchants. Something of this singular character was echoed in the old jibe about 'Manchester men and Liverpool gentlemen', or in the counter-jibes of Manchester's popular songs of the 1820's, alluding to the parasitical nature of employment in Liverpool.[101] At a different level it can be heard again in the opinions of serious writers on Liverpool's history, like Thomas Baines.

There can, at all events, be no doubt that contemporary citizens watched Liverpool's privileges with jealous eyes. In 1839 when Poulett Thompson's Bill to extend the privilege of Bonded Warehouses to inland towns was put forward, the proposed change caused an immediate and nervous reaction from the Liverpool Association of Land and Warehouse owners; and the matter came up for earnest discussion in the Council on 3 and 8 July.[102] Whether or not valid grounds for them existed, there were fears that Liverpool might, under a régime of Free Trade and open docks, become no more than an outport for Manchester. The arrival of the railways presented the mercantile community with the same spectre in still more alarming form.

There is evidence for this in the attitudes expressed over two railway schemes which would have completely changed the conditions of competition in the 1850's. The first, which remained merely a subject for discussion, was John Grantham's Strand Street project of 1856; the second, which was formally presented to Parliament and approved by them, was J. M. Rendel's £400,000 plan for the development of rival docks on the Birkenhead side of the Mersey, with direct railway access. Both met with severe criticism and the Rendel scheme with determined opposition, for the same reason—that they appeared to reduce the local benefits deriving from warehousing and trans-shipment, by drastically improving railway access from the interior directly to the Mersey.

Grantham's plan was for a high-level station, to be situated near the Customs House at Strand Street, which would both give an internal through-route for goods and passengers, combined with direct access to the docks, waterside tracks, and direct loading by steam cranes.[103] Such a

[100] T. Baines, *Liverpool in 1859* (1859), 4–6.
[101] George Chandler, *op. cit.* 353.
[102] LRL Council Books, 3 and 8 July 1839, pp. 212–4.
[103] Originally it was intended as a dock railway, but later grew to a proposed main-line station. J. Grantham, *Trans. of Liv. Poly. Soc.* (1853), 28–9, (1856), 209–11.

system, he argued, was not impracticable; and in this he received support from an unexpected quarter. Samuel Holme, the Mayor, who was present, had noted something of the kind working at Cardiff, and commented, 'It is certainly a matter of surprise, that when steam is employed in making clogs and cutting nails, it should not be employed in working the Liverpool docks.' Further, more outspoken, support came from Alderman Bennett, and from the L. & N.W. Goods Manager, Braithwaite Poole. Poole spoke very critically of the current inadequacy of the dockside rail or tram-way system, 'suitable merely for earth moving', and compared it with the more efficient systems operating at Hull, Dundee and Gloucester. Progress was most rapid, he asserted, when the dock estates were united with the railways. Alderman Bennett made explicit the implied corollary, 'Let the railway be made and both docks and warehouses be made subservient to it.' 'How many great points had been missed', he added, 'through the want of unity amongst the railway companies, and through the unwillingness of the Dock Committee to work in concert with them?' Since Grantham's plan had first been published, he added, 'How many buildings have been erected solely for the purpose of preventing that plan being carried out?' In particular (as Grantham specified during the discussion) the Dock Committee's projected warehouses at Princes' Dock 'would have stopped the railway as effectively as if a pyramid had been placed there.'[104]

These radical views did not pass unchallenged. J. B. Smith, a member of the Dock Committee, flatly stated that in his opinion the town was not prepared for a high level railway; Bramley-Moore, the ex-Chairman of the Dock Committee, attacked the L. & N.W.'s own record. But it fell to James Newlands, the Borough Engineer, and Councillor James Holme, to make the most damaging criticisms of the scheme. Taking six ships at random, Holme showed that their cargoes required division amongst seventy-five different consignees; one vessel alone, the *Mary Cannon* had a mixed cargo to be divided on arrival between nineteen consignees. Grantham answered this objection by arguing that a hundred and fifty railway trucks could remove the cargo of the *Mary Cannon*, and at the same time provide convenient units for sorting out consignments. He had no reply, however, to the other objection to his scheme: that it 'is only suitable for the traffic from the docks to the interior of the country and *vice versa*, and is not suitable to Liverpool. It has nothing to do with Liverpool and is, in fact, a *Manchester* railway.'[105]

The same views were given a public airing again, during the final crisis in the Dock Committee's affairs, in 1856–7, which culminated in

[104] *Ibid.* 10 March 1856, 212–6.
[105] *Ibid.* 14 March 1853, 40 *et. seq.* 28 February 1853, 37.

the dissolution of the direct link between the Corporation of Liverpool and the Dock Estate. At the height of this crisis, Parliament and the country were treated to the extraordinary spectacle of a combination between the Town Clerk of Manchester and the Great Western railway company to promote a Bill to break Liverpool's exclusive control over its own docks.[106]

There were two principal objections to the monopoly control which Liverpool had managed to retain over the docks in the Mersey. The scale upon which dues were levied was criticised as a tax upon imported raw materials and exported goods; and further resentment was caused by the fact that out of these dock dues, an annual payment averaging £120,000, known as the Town Dues, was made to the Corporation of Liverpool, and used by them to lighten the incidence of local rates. 'Robber barons' was the epithet Harriet Martineau used to describe the Liverpool Corporation.[107]

Since the Great Western railway company was excluded from Liverpool by the actions of its rivals, and the City of Manchester was paying a good portion of Liverpool's dock dues, they formed natural allies in the task of monopoly-breaking.[108] And although—as counsel for the Corporation of Liverpool argued—there was no precedent in statute law for the transfer of property from the hands of a body which had not been charged with specific mismanagement, this is precisely what was authorised by the Mersey Conservancy and Docks Act of 1857. The old Town Dues were commuted to a lump sum of £1,500,000 payable to the Corporation of Liverpool, and a new Mersey Docks and Harbour Board set up, with the obligation to take over management of the docks on both sides of the river, and to complete J. M. Rendel's scheme for direct rail access at Birkenhead; 'in appearance,' wrote Brian D. White, 'a triumph of outside interests over Liverpool as a whole.'[109] In fact the course events took, as White recounts, were to reveal that it was a constitutional triumph only. The dock dues were not substantially reduced, nor was the scheme for rail access carried out on anything like the scale contemplated.

The dock users, and the railway companies serving Liverpool, found answers to the problem over the next generation in their separate ways. The answer to monopoly dock dues, as to monopoly railway charges, was the unique Manchester Ship Canal; and it is noteworthy that the

[106] 'In the heat of that memorable conflict all that Manchester appeared to thirst for was the humiliation of Liverpool', *Daily Post*, 12 August 1867.

[107] There is an interesting short account in B. D. White, *A History of the Corporation of Liverpool, 1835–1914* (1951), 71–4.

[108] *The Corporation of Manchester: an Historical Record* (Manchester, 1894), 9–11. 'Liverpool Corporation desire to lessen the local charges or rates of Liverpool at the expense of the Dock Estate'.

[109] B. D. White, *op. cit.* 78–9.

capital and impulse for this scheme came entirely from Manchester.[110] The Liverpool docks were effectively by-passed, or exposed to competition. The railway companies serving Liverpool turned increasingly to the development of their own ports, where the installations, though more modest, were their own creations, and gave the direct access which Rendel's and Grantham's schemes had promised, but failed to achieve. Liverpool remained unchallenged as the largest West Coast port, but her proportion of the United Kingdom trade declined from the 45% achieved in 1857. The smaller harbours, to which some of Liverpool's trade was siphoned off by the railway companies, had inferior positions compared with the Mersey, and their facilities were often exiguous, hardly more than marine equivalents of a railway goods station. These drawbacks were offset, however, by the gains which came from direct control of the docks' operation and scale of charges, and from the absence of established and wealthy mercantile patriciates with strong local interests.

[110] A. Redford, *Manchester Merchants and Foreign Trade* (Manchester 1956), II, 165–6, 184.

VIII

Glasgow

1. *The property ownership pattern*

THE original patterns of landownership in Glasgow, as in London, were substantially laid down during the Reformation. At that time many of the 'rentallers', who had managed ecclesiastical lands in Glasgow, became their feuars, or permanent owners. Some of these families had acted as rentallers for a long time before 1560—a reputed two hundred years in the case of the Andersons of Stobcross—but after they secured full title to their suburban estates the way was opened to wider enterprise, in which overseas trade, land ownership and civic office were inextricably combined. The Andersons, the Bells of Cowcaddens, and the Campbells of Blythswood interchanged the office of provost amongst themselves twenty-two times in the second half of the seventeenth century.[1] And they, together with Walter Gibson (another member of a family of ex-rentallers turned provosts), the clients to whom portions of their estates were sold, and the merchants, newly rich in overseas trade, came to form a system of social 'sets' which bears more than a passing resemblance to that in Liverpool. Matthew Crawfurd, Robert Bogle, Alexander Oswald, John Orr of Barrowfield all bought ex-rentallers' land; and the Wills and Sederunt Books of Bogle, Ingram and Carrick show the typical pattern of their holdings—a few ships, or shares in ships, a share in one of the early banking companies, in a printfield or an overseas plantation, some urban tenements, and a landed estate.[2]

The emergence of these prosperous merchants and *rentiers*, in the late seventeenth and the eighteenth centuries, provided the most

[1] *Regality Club* (Glasgow, 1893), 109–11. (1912), 187–8, GRL B475256.
[2] GRL, Bogle Papers, Nos. 13 and 86. Baillie's Institution Library, *The Sederunt Book of Archibald Ingram's Trustees*. J. O. Mitchell, *Old Glasgow Essays* (Glasgow, 1905), 164 *et. seq.*

characteristic feature in the pattern of Glasgow's landownership, and the names of Bell, Crawfurd, Oswald and Campbell of Blythswood, can still be seen on the sketch map at the time the railways arrived. There was no exact equivalent to landed aristocracy or gentry, of the type common in the major English cities, except perhaps in the persons of the Maxwell family. They had been very considerable landowners south of the river for many years (a Sir George Maxwell had allegedly been

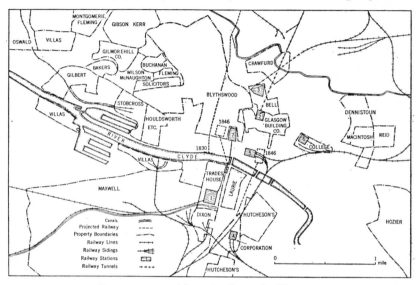

Property ownership and railways in Glasgow.

bewitched in 1677); and by the early nineteenth century their holdings had been increased by the purchase of the Town Moor.[3]

Sir John Maxwell, and Sir William Stirling-Maxwell, adopted an attitude similar to that of Lord Calthorpe in Birmingham, whose estate their own in some ways resembled. Parts of it, at any rate, were laid out in parkland and studded with villas; some three hundred by the end of the century, constituting the nucleus of the prosperous inner suburbs of west Pollokshields.[4] Sir John Maxwell opposed the Glasgow, Paisley, Kilmarnock and Ayr and the Glasgow, Paisley and Greenock railway companies' plan for a joint station in 1837 (No. 1 on sketch map). One acre of his land was to be taken for the Cook Street depot, and his

---

[3] Andrew McCallum, *Pollokshaws, Village and Burgh* (Paisley, 1925), 17.

[4] George Martin, *Map of the City of Glasgow* (1842), shows the original site for villa development, just east of the name 'Maxwell' on the sketch map. The actual development was south of the G.P.G. railway line. John Bartholomew, *Map of Glasgow* (P.O. Directory, 1897–8).

estate traversed; but the estate itself was at such an early stage of development that only a map of the 'intended improvement' could be offered as evidence. 'There is nothing of the kind on it at the moment', the G.P.K. & A.'s valuers were able to claim; and Maxwell was neither able to prevent the railway, nor to obtain a particularly high price for his land.[5] The severance produced by the railway was somewhat reduced in extent, but made still more concentrated in effect, by John Miller's selection of a route close to the Ardrossan canal (see sketch map). Maxwell's counsel was equally unsuccessful a few years later when the Glasgow Harbour scheme, to provide access to the river, was projected northwards through his land. Once more the plans were produced of streets 'laid out ready to be made'; and once more the rejoinder was made 'they are invisible yet.'[6] Thomas Binnie, the builder and valuer, testified to the good quality of the houses which had already been built, but the Select Committee took the view that this was a matter which could better be met by compensation than by rejecting the whole scheme. However, the Maxwells did not lose absolutely by the arrival of the railways, for when the small Glasgow, Barrhead and Neilston Direct railway was formed, Sir John Maxwell was sufficiently pre-disposed by what he had experienced, to join the company, alter the avenue to Pollock House, and specify that trains should pass 'by or through or near Pollokshaws'.[7] The Barrhead and Neilston railway was too small to survive for long, but in 1849 the shareholders' problems were solved when the Caledonian railway company took it over, by means of a 999 year lease at a guaranteed $3\frac{1}{2}\%$ to $4\frac{1}{5}\%$. Twenty years later, when the Caledonian put forward its Central station scheme their counsel was able to announce, 'We have agreed with Sir William Stirling Maxwell . . . and I think we are exceedingly fortunate, going through this valuable property, where the property added to the engineering costs more than a million of money, that we have no opponent.'[8]

With the exception only of the Campbells of Blythswood, most of the other large personal owners of land came to an arrangement sooner or later with the railway companies, withdrew opposition, and took their compensation; or they even, like the Maxwells, chose the opportunity to invest and, in course of bargaining, to specify that certain accommodation works, or provisions of intermediate stations should be made on their land if they should require it in the future. J. G. Oswald, the proprietor of Scotstoun (see sketch map) was one of these. He was himself resident at Menton in France for most of the time, and his rental was

---

[5] H.L., 1837, III, 30 June, p. 149, 4 July, p. 207.
[6] H.C., 1846 (267) XII, Q.1136.
[7] Andrew McCallum, *op. cit.* 173–4.
[8] BTHR PYB 1/579, 6 May, p. 18.

drawn from the thirteen tenants who farmed his 930 acre estate; but he had declared the intention of breaking the entail upon his land and feuing it for building purposes.[9] Consequently the argument between himself and the North British railway company in the 1860's and 1870's dwelt upon the provision of accommodation works and a station as much as upon the question of compensation. What would happen to the projected roads on his estate which the N.B. line would cross? Was the railway company prepared to build bridges for non-existent roads? Mr. Oswald would not merely require this, but (his solicitors made clear) he would require a station to be built at a point of his choosing, 'traffic or no traffic', to develop his estate. Although not prepared to commit itself to indefinite accommodation works and bridges, the railway company offered to undertake to open a station in the Jordanhill area when twenty-five feus had been completed; but when Oswald turned down even this offer, the line was cut through his land, and argument left to the solicitors.[10]

Amongst the other landowners, varying shades of enthusiasm for the railways can be observed. In general, the most eager to assent, or to subscribe, were those whose land was least likely, for various reasons, to suffer from the effects of intersection or deterioration: perhaps because it was further out of town, where the railways had more room for manoeuvre, and could skirt estates if need arose; perhaps because it was off the main route, or even more centrally situated than the terminal itself; or because it was already industrial in character, and therefore with little to lose in the way of amenity and much to gain from linkages. Examples of all these attitudes can be found amongst Glasgow property owners.

It is noticeable, in the first place, that landowners who were further out, and could be avoided more easily if they were unreasonable, tended to assent more readily and to bargain less closely over the price. Indeed the *Books of Reference* for the early lines record, in M.S., favourable extracts from the owners' letters. Similarly, those whose estates lay off the routes either adopted a neutral attitude, like James and Alexander Dennistoun or James Hozier (see sketch map), or gave their active support as investors, like Dugald Bannatyne of the Glasgow Building Company, or John Fleming of Clairmont.

Examples of the type of landowner more concerned with *industrial* than residential development are provided by the Houldsworth and Dixon estates (see sketch map). Henry Houldsworth's concerns lay

[9] *Regality Club* (1893), 95.
[10] G.U. Collection Solicitors' Papers, Box 2, Glasgow, Yoker and Dalmuir Railway.
[11] HLRO, B.Ref., 1837, Edinburgh and Glasgow Railway. 'I welcome anything which will give greater facility in feuing.'

chiefly with cotton mills, and with the Anderston Foundry, but he also held villa land at Cranstonhill; and William Dixon was primarily a colliery owner and ironmaster, but also a substantial landowner south of the river.[12] During the early stages of railway building, in the 1830's and 1840's, until others took up the railway interest, industrialists of this type lent their capital and assistance even more wholeheartedly than their fellow landowners—the speculative builders, solicitors and *rentiers*. Even Dugald Bannatyne—though he invested personally, and his legal firm A. & D. J. Bannatyne handled more railway business than any in Scotland—could not quite equal the record of William Dixon, who contributed to the projected Glasgow, Airdrie and Monklands Junction railway, was the sole proprietor of the small Pollok and Govan line, and was the originator and the largest shareholder in the Clydesdale Junction railway.[13] Possibly Dixon's view of a railway's function might be criticised as rather narrow in conception. Like most industrialists he thought of the railways in terms of minerals, raw materials, heavy manufactured goods—indeed, virtually as an extension of his colliery and ironworks. However, there could be no doubt concerning the energy and effectiveness of his part in promoting railway building. Although small, his two small lines were incorporated into a larger network by the Caledonian railway company, which bought them up for a 6% annuity on an assumed capital of £450,000.[14] A generous price, not uninfluenced by the land sales Dixon also made to the Caledonian company in connection with their South Side station (No. 4 on sketch map.)[15]

Amongst the landowners whose attitude towards the railways was less enthusiastic, may be counted the Lauries, William McLean and Moses Stevens, W. S. S. Crawfurd, Mrs. Graham Gilbert and the Campbells of Blythswood (see sketch map). David and James Laurie had laid out, between 1800 and 1830, an estate of high social pretensions between the two bridges, south of the river; and the effect of railway encroachments upon the area has been discussed in some detail elsewhere.[16] After James Laurie's death, his nine heirs and successors were even less capable than he had been of repelling the railways and maintaining the intended elegance of Abbotsford Place.[17] Similarly at Heatheryhall, Clydeville, Cessnock Bank, Mavis Bank, Green Bank and Plantation ('villas' on sketch map), south of the river, the new docks, and the General Terminus railways company's yards and coaling

---

[12] *Memoirs and Portraits of 100 Glasgow Men* (Glasgow, 1886) I, 166.
[13] *Ibid.* I, 26, 105.
[14] H.L., 1847, XL, 26 April, p. 123.
[15] HLRO, Min., H.C., 1846, 7 July, p. 155, S.C. on Caledonian Railway.
[16] *Infra* Ch. 10, sec. 1, and John R. Kellett, 'Property Speculators and the Building of Glasgow', *Scot. Jour. of Pol. Econ.*, VIII (1961), 211–32.
[17] HLRO, P & S, B.Ref., 1864, Union Railway, Railway No. 1.

quay, produced a striking change of character. In the 1820's the area had been described as 'snug' by contemporaries; 'Mavisbank, Green-bank, Plantation, the very names seem to breathe a spirit of retired quiet.'[18] Such a spirit proved very fragile in the railway age, and the only remedy for these smaller proprietors was, like Laurie's successors, to make the most they could out of the financial compensation.

North of the river the entailed estate of W. S. S. Crawfurd lay in the path of the Buchanan Street and Queen Street termini (Nos. 3 and 2 on sketch map). At first his dealings showed a certain ineptness or ingen-uousness. The Glasgow and Garnkirk railway company, for example, was able to buy 16 acres from him for a mere £807 in 1836; and the Edinburgh and Glasgow railway company only paid £3,000 for his Colston and Broomhill lands.[19] His estate spread along the southern bank of the Forth-Clyde canal, with a smaller extension to the north of it. It mostly comprised arable land, Broomhill Nursery and other market gardens, a coal depot and a few houses. There were no covenants restricting land use, and, indeed, the area was already taking on an industrial character at the time of George Martin's map (1842).[20] One might well have expected a person on whose land soda and chemical works were being built to welcome railway linkages; but Crawfurd's name does not appear on the *Subscription Contract* of the Edinburgh and Glasgow company (1837, No. 2 on sketch map), though it does appear in the Lists of Dissents from landowners.[21] It may well be that Crawfurd, and his factor Gilbert Kennedy, intended to develop the property for residential uses and wished to keep the railways out. This is the impression one gathers from the Private Act of Parliament which Crawfurd obtained in 1842, to enable him to apply funds from the entailed estate to lay it out for feuing, and to purchase further parcels 'to enable Mr. Crawfurd to continue his plans of feuing and to make other improvements for the benefit of the estate.'[22] It might also be possible—and this hypothesis is complementary rather than alternative to the one just put forward—that Crawfurd's feuing plans were intended to establish a new platform for the selling price of his lands.

Mrs. Graham Gilbert (see map), whose lands lay to the west, also adopted procedures to enhance the price commanded by her land near the North British railway company's goods terminal at Stobcross.

[18] Owned by Messrs. Blair, Hamilton and McLean. *Memoirs and Portraits etc.* (1886) I, 35.

[19] 'The Milton Estate of William Crawfurd', GRL, *Lanarkshire Topographical Collections*, V, 8–9.

[20] George Martin, *Map of the City of Glasgow* (1842). S. G. Checkland, 'The British Industrial City as History: the Glasgow Case', *Urban Studies* I (1964), 46.

[21] HLRO, B.Ref., Books of Dissent, Subscription Contract, 1837, Edinburgh and Glasgow Railway.

[22] 5 & 6 Vic. c. 36.

Since the complete set of solicitor's records have survived for this line it is possible to trace in unusual local detail the course of litigation, and the issues raised. Mrs. Gilbert, though married, held land in her own right, which she had inherited under strict entail from her uncle. Her plan to assure what she considered the full value of her land was complicated and timed to the last hour.

The land itself was, indeed, of great intrinsic value, two miles only from the Exchange and ¾ mile from Finnieston, where the built-up area stopped. It commanded the very entrance to the large site secured by the N.B. railway company for their riverside terminus and marshalling yard. Between these Stobcross/Overnewton lands already bought by the N.B. railway company and the Kelvin lay Mrs. Gilbert's two decaying mansion houses, Yorkhill and Thornbank, with a 75 acre estate attached. She elected to by-pass the arbitration procedures laid down and to call a Jury Trial to settle her claim.[23]

There were several strings to her bow. First, the land was laid out in a series of elegant crescents and streets, none existing, except on paper and as imaginary lines crossing her rambling property. Secondly, it was contended by her agents, her land, if not devoted to these purposes, would undoubtedly receive very profitable employment before long for an extension of the dock facilities already projected or commenced at Stobcross.

The 'elegant estate' argument, in this unrestricted and increasingly industrial riverside area, was not taken very seriously by either side; but carefully-drawn plans of the streets and houses were submitted and are preserved amongst the solicitor's papers. Counsel for the N.B. railway company contemptuously swept aside arguments based on this plea. 'As to the noise of the engines, the locality is one so surrounded by Shipbuilding Yards, Boiler Works and Manufactories of every description, producing incessant noise, that any injury arising from this cause will be hardly perceptible.' 'The Railway is no doubt visible from the ground; but in a locality of that kind, in place of being an injury, it will be a benefit, by shutting out the view of the ship-building yards.' The second plea, that docks would soon be formed, was opposed with more careful and detailed evidence led by the N.B. railway company. Quoting the reports, adducing the personal testimony of Mr. Reith, the General Manager of the Clyde Trust, and producing voluminous figures for the growth of maritime traffic, they attempted to show that it would take 30 years before Mrs. Gilbert's lands were urgently required for dock facilities; and, even then, 14–20s per square yard would be the utmost she could realise.

[23] The four paragraphs which follow are based upon the solicitors' Briefs, Memoranda for Witnesses, Valuations and Reports and Statements and Claims for the Yorkhill Jury Trial. G.U. Coll. Sol. Papers, and John R. Kellett, *JTH*, VI (1964), 234–5.

However, Mrs. Gilbert outmanoeuvred the N.B. railway company by a third plea, which they themselves admitted, 'is most ingeniously framed.' She began negotiations with the Clyde Trustees late in 1865, a year after the railway plans had been authorised. In October 1865 her agent visited the railway company's solicitors to find out what line was intended and persuaded their surveyor to mark it in pencil on an ordnance map. On 6 and 18 December 1865 and on 3 January 1866 (the very day the notice of compulsory purchase was served) she signed missives with the Clyde Trustees selling her river-front property at 25s per square yard, together with 'the whole land to the South of whatever line the Railway Company may adopt up to the most Northern limits of deviation shown on the Parliamentary Plans.' She then argued that these missives of sale 'fix conclusively the value to the claimant of the whole land up to the most Northern limits of deviation.' The Clyde Trustees themselves expressed dismay at the turn affairs had taken. They had not intended, they said, either to commit themselves to a purchase of indefinite size or to establish a precedent the N.B. railway company should follow.

The railway company attempted to argue that the price was 'an advantage which might have accrued to her if the company had chosen to deviate northwards; but if they did not choose the Claimant has not been deprived of anything to which she has a right', but Mrs. Gilbert was awarded £42,791 for the 9,500 square yards required and adjacent deterioration, nearly three times the railway company's offer.

The Campbells of Blythswood, who owned 590 acres of central land, were the most extensive and successful of all Glasgow's central land-owners and the only proprietors sufficiently powerful and well situated to defeat the railways.[24] Their estate, which had been acquired by Colin Campbell, a provost in the seventeenth century, was entailed in 1739; the entail was broken and Trustees set up in 1792.[25] Under Major Archibald Campbell the feuing of lands had proceeded rapidly until, by 1830, 457 acres had been feued under strict covenants forbidding any nuisances or industrial uses, and Blythswood was beginning to attract central business users. This was reflected in extremely high rentals, £74,000 *per annum* by 1830.[26] Consequently when the Edinburgh, Glasgow and Leith railway, conceived by Grainger and Miller, proposed to tunnel under Main Street and Blythswood Square to reach a butt-end terminal at Broomielaw, on the north bank of the river (see sketch map), the Blythswood Trustees were able to argue successfully

---

[24] Robert Renwick, *Extracts from the Records of The Burgh of Glasgow* (Glasgow, 1916), VII, 679.

[25] *Glasgow, Past and Present* (Glasgow, 1884), I, 316–20.

[26] The Blythswood Trustees against the Edinburgh, Glasgow and Leith Railway (1830), GRL, *Miscellaneous Railway Pamphlets*, B53157.

that the whole capital of the railway company was insufficient to compensate for intrusion into such central land. The project was defeated, not merely because the railway was small, under-capitalised, and extremely early, but for more lasting reasons. The West of Scotland Junction terminus, planned in 1846 to link the Edinburgh and Glasgow and the G.P.K. & A. railways, also intended to tunnel through Blythswood, this time under Wellington Street (see sketch map); and there could be no doubt that this scheme, with two established companies behind it, was adequately financed.[27] Five acres had even been purchased in advance of the scheme to reserve an unbuilt space [28] Yet this scheme also folded up, for reasons discussed below. By the time the Caledonian railway company reconnoitred the Blythswood Holme station scheme again, in 1866, the few acres of Campbell land required, the approaches, compensation, and engineering works, would have cost a total of £3,000,000; and so the alternative Central station (No 7 on map) was sketched out by George Cunningham and John Hawkshaw [29]

The remaining proprietors were corporate bodies; and they performed a larger rôle in Glasgow, during the period of railway building, than in any of the other major cities There was one canal company, the Eglinton-Ardrossan, which was taken over and used (as in Birmingham) for its approach routes and basin [30] Three property copartneries had been formed: the Glasgow Building Company, which dated back to the 1780's, and played a key rôle in the building of the central commercial and administrative district; and two speculative mid-nineteenth century foundations, the Gilmorehill land company and the Stobcross proprietors, both of which figured largely in the transactions of the Union and the North British railway companies in the 1860's The old College, or University of Glasgow, also gave its name, and its 26 acre site east of the High Street, to the College goods yard in the 1860's; the municipal Corporation of Glasgow played a significant and permissive part in admitting the Union railway company, and in selling house property to it; and both the Trades House and Hutcheson's Hospital made available large acreages of land south of the river to the Glasgow and South Western and to the Caledonian railway companies.

Hutcheson's Hospital, in fact, had played a dominant part in the emerging landownership patterns of Glasgow during the period of

[27] Although John Miller's estimate of £200,000 was optimistic. HLRO, P & S, 1846, West of Scotland Junction, and Min., H.C., 1846, 20 March, p. 88.

[28] W. H. Marwick, *Economic Developments in Victorian Scotland* (1936), 38.

[29] HLRO, Min., H.C., 1873, 6 May, p.43, S.C. on Caledonian Railway (Glasgow Central Station).

[30] 44 & 5 Vic. c. 149. GRL B53152 (Grainger and Miller's Report on Ardrossan canal railway, 1831), GRL C51395 (Carrick's Report on Parliamentary Bills, 1880–1).

rapid growth in the half century before the coming of the railways, and had already disposed of large blocks of its estate by 1830.[31] Nevertheless it still retained enough to be described as 'the largest proprietor on the south side of the Clyde' in 1873. The Hospital's factor, Andrew Hoggan, claimed at that time that 100 acres were still left to feu, and the Caledonian railway company was able to purchase 40,000 square yards of this. 'At a price that you are satisfied with?', enquired counsel for the G. & S.W. 'Well, I would have liked more', Mr. Hoggan replied; but the sum was evidently sufficient to persuade the Hospital to withdraw its opposition.[32] Counsel for the G. & S.W. was not content with this answer but pressed his enquiry concerning the land price further, presumably to cast doubt upon the disinterest of the Patrons' motives for withdrawing their opposition to the Caledonian Central station Bill. His cross-examination was interrupted by counsel for the Caledonian company, who protested in words which substantiate and explain ones' suspicions regarding the paucity of official estimates on land costs—'My friend is not entitled to ask the price that is to be paid for the land, because it would be manifestly inconvenient that their figures should be in print. That could affect every compensation that might subsequently be held under the Bill.'[33]

The Caledonian railway company also depended for its operations south of the river, upon the land owned by the Corporation of Glasgow. During the division of the Barony of Gorbals estate, in 1789, the Corporation had acquired a large tract at Gushetfaulds, a little too far out to be immediately attractive for building purposes; and this vacant land was sold for part of the Caledonian's South Side station in 1845 (No. 4 on sketch map).[34] Some twenty years later, the approaches and triangle junction for the Glasgow and South Western railway company's St. Enoch station (No. 5 on sketch map) also ran through a good deal of Corporation property; though in this case the property was not part of the city's old patrimony, but had been very recently acquired, house by house, by the City Improvement Trust, as part of its pioneer programme of slum clearance.[35]

The old College, with extensive grounds east of the High Street (see sketch map), also presented a large and tempting block of land for railway speculation, and the Principal and Professors were more than

[31] John R. Kellett, *Scot. Jour. of Pol. Econ.*, VIII (1961), 213–5. The brothers Thomas and George Hutcheson who founded the Hospital in the seventeenth century were 'writers' (i.e. solicitors) and sons of a rentaller. *Glasgow, Past and Present* (Glasgow, 1884), I, 526.

[32] BTHR PYB 1/579, 8 May, QQ.648–51.

[33] *Ibid.* Q.671.

[34] *Glasgow, Past and Present* (Glasgow, 1884), I, 347, 540. *Memoirs and Portraits etc.* (Glasgow, 1886), I, 34.

[35] HLRO, Min., H.L., 1864, 14 July, p. 17, S.C. on Union Railway.

anxious to move. By the 1840's the area around the College had become appallingly decayed and overcrowded. The evening law classes had been abandoned because of the nightly pandemonium of screams and policemen's rattles, and the inexpediency of bringing young men through the parade of women of the town in front of the College entrance.[36] The adjacent area, in which the students were to find lodgings, included the notorious Vennel and Havannah slums, inhabited by rag dealers, thieves, prostitutes and receivers of stolen goods. The first scheme to demolish the College and build a station on the site miscarried in 1846, however, because of the delays and complications involved in the three-cornered dealings between the College, the Treasury, and the Glasgow, Airdrie and Monklands Junction railway company. But in the 1860's a similar plan was revived by the North British railway company, as part of the Union scheme (No. 6 on sketch map), and the University was removed to a more westerly site. At Gilmorehill a land company had bought a sixty acre estate from Archibald Bogle in 1845, the year in which the G.A. & M.J. railway company was floated.[37] After that company's scheme miscarried, proposals were made to spend £20,000 to turn the area into an ornamental walk and cemetery for people of the higher classes, but essentially the ground lay idle until 1864, when the Union railway company bought it to exchange for the old College site on the High Street. Since the land had appreciated from £12,000 to £82,000 whilst laying vacant for eighteen years, the Gilmorehill land company had no cause to feel dissatisfied with the result.[38]

The Stobcross proprietors (see sketch map) also had cause to congratulate themselves upon their timely speculation. Operating under the more liberal Scottish law concerning joint-stock companies, they had raised £58,000, in 1844, to purchase sixty acres from the Trustees under John Phillip's will.[39] The sale of a mere quarter of the estate to the North British railway company for their Stobcross goods station, in 1864, was enough to repay all the capital laid out.[40]

The Trades House (or association of craft gilds) was also a considerable supplier of land to the railway companies; and its finances benefited from the railways' effect on the land market both directly and indirectly. Its title to land originated in a loan of £1,743 raised as a quarter share towards purchasing the Barony of Gorbals from Sir Robert Douglas in 1640. In 1789, as already mentioned, the Trades House, Corporation and Hutcheson's had decided to divide the land

[36] HLRO, Main Papers, 1846, Glasgow College (MacFarlane's Estate), H.L., 6 July, pp. 191–3, H.C., 10 August, pp. 43–6.

[37] *The Old Country Houses of the Glasgow Gentry* (Glasgow, 1878), 122–3.

[38] HLRO, H.C., 1864, 23 May, pp. 1–10, S.C. on Union Railway.

[39] *The Old Country Houses etc.* (Glasgow, 1878), 244–6.

[40] *Glasgow, Past and Present* (Glasgow, 1884), I, 197, III, 451.

and take direct possession of it; and some eighty acres fell to the Trades House south of the river (see sketch map). A modest beginning at the feuing of steadings facing Bridge Street was made in the early 1790's, and by the time the Glasgow, Paisley and Greenock, and the G.P.K. & A. railway companies sought a site for their joint terminus, some 150 steadings had been laid out.[41] The feu duties payable on them came to £2 8s to £5 per steading, and the effect of the railway's arrival in 1837 was clearly marked. Some 22 properties were demolished for the approach line, and for the small annexe passenger station at Bridge Street; and further unfeued ground was set aside for the goods sidings, sheds and workshops (No. 1 on sketch map). For these portions, totalling 38,082 square yards, the annual feu was £1,257—or approximately four times the amount brought in by the land which the Trades House had laid out for building, although the area covered by the railway was only a third or a quarter as great.[42] 'The establishment of railways in the neighbourhood aided most beneficially', wrote a contemporary historian of the Trades House, 'in promoting the rapid enhancement of the value of these lands.'[43]

The members of the Trades House were so delighted with the results of their land speculation that they decided to invest elsewhere, and attempted first to settle the principles upon which their investment should be made. Their discussions are reported unusually fully and frankly, and they raise important questions which affected the policies of corporate and charitable bodies in all the major cities.

'Under this great prosperity, several members of the House met occasionally in private, without any formal appointment, and talked over the propriety of purchasing lands, in the neighbourhood of Glasgow, as an investment for the funds of the House. The view entertained by those gentlemen was, that the land purchase should be capable of being soon feued, and of thereby becoming available, in twelve or fifteen years, as a source of increased revenue. Another view was suggested to them, namely, that the lands purchased should be bought at little more than their agricultural value; consequently, that they should be situated beyond the present feuing district, but capable of yielding an agricultural rental in the meantime, which would be sufficient for all the wants of the House. This scheme contemplated the retention of the lands for a long period, under cultivation, until the expansion of Glasgow should place them within its buildings, and enable the House to realise a larger income at a distant time, as was exemplified in the case of the Gorbals lands, and as was also exemplified in the case of Heriot's Hospital of Edinburgh, and in the case of the extensive suburbs in the west end of London. In those suburbs lands which, at the close of the last century, were under cultivation at agricultural rents, now yield enormous ground rents,

[41] Masons' Incorporation, Minute Books (1772–1817), 26 November 1790.
[42] George Crawford, *A Sketch of the Trades House* (Glasgow, 1858), 187–97.
[34] *Ibid.* 188.

well secured by the elegant mansions now erected on them. A wealthy corporation, which never dies, and whose lands need not be sold for distribution among heirs, or burdened for younger children, can alone afford to take this course.'[44]

The choice was, simply, to buy at a low price and hold for fifty years, or to buy at a high price and hold for twelve or fifteen years; and the latter course was preferred. The first selection of a promising estate in which to invest the surplus funds was that of Stobcross, but these lands were bought by a syndicate, 'at a mere trifle above the price at which the members of the House had agreed.' If the Trades House had been a little quicker, or offered a little more, they would have been able to repeat on the north bank their highly successful dealing with the railway companies south of the Clyde. As matters fell out they decided to bid instead for Dr. Rae Wilson's villa and grounds at Kelvinbank, and for the adjacent area of Sandyford (Wilson/McNaughton on sketch map). At this stage the corporate spirit evident in their private discussions broke down, and one of the Trades House members, Archibald McClellan, bought Kelvinbank himself; he also, in association with James Smith—who was not even a member of the Trades House—bought Sandyford. Soon after, they either repented, or experienced some difficulty in actually raising the £30,000, and the Trades House took over the purchase, sending out a letter to be read at the meetings of its component gilds speaking of the 'fair prospect that the purchases by the House will promote its future prosperity as the purchase of the Gorbals lands has hitherto promoted the prosperity of the House and incorporations.'[45] The railways, however, were not such liberal contributors to the Trades House's prosperity on this occasion.

2. *Conditions of competition between railway companies*

Glasgow was the theatre for a bitter conflict between three rival railway groups which lasted from the mid-1840's until the end of the century, and was protracted by the even balance between the companies engaged, which at times produced a perfect deadlock, at other times long and obstinate arguments. The endless repetition of grievances, and the taking up of uncompromising positions could not be better illustrated than during the ten year correspondence which took place after the Glasgow and South Western railway company had managed to secure St. Enoch's station (No. 5 on sketch map) and effectively to exclude its rival, the Caledonian, from a full share in the growing passenger traffic. 'Whoever conducted the correspondence for them,' Mr. Aspinall Q.C. said to a Commons' Select Committee in 1873, 'did with con-

[44] *Ibid.* 205.
[45] Mason's Incorporation, Minute Books (1817–66), 28 May 1847.

siderable skill write his letters as though he was wanting hostile answers and wished to excite that feeling to the greatest possible extent.'[46] There is, indeed, something intransigent and personal about the tone of the exchanges between J. G. Wood, Secretary to the Union railway company, and Archibald Gibson, Secretary to the Caledonian railway company, which may help to explain why accommodation or compromise was never seriously considered between the two companies.[47] As John Fowler put it, 'I never remember an occasion in which the Union company have been in Parliament on which the Caledonian have not been opposite.'[48]

If the minor lines, absorbed by amalgamation or leasing, and the speculative terminal company, the so-called 'Union Railway', be set aside, there were three main protagonists, whose rivalry essentially sprang from the three trunk routes which they controlled from Glasgow southwards to the Border. In the west, was the short distance line from Glasgow to Paisley, Kilmarnock and Ayr, authorised in 1837, to which an extension through Cumnock and Dumfries to Carlisle was later added. Its *forte* was, to an unusual extent, mineral and goods traffic, differing little from summer to winter; and revenues from these sources were consistently larger than passenger receipts from all classes. It was only in the 1870's that the passenger receipts began to rise really markedly, quadrupling in seventeen years, whilst the mineral and goods receipts only doubled. The passenger traffic included a good deal of seasonal excursion and holiday traffic to the coastal resorts, fifty trains a day being run during the peak week-ends by the mid-1860's; but it also included a good deal of regular, all-the-year-round, short-distance passenger traffic, as the *Dumfries Courier* had foreseen when the line was first projected.[49] 'It is what we call the "far ends" that pay coach proprietors both as to parcels and passengers, and we suspect the same rule applies to railways, whether traversed by locomotives or common wagons. What Dumfriesshire could not do as a principal she may manage to achieve as a zealous auxiliary.'[50] The short-distance traffic, upon which the G.P.K. & A. railway was based (and that of its successor, the Glasgow and South Western) was lucrative—the company paid annual dividends which were regularly over 8% between 1850 and 1880 —and kept the small passenger terminus at Bridge Street, and the Cook Street goods depot, fully occupied even from early days. On the other hand, a perpetual disadvantage of the local and short-stage nature of

[46] BTHR PYB 1/579, 13 May, p.6.
[47] Some of the correspondence was submitted to the S.C. on Caledonian Railway (Glasgow Central Station), HLRO, Min., H.C., 1873, 6 May, pp. 77–96.
[48] HLRO, Min., H.C., 1872, 6 May, p. 97, S.C. on Glasgow Union Railway Junction with Glasgow Kilmarnock Joint Line and Caledonian Railway.
[49] HLRO, Min., H.C., 1864, 12 May, p. 146.
[50] W. McIlwraith, *The Glasgow and South Western Railway* (Glasgow, 1880), 10.

the G. & S.W. system was that it lost twenty miles, and one hour, on the direct Carlisle to Glasgow route compared with its rival, the Caledonian company; and it was the desire to compensate for this by offering superior and more central station facilities in Glasgow which predisposed its directors to accede so readily to the St. Enoch scheme when it was put to them by James Ferrie Blair, John Fowler, and Morton Peto.

The east coast trunk route into Scotland, from Berwick to Edinburgh, was controlled by the grandiosely named North British company, floated in 1843; and it was possible to reach Glasgow by the North British metals, changing at Edinburgh to the Edinburgh and Glasgow railway company's lines—though such a devious route would only be taken by those who had business in both cities. The Edinburgh and Glasgow company itself was one of the older lines, authorised in 1838, and was wholly committed to the traffic between the two major cities. Attempts were made to absorb the Edinburgh and Glasgow into the Caledonian system, in 1849, 1860, 1861 and 1864, but all failed, for different reasons; and if they had succeeded the Caledonian would have been placed in a position of quasi-monopolistic power in Scotland.[51] As it turned out, it was the smaller North British line which merged with the Edinburgh and Glasgow in 1865, and added the College station (No. 6) to the old Edinburgh and Glasgow company's terminus at Queen Street (No. 2 on sketch map).

The central, and shortest, railway from the Border followed the hilly and difficult Annandale route *via* Beattock summit to a point approximately half way between Glasgow and Edinburgh. Its basic pattern was, therefore, very similar to that of the Grand Junction railway, which also was built to provide the vertical shaft of a capital letter T; and the Caledonian railway was, in fact, conceived by Henry Booth, the Secretary of the Grand Junction railway company, and by Joseph Locke, their engineer. It was also financed to a considerable extent by investors from England; and from London in particular. When the company's finances were subjected to serious criticism in 1850, it was a London committee of shareholders which forced Hope-Johnstone's resignation from the chair; and it has been suggested that the name 'Caledonian' was partly chosen to conceal the fact that the company was so largely financed by capital from outside Scotland.[52] Although it had one or two notable West of Scotland directors, like John Houldsworth of Cranstonhill, or James Lockhart, M.P., it did not enjoy the broad local basis of support which the G. & S.W. could claim—over 70% of the latter company's capital being raised locally, and the company chaired, in succession, by three Glasgow Lord Provosts. On the other

[51] O. S. Nock, *The Caledonian Railway* (1962), 34, 43.
[52] *Ibid.* 16.

hand, although it may have originated with London capital and Liverpool ideas, the Caledonian soon became inextricably dependent upon the network of small local lines in central Scotland.[53] After the failure of its attempted merger with the Edinburgh and Glasgow, although the Caledonian company continued, for a time, to use its grant of running powers on the Edinburgh and Glasgow railway to send its expresses from the south into Queen Street station (No. 2), it adopted the policy of buying up small companies, ex-mineral lines (some with 4' 6" narrow gauge), and using their approach routes to Glasgow. The Glasgow and Garnkirk, the Monkland and Coltness, and the Monkland and Kirkintilloch were all bought up, with guarantees of 8% to 10% upon capitals which were generously stated. These railways, between them, provided the Caledonian with an approach into Glasgow from the E.N.E.; and the Glasgow and Garnkirk company also brought with it the invaluable Parliamentary authorisation of an unopposed station at Buchanan Street (No. 3 on sketch map).[54] The Caledonian's approach to the General Terminus dockside station and to the Southside goods and passenger terminus (No. 4 on sketch map), was also secured by equally complex purchases; the Clydesdale Junction company (from Motherwell to Rutherglen); and thence the Pollok and Govan company to Southside.[55] Both of these companies, together with the Glasgow, Paisley and Greenock, which was also purchased, in 1847, were given guarantees upon their entire capitals of 5% or 6%—terms which a Caledonian shareholders' *Report* of 16 October 1849, described as 'exorbitant'; and a great deal of the Caledonian company's financial difficulty in 1850 can be directly assigned to these over-generous bargains with small local railway companies.[56]

The extensive facilities which it had purchased, however, and its large traffic and capital, placed the Caledonian railway company in a position of unchallengable influence in the Glasgow area; and from the time of its formation, in 1845, the G. & S.W. and the Edinburgh and Glasgow, or later the G. & S.W. and the North British, formed what counsel for the Caledonian sarcastically described as 'a happy family'.[57] It was not a formal alliance, and did not preclude arguments between the G. & S.W. and the N.B which were bitter enough to take both parties before the Solicitor General: but in Glasgow, at any rate, there was a tacit

[53] G. Robin, 'With the Caledonian Railway from Hamilton', *The Railway World* (1955), 45–7.
[54] H.L., 1847, XL, 124, 363.
[55] H.C., 1846 (212) XII, QQ.314–5, 388–400.
[56] BTHR (Edinburgh) RAC(S) 1/3. The G.P. & G. also had as engineer Joseph Locke and as secretary Mark Huish, who later moved to the Grand Junction railway company.
[57] BTHR PYB 1/579, 13 May, Q.26.

understanding that the two companies would both throw their weight in the balance against the Caledonian.[58] This concerted hostility to the Caledonian may have been assisted in its earlier stages by the fact that the North British and the G. & S.W. served different regions and, although they met at Glasgow, they did not compete there to any marked degree. Nor was their friendship put to the strain of sharing station facilities until 1876; although it withstood even this test at St. Enoch's.

The result of this even balance between the Caledonian company and its opponents was a competitive struggle for traffic, for urban space, and for local influence which lasted for sixty years. The operational rivalry between the three companies extended from the trunk routes across the Border to the railway-owned steamboat services in the Clyde, and afforded spectacular, and occasionally dangerous, races—a source of intermittent benefit to contemporary travellers, and of continuous delight to railway historians. It was also reflected in urban affairs; and in Glasgow the siting of termini, the number provided, and the timing of their construction, can be shown to depend in large measure upon the precise relations existing between the three companies, and their relative success in canvassing their schemes.

In 1846, for example, no fewer than three schemes for large terminals were laid before Parliament, with full preparation and at great expense; apart from other schemes, as seriously intended perhaps, which were discussed but not formally presented. Yet not one of these schemes succeeded; all were defeated by the combined opposition of other parties. The College Goods station scheme (overlaid exactly by No. 6 on sketch map), although it was generously supported by Colin Dunlop, John Wilson, J. B. Neilson, William Dixon and Andrew Buchanan (the largest coalowners and ironmasters in the West of Scotland), was obviously conceived in far larger terms than a mere mineral line. In fact the intention was to join the eleven mile railway with some other small mineral lines, and offer the whole package to the Edinburgh and Glasgow company, as a terminal company.[59] There was no other reason why a twenty-six acre station site and £400,000 capital should be proposed for a railway which was only eleven miles long. Surely 'it is a little strong', counsel for the Caledonian railway company suggested, 'to take so much land at the station for so short a line?'[60] The Caledonian, suspecting the intentions of the new project, strenuously opposed it in Committee; although the failure of the Glasgow, Airdrie and Monklands Junction railway company was due to other factors, outside the Caledonian's control.

[58] *Ibid.* 12 May, Q.697.
[59] With a guarantee of 4% on its £400,000 capital. HLRO, Min., H.C., 1846, 20 May, pp. 90–100, S.C. on Glasgow, Airdrie and Monklands Junction Railway.
[60] HLRO, Min., H.L., 7 July, p. 55, S.C. on College of Glasgow.

The Caledonian company was also in opposition to the second major scheme for a new urban terminal to be discussed in 1846—the West of Scotland Junction project, sponsored by the G.P.K. & A. and the Edinburgh and Glasgow railway companies ('1846 dotted square' in Blythswood land on sketch map). Their counsel Serjeant Wrangham, four Q.C's, Austin, Talbot, Hope and Forsyth, and the counsel for the Caledonian's satellites, the General Terminus, the Glasgow, Paisley and Greenock, and the Glasgow, Barrhead and Neilston Direct railway companies, were able to lead extremely damaging evidence concerning the proposed high level tubular steel bridge 'on the principle about to be adopted by Mr. Stephenson for crossing the Menai Straits', and on the effect of the proposal upon their own system. Added to this was the opposition by the Blythswood Trustees, the Clyde Navigation Trust, the Corporation of Glasgow, and the Tidal Harbours Commission. Not surprisingly, the result was a defeat for a scheme which, in fact, had many advanced features about it, and which anticipated the cross-town linkage made, twenty years later, and at vastly increased expense, by the same companies. The G.P.K. & A. and the Edinburgh and Glasgow companies did renew the Blythswood scheme for two Parliamentary sessions, but its rejection in 1846, at a moment when prospects in the railway investment market were rapidly deteriorating, caused the scheme's final and permanent abandonment.[61]

The same fate overtook the third and biggest proposal put forward in 1846 by the Caledonian itself. This also involved crossing the river, though a little further upstream, almost on the site of the later St. Enoch scheme ('1846 dotted square' near No. 5 on sketch map). The terminus to be established was fiercely criticised by the G.P.K. & A. and the Edinburgh and Glasgow companies' counsel, on a variety of grounds—disturbance to property, congestion of traffic in the central streets, interruption of navigation in the river, and failure to effect a junction between the railway systems north and south of the river.[62] Their principal witness was the engineer of their two companies, John Miller, but A. & D. J. Bannatyne, the solicitors for the G.P.K. & A., were prepared to pay expenses for any witnesses hostile to the scheme.[63] John Carrick, who in fact favoured a scheme further east where it would be of greater sanitary and social benefit to carry out demolition, was brought down to London by Bannatyne's.[64] David Dreghorn, a

---

[61] The Edinburgh and Glasgow railway bought the plot for £75,000 or thereabouts, and sold it, when their project fell through, to James Scott for £37,000. HLRO, Min., (W. of Scotland Junc. Rly.), H.C., 1846, 26 March, pp. 88, 145–85, and *Glasgow Past and Present* (Glasgow, 1884), I, 161.

[62] HLRO, Min., H.L., 1846, 7 July, pp. 1–15, 9 July, pp. 196–234, S.C. on Caledonian Railway (Dunlop Street Station).

[63] *Ibid.* 7 July, pp. 272–305.

[64] *Ibid.* 7 July, p. 319.

Bridge Commissioner and Town Councillor, was also called as witness to discredit the Caledonian scheme, and even to impugn the motives of the Clyde Trust and its engineer for supporting it. 'You believe the River Trustees are prepared to sacrifice public interest to railway considerations and that Mr. Walker, their engineer, would lend himself to that object?', he was asked, in cross-examination. He repeated that Walker was a man of high honour, but not sufficiently independent to give a judgment. 'I am not prepared to say either that the Trustees are prepared to sacrifice the public interests or that Mr. Walker would lend himself to it, but I say that one section of the Trustees are in favour of the West of Scotland Junction scheme, another section of them, who are Directors in the Caledonian are using their energies to promote the present scheme, and probably another section connected with a third scheme will be seeking to promote that. I say that those are not the men to say which is the proper place.'[65]

The net result of this criticism, reported in over a thousand pages of MS notes, was to cause the rejection of the Caledonian scheme. The companies involved had shown themselves masters of the art of tactical opposition, using every means to discredit a scheme one year, putting forward closely similar schemes themselves the next. The resulting deadlock in 1846 meant that no one succeeded in effecting a river crossing or establishing a new central terminus, and major urban projects were shelved until the 1860's.

The years of recovery from the aftermath of railway mania, the early 1850's, proved in the West of Scotland, as in other areas, a period of the most unrestrained operational competition. Between 1854 and 1855 the Caledonian launched 'an attack' (in the Edinburgh and Glasgow directors' words) in central Scotland, running seventeen daily trains (including eight expresses) at a 3rd class fare of only 1s from Glasgow to Edinburgh, and later reduced the fare still further to 6d. The total passenger receipts on the E. & G. fell drastically, in the half year ending January 1855; and although fare reductions on their part brought a marked increase in the numbers carried in the next six months, the money receipts fell by a further 25% and the proportion of working expenses to receipts rose from 37% to 50%. 'Is there any prospect of a termination to such wasteful proceedings?', the Edinburgh and Glasgow board asked; and the following year a ten-year agreement on a joint purse was reached with the Caledonian, under the guidance of an arbiter.[66] A similar cut-throat contest on the trunk routes from Carlisle to Glasgow, between the Caledonian and the G. & S.W., likewise terminated, at about the same time, in a Traffic Sharing Agreement.[67]

[65] *Ibid*. 9 July, p. 242.
[66] BTHR (Edinburgh) RAC(S) 1/73.
[67] HLRO, Min., H.C., 1864, 13 May, pp. 30–1, S.C. on Union Railway.

By the agreement the Caledonian allowed its smaller rival 40% of the goods and 15% of the passenger receipts out of a joint purse. The percentage allowed for goods was a reasonable estimate but the passenger figure was not. The G. & S.W.'s route through Nithsdale was longer than the Caledonian's, and so, although collecting 15% of the joint passenger receipts, the G. & S.W. only carried, in fact, 5% of the passengers.[68] William Johnstone, the G. & S.W's manager, in admitting the existence of such an agreement to the Commons' Select Committee in 1864, added that his company felt a 'strong moral obligation not to break the agreement until it expired' (in 1874).[69] This did not preclude him, however, from using the period of this profitable truce to strengthen the G. & S.W.'s position, and the new Union Railway terminal scheme of 1864 was devised to give the G. & S.W. several decided advantages when the agreement expired.

In fact, the effect of the 10-year and 21-year Agreements was similar to that noted in other cities—to shift the emphasis in competition from fares to accommodation and facilities. The proposals of 1846 were revived, in slightly modified form, and the old battles in Select Committee fought again, between the Caledonian on one side and its rivals, the G. & S.W. and the North British, on the other. By the 1860's, however, the evidence in favour of some river crossing and link railway scheme was incontestable, and the Union project was not allowed to fade away a second time—although the political upheaval it caused has been noted elsewhere.

A condition promised by the companies which sponsored the Union station (St. Enoch's, No. 5 on sketch map), and the revived College Goods station project (No. 6 on sketch map), was that they would be 'an open railway for all comers.'[70] This undertaking cannot have been seriously intended, for one of the objects of the scheme had been to gain competitive advantages in passenger and goods services, and in all types of traffic: the through traffic would virtually be captured, since no other cross-town linkage existed; trunk traffic would be attracted by the large new central station; and there would be gains even in local passenger traffic, as a result of the increased handling capacity and more central location. All these would be lost if the Caledonian railway company were admitted on equal terms; and, in spite of its fierce opposition to the scheme, the Caledonian immediately applied for running powers, as soon as the Bill received the Royal Assent.

Although, in view of the 'open station' promise, the Caledonian company could not openly be excluded from St. Enoch's, conditions

[68] *Loc. cit.* pp. 34–7.
[69] *Loc. cit.* p. 45.
[70] H.C., 1864, XXI, 165 (Board of Trade Reports). HLRO, Min., H.C., 13 May, p. 216, S.C. on Union Railway.

could be laid down which were sufficiently onerous to produce the same effect. One remote and inconvenient platform could be assigned to them; a toll of 6d per passenger levied (which would effectively price the Caledonian out of the local traffic); preposterous limitations could be insisted upon, by which, for example, all Caledonian passengers who had travelled from further afield than Hamilton should be turned out at the Southside station, and not allowed to travel in to St. Enoch's; it could be specified that a lump sum contribution of £250,000, and an annual levy of £25,000 must be paid by the Caledonian, in addition to its passenger tolls, and that, in return, they would be allowed two of the nine seats on the joint board; the Caledonian could be forbidden to use the College station at all, yet at the same time required to contribute towards their rivals' Parliamentary expenses in securing the Bill.[71] When such conditions were laid down it was difficult for the Caledonian directors not to feel that they were merely being trifled with.

So the St. Enoch station itself became a further pawn in the competition between the three companies. Left to themselves to finance the project, the G. & S.W. and the North British proceeded very slowly, dragging out the construction of the St. Enoch station over twelve years (1864–76).[72] The difficulties encountered in clearing away a vast tract of slum housing—the so-called 'Wynds'—and the strain placed upon the contractors who had offered to stand behind the scheme, suggest further reasons for the delay in building and opening the new station. Throughout this period the Caledonian kept up the acid correspondence already referred to, and harassed the G. & S.W. and the North British, by opposing all their supplementary Bills to re-route their southern approaches, and by putting forward awkward and obstructive link lines of their own.[73] Even before the St. Enoch station was opened the Caledonian company had returned to the idea of a second independent terminus of its own, deliberately reduplicating the facilities at St. Enoch's. Tension between the companies was heightened by rumours, in 1872, of possible mergers between the long-distance English amalgamations and the Scottish companies.

It was against this background that the Caledonian Glasgow Central Station Bill was put forward in May 1873. At first the Caledonian had re-examined the Blythswood Holm station project, which had been

[71] HLRO, Min., (Union), H.L., 1864, 11 July, pp. 90–6, Min., (Union), H.C. 1864, 13 May, pp. 77–9. Min., (Central), H.C. 1873, 6 May, pp. 96–9.

[72] 'They still have not finished, and will need to spend £2,100,000.' HLRO, Min., (Central), H.C., 1873, 6 May, p.30 (George Cunningham). A Temporary station was used from 1870–6.

[73] HLRO, Min., H.C., 1872, 6 May, pp. 80, 112, S.C. on G. Union Rly. Junction etc. The most obstructive line of all, however, was a proposed surface link in 1873 from St. Enoch Station to Stobcross (see sketch map), which would permanently have excluded the Caledonian from central Glasgow.

originated by its rivals in 1846, but the rise in land values in that area had now inflated the project's cost to a prohibitive £3,000,000.[74] The property selected at the alternative Gordon Street site, proposed in 1873 by the Caledonian railway company, was still expensive, but came as near to constituting an enclave of low values as could reasonably be expected in such a central district. Instead of offices there were half-a-dozen 'photographic galleries', some vaults and warehouses, and a few stables and grain stores.[75] Working on the opinions of 'two or three experienced valuators'—theirs were the estimates which now counted for most, not the engineers'—the Caledonian estimated that £967,000 would cover the mile and a quarter extension, provided that the street frontages acquired in the schedule could be re-sold, and only the back portions used for the station premises.[76] Once again, expert counsel was engaged, *Plans and Sections* and *Demolition Statements* submitted, witnesses brought down to London. One of them was the same John Carrick (now the City Architect and Master of Works) who had given evidence twenty-seven years earlier. 'Why are we, in 1873, enquiring into station accommodation at Glasgow?', he asked the Committee. 'For this reason, that the companies cannot agree—it all comes back to that. It is the jealousy and mutual distrust which they have of one another, which has driven the Glasgow Corporation here to oppose these Bills.'[77]

3. *The development of railway facilities: a chronological sketch*

Since the competitive postures just described were not taken up until the mid-1840's, when the Caledonian company came into existence, the earliest railway schemes in Glasgow—the Bridge Street and Queen Street termini (1837, Nos. 1 and 2 on sketch map)—were located with simpler considerations in mind. Prominent amongst those was the problem of land acquisition. This was not, as later became the case, because the price of land, and the scope for acquiring space without extensive demolition of existing buildings, restricted the opportunities for the exercise of railway enterprise to narrow confines. It was primarily because the railways were themselves undercapitalised even for the relatively small scale of their operations, and, as a result, needed to get their services into operation, and receipts flowing in as soon as possible, even if this involved the use of temporary and unsatisfactory terminals

---

[74] HLRO, Min., (Central), H.C., 1873, 6 May, p. 43.

[75] *Ibid.* P & S, B.Ref.

[76] *Ibid.* 6 May, p. 107. As an afterthought Cunningham rounded the figure off to £1,200,000.

[77] BTHR PYB 1/579, 27 May, Q.94.

It was also because, in the 1830's, there were still no reasonable precedents established upon which the railways could expect to purchase land; and this continued to be a problem for railway companies in all the major cities until a *corpus* of experience in land dealings had been built up.

The inaccuracy of the early railway companies' first estimates on traffic was soon apparent. At the Select Committees, estimates of existing traffic were produced, on the various routes from Glasgow to Kilmarnock, Ayr, Paisley, Edinburgh and intermediate points, divided into various classes—coaches, gigs, vans, carts, steam-packets, and canal boats. The statistics were based upon the numbers of vehicles plying per week in 1837, and upon arbitrary loading factors. There was also, clearly, a great deal of latitude for interpretation, and possibly for double counting, in the lists of intermediate points from which traffic originated. However, for what they are worth, these were the statistics upon which the two earliest large railways to Glasgow attempted to persuade Parliament to authorise, and shareholders to invest in their project; and upon which they based their own estimated requirements of terminal space, and assessed their own revenue earning capacity.

The expectations of the Edinburgh and Glasgow company were that it would be able to count on carrying half as many passengers as the canal fly boats, and twice as many as the coaches and other road vehicles. They did not state whether this traffic would be newly generated, or merely would be drawn away from their competitors.[78] The G.P.K. & A. were more explicit about this point, and also more modest about their claim. They assumed that they would be able to take away 25% of the existing traffic from the roads and canals, and to add to that an equal quantity for newly generated traffic.[79] In fact, both companies underestimated, by a factor of two to three, the power of the railways to generate new traffic. The figure of 340,000 passengers, expected on the Edinburgh and Glasgow railway each year, once they had settled down to steady operation, was achieved within the first six months; and the G.P.K. & A. also found that its actual traffic was between two and three times as great as had been expected originally. The further annual growth which then took place did so from these higher initial levels. It is worth a short digression to note and illustrate the nature of early traffic estimates, for such understatements were not peculiar to Glasgow. In most large cities the initial calculations of terminal space requirements in the 1830's were based upon some rule-of-thumb calculations of the sort just described.[80]

[78] HLRO, Min., H.L., 1838, 1 June, p. 21.
[79] Prospectus, G.P.K. & A. in W. McIlwraith, *op. cit.* 20.
[80] H.L., 1836, XXXIII, 257. 'This is the usual principle, to double the passenger traffic'.

A similar lack of experience, both on the part of valuers and of vendors of property, is apparent in the 1830's, and until the procedures for land acquisition were systematised, in 1845. Some of the early claims against the Edinburgh and Glasgow, and the G.P.K. & A. companies were so ill-founded that it is hard to explain them except upon the basis of novelty. For instance, the tunnelling to Queen Street (No. 2 on sketch map) took the Edinburgh and Glasgow railway under the grounds of the Town Hospital, or Lunatic Asylum, and the claim made on behalf of the institution was so wild that it might have been prepared by the inmates rather than the Trustees; £44,000 later reduced to £10,000, and finally settled for £873.[81] The Minute Book of the Edinburgh and Glasgow railway company's Committee on Lands and Works gives other examples, hardly less inflated. The Union Canal claimed £28,200, of which £25,000 was for damages, for property which the railway company's valuers placed at £1,020. And other proprietors, like James Campbell of Possil (to the north of Glasgow), put in a claim 'which the committee have considered not merely exorbitant in itself, but as offering a precedent to which other parties would appeal in dealing with the company.'[82] Actually Campbell's claim, for a price based upon 40 years' purchase, although it shocked the committee, was not too far removed from the general level of claims to which, in the 1840's and thereafter, the railway companies would have to begin to accustom themselves.

An example of the early type of claim which was more representative than that submitted by the Lunatic Asylum may be chosen from the arbitration cases on the pathway of the G.P.K. & A. (No. 1 on sketch map). The site in question was a Methodist Chapel and its grounds in Eglinton Street for which the railway company offered £3,000, a sum which seemed reasonable in view of the Methodist Trustee willingness to sell it a few years earlier for that precise sum.[83] The Trustees in their Memorial & Claim to the arbiters admitted that 'the Methodist Society some years ago had serious thoughts of disposing of their property'. Now, however, 'the long delayed deepening of the river and the construction of a more commodious bridge' had taken place, resulting in a 'gradually increasing demand for warehouse, counting-house and dwelling-house accommodation'. The Society's property, they concluded, was 'only now coming to its full value.'[84] In other words, even though they were, no doubt, 'the gratuitous and disinterested representatives of a religious body' as they claimed, nevertheless they

[81] F. S. Williams, *Our Iron Roads* (1852) 87.

[82] BTHR (Edinburgh) EGR, Committee on Lands and Works, Minute Book I, pp.19, 25.

[83] G.U. Coll. Sol. papers. Correspondence between Messrs. A. & D. J. Bannatyne and the Society of Methodists, October–December 1838.

[84] *Ibid.* Memorial and Claim, 1 February 1839.

expected a price which was not based upon the original cost of site and buildings, but upon the development price (or in their words 'the full price') which, they successfully claimed, was more than double the sum offered by the railway company.[85] If this was the attitude of a religious body, proprietors of commercial and industrial sites and private owners could be expected to bargain even more obstinately. The result, in Glasgow, was a steady and rapid rise in the price paid for the urban land on which the terminal lines and buildings were laid out.

The awakening of urban proprietors to the new value of their lands, together with the modest traffic expectations and the small resources of the early railway companies, led to half-hearted and inadequate terminus facilities. These consisted, at Bridge Street, of a minute platform, a mere outpost for passengers on the river's south bank, and a goods depot, at Cook Street, which required expensive cartage to most points of collection and unloading, and was too remote to allow a direct approach to the quayside. At Queen Street the station was well situated, but also too small, and very difficult to enlarge. Yet both companies found that they had exceeded their estimated costs; of £850,000 for the Edinburgh and Glasgow, £623,000 for the G.P.K. & A. However, the surprisingly large number of people with motives for travel, and the ability to pay, provided the answer to both of the problems characteristic of railway building in the 1830's. The meagre provisions could be supplemented, and the rise in the price of land overtaken, if the public were persuaded, by the railway's obvious success, to press forward with investment capital on the required scale.

In the mid-1840's, therefore, one might well have expected that the proffering of large funds for railway projects would lead to a series of comprehensive schemes, to augment the early railway termini at Bridge Street and Queen Street, and to bring the railways more fully into Glasgow. Indeed, but for the competitive factors referred to in the previous section, this might well have been the case, for there was certainly no shortage of schemes which were large in conception. Glasgow was distinguished amongst nineteenth-century cities by being the only one, apart from London, which required a Royal Commission to analyse the multiplicity of urban railway projects.[86] It seemed, in 1846, that the centre of the city would be violently transformed by the projects, clamorous in advocacy, and inconsistent in intention, which the rival companies were simultaneously canvassing.

All the major passenger station and through-railway schemes put forward in 1845/6 were frustrated, however, and only two second-string termini, the Buchanan Street and the Southside stations (1849, Nos. 3 and 4 on sketch map), and the General Terminus scheme (sidings on

[85] *Ibid.* Memorial of Arbiters' Settlement, 19 November 1839.
[86] H.L., 1847, XL, 361–6.

south side of harbour), survived the decade's self-destructive competition. Even the Harbour scheme produced its casualties, for there were three simultaneous projects laid before Parliament, the General Terminus and Glasgow Harbour Railway (G.T.) the Glasgow Harbour Grand Junction Railway Terminus (G.J.) and the Glasgow Harbour and Mineral Railway (G.H.). The difference between them lay in the cost and position of the site they selected, but even more in the amount of preparation and support they had secured. The G.H. system, which proposed to build a dock two miles to the west of Glasgow, would seem to be least likely to interrupt the general trade of the harbour; but it was further downstream, which would itself add the crucial two or three pence per ton to the charge, apart from the fact that ships bunkering would need a steam tug.[87]

There was less to choose between the other two central schemes; indeed, they overlapped for 900 feet of their frontage. The G.J. scheme was slightly more easterly and so the objections to coaling operations in the harbour for general trade would apply rather more strongly. But, on the other hand, the land to be acquired would be available more cheaply, and provide a larger storage depot.[88] All of the schemes came under the general objections made against the specialised coal trade. At London, Hull, Liverpool and Bristol, where the trade was general, no such mineral railways had been authorised; and any collier which applied to the West India dock, for example, would have been scouted immediately. In Glasgow, the objection was similar; the dust raised as coal was hurled down into the vessels, 'would ruin the Paisley shawls and muslins, and other general merchandise awaiting export on the quay.'[89] Since coal was also a bulky, low-value trade, there was also an objection to staiths occupying the 'most valuable and convenient part of the quays of the harbour, to the serious injury of the general trade of the port.'[90]

It is difficult to escape the feeling that the determining factor in the rejection of two of these schemes was the attitude of the Clyde trustees, who withdrew their objections to the laying of rails on their quays by the G.T. on the morning of 25 March, after a session which had lasted eight days. Later the same day the preamble of the General Terminus Scheme was proved. What had happened in the two years since their resident engineer had condemned joint-stock coaling schemes in principle was revealed in the course of interrogation by hostile counsel. Mr. Charles Gray, deputy chairman of the Clyde Navigation Trust, who had strongly supported the General Terminus scheme, was compelled

[87] H.C., 1846 (267) XII, QQ.939–43.
[88] *Ibid.* QQ.1068, 1092–3.
[89] *Ibid.* QQ.31, 976–87.
[90] *Ibid.* Q.1045.

1*

to admit that he had, in fact, become a shareholder in the company, and that the shares had risen appreciably in value when the Trust's forthcoming support for the General Terminus bill was announced. Five other trustees who held shares were also named.[91] Apart from this personal interest, the Clyde Trust itself stood to benefit, as a corporation; for the Terminus Company was in course of selling to them, on special terms, 37,000 square yards out of the land it had already purchased for their use in excavation and harbour-making.[92]

Neither the successful Harbour scheme, nor the Buchanan Street or Southside station—which were all that emerged from 'railway mania'—could be argued to serve central railway functions. The General Terminus was purely for goods and minerals, and both the other stations handled goods as well as passengers. The Buchanan Street station was approached by passengers from England *via* the Gartsherrie junction upstream, and they arrived in reverse down a three and a half mile gradient. The station itself was on the seedier fringes of the central district.[93] The Southside station was still remoter and more unpopular, 'a discredit to the city'.[94] Dingily situated, it left passengers with a mile to travel and the crowded bridges to cross to reach the business centre. 'It is like delivering passengers at Birkenhead for Liverpool', the Caledonian's counsel explained.

The belated assault upon the city centre, which resumed in the 1860's, focused upon the Union railway scheme. Originally this project was scheduled to cost £900,000, but this was added to by Supplementary Bills in 1872 (£400,000), 1874 (£250,000) and 1876 (£550,000).[95] This total of £2,100,000 put the Union scheme in the same class as the contemporary Liverpool Street terminus in London, and there were suggestions in Select Committee that when the final bill was presented it would greatly exceed even £2,100,000. The Union scheme included both the College station and that at St. Enoch (Nos. 5 and 6 on sketch map).

As already mentioned, the twenty-six-acre site of the old College and grounds had already attracted the interest of railway projectors in 1845, when the *Citizen* had remarked, eloquently but somewhat prematurely,

'The proposal to blot out our ancient University and erect a grand railway terminus in its stead, has a boldness in it that is apt to upset minds of ordinary

[91] H.C., 1846 (212) XII, QQ.214–35.

[92] *Ibid.* QQ.42–3.

[93] 'Surrounded by mean streets and tenements', J. F. Gains, 'Buchanan Street Station', *Railway Magazine* (1928),1.

[94] HLRO, Min., (Union), H.C., 1864, 12 May, p. 51

[95] BTHR PYB 1/579, 1 July, p. 1.

[96] W. MacAdam, *Birth, Growth and Eclipse of the G. & S.W. Railway* (Glasgow, 1924), 43.

calibre. It is strikingly characteristic of the irreverent audacity of the railway system—which skims over every hollow and cuts through every obstacle—which penetrates or lays open granite mountains with an earthquake's power.'

'Whatever comes in its way will inevitably be crushed and trampled down. It cares as little for old associations as it does for old houses, and offer what opposition we will, every year that passes will see iron lines dashed with remorseless sweep, through the faded handwriting which bygone ages have left on the earth's surface.'[97]

In this particular case, however, it was the railway company which was trampled underfoot. A separate Bill had had to be obtained to enable the College to sell its corporate lands, and clauses in this required the Treasury to approve the new buildings at the proposed site in Woodlands (Buchanan on sketch map). The designs for the proposed University, by John Baird, were sent back, after a lengthy delay, with criticisms by Pugin and Barry, to whom they had been referred.[98] For two years the plans were amended, despatched, discussed by delegations. Finally the Treasury gave its consent in July 1848, but in August of that year the railway company repudiated the whole deal because of the delays and losses. It was successfully sued by the University and went into liquidation in 1849.[99]

The University's grounds, however, were placed on the market again in the 1860's and formed the only large single block of property scheduled in 1864 for the Union scheme. All the rest was in extremely fragmented ownership. South of the river the elevated approach lines from Southside station, and from Shields Road, passed through bleaching greens, dwelling houses with back courts containing pig sties and hen houses, timber yards, sawpits and other low-grade properties.[100] North of the river the line forked, the left-hand branch curving westwards into a station situated in roughly the same area as the 1846 Caledonian Dunlop Street (see sketch map); the right-hand branch proceeding to a junction with the College station, and bridging the main thoroughfares of Saltmarket and Gallowgate. Both of these branches swept through densely packed dwelling houses, with backcourts and ashpits, usually owned singly or in twos and threes, quite often by women, and let out to tenants on a one year basis.[101] Railway No. 6 (as the branch to Stockwell Street and St. Enoch Square is designated on the *Plans and Sections*) ploughed through territory which was low-grade residential in charac-

[97] *Citizen*, 1 November 1845. In *Lanarkshire Topographical Collections*, VI, GRL 51366.

[98] Glasgow University Archives, OCB/R 10745.

[99] *Ibid*. OCB/R 10710.

[100] HLRO, P & S, B.Ref., 1864, Union Railway. Railways Nos. 1 and 4.

[101] 55% of the properties scheduled were owned singly, 30% owned in twos, 15% in groups of three or more. *Ibid*. Railways Nos. 1 and 6.

ter, but included also a number of spirit houses and stores, warehouses, cart sheds and a few business premises. Agnes Oswald, who had owned thirty properties scheduled by the Caledonian in 1846, had died, but her trustees had infilled her wood, stone, slate and firebrick yards with dwelling houses. Sir Andrew Orr, an ex-provost and ex-Chairman of the Glasgow and South Western railway company, was a new owner who had moved into the district, and his name recurs frequently; sometimes on his own account as sole owner, sometimes with groups of trustees, or with other individuals. In this area, and that covered by Railway No. 7, which took in three hundred properties in an even older part of the town, the owner-tenant relationships were sometimes of extraordinary complexity. One corner site at Princes Street, for example, comprised a group of shops, dwelling houses, a pawn office, a singing saloon and some cellars, owned by ten people as individuals, together with three sets of trustees (twenty-three people in all); the whole parcel was leased to one man, and was occupied by forty tenants.

All this was erased by the demolition operations carried out in the mid-1860's, but this incursion into the city was not to be the last. For reasons already explained, the Caledonian refused to share the St. Enoch's station and took on the task of further demolition anew in the 1870's. George Cunningham's plan for a large butt-end terminal (No. 7 on sketch map) did not involve such extensive bridging, demolition and closures as the Union scheme, and, as already mentioned, it used the high level approach to economise with street frontages, but the scale of disturbance was still very large. At the station site itself only six of the owners gave their assent, and over half of the eighty affected took the trouble to record their dissent. The occupiers, whose names cover some seventeen pages in the Parliamentary records, felt even more strongly hostile; only forty-two, out of nearly six hundred, agreeing to the station scheme.[102] The buildings in this area were poor, but their situation good, according to Thomas Binnie, and a larger proportion of them were commercial premises, occupied by their lessees, than had been the case with the Union scheme, further east.[103] This, no doubt, partly explains the tenacity of their opposition. However, once the preamble to the Caledonian Bill was proved, on 27 May 1873, the only remaining opposition could be on clauses, or over compensation.

4. Summary and general considerations

The outcome of the decisions recorded above was unsatisfactory on many counts. The city was served by means of a series of make-shift

[102] HLRO, Books of Assent and Dissent (Owners), 1873, Caledonian Railway (Glasgow Central Station). *Ibid.* (Occupiers).
[103] HLRO, Min., (Central) H.C., 1873, 12 May, p. 62.

facilities for a generation (from 1846–76), and the Corporation, land-owners and private citizens kept in a state of suspense, or of unfulfilled expectation. Nor did the projects which were abandoned fail because they outran potential traffic needs, or because of some flaw or weakness in their conception. Glasgow provides an excellent example of a city with an urban history which is littered with schemes which, although technically feasible and adequately backed, miscarried as a result of opposition which was essentially tactical in origin. London in the 1840's provides a similar example of a city where competitive checks and official intervention caused the frustration of a large number of imaginative projects; but in Glasgow the number of survivors was even smaller, and the delays before replacement schemes were sponsored was even greater.

In view of the extremely important part which was played by the Royal Commission of 1846 in determining London's future railway communications, perhaps it is worth glancing for a moment at the effect of the other Royal Commission of 1846, which investigated railway communications in Glasgow.[104] The two Commissions were very different in composition and remit. That in London was composed of senior administrators, Lords Canning and Dalhousie, John Johnson (the Lord Mayor of London), J. C. Herries and J. M. F. Smith, and had wide powers 'to investigate the various Projects for Establishing Railway Termini within or in the immediate Vicinity of the Metropolis.'[105] Its main recommendation was that railways should be excluded from the central area; and the profound effect of this ruling is discussed elsewhere. The Royal Commission in Glasgow was, by comparison, made up of engineers, and chaired by a Captain in the Corps of Engineers. Its commission was also narrower in scope, to 'consider and report upon the advantages or otherwise of a Central Railway Terminus in Glasgow'. Its main practical recommendations—that the Caledonian railway company's proposed Dunlop Street terminus ('1846 dotted square', adjacent to No. 5 on sketch map) should be preferred, and that the College station project 'may be made a very convenient depot for the general safety and arrangement . . . with reference to goods'—were dead letters; the Caledonian Bill had already fallen in Committee before the combined attack of other interested parties three months before the Royal Commission published its *Report*, and the Commission's approval did nothing to help the ill-starred College station project.[106] Nor was the *long-term* policy conclusion which the Commission recommended any more effective. It decided that plans to form a central station linking railways north and south of the

---

[104] H.L., 1847, XL, 361–6. Although dated October 1846 its publication fell in the sessional year 1847.
[105] H.C., 1846, XVII, 3.
[106] H.L., 1847, XL, 365–6.

Clyde was 'neither desirable nor practicable'; but the Commission's ruling did not perceptibly stem the flow of ambitious projects with this very end in view, nor inhibit Parliament from sanctioning one of them.

One may take as example of the sturdy indifference to the Royal Commission shown by railway projectors the long run of life accorded to G. W. Muir's 'Plans for a Glasgow Junction Railway terminus at Trongate'—a scheme which has not previously been mentioned.[107] Since the plan was free-lance—like Charles Pearson's in London—and was never formally submitted to Parliament, with *Plans and Sections*, *Books of Reference*, etc., it has not been shown on the sketch map accompanying this chapter; but it was located immediately north of, and partly overlapping, the triangle junction later built in connection with the Union scheme (No. 5 on sketch map). For the same reason, *viz.* that it was an unsponsored scheme, Muir's project was never directly discussed by a Select Committee; although more than one indirect reference to it was made during the discussion of Bills for other projects. The fact that it had not been formally prepared and presented to Parliament, however, did not prevent the Royal Commission, with its more flexible procedure, from examining Muir's scheme. The Commissioners did not object to its southern approach route, but took exception to the bridging of three main thoroughfares which its northern exit would involve. The alleged public merit of a scheme which would remove part of the Wynds, and put the area to 'better employment as a Railway than producing cholera or typhus', left the Commissioners unmoved. They agreed that the buildings and alleys there formed 'a hotbed of disease and crime', but added, shrewdly, 'We think it is by no means certain that the removal of the Wynds, by simply dispossessing the present occupiers would effect a sanatory (*sic*) improvement of the city, as it formed no part of Mr. Muir's scheme to provide other or better abodes for them; besides, improvements of this nature are more properly the business of the authorities and guardians of the city than of railway companies.'[108] The city authorities, however, were in no position to fulfil that duty in 1846, and indeed it was not until 1862 that they began to gather the necessary information, 1866 when they secured statutory powers to carry out improvement. George Muir, however, was undeterred by the Commission's rejection of his central terminus scheme, and it was once more canvassed at public meetings in 1864, and introduced into the evidence being heard by the Select Committee on the Union railway company's Bill.[109]

The Royal Commission in Glasgow then, unlike that in London, left

[107] G. W. Muir, 'A Plan etc.' (1846), *Bibliography of Scottish Topography* (ed. A. Mitchell and C. G. Cash, Edinburgh 1917), I, 318.

[108] H.L., 1847, XL, 362.

[109] HLRO, Min., (Union), H.C., 1864, 23 May, p. 157.

little mark on the city's pattern of rail communications, and failed to guide or to expedite the provision of additional passenger and goods facilities. Even the growth of traffic, and of demand pressures, seemed to have less effect upon the provision of added facilities than might be expected. The Caledonian railway company's annual passenger traffic rose from one million to nearly four millions in the period 1848–64; and of these, two-thirds were passing through the Glasgow terminals at Buchanan Street and Southside, the make-shift nature of which has already been mentioned. The Glasgow and South Western railway company's traffic doubled between 1848 and 1862, from a total, on their whole system, of three-quarters of a million passengers *per annum*, to one and a half millions; of which, according to a separate count, nearly half a million were arriving at the tiny Bridge Street station.[110] In addition, a further three quarters of a million arrived *via* the Joint line, worked by the Glasgow, Paisley and Greenock railway, in conjunction with the G. & S.W.; all of these passengers disembarking on a platform only 260 yards long and 20 feet above street level.

The Edinburgh and Glasgow railway company's traffic over the same period also increased, from one to two millions, and three-quarters of these arrived at, or departed from, Queen street.[111] This was an undue number for a station only a little over two acres in size to handle safely; and safety standards were allowed to decline. J. D. Marwick, the Town Clerk, conducted a lengthy correspondence with the North British company, the Home Secretary and the Board of Trade, complaining of passengers being 'jostled off the platforms, crushed between piles of luggage, having to alight in the tunnel and make their way into the station along a narrow ledge.' 'Only two platforms of very limited size are available for all the passenger traffic.' Marwick continued, 'and when a large train is about to start, or when two or more trains of ordinary size leave in quick succession, the utmost confusion and danger prevail.'[112] Weiland, the Secretary of the N.B. railway, replied laconically that the only accidents reported to him appeared to have been caused 'by want of reasonable care on the part of the passengers themselves.' The Board of Trade sent their inspector, Captain Tyler, in December 1873, to make a report, and he also wrote that it was impossible to emphasise too strongly 'the urgent necessity that exists for removing the Goods traffic elsewhere'; but their report was ignored by the North British company, in spite of urgent letters throughout the whole of 1874 from the Town Clerk. The Secretary to the Board of Trade, to whom the

---

[110] BTHR (Edinburgh) RAC(S) 1/3. HLRO, Min., (Union) H.L., 1864, 11 July, p. 163.

[111] *Ibid.* RAC(S) 1/73.

[112] GRL MS. Correspondence D397154, 25 September 1873. The other quotations in this paragraph are from the same source.

239

Town Clerk appealed, made his own position clear: 'Your Corporation should understand distinctly that the Board of Trade have no power to make any order upon a railway company.' The most he could do for Glasgow, or any other municipal corporation dissatisfied with the railway services it was getting, would be to give a certificate under Sections 11 and 13 of the Regulation of Railways Act, 1873, which would allow the Corporation to bring the case before the Railway Commissioners. Even the Home Secretary, Richard Cross, to whom the Town Clerk also appealed, professed himself to be powerless in the matter.

So the Corporation was no more effective in its complaints than individual passengers. There was nothing which could be done to *compel* the railway companies serving Glasgow to provide facilities which kept abreast of demand. If they wished to do so, or if they were swayed by calculations of the prospective cost and opposition any proposal of a new station would arouse, they could simply allow the transport system to burst at the seams. Alternatively, the traffic itself could effectually be tailored to fit the facilities, by the type of fares policy and the frequency of services adopted.

It is difficult to make a firm generalisation upon this point, for two reasons. In the first place, there is a distinct shortage of comparable statistics. What is required, of course, is not the overall passenger figures for railway companies, but specific passenger counts at the individual urban termini, or at one given city; and these figures, because of the technical difficulty of compiling them, only exist fortuitously and at irregular intervals, rather than in series. Even the Select Committee documents—which one would have thought might reasonably be expected to contain compilations and estimates of the passengers handled, or anticipated, at the urban termini under discussion—only contain statistical information from time to time. However, reasonably full estimates, which cross-check between the different companies originating them, exist for Glasgow in 1863, on the eve of the new central terminal plans.[113] The whole passenger traffic for the city was then approximately five millions; and from the further local break-downs of traffic supplied in 1873 we may deduce that it had doubled in the intervening decade.[114]

Arrivals and Departures at Glasgow termini, 1863

Caledonian		2,743,000 *per annum*
	(of which)	1,128,000 local traffic from Greenock

[113] HLRO, Min., (Union), H.C., 1864, 12 May, pp. 143–55. *Ibid.* H.L., 1864, 11 July, pp. 98–106, 112–7, 13 July, pp. 77–90.
[114] HLRO, Min., (Central), H.C., 1873, 7 May, pp. 243–5. BTHR PYB 1/579, 16 May, QQ.471–3.

Glasgow and South Western	779,000 *per annum*
(of which)	355,000 Joint Line
	(G.P.K. & A. and
	G.P. & G.) passengers
Edinburgh and Glasgow	1,575,000 *per annum*
TOTAL	5,097,000

Arrivals and Departures at Glasgow termini, 1873

Caledonian	5,500,000 *per annum*
(of which)	2,000,000 local traffic from
	Greenock
Glasgow and South Western	2,027,000 *per annum*
(of which)	512,000 Joint Line
	879,000 Dunlop Street annexe
	for St. Enoch's.
North British	3,000,000 *per annum*
(by extrapolation)	
TOTAL	10,527,000

The North British company, in fact, did not provide the Select Committee with any statistics in 1873, and in view of the fact that this was the year in which their acrimonious correspondence with the Town Clerk began, perhaps this is not surprising. William Johnstone, the General Manager of the G. & S.W., submitted figures which were in themselves misleading; and also, when directly taxed as to the value of his passenger traffic into Glasgow was compelled to reply, 'I am afraid I have no statistics to show the money that we get.'[115] He would guess that it was something in the order of £1,000,000 (obviously including the longer distance travellers)—an extraordinary admission, one might think, from the manager of a company which had just undertaken to invest over £2,000,000 in providing new station facilities; but, as illustrated elsewhere, this intuitional method of approach to business decisions was not uncommon.

Some figures were also produced for Goods traffic, but these were even more fragmentary and unsatisfactory. If, however, one takes the passenger arrival and departure figures as a guide to the scale and adequacy of rail-transport provisions in Glasgow, then a second obstacle to forming a retrospective judgment arises. With what are the

[115] *Ibid.* 16 May, Q.663.

figures of five, or ten, million passengers per year for Glasgow to be compared, since they are virtually meaningless standing in isolation? If they are compared with the most satisfactory available figures for urban terminal receipts—those for London—certain obvious difficulties arise, concerned particularly with regional differences in social structure, income levels, employment patterns, and residential habits and opportunities. For example, the entire Glasgow passenger traffic in 1863 would only have occupied one-third of London Bridge station's capacity.[116] Admittedly, London Bridge was a station which specialised in relatively short-distance journeys, of the kind seen on a much smaller scale at the Bridge Street terminus in Glasgow; but even the station at Waterloo handled four million passengers *per annum* in 1858; and (it may be supposed) this one London station was handling a number of passengers similar to the annual turnover at all Glasgow's termini in 1863. The Fenchurch Street and Shoreditch termini in London, which also specialised in short-distance traffic, were handling some ten million passengers between them, even in 1855; but, on the other hand, the long-distance stations, Euston, Paddington and King's Cross, only handled a total of three millions at that date.[117]

Speculation upon the question of how greatly the rail facilities which were actually provided in Glasgow may have lagged behind the demand must inevitably encounter such difficulties as these. How many potential work-journeys—given the unusual character of the city, mentioned elsewhere—could the Glasgow region be expected to develop? What proportion of traffic was long-distance? What would be the local equivalent to the fares prevailing in the London area, and what social classes might, potentially, be tapped by railway company offers? The shaping of travel patterns in the West of Scotland region was not a matter which lay entirely within the disposition of the railway companies. Yet, on their cheapest service,—the Joint Line from Greenock, which offered the only fares to compete ($\frac{1}{10}$d per mile) with those of the Great Eastern railway company in London—the response was proportionately impressive. When, after the long rivalry between the companies to whom Glasgow was an arena had finally produced a new and belated equilibrium in the late 1880's, the effects of the closing of Bridge Street and the re-routing of its traffic to the Caledonian Central Station was as remarkable an example of traffic growth as can easily be found in any city. In 1880 the Caledonian's 173 trains per day carried 4,750,000 passengers to and from the new 'Central Station' terminus; a number which was already beginning to approach that from

[116] T. C. Barker and Michael Robbins, *A History of London Transport* (1963), 139. H. P. White, *A Regional History of the Railways of Great Britain, Vol. III, Greater London* (ed. D. St. J. Thomas, 1963), 25. Edwin Course, *London Railways* (1962), 48.
[117] H.C., 1854–5, X, App. p. 215, Table II.

all Caledonian termini as recently as 1873. By 1888 and 1897 these figures had multiplied to 9,250,000 passengers in 300 daily trains, and 15,750,000 passengers in 486 daily trains. The loading factors had also increased from an average of 78 passengers per train in 1864, to 90 in 1880, and to 105 in 1897.[118]

These traffic figures from the Caledonian's new station offered, in the last decade of the nineteenth century, genuine comparison with those of individual London termini at the same date; they were greater than the annual arrivals and departures from Charing Cross or Cannon Street, and half as large as those at Waterloo or Victoria stations.[119] A major point left for analysis is the relative elasticity of social response in different regions of Great Britain to the transport services offered; but this itself might be subjected to historical influences over periods of three or four decades. In Glasgow there can be little doubt that the course of events in mid-century encouraged, even more than might otherwise have been the case, the provision of services which lagged behind potential demand.

[118] HLRO, Min., (Union), H.L. 11 July, pp. 80, 118. O.S. Nock, *The Caledonian Railway* (1962), 112.
[119] H.C., 1905, XXX, 614–5.

IX

London

1. *The property ownership pattern*

Introduction

In London the study of land ownership patterns presents many problems which are essentially those of scale—the area covered by the buildings and immediate fringes of the cities of London and Westminster was so large, even in the early nineteenth century; the recorded history of transactions in central land so long and complex. Yet comparisons and contrasts may be drawn between the metropolis and the great provincial cities.

In London's environs, as in those of Manchester, Birmingham, Glasgow and Liverpool, the same remarkable transition from field to suburb could be observed within a generation. On the other hand, the process was of longer standing, took place upon a proportionally larger scale in London than in the other major cities, and the landholders tended to be recruited from the wealthiest and most firmly established families of the day. They were not local aristocrats with traditions which were essentially agricultural in nature, and who might have experienced windfall acquisitions of suburban acreage beyond their means, almost fortuitously, from an Enclosure Bill or the spoils of local government; but included families who were amongst the wealthiest in Britain, and who, like the Russells and Grosvenors, had already had several generations of experience of managing urban estates by the time the first railway approach routes were cut. Their ranks were reinforced, not as in the provinces, primarily by speculative solicitors, builders and land agents, but also by wealthy placemen from the central government or the legal professions.

A further contrast which might be drawn between the patterns in London and the great provincial cities stems from the long history of London's territorial expansion, and from the resources of the select families who held title to the land over which expansion took place. Because of their considerable resources, and the protracted nature of the demand for building sites, the inner estates tended to remain

244

intact to a surprising extent. There was no tendency for the estates to be dissolved as they were covered with buildings, In the provinces the largest central estate holders (with the exceptions which have been noted) tended to own only a street, or a few valuable but scattered blocks of property. The difficulties of financing larger central developments, and the temptations presented by rapidly rising values, ensured that the landholders least affected by the transformation of their land from fringe to central, would be the corporate, ecclesiastical, and charitable bodies—which were often constitutionally incapable of divesting themselves of their heritages.

The consequence of this, observable to differing extents in the major provincial cities, was a 'ring' effect in the tenurial patterns. Large ex-manorial tracts of land were held in the immediate environs of the city, forming an inner suburban ring of large holdings; but as the tide of building advanced it tended to wash away the larger boundaries. In London this was far less marked, and the large estates retained their unity to an unusual extent. Partly, as has been suggested, this may be explained by the gradual nature of the urban expansion over the previous two centuries. The development of the Russell estate, for instance, went back to the early eighteenth century; a time when Glasgow and Liverpool had populations which had only just reached five figures. The long history of the Russell estate's development, in the years before the urban population explosion, meant that batches of the twenty-one year Repairing Leases, and even of the longer Building Leases, had had time to fall in; and the fines on their renewal formed, in Scott-Thomson's opinion, 'a very pleasant capital account for the Duke of Bedford'.[1] Further sums to capitalise the crucial early stages of urban estate development without splitting or alienating the estates came from the substantial rent-rolls from improved agricultural land which families like the Russells could command. In an emergency, as under the improvident third Duke of Bedford, the timber on the Woburn Abbey estates could be sold to prevent the sacrifice of city properties.[2] Or the funds to retain integrity of holding could come from the infusion of capital gained in other fields; and in no other city were these fields so numerous as in London.[3]

Whatever the reasons, more large tenurial units survived in London's inner district—between the central district and the suburbs—both absolutely, and even proportionately, than in the other four cities studied, and this fact was of great importance to the course of railway development in the capital.

[1] Gladys Scott Thomson, *The Russells in Bloomsbury* (1940), 186–7.
[2] *Ibid.* 58, 188.
[3] *Ibid.* 298–311. Perquisites and salaries in the central government were not the least of these.

The north and west

It had particular force, as may be seen from the accompanying sketch map, in north-west London, where the major trunk route approaches were dominated by the holdings of a few large landowners. From the first purchase by the London and Birmingham railway company in the 1830's, to the Great Central's dealings with Viscount Portman sixty years later, the main-line companies' plans were influenced by the existence of large blocks of property in the north-west. 'All the land we bought in London', the London and Birmingham company's Law Agent declared, 'was entirely the property of Lord Southampton, and then we got into Eton College property. Up to the river Brent, six miles from London, there were scarcely more than 6 or 8 proprietors.'[4]

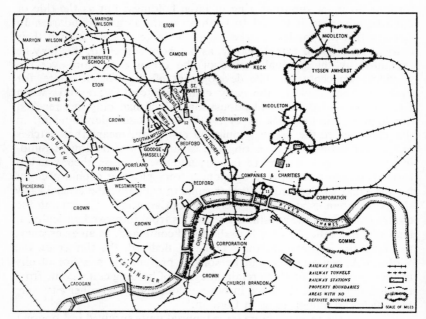

Property ownership and railways in London.

Southampton was one of three commoners connected with the central government who established title to land when the prebendal manors of Cantelows, Tottenhill and St. Pancras were sold to their tenants in the eighteenth century. Charles Fitzroy, brother to the Prime Minister, the Duke of Grafton, rented some 255 acres, the manor of Cantelows (in the Kentish Town area), for £300 *per annum* from the

[4] H.C., 1845 (420) X, 29 May, Q.5.

Dean and Chapter of St. Paul's.[5] In 1768 the purchase was carried through, the estate settled upon the Fitzroy family, and Charles was created Baron Southampton in 1780.[6] His estate was at first developed upon the basis of forty-year leases; a short period, which together with the out-of-the-way situation of his estate, north of the New (later the Euston) Road, led to a marked reluctance on the part of builders to take up leases except for low quality houses.[7] The houses on Southampton's lands were officially described in the leases of 1809 as 'third-rate'; other epithets were applied to them within a few years. John Nash described them as 'mean', and a disgrace to the north-western apex of the metropolis; John White categorised the first of the five hundred houses to be finished as inferior, 'miserable modern erections'.[8] Since the fate of a successful and elegant estate did not hang in the balance, the result was, in 1835, that Southampton did not offer the same determined opposition as the Duke of Bedford to the route and terminal plans proposed, on behalf of the London and Birmingham railway company, by Robert Stephenson.[9] No restrictive clauses were insisted upon to limit the railway company's free use, for forges, workshops or manufactories, of the land it purchased for its rights of way.[10] The chief grounds of debate were over the allowance for severance and compensation, and the settlement of such claims finally came to half the company's disbursements.[11]

Adjacent to the lands acquired by Charles Fitzroy were the Church estates acquired by Charles Pratt, created Earl Camden in 1786, and those of Charterhouse bought by Charles Cocks, M.P., whose son was created Baron Somers in 1784.[12] The Camden, or Camden Town estates, though originally laid out, under an Estate Bill in 1788, to provide suburban dwellings for the industrious artisan, declined even from this modest intention into an area of fourth-rate residences, public and boarding houses.[13] The neighbouring estate at Somers Town was even more notorious. Optimistic miscalculations marred the initial development of the area by Somers and Jacob Leroux during the war

[5] *The Survey of London*, XIX (1938), 12.

[6] Euston Hall, hear Thetford, was the seat of the Dukes of Grafton, and it was this family link which gave the square and station on the New Road its name. J. Bateman, *Great Landowners of Great Britain* (1883), 190.

[7] Frank Banfield, *The Great Landlords of London* (1890), 19–20.

[8] Hugh C. Prince, 'North-west London, 1814–1863', *Greater London* (ed. J. T. Coppock and H. C. Prince, 1964), 95–6.

[9] HLRO, P & S, B.Ref., 1835, London and Birmingham Railway Extension. Properties numbered 3–110.

[10] 5 and 6 Wm. IV, c. 56. Donald J. Olsen, *Town Planning in London* (1964), 151.

[11] H.C., 1845 (420) X, 29 May, Q.30.

[12] *The Survey of London*, XXIV (1952), 118.

[13] HLRO, Main Papers, H.L., 20 May 1788, Earl Camden's Estate. Donald J. Olsen, *op. cit.* 63. Hugh C. Prince, *loc. cit.* 97.

years: 'some unforeseen cause occurred, which checked the fervour of building, and many carcasses of houses were sold for less than the value of the materials.'[14] After this setback builder's were 'allowed to build such houses as they pleased', so that by 1826 the Duke of Bedford's agent felt it necessary to erect gates 'so as to shut out the low population of Somers Town.'[15]

Neither Camden nor Somers, therefore, had apparently much to lose by direct deterioration of their property. Moreover the decisions concerning this area were made between 1833 and 1835; and it is doubtful that they, or anyone else, could have foreseen at this early date the drastic effects which the London and Birmingham, the Great Northern, and the Midland railway companies were to have upon the great tract of land bordered by the New Road, Regent's Park and Hampstead Heath. The mean half-formed streets of fourth-rate cottages, the dilapidated summer houses, clay pits and carpet-beating grounds, described by Dickens, were intersected and isolated, and although rapid building took place after the first railway arrived, it was all dominated by the lines leading to the station; and by the station itself, where the engines stood 'bubbling and trembling, making the walls quake, as if they were dilating with the secret knowledge of great powers yet unsuspected in them, and strong purposes not yet achieved.'[16] The main streets of Camden Town were given over to railway hotels and boarding houses, cabstands and omnibuses, even 'railway patterns in its draper's shops and railway journals in the windows of its newsmen.'

The other estates in this immediate area, north of the New Road, belonged to St. Bartholomew's Hospital, the Brewers' Company, and the Church; and their attitudes towards the railway companies were also influenced, in a similar way to Camden's, Somers' and Southampton's, by the nature of the building which had already taken place, and the probable development prospects of their remaining land. The Brewers' Company had begun the development of its estate, in 1811, by securing an Act enabling the borrowing of £50,000 to provide streets and pavements for ground to contain 700 third and fourth-rate houses; but by the 1840's their estate was almost as bad as Somers Town, and the presence of an evergrowing maze of yards and approach tracks precluded any rehabilitation of the area over the next twenty years.[17]

[14] *The Survey of London*, XXIV (1952), 118, 134.

[15] Donald J. Olsen, *op. cit.* 64–65, 148.

[16] Charles Dickens, *Dombey and Son*, Ch. 6. Other quotations from this chapter may be seen in W. G. Hoskins, *The Making of the English Landscape* (1957), 202, Hugh C. Prince, *loc. cit.* 110.

[17] HLRO, Main Papers, H.L., 30 May 1811, Brewers' Company, St. Pancras Paving Bill. The houses were to rent at £30 *per annum*.

By the time of the Midland railway's St. Pancras scheme, in the early 1860's, the Brewers' Company's property, and that of the Skinners' Company adjoining it, had come to form an unattractive zone of intermingled craft and service industries, and of low grade rented houses The area of Skinner Street and Brewer Street, demolished for St Pancras station, was covered with packing sheds, small workshops, wine vaults, slaughterhouses, and cheap cottage properties. But it is noticeable, in the *Books of Reference*, that the property held by the Brewers' Company was rather unusual, in that a majority of tenants held only one house and were resident in it themselves; which one may take to have been a sign of respectability of a sort.[18]

The Church and St. Bartholomew's Hospital holdings (see sketch map) were far more retarded in their development than the estates so far mentioned. They had only reached the stage—customary in all rapidly expanding cities—of exploitation for their building materials. This was the area described by Thomas Milne, in 1800, as the zone of clay-pits, where the earth was removed and baked into bricks on the spot, at the rate of four million per acre.[19] Even at the time the Great Northern railway company projected its entrance route and station at King's Cross, in 1845, the approach ground was still covered with 'Tile kilns, brick and tile sheds, clay pits and brickmaking grounds.'[20] Much of the rest consisted of large open fields, and of what were euphemistically described as 'pasture and ornamental grounds'.[21]

East of the Gray's Inn Road, and bestraddling the Pentonville Road, lay the Clerkenwell properties of Lord Calthorpe and the Marquis of Northampton. Neither of these estates was of first-class residential status. The Northampton leases, granted from 1815 or 1818 onwards, were mostly taken up by middlemen, who were not prevented from infilling the internal yards and courts with cheap houses.[22] The Calthorpe properties, were owned by the same family—the Goughs—who were currently developing a residential estate of the highest quality at Edgbaston, in Birmingham; but they stood in marked contrast to that area.[23] An Estate Bill of 1814 had proposed to treble the rents of the Calthorpe land by paving it, and laying it out for building; but the final result was low grade mixed commercial and residential develop-

[18] HLRO, P & S, B.Ref., 1863, Midland Railway Company, Extensions at St. Pancras.

[19] G. B. G. Bull, 'T. Milne's Land Utilisation Map of the London Area in 1810', *Geographical Journal*, 122 (1956), 25–30.

[20] *Ibid.* 28.

[21] HLRO, P & S, B.Ref., 1845, Direct Northern Railway. Properties numbered, 7, 36, 38, 71 and 77.

[22] H.C., 1887 (260) XIII, 339, S.C. on Town Holdings. D. J. Olsen, *op. cit.* 103.

[23] *The Survey of London*, XXIV (1952), 27.

ment.[24] By the time the Metropolitan, Great Northern, and London, Chatham and Dover railway companies intruded, in the 1860's, the district was not one which required skirting on grounds of amenity; although, even so, expensive tunnelling was used for a good part of the way from Ludgate Hill and Farringdon Street through to King's Cross.[25]

The other estates in the north-west/central area, belonging to the Crown, Eton College, and the Duke of Bedford, fell into a very different category. The Crown land was primarily reserved as open park, but John Nash's plans for it, in 1815, also included spacious terraces and villas for 'the first class of society', and this, together with its royal patronage, preserved the area absolutely from incursions by railway companies.[26] The projected North London Junction and Regent's Canal railways, which would have infringed upon the estate in the 1840's, failed to secure authorisation; and the Great Central's Marylebone station extension line skirted the western flank of the park.[27] Eton College's lands were likewise laid out for residential development in 1824, but on a far less ambitious scale. The buildings were 'inoffensive, deliberately undistinguished houses . . . built to please respectable but undiscerning clients'.[28] Nevertheless they were villas of middle-class type, and Eton College therefore insisted upon clauses in the London and Birmingham Bill of 1833 which involved extensive tunnelling to preserve the district's future amenity. The Bedford estates, which have attracted detailed historical study, were also residential areas of high social pretensions. This had been true even of the smaller Covent Garden estate in the early eighteenth century, though by the 1840's that area was mostly occupied by what the Duke's steward, Christopher Haedy, described as 'a very poor and low class of persons'; market porters, shoe menders, jobbing tradesmen, laundresses, charwomen and labourers'.[29] The Bloomsbury estate, on the other hand, had successfully resisted such deteriorating pressures. It had, on its eastern fringe, a colony of ill-housed poor, many in domestic service; but the squares of central Bloomsbury formed for a time probably the most fashionable central residential area with such close access to the City and Inns of Court. John Bourne and Christopher Haedy, the Duke's agents, pursued a rigorous policy of excluding nuisances; even the opening of a genteel bookshop was subjected to close scrutiny.[30] Construction of James Burton's and Thomas Cubitt's fine terraces, which had hardly

[24] HLRO, Main Papers, H.L., 11 May 1814, Lord Calthorpe's Estate.
[25] T. C. Barker and Michael Robbins, op. cit. 130.
[26] H.C. Prince, loc. cit. 97, 100–1.
[27] H.C., 1846, XVII, Report, p. 11.
[28] H.C. Prince, loc. cit. 105.
[29] D. J. Olsen, op. cit. 139–41.
[30] Ibid. 113

faltered, even during the Napoleonic Wars, received a check, however, in the 1820's.[31] The main cause, in Haedy's opinion, was the successful competition of rival houses of the first class, many built by Cubitt himself, further west, on the Duke of Westminster's estate, in the Hyde Park Gardens and Belgrave Square area. 'If Mr. Cubitt, when he commenced building on this part of your Grace's estate', Haedy wrote to the Duke of Bedford, 'had foreseen that rivalry, he would no doubt have erected houses which would have been less subject to its influence. . . . The consequence of his not having done so was that the houses he built were rather too large and expensive for the locality, and the difficulty he found in procuring purchasers and tenants for them made him hesitate to proceed with the erection of houses of a similar kind, whilst at the same time he felt that to build houses of a smaller kind and lower price would tend to lessen the value and interfere with the sale and letting of those he had already built.'[32]

This was the dilemma in which the Duke's agents and builders found themselves on the Bloomsbury estate at the time the railway arrived. The opening of the Euston, and later the King's Cross and St. Pancras terminals exacerbated the problem in two ways. In the first place it is possible, as D. J. Olsen has suggested, that by unlocking new building lands suitable for suburban residence and daily commuting to the City, the railways may have 'seriously diminished' the element of monopoly which the landowners of central districts had enjoyed.[33] The building of exclusive mansions and villas in the outer suburbs in the 1840's and 1850's may have been undertaken for those who failed to take up the fine town houses in Bloomsbury. It is hard to say; although since it took forty years to complete one Bloomsbury Square, one is inclined to suspect that there must, quite apart from the railways' effect upon demand, have been serious miscalculation of the market for houses in the central area. Free railway tickets were certainly offered as an inducement to those purchasing villas with a rent of over £50 *per annum* in Middlesex, but only a few were claimed; and of the three railway companies with terminals in the New Road, only the Great Northern railway made any serious attempt to cater for short-distance traffic.[34] Even the Great Northern's suburban services were described as 'quite a small affair' in the 1860's, and still fewer suburban trains ran into the L. & N.W. station at Euston.[35]

[31] *Ibid.* 55.

[32] *Ibid.* 40.

[33] *Ibid.* 150

[34] Merlyn Rees, *The Economic and Social Development of Extra-Metropolitan Middlesex, 1800–1914,* (London, M.Sc. thesis, 1954), 55. T. C. Barker and Michael Robbins, *op. cit.* 53, point out that only 60 of these passes had been issued by 1857, and fewer than 100 on the Eastern Counties routes.

[35] C. H. Grinling, *The History of the Great Northern Railway, 1845–1902* (1903), 202.

Whether the neighbouring railway stations were responsible for the scarcity of potential tenants in the 1840's to 1870's or not, there can be no doubt that the road traffic generated by the stations had a most unwelcome effect upon Bloomsbury's residential amenity. A partially successful attempt was made to bar the estate to north-south passage by carts, omnibuses, empty hackney carriages, and to all vehicles after 11 p.m., by erecting gates along the northern boundary. In this way some of the heavy traffic flow to the stations was diverted round three sides of a block, to skirt Bloomsbury; and the Duke of Bedford retained this privilege until 1890, despite public opposition and inconvenience. 'I am a constant passenger by the Great Northern Railway,' the Prime Minister complained in 1890, 'and I must say that I have never passed the *Sacred Gates* in going to the Great Northern Station without mental imprecations against the persons who originally set them up and the persons who have since maintained them there.'[36] However, though the main stream of traffic may have been diverted, the functional influence of three large trunk railway termini was still reflected in the Bedford Office's losing battle to restrain the conversion of houses in the Bloomsbury estate into private hotels and boarding houses during the late nineteenth century.

In the smaller Bedford estate, at Figs Mead, north of the New Road, the effect of the railways was still more direct. The area was intersected, at Ampthill Square, by the final approaches of the London and Birmingham railway to its terminus at Euston, and what had been laid out as an estate of third and fourth-rate houses for 'the higher class of merchants', bankers' and counsels' clerks, attorneys' managing clerks, clerks in the law offices, and persons in trade' steadily declined between the early 1840's and the 1880's.[37] Here the deteriorating effect of a main-line surface railway upon a residential neighbourhood with even modest social pretensions was demonstrated, and the Bedford Office subsequently deterred or blocked all further attempts to drive lines through the main estate. In the plethora of railway schemes in 1846, for example, no extension from the London and Birmingham terminus was projected, although both the Direct Northern and Direct London and Manchester railways both submitted schemes for southward extensions to Holborn.[38] Later schemes, submitted in 1861 and 1871, for an underground link joining Euston and St. Pancras main-line stations to Charing Cross likewise skirted the Bedford estate, by adopting a cut-and-cover route down Tottenham Court Road.[39] Further west upon the New Road lay the Portland and Portman

[36] D. J. Olsen, *op. cit.* 149. Mark Searle, *Turnpikes and Toll Bars* (n.d.), II, 724.
[37] D. J. Olsen, *op. cit.*, 67-9, 151.
[38] *Supra* Plate 1, and H.C., 1846, XVII, Report p. 11.
[39] BTHR PYB 1/535, 23 March 1871, pp. 1-4.

estates, with the Eyre estates a little to the north; and south of them, bordering Crown parkland, lay the Duke of Westminster's property. All were similar in quality to the Bedford estate, and apart from the Metropolitan underground works carried out along the New Road in the 1860's, remained immune to railway intrusions until the closing decade of the century. The houses and villas which had been laid out, in 1794, upon land which had been in the Eyre family since 1732, were by no means cramped in style, but like Somers Town they were treated to street closures by their more elegant neighbours to prevent inter-communication.[40] The neighbouring estate belonged to Edward Berkeley Portman, descendant of a sixteenth century Lord Chief Justice; and between 1780 and 1815 the building had commenced, in the Baker Street/Bryanston Square area, of a first-rate series of squares, streets and fine terraces upon Portman's property.[41]

Two such estates presented a formidable barrier to the last and most expensive urban terminal scheme in London, that proposed by the Great Central. Their first Bill in 1891 was, in fact, thrown out on the grounds of damage to property; and the modified Bill, in 1893, agreed to comply with burdensome and expensive restrictions. A lengthy tunnel was to be constructed, eight-foot walls erected to conceal the trains, no advertisement hoardings were to be erected, nor dwellings for re-housing the working class in Marylebone or St. John's Wood, coal yards were to be roofed in, and railway buildings to be 'reasonably ornamental' in character.[42]

The Portland, and northern-most Westminster estates, may be mentioned very briefly, since, as may be seen from the sketch map, they lay altogether out of the route of railway schemes. Even the Metropolitan underground only ran along the northern border of the Portland properties at the New Road. The Portland properties had been laid out as early as 1717 by Edward Harley, second Earl of Oxford and Mortimer. The property was then transferred with his only daughter, as her settlement, when she married William Bentinck, second Earl of Portland.[43] In the 1760's and 1770's Robert Adam and John Johnson laid out further squares with houses of the first-rate, worthy of the aristocracy, 'judges, generals and Irish bishops' who occupied them.[44] Here, perhaps as clearly as anywhere in England, one can see the tangible signs of the landed aristocracy's important role in moulding urban growth. Indeed the *Street Directory* can be read in conjunction

---

[40] W. Besant, *London North of the Thames*, (1911), p. 337. H.C. Prince, *loc. cit.* 133–4.

[41] *Ibid.* 87.

[42] *Ibid.* 133–4.

[43] W. Besant, *op. cit.* 337–8.

[44] John Summerson, *Georgian London* (1962), 164.

with *Burke's Peerage*. Harley, Cavendish, Vere and Holles Streets, the family names; Oxford, Portland and Mortimer, the titles; Henrietta and Margaret, two of the heiresses; Wigmore and Welbeck, the country seats.

The Westminster estate was equally aristocratic. Sir Thomas Grosvenor had acquired the ex-manorial lands of Ebury and Neyte by marriage to Mary Davies in 1676, and building in the Grosvenor Square area had started by 1695. Sir Richard Grosvenor, one of Pitt's electioneers, received the titles Viscount Belgrave and Earl Grosvenor; the titles of Marquess of Westminster and Duke of Westminster were added to the family later.[45] Although the Mayfair estate lay in the shelter of the Crown lands of Hyde and Green Parks and was never at any time included in railway projectors' schedules for compulsory purchase, the same cannot be said of the Grosvenors' estates further south. Admittedly the southern properties were later and less fully developed. In Rocque's map (1746), although Grosvenor Square is completed and Berkeley Square commenced, on the Mayfair estate the southern holdings were still vacant land.[46] Tothill fields, later Belgravia, were covered, at this time, with Neat (i.e. Cow) Houses and market Gardens; Lord Grosvenor only secured an Act to enable the draining of the area in 1826.[47] But open fields which lay within a mile of Parliament itself had a very high intrinsic value. This was by no means one of the paper estates for which plans were sometimes conjured up when the railways entered the land market, but a *bona fide* speculation with first class prospects. Thomas Cubitt's and Seth Smith's houses were finding ready lessees at the time London's first railway, the London and Greenwich, nosed its way into the southeastern suburbs.

The scale and quality of the Grosvenor's developments in Westminster and Belgravia were reflected in the appreciation of land values which, one might have thought, would be enough to deter even the hardiest railway speculators. The major companies themselves, approaching London from the north-west and west, had not had the problem of severing a first class residential estate or even of driving extensively through a built-up area. Those companies approaching from the east, which had proceeded through a greater amount of built-up area had found themselves financially embarrassed, even though the housing demolished was of low quality.

[45] Charles T. Gatty, *Mary Davies and the Manor of Ebury* (1921), I, 28–9, 200. Frank Banfield, *The Great Landlords of London* (1890), 53. W. Besant, *op. cit.* 155–6. Michael Harrison, *Lord of London: a Biography of the 2nd Duke of Westminster* (1966), 19.
[46] John Rocque, *A Plan of the Cities of London and Westminster* (1746).
[47] W. Besant, *op. cit.* 184.

Yet in 1846, an elaborate, if somewhat unrealistic, project for a railway passing through the centre of the Grosvenor estate in Westminster was submitted to Parliament. It was to work on the atmospheric principle, and to form a 'railway street', 160 feet wide to accommodate four lines of traffic, having rows of trees along each side, and following the route shown in Plate 1.[48] Land for a station would be taken at the mews behind Westminster Hospital.[49] The promoters of this scheme, known as the 'Great Western, Brentford, and Central Junction Terminus Railway', estimated £1,100,000 would cover the cost of the section from Westminster out to the Great Western railway company's track at West Drayton. The Commissioners rejected the scheme in favour of the South Western railway company's terminus at Nine Elms, south of the river, and its Waterloo extension, newly sanctioned. 'We are not disposed to recommend the establishment of a Terminus in the heart of Westminster, at the expense of much interference with property, and probably with future improvements, in that part of the Metropolis.'[50]

Yet, absurd though the scheme might seem, in fact it anticipates in many ways the railway pattern which later emerged, at great expense and after twenty years' pressure by established companies. The route followed—along the Embankment from the City, south-west through Westminster, curving north-west at Sloane Square— bears more than a passing resemblance to that adopted by the Metropolitan District underground railway twenty years later; and the ambition of a connection between the Great Western railway and a new West-End terminus was also realised at the same time, in 1863, with the opening to traffic of the Victoria joint station (No. 9 on sketch map).[51]

The costs of these railways through the Grosvenor estate, cut in the 1860's, although not as excessive as those incurred at Marylebone by the Great Central, were nevertheless extremely heavy. The Metropolitan District railway was involved in street widening and slum clearance at Tothill Street, and a great burden of compensation payments and accommodation works. Over £3,000,000 was expended on the three miles from South Kensington to Westminster.[52] The subsequent traffic could not bear such heavy charges and show any worthwhile profit. For a time the Metropolitan District managed to meet the guaranteed payment on its 5% Preference Shares, but the Ordinary Shares paid nothing, or an occasional 1%. The later completion of the eastern portion of the Inner Circle route, to link up with the Metro-

---

[48] H.C., 1846, XVII, Report, p. 14.

[49] Westminster Hospital was then in Broad Sanctuary, opposite the Abbey. I am indebted to Dr. F. W. H. Sheppard for this information.

[50] H.C., 1846, XVII, Report, p. 15.

[51] Edwin Course, *op. cit.* 97. H. P. White, *op. cit.* III, 33 and T. C. Barker and Michael Robbins, *op. cit.* 150.

[52] *Ibid.* 152.

politan underground railway, reduced even the payment on Preference Shares to $2\frac{1}{2}\%$.[53]

The remaining West End terminal to be noted (No. 3 on sketch map) was the much earlier station belonging to the Great Western railway company, and located in Paddington, upon land belonging to the Bishop of London. Originally the whole manor had belonged to the Bishop of London, and the Dean and Chapter of Westminster, but as time passed large portions had been alienated to the Thistlethwaite family, and the Pickering estate.[54] Very little building of any sort had been completed at the time the Great Western railway arrived, except along the Edgeware and the Uxbridge roads; although a pattern of streets had been laid out, oriented N.N.E. in a slightly tilted grid-iron pattern—Spring Street, Westbourne Street, Ranelagh Street, Praed and Conduit Streets. Within a few hundred yards of its terminal, however, the Great Western passed through fields and parkland; and the terminal site itself was described as 'a certain field lying between the Paddington land and the Turnpike Road.'[55] For these reasons the land was inexpensive, and the company was even able to buy sufficient land to begin building before compulsory purchase powers were granted in July 1837; it was also able to extend later to an enlarged station, designed by Brunel and Digby Wyatt, with very little difficulty. The greater part of the necessary land was already in their possession before 1851, when the company's board sanctioned the extension.[56]

The Great Western railway company's land dealings, therefore, were early, simple, inexpensive, and in marked contrast to some of the other metropolitan-based companies. But one of the reasons for this was the rather remote situation chosen, and attempts to gain a closer approach to the Cities of London and Westminster, and even to the West End, led the Great Western to adopt an unusually active role in the development of an underground link railway.

The south and east

South of the river the pattern of landownership bore many resemblances to the outer western approaches. Like them the area was relatively undeveloped. Along the southern bank of the river, and along the roads leading back from the main bridges, building had taken place, particularly densely along the Borough High Street of Southwark and in the Mint district. It was, however, very mixed in type, chaotic in

[53] *Ibid.* 175.
[54] W. Besant, *op. cit.* 143–50. D. A. Reeder, *Capital Investment in the western suburbs of Victorian London* (Leicester Ph.D. thesis, 1965), 266. John Britton, *Map of St. Marylebone* (1837).
[55] E. T. MacDermot, *op. cit.* I, 13.
[56] Edwin Course, *op. cit.* 189–90. H. P. White, *op. cit.* III, 110.

layout, and poor in quality; riverside trades, timberyards and rope-walks, warehouses and cheap cottages.

As in western London the Church was the principal landowner. In Southwark the Bishop of Winchester had extensive holdings, including a 58 acre estate laid out for 1800 houses.[57] To the south-east, in Bermondsey and Rotherhithe, ownership was fragmented, apart from Sir William Gomme's holdings.[58] In this district, however, building had not ventured very far from the riverside, so that it was possible for the London and Greenwich railway to approach to within four hundred yards of its London Bridge terminus through open fields, and to purchase spare land alongside the terminus for expansion.[59] The Bricklayers' Arms extension and station was likewise laid out on open ground, north of the Old Kent Road.[60]

The manor of Lambeth also belonged to the Church—in this case represented by the Archbishop of Canterbury. To these very extensive lands (some 1500 acres) more was added by an Enclosure Act of 1806; and in 1820 the granting of long building leases was negotiated.[61] To enable this a private Estate Act, citing the convenience of Lambeth for 'houses, warehouses, and other buildings', was secured and small local firms of builders, most of them operating within a mile of their yards, began to develop large tracts of south London for 'clerks, shopkeepers, skilled artisans and the rank and file of the commercial world'.[62] 'Despite the wide variety of meaning which the term "manor" could imply, particularly in the eighteenth and nineteenth centuries,' F. H. W. Sheppard writes, in The Survey of London, Vol. XXVI, 'the manors still exercised an exceedingly important influence on the development of their areas.'[63] The length of lease granted, and the scale of fines for renewal, could be used as instruments to control the type of housing erected. If the worst came to the worst, the ultimate step was occasionally taken of pulling down the existing buildings when the reversion of a leasehold fell due.[64]

These instruments of control assumed, however, that the Church had a consistent policy to pursue regarding housing on its lands, and there is little to suggest that this was the case. It may be that the Church deliberately eschewed the attempts to set up socially select residential estates, and felt that it would be inappropriate for such a corporate

[57] The Survey of London, XXII (1950), 45.
[58] W. Besant, London South of the Thames (1912), 152.
[59] T. C. Barker and Michael Robbins, op. cit. 46.
[60] Edwin Course, The Evolution of the Railway Network of South-East England (London Ph.D. thesis, 1958), 314.
[61] 46 Geo. III, c. 57; 1 Geo. IV, c. 48.
[62] The Survey of London, XXIII (1951), 4, XXVI (1956), 10–12.
[63] Ibid. XXVI (1956), 3.
[64] Ibid. XXV (1955), 56.

body to seek to exclude the poor by a rigorous covenant policy, of the type followed by J. R. Bourne or H. T. Boodle on behalf of the aristocratic owners north of the river.[65] It may simply be that the district's location and the nature of its pre-existing zoning precluded any concerted attempt to lay out better-class properties. The result, at all events, was that in south London the railways, when they sought for closer approaches to the City and West End, or even for surface links with each other, were able to deal with one or two major ecclesiastical proprietors only. This, together with the generally poor quality of the buildings scheduled, exempted the southern schemes from the general restriction imposed by Parliament upon railway schemes in inner London in 1846. 'The property to be disturbed,' the Commissioners had reported, 'and consequently the cost of furnishing the accommodation to the public would, on this account . . . be proportionately smaller.' Other factors, it should be mentioned, also helped to persuade the Commissioners 'to look upon the close approach of the Southern railways to the eastern and western bridges of the Metropolis in a more favourable light': there would be less disturbance to traffic, or to the improvement of thoroughfares; and Surrey and Kent had a greater number of people 'having occupations in London, and are more frequented for occasional relaxation than the corresponding parts of Essex, Middlesex or Hertfordshire.'[66]

The wide areas of the clerical manors, which made it possible to advance from Nine Elms to Waterloo, from London Bridge to Charing Cross and Cannon Street, over property which belonged almost entirely to the Bishops of Winchester, Rochester and London, and to the Archbishop of Canterbury, undoubtedly reduced the delay, litigation and expense similar schemes encountered in east and north-east London. The Church offered no opposition to the schemes, possibly because, in common with the Police Commissioners, it viewed some of the properties which it owned with very mixed feelings; and indeed in some parishes the odd situation arose of vestries opposing schemes to which the Church, as principal proprietor, had given assent.[67]

From the railway companies' point of view the result was to bring within the bounds of practicality certain schemes for surface railways which could not have been contemplated in other parts of the Metropolis so near the central district; but although the expense was reduced,

---

[65] Ralph Clutton was the agent for the Ecclesiastical Commissioners, and spoke of the 'great tendency on the part of the people who have building estates rather to seek to develop them for dwellings for the middle class'. H.C., 1884–5, XXX, 211, and D. J. Olsen, *op. cit.* 21. The ecclesiastical policies are discussed in G. F. A. Best, *Temporal Pillars* (1964), 480–98.

[66] H.C., 1846, XVII, Report p. 4.

[67] *Ibid.* QQ.3029–3100 and App. I, p. 249. The church wardens of St. Saviours' Southwark petition against the L. & S.W. railway company.

it cannot be said that the schemes were cheap. The one mile and a quarter by viaduct from Nine Elms to the derelict pleasure gardens which occupied the site of Waterloo station, was estimated to cost £800,000—a very fair sum for 1846.[68] Moreover Charles Lee, the surveyor and valuer, who purchased the land for the London and South Western railway company, admitted later that it had finally cost them £1,250,000.[69] The South Eastern railway company's extension from London Bridge to Charing Cross, planned in 1858, was estimated in John Hawkshaw's and Samuel Smiles' report to the Directors, to cost £1,070,000. This was discreetly reduced to £800,000 in the estimates laid before Parliament; but the final bill came to £3,000,000.[70]

North of the river, in the eastern fringe of the City into which the railways penetrated, the same problems recurred in aggravated form. Here the largest owners were the historic Companies of London and the Corporation itself. The buildings included many which were of low quality, like those on the south bank; but since they were contiguous to the expanding commercial district their values tended to rise even more rapidly and prohibitively. They also differed from the southern railway approaches in another respect. Strict legislative boundaries were set in the eastern outskirts in 1846, partly as a consequence of the considerable interference with property and traffic already evident from the cutting of routes and stations carried out in the late 1830's by the Eastern Counties (Bishopsgate, No. 5 on map) and London and Blackwall (Fenchurch Street, No. 4 on map) railway companies. Thereafter, although G. P. Bidder repeatedly urged schemes for an advance to the Artillery Grounds, or Finsbury Circus, no further encroachments were allowed until the Broad Street and Liverpool Street schemes in the early 1860's.

Even the two earlier viaducts through the eastern outskirts, though they had not encountered unexpected opposition, had certainly encountered unexpected expense, stemming from the property transactions involved.[71] In the Eastern Counties' case there were also technical difficulties 'consequent upon passing through crowded building property, intersected with sewers, old ditches and numerous cesspools'; but the main charge was that for land.[72] John Duncan, solicitor to the Eastern Counties company, complained of prices based upon 26 years' purchase being allowed, even on 'houses of a very low description, not worth above 14 or 15 years' purchase.'[73]

The London and Blackwall railway company also encountered

[68] W. Besant, *London South of the Thames* (1912), 10.
[69] BTHR PYB/112/6, 19 July 1860, p. 115.
[70] Edwin Course, *op. cit.* (1958), 251.
[71] Jack Simmons, 'Railway History in English Local Records', JTH, I (1954), 163–4.
[72] BTHR EC 1/5, 6 September 1842, and *Survey of London*, XXVII, 252–3.
[73] H.C., 1845 (420) X, 29 May 1845, QQ.80, 84.

difficulties connected with the purchase of property, which went further than it was prepared to admit publicly. In 1840 the Chairman put a bold face on his company's negotiations with landowners. 'The progress making, in regard to the extension of the line, although not apparent to the eye, is considerable; the claims of the several parties whose property is destined to be removed have been duly considered, and negotiations are advancing for the purchase of the same. The Freeholds are, in a great measure, in the hands of the Corporation of London, and they have already been agreed for.'[74] This cheerful progress report failed to reveal the considerable embarrassment currently being caused by the number of other residuary interests clamouring for compensation: the various leaseholders and the tenants, many of whom were running small businesses on the premises and put in claims for loss of business connections. Moreover, there was also a great deal of other property in fragmented ownership, which William Routh had tactfully left out of account in his *Report* to the half-yearly General Meeting.

Similar problems of land purchase recurred two decades later, when the newly constituted Great Eastern attempted to improve upon the Bishopsgate facilities. G. P. Bidder had, in fact, been Robert Stephenson's assistant in the London and Blackwall railway company when the extension was made to Fenchurch Street; but he still based his decisions in the 1860's upon two miscalculations.[75] The first was that Robert Sinclair's estimate of £1,363,000 would be reasonably accurate; in fact the total expenditure came to between two and two and a half millions.[76] The second was that it would be possible to write off the whole Liverpool Street project as a general contribution to his company's traffic prospects. No additional fare for the extension would be charged at all, the benefit would come indirectly, he told the Parliamentary Select Committee, from the 'suburban gentlemen' who would patronise the line.[77]

The growth of traffic materialised, on a scale far larger than that anticipated, but no one would have used Bidder's epithet 'suburban gentlemen' to describe the 20,000 2d-fare travellers who poured daily into Liverpool Street by the early morning workmen's trains. Within three years the Great Eastern was compelled to approach Parliament for powers to raise a further £3,000,000 to set the company on its feet.[78]

Adjoining Liverpool Street was the North London railway company's extension line and terminus (Broad Street), authorised in 1861. Indeed G. P. Bidder's first hope had been to share the facilities and expenses by

[74] Six-monthly Report, 26 August 1840, London and Blackwall railway company.
[75] HLRO, Min., H.L., 1864, 19 July, p. 32, S.C. on Great Eastern (Metropolitan Station and Railway).
[76] *Ibid.* p.36. Cecil J. Allen, *The Great Eastern Railway* (1955), 58.
[77] HLRO, Min., H.L., 1864, 19 July, p. 11.
[78] W. M. Acworth, *The Railways of England* (1900), 409.

bringing the Great Eastern in to the same site; but the Great Eastern company's bill proposing this had been thrown out in 1862.[79] The North London line was the successor to the East and West India Docks and Birmingham Junction railway company, planned by Robert Stephenson and Henry Martin to give access from Camden Town, on the L. & N.W. line, to the riverside docks. Naturally, it was expected, with such a route, that the main traffic would be in goods; but, in fact, it proved popular with a large number of passengers, who travelled round the semicircle and along the spur to Fenchurch Street station.

Its building had been attended by the usual miscalculations concerning land purchase. Stephenson's estimate of 1845 had stated £600,000 would cover the eight miles of track and the cost of land; in fact the land purchase alone came to £569,000.[80] Nevertheless its construction, along what was the frontier of building development in the mid-1840's, was extremely timely, the 8d or 1s return fare gave a reasonable return, and the company had no terminal expenses except the burdensome toll for using Fenchurch Street station.[81] One might say that it was one of the few urban railways constructed at a bargain price, and its unusual dividend performance—a steady five to seven *per cent*—reflected this.[82] In 1861 Henry Martin, on the instructions of the North London railway company, prepared a plan for a direct extension southwards into the City, following a route parallel to the Kingsland Road; and over the next four years the line and terminal were cut, at a cost of £1,000,000.[83]

The property through which these inter-related railways in the 1840's and 1860's passed in north-east London, was not divided into large estates, controlled by strict policies. The largest holdings were those belonging to the Tyssen-Amherst family, descendants of the Francis Tyssen who had bought the manor of Hackney; but William Amhurst Tyssen-Amherst himself did not hope to pursue an exclusive estate plan.[84] There was, his agent told a Select Committee in 1887, plenty of scope for building houses of different classes, for artisans as well as the wealthier classes.[85] Consequently, like Southampton, Somers or Camden, he raised no difficulties when 250 of his properties were scheduled in 1845 for the E. & W.I.D. & B.J. link line, 290 for the

[79] HLRO, Min., H.L., 1864, 19 July, p. 4.
[80] HLRO, P & S, 1846, E. & W.I.D. & B.J. Railway.
[81] Six-monthly Report, 24 February 1852, London and Blackwall railway company. Tolls from the E. & W.I.D. railway opened 'a new era' in the Blackwall company's finances.
[82] T. C. Barker and Michael Robbins, *op. cit.* 52, 174. The company was renamed 'North London' in 1853.
[83] *Ibid.* 163.
[84] W. Besant, *London North of the Thames* (1911) 546.
[85] D. J. Olsen, *op. cit.* 21.

Broad Street extension of 1861, and 100 for the Liverpool Street extension of 1864.[86] Likewise Sir William Fowle Fowle Middleton, who held extensive lands in the same areas, was not amongst those landlords objecting before the Select Committees.

Unlike Tyssen-Amherst and Middleton, the Corporation of London, which held a relatively small number of properties on the Liverpool Street extension line, did take steps both to petition against the line, and to send counsel to represent them; although, to judge from the Common Serjeant's cross-questioning, their primary objection was to the viaduct itself rather than to the sale of property. Amongst the City Companies in the path of the Broad Street extension were the Goldsmiths, Skinners, Merchant Taylors, Poulterers and Carpenters, holding 14 to 22 parcels of land each. On the Great Eastern's route to Liverpool Street, the Carpenters, Poulterers, Merchant Taylors, Grocers, Skinners and Goldsmiths held similar portions.[87]

Moreover, as the *Plans and Sections* and *Books of Reference* show, these properties held by City Companies and large landowners constituted only a relatively small proportion of the 3,300 parcels purchased for the Broad Street/Liverpool Street schemes. The ownership of the rest was extremely fragmented; a feature which at the same time rendered it possible to ignore possible opposition, and enhanced both the direct compensation charges, and the legal costs associated with the purchase of multiply-owned properties. Or—even more ominously— the properties had been gathered into groups of twenty or thirty by solicitors, or by trustees under wills, who, since similar schemes had been projected as early as 1846, can hardly have been unaware of the possible windfall increments railway purchase might bring.

2. *Conditions of competition between railway companies*

The competitive schemes for urban railways and terminals in Victorian London were influenced by exclusive features peculiar to the metropolis. As already mentioned, in Chapter 2, strict limits to the scope of railway encroachment were laid down, in 1846, and re-affirmed in modified form in 1863. From this legislative intervention sprang many of the special issues of London's railway politics: in particular, the inner link railway and central station controversies; and in general, the failure of competition to develop between the large companies serving London from the north and the south. Competition, of a fluctuating but at times vehement nature, existed between the railways with southern

[86] HLRO, P & S, B.Ref., 1846 (E. & W.I.D.), 1861 (North London Extension to City), 1864, (Great Eastern, Metropolitan Station and Railways).
[87] In each case the City Company holdings were concentrated most heavily in St. Botolph's, Bishopsgate. *Ibid.* 1861 and 1864.

approaches: the South Eastern, the London, Brighton and South Coast, the London Chatham and Dover, and the London and South Western railway companies. It also existed to a certain degree between the major main-line companies approaching London from the north: the London and North Western, the Great Northern, the Midland, and the Great Central railway companies. The river Thames, and the urban bulk of London itself, however, remained an impenetrable barrier to the development of competitive through-routes to a degree which requires further explanation.[88]

To attempt to give a blow-by-blow account of the rivalries of the different groups, and to trace the genealogies of the pioneer, client, and main-line building companies would expand the present *Case History* to unreasonable length. Fortunately there is no need to do this to establish the necessary points of analysis, for although London was the focus of activity for so many railway projectors in the nineteenth century, a corresponding interest in the affairs of the capital and of its railway network has been shown by historians. The chronicles of individual companies by the railway historians tend naturally to converge on London: Williams and Barnes (Midland), Grinling (Great Northern), Steel (London and North Western), MacDermot (Great Western), Allen (Great Eastern), Dow (Great Central), Marshall (Southern railways). In addition, London's railways have been the subject of a large number of detailed full-length studies (of which the most notable are those by Course and White); of original monographs (notably by Baker, Dyos, Hall, Lee, Nock, Robbins and Sekon); and also of a modern bibliography (Ottley), and a modern history (Barker and Robbins), which come as near to being definitive as can reasonably be expected. To these writings, listed in a footnote, the reader may be referred for a detailed narrative of the rivalry between companies.[89]

[88] *Infra* sec. 4.

[89] F. S. Williams, *The Midland Railway, its Rise and Progress* (5th ed. 1888). E. G. Barnes, *The Rise of the Midland Railway, 1844–1874* (1966). C. H. Grinling, *The History of the Great Northern Railway, 1845–1902* (1903). W. L. Steel, *The History of the London and North Western Railway.* (1914). E. T. MacDermot, *History of the Great Western Railway* (1927–31, and C. R. Clinker revised ed., 1964). C. J. Allen, *The Great Eastern Railway* (1961). G. Dow, *Great Central* (1959 and 1962). C. F. Dendy Marshall, *A History of the Southern Railway* (R. W. Kidner revised ed., 1963). Edwin Course, *London Railways* (1962). H. P. White, *A Regional History of the Railways of Great Britain, Vol. III, Greater London* (ed. D. St. J. Thomas, 1963). J. C. Y. Baker, *The Metropolitan Railway* (Lingfield, 1960). H. J. Dyos, *JTH*, I (1953), 3–19, II (1955), 11–21, 90–100, III (1957), 23–30. Peter Hall, 'The Development of Communications', *Greater London* (ed. J. T. Coppock and H. C. Prince, 1964). Charles E. Lee, *The Metropolitan District Railway* (Lingfield, 1956). O. S. Nock, *British Steam Railways* (1961), Ch. 8. R. M. Robbins, *The North London Railway* (South Godstone, 1953). G. A. Sekon, *Locomotion in Victorian London*, (1938). G. Ottley, *A Bibliography of British Railway History*, (1965). T. C. Barker and Michael Robbins, *A History of London Transport*, I, (1963).

The general consequence, already observed in other cities exposed to competition, was the re-duplication of stations and of connecting lines, and/or violent disagreements over the use of shared facilities. Similar results can be observed on both sides of the river, but perhaps it was to the south, where greater latitude was allowed by legislation and landownership patterns, that the effects upon the urban map were more pervasive and lasting. Apart from the London and South Western railway company's straightforward advance from Nine Elms to Waterloo (No. 7 on sketch map), all the other principal stations established as a result of the southern railway companies' activity—London Bridge, Bricklayers' Arms, Victoria, Charing Cross and Cannon Street, (Nos. 1, 6, 9, 10, 11 on sketch map) fit precisely into the framework of the competition between companies. Indeed, it is impossible to set forth any rational explanation of the location and timing of these major termini which does not take into account the changing relationships between the four major companies involved.

The building and constant re-building of the earliest London terminal, at London Bridge, is a case in point. Authorised in 1833 and opened in 1836 by the London and Greenwich railway company, which operated a mere four miles of track, the site was soon expanded as larger toll-paying railways (the London and Croydon, the London and Brighton, and the South Eastern railway companies) began to use the viaduct and station.[90] An adjoining station was built on spare ground to the north, in the late thirties, by the Croydon company; but exchanged, after a few years, for the London and Greenwich's original site, where a new and enlarged joint-station was constructed. Quarrels about facilities and about the toll (of $4\frac{1}{2}$d per passenger) charged by the London and Greenwich led, first of all to the building of a 'secessionist' station at Bricklayers 'Arms (No. 6 on map) by the South Eastern, and later to the leasing of the Greenwich Company by the South Eastern. Bricklayers' Arms remained as a type of 'folly', fulfilling a function as a goods station (to which it was re-classified in 1852) but built in a style sufficiently grandiose to make a suitable reception point for Napoleon III.[91] A further merger—between the London and Brighton, and the London and Croydon companies, which became the London, Brighton and South Coast railway company in 1845—reduced the number of protagonists at London Bridge from four to two in the late 1840's; but the competition between the two remained as intense, and was given physical expression in August 1850 by the construction of a dividing wall down the middle of the station.[92] Both the L.B. & S.C. and the South Eastern continued, over the next twenty years, to pursue

[90] Edwin Course, *op. cit.* 19 *et seq.* H. P. White, *op. cit.* 22 *et seq.*
[91] Edwin Course, *op. cit.* 72.
[92] *Ibid.* 37.

policies of securing separate bridge-head stations on the north bank; policies finally realised at Victoria (L.B. & S.C.) and Charing Cross (S.E.). This competitive extension of the southern lines was further stimulated by the emergence of a third major company in the late 1850's—the London, Chatham and Dover railway company.

The London, Chatham and Dover company was an energetic late-comer to the scene, which played a role in south London similar to that which the M.S. & L. played in Manchester and Liverpool; and in view of its ambitious urban railway building projects it is not surprising that its dividend performance was as poor as that of the M.S. & L.[93] Originally authorised in August 1853 as the modest, 48½-mile, East Kent railway company, within five years the L.C. & D. had built extensions and secured running powers which took it across the other southern companies' territory to a new shared terminal at Victoria (No. 9 on sketch map).[94] At first it had drawn a good part of its support from local speculative builders or landowners, but when the railway contractors Morton Peto and Edward Betts lent their backing to the company its affairs took on a new impetus, and its projects in south London became more ambitious. This phase in its affairs received a set-back in 1866, when the collapse of the banking house of Overend and Gurney brought down Peto and Betts (who left debts of £4,000,000 outstanding), but by that time the shared station at Victoria and the L.C. & D. extension across the river to Farringdon Street had already been opened. The typical L.C. & D. strategy, in O.S. Nock's words, was to share stations and to make link lines 'connecting with every-thing possible, in every direction'.[95] The resulting L.C. & D. linkages with the Great Western, L.B. & S.C., G.N., Midland, L. & S.W., and Metropolitan companies produced an incredibly complicated and space-consuming system of connecting lines and intersecting train services. The L.C. & D. was a major contributor to the 'Battersea Tangle' in the south west; and even in the central district the L.C. & D. carved out a triangle junction to allow through connection with Moorgate and King's Cross via the so-called 'Widened Lines'.

Victoria, Charing Cross and Cannon Street stations took their place in this competitive pattern. The Victoria Station and Pimlico Railway in 1858 was a promotional company of the type with which John Fowler was associated in London, Liverpool and Glasgow. As already mentioned, the L.B. & S.C. company was anxious to extend beyond the shared station at London Bridge, and therefore put up £450,000 of the promotion company's capital of £675,000 in 1858. After an

[93] H. P. White, *A Regional History of the Railways of Great Britain, Vol. II, Southern England* (ed. D. St. J. Thomas, 1961), 39 *et. seq.*
[94] T. C. Barker and Michael Robbins, *op. cit* 142, 151.
[95] O. S. Nock, *op. cit.* 110-3.

K*   265

unsuccessful attempt to take over entire control in 1860, it continued to share Victoria with the L.C. & D., and with those companies running through the West London Extension line or the L.C. & D. Farringdon Street branch; i.e. the Great Western, and even, occasionally, the Midland or Great Northern companies.[96] Once the promotion of Victoria had succeeded, Parliamentary Committees found it difficult to refuse a similar concession to the South Eastern railway company, and the Charing Cross and Cannon Street stations were authorised one and three years respectively after the Victoria Station and Pimlico Railway was incorporated.[97]

Rivalry between the companies operating north of the river also played a part in determining the number and the timing of station provision in London, though perhaps to a less conspicuous degree. Paddington remained the sole property of the Great Western railway company, relatively isolated from the currents of inter-company rivalry; and the same could be said of the other trunk pioneer's headquarters, those of the London and North Western railway company at Euston (Nos. 2 & 3 on sketch map). The fierce battle which preceded the authorisation of the Direct Northern Railway (or Great Northern), and its 'frightful expense'—£590,000 in Parliamentary expenses alone—is a story which is too well known to be repeated here.[98] From the struggle emerged a new trunk line and terminal at King's Cross (No. 8 on sketch map), which was not, in practice, as directly and rigorously competitive with the London and North Western as had been originally anticipated.[99] The King's Cross terminal was soon shared between the Great Northern and the Midland, as a consequence of an Agreement negotiated in 1857 between James Allport and Seymour Clarke. By it the Midland was allowed to install its own clerks and guards, build sheds for twenty-four locomotives etc., but in return agreed to a scale of tolls which rose, within five years, to £60,000 *per annum*, and agreed also to concede priority to Great Northern trains at the signals.[100] The resulting expense, delays and even accidents persuaded the Midland company to undertake in 1863, the ambitious and costly programme of constructing, at St. Pancras, (No. 12 on sketch map) goods (opened 1867) and passenger (opened 1868) stations. Here was a case of a business accommodation, at first to both partners' benefit, becoming less and less satisfactory as the traffic grew, until the 'guest' company withdrew, and undertook the expensive reduplication of terminal facilities.

[96] BTHR PYB 1/107, 20 March 1860, p. 3 (Hope Scott Q.C.).
[97] 22–3 Vic., c. 131 and 24–5 Vic., c. 93.
[98] H.C., 1857–8, XIV, QQ.1730–33.
[99] Jack Simmons, *The Railways of Britain* (1961), 115.
[100] E. G. Barnes, *op. cit.* 164.

This risk was avoided at Liverpool Street and Broad Street, the other northern terminals authorised in the 1860's. For although a proposal was laid before Parliament, in 1862, by the Great Eastern railway company, that the expense of a city site should be shared, the North London railway company, and its sponsor the L. & N.W., strongly opposed the Bill and secured its rejection. Here again the result was the construction of duplicate facilities—the Broad Street (1865) and Liverpool Street (1875) passenger termini, almost adjacent to each other (No. 13 on sketch map), and each carrying a large short-distance traffic, but with widely different fares policies and catchment areas.[101]

It is, of course, extremely difficult to isolate the effect of inter-company competition from the other factors, of a legislative, financial or social nature, which affected the timing and distribution of railway provisions in London. From the examples cited, however, it would seem that the principal direction it gave was to stimulate the quest for autonomous stations, regardless of expense. The very high cost of metropolitan land pulled one way, suggesting a commonsense and co-operative approach to the problem of terminal costs—which took on unusually formidable proportions in inner and central London. Given such land costs the obvious solution was to share sites. On the other hand, business ambitions, and the practical disharmony created by day-to-day operations pulled in the opposite way, strongly suggesting that separately controlled stations were the only satisfactory solution; and the policies of the Midland or the South Eastern railway companies can only be explained in this light. These conflicting pressures gave rise to a tendency towards the proliferation of termini (as seen on a smaller scale in Manchester); a trend further accentuated by the action of speculative or promotional companies, catering for and playing upon the rivalries of established railways. Whether the station companies were old established toll-charging companies, like the London and Blackwall, or the London and Greenwich (Nos. 4 and 1 on sketch map), or opportunistic speculations like the Victoria Station and Pimlico Railway company (No. 9 on sketch map), they found no shortage of bidders at the prices they asked.

Only the L. & S.W., L. & N.W. and G.W. companies pursued policies which were, on the face of it, relatively uncomplicated by terminal politics. Each built and owned its own terminal, established it early, and did not share it. The Great Western enlarged Paddington (No. 3), as already mentioned. The L. & N.W. and the L. & S.W. carried out operations which, though expensive to execute, and marked in their effects upon the urban fabric, were operationally simple: the advance

[101] H. P. White, *op. cit.* III, 78. T. C. Barker and Michael Robbins *op. cit.* 131.

from Camden Town to a new passenger station at Euston (No. 2), by the L. & N.W., being mirrored by a similar movement from Nine Elms to Waterloo (No. 7), by the L. & S.W. Yet, if one looks more closely, even these companies were more influenced by competition than their straightforward building programmes would suggest. Both the L. & N.W. and the G.W. became involved in the inner 'ring' or underground railways—i.e. the North London, the West London Extension, and the Metropolitan railways; responsibilities which were undertaken partly as a substitute for further and more complex urban railway building under their own direct management. Moreover, both the L. & S.W. and the L. & N.W. entertained plans at various times—1845 and 1864 respectively—to push their passenger stations further in to the centre (in fact to the same site at Charing Cross), though the schemes in each case miscarried.[102] So it does not require any great stretch of imagination to see even these orthodox companies, the L. & N.W., L. & S.W. and G.W., as possible station sharers. The pull of a more central location was in these cases offset by the fact that each company had a secure base from which to appraise the attractions and the disadvantages of a shared junction. The general impression which is left, however, both north and south of the river, is that the loosely spaced ring of fourteen major surface stations only makes sense under the conditions of sectional or isolated competition which prevailed in London after 1846.

3. *The development of railway facilities: a chronological sketch*

Fourteen major central stations are listed on the sketch map accompanying this chapter, and Broad Street/Liverpool Street are merely shown as one unit for reasons of scale. If, to this fifteen, the further central stations deserving treatment be added—Ludgate Hill, St. Paul's, Farringdon Street, Moorgate, Nine Elms etc.—no doubt the complete list could be exended to a score or more. To attempt to present a summary of the information contained in the *Books of Reference* and *Plans and Sections*, or the arguments which attended the authorisation of each of these stations by Parliamentary Select Committees, as in previous *Case Histories*, would extend the present section to overwhelming length. Moreover, as previously mentioned, the metropolitan railway system has been unusually fully covered in the books already listed, so that extensive and detailed treatment would be gratuitous as well as lengthy. Therefore it seems reasonable to refer, in chronological order, but *selectively* to the London's urban lines and stations, emphasising and illustrating the recurring themes which are treated analytically elsewhere—in particular, the exorbitant costs of

[102] E. G. Barnes, *op. cit.* 252. H. P. White, *op. cit.* III, 40.

metropolitan stations, the possible reasons for the scale of these costs, and their operational and financial consequences.

The earliest terminal, at London Bridge, presents a straightforward type of land purchase operation. The approach route ran through a good deal of undeveloped, open land, and at the site large parcels of low value were in Church hands. At this early date, before the railway's own activities had caused values to appreciate, and before the precedent of steep payments had been established, the costs were not unreasonable. Admittedly the London and Greenwich railway company had to approach Parliament for permission to supplement the original £400,000 capital and £133,333 mortgage loan, authorised in 1833, but this was partly because of the novel expense accompanying viaduct construction.[103] The total capital of the London and Greenwich railway company stood at about £1,000,000 in 1845, when the South Eastern took out a lease upon it; and the S.E.'s annual rental of £45,000 assured a steady $4\frac{1}{2}\%$ dividend for L. & G. shareholders. Further extensions, including the northern station, and the extensive re-building in the early 1850's after the terminal had been divided, increased the total costs of the site considerably; but on the other hand London Bridge from its early days carried a traffic which, although short distance, was not notably cheapfare, and was very heavy in volume. In the 1850's the daily arrivals rose from something in the region of ten to over twenty thousand passengers, and by the end of the nineteenth century fifty thousand arrivals per day could be counted. In spite of the complaints by the Chairman of the London and Croydon railway company, and Charles Knight's reference to the 'immense cost' and the 'bickering between companies', the expenses incurred at London Bridge station were not at all unreasonable, and were satisfactorily discounted when set against its long and useful life.[104]

The same might also be said of the two of the other large terminals constructed in the 1830's, Euston and Paddington. In spite of the considerable inflation of estimates, particularly at Euston, the sites provided permanent footholds for two great trunk companies, were timely in construction and, retrospectively at any rate, they must have been viewed as enviable bargains. In each of these cases, as already mentioned, the land was in the hands of the Church, or a few large proprietors, and in a very early stage of development.

The cost of the Fenchurch Street (No. 4) and Bishopsgate (No. 5) terminals opened in the early 1840's was not so unexceptionable in relation to their traffic.[105] The difficulties and expenses encountered by the Eastern Counties railways company at Bishopsgate have already

[103] Edwin Course, *op. cit.* 20, 31.
[104] Charles Knight, *Pictorial Half-Hours in London* (1851), 232.
[105] *The Survey of London*, XXVII (1957), 252–3.

been mentioned, and brief reference has been made to the London and Blackwall railway company's constructional and land purchase problems. Fuller details of the expenses to which this had given rise, even before June 1841, were set forth in a confidential letter to the Directors from two of the firms of solicitors employed. The direct land costs themselves totalled £122,840, as against the £207,700 claimed by the vendors, for the group of properties under consideration by their two firms. Since the total land costs up to August 1842, were elsewhere stated to be £526,000 it may be judged that the two firms handled only a portion of the total.[106] What is interesting and worthy of note, however, is the explanation which the solicitors felt obliged to attach to their bill.

'It has been imagined', they wrote, 'that the legal expenses should bear a proportion to the length of a Railway. We submit that they ought rather to be considered in reference to the district through which it may pass; this, in the present instance, as you well know is for the greater part the most densely populated of any in London, mostly by tradesmen and manufacturers, and almost every house owned by a different landlord, with various derivative leases, all of which have to be separately purchased and conveyed.' The result of this, and of the claims for the goodwill lost by enforced removal, was to produce demands, they explained, which were complex and extortionate.

All this has already been referred to, and illustrated, in other contexts and other cities. What takes the breath away in this case is the full and detailed breakdown of the solicitors' own charges in dealing with the £122,840 worth of property they had purchased.

	£
To attending counsel in Parliament, 137 days	25,010
Stamp duties, court fees, charges for jury cases	37,342
Payments to vendors' solicitors for conveyances	25,911
Engineering and surveying charges, parliamentary agency, salaries of clerks, rents, taxes and advertisements	28,123
	116,386

This sum excluded, of course, the charge made by counsel themselves in Parliament; and the engineers referred to were the solicitors' engineers, not the company's consultant or resident engineers. Even if one limits the solicitors' charges to those directly connected with the land transfer, they come to £63,253; or approximately half as much as the total purchase price awarded.

[106] Six-monthly Report, 30 August 1842, London and Blackwall railway company.
[107] BTHR RAC 1 227A, Letter dated 28 January 1843.

Partly as a result of these, and other similar expenses, the Blackwall railway company's affairs were in so precarious a state by 1843 that a shareholders' Committee of Investigation was set up, and professed itself 'alarmed at the great outlay'; two years later the company was saved by being absorbed by amalgamation with the Eastern Counties.[108] The Eastern Counties itself however was hardly in a better financial state than the Blackwall, and for much the same reasons. It crashed financially in 1848, and the rolling stock at Bishopsgate station was seized for debt.

The three stations authorised in the mid-1840's (Nos. 6, 7 and 8) formed a mixed bag, but shared one feature in common; they all cost more than had been anticipated. The 'Grand West End Terminus' at Bricklayers' Arms (1843–6) finally cost £1,000,000 instead of the £400,000 estimated, and passengers could only be induced to alight at such an inconvenient station by a substantial differential in the fare.[109] Croydon to London Bridge cost 2s 3d, to Bricklayers' Arms only 1s 3d; so on strictly financial grounds it made no sense to build such a terminus to escape the 4½d toll levied by the London and Greenwich. From a tactical point of view, however, the £1,000,000 spent upon Bricklayers' Arms served the purpose of bringing the smaller company to terms.[110] 'All attempts to create a passenger traffic (at Bricklayers' Arms) have failed', Charles Knight later reported; and in 1852 the station was reclassified as a goods terminus.[111]

The L. & S.W.'s advance from Nine Elms to Waterloo (1846–8), by contrast, was no folly, produced by the tactical needs of a passing phase of railway politics, but an obvious and logical extension of existing facilities. Although the cost came to £1,250,000 instead of £800,000, even this was still not unreasonable, and was accounted for by the extensive swathe cut through residential property. The 1,600 cottages and parcels of land, hop warehouses, coach sheds and yards, were mostly in ecclesiastical ownership, and had been leased in unusually large batches; not the customary half dozen or dozen per person, but up to a hundred or a hundred and fifty properties being held by individual lessees, not infrequently in conjunction with other individuals whose names recurred elsewhere in the same *Book of Reference*, and who formed a series of shifting partnerships or syndicates. These large leaseholdings, together with the small number of proprietors, should have made for relatively cheap land transactions; yet the 1¼ mile Waterloo extension accounted for almost 25% of the L. & S.W.'s

[108] W. M. Acworth, *The Railways of England* (1900), 408–9.
[109] Edwin Course, *op. cit.* 71.
[110] 'Making Bricklayers' Arms was a matter of compulsion in driving the Greenwich people to reasonable terms' (Vignoles), C. F. Dendy Marshall, *op. cit.* 31.
[111] Charles Knight, *Pictorial Half-Hours, etc.* 233.

entire capitalisation in 1849—a large proportion, but nothing that could not be digested by a company with growing traffic and competitive premises.

At King's Cross station (1846–52), the land ownership pattern, likewise, was not unfavourable. There were one or two unusual complications; for example, the relationship between owners and tenants was diametrically opposite to that just cited for Waterloo. Instead of one owner leasing property to syndicates of tenants, a syndicate of thirteen owners leased their property to a single lessee; but only thirty properties were affected in this way.[112] The greater part of the site was given over to a smallpox and fever hospital, there was a good proportion of open ground, and the approaches through Islington were largely owned by St. Bartholomew's Hospital, by George Keck (110 parcels of land), and by Henry Tufnell (150 parcels of land). From the way in which the estimates were drawn up it is not possible to extract a figure for the King's Cross project as a whole; and later estimates as to the actual cost vary, but it seems likely that here again a station was established, at a cost around one million pounds, which formed a substantial asset rather than a burden upon the operating company.

The timing of the stations mentioned so far was clearly of cardinal importance. The first three major stations, projected and built in the 1830's, had all proved sound propositions. The Fenchurch Street and Bishopsgate termini, a little later, ran into serious difficulties. Although there might, superficially, appear to be no reason why railways setting off from London in any compass direction should not stand an equally good chance of making a profit, there were marked differences in prospects. In the east the combination of short-distance runs through lightly populated rural areas, and lengthy viaduct approaches through crowded urban districts, in fragmented ownership, and against a background of rapidly appreciating land values, had severely strained the finances of both the Eastern Counties and the Blackwall railway companies. In spite of these clear indications of the way in which prices for terminal sites were increasing, however, the next three stations (Nos. 6, 7, 8), built in the mid or late 1840's were all viable as business enterprises in themselves—even Bricklayers' Arms, in all likelihood, once it had been converted to a more appropriate use—and they did not require justification solely upon strategic or competitive grounds. Yet already this aspect of their construction was assuming greater importance. The Railway Department of the Board of Trade, reporting on railway schemes in Kent in 1845 had laid it down as a guide to selection that 'preference should be given to those with established termini', and on these grounds had recommended the South Eastern

[112] HLRO, P & S, B.Ref., 1846, Direct Northern Railway Properties 38–68 in St. Mary, Islington.

railway company since 'it has the Bricklayers' Arms, or a proposed extension at Hungerford Bridge.'[113] By the time the building of the terminals planned in the 1840's had been completed, the advantages of a secure foothold in London had become still more marked. Even shareholders had come to doubt the prospects of return upon the huge sums required for metropolitan terminals; as John Bright was flatly told in 1852, when he asked the Secretary to the Railway Department whether there was any chance that a direct Manchester to London railway and terminus might be constructed. It was ruled out, Samuel Laing replied, because 'the expense of getting a metropolitan terminus is so enormous, and is probably increasing so much every day, that unless a rival scheme is grafted upon some existing company, there is no immediate probability, in the present state of the money and railway markets, of having it carried out.' It would be more economical, he added, in reply to a later question from the chairman of the Select Committee, to lay down four lines along existing routes than to construct a new approach, 'the great expense is the terminal stations and getting into London.'[115] The expense was enough, in fact, to cause the pidgeon-holing of several interesting and ambitious schemes for railway building put forward in the mid-1850's, and railway terminal building was not renewed until the closing years of the decade, with the Victoria station project in the middle of the Marquis of Westminster's estate (No. 9 on sketch map).[116]

The building of a terminal in such an area might well seem to have offered insuperable difficulties, both in terms of expense and the opposition which might be aroused; but an ingenious and relatively inexpensive way of reducing costs and disarming opposition was discovered by John Fowler. Fowler was backed, in his formation of an independent Terminal Company, the 'Victoria Station and Pimlico Railway', in 1857, by Betts, Peto and Kelk, who gave credit and also became large shareholders, and by the London, Brighton and South Coast railway company, which subscribed half the capital required for this speculative venture.[117] He was also assisted by two fortunate chances: the construction (1853–8) of a short (6-mile) spur railway— 'the railway to a turnstile'—from the Crystal Palace's new site at

[113] H.C., 1845, XXXIX, 13 February, pp. 4–5, 7.

[114] H.C., 1852–3, XXXVIII, Q.110.

[115] *Ibid.* Q.250.

[116] The most ambitious and expensive of which was Paxton's Great Victorian Way, proposed in H.C., 1854–5, X, QQ. 711–850. 'The scheme I then projected was to form an internal girdle of railways', Paxton said later. 'It was at the time of the Russian war and I had not then the opportunity of submitting it fairly before the public in order to bring it out.' The estimated cost was £34,000,000. HLRO, Min., H.L., 1861, 11 March, pp. 4–7, S.C. on Charing Cross Railway (City Terminus).

[117] H. P. White, *op. cit.* III, 32.

Sydenham, to what was grandly called a 'West End terminus' on the south bank of the river, in Battersea; and the existence on the northern side of the bank, of the 'Grosvenor Canal'.[118] The one-mile long Grosvenor canal was not, in origin, a canal at all, but part of the old Chelsea Waterworks and reservoir, which had been constructed in 1725 to provide water for domestic purposes, but later converted to take barge traffic.[119] In 1857 conversations took place between the Marquis of Westminster and the Victoria Station and Pimlico Railway representatives in which it was suggested that the unattractive and virtually submerged route and basin of the Grosvenor canal should be used. 'In approaching it,' Morton Peto observed, in his evidence to the Select Committee, 'you avoid any large viaduct across an expensive building property by using the canal . . . the wide thoroughfares are not likely to be surcharged with traffic—and long platforms will be possible.'[120] Special features to preserve the amenity of the district included the planting of shrubs on the approaches to the bridge, and the banning of goods trains, the roofing over of the station approach, the insertion of rubber underlays beneath the sleepers to deaden the sound, and the building of bridge parapets to an aesthetic standard judged satisfactory by the First Commissioner of Works.[121] Even with these features, however, the estimated cost came to only £675,000; a very reasonable sum for a mile and a quarter through such a district, and there can be little doubt that a contributory factor was the favourable attitude of the Marquis of Westminster. He owned all the property, including the canal basin, except for a couple of dozen parcels of land, houses and a shop, which belonged to William Stanley.[122]

One can only speculate as to why he gave his assent to the scheme, for, in spite of the precautions taken, it did tend to reduce the residential attractiveness of the immediate area. On the other hand the new Victoria Street had already opened in 1851, and the character of this quarter of Belgravia was beginning to change from residential to that of a more vigorous mixed zone, of shops, offices and places of professional and other business. The canal site was also obsolete for transport use, and an Act of 1852 had forbidden the extraction of water for domestic purposes. In 1854, moreover, a company called the Westminster Terminus Railway had secured authority to cross the river to the site of the Grey Coat School on Horseferry Road; though

---

[118] *The Survey of London*, XXVI (1956), 6–7.
[119] Edwin Course, *op. cit.* 95.
[120] HLRO, Min., H.C., 1858, 7 May, pp. 4–5, Victoria Station and Pimlico Railway.
[121] HLRO, Min., (Vic. Stn. & Pim. Rly), H.L., 1858, 5 July pp. 41–52. Edwin Course, *op. cit.* 96.
[122] HLRO, P & S, B.Ref., 1858, Vic. Stn. & Pim. Rly. Properties 32–47, 66–75.

it had not, in fact, followed up the scheme.[123] Presumably, under these circumstances, it may have seemed wise to settle for £3,000 *per annum* chief rent, and for an undisclosed portion of the £675,000.[124]

A contemporary scheme, proposed at the same time, and authorised in 1859/61, was the twin Charing Cross and Cannon Street extension (Nos. 10 and 11).[125] This differed from the Victoria Station and Pimlico Railway, in that it was directly and wholly sponsored by one large parent company—the South Eastern, but it is interesting to note that the same business technique of a separate terminal company was used. Originally estimated to cost £1,070,000, the Charing Cross railway company had expended £3,000,000 by the time it was wound up, in August, 1864.[126]

Although not, perhaps, as irredeemably beyond the margins of profitability as the later Marylebone scheme, instanced below, it is very dubious whether the Charing Cross scheme ever broke even. On their own assessment of £1,070,000 the South Eastern had optimistically hoped for a return of $7\frac{1}{2}\%$; a surcharge of 3d per head on 8,000,000 passengers who would travel the extra distance instead of alighting at London Bridge.[127] In fact the scheme cost three times the estimate, and the traffic, for many years, remained far below that expected. Only by 1903 was the figure of 10,000,000 passenger journeys to and from Charing Cross realised. Moreover it is not clear whether, in his estimate for running expenses, the secretary, Samuel Smiles, included a sufficient allowance for the heavy charge of staffing and maintaining a new station, or of paying municipal rates and other expenses.[128] Certainly the direct costs of operating the engines and rolling stock were increased far beyond those anticipated by the failure to take a realistic view of the amount of siding space likely to be available at the station; and Smiles' estimate of operating costs (which equalled 25% on revenue for the terminal and short line) seems unduly sanguine, in view of the 47–49% operating costs returned on the national rail network as a whole at this time.[129] Altogether it is likely that the new line and station did

[123] T. C. Barker and Michael Robbins, *op. cit.* 141. C. E. Lee, 'The First West End Terminus', *Railway Magazine* (1958), 164. Peto and Brassey also sponsored this project.

[124] HLRO, Min., (Vic. Stn. & Pim. Rly), H.L., 1858, 5 July, p. 71.

[125] Edwin Course, *op. cit.* 51.

[126] Six-monthly Report, 25 August 1864, Charing Cross Railway, BTHR RAC 1 378.

[127] The simple calculation ran: 8 million $\times$ 3d = £100,000 + £5,000 for rent of premises beneath viaduct, — £25,000 running expenses = £80,000, or 8% on £1,070,000.

[128] H.C., 1905, XXX, 614–5. Edwin Course, *London Railways* (1962) 48, *idem*, *The evolution etc.* (London Ph.D. thesis, 1958), 251. T. C. Barker and Michael Robbins, *op. cit.* 224.

[129] H.C., 1890, LXV, 680–1.

not return enough additional revenue even to service the heavy capital expenditure; and certainly not enough to pay for the scheme and show a commercial profit.

The question, therefore, arises as to why, even under the favourable conditions of landownership which made such schemes feasible in south London, the expense should be so exorbitant. One answer lies in the fact that in the 1840's and certainly by the late 1850's, the area was very densely built up; and the expense of cutting a swathe, even through poor property, should not be underestimated in such circumstances. William Tite, who was both architect to the London and South Western railway company and a Governor of St. Thomas's Hospital (due for demolition by the Charing Cross scheme) revealed to the Commons' Committee that his own company, the South Western, had contemplated a similar scheme but had been deterred by the expense. For some years, he stated, an Act had been drawn up 'for the continuation of a railway which was to a certain extent identical with this . . . (but it had been abandoned) . . . at the instance of all the old proprietors in Liverpool and Manchester on the ground that it would not pay for executing the work.'[130] In the late 1850's less cautious calculations prevailed, however, than those enjoined on the South Western company's management by their provincial shareholders.

A large part of the sums expended on property by the southern railway companies went to the Church, in respect of their ground rents, or improved ground rents; but the total was swollen by other payments in compensation, in the way described by land valuers like Francis Fuller. 'In London property there are frequently numerous interests, that is to say there are so many as two or three leaseholders, besides the tenant from year to year or the tenant at will. . . . In the same property? —In the same house. . . . Those interests I suppose must be compensated? At what do you put them? Take the actual tenant's interest without reference to the leasehold—I divide them this way. I take the tenants first of all and I put them down at 5% upon the cost. Then 5% for the interest of the leaseholder, equals 10%, plus 10% for compulsory sale.'[131] Another 10% was added for conveyance and surveyors' charges, and 10% as a 'safety fund'. This increase of 40% was allowed, in an experienced valuer's back-of-the-envelope calculations, over and above the cost of purchasing the ground landlord's interest, and the buildings and outstanding years' interest held by the leaseholders or groups of leaseholders. Those most directly affected by the scheme, the sub-tenants, lodgers and other occupants, received nothing by right, unless a small inducement to move quietly were paid, presumably out

[130] HLRO, Min., H.C., 1859, 28 March, p. 275, S.C. on London Bridge and Charing Cross Railway.
[131] BTHR PYB 1/112/6, 18 July 1860, pp. 76–8.

of the 5% extra for the 'tenant's interest'. Nevertheless even with the additional 40%, the estimates were grossly understated; not perhaps upon the real current value, but upon the value which sympathetic juries or arbiters were likely to award. It is clear that where calculations of an engineering and structural nature were concerned the estimates bore some resemblance to the ultimate costs; but where the purchase of property was at issue the estimates bore little relationship to reality or to past experience.

The two major schemes executed in the 1860's, St. Pancras and Liverpool Street (Nos. 12 and 13), both cost far more than the parent companies could properly afford. The Great Eastern was, in fact, brought into Chancery by the effort of constructing Liverpool Street. Even such a short extension—under a mile from Bishopsgate—cost over £2,000,000; and the attitude of the Great Eastern managers towards it has already been described. The Midland railway company's finances were much sounder, and its traffic more firmly established at the time it planned the St. Pancras extension, and yet the undertaking lopped two *per cent* off the company's dividends.[132] Liddell and Barlow's original estimate of the cost of the London extension, in 1862, had totalled £1,750,000, but by 1867 a special general meeting had to be called to raise a further £2,150,000. 'It has, in fact, been found,' a Midland circular to shareholders announced, 'that the value of property required and the amount of compensations have been enormously in excess of what was anticipated, and it would seem that *the cost of carrying the works of a railway into London is such as to defy all previous calculation.*'[133] W. E. Hutchinson, Chairman of the Midland railway company, enlarged upon this theme at the special meeting in January, 1868, giving as the main cause for the increase in estimates 'the steep rise in property values after 1862, which had also affected the rates of compensation paid for land taken for the company's purposes.'[134]

One final scheme remains, the belated entry of the company which had already played an important role in re-shaping railway provisions in Manchester and Liverpool—the M.S. & L., now, with a suitable change of name, achieving metropolitan status. The formidable nature of the property enclave into which entry was required for the Marylebone station (No. 14 on sketch map) together with the extra accommodation works required (although these, at least, could be calculated), and the fact that almost half the lessees were occupiers, increased the cost beyond all reasonable estimation.[135] Charles Niddell had only been

[132] E. G. Barnes, *op. cit.* 187.
[133] Circular to Shareholders, 17 December 1867, Midland railway company, H. C. Prince, *loc. cit.* 127. My italics.
[134] E. G. Barnes, *op. cit.* 261.
[135] HLRO, P & S, B.Ref., 1892, M.S. & L. (Extension to London).

prepared to say that the station would probably cost about £400,000; and total works would be approximately a further £2,525,000, of which £1,427,000 could be for land purchase.[136] In fact the final cost of the railway scheme came to over £6,000,000; a sum which, on any rational basis of calculation, meant the surcharging of all terminal traffic at the rate of over £100,000 per mile *per annum*. Perhaps one might say that it is at this point that the railways were, beyond all doubt, overtaken by the rise in land values.[137] Schemes had become increasingly expensive—the St. Pancras, Liverpool Street and Charing Cross/Cannon Street schemes, had all been approaching the margin in the 1860's—but the Marylebone terminal and approach required justification, if it were at all possible, upon other grounds than those of profitability. On the basis of the traffic running into Marylebone Station ten years after its opening, an extra 12s should have been levied upon each passenger to meet the interest charge alone on the works necessary to bring him the last two miles of his journey.[138]

4. *Summary and general considerations*

There is one unusual feature of London's railway pattern emerging in the course of narrative which perhaps merits closer examination. Apart from limited exceptions, noted below, London was never completely traversed by any single main-line company. The northern and southern groups of railway companies did not merge into cross-river amalgamations. London remained a species of watershed from which railways flowed separately to the north and the south.

Indeed, it may appear to require no explanation or comment that London should have presented a barrier to the amalgamation of railway companies. Yet much more elaborate and unlikely mergers took place, and the long-distance main line companies demonstrated a keenly competitive spirit over the extension of their services northwards. The compulsion to seek trunk running arrangements even crossed the Border, in the 1870's, in the form of traffic alliances between the L. & N.W. and the Caledonian, the Midland and the Glasgow and South Western, the Great Northern and the North British companies.[139] It would seem no more than logical that the great trunk lines from the north should seek to run from coast to coast; and there is, in fact,

---

[136] *Ibid.* Railways Nos. 6–12.

[137] 'Immense compensation' had been paid to the Marylebone proprietors, W. Besant, *London North of the Thames* (1911), 342.

[138] H.C., 1905, XXX, 614–5. Passengers to and from Great Central terminus totalled 500,000 in 1903. The interest charge on the total capital expended for the Marylebone scheme (at 5%) = £300,000.

[139] O. S. Nock, *Scottish Railways* (1961), 9–10. HLRO, Min., H.C., 1873 7 May, pp. 18–20, S.C. on Caledonian Railway (Glasgow Central Station).

evidence that such an ambition crossed the minds of some of the main-line companies' managers, although the field was given over to speculative gestures rather than convinced business strategy. To take first of all the most likely candidate—Edward Watkin. As Chairman of the M.S. & L., the Metropolitan and the South Eastern railway companies, Watkin would seem to have been almost ideally placed for executing a through linkage from Northern England to the South Coast; or even (as Cleveland-Stevens suggested) from the north of England to Europe, if the projected Channel Tunnel scheme had come to fruition.[140] There is, however, no direct evidence that such a scheme seriously entered Watkin's calculations. Watkins 'did not confide his policy to many people', or disclose any set programme—even to his own General Manager, John Bell. Moreover the last link in the connection, that of the Great Central's entry into London, was only executed on the eve of Watkin's retirement in 1894, and, in Harold Pollins' opinion, may not have been in Watkin's mind before the late 1880's. Even after the entry to London had been effected, it is difficult to see how direct express connections across London could take place between the Marylebone/Baker Street and the South Eastern railway system.[141]

There is, however, some direct evidence from other quarters of main-line schemes for crossing London. At the time of the Cobden Treaty liberalising trade with France (1860), both Seymour Clarke of the Great Northern railway, and James Allport of the Midland pressed forward schemes for a through linkage. The Midland hoped to join the southern railways at Charing Cross, 'to avail themselves of the bridge there.'[142] Already, Allport pointed out in 1863, the French Treaty had had the effect of increasing the continental traffic, and he expected it might increase fivefold 'in a few years'. The Midland railway company, which already passed 100,000 tons of goods through London, wished to share in this rapidly growing traffic.[143] The Great Northern, likewise, experienced a similar anxiety to claim a share of the continental trade, conducting specific and detailed negotiations with the London, Chatham and Dover, the company which constructed the only through line in central London, that over Blackfriars Bridge (centre of sketch map).

Seymour Clarke's primary motive for seeking the connection was to reduce the cross-town cartage, which was costing the Great Northern £50,000 *per annum*, and necessitated the stabling of five hundred horses.[144] If the demand for trunk passenger bookings from Dover to the north or *vice versa* rapidly increased, however, then the under-

---

[140] H. Pollins, 'The Last Main Railway Line to London', *JTH*, IV (1959), 85–95.
[141] T. C. Barker and Michael Robbins, *op. cit.* 211.
[142] H.C., 1863, VIII, Q.504.
[143] *Ibid*. QQ.510–23.
[144] *Ibid*. QQ.367–80.

standing with the London, Chatham and Dover company would be doubly useful. On his side J. S. Forbes, the General Manager of the L.C. & D. railway company, shared the same hopes. He had at one time been the manager in charge of stabling and carting for the Great Western company, and was, therefore, unusually interested in the trans-shipment problems caused by the break in connection. It cost, he estimated, an additional five or six shillings per ton to transfer the freight from the Great Northern to the L.C.D. lines, apart from the burden of running a large carting establishment. The employment of agents, such as Pickford's or Chaplin and Horne's, could reduce this burden, but only at the cost of raising further problems of accommodation and status.[145]

It must be admitted that the other managers of the southern railway companies did not share Forbes' enthusiasm. Cornelius Eborall, of the South Eastern railway company, dismissed any idea of a central junction at Charing Cross with the northern companies as 'a perfect Babel'. 'There is much more to be done in widening the streets', he asserted, 'than can possibly be done by railway communication.'[146] Frederick Slight, of the London, Brighton and South Coast railway company, which was still digesting the effects of its move to Victoria, also held the view that no north-south linkage, other than that provided by the West London line upstream, was advisable. Yet a union of the Great Northern and the London, Chatham and Dover companies might have caused a reconsideration of these views.

Colonel Yolland, Inspector on the Railway Department of the Board of Trade, who was asked to draw up a general plan (much to John Hawkshaw's disgust), certainly spoke of the anxiety felt by all three of the northern main line companies in the early 1860's; and the solution he suggested was that the L. & N.W., the Midland, and the Great Northern companies should all be allowed to make a junction with the southern railways at Charing Cross, where the levels would be suitable, and the river bridge already under construction.[147] Seymour Clarke, perhaps the most ardent supporter of the idea of a north-south route, went even further, and suggested that *two* large new central termini should be built; one on the south bank to which the northern companies would have access, and one on the north bank for the southern companies.[148]

However, these grandiose notions of railways spanning London came to nothing, with the exception only of the London, Chatham and Dover

---

[145] *Ibid.* QQ.848–51. Some of the goods, such as the iron masts from the north for Chatham dockyard, caused serious carting problems.
[146] Ibid QQ.659, 670–6.
[147] *Ibid.* QQ.193, 218–27, 1092 (James Booth, Col. Yolland, John Hawkshaw).
[148] *Ibid.* Q.350.

company's metropolitan extension to Farringdon Street and Holborn, authorised in 1860. Apart from this, the only other line across London sanctioned by the Joint Select Committee of 1864, after careful consideration of the public issues involved, was a cut-and-cover scheme which offered to construct contemporaneously three important new streets from Tottenham Court Road down to the Embankment, and to carry out extensive demolition in the notorious slum districts at Seven Dials, and High Street, St. Giles.[149] The expense which this public aspect of its construction involved resulted in the indefinite postponement of the scheme—the 'Hampstead, Midland, North Western and Charing Cross Junction'; and the same fate overtook the Central London Railway in 1871, and other similar projects.[150]

Linkages were made outside the central area, both upstream, by the West London, and downstream, by the East London railway and tunnel; but in each case the small companies concerned became 'service' railways—meeting grounds for all interested parties rather than links between specific companies. The East London line (1869–76) came under the joint management of six companies—the L.B. & S.C., the L.C. & D., and the South Eastern companies to the south of the river, the Great Eastern to the north, and the two Underground companies.[151] The West London Extension railway across the river (1859–63) was owned by four railway companies and offered facilities to the London and South Western and the L.B. & S.C. south of the Thames, and to the L. & N.W. and the G.W. north of the river. Both the East and West London connections were useful for the transfer of freight, but their development of through passenger traffic was belated and insignificant.[152] Essentially London remained a city where the journeys were broken, traffic was transferred by street from one main-line terminus to another, and the railway companies changed.

This topic has been discussed in some detail because, on at least two occasions, the barrier to competition seemed likely to be swept aside. In 1846 and in 1863 it appeared almost inevitable to contemporaries that London was about to be served in the same way as the other major cities. 'It seems that we are to be allowed no rest from railway engineering operation', wrote John Hollingshead in 1862, 'until the great idea of a central station in the City of London is made to take material shape. Every railway, at present condemned to have its terminus in the outskirts, is looking wistfully towards that coveted spot within the shadow of St. Paul's, and making signs to its brethren

[149] P. J. Edwards, *History of London Street Improvements, 1855–1897*, (1898) 61. H.C., 1864 (87) XI, 2–3.
[150] BTHR, PYB 1/535, 23 March 1871, pp. 1–4.
[151] T. C. Barker and Michael Robbins, *op. cit.* 145. H. P. White, *op. cit.* III, 94–5.
[152] T. C. Barker and Michael Robbins, *op. cit.* 229. H. P. White, *op. cit.* II, 125–7.

281

to join hands in drawing the circle together. The Eastern Counties is not content to remain at Shoreditch; the Great Western is dissatisfied with Paddington; the North Western and the Great Northern are not happy at Euston Square and King's Cross; the Brighton railway is discontented with Southwark, although it has stretched out in a roundabout direction and has succeeded in crossing the river at Battersea, and in reaching Pimlico; the South Eastern has already taken steps to push on to Hungerford Market by way of the suspension bridge, where it expects to be joined by the South Western railway, which is fretting down in the hollow of the Waterloo Road; and the Greenwich, Chatham, Southend and other lines are all directing their eyes to one common centre.'[153]

Hollingshead was a professional journalist, a *protegé* of Charles Dickens, and a shrewd observer of many different aspects of London life; and in his view the junction of the main-line companies seemed not speculative but imminent. His views were exactly echoed, thirty years later, by another well-informed observer, Charles Booth, to whom the impenetrable nature of the metropolis seemed a matter for wonder.

'Reaching London from north, west and east, the railways for the most part touch, but do not cross, this semi-circle; and the southern lines, with one exception, are content if they can deliver their passengers on the northern bank of the river. The one exception, which passes its trains under the very shadow of St. Paul's, and discharges its passengers at Holborn, was most dearly paid for. Even tramcars infringe but little on this charmed circle; within it plies the omnibus, but it is still more essentially the sphere of the hansom cab.'[154]

The failure of the main-line companies to break this 'charmed circle' profoundly changed the pattern of railway construction, and influenced its functional efficiency, in the whole London area. 'The necessity imposed on all the railways of making their connections without infringing on the central area however' the Royal Commission on London Traffic of 1905 concluded, after its detailed survey, 'has had an unfortunate effect on the railway system taken as a whole. The connections which have actually been made are not nearly so useful for local traffic, or so convenient for connecting purposes, as they might have been, if the central area had not been barred, nor do they harmonise so well with comprehensive urban and suburban railway schemes designed to meet modern needs.'[155] This oval of prohibited ground—four miles from east to west and one and a half from north to south—not merely distorted directly the pattern of railway building, but also exercised an arbitrary and indirect influence upon the conditions of

[153] J. Hollingshead, *Underground London* (1862), 204.
[154] Charles Booth, *Life and Labour of the People of London* (1892), I, 189.
[155] H.C., 1905, XXX, 609.

competition between companies. The central government's unique exercise of a legislative *veto* combined with metropolitan central land values to erect a barrier around the core of the city which was virtually impassable to surface railways.

Part Three

*The Impact of Railways
on Victorian Cities*

X

The railway as an agent of internal change in Victorian cities; the city centre

1. *Introduction*

THE rapid growth of the major Victorian cities was accompanied by internal changes in communications which, though not as dramatic as the arrival of the railways, were essential to sustain continued expansion throughout the nineteenth century.

The greatly increased internal circulation of people and goods, by day and night, in the expanding cities, had to be accommodated by expensive street re-alignments and improvements. The alterations in each town required no new techniques, and make a dull chronicle, but neither the investment effort nor the results should be underestimated. The sums involved in cutting new streets in Birmingham and London, where the most drastic alterations took place, ran to a million and a half per scheme in the 1870's; operations comparable in nature if not in total scale, with the urban railway works. The improvement of Victorian cities' internal roads kept pace, though only by the narrowest of margins, with the growing numbers of road vehicles, and provided them with variable routes for transit at approximately one third to one half of modern urban road speeds.[1] The new variety and number of public cabs and omnibuses, and the volume and increasingly specialised types of commercial vehicle which thronged the streets in mid-century, reflect a service industry which was growing as rapidly as any in Victorian cities.[2]

In London, for example, although the numbers employed in regular

[1] From 3·28 to 4·55 m.p.h. (H.C., 1863, VIII, QQ.1226–8) to between 5 and 10 m.p.h. effective speeds. R. J. Smeed, 'The Traffic Problem in Towns', *Town Planning Review* 35 (1964–5), 133–58.

[2] John Hollingshead, *Odd Journeys in and out of London* (1860), 182–6, describes the great range and variety of horse drawn vehicle seen on the streets.

service for the railways, as clerks, porters, guards, drivers and other officials, roughly trebled between 1861 and 1891 (from 8,300 to 24,800), the numbers employed as carmen and carters also trebled (from 14,700 to 43,800). The employment offered by the passenger cabs, omnibuses and coaches in 1891 added a further 48,200, so that the totals engaged in horse-drawn urban transport of passengers and goods were more than three times as large as those in regular metropolitan railway service. With their families and dependents they numbered, according to Charles Booth's calculations, some 260,000 people—one of the largest occupational groups in London.[3] It is true that many of the carters, cabbies and omnibus drivers were engaged upon cross traffic and feeder services connected with the railways, but others provided services which were sturdily competitive. Within a ten mile radius of London by far the greater part of retail distribution was in the hands of the carters. Even Mr. Seymour Teulon, an ex-director of the South Eastern railway company, who lived twenty-one miles out of town, found it more convenient to use a carter in the 1860's; and in 1900 the vans and carts had a virtual monopoly, 90% or more, of the merchandise and shop goods, over a two-hour journey or ten-mile radius.[4] On the streets of London's inner district the horse buses, given a new profitability by the fall in imported feeding-stuffs, gained passengers at a faster rate than the railways in the fourth quarter of the century.[5]

The last quarter of the nineteenth century also saw the belated application of the railway principle to urban street traffic. Although at first introduced experimentally—in Glasgow, for example, the first horse tramways were intended to move coal and other goods by night and passengers by day—they were soon established as the only practical method of improving upon orthodox horse-power; doubling the stage lengths and trebling traction.[6] Using very limited technical means the street tramway provided the most substantial of all contributions to the Victorian cities' internal transport problems, conveying, by the end of the century—even in London, where the lengths of run favoured the railway—forty five *per cent* more passengers annually than local railways.[7] The tramcar played a role which was important enough to survive for many decades into the age of electricity and the petrol engine. It shared the drawbacks of a fixed-route system, seen so clearly in the urban surface-railway lines; but the force of these drawbacks was greatly reduced by the fact that the stops were frequent and easy

---

[3] Charles Booth, *op. cit.* VII, 284.
[4] H.C., 1867, XXXVIII, Q.16441 (Teulon); H.C., 1904 (305) VII, QQ.113–4.
[5] T. C. Barker and Michael Robbins, *op. cit.* 243, 261, 271.
[6] HLRO, Min., H.C., 1872, 3 June, S.C. on Glasgow, Coatbridge and Airdrie Tramways.
[7] H.C., 1905, XXX, 570.

PLATE 5   London's traffic in 1872 as seen by Gustav Doré:
London Bridge (see p. 313)

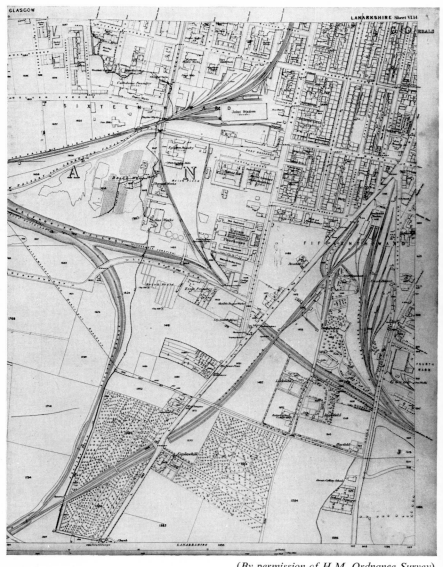

PLATE 6   South Laurieston, Glasgow, 1858 (see p. 292)

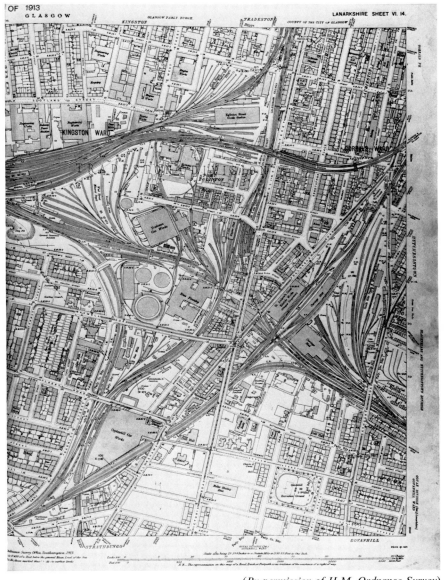

PLATE 7   South Laurieston, Glasgow 1913 (see p. 292)

PLATE 8 London traffic in 1872 as seen by Gustav
Doré: a traffic jam (see p. 316)

of access, and the routes widely and cheaply dispersed.[8] In these ways the growing internal traffic of Victorian cities was accommodated, using simple techniques which had been available at the time early horse-railway pioneers like Thomas Hill had canvassed their ideas in the 1820's.[9]

2. Railway land hunger and the Victorian city

Yet still, even after the other internal transport changes have been given their due weight, the most revolutionary of all the novel features of the mid-nineteenth century city were its new railway stations, and they exercised, over each city, both a general and a local influence. In the first place, the railway station stood as a symbol of the most recent of major advances in technology; the extension, to locomotion and distribution, of steam power, which had already revolutionised substantial sectors of industrial production. In the environment of the Victorian city the modernity of the railway station was outstanding: one arrived by mechanical transport, in a manner which differed only in degree from that of today, before stepping out into a world of horse-drawn vehicles. 'Wonderful Members of Parliament,' wrote Charles Dickens, 'who little more than twenty years before had made themselves merry with the wild railroad theories of engineers, and given them the liveliest rubs in cross examination, went down into the north with watches in their hands, and sent a message before by the electric telegraph to say that they were coming.'[10]

The Victorian railway was also the most important single agency in the transformation of the central area of many of Britain's major cities. Unlike the ubiquitous horse omnibus, cab or tramcar, operating cheaply upon the public thoroughfare, it could only function if large areas of the town were exclusively set aside for its fixed routes and separate rights of way. Nor could its equipment be dispersed at night into scores of small yards and stables, located wherever a cheap and convenient space presented itself. Although, like the horse-drawn traffic, the railway was called into being primarily to serve the traffic needs of established business and residential areas, it was a noisy and obtrusive servant. Soon the space it required was comparable with that of any other single group of commercial or industrial land users.

It is not easy to present an undistorted measurement of the impact

---

[8] Cost per mile: Tramways £40,000 (without street widening)
              Tubes £250,000—£300,000
           Railways £1,000,000 (cut and cover)
  H.C., 1905, XXX, 590.
[9] MRL, Political Tracts, P 3411, P3486.
[10] Charles Dickens, *Dombey and Son*, Ch. 6.

L

of railway land-hunger upon Victorian cities. For example, there is, as yet, no standard classification of the central business districts of British cities comparable to that carried out in the United States by J. E. Vance, R. E. Murphy and B. J. Epstein.[11] Nor are there, as yet, any published series of historical land use maps; although some work is now being undertaken in this field. Under the circumstances the most simple and practical definition of the comparable central districts of the five major Victorian cities has seemed to take the built-up area in 1840, when detailed maps of each are available, and to measure planimetrically the intrusions into this area made by the railways during the rest of the century.

Worked out upon this basis the central space requirements of the railways up to 1900 can be seen to vary between five and a half *per cent* for London (where the legislative policy of exclusion has already been described) to seven and a half or nine *per cent* for the port and terminal cities, Glasgow and Liverpool.

	Built-up area in 1840 (acres)	Railways in central zone in 1900 (acres)	% of central zone owned by railways in 1900
London	14,453	776	5·4
Birmingham	1,439	75·5	5·3
Liverpool	1,673	151	9·0
Manchester	1,886	137	7·3
Glasgow	1,117	84·5	7·6

Given the necessary correction factors, these results accord reasonably well with Harland Bartholomew's work on fifty-three cities in the United States, where the average land use claim staked by the railways was 4·86%, rising to 12·76% for a transfer point like Kansas City.[12] Bartholomew also reported, though unfortunately it is not possible in the present state of urban studies in this country to parallel his figures, that on average the American urban railways were second only to commercial and trading land users in the central area, and consumed

[11] Raymond E. Murphy and J. E. Vance Jnr., 'Delimiting the Central Business District', *idem* 'A comparative Study of Nine Central Business Districts', *idem* and Bart. J. Epstein, 'Internal Structure of the Central Business District', *Economic Geography*, 30 (1954). 189–222, 301–336, 31 (1955), 21–46.

[12] Harland Bartholomew, *Land Use in American Cities* (Cambridge, 1955) 58–9. An example of the correction needed may be illustrated from a British city. J. Cunnison and J. B. S. Gilfillan, *The Third Statistical Account of Scotland: Glasgow* (Glasgow, 1958), 47, Table IV, gives modern land use figures, according to which 4·5% of land within the City Boundary was used by railways in 1944–5. But the area included covers 39,725 acres, of which 40·3% was undeveloped, 10·9% open land. This is not inconsistent with the figure cited in the text above.

approximately three quarters as much area as heavy and light industry combined. In view of the absence of comparable information here no similar relationship between the railways and other central land users can be demonstrated, but it is perhaps reasonable to suggest, on *a priori* grounds, that proportions of at least a similar order might be expected in the major British cities.

The railways' land-hunger, however, could be seen to the greatest effect in the peripheral areas outside the central district of each city. Here land was consumed for marshalling yards, locomotive and carriage works and sheds, link and cut-off lines, and circumferential railways, at a prodigal rate. By 1900, for example, taking an average track width of 22 yards, as the amount usually allowed for the limits of deviation, Glasgow's urban lines and terminals, and the railways skirting the city, together with their associated yards and sidings, occupied over 820 acres—an area equal to three-quarters of the built-up acreage of the whole city in 1840.[13] In Liverpool and Manchester also, the lands in railway ownership in 1900 were half as large as the built-up areas of each city sixty years earlier; although in Birmingham, for reasons already suggested, and in London, where the city area was already very large by 1840, the railway's land acquisitions were not so disproportionate.

Reference to urban maps illustrates and explains this remarkable land hunger. In Glasgow the St. Rollox—Sighthill—Springburn complex of engine works and goods yards covered over one hundred and ninety acres to the north-east of the city; to the south, the Caledonian railway company's various coal depots, carriage sheds and marshalling yards covered another hundred and sixty. North of the river, link railways skirted the town from east to west in a great semicircle. In Birmingham the Curzon Street and Vauxhall yards covered a hundred and twenty acres to the east of the city. In Manchester the Ardwick yards covered nearly ninety acres, and the Central and Ship Canal yards covered a further thirty and fifty acres respectively; a hundred acres more was laid out for the Lancashire and Yorkshire and L. & N.W. goods sidings, and the Windsor Bridge cattle yards in Salford; and a link railway skirted the east of the town to Miles Platting, where sidings and yards covered another hundred and twenty acres. In Liverpool the northern dock sidings, and those at Kirkdale and Sandhills covered seventy-five and fifty-five acres respectively; with the Aintree sidings, also to the north but a little further out of town, adding a further forty acres of marshalling yards. A link railway running from

---

[13] F. S. Williams, *Our Iron Roads* (1852), 93, 'exclusive of cutting or embankment'. The official view was that 34 yards, or 12·97 acres per lineal mile should be allowed, and even this was probably an underestimate on the urban approach lines. H.C., 1867–8, LXII, 275.

Garston in the south skirted the built-up area, before curving in towards the coast again to the north of the town, connecting *en route* with the enormous sidings at Edgehill, which covered a hundred and fifty acres. These features, as with the other towns mentioned, are so large as to stand out, even in the diagrammatic maps accompanying Chapter 1.

In London, north of the Euston Road, a series of depots and yards covered over three hundred acres; and similar, though smaller, groups of railway depots, servicing, storage and marshalling areas marked the other major exit routes. As in the other cities, peripheral railways also skirted the town; the spectacularly unsuccessful West London (Punch's) railway; the timely and successful North London, which had started life as a mere dockside line with the northern trunk routes; and the East London, a contractors' line built by John Hawkshaw, Samuel Brassey and Lucas brothers.[14] In some of these cases the lines had originally run along the fringe of the urban frontier, but had later been surrounded by buildings; otherwise they were the nearest surface railway equivalents to the *ceintures* of the northern cities.

The space consumed by these yards, for loading, storage, shunting, servicing, and even for building the engines and rolling stock, requires little comment or explanation, except once more to stress the very large total acreages set aside for this specialised use in each town's outer districts, and the barrier effect of these great unbridged urban clearances.

Examples of the barrier effect could be cited for any city but are difficult to discuss without illustration. Indeed the large-scale Ordnance Maps give a more graphic impression than any words of the effect of severance and isolation the intrusive railway sidings and ever thickening through routes had upon the districts in which they were located. The illustrations (Plates 6 and 7), which could easily be matched for any of the other four cities, show a small part of the development of southern Laurieston and Tradeston, a district which was intended to be one of the finest residential areas in Glasgow by its projectors David and James Laurie; but which fell a victim to encroachments by industrial users, and was given the *coup de grâce* by the Caledonian, and the Glasgow and South Western railway companies.[15] Although only 1–1¼ miles from the Exchange and central business district, it was cut off, a resident complained, 'as if it were a walled city or something like that.'[16] Laurieston rapidly deteriorated between 1840 and 1900 into a slum annexe to the Gorbals; a useful overflow district (for some of the

[14] T. C. Barker and Michael Robbins, *op. cit.* 217 (Punch's); Michael Robbins, *op. cit* (1953) (North London); *The Builder*, XXVII (1869), 630 (East London).

[15] John R. Kellett, *Glasgow: a Concise History* (1966), 14–18.

[16] HLRO, Min., H.C., 1846, 9 July, p. 272, S.C. on Caledonian Railway (Dunlop Street Station).

thousands displaced by more central railway demolition) with large houses capable of subdivision into warrens housing a hundred and fifty people under one roof.

It would be an over-simplification to ascribe Laurieston's dilapidation to the railways alone. Anderston, at a similar distance to the west of the city centre, developed a similar pattern of shabby mixed zoning and gross residential overcrowding during the same period, although the railways were excluded from the district. Clearly, the evolving 'twilight zones' of Glasgow, east London, and other Victorian cities, were no mere by-product of the railways' approach routes and sidings. The root cause, as those who took an interest in the urban working class from Pearson to Booth or Costelloe pointed out, was the usurpation of central space by business, commercial and railway users, combined with the sustained demand for casual labour in the central district. 'A slum, in a word,' said Costelloe, 'represents the presence o a market for local casual labour.'[17] There were in London half a million who had to live close at hand to be 'on the spot at the lucky time'; in the Drury Lane slums for the Covent Garden market, at Tower Hill for the docks, in Soho for the West End tailoring trade.[18] Even in the skilled craft industries—where equipment might have to be borrowed three or four times per day—the pull of the central district was almost as strong as in the casual labour market. The opportunities for cheaper food on credit from local shopkeepers, and for the part-time employment of womenfolk in the central area, were amongst the other factors contributing to the overcrowding of the central area listed by the Royal Commission on the Housing of the Working Classes.[19] These factors applied with similar force not merely in London but in the other major Victorian cities.

The making of a slum is too large and general a process to be ascribed to the railways alone, but it is noticeable that districts divided and confined by the railways tended to be cast finally and irretrievably into the now familiar mould of coal and timber yards, warehousing, mixed light and heavy industrial users, and fourth-rate residential housing.

Apart from the yards and sidings, which filled an obvious operational purpose, however, there were also large tracts of cross-overs and connecting lines, the utility of which was far more questionable. Although built, on occasions, to serve an ephemeral or tactical purpose,

[17] B. F. C. Costelloe, *The Housing Problem* (1899), 48–9. A Reprint of pp. 41–63 of *Trans. Manch. Stat. Soc.*, 1898–9.

[18] *Ibid.* 48. For these reasons those working in Shoreditch declined the offer of a cottage and garden at Potters' Bar on the railway which had trains running into a terminus near their old houses. 'They were offered housing and railway facilities for the same rent they paid in the slum. Yet not 5% of them would even look at the offer.'

[19] H.C., 1884–5, XXX, 22–3.

these products of rivalry were just as permanent and immoveable as the sections of track with a durable function. They could not be rolled up when the occasion which had prompted them had passed; and yet the statute book is full of these short links and extensions, often grouped wholesale under a discreet 'Additional Powers' bill. They were listed, at the close of the year in *The Times*, but in the smallest advertising type, and the driest legal style; 'and the result', John Hollingshead complained, 'is that projects more revolutionary in their effects upon persons than an Indian rebellion or a Parisian riot, are able to give that "preliminary notice" of their birth which is required by parliamentary regulations, without disturbing even the timidest and oldest inhabitant amongst us.'[20]

Every town can produce examples of these cross-overs, triangle junctions and link lines, but the most spectacular are the 'New Cross tangle' and the 'Battersea tangle' in south London. Originating at the time of the Victoria, and Bricklayers' Arms stations, and added to in succeeding generations, these networks of lines consumed over three hundred acres of inner suburban land. They are large enough to stand out on any aerial photograph of London, and are indicated, lower right, and lower left, in the diagrammatic map of London accompanying Chapter 1. Their complexities have inspired chapters in two recent books by O. S. Nock and Edwin Course, which unravel the historical intentions of each addition to the track in this vast network.[21] In this attempt they have been bolder than Mr. Serjeant Sargood, who, perhaps speaking with the assumed ingenuousness which counsel sometimes affected, abandoned all attempt at explanation. 'There is such a network of railways I do not think there is any one person in England, unless it is perhaps Mr. Allport, who knows what the different lines are. They run in such innumerable directions, and engines are passing along them at such angles at such various speeds, and with so much complication, that I do not think anybody who did not know that they will all be arranged safely but would suppose that they must all come to a general convergence and wreck, and that it will be the end of them all.'[22]

The railway companies engaged in the struggle for Britain's major cities were not deterred by any such apocalyptic visions from pursuing a policy of building, at all costs, their own linkages. John Hawkshaw explained the very strong feelings upon this subject entertained in railway boardrooms.[23] There were four clear categories of railway

[20] J. Hollingshead, *Underground London* (1862), 203.
[21] O. S. Nock, *British Steam Railways* (1961), 109–26. Edwin Course, *London Railways*, (1962), 63–81, 105–117.
[22] HLRO, PYB 1/579, 27 May 1873, p. 7.
[23] HLRO, Min., H.L., 1866, 13 July, p. 227, S.C. on M.S. & L. (Central Station and Lines).

independence. First, the ideal for which each company strove, was a line built, staffed and controlled by the promoting company. Second, a joint line, regarded as a poor substitute for autonomy.[24] Even the Cheshire Lines Committee, supposedly an alliance, needed arbitrators to settle the disagreements which constantly arose between the constituent companies; and the extreme in disharmony was demonstrated on joint workings such as the Manchester South Junction line.[25] The operation of this urban link railway was controlled by a joint committee composed of an equal number of directors from the M.S. & L. and the L. & N.W., with chairmen alternating from each company. Since the directors' votes invariably cancelled each other out, it was by the casting vote of the chairman that decisions were made, and last quarter's decisions invariably countermanded.[26] Third in order of preference came the granting of running powers. This was essentially the action of a company whose own intentions had been frustrated, and had sought the alternative of an expensive appeal to Parliament for statutory rights to use sections of a competitor's track or station. Powers wrested by statute from a grudging competitor in this way tended to be greatly diminished in practice by the day-to-day possibilities for operational obstructiveness. Finally, and lowest on the scale, was the mere 'grant of facilities' on sufferance.

Given conditions of competition, and the fluctuating hot and cold relationships even between allied companies, it was inevitable that each railway company should, in addition to its immediate space requirements for running and marshalling, seek to make urban links, under its own direct control, duplicating competitors' approach linkages just as it duplicated their stations.[27]

3. *The function of the central business district, land values, and the arrival of the railways*

There is, despite architectural differences, an essential similarity in the character of the central business districts of Victorian Britain's five largest cities which gives a key to the feature to which, in substantial measure, they owed their pre-eminence: the highly developed exchange

[24] Although it was better than nothing, and O. S. Nock describes it as 'a typical London, Chatham and Dover strategy' to induce large companies to share expenses. In this way the L.C. & D. became involved in line or station sharing with six major companies. However the result, once more, was 'an incredibly complicated series of connecting lines.' O. S. Nock, *op. cit.* 111.

[25] HLRO, Min., (M.S. & L.), H.L., 1866, 13 July, p. 229.

[26] *Manchester City News* (1881-2), 24, 'Notes and Queries' Supplement, MRL 9427 M 9 A.

[27] For examples of this in London and Liverpool referred to by a railway manager see H.C., 1872, XIII, QQ.6681-3 (Cawkwell).

and market services they carried out for their extensive hinterlands. In the case of the metropolis and of the cities whose rapid eighteenth-century growth had been associated with mercantile trade—Liverpool and Glasgow—the point may seem so obvious as to be a truism; but it is equally true of Manchester and Birmingham, which might, at first sight, appear to be essentially manufacturing cities. In their central districts also, and to the same extent, were concentrated the apparatus of accounting and credit, of storage and selling.

Visitors to Manchester in the nineteenth century who had expected the centre of the cotton textile industry, 'Cottonopolis', to be nothing more than a great factory district, were surprised to find a town of warehouses and banks, as quiet at night as the City of London.[28] The factories from which the greater part of the goods dealt with on the Royal Exchange came were not in Manchester, but at Stalybridge, Bolton, Stockport, and other manufacturing towns and villages.[29] Manchester's primary function, evolving even before the railways were built, was as a market, banking, business and distributing centre.[30]

This central land use was not merely prior in time to the railways, it also preceded them, logically, in importance. Although for a time their immense size and capitals enabled railway companies to compete for sites in, or verging on, the commercial core of the city, it must be stressed that the railway and the telegraph were only the instruments by which these marketing functions were accelerated, and extended in area. The railways existed to carry the traffic generated by the daily transactions which were undertaken in the business district. For example (to continue to use Manchester as illustration) the number of subscribing members of the Royal Exchange during the Napoleonic Wars was about 1500, rising to 2000 merchants and manufacturers by the early 1840's. As the railway linkages with the Lancashire factory towns were completed this number rose, to 3000 by 1850, 4000 by 1860, and 7500 by 1885.[31] Only a certain, debatable, proportion of this increase can be assigned to the railways; other factors, both in the international economy and industrial technology acted as equally important joint causes. The more limited and useful point that may be made here, however, is that the railways were closely, if not indispen-

---

[28] 'The centre of the town is, like all centres of modern towns, wholly given up to business. Hardly in London itself is there a more utter absence of residential life than on Sunday exists for a mile or so around the Exchange at Manchester.' George Saintsbury, *Manchester* (1887), 193.

[29] James Tait, 'A Brief Sketch etc.', *Manchester in 1915* (British Association, 1915), 6, and Chap 6, sec. 4 *supra*.

[30] T. W. Freeman, 'The Manchester Conurbation', *Manchester and its Region* (British Association, 1962), 49–50.

[31] D. A. Farnie, 'The Commercial Development of Manchester in the later Nineteenth Century', *The Manchester Review*, VII (1956), 332.

sably, associated with the marked increase in the number of transactions in the central business district, which this increased membership represented. The manufacturers who came up to the Exchange used, as a matter of course, the telegraph to receive advance information, and railway contract tickets for the journey.[32] By the 1880's, in fact, every important firm in the Lancashire cotton industry was represented by an office or an agent in Manchester, and three-quarters of Britain's cotton yarn and woven cloth was marketed there. These offices, exchanges and warehouses, although they might, individually, be elbowed out of the way for sites, were the railways' *raison d'être*.

The point has been made emphatically because it is reflected in the pattern of land values in the central business district, with which the railways had to contend at every stage of their development. In each city land values in the central district were based upon the rents at which premises could be let. It was this which made high density building profitable and which gave the actual ground its value. The rent offer was highest in those areas which were central in relation to established market and exchange uses and to existing transport facilities, and it changed as these factors changed.[33]

At the time the railways arrived, however, the central land values were established upon an extremely narrow compass; a few paces could make a difference of several hundred *per cent* in the value of land. And the inertia of this pedestrian scale of values continued after the railways arrived, because the internal traffic problem within the central districts of the great cities was not amenable to solution by steam transport. Around the Exchange in London, for example, land fell off so rapidly in value that sites at the far end of Cornhill were only worth a third of those nearer the centre; and there was a marked difference in the value of land even between the north and the south sides of King William Street. In general, values fell off in mid-Victorian London, from a peak central figure of 20s (rent, per superficial foot, *per annum*), to 10s extremely quickly (even in the length of one street), and only slightly more slowly to 1s. South of the river no land was worth more than 1s a foot, and the offer rapidly declined to 6d if the site was at any distance from the riverside. In the central business district of Manchester, values were not far short of those in the City of London and the gradient of rents demanded was equally steep.[34]

---

[32] 'Railway contract tickets' were the reason why the *Manchester Guardian* stopped reporting local Blackburn yarn prices. Nine-tenths of the subscribers to the Royal Exchange used Victoria station (No. 4 on sketch maps). *Ibid.* 331, 333.

[33] For a theoretical discussion of these and of the other major factors which affect urban rents see R. H. Turvey, *The Economics of Real Property* (1957), 1–52.

[34] *The Builder*, XXIX (1871), 3 June, 420–1.

Many factors played a part in producing these central values: the amount of land available in one lot, its aspect and light, whether it was on a corner site, its convenience of access, suitability for specialised building, non-liability to interference by adjacent owners, and its geological characteristics.[35] But the basic platform from which the values commenced was given by proximity to established market functions. 'To be in a market is, we all know, of great importance,' remarked Mr. Edward L'Anson, in 1871. 'It is something to be in London, itself one vast emporium and mart, but it is more still to be in the great market itself.'[36]

Similar views have been discussed and amplified more recently in this country by Ralph Turvey and Nathaniel Lichfield, and in the United States by Richard L. Meier. 'The urban core', writes Meier, 'provides the institutions and services which enable the making and breaking of contacts at a high rate. . . . The daily migration to the centre of the city is an attempt to maximise the transaction rate.'[37] Perhaps the most important factor in maximising the transactions upon which the city depended, suggests Meier, is the face-to-face meeting, 'with the conversation tugged this way and that in order to discover the bases for co-operation and the grounds for conflict', terminating with the handshake or signature. Although Meier is speaking of modern American experience, his observations find very apt illustration in the historical functions of central business districts in British cities. In the Manchester Exchange, for example, 'transactions of immense extent,' wrote Leon Faucher in 1844, 'are concluded by nods, winks, shrugs or brief phrases. . . . There is perhaps no part of the world in which so much is done and so little said in the same space of time. A stranger sees nothing at first but a collection of gentlemen with thoughtful, intelligent faces, who converse with each other in laconic whispers, supply the defects of words with nods and signs, move noiselessly from one part of the room to another, guided as if by some hidden instinct to the precise person in the crowd with whom they have business to transact.'[38]

Because they set in motion a whole chain of operations in manufacturing, warehousing, transporting and selling, and because they depended to such a marked extent, even in the days of the telegraph

[35] The list could be extended, of course, to include questions of the goodwill or prestige of a site (often very important) the right to use without restrictions, etc. For a discussion see Nathaniel Lichfield, *Economics of Planned Development* (1956), 67–83.

[36] *The Builder*, XXIX (1871), 3 June, 420.

[37] Richard L. Meier, *A Communication Theory of Urban Growth* (Cambridge, Mass., 1962), 64–5.

[38] Leon Faucher, *Manchester in 1844* (Manchester, 1844), 21, and D. A. Farnie *loc. cit.* 331.

and efficient postal service, upon the personal meeting, the dealers on the Exchange, and their associated offices and credit agencies, were able to bid for central location against all comers. Land values in the City of London were six to eight times as high as even the most elegant West End residential addresses. They were even two or three times as great (for the smaller sites required) as the prices the railways were able to bid for central land. The core of the central business district, therefore, must be taken as immovable by direct railway pressure.[39] Residential areas, historic buildings, graveyards, hospitals, craft workshops, even, where necessary, factories, could be traversed or swept away, but not the central Exchange area.

Other subdivisions within the structure of the central business district, however, were not so invulnerable, and came lower in the rent paying hierarchy. The railways in the five cities studied were able on occasions to drive wedges into the central business district, or to define and circumscribe the area; but it must be frankly stated that their perceptible effect, even in the long term, upon the location of central business district functions was smaller than has sometimes been suggested.

In London the City remained the principal resort and exchange, but the westward spread of some business functions was under way a century before the West End Stations were built. Indeed London had always had two nuclei, the City and Westminster; and the area between them, the so-called West End, had formed a zone into which some business functions had begun to migrate in the seventeenth or even the late sixteenth century. 'The City of London gradually removes Westward,' wrote John Graunt, in 1676, 'and did not the Royal Exchange and London Bridge stay the Trade, it would remove much faster.'[40] The trades, specifically, which were migrating westward at that time were drapery, from Canning and Watling Street to Ludgate Hill, mercery from Cheapside and Lombard Street to Paternoster Row. Leadenhall Street and Fenchurch Street were losing other retail trades.

In the eighteenth century these retail trades tended to move still further westward. Shops left Paternoster Row for Fleet Street, or moved along Holborn and St. Giles, *en route* to the Regent Street, Bond Street and Oxford Street locations of the early nineteenth century. To a certain extent their migration may be attributed to a strong attraction towards the aristocratic quarters of Mayfair and Belgravia, whose residents provided their clientele. To a certain extent the retailers may also have been speeded in their departure by the willingness of

[39] Louis K. Loewenstein, 'Location of Urban Land Uses', *Land Economics*, 39 (1963), 411, suggests that a host of ancillary services, printers, restaurants etc. also helped to make this central district 'relatively impervious to change.'

[40] John Graunt, *Natural and Political Observations on the Bills of Mortality* (1676), 75.

other fringe activities of the central business district to step into their premises. Mercery, for example, was virtually chased into the West End by the expanding printing business; first the professional publishers of legal and other documents in Paternoster Row, then the newspapers of Fleet Street.

Whatever the reasons, the result by the early nineteenth century was that the principal shopping functions had detached themselves from the rest of the central district by a greater distance than in the other cities, and had begun to form a more westerly zone of their own.[41] The building of West End stations at Victoria and Charing Cross was no more than a recognition and (one might say) reinforcement of the changes in land use which were already under way.

The exchange functions in London, as in most of the five cities, remained firmly rooted in the oldest part of the town. 'The City,' in its modern sense, covers almost exactly the old walled city of London. In Liverpool, likewise, the office, banking and exchange quarter corresponds closely to the earliest part of the town. 'The first fact which strikes a historian, on studying the map,' wrote Ramsey Muir in 1910, 'is that the office area includes the whole of the original town of Liverpool as laid out by King John, and very little more.'[42]

The establishment of this central location for the essential exchange functions need not be the product of as long a history as that of London or Liverpool. In America the same tendency has been remarked by Warren R. Seyfried, who explains it in organic terms: cities, like other organisms, 'were born small', the developing transport system converged towards the original nucleus, and the market was fixed (with appropriately high rents and land values) where convergence was greatest.[43] The remaining land uses, and any prospective alterations and improvements in the transport system, had the option of naturally conforming to the established pattern, or of waging an uphill and unprofitable struggle to break it down and establish a series of new locations. In all five Victorian cities selected for study here, the choice was taken to conform.

In London it is noteworthy that although the major national trunk routes terminated there, one has only to glance at the traffic figures in 1855, or even 1905, to see the quite disproportionate role in urban

[41] D. F. Stevens, 'The Central Area', *Greater London* (ed. J. T. Coppock and H. C. Prince, 1964) 170–1, and A. E. Smailes, 'The Site, Growth and Changing Face of London', *The Geography of Greater London* (ed. R. Clayton, 1964), 20–33.

[42] Ramsay Muir, 'Liverpool, an Analysis of the Geographical Distribution of Civic Functions', *Town Planning Review*, I (1910), 37–40. 'Office Liverpool is very obstinate and very conservative. . . . It has chosen its centre and no power will remove it.'

[43] Warren R. Seyfried, 'The Centrality of Urban Land Values', *Land Economics*, 39 (1963), 276.

traffic played by termini which had relatively minor roles in the trunk route system; such as London Bridge, Fenchurch Street, and Liverpool Street stations. Though comparatively little used by long distance travellers then, or now, they secured the greatest degree of convergence upon the heart of the central business district, and with this the reward of dense business traffic. If the Great Northern and the London and North Western railways' plans for extensions into the Holborn/Fleet Street area, described earlier, had been sanctioned in 1846, the northern main-line routes might have enjoyed equally close access to the business district, whilst retaining their outer termini at King's Cross and Euston for trunk traffic. The increased convenience of their projected termini in Farringdon Street might have led to the exercise of increased demand pressure, as early as the 1850's and 1860's, upon the respective railway companies, and upon the landowners to the north and north-west of London, to give accommodation to a wider range of business, professional and clerical commuters. On the other hand it would have driven a wedge down from the north between the City and the expanding West End. The sheer expense of competing for land on such a scale with central business users, and the drastic interruption of east-west street communications which these northern schemes involved, gave a decisive advantage to the railways with approaches through the relatively undeveloped district of cheap residential housing south of the river. The City and West end remained relatively undisturbed, by the railways, except for the underground Metropolitan and Circle lines of the 1860's and 1880's; the westward spread of some of the business functions towards, and finally into, the high-class residential area continued uninterrupted.

In Glasgow a similar westward shift of some of the leading commercial premises from Buchanan Street and the Exchange was also in progress in the second and third quarters of the century, and was not diminished by the shortage of railway accommodation in that area. Although one might have expected the Bridge Street, George Square and Buchanan Street stations (Nos. 1, 2 & 3 on map), which were the most central termini in Glasgow until 1873, to exercise a contrary attraction, pulling the commercial premises back to the centre and south, the march of business into Blythswood and into the West End of Glasgow continued unchecked.[44] The key factor in this case, as it probably was in London's, seems to have been the availability of land and premises in units of the right size, character and price. These considerations quite outweighed the locational pull of the railway

---

[44] D. R. Diamond, 'The Central Business District of Glasgow', *Proceedings of the I.G.U. Symposium in Urban Geography* (Lund, 1962), 525–34. Unpublished historical land use maps by W. Forsyth of Glasgow University for 1825, 1850 and 1875, founded upon city directory material, illustrate the movement in progress.

termini. After all, as the *Case Histories* frequently illustrated, the opportunities presented by the evolving pattern of land values and land ownership were also a major factor in determining the location of many of the railway termini themselves. By moving into the spacious and well-kept sites offered by the once high-class residential area of Blythswood, commercial users were merely responding to similar opportunities.

Since the westward march of business was not retarded by the construction of the early terminus at Bridge Street, Glasgow, the obvious step was, as in London, to plan more westerly stations; and one such station, to be situated in Blythswood Holm, was contemplated, and some of the land for it acquired, as early as the 1840's. By the late 1860's, however, when the Caledonian company returned to the scheme, the designated site had appreciated so greatly in value that the land costs would have been prohibitive, and the railway company had to content itself with a slightly less central location.[45] When it came to a contest with business users over the few hundred yards of most highly prized central space the railways had to retreat.

In Birmingham the two main central stations were established unusually early, yet a high degree of specialisation in the central district already greeted the railways on their arrival, with clearly defined jewellery and gun quarters, public offices and retail centre. Indeed the Snow Hill and New Street projects went to great lengths to establish locations for themselves which were convenient for already existing functions. Several hours of the Select Committees' time on the rival bills was taken up hearing detailed evidence regarding the precise walking distances to the principal warehouses, the Post Office, the Royal Hotel, the professional quarters and the banks.[46] Indeed the New Street committee's patience was so tried by a clash between opposing counsel over the relative distances to Spoon and Attwood's Bank, that the chairman intervened; 'This is not very important. Might we not move on?'[47] As in other cities, there was a tendency to take it as read when counsel showed a tendency to particularise too greatly over the internal structure of the central district.

However, it is clear that, both in Birmingham and Glasgow, there was a tendency for the railway stations, and the short distances of their approach lines which fell within the central area, to act as outer boundaries for the central business district, and even to sever from the main

---

[45] According to Thomas Binnie's valuation even this site (No. 7 on sketch map) cost, at £100,000 per acre, five times as much as the Blythswood Holm site in 1846. HLRO, Min., (W. of Scot. Junc.), H.C., 1846, 26 March, p. 88 *cf.* BTHR, PYB 1/579, 12 May 1873, Q. 136.

[46] HLRO, Min., (B.W. & D.), H.C., 1846, 24 June, p. 232. HLRO, Min., (L. & B. Ext.) H.C., 1846, 11 June, p. 9.

[47] *Ibid.* 11 June, p. 35.

body some central space users of less exalted status. In Glasgow, at the time of the abortive Caledonian Dunlop Street scheme in 1846, evidence of such severance had been submitted. Some of the humbler business functions had been left behind in the westward march. The principal packing places and calenderers (who operated steam presses and mangles) had remained in their old locations near the High Street; the 'servants' hiring market' was still further east in Gallowgate.[48] The provision of a large terminus and viaduct between them and the Blythswood offices, it was suggested, might isolate them still further. Likewise in Birmingham, the early and extensive railway land requisitions tended to form a barrier, in this case to any eastwards extension of the central business district, a point Elrington and Tillott have commented upon; and also to throw the small severed portion of the east central area into the new industrial belt, which rapidly spread between 1860 and 1900 along the Rea and Thane valleys towards Salford Bridge.[49]

It is difficult to believe that the railways did more than underline the differentiation which was already developing within the inner districts of Glasgow and Birmingham. However, to be on the wrong side of the tracks, or at the back of the station, in the small central areas severed, placed an end to hopes of future expansion. Moreover it was in some cases aggravated by the road closures which the approach lines or viaducts involved, or by the noise, nuisance, heavy traffic and damage to goods associated with the fringe industrial activities which, apart from the railways, now became the only neighbours for those cut off in this way.

Apart from this limited measure of severance in east central Glasgow and Birmingham, neither city shows any marked reorientation of the central business district which can be assigned to the direct influence of the railways' terminal site selection. In Glasgow the westward movement already in progress continued unchecked. In Birmingham the centre of the specialised business district hardly moved. Indeed since the original projectors had gone to such lengths to establish proximity in Birmingham it would be suprprising if such re-location had occurred; although Conrad Gill opens a line of speculation which is particularly interesting in view of the Street Commissioners' projected street plans in east Birmingham in 1838. 'If Curzon Street had remained the principal station for some time longer those (new) streets would

---

[48] In Candleriggs, Brunswick and Wilson Streets. HLRO, Min., (Caled. Dunlop St.), H.L., 1846, 8 July, p. 117; *loc. cit.* p. 170–2.

[49] C. R. Elrington and P. M. Tillott, 'The Growth of the City', *A History of the County of Warwick* (Victoria County History, 1964), VII, 4–26; M. J. Wise and P. O'N. Thorpe, 'The Growth of Birmingham 1800–1950', *Birmingham and its Regional Setting: a Scientific Survey* (British Association, 1950), 222–4.

certainly have been made', he writes, 'and the commercial centre of the town would have been drawn to the East.'[50]

In Liverpool there was, perhaps, more evidence than anywhere else of a re-centering of certain elements in the central district, although the heart of the central business district—the exchange and office area—

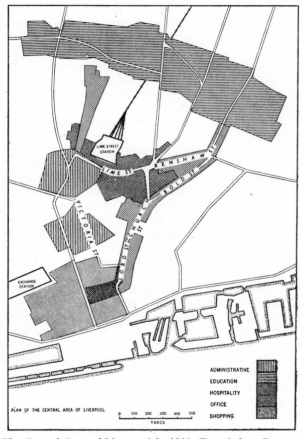

The Central Area of Liverpool in 1910. Founded on Ramsay Muir, 'Liverpool, an analysis of the geographical distribution of civic functions', *Town Planning Review*, I, 304 (1910).

remained impregnably fixed in its old location inland from the Pier Head and Castle Street. 'From the peculiar position of the business parts of Liverpool, *viz.* their congregation on the banks of the river,

[50] Conrad Gill, *The History of Birmingham* (1952), I, 338.

the land in that neighbourhood is raised to a most extravagant value', wrote the reformer Joseph Boult, in 1846.[51] These values displaced thousands from the water front areas over the next twenty years, and drove them inland (eastwards) to the newly run up cottage properties of Everton and West Derby. Those who, as William Trench, the Medical Officer of Health put it, 'preferred to crowd into the restricted area of contiguous streets rather than, at the expense of a morning and evening walk, seek better air in the outskirts of town', moved only a few hundred yards to the overcrowded, cholera-ridden slums of Vaux-hall Road and Marybone.[52]

As the central business district expanded it could only move inland, of course, and as land values rose in the exchange district, not only residents but even some of the central functions—administration, retail shopping and the restaurant/entertainment trade—began to move out of the old town. Partly they may have been expelled by site competition rather than attracted by the railway stations. But the retreat inland from the waterfront still permitted building and purchase over a 180-degree arc; and yet all the lesser functions directed their growth towards Lime Street station, with a unanimity which it is hard to assign to coincidence.

The shopping area, which ran along the Lord Street/Bold Street axis, south eastward from the waterfront, added a wing or extension reaching back northwards along Renshaw Street towards Lime Street. The hotel and entertainment area, at the end of its regrouping, was also concentrated in an unusually narrow compass around Lime Street. An even greater change took place in the location of the administrative area—the law courts, municipal and public buildings, the Post Office—as expansion and reconstruction took place in the mid and late nineteenth century. Once again it was oriented towards Lime Street, forming a species of platform or avenue between the office and exchange quarter and the terminal which, for many years, was the only exit for Manchester, Birmingham and London passenger traffic.

The deliberate nature of the choice made, in one case at any rate, is attested by the letter received by the corporation from C. B. Banning, the postmaster, in 1847, asking 'Whether the Corporation of Liverpool have any lot of land containing about 1,500 sq. yds. situated somewhere near the Railway Station in Lime Street, or between that building and the Exchange, which they will be willing to let the Government have as a site for the new Post Office.'[53] The site was eventually combined with

[51] Joseph Boult, 'On the Improvement of Tenements in Towns', *Trans. of the Liv. Poly. Soc.* (1846), 85.

[52] LRL, Council Minutes, 1863–4, 518, Report by M.O.H.

[53] LRL, Council Books, XX, 4 August 1847, Finance Committee Minutes XII, 6 and 13 August 1847.

the cutting of a new thoroughfare, Victoria Street, the nearest equivalent in the Victorian cities studied to a continental *Bahnhofstrasse*.

The original suggestions for the scheme had been laid before the
Liverpool Polytechnic Society, an unusually influential town forum,
in 1843 by Samuel Holme, later mayor.[54] The advent of the railways,
Mr. Holme suggested, should be taken as an opportunity to demolish
the dilapidated old Islington market and use the site for magistrates'
courts and a police station, to match the assize court and 'form a
splendid quadrangle with the assize courts on one side and the grand
facade of the railway station on the other.' The station in question was,
of course, Lime Street, and the corporation's pride in the façade was
understandable since it had contributed generously towards completing
the building; an act of unique and unrequited civic generosity.

A major suggestion, partially realised later, was the demolition of
the fever-ridden dens south of Dale Street, and the construction of a
60-foot wide street (on the line of modern Victoria Street). 'Being in
line with Brunswick Street,' Mr. Holme wrote, 'it would be most
valuable for shops or places of business, *which would tend to concentrate
trade in the very heart of the town and give a direct passage to the railway
station.* . . . Much would be gained by the thousands who every day
walk round this neighbourhood instead of walking through it, and the
property between this new Street and Dale Street would be materially
increased.'[55]

Here Mr. Holme touched upon one of the primary reasons for the
inertia of the central district, and the suspicion under which schemes
likely to reorient it fell. Quite small movements in fashion and convenience were reflected by very marked differentials of land value, as
already indicated; so rather more was at stake in altering the balance
of a city than might at first appear. However where, as in this case, or
as in the case of some London realignments, the property was derelict
and everyone (except those evicted) stood to gain, the principal obstacle
was shortage of corporate funds.[56]

In Manchester, as in London, Glasgow and Birmingham, there was
no perceptible re-location of the central business district as a whole
which can be assigned to the presence of the railway stations. The
centre of the warehouse district, however, did migrate southwards by

[54] S. Holme, 'Upon the Public Improvements of Liverpool', *Trans. of the Liv.
Poly Soc.* (1843), 30–4.

[55] *Loc. cit.* 33. My italics.

[56] Northumberland Avenue in London, is possibly the nearest equivalent to
Victoria Street, Liverpool, but only ran from Charing Cross station to the Thames
Embankment, rather than to a central point. It was also planned and constructed
contemporaneously with the station. Its net cost, after the re-sale of land was
£600,000. P. J. Edwards, *History of London Street Improvements, 1855–1897* (1898),
61.

up to half a mile, from the Cannon street area, where nearly 400 were located in 1820, down towards Portland Street—which was described as 'the essential Manchester' by the 1860's.[57] 'Poor Cannon Street—almost deserted', depreciated greatly in value, and became a convenient site for country manufacturers at lower rents. This southward shift was partly accounted for by the growth in number and value of warehouses—many of the Portland Street/Mosley Street warehouses were completely new; but many Cannon Street firms, such as Potters and Norris, E. & J. Jackson, J. S. & J. Watts, thought it worth while to uproot themselves from established premises, and move the few hundred yards involved.[58] In doing so the later migrants were actually moving away from Victoria station, which is only a stone's throw from Cannon Street, and they were not moving directly towards the London Road station but, if anything, to a point equidistant between the two main stations, and as far away from them as they could be without actually moving out of the central business district altogether. Nor does it appear that wider access roads or lighter traffic could have compensated for the increased distance. Portland Street was described by John Pendleton in the 1890's, as so crowded with drays and carts piled high with Manchester goods moving slowly stationwards that 'it required quite an acrobatic feat to cross such a maze and struggle of traffic.'[59]

There seem to have been two main reasons for this contrary drift of the commercial element in Manchester's central business district away from the stations. First, the Manchester warehouses were no mere transit sheds, but were used for display and sale by sample. 'The best and handsomest buildings in the City of London are only ordinary representatives of the warehouses now built in Manchester', claimed Mr. J. F. Bateman in 1866; and others spoke of the 'unsurpassed and palatial' nature of the buildings, designed at great expense by some of the most eminent Victorian architects.[60] A spacious and airy setting was essential for buildings of this character. Secondly, these wider spaces were available at reasonable rents in the southern arc of the business district, within the limits defined by the Manchester South Junction viaduct. The opportunity presented by the pattern of land

[57] D. A. Farnie, *loc. cit.* 328–9.

[58] *Manchester as it is* (Manchester, 1839) 173 *et. seq.* Even at this early date the movement was under way. Potters and Norris had moved to George Street, A. & S. Henry had opened 'imposing' premises in Portland Street, and Hargreaves had built a 'beautiful' warehouse at Meal Street. Portland Street was 'rapidly converting to warehouses'.

[59] John Pendleton, *Our Railways: their origin, development, incident and romance* (1896), I, 130.

[60] BTHR PYB 1/383, QQ.3288–9; C. Stewart, *The Architecture of Manchester* (Manchester, 1956), 41–55, *idem, The Stones of Manchester* (1956), 67–8.

values and land ownership was of more immediate importance than transport facilities. Bateman, who was a civil engineer with thirty years experience of Manchester, explained the warehousemen's feelings on the subject as follows. 'Within certain limits a station may be an improvement, but a person establishes a warehouse not with reference to the station but with reference to the general convenience of his trade: but if there were two places, one a mile and the other half a mile off from a station, he might take the one that was only half a mile off the station.'[61]

As in the Blythswood area of Glasgow, functional competition for land developed by the 1860's between the railways and business men; and, as in Glasgow, the railways lost the contest. James Lynde, city surveyor, in his evidence, stressed the reluctance of first class warehouses to come within a considerable distance of the railways, and asserted that if the M. & S.L. trans-urban viaduct, projected in the 1860's, were allowed to run, adjacent and parallel to Portland Street, across the central business district, no further business expansion would be possible, and that a large segment would be severed to the south-east from the valuable central land. He and Bateman were pressed to enlarge their views upon the subject, which are, perhaps, worth quoting more fully.

'With regard to what you say about depreciating the property for warehouses,' Lynde was asked, 'I presume that if it becomes necessary for the trade of Manchester that there should be increased warehouse accommodation, and that more warehouses should be built, they will be built somewhere?—Yes, they will be built somewhere, but there is no district in which they could so conveniently be built as the district now proposed to be cut up.'
'If they cannot go there, then they must go to some other part of Manchester?—It follows as a matter of course.'
'Then after all it is a balance, one part of Manchester being deteriorated and another part improved?—It is so to a certain extent, but certain trades go to certain districts, and if you cut off one half of the trade from the other it is very inconvenient.'[62]

The severing effect of a viaduct in the central business district could not be overstated, Lynde believed. As City Surveyor it was part of his job to examine streets, pavements and bridges, and he found the greatest nuisances in the city were in the region of the Manchester South Junction viaduct. No foot pavements were possible because of the arch entrances, the arches were heaped with lumber, and the streets congested with the horses and carts of merchants of inferior trades, parked at right angles to the traffic. 'Parties willing to occupy warehouses alongside the viaduct could not be found'; instead they

[61] BTHR PYB 1/383, Q.3341.
[62] *Ibid*. QQ.3258–60.

only brought 'a low class of person into the neighbourhood.'[63]
The objection was not to the station itself—which might well,
Bateman estimated, increase values within a radius of about half a
mile—but to the approach routes, particularly viaducts, and particularly
if they crossed the city centre. 'Can you fix any limits in reference to
the viaducts? How far on each side of the viaduct would any harm be
done by it?—I do not think it would be a limit of distance; it would
rather be a limit of time. The result in my mind would be this: that if
that railway (the M.S. & L. Central) were made, the property which
now, if the district were left alone, would be rapidly absorbed for
warehouse purposes, would cease to be absorbed, so that the warehouses to be built would find other places in which to be built in
preference. And, finally, when the whole of that property was covered
with warehouses, and they were obliged to resort to the part near the
railway, they might fill up the intervening space.'[64]
These were opinions not facts, of course, as Mr. Denison, Q.C.,
counsel for the M.S. & L., quickly pointed out. But they do fit the
apparent shifts in the internal structure of the central business district;
and the chairman of the M.S. & L. himself, though giving evidence
expressly to promote the scheme, virtually conceded the point when he
stated that his company's anxiety to proceed at once with the scheme
partly sprang from the fact that 'in two or three years' time the area
will be covered with warehouses.'[65]
In Manchester, then, the warehouses may be seen as rivals, not
merely clients, to the railways. How far this experience may have been
general remains a matter of some doubt. During the hearing on the
M.S. & L. bill counsel attempted to demonstrate that there was no such
repulsion or antipathy between the two land uses in Liverpool, where
the Lancashire and Yorkshire railway approached its station (Exchange,
No. 3 on map), by a high viaduct running close to large warehouses,
many of which had been built after the line was completed; in London,
likewise, many examples could be found of warehouses seeking to
move into the fringe of residential dilapidation which ran along the
routes of urban viaducts.[66] Writing quite independently on this topic
in 1861, with close first hand experience of London, William Denton
also referred to the 'natural association' of railway and warehouse,
causing a dual effect upon working class housing: first by the railway
demolitions, then 'add to this that the making a great railway station
leads naturally and inevitably to the conversion of dwelling houses

[63] *Ibid.* QQ.3183–3269.
[64] *Ibid.* Q.3328.
[65] HLRO, Min. (M.S. & L. Central Station), H.C., 1866, 9 May, p. 135.
[66] BTHR PYB 1/383, QQ.3319–25, 3331.

into warehouses and other uninhabited houses.'[67] In view of this and other similar evidence, it seems reasonable to deduce that a critical factor was the character of the warehouse, and the purpose for which it was intended, whether exhibition and sale, or mere storage; but that even this was subordinate to site opportunities.

Apart from this movement, in which the railways played an unusual role, there was no substantial re-location of the other functions of the central business district in Manchester which cannot be accounted for by the process of growth and site opportunities. The exchange, office and banking centre expanded, but retained its location north of the King Street/Spring Gardens axis; shopping continued to grow outwards from St. Ann's Square and Market Street.[68]

Once again, as with Birmingham, this apparent lack of disturbance to central functions should give no grounds for surprise, in view of the original location of Victoria and London Road stations; which were planned, within the limits of available capital and sites, to serve and reinforce the already established functions. This intention had been clearly brought out during the public controversy in 1842 between the rival railway companies engaged. At the twentieth half-yearly meeting of the Liverpool and Manchester railway, the company's directors, entreated shareholders to 'take the map of Manchester in their hands, and form their own judgement of the comparative merits of Hunt's-Bank and Store-street' (i.e. Victoria and London Road stations Nos. 4 & 3 on map) 'for a central junction station; bearing this important fact always in mind, that with the probable increase of Manchester and the surrounding districts, in the ratio and in the direction witnessed in the last twenty years, the Store-street station will become, year by year, more central and more convenient for all the great purposes of business and general intercommunication; whilst the site of Hunt's-Bank, already in a comparatively distant quarter of the town, seems likely to become, in the course of years, still more remote from the great central localities, whether of business or general and miscellaneous resort.'[69]

The Liverpool and Manchester case was exaggerated, but it establishes the point that consideration was given, in the early days when routes and sites were still being chosen, to proximity to the existing business district. In a counterblast, the Manchester and Leeds directors argued, 'The superior convenience of Hunt's-Bank as a central station is attested by the fact that of the 28 inns and hotels in Pigot's Directory

[67] W. Denton, *Observations on the Displacement of the Poor by Metropolitan Railways and by other Public Improvements* (1861), 10.

[68] D A. Farnie, *loc, cit.* 336. T. W. Freeman, *loc. cit.* 49, and Fig. 15 *Idem, The Conurbations of Great Britain* (Manchester, 1959), 187.

[69] Six-monthly Report, 26 January 1842, Liverpool and Manchester Railway.

for 1841, 19 are nearer Hunt's-Bank, 2 are equidistant, 7 are nearer Store-street.'[70]

All things considered, there was, in fact, little to choose between the two sites. The enquiry conducted by the council to decide the best location for the General Post office concluded that the 'centre of great business' was equidistant between the foot of the High Street and the Exchange; a choice which was settled by Sir Oswald Mosley's offer of a suitable site in this area for the Post Office.[71] This location favoured Victoria, but only by 200 yards.

Only in Liverpool, therefore, is there any historical evidence of the marked gravitational influence which has occasionally been ascribed to railway stations. In Japan and Denmark, for instance, Peter Schöller and Aage Aagesen both report 'influence on [the structure of the city' and a 'trend towards the station for market sites'; in Newcastle, M. R. G. Conzen detects a tendency for the central business district to be drawn southwards; and in Portsmouth, A. E. Smailes writes of 'significant re-centering of the town'.[72]

It may be that when an adequate series of historical land-use maps have been constructed for the five great Victorian cities, more evidence will emerge of the gravitational influence of railway stations upon their business districts. On the other hand, it must be borne in mind that in the five cities chosen, the growth of business, credit and exchange facilities had been a feature of urban history for a century or more, and had been enormously accelerated over the fifty years after 1780. By the time the railways arrived in the 1830's the five cities had populations ranging from 200,000 to 1,500,000. The complexity of their land ownership and land value patterns, and the already well developed localisation of their central business functions, ensured that they would not provide simple arenas for the free play of any single economic agency, no matter how powerful.

4. *The railways' effects upon traffic and land uses in the central business district*

a. *Traffic*

In spite of the shortage of detailed traffic figures for the major Victorian

[70] *Reply of the Directors of the Manchester and Leeds Railway Company . . . on the subject of the proposed junction line through Manchester* (1842), MRL, Miscellaneous Tracts, P2896.

[71] MRL, Council Proceedings, 1838–42, pp. 100–1.

[72] *Proceedings of the I.G.U. Symposium in Urban Geography* (ed. Knut Norborg, Lund, 1962), 586–7 (Schöller), 597 (Aagesen), 392 (Conzen). A. E. Smailes, *The Geography of Towns* (1964), 122.

cities there can be no doubt, from eye-witness accounts, that street traffic reached, by the 1860's, levels which were unexampled in all the cities and almost intolerable in the Metropolis. 'In the City,' one businessman testified in the mid-1840's, 'we make no appointment when we have occasion to use a carriage; the whole place is stuffed up to such a degree.'[73] During the next ten years it was to become even worse.

A wide variety of land uses played their part in generating this urban traffic, but from no point did so much originate as the railway stations. Charles Pearson, at one stage of his evidence to the Select Committee on Metropolitan Communications attempted to set down some sort of list of 'those establishments which occasion the presence of persons from the Metropolis and from the provinces daily in the City of London to such an enormous extent.'[74] Moving from east to west in the City he enumerated: the Customs House and India House, the Bank of England, the Royal Exchange, Lloyds', the great banking houses, the Clearing House, private banks and joint-stock banks, the various insurance companies, life, marine and fire, the Australia, Canada and Levant companies, the Coal Market and Corn Markets, the wholesale fish, poultry and meat markets catering for nearly two million people, the linen, cotton, silk and wool offices in Gutter Lane and Wool Street, those for colonial produce in Mincing Lane, for iron and paper in Thames Street, the Post Office, the Paternoster printing firms, the Bankruptcy, Wills and Administrations, Central Criminal, and the Admiralty Courts. All of these buildings generated endless daily comings and goings on foot, by cab and omnibus. The position was similar, on a smaller scale, in the central districts of all the provincial cities.[75]

No single central business district function attracted and focused more traffic, however, than the railway stations. They were the originating points of a great part of the cab traffic, and their names figured on the destination boards of many of the new horse omnibuses which replaced the short-stage coaches in London in the 1830's. Existing omnibus companies, Adam Shelford, Inspector of City Police testified, extended their routes 'wherever a railway station or terminus opened some distance off', and extra police had to be detailed to control the increased traffic.[76] The heaviest traffic in London by the late 1850's, in fact, was over London Bridge, where traffic had increased more than

[73] H.C., 1846, XVII, Q.1541 (Chaplin).
[74] H.C., 1854–5, X, Q.1349.
[75] For a modern attempt to measure the number of trips by employees, callers and vehicles generated in part of the central business district of a major provincial city (Deansgate, Manchester) see Franklin Medhurst, 'Traffic induced by Central Area Functions', *Town Planning Review*, XXXIV (1963–4), 50–60.
[76] BTHR PYB 1 112/6, 18 July 1860, pp. 43–4.

tenfold in a decade; a flow of 1700 vehicles an hour at the 9–10 a.m. and 4–5 p.m. peaks. This increase John Hollingshead attributed largely to the joint station at London Bridge. 'From the day of steam encroachment my tranquillity was at an end.'[77]

The Select Committee on Metropolitan Communications of 1854/5 listed the total number of those arriving and departing from the principal stations daily as 75,000; of whom 8,500 came to, or left, Paddington, Euston and King's Cross stations—all far enough from the centre and from the southern terminals to necessitate transport.[78] The arrival of long-distance passengers, with their mountains of luggage, caused a disproportionate amount of confusion and congestion on the approach roads to these main-line terminals. Most of the railway arrivals from these, and other, stations dispersed throughout the town, but there was a certain amount, estimated at about 10%, of interstation traffic; enough, later in the century, to persuade the Great Northern, the London and North Western, and the Midland companies to run special inter-terminal omnibuses, either under contract or under their own direct management.[19] By 1906 the numbers of omnibus routes using railway stations as their termini came to dozens, and the departures and arrivals varied from one to four per minute.[80]

More marked still was the quantity of heavy cartage which originated or terminated at the railway stations. Hundreds of waggons, carts and vans could be seen at any of the major termini by mid century; nearly a thousand at Camden Town and Euston and equivalent numbers at Nine Elms, Paddington and the other depots.[81] At Camden Town could also be found the depot of Messrs. Pickfords, specialised carriers, with its steam cranes, steam hay cleaner, steam cutters, and gas lighting for night work, the pride of the *Penny Magazine* and the *Quarterly Review*.[82]

Pickfords, who had run a profitable trunk service of their own by express van from London to Manchester between 1818 and 1825, were only one of the large carters who found, when they had acclimatised themselves to railway competition that, if they turned their

[77] John Hollingshead, *Odd Journeys in and out of London* (1860), 177.
[78] H.C., 1854–5, X, Tables II and IV, App. pp. 215–6.
[79] T. C. Barker and Michael Robbins, *op. cit.* 262.
[80]

Number of omnibuses per hour			
Victoria	215	King's Cross	69
Liverpool St.	208	Waterloo	59
London Bridge	72	Charing Cross	50

H.C., 1906, XLI, 145, App. 6, Table 14.
[81] H.C., 1846, XVII, Q.1770 (Bevan).
[82] BTHR PIC 4/1; the *Penny Magazine*, 20 August and 8 October 1842, *Quarterly Review*, December 1848.

attention to urban carting and railway feeder services, the annual volumes of their business could be more than sustained at the pre-steam levels.[83] Chaplin and Horne, Sherman, and Dibbin, all took over old inn-yards, which had been deserted by the long-distance traffic, for use as receiving houses for railway goods.[84] 'These houses and yards are chiefly in the very narrowest and most confined streets,' wrote Charles Pearson, 'they answered well enough when the arrivals of coaches and waggons were few and far between; but now, when they are converted into suction-pipes, drawing together the whole trade of the City to the stations in carts and waggons, they create the most serious interruption to regular trade.'[85] At these carriers' yards the small loads were accumulated, two or three chests of tea in one van, a bale of goods or a couple of tons of iron in other carts; then later in the day they were transshipped and taken to the terminus in leviathan waggons, for the appropriate departure time. On other occasions, as when the processing of goods intervened, the number of cart journeys before despatch could rise to four or five. The Directories of provincial cities reveal similar activity amongst the carriers in each city.

In Glasgow, for example, the carrier's quarters (as in London) were situated in the narrow streets—in this case the small streets leading from Gallowgate and Trongate—and collected goods for distribution around the three districts into which the town was divided.[86] The goods collected at the railway stations also ran the additional hazard, at Jamaica Street Bridge, of conflicting streams of extremely heavy harbour traffic. Large carts, loaded with boxes, bales, coal and pig iron, in course of movement from the south bank (which took two-thirds of the export trade) to the north bank (where the import and bonding warehouses were situated), clashed with the carts making their way into the town from the Bridge Street goods terminus and with those making their way from the industrial quarter at Port Dundas, in the northern outskirts, down to the south bank of the river.[87]

This confusion between the dock, railway, and through traffic also arose at Liverpool, where bitter complaints led, in 1856, to the first discussions about a high-level rail or tramway, to separate the traffic flows. At Glasgow, however, since the traffic between the main southern goods terminal and the town, and between the two sides of the harbour, was all funnelled down one thoroughfare, the effect was greatly magnified. Jamaica Street by the 1870's with 900 vehicles per hour, was 'as crowded as Cheapside or London Bridge', in the opinion of the manager

[83] S. Salt, *Railway Commercial Information* (1850), 11, 18.
[84] H.C., 1846, XVII, Q.2834.
[85] *Ibid.* App. 23, p. 283.
[86] *Post Office Directory, Glasgow*, 1852–3, 60.
[87] John R. Kellett, *Ec.HR*, XVII (1964), 359.

of the London General Omnibus Company.[88] As in other cities, no small part of the congestion was caused by the unwieldy vehicles dispersing the railway goods, collecting them for delivery to the station, or carrying out inter-terminal transfer. Pickfords, Camerons, and Wordie, who carted for the different companies, all complained, by the early 1860's, of the great delays encountered both in loading goods and in moving them to and from their quarters.[89]

As with the goods cartage, so the increased passenger traffic in Glasgow also focused upon the railway stations. The numbers of cab-stands increased five-fold in the two decades after the passenger terminals opened, and more than half of them were at, or outside, the stations. Catering for passenger arrivals offered a sufficiently large and assured business by the 1860's to form a valuable concession, and attract larger, multiple-cab operators. John Walker, for example, stabled and paid tax on 366 horses in the mid-1860's, and bid £500 for the concession at Buchanan and Queen Street stations.[90] At the average cab-fare, and assuming a profit of 25% to 33%, this would mean that he must cover 40,000 journeys to break even. In fact his cabs probably made at least 75,000 to 90,000 journeys *per annum*. In a good month they made 225 daily trips from Queen Street and 75 from Buchanan Street stations.[91] In addition to the station cab service, horse omnibuses were running every two and a half minutes through the main streets outside the railway termini by the 1870's.[92]

Since, as already mentioned, the major companies in Glasgow frustrated each other's efforts to secure a central terminal in the 1840's, the problem of street traffic congestion was already acute when the second wave of railway projects broke in the 1860's. The basic idea of the rival Glasgow and South Western, Caledonian, and North British schemes was in each case to approach more closely the central business district; and this obviously would lead to the debouching of still more traffic onto Argyle Street, and other overloaded central thoroughfares. In view of this, the rudimentary nature of the provisions at the projected Union station were strongly criticised by the Dean of Guild Court. Provided the traffic could actually get on and off their premises without blockage, the Union company were quite satisfied with the result. What their plans would be likely to do, however, the Dean of

[88] HLRO, Min., H.C., 1872, 28 May, pp. 122–30, 156–92, S.C. on Glasgow and District Tramways.

[89] Pickfords were agents for the G. & S.W., Camerons for the Caledonian railway company. HLRO, Min., H.C., 1864, 13 May, p. 85, S.C. on Union Railway.

[90] HLRO, Min., H.C., 1866, 8 May, p. 8, S.C. on Glasgow Police. He owned 45 licenced and 55 job cabs.

[91] HLRO, Min., (Union), H.L., 1864, 12 July, pp. 114–5.

[92] HLRO, Min., H.C., 1872, 7 May, pp. 51–61, S.C. on Glasgow Corporation Tramways.

Guild Court pointed out, was simply to cause a jam twenty or thirty yards down the street from the station, where traffic joined the main-east-west stream.[93]

What was obviously desirable, especially for the later, more central stations built in the 1860's, was the extensive realignment of approach roads, in co-operation with the local authorities or statutory bodies, and with the expense shared between them and the railway company. In London a number of schemes of this sort were carried through, though the railway companies' contributions were not as generous as some would have liked. There are examples on a small scale from Manchester, Liverpool and Birmingham of street re-alignment. In Glasgow, however, there was no such accommodation, partly for reasons already suggested, partly because of the inflexible grid-iron street plan laid down in the 1770's and 1780's for the district into which central business functions were now migrating.

In all the other cities the contribution of the railways to urban traffic was similar in kind: square yard for square yard, the railway stations generated more traffic than any other buildings. Yet although Birmingham, Liverpool and Manchester had their own nineteenth century traffic problems, which merit more detailed separate study, none of them appear to have produced the sustained blockages typical of the river crossings at Glasgow and London.

Hopes that the railways might also supply the solution to the problem which they had so largely augmented were realised very imperfectly during the nineteenth century, even in London. It was in the capital, where, by the 1860's, one could 'walk over the roofs of vans and buses as readily as over the united up-raised shields of the Roman soldiers outside the walls of some beleaguered city', that the idea of a 'railway amongst the sewers' was put forward as a solution to street traffic congestion.[94] Henry Mayhew describes how the idea was first shadowed out by the late City Solicitor (Charles Pearson). 'We knew him well, and while discussing our joint schemes for the utilisation of convict labour, have often smiled at the earnestness with which he advocated his project for girdling London round with one long drain-like tunnel, and sending the people like so many parcels in a pneumatic tube, from one end of the metropolis to the other.'[95]

If a reformer like Henry Mayhew found time to smile, whilst discussing convict labour, at Pearson's visionary ideas, the public reaction can easily be imagined. 'It shook its head and laughed at the idea of a

[93] HLRO, Min., (Caledonian Central Station), H.C., 1873, 9 May, pp. 90–160.
[94] Henry Mayhew, *The Shops and Companies of London* (1865), 145.
[95] *Ibid.* 144.

railroad amongst the sewers', John Hollingshead wrote, 'The omnibus and cab interests, as represented by their drivers, were particularly facetious on the subject, forgetting what their predecessors, the stage-coachmen, had predicted of railroads in general, and how signally their prediction had failed.'[96]

London's traffic congestion in the 1860's, however, had reached crisis proportions. Transit from one end of the metropolis to the other was as difficult and slow as at the time when no roads at all existed. The primary agency of this increase, in Mayhew's opinion, was the arrival of the railways. 'The increased flood of immigrant passengers from the provinces and torrent of goods that kept pouring into the great emporia of the capital . . . caused an utterly new phase of traffic.'

The building of the Metropolitan underground line, to relieve this street congestion, could well stand as the epitome of Victorian urban railways. The scheme originated in 1837 in the mind of Charles Pearson, the City Solicitor, who, in spite of his prosaic office, was an idealist and visionary. 'Thousands of hours and thousands of pounds of my money and time have gone to the prosecution of this scheme, as to which I desire nothing but to see success, and do not seek for any remuneration.'[97] He had a special model, 'not a toy; it has been got up by professional men employed by myself', of his underground railway and central terminal schemes, which he offered to lay out in the dining-room of Guildhall for the members of the Royal Commission of 1846 to inspect. Nine years later the Select Committee on Metropolitan Communications was also badgered to inspect his model, and peruse his memoranda and coloured plans. He lived to see an underground railway based upon the scheme which he had conceived, begun in 1859, though it was still not opened to traffic at the time of his death.

The scheme was carried through, however, by a group of men who, though less far-sighted and disinterested than Pearson, brought together the necessary elements for re-making a city.[98] The engineer was the brilliant but avaricious John Fowler, concerned, as his record with the Metropolitan District later showed, rather with personal achievement than sound business; but capable of sustaining the confidence of others in the scheme—even when the Fleet river burst into the workings. Another director was the solicitor William Burchell, who arranged half the total expenditure (the part concerned with land purchase and compensation), without obtaining prior agreement, or keeping proper books. Burchell also connived at the payment of a quarter of the

[96] J. Hollingshead, *Underground London* (1862), 205.
[97] H.C., 1854–5, X, Q.1357.
[98] The following paragraph is based upon T. C. Barker and Michael Robbins, *op. cit.* 99–126.

declared dividends out of capital, a practice which had been considered dubious since George Hudson's disgrace in 1859; and he was connected with the contracting firm Peto and Betts, whose associates Thomas and Solomon Tredwell became joint builders of the line, and large shareholders in it. The chairman of the company was William Malins, who floated the scheme by persuading the bankers Heywood, Kennards & Co. to advance the necessary deposit to comply with Standing Orders, in return for appointment as the Metropolitan's bankers. His skill in presentation before the Select Committees earned a tribute even from Parliamentary counsel. In Myles Fenton the Metropolitan gained a general manager of unusual ability: and finally, in Edward Watkin, a new chairman who set the company on its feet as a business proposition when irregularities had brought it to the verge of bankruptcy.

The Metropolitan was such a remarkable success operationally as to precipitate the rush of urban railway projects in 1863 described in an earlier chapter. Its services, at five to ten minute intervals, represented a new approach to railway transport, and were more popular than anyone had dared to hope. This was reflected in the margin by which its weekly receipts of £720 per mile exceeded the average (£30 to £40) per mile per week for the major trunk routes.[99]

Its effect upon traffic congestion, however, was not as marked as might be supposed. For a time the New Road omnibuses, with which it directly competed, were reported to be running almost empty, in spite of halving their fares, but once curiosity about the new underground railway had died down their seats filled up again. Although by the end of the 1860's the Metropolitan was carrying twenty-five million passengers per year, and extending its works through the City, the London General Omnibus Company still carried forty million passengers per year, as it had before the underground railway was constructed. Once again the railway's role had been to create, or stimulate, additional new traffic.

b. *Land uses adjacent to the central stations*

As already mentioned, up to 9% of the old inner area of the five largest Victorian cities was directly purchased and taken over for railway uses; and by definition something in the order of a fifth of central land users found themselves neighbours, perhaps involuntarily, of the railway companies. Although the railways repelled the specialised display warehouses, and the new department stores of the 1860's and 1870's—which sought the carriage trade and objected even to street tramways—they attracted other land users.[100] Places for refreshment and entertain-

---

[99] Henry Mayhew, *op. cit.* 146.
[100] *Street-Railways or Street-Tramways* (1868), BM 8235 ee 31.

ment, for eating and lodging, and for retail shopping, gathered conveniently around the terminus. The lock-up shops under central railway arches always let readily, unlike the arches under the viaducts in the outskirts; and the squares or streets where the main passenger terminals were situated presented an obvious confluence of people and traffic, which resulted in a rising demand for sites of all descriptions around the stations.

The larger passenger stations acted as magnets for hotels, in particular, as the numbers breaking their journey or visiting each city increased, and the small inns at which travellers had arrived were converted to carriers' quarters or non-residential public houses. The increase in inter-city traffic was quite beyond the capacity of the traditional inns and lodgings to accommodate, and entirely new and greatly enlarged premises had to be built to cater for it. According to one estimate the national total of coach and mail passengers in 1833 was 2,688,000; to this should be added a further twenty-five or thirty *per cent* for arrivals by post horses, canal boats & etc., giving three and a half million travellers.[101] Thirty years later the number of rail travellers was 204,635,075; an increase, in relation to the larger population, of about forty-fold.[102]

The railway companies themselves provided large hotels at each of the great towns, all on a large scale. The railway hotel at St. Pancras, designed by Gilbert Scott and, in his words, 'possibly too good for the purpose it is to serve', was the largest hotel in Britain at the time it was built.[103] With such assured increases of passenger traffic there was hardly any speculative element at all in the building of hotels at the station sites; and this extension of land use by the railways into an associated field was never questioned either by shareholders or by the legislature. Other hotel promoters, large and small, made haste to follow in the middle years of the century.

In London a small group of hotels grew up in Pimlico, associated with Victoria station.[104] The same thing occurred, on a larger scale, in Paddington and Bayswater, near the main arrival point for travellers from the West Country, and in Bloomsbury, associated with the northern main line termini.[105] In Liverpool the hotel quarter also redistributed itself, over the same period, from the old town to the neighbourhood of Lime Street, the main terminal for overnight

[101] T. Baines, *Lancashire and Cheshire, Past and Present* (1868), II, p. lii.

[102] H.C., 1890, LXV, 681.

[103] Sir G. Scott, *Personal and Professional Recollections* (1879), 271 quoted in Jack Simmons, *op. cit.* 92.

[104] D. F. Stevens, 'The Central Area', *Greater London* (ed. J. T. Coppock and H. C. Prince, 1964), 192–3.

[105] D. J. Olsen, *op. cit.* 113–4.

passengers; and the other cities witnessed a similar, though perhaps less marked, re-location of hotels and the services associated with them.[106]

If one turns from these arrangements made for the local reception of travellers to those made for the reception and storage of goods, the urban railway terminals may be observed exercising a similar, if weaker, attraction. Once again—and this can surely be taken as a guide to the assured and unspeculative nature of the enterprise—the railway companies themselves laid out capital, which might well have been put to other uses, in providing specialised markets incorporated into their terminals in the major cities. London had two wholesale potato markets at railway terminals. That which the Great Northern railway company constructed at King's Cross had thirty-seven small covered warehouses, each with a short line of rails. They could be leased for sums of £35 to £65 *per annum*; or a 2d per ton surcharge could be paid if the consignee preferred to operate without leasing a warehouse.[107] In Liverpool the L. & N.W. railway company had a potato depot at Crown Street, and the Lancashire and Yorkshire company one at Great Howard Street.[108] In Manchester the Lancashire and Yorkshire railway had a carrot and potato market at Oldham Road station where it sold only the goods which it had transported, paying the Corporation £1,000 *per annum* for the licence.[109] In Glasgow and Birmingham perishable foodstuff markets were not incorporated in the station yards, but were situated very near them. Indeed proximity, or convenient access, to railway stations became one of the most important considerations in the siting of the new and enlarged central wholesale markets for perishable foodstuffs in the mid and late nineteenth century.

The traffic soon extended to a far wider range than the root crops which had at first formed the staple. Cattle trucks brought meat, by the mid 1840's; the fish trade was, in the words of a wholesale fish dealer, 'entirely changed since the introduction of railways and telegraphs.'[110] By the 1880's a city like Manchester could draw upon spring cabbages from Evesham and Lincolnshire, broccoli and cauliflowers from Northamptonshire, green peas from Nottinghamshire, or even

[106] W. Smith, 'The Urban Structure of Liverpool', *Merseyside: a Scientific Survey* (British Association, 1953), 192–3.

[107] LRL, Council Minutes, 1863–4, p. 583, Report of Town Clerk on London Markets.

[108] *Loc. cit.* pp. 587–93.

[109] *Manchester of Today* (Manchester, 1888), 74.

[110] The early cattle trucks were 'to be fitted with spring buffers and drawbars, to answer occasionally for passengers.' Jack Simmons, *op. cit.* 143. LRL, Council Minutes, 1872–3, pp. 563–8, Conference between Markets Committee and Wholesale Fish Dealers.

JOHN F. CLARK, C.E.
WILLM. WILSON, Assistant Engineer.

PLATE 9
Original plan of area
scheduled for purchase
and demolition at
Victoria Station,
London, 1858
(see p. 327)

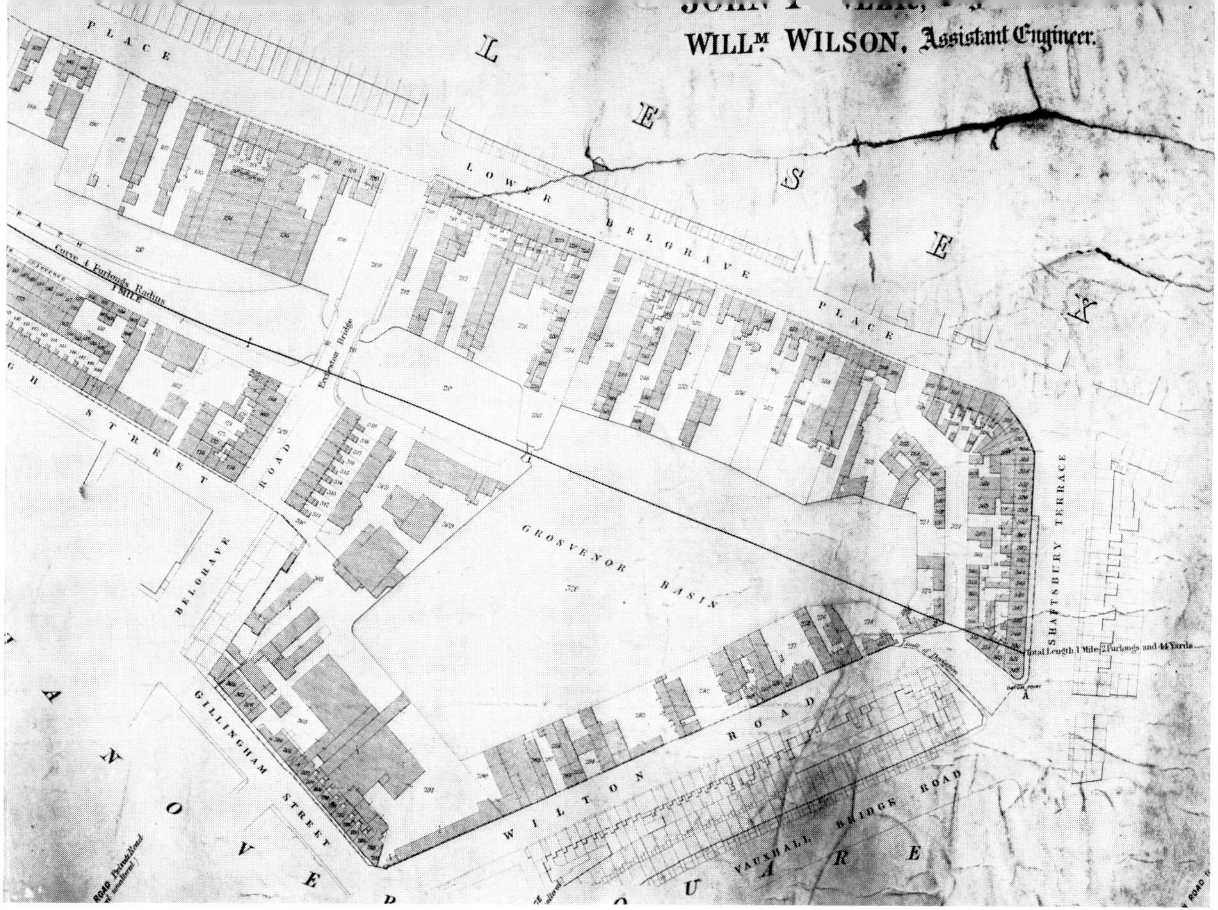

(By permission of HLRO)

PLATE 10 Housing conditions and land use in Manchester, 1904 (see p. 337)

(see p. 337)

KEY Lighter shading shows offices, warehouses, commercial buildings

PLATE 11   The railway arches: paupers at night
(see p. 345)

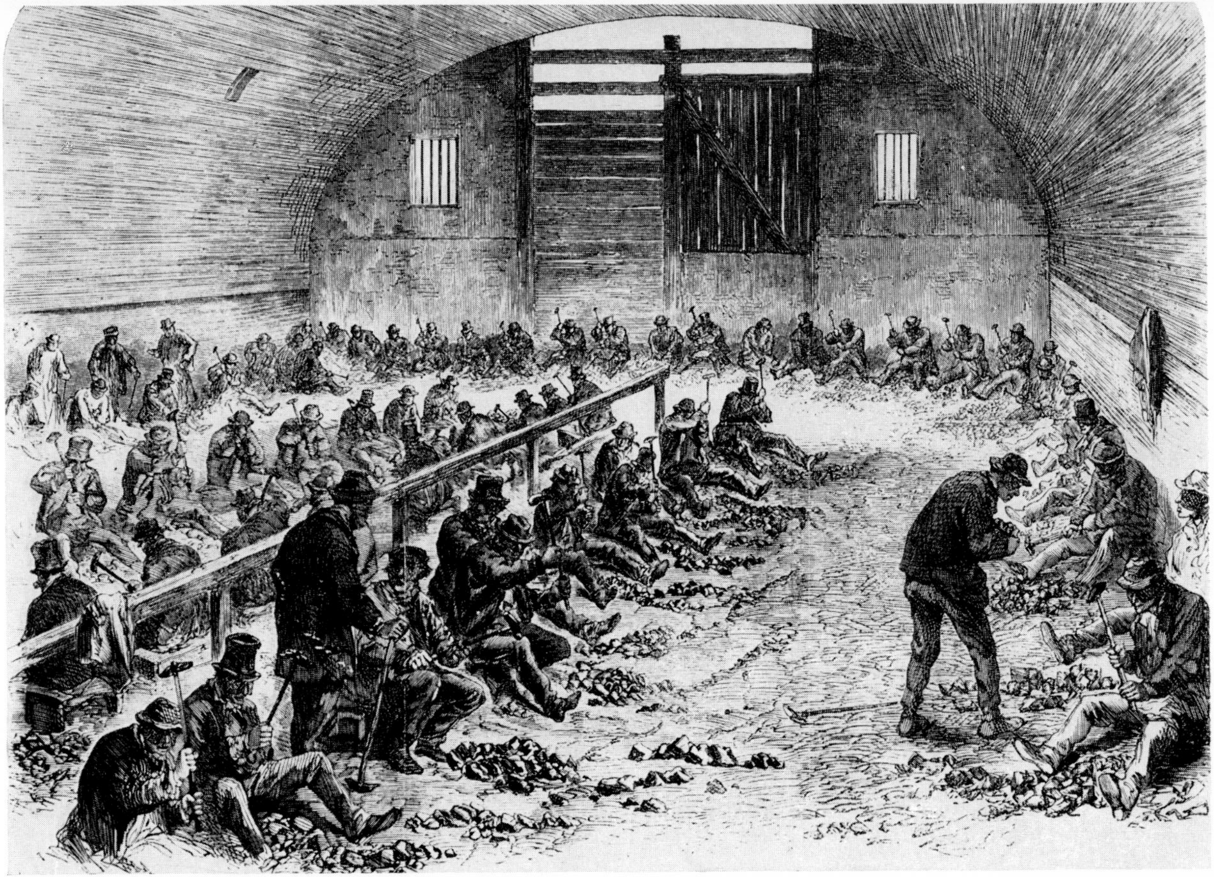

PLATE 12 The railway arches: unemployed by day
(see p. 345)

(By permission of 'Illustrated London News')

France, potatoes from Lancashire, Yorkshire, Lincolnshire and Jersey, carrots from the Midlands and France, cucumbers and onions from Bedfordshire, soft fruit from Kent, and imported apples from Liverpool.[111] Those dealing wholesale in these commodities in the central area, though not tied to exact locations, clearly would consider easy access to a station a positive advantage, and be prepared to pay for it. Even if the important coal traffic, which grew so rapidly after the 1860's, be excluded (since it was largely distributed from outlying stations) the list of centrally distributed commodities could be extended. There were the famous vaults at St. Pancras which contained thousands of gallons of Bass; the facilities for storing and distributing milk from Euston, St. Pancras, Paddington and Vauxhall. 'City cows', writes Hamilton Ellis, 'vanished like the scavenging pigs of earlier centuries.'[112]

One would imagine that the establishment of all these wholesale outlets for the cities' daily needs would itself generate a great deal of traffic. So it did, but the traffic was merely originating from new points rather than new in itself. Carting to the markets, large and small, throughout the cities, had always been heavy, but had tended to converge from the surrounding countryside. At least one Borough Engineer came to the conclusion that the concentration which railway delivery afforded actually 'diminished greatly the number of vehicles proceeding to the markets through the streets.'[113] What was clearly happening, if his observation was correct, was that wholesalers were congregating around the termini to take advantage of the short journeys, full loads and speed of turnover.

The amounts which the wholesaler, or, for that matter, the large hotelier, or the small well-sited retailer, were prepared to bid for proximity to the inner stations, or for vantage points in the traffic streams which the stations generated, were reflected in rising land values. The appreciation of site values around the city terminals was so marked, in fact, as to present an embarrassment to those companies which had at first underestimated their land requirements. After his early experience in this field Robert Stephenson was one of those who enjoined upon his board the policy of erring on the side of extravagance in scheduling land for compulsory purchase. 'Mark me, Mr. Glyn, you require it all,' he said at the time of his land purchases from the Earl of Southampton at Camden Town, and the Duke of Bedford at Euston, 'but if you did not require it, the value of property

[111] *Manchester of Today* (Manchester, 1888), 73.
[112] E. G. Barnes, *op. cit.* 253; Hamilton Ellis, *British Railway History* (1954), I, 407.
[113] James Newlands, in his report on Paris Markets to Liverpool Corporation, LRL, Council Minutes, 1863–4, p. 613.

in the neighbourhood will be so enhanced that you will be able to part with it to advantage. . . . In my whole experience I have never known a case where the railways have caused the value of property to fall.'[114]

To this extent the railways were their own enemies, causing a rise in the price of land which they themselves might later come into the market to purchase; and nowhere was this more evident than in the land around the city terminals. In spite of making what, on Stephenson's advice, was considered to be a sufficient purchase at Euston in 1835, the Chairman of the L. & N.W. was compelled to admit, in 1848, 'we have since then been obliged to buy streets—*streets*, gentlemen—to give the public the accommodation they require.'[115] Both the Midland railway, in its St. Pancras operations, and the Metropolitan railway in the 1860's, went to extremes to anticipate future space requirements, in order to avoid the ransom prices which they might be charged for any extensions.[116] In one case, virtually a whole parish was demolished, using techniques of deception and force which reflected grave discredit on the Midland company, and provided reformers with an example of railway clearances which was cited for twenty years.[117] In the other case, the Metropolitan company found itself the owner of nearly a thousand urban properties, on lands surplus to its requirements, and was obliged, before its Acts expired, to set up a special Surplus Lands Company to deal with the properties it had retained.[118]

Part of this rise in land prices was undoubtedly due to the impact of the railways themselves upon the land market. Adroit purchases fringeing likely areas of expansion, or lying across possible urban extensions, undoubtedly helped to send up the value of land. There were ingenious techniques, described elsewhere, which could be used to take advantage of the railway companies' appearance in the land market; and, where there were no alternative choices of route or site, the railways often paid twice the average amount agreed upon by independent valuers.[119] Since the railways, wherever possible, made their approaches to the urban core through working-class housing, this gave the owner of slum property yet another chance of speculative gain.

On the other hand, part of the appreciation of property values around

---

[114] Samuel Salt, *op. cit.* 95–6.

[115] Six-monthly Report, L. & N.W. railway company, 18 February 1848.

[116] Six-monthly Report, Midland railway company, 15 January 1868. W. E. Hutchinson (Chairman) states 407 acres had been bought near London, instead of 209 'to forestall rising land costs.'

[117] H.C., 1874, LIX, 159–62. H.C., 1884–5, XXX, *passim.*

[118] Six-month Report, Metropolitan railway company, 25 July 1885.

[119] This is a conservative estimate. Some railway directors, like G. P. Bidder, believed that, on the average, railway companies paid four times the value of given land. H.C., 1867, XXXVIII, Q.17170.

the terminals was genuine; not induced by the prospect of ransom sale to the railway companies, but the product of *bona fide* alternative land use demands. Between the 1840's and 1880's the larger Victorian cities regularly experienced a $2\frac{1}{2}\%$ to $3\frac{1}{2}\%$ annual increase in central land values, but it is not easy to say what proportion of this should be assigned to the direct agency of the railways. Modern work in the United States, attempting to relate land values to transport facilities, came to the conclusion that, in New York at any rate, the trend of values was 'largely influenced by factors other than transit developments.' But the analogy may be misleading, and other economists, speaking more directly from British nineteenth century experience, have taken the view that the sustained rise in urban site rents— which exceeded the rise in the national income throughout the nineteenth century—was symptom of rail transport's inherent tendency to 'freeze', and densely to concentrate, both population and industry.[120]

Until further work is carried out to illuminate the complexities of site use and value in the central districts of Victorian cities, perhaps the most that can be said, by way of generalisation, is that values can be observed to rise quickly in the area between the termini and the most favoured street intersections of the central business district, for a variety of causes, amongst which a major new contributor by the 1840's was the locational advantage bestowed by a station's proximity. Although the nucleus of the central business district continued with its own processes of assimilation and discard, influenced more by established uses and by land supply than by the railways, the areas between it and the stations now experienced a new inflationary factor. It was, it must be stressed, still only one factor amongst many; but 'distance from the railway station' was an important and *novel* consideration to which at least a part of the increment in inner land values should be attributed.

William Tite, the engineer and valuer responsible for the extension

---

[120] The total rise in rental values in the central area of Manchester, for example, was 35–40% per decade 1861–81.

	1861 Rental values	£972,894
1871	,, ,,	£1,362,164
1881	,, ,,	£1,803,000

H. Baker, *Trans. Manch. Stat. Soc.* (1868–72), 92–4, (1881–5), 9–13. This was reflected in central land values exceeding £200,000 per acre by 1880. H. Baker, *loc. cit.* (1868–72), 94, W. Ashworth, *The Genesis of Modern British Town Planning* (1965), 100.

For American experience see E. M. Spengler, *Land values in New York in relation to Transit* (New York, 1930), 129–31, and Paul F. Wendt, 'Theory of Urban Land Values', *Land Economics*, XXXIII (1957), 234. For 'concentration' see Colin Clark, 'Transport—maker and breaker of cities', *Town Planning Review*, 28 (1957–8), 245–8.

from Nine Elms to Waterloo (No. 7 on map) described the railway's primary effect as that of 'giving new frontages and new opportunities for building'. 'There is no doubt that the advantages which you describe might result from placing the railway there, but the question is,' he was asked, in cross-examination, 'whether the public so far appreciate those advantages as to show it by giving a higher price for the land?— They would, of course,' Tite replied, '*where the railway brings direct advantage as a station.*'[121]

Here Tite had touched upon a most important qualification. Around the terminal the attractions were apparent to some, if not all, categories of land user. But no one, except heavy industrial firms with their own sidings, wanted to be placed alongside the railway line at distances of half a mile or more down line; so that from this point outwards, the railway routes tended to run through belts of dereliction. Of course, though everyone might wish to be located by a terminus rather than an unbroken, possibly elevated, stretch of line, in the nature of the case this was impossible. With each terminus were associated many acres of approach routes, and even those railways which had tunnel exits and entrances did not continue their tunnels clear of the town, but emerged at ground level in the so-called 'inner districts', adjacent to the business centre.

c. *Demolition*

There was another problem of growing magnitude in the mid-Victorian city centre to which the railways contributed substantially, without being able, or willing, to provide a remedy; that of demolition in the central areas. In many ways it was a more serious and intractable problem than that of traffic, certainly in its social and sanitary aspects; and once again it was hoped that new types of short distance underground railway might solve the problem. At a public meeting in December 1858, chaired by the Lord Mayor of London, Charles Pearson and Lord John Russell spoke in favour of a central terminal combined with a cheap fares policy, and persuaded the meeting to pass two resolutions; the first complained of the overcrowding of the streets, the second of the overcrowding of the dwellings of the poor. The two were associated and to be solved by the same means—the use of the railways as 'an outlet' for the pressures both of population and traffic.[122]

It will be clear from what has been said earlier, that the intense overcrowding in those working class houses which remained intact in the 'City without the Wall' parishes in London, and in the central and inner districts of the provincial cities, was the product of a number of

[121] H.C., 1846, XVII, QQ.405–7. My italics.
[122] *Illustrated London News*, 4 December 1858, 524.

economic forces, of which the railways were only one. 'Now and again' wrote H. Baker in the *Transactions of the Manchester Statistical Society* (1871), 'complaint is vocal at the so-called "wholesale" eviction of population, and demolition of dwellings consequent upon railway enlargement; but scarcely even a passing notice is taken of the continuous pushing out of the population from the central sub-districts of the city by the centric aggregation of trading interests.'[123] The conversion of the central area to warehouses and offices, though less spectacular than the railway intrusions, and rarely affecting such large units of territory, was undoubtedly responsible for as many evictions in total as the railway companies. Large though they were, the railway clearances can hardly explain, as sole cause, the phenomenon observable to varying degrees in each city: the emptying of population from the central areas, beginning in London, Birmingham, Manchester and Liverpool from the 1850's, and Glasgow from the 1860's. Nor, if we take into account the orders of magnitude of population movement involved, does railway demolition, even if we assign to it the very large numbers suggested below, do more than partially account for the exodus. But it was a conspicuous, abrupt and direct agency and, like the demolitions by the school boards and street improvement committees, it attracted note.[124] The more gradual process of commercial replacement as leases fell in, or by piecemeal purchase, though perhaps more far-reaching over a long span of time, was not as concentrated, nor did it make use of compulsory powers and such urgent methods: blocking streets, unroofing houses to get the occupants out, and reducing the inhabitants of whole working class districts like Somers Town to the state, in Lord Shaftesbury's words, of 'people in a besieged town, running to and fro, and not knowing where to turn.'[125]

The social effects of these violent and sudden demolitions, and the contemporary comment upon them, has already been made the subject of a comprehensive and illuminating study for the London area.[126] The same problem also recurred in the provinces, where it excited similar comments. 'Demolition Statements' were also returned under Standing Order 191 in the provincial cities, ludicrously understating the numbers of members of the working class likely to be dishoused: 1,275 people in the 255 cottages due for demolition under the 1866 Manchester Central Bill; 540 in 135 houses to make way for Liverpool Central; 6,142 in 443 of the larger Glasgow tenements for St. Enoch's station, and a further 2,178 people and 141 houses for the Caledonian Central station

[123] H. Baker, *Trans. Manch. Stat. Soc.* (1868–72), 87.
[124] H.C., 1884–5, XXX, Report p. 19.
[125] *Loc. cit.* p. 25, and Hansard, CLXI (1861), 1069.
[126] H. J. Dyos, *JTH*, II (1955), 11–21, 90–100.

a few years later.[127] To judge from independent comment, and from estimates by local officers of health and other witnesses, it is clear that these figures are no reliable guide, and, indeed, would hardly explain the public attention attracted by railway demolitions.[128] But they were, of course, returns made by the railway companies themselves, the very 'people who have every motive for under-stating the number that they displace.'[129] Since census returns cannot be used, for a variety of reasons, to show short term local migrations of population, we are thrown back upon the informal guesses of contemporaries, and these multiply the numbers officially returned by a factor varying from threefold to tenfold. Alternatively, the proportions of the built-up area of each town demolished, mentioned earlier (*viz.* $5\frac{1}{2}\%$ to 9%) may serve as a guide. For example, $7\frac{1}{2}\%$ of the central area of Glasgow in 1840 contained roughly 20,000 people, and this number is far likelier to reflect the real number displaced than the official return of 8,320.[130] But though more plausible than the official figures, even these estimates probably err on the side of understatement; for it was not just any $7\frac{1}{2}\%$ of the town that was chosen for the railways' route. In Glasgow, and in the other towns without exception, the areas which were invariably selected for demolition were populous working class districts. The thinly inhabited commercial or industrial areas were meticulously avoided, for reasons to which reference will be made later.

However, although the social problems of demolition recurred in the northern cities, in much the same form, the problem was particularly acute in London. The Royal Commission on the Housing of the Working Classes decided, 'The compulsion to live close to work is not such a difficulty in provincial towns as it is in the metropolis.'[131] A somewhat complacent view, which does not accord with the findings of William Trench in Liverpool, or John Leigh in Manchester, but one

---

[127] References for these have already been given in the *Case Histories*. The companies building Snow Hill and New Street Birmingham, Lime Street and Exchange Liverpool, or indeed, any stations built before 1853, were not required to submit demolition statements. The Demolition Statement for the C.L.C. 1872 plan—the present day Manchester Central—is missing, though the Lords' Committee mentions 312 houses, occupied by 1,663 persons of the labouring classes, in the area due for demolition.

[128] The Midland railway company's operations in the 1860's, for example, were only stated to be 4,347, but contemporary estimates put the figure at 20,000 to 32,000. Similarly, there was no Demolition Return for one of the largest projects— the Great Eastern's Liverpool Street extension (see H. J. Dyos, *JTH*, II (1955), 12, III (1956), 26–9), whereas 7,000 people in 450 houses were affected by the demolition. H.C., 1884–5, QQ.10164–5, 10181–5.

[129] H.C., 1884–5, XXX, Q.9110.

[130] Or if one takes the average for central land absorbed by the railways and multiplies it by a factor of 300 (300 to 400 per acre being a common density in working class areas) the comparable result is 22,500 displaced.

[131] H.C., 1884–5, XXX, Report p. 23.

takes the Commissioners' point.[132] It was essentially a Metropolitan problem, because of the scale, both of the demolitions and of the distances, displacement might involve.

In London, something of the order of 800 acres of central land was taken for railway uses in the course of the nineteenth century: an area sufficient for a fair-sized town in itself. The numbers displaced, came to over 76,000 between 1853 and 1901, according to H. J. Dyos—who makes it clear that this figure represents an absolute minimum on which to base estimates and is in no real sense an accurate count.[133] This number spread over the area involved would, in fact, work out at 95 per acre. According to Dr. Lethaby's estimates in 1861 the average in the central parishes was nearer 150 per acre, rising to as high as 300 per acre in some districts. The lower of these two figures would give 120,000 people affected by displacement in the period from 1840–1900; and taking $5\frac{1}{2}\%$ of the population of the central parishes produces a similar total.[134] There are two further reasons for expecting the total count of those evicted by the railways in London to reach at least 120,000. The returns under Standing Order 191 only started in 1853, and so exclude the considerable displacements connected with the building of the several stations at London Bridge, Fenchurch Street, Shoreditch and Waterloo, and the lesser displacements at Paddington and Euston. They also referred only to the houses of the 'labouring classes', so that the returns were not even intended to be full 'Demolition Statements', but only partial statements of the demolition of those houses which it was necessary to classify as belonging to the 'labouring classes'. The result was a further paring down of the quantities involved; as two examples, one from London, and one from the provinces, may illustrate. The Victoria and Pimlico railway and station scheduled several hundred properties owned by William Stanley and the Marquess of Westminster, some of which may be seen in the accompanying illustration (Plate 9): yet since the social and occupational categories of the occupants was not established as 'labouring classes', the *Plans* and *Sections* were endorsed, 'Not 30 in any one parish to be taken'.[135] The demolition involved, however, was still quite considerable. Or in Liverpool, the first M.S. & L. scheme for the Central Station stated that 135 houses, containing 545 members of the labouring classes, would be scheduled for demolition; but the full number of properties— whose inhabitants were no less real for not being the subject of

[132] LRL, Council Proceedings, 1871–2, 702–17. MRL, Reports of the M.O.H., March 1884, pp. 22–7.

[133] H. J. Dyos, *JTH*, II (1955), 13, 98–9, *JTH*, III (1957), 23–30.

[134] Dr. Lethaby's report, dated 22 June 1861, is quoted in H. D. Davies, *The Way Out* (1861), 7–8.

[135] HLRO, P & S, 1858, Victoria Station and Pimlico Railway. The plans were deposited, as usual, in November of the preceding year.

philanthropic statistics—came to over 800.[136] If one wishes to form a picture of the total amount of demolition, therefore, some addition should be made for those not falling within the definition 'labouring classes' whose houses were taken. Altogether it would be surprising if the true number of those who lost their homes were not upwards of 120,000.

In case this estimate may seem unwarrantably large, it is perhaps worth rehearsing additional reasons for increasing so substantially the numbers contained in the Demolition Statements. First of all, the statements were not official in any real sense except that they were filed with official papers. The census was taken by the companies themselves and was not subjected to any official checking other than that of formal record. The railway companies concerned with persuading Parliament to sanction the taking of property and eviction of tenants, were hardly likely to submit, in the November before their bill was heard, a return which might cause alarm to Select Committees.

However, the inaccuracy of the Demolition Statements goes further than this. The railway companies gave unequivocal signs by the practices they pursued, that they were not merely concerned to minimise the likely results of their schemes by taking the lowest reasonable estimate. There was a deliberate intention to mislead. Schemes were broken down into parts so that each slice did not seem excessive.[137] Properties in the route of projected advance were also bought up privately by agents before the scheme was announced so that the question of consent or displacement did not arise; and there is evidence to suggest that this was a practice further extended in the second wave of projects in the 1860's than it had been in earlier days. There was even an attempt, of doubtful legality, by the Midland railway company, in the early 1870's, to carry out wholesale pre-demolition of 700 cottages by means of a separate company, from whom the land was later to be leased.[138]

Advance purchase had three beneficial results: it was cheaper to

---

[136] HLRO, P & S, 1862, M.S. & L. Liverpool Central Station Railway; P & S 1864, Liverpool Central Station Railway. The first deposited plans of the M.S. & L. scheme of 1862 contain no Demolition Statement, nor any reference to one, nor do the registers at HLRO refer to one—a strange breach of procedure.

[137] As in the Central Station project at Liverpool just cited, or the Union project at Glasgow, where the College Goods station was left out of the Plans and Demolition Statements.

[138] 'In conversation with one of the Midland Directors, I was informed that the Company had in fact actually acquired the land, had bought up nearly all the leasehold and occupiers' interests, that they had pulled down a number of the houses, and had vacant possession of a still larger number; that the Railway Company intended to carry out the proposed scheme by means of a separate company from whom they would lease the undertaking when completed.' Sir Sidney Waterlow M.P. to Richard Cross, Home Secretary, 20 May 1874, H.C., 1874, LIX, 159–62.

purchase before the railway company came openly onto the market; it enabled sizeable private profits to be made; and it meant that the untenanted houses did not appear in the Demolition Statement. Sometimes if the purchase could not be made privately, a hint was dropped that compulsory powers were to be applied for in a future session to add pressure to persuasion. Miss Octavia Hill described the process in detail.

'Usually the railway company communicate with the landlords, and tell them, "We are going to take your property"; the landlord gives the ordinary weekly or monthly notice to the tenants, and long before the railway comes the tenants have been got rid of; so that the landlord pockets the compensation, and that is what is taking place I am told and in spite of the advice of my fellow workers, in Albert Buildings. In Albert Buildings, Lambeth, the tenants are told by the agents of the railway company that they will have to move, and that their best plan is to get out soon. This is before the Act is obtained. The companies, therefore, can go before Parliament, and say, "We do not displace people; there is nobody there".'[139]

In other words they displaced a great number of people unofficially and only counted those who were left. Apart from the pressures Miss Hill described, the railway companies were not above bribing tenants to leave, Joseph Chamberlain alleged; and the Medical Officer of Health for St. Pancras, S. F. Murphy, gave evidence that the railway companies paid more for a house handed over to them empty.[140] Even in the actual counting there was further scope for whittling down. As William Denton pointed out, the term 'artisan' used in the Standing Order could be given a very narrow interpretation, to include mathematical instrument makers, but exclude tailors, shoemakers etc.[141] Moreover the railway companies, in their evidence, were apt to refer to 'tenants' who were usually heads of households; taking no account of subtenants, lodgers and other members of the family. For this reason alone it was suggested (and agreed to by Edward Watkin) that the figure should be multiplied by four to give occupants.[142]

Supporting evidence, not to labour the point, was put forward by the Assistant Secretary to the Board of Trade, the Clerk of Public Bills in the House of Lords, and the Surveyor for the Metropolitan Board of Works, all to the same effect: the Standing Order, even after it had been reinforced in 1874, was 'systematically evaded' and the returns were, in Joseph Chamberlain's words, 'grossly inaccurate'.[143]

[139] H.C., 1884–5, XXX, Q.8841.
[140] *Ibid.* QQ.12432, 1578–1674.
[141] *Ibid.* Q.10722.
[142] *Ibid.* QQ.10643–5.
[143] *Ibid.* QQ.9974–10061, 10740–3, 9943–54: Report p. 52, 'The evidence was unanimous that the Standing Orders were either evaded or were insufficient.' Q.12432 (Chamberlain).

M*

The railway companies' Demolition Statements could not, in fact, bear even the slightest critical examination. Drawing them up was an essay in deception, and probably the best attitude to adopt towards them for a conscientious manager, who wished to keep his hands clean, was Edward Watkin's affectation of lordly indifference.

'There is a Standing Order of the House of Lords directing a return of the number of persons evicted by railway companies, is there not?— I really do not know. You know better than I do, but very likely that is so.'[144]

Apart from its direct impact, demolition produced a second effect, which was perhaps still more important from a social point of view: the overspilling of those evicted into adjacent areas. 'The poor are displaced,' said *The Times*, in 1861, 'but they are not removed. They are shovelled out of one side of the parish, only to render more over-crowded the stifling apartments in another part. . . . But the dock and wharf labourer, the porter and the costermonger cannot remove. You may pull down their wretched homes: they must find others, and make their new dwellings more crowded and wretched than their old ones. The tailor, shoemaker and other workmen are in much the same position. It is mockery to speak of the suburbs to them.'[145]

Because of the increased demand for house space from these unfortunate refugees, not merely were the surviving slums packed even more densely than before, but rents in the vicinity rose by up to 50%. Those evicted from their squalid courts moved on, with their half crown or guinea compensation, to the areas described two years later in the *Illustrated London News*. Countless houses of 'precisely the same original bad quality as those which had been pulled down, but made infinitely worse, while being proportionately dearer through those very improvements.'

'They enter upon a new and terrible competition, which is for the most part finally settled by fresh discoveries in the art of huddling the largest number of human beings into the smallest possible spaces.'[146]

The leading article just cited concluded upon a note of premature optimism. 'Lord Derby—to his honour be it recorded—has taken the lead in enforcing the novel but obviously right and necessary role that the promoters of such improvements shall make due provisions for the people they displace.'[147] Making provisions, however, raised further

[144] *Ibid*. Q.10448.
[145] *The Times*, 2 March 1861.
[146] *Illustrated London News*, 17 January 1863, 83.
[147] Derby introduced the petition on 28 February, referring particularly to the North London railway company's operations at Broad Street. 'In the whole parish there is not a single gentleman's house, or even a large shop.' Costermongers and dockworkers with their families, living at a density of 10 or 11 per house, were the chief sufferers. Shaftesbury also spoke in support. *Hansard* CLXI (1861). 1063–9. 1698–9.

problems. Re-housing could hardly be carried out by building new replicas of the appalling slums demolished, yet there was no other way to produce low rents in such central districts. The nearest approach was by barrack-like workmen's dwellings, but even in these the rents were often beyond the means of those displaced. If the building problems were solved, how could it be ensured that the same tenants would be re-admitted? Would the railway companies act in good faith, moreover, or would the improved dwellings be quietly removed later to make way for warehouses? Were railway companies to be tied, in perpetuity, not to sell or convert their property to other uses? These difficulties ensured that the attempts to tighten up legislation on re-housing came to little. The alternative solution, really cheap transport, although an issue pursued by reformers with great vehemence, also fell short of the goals intended for it, for the reasons suggested elsewhere; but it was in 1861, in the aftermath of Derby's speech on demolitions, that the first clauses for cheap workmen's services were secured.[148]

One further question concerning the fabric of the city centre, and the effect of railway demolition, remains. Why did the railways always choose to smash their way through the densely packed working class residential districts? A glance at the *Plans and Sections* of the twelve major schemes affecting London, which were listed by the Assistant Secretary of the Board of Trade, shows that residential demolition was, in fact, the invariable practice, unless some open space which had miraculously survived—an old pleasure garden or open-air market—presented itself.[149] Given the necessity to schedule buildings, the railway promoters always chose slums, even after the grave social costs this policy incurred were apparent. In the popular view it seemed almost as if the railways were directed either by utter heedlessness of consequences or by sheer malice. The 'Goths and Vandals Railway' was *Punch*'s satire in 1861; 'Attila in London' the title of an article in Dickens' *All the Year Round* magazine in 1866; and there was, more generally in literature, a rapid movement of opinion in the 1860's away from the enthusiastic and uncritical reception the railways had received twenty years earlier.[150] For this change of attitude the daily spectacle of demolition and eviction in the great cities was partly responsible. Yet the demolition of residential housing was no idle or callous choice. There were three basic reasons why this class of property was selected.

[148] The North London railway company's Broad Street extension, and the Metropolitan railway company's Finsbury Circus extensions, 24–5, Vic., c. 196, and 24–5 Vic., c. 233. Three years later the important Great Eastern, Metropolitan and Metropolitan District, and London, Chatham and Dover clauses followed. H.C., 1872, XIII, Q.7383.

[149] H.C., 1884–5, XXX, Q.9974.

[150] H. J. Dyos, *JTH*, II (1955), 14–6.

The first was simply that, however aggrieved they might feel about it, tenants had no legal standing to object. Their interests were supposedly covered by a lump sum in compensation for removal.[151] If they were awkward and vocal enough, or could enlist the help of a local clergy-man, or another philanthropic member of the middle class on their behalf, they might cause this sum to be increased. But that was the end of their rights, and until the national and municipal franchises were extended there was nothing further they could do about it. William Denton believed it was the legal impotence of tenants which swayed the railways' route-makers. 'Much of the injury which new lines of railway cause could be prevented if the shortest and best routes were considered, and not merely whether the people on a given spot were or were not able to offer effectual opposition to the scheme proposed.'[152]

No doubt this legal consideration entered into the companies' choice of routes, especially in the haste and delicate balance of Private Bill procedure, where the absence of opponents with legal standing deprived hostile counsel of one of their principal opportunities to tip the scales against a bill. Railway companies, however, obviously be-lieved that their routes, if not always the shortest, were the best avail-able.[153] Yet exigencies of competition could arise under which it would be true (as Parliamentary witnesses suggested) that 'the parties care very little whether the line they have adopted is exactly the cheapest and best.'[154] Departures from first choice might be forced upon a company by competitors' blocking schemes or pre-emption of land, or simply by the need for speed of action.

The practical restrictions upon an urban railway promoter's freedom to choose his route must not be exaggerated. It was possible, if the timing of a bill were properly managed, even to plan a line overlapping with rival schemes for a great part of the route, and to rely upon adroit counsel, and the reputation of the engineers and company concerned, to secure preference. It was also possible, though more difficult, after a competitor had bought land which successfully gave monopoly access and obstructed other approach routes, to persuade Parliament to allow one railway company to take and demolish the buildings of another company. When the Caledonian railway, for example, applied for a

[151] Or the payment of rent-arrears outstanding. The weekly tenant had no claim to compensation whatsoever. Dyos, *loc. cit.* 95–6.

[152] William Denton, *op. cit.* (1861), 25.

[153] In the equation land costs, and the probable operational cost, weighed on the one side, the minimum length of approach route on the other. A slightly longer route which avoided awkward curves and gradients on an approach to a city termi-nus, or gave more space for the subsequent handling of traffic might be preferred. 'Choose that which is the least expensive even though it should not always be the most direct', advised Robert Stephenson, quoted in E. A. Course, *op. cit.* (1958), 5.

[154] H.C., 1836, XXI, QQ.356–76.

direct route of their own into Glasgow, 'to avoid' as their counsel put it, 'going by a *circumbendibus* through someone else's station', property belonging to the opposing Glasgow and South Western railway lay on their route.[155] They proposed to take part of it and miss the G. & S.W.'s Board Room, in Bridge Street, by a few yards, so that the noise of the Caledonian engines thundering past, the Select Committee was told, would make it exceedingly difficult for the G. & S.W. directors to conduct their business. 'If they want another Board room,' said George Cunningham, obviously savouring the moment, 'there is no difficulty in giving it to them—the whole offices are very small.'[156]

The successful conclusion of such clashes, and the imposition of a further compulsory purchase schedule over a part of land which, only a few years before, had been exclusively granted by Parliament, was very rare however; more frequently the successful establishment of a statutory claim had the effect of excluding competitors, or forcing them to choose an inferior route. To this extent Denton's allegation that railways did not choose the shortest and best routes was correct, but it does provide a full explanation of the railways' selection of sites and routes.

The second, and more important explanation, lies in the pattern of land ownership on the periphery of the great cities. As suburban manorial or ecclesiastical units of tenure broke up, and came on to the market, great proprietors emerged, as traced the *Case Histories* above. There were very obvious advantages, in terms of speed and simplicity, to negotiations with these great proprietors; and the railways always, for preference, dealt with them rather than with a multiplicity of small owners.[157] On the great landed estates residential houses were held under a variety of leases, ranging from the complicated three lives and twenty one years system in Liverpool, to the repairing, or building, leases of twenty-one to ninety-nine years in London. What is noticeable, however, is that with certain exceptions, the large estates tended to favour residential land uses. On the whole, industry and commerce were less than proportionately represented on the great proprietors' land, either as a consequence of estate policy, or because the larger industrial and commercial users themselves preferred to purchase free-hold. The objection to using rented premises was not so marked in trade and commerce, but the *Books of Reference* suggest that most

[155] BTHR PYB 1/579, 27 May 1873, p. 8.
[156] HLRO, Min., (Caledonian Central), H.C., 1873, 7 May, p. 73.
[157] Although the weekly and the yearly tenants did badly, on the whole, from demolition, the tenants with longer interests, the lessee and the freeholder, were in a stronger position. Manuals of advice—'Never delay or let the time for improvements go by because a railway . . . is coming that will take your property'—instructed them as to the best course to take to secure full compensation. T. H. Hovenden, *New Railways and New Streets* (1872), 13.

manufacturers preferred to become proprietors of their own sites.

The great estates, lay and clerical, which offered the convenience of dealing with one landlord, ten or a dozen middlemen and an amorphous group of tenants (many of whose leases might be due to fall in), were predominantly residential in character.[158] Added to the convenience and legal simplicity of dealings with them, was the sheer cheapness of the transaction. Even though a price perhaps several times the value of the crumbling courts and terraces might be paid to secure consent, it was still by far the cheapest method.[159] The buildings themselves were low in value compared with business or industrial premises, and by selecting this route two further economies were achieved. By it was avoided the expensive litigation over the value of land and buildings which endlessly reduplicated dealings with small proprietors could involve. Also avoided were the exorbitantly large awards sympathetic juries often gave, in addition to land and building awards, for the loss of shadowy 'goodwill' and business connections attached to small proprietors' premises.

To find such a parcel of dilapidated residential properties and exploit them did not seem heartless to the railway entrepreneurs, but merely sound business; and many of the conceptions for urban schemes originated with the discovery of a route through such properties. It was no conspiracy, merely commonsense, though even *The Times* voiced contrary suspicions. 'The special lure to capitalists offered by railway projectors, is that the line will pass only through inferior property, that is through a densely populated district, and will destroy only the abodes of the powerless and poor, whilst it will avoid the properties of those whose opposition is to be dreaded—the great employers of labour.'[160]

Circumstances could conceivably alter the magnetism which slum districts exercised over railways seeking access. If, for example, the re-housing Standing Orders of the closing decades of the century had been made effective, and railway companies had been compelled to provide, in anticipation, and by stages, replacement housing for the slums demolished, it would have put an end to this type of urban railway enterprise. The difficulties which reaccommodation involved were illustrated when Edward Watkin persuaded his fellow directors on the Metropolitan railway to carry out a pilot re-housing scheme at the

[158] Information from a landowner's estate office was itself of value, as Watkin revealed. 'We have completed purchases where there was any chance of new leases being set up.' H.C., 1884–5, XXX, Q.10572.

[159] This was the point stressed in the 1884–5 Royal Commission's Report, and in the questioning of some witnesses. 'The reason why railway companies often schedule and take the poorest properties . . . is that they have hitherto been the cheapest to obtain.' H.C., 1884–5, XXX, Report, p. 20, QQ.863–4.

[160] *The Times*, 2 March 1861.

Minories in central London in the early 1880's. The land, though worth £10 per square yard, had to be written down at a nominal price; and with this favourable start the 750 rooms at one shilling or one and sixpence per week were to bring in 2% or 3% return. 'I would say that we are thoughtful people, and anxious as far as we can to make our work answer, not merely as a matter of profit and loss, but as a fulfilment of what we consider to be our duty.'[161]

Watkin's scheme, like all other attempts at central re-housing, failed before the same difficulties of rapidly appreciating central values which defeated private builders and even the L.C.C.; but it suggests the third cause for the railway choice of residential properties for demolition. In the period between 1840 and the mid-1860's the first and greatest task in Britain's cities seemed to be to get rid at all costs of the cholera-ridden slums, and to 'ventilate' the city centres. Mr. Simon, the Medical Officer of Health for the City of London, expressed, in a report to the Corporation in 1855, opinions which were echoed by men in his profession in all the major cities.

'There are many parts of the City where great and immediate advantage would arise from an expenditure of money *applied solely to the purpose of destruction*; parts, where the purchase of an entire court, or series of courts, for the sole object of pulling down houses, and leaving open spaces in their stead, would be the cheapest as well as the most effective manner of dealing with their sanitary difficulties; and I have earnestly to suggest for your consideration that proceedings of this nature will require to be pursued to a very great extent, and at a large annual expense, within the City.'[162]

No one who had entered these squalid courts could feel the slightest regret or sentiment at their demolition. Demolishing them seemed to fall into the same category as prohibiting unsound meat or grossly adulterated bread, and there were many who applauded the railways for their work. By the following decade, however, more sceptical voices were raised. 'The railway locomotive', wrote Henry Davies in 1861, 'has a giant's strength, but is no better than a blind and undistinguishing Polyphemus when he is called in as a sanitary reformer.'[163] After the 1860's 'reformers hopes were pinned', as H. J. Dyos has pointed out, 'to more general solutions of London's housing problems—particularly to the Lodging Houses and the Torrens and Cross Acts.'[164] Yet even these measures evinced something of the same negative spirit in their attempts to cure slum conditions by demolition, or by the simple

---

[161] H.C., 1884–5, XXX, QQ.10475–8, 10601–10.
[162] H.C., 1854–5, X, 167. My italics.
[163] Henry Davies, *op. cit.* 27.
[164] H. J. Dyos, *loc. cit.* 18.

prohibition of overcrowding and sub-standard housing. Unfortunately time showed that it was one thing to condemn meat or bread, where better articles of the kind were speedily forthcoming, but quite another to condemn houses.

XI

◇◇

The railway as an agent of internal change in Victorian cities: the inner districts and the suburbs

◇◇

1. *Physical effects upon the inner districts of the city*

THE main effects of railways in the centre of the Victorian city were to add to the congestion of traffic and the overcrowding of working class housing, and to contribute, both directly and indirectly, to the changes in land use and the rapid increase in land values. Their characteristic effects in the inner districts were to compress the areas which were within walking range of the city centre, to interrupt communications between them, to stabilise their land values for residential uses and reduce their improvement prospects. The fringe of the central district, comprising the inner areas of cheap housing, small trades, storage yards and dumps, into which the working classes overspilt in the 1860's, formed a region where the effect of urban railway building seems, at close quarters, to be more far-reaching than might initially be expected. Not merely did the many-tracked urban routes, with their fringe lands, act as formidable physical barriers, but they also produced a curious effect upon the inner districts through which they passed, freezing their value, and confirming their dereliction.

Two detailed examples may serve to illustrate the effect. The map (Plate 10) is reproduced from a *Report for the Citizens' Association for the Improvement of Unwholesome Dwellings*, Manchester, 1903.[1] Inspired by Booth's and Rowntree's surveys of London and York, it attempted to describe the situation of the 200,000 poor in Manchester, 75,000 of whom were living below the level of 'primary poverty', as defined by Rowntree. Their map summarises available evidence at

[1] T. R. Marr, *Housing Conditions in Manchester and Salford, 1903* (1904), Frontispiece.

337

the end of the nineteenth century concerning the location of back-to-back houses, (the worst of all surviving slum properties), bye-law houses, industrial and commercial properties. 'Our purpose', wrote their secretary and editor, T. R. Marr, 'has been to get information which would enable those who reach Manchester by train to realise the condition under which people live in these streets.'[2]

The striking way in which the railways served to delimit the central business area by 1900 is clear enough from the map to need little underlining. Except for a small quantity of dilapidated housing squashed between the new Cheshire Lines Committee Central Station, the Great Northern railway goods depot, and the old Liverpool Road terminus of the Liverpool and Manchester railway (now converted to a goods depot), and a few back-to-back houses between the approaches to Exchange station and the river Irwell, the whole central district of warehouses, shops and offices was by 1900 delineated by the railways running south-west from Victoria, and west from London Road stations. Less distinctly, the eastern boundary was defined by the area of mixed industrial and residential zoning running between the Lancashire and Yorkshire railway's Oldham Road, and the Midland railway's Ancoats, goods stations. Here, apart from a few shopkeepers in Ancoats Sanitary District No. 1, and some clerks, mechanics and artisans in the 11th district, lived the porters, labourers, hawkers, tramps, hurdy-gurdy men and people of no definite occupation, sandwiched between the railway sidings, dye works and cotton mills, iron and boiler works, gas and sanitary installations, and works making oil and grease.[3] The houses were of the cottage type with stone flags resting directly on a clay subsoil, unventilated, with defective drainage, a third of them occupied by more than one family. Altogether a particularly bad example of the type of no-man's land created by speculative building in the areas between railway sidings and industrial users on the outer fringe of an urban central district. 'In no other district do we find,' reported the Manchester and Salford Sanitary Association, 'such an aggregation of extremely old, low, damp, filthy and dilapidated dwellings, nor any houses arranged so as to enclose so much that is noxious and offensive.'[4]

The railways cannot directly be blamed for creating or perpetuating these conditions. An extraordinarily detailed survey carried out in the 1880's by John Leigh, the Medical Officer of Health, illustrated the causes of acute distress amongst the working class in 'twilight zones' like Ancoats, and his evidence accords exactly with that of Charles

[2] *Ibid.* 64.
[3] MRL, Reports of the M.O.H., 1884, p. 48 *et seq.*
[4] *An Enquiry into the causes of Excessive Mortality in No. 1 District, Ancoats* (1889), 38. MRL 614 RE 1.

Booth. They were places of resort for poorly paid casual labourers who were unable either to move from the district or to pay higher rent; therefore they were accommodated in shoddy and cheap housing, with defective sanitation and cramped space; finally, the precarious balance which might be maintained whilst in employment, good health and spirits, was upset by loss of work, sickness, bereavement or intemperance. Although there were some complaints to him about dense smoke and other industrial nuisances, the railways were not mentioned as a major factor in their discomfort.[5]

Yet the railways played an indirect part in concentrating population in these areas and in determining their locations. Their extensive central demolitions contributed to what a contemporary member of the Manchester Statistical Society described as 'the summary elbowing out' of residents into the outer areas.[6] Moreover, it can be demonstrated that the railways themselves marked out the inner districts through which they passed as suitable overspill areas for those 'elbowed out' of the centre.

Amongst the Medical Officer of Health's Reports in Manchester is a most unusual series of maps drawn by Richard Bastow, probably founded on Adshead's land-use map of 1850, which is itself remarkably detailed. Bastow's maps show on a large scale, for all the central rating zones, not merely land uses, but also the varying ages of residential housing.[7] With their help it is possible to analyse the physical effect of the urban termini, and their approach and link lines, upon the surrounding urban fabric in greater detail for Manchester than for any other of the major cities chosen for study.

They show clearly, as is already well known, that once the demolitions which accompanied the driving of the railway into the city were over, the routes, for a considerable margin along both sides, tended to attract thick belts of industrial users, storage and constructional businesses and the like. They also show, however, that where residential housing was left standing, it was never renewed. Bastow's age groupings for houses are '*1850–1870*', '*1830–1850*', and '*Before 1830*'. In the whole of Manchester and Salford there was, with the exception only of the Miles Platting district, not one substantial area through which the railways ran which showed housing built or rebuilt after 1830; and many of the cottages past which the railways rattled at roof top level were a hundred years old at the time the Medical Officer wrote, derelict properties

[5] Reports of the M.O.H., 1881–6 *passim*.

[6] H. Baker, 'On the Growth of the Manchester Population, Extension of the Commercial Centre of the City, and Pressure of Habitation, 1871–81', *Trans. Manch. Stat. Soc.* (1881–5), 9.

[7] MRL 614.0942 M 4.

dating back even to the 1780's.[8] It is conspicuous that where the railways passed no residential replacement took place. They were frozen, as far as renovation or improvement was concerned, as completely as if time had stopped in 1830. Capital sunk in replacing residential housing in such an environment with a more up-to-date equivalent was obviously considered capital wasted. The best plan for a proprietor was to patch the properties up, accept a lower class of tenant, and wait until a further major alteration made it possible to abandon residential use altogether: until a commercial or business offer was made, a corporation clearance or street widening scheme swept the district away, or the railways themselves enlarged their approaches.

Richard Bastow's unique series of maps shows only one prominent area in which modern cottage properties, under 20 years old, had been erected in substantial numbers adjacent to railway lines; those bordering on the Lancashire and Yorkshire railway at Miles Platting, occupied, in large part, by the relatively well paid railway workers.[9] Miles Platting, however, one and a half miles from the centre, was almost far enough out to be called a suburb, and was newly-built. 'Whilst healthy zones of new growth match the annual expansion of the city, the rottenness at the core increases,' wrote a contributor to the Manchester Statistical Society in 1871. 'Moreover it is not practicable,' he continued, 'that all the labouring classes should live in the suburbs.' For the casual labourer in the city a walk of 4 or 5 miles a day would be 'a tax too burdensome to be borne.'[10] Given the demand for casual labour, the labourer's need for easy access to the daily-changing opportunities for employment, and reluctance to move away from the home meals and short walks of the inner districts, the house farmers found no difficulty in letting rooms there, no matter how dilapidated and ramshackle the buildings might be.

One is reminded of the passage in which Dickens describes the view from the viaduct as Mr. Dombey's railway journey draws to its end. 'Everything around is blackened. There are dark pools of water, muddy lanes, and miserable habitations far below. There are jagged walls and filthy houses close at hand, and through the battered roofs and broken windows, wretched rooms are seen, where want and fever hide themselves in many wretched shapes, while smoke and crowded gables, and distorted chimneys, and deformity of brick and mortar pinning up deformity of mind and body, choke the murky distance. As Mr. Dombey looks out of his carriage window, it is never in his thoughts that the

[8] District No. 2, the area around Victoria station fell into this category. The warehouses were replaced, or they chose to remove, but some of the housing surviving off Hanover and Mills streets dated back to 1780.

[9] *Ibid.* Report, March 1883, 31.

[10] G. T. Robinson, 'On Town Dwellings for the Working Class,' *Trans. Manch. Stat. Soc.* (1868–72), 69.

monster who brought him there has let the light of day in on these things: not made or caused them. It was the journey's fitting end, and might have been the end of everything; it was so ruinous and dreary.'[11]

Dickens was perfectly correct to point out that the railways let the light of day in on such living conditions, by holding them before the eyes of those of the travelling public who looked out of the window as they approached the terminal. The railways did not cause the deficiency in the supply and quality of housing, nor the illness, intemperance and unemployment which marked the residents in these quarters. But similar views from the viaduct were all too characteristic of the final approaches to termini in most of the great cities. Indeed, to move on to the second detailed example, Charles Dickens himself has left a vivid description of an equally wretched area, isolated between the approach routes of the London and North Western and Great Northern railways at Euston and King's Cross. Agar Town and Somers Town formed an area of short leases and intermingled residential and industrial uses, dominated by the approach lines of railway termini, similar to Birmingham's Saltley, Manchester's Ancoats, Glasgow's South Laurieston or Liverpool's South Scotland and Vauxhall wards.

The north London area of dereliction differed from that of Ancoats, just described, in two ways. First, the houses were new and their life span only twenty-one years, instead of the fifty or more years for which the ramshackle terraces and back-to-backs of Ancoats had to serve.[12] But they were even more dilapidated, consisting of sheds and hovels run up by journeymen bricklayers and carpenters working on Sundays and in their spare time, an 'English Suburban Connemara', as Dickens described it. 'There were the dog-kennel, the cowshed, the shanty, and the elongated match-box styles of architecture. To another, the ingenious residence of Robinson Crusoe seemed to have given his idea. Through an opening was to be seen another layer of dwellings at the back: one looking like a dismantled windmill, and another perched upon a wall, like a guard's lookout on the top of a railway carriage. Every garden had its nuisance—so far the inhabitants were agreed— but every nuisance was of a distinct and peculiar character. In one was a dung-heap, in the next a cinder-heap, in the third, which belonged to the cottage of a costermonger, was a pile of whelk and periwinkle shells, some rotten cabbages and a donkey: and the garden of another exhibiting a board inscribed with the words "Ladies School" had become a pond of thick green water.'[14] The centre of the district was

---

[11] Charles Dickens, *Dombey and Son* (1869), 176, Chap. XX.

[12] An attempt was made to extend the leases, as John Hollingshead discloses, 'expecting no doubt to profit by the advance of railways on the metropolis.' John Hollingshead, *Ragged London* (1861), 130.

[13] Charles Dickens, *Dombey and Son*, Chap. 6, quoted H. C. Prince, *loc. cit.* 111–12.

occupied by the mountains of refuse from the metropolitan dustbins, and by the small scale trades associated with such an area: rag collectors, knackers' yards, bone boiling, manure making, and soap manufacturing works, brick kilns and a gas works.

The 'Ladies School' notice was a reminder of earlier days when a few larger houses, market gardeners and dairymen had occupied the area, which was owned by the Church Commissioners. In 1841, a couple of years after the Euston railway station had been opened, William Agar, a lawyer who had taken a lease from the Church Commissioners, parcelled out the estate indiscriminately into twenty-one year building leases. When these fell in again in 1862 the whole area was demolished to make way for the St. Pancras station of the Midland Railway company—which, because its scheme fell just outside the defined limits of the Metropolitan area, was allowed full powers of demolition without even the *quid pro quo* of cheap workmen's services, imposed in the same year upon the Great Eastern company in the terms of its Liverpool Street Station Act.[14]

The second way in which Agar and Somers Towns differed from Ancoats was that the former areas did not merely front the terminal approaches, they were actually sandwiched, after Thomas Brassey had completed the Great Northern's works to King's Cross (1852), between two of the largest terminal approaches for a distance of a mile and a half, up to Camden Town. This overlapping of the areas of dereliction left a zone, or wedge, in which all development was paralysed, and which formed a convenient and obvious route for the third great company to drive in its northern approach.

To a certain extent such densely occupied and makeshift inner suburbs were a product of the rapid growth of urban population itself, including the growth of a large class unable to pay for anything better, and were not the result of any action by the railway companies; but the railways might be said to have worsened the situation in two ways. First, they added substantially to the stream of dispossessed leaving the central district, without either providing alternative accommodation or really cheap fares. By these actions they produced the very opposite effect to that commonly ascribed to the railways; they increased the degree of overcrowding and compressed the mid-Victorian city rather than assisting it to expand. The immediate results of this pressure of overcrowding can be seen in the subdivision of existing tenements, the occupation of empty houses where these could be found, and the running up of 'temporary' housing of the type small builders or weekend entrepreneurs were prepared to supply, no matter how short the building lease. In areas where houses had stood untenanted the empties were taken up; and this side-effect of demolition was one which larger

[14] H.C., 1905, XXX, 568–9.

builders with stocks of empties on their hands openly welcomed. In fact the clearest way to trace the movement of population caused by railway demolition, John Leigh, the Manchester Officer of Health, suggested, was to note the rate at which empty houses were taken up in the adjacent reception areas. He quotes, from his own experience, the example of how, after the destruction of the old three-storey houses which had occupied the site of the C.L.C.'s Central Station in Manchester, two or three of the sanitary areas in the upper part of St. George's district began to show a marked increase in mortality.

'This led to a house-to-house visitation, for there was no epidemic at this time, nor apparent reason why the mortality should be of a higher rate than usual, or higher than in the neighbouring sanitary districts. It was ascertained that a considerable number of persons who had been displaced from some of the worst streets off Deansgate by the operations for the Central Station had migrated to these sanitary districts, carrying, of course, with them their bad habits and deteriorated health. They had been led to these localities by the fact that a number of the houses had long been empty, and were available at low rents. They raised the rate of mortality of the districts, but, benefiting by the change, had lowered their own.'[15]

These reception areas were scattered, within walking distance of the casual labour markets, around the inner areas of the city, sometimes in the shadow of the station, sometimes in some other area of low residential amenity: on occasions the inflow was even accommodated by the rookeries surviving in the central area. But, and here was the second influence of the railways, they cramped and confined the inner districts into which migration from the centre took place, by their network of main lines, viaducts, yards and works, and, as it were, *suggested* areas where, because residential values had been frozen, the overflow might accumulate. Unlike other areas, for which the process of gradual improvement and residential replacement was always a possibility, however remote, the inner districts intersected by the railways were fixed in dereliction.

The effect upon amenity was combined with an effect upon communications. Ancoats was particularly bad in this respect. 'With a population equal to that of a large city', wrote John Leigh, 'it has not a single road or street enabling that vast population to communicate in a fairly straight line with the city with which its business chiefly lies. A series of zig-zags, along narrow streets, form its avenues to the city. Every year adds to its dismal character, and lessens the enjoyment of its inhabitants.'[16] Like the inhabitants of Saltley, the equivalent area in east Birmingham, the 48,000 inhabitants of Ancoats suffered from an interdiction of communications by the railway workings. Apart

[15] MRL, Reports of the M.O.H., March 1884, 120.
[16] *Ibid.* March 1884, 48.

from the sheer difficulty and expense of bridging railway land, the routes themselves were often raised on embankments or viaducts, crossing the street pattern at angles, with the minimum headroom and width; so that where road communications were poor, or incompletely formed, the possibilities of future widening and realignment were drastically curtailed.

In London similar effects were produced, both in the east and in the south, by railway approaches through the inner districts. Petitions against the London and South Western railway company's projected route from Waterloo to Thames-side at Clink Street summarise the objections. 'It will run direct across all the southern entrances to London, crossing at a low elevation, the important and leading thoroughfares of Waterloo Road, Blackfriars Road and Southwark Bridge Road, and enclosing as it were the southern part of the metropolis with a brick wall and preventing all future improvements.'[17] Such destruction of communications between the inhabitants and the central district was 'contrary to the feeling which has abolished city walls and gates as obstructions to business and recreation.'[18] Mr. Charles Stephens, owner of a hundred and fifty acres freehold in Camberwell, and a hundred more in Lewisham, described a landowner's anxiety to the Royal Commission of 1846 in these words.'Such a railway will place an impassable and hideous wall between the most important and populous parts of this parish—and will induce the building of houses, wherever that event shall take place, in a confined manner and of an inferior class.'[19]

Although on this occasion the protests were timely and effective, in other areas representations were not organised, were too late, or were directed to bodies not competent to deal with them. A few hundred yards from the line just rejected, the London and South Western company completed a viaduct to Waterloo, which caused, almost at once, the very effects predicted by the petitioners of St. Saviour's, Southwark, and St. Giles's, Camberwell.[20] 'A rapid deterioration followed the coming of the railways to Lambeth,' writes the Survey of London. 'Streets were cut up and buildings torn down or dismembered, while the series of dark, damp arches under the lines encouraged the more disreputable element of the population.'[21]

[17] H.C., 1846, XVII, App. 1, p. 249.
[18] Loc. cit. p.256.
[19] Ibid. Q.2810.
[20] 'This is an evil . . . in connection with the impassable boundaries of railway lines, as will be seen on the South Western map by tracing the course of the railway from Nine Elms to Clapham Junction.' 'The worst elements have for the most part taken refuge in blocks of houses isolated by blank walls or railway embankments or untraversed by any thoroughfare.' Charles Booth, op. cit. (1892), I, 265, 281.
[21] The Survey of London, XXIII (1951), 1.

The railway arch was, of course, a functional necessity for many of the approach routes, if they were to avoid the wholesale street closures and level crossings, against which Parliament had set its face. All the early hopes that arches might be turned to advantage miscarried, however, and within a few years they became symbols of all that was shabby and down-at-heel in Victorian urban life. Some of the central arches were let to people who lived on the premises, in spite of 'the difficulty of providing chimneys and such other little difficulties', and carried on a low class of trade.[22] Some of the arches of the Blackwall railway were bought by 'a very benevolent person, who has fitted them up as houses for the poorer class of people': and near the Minories station a clergyman's application for the use of the arches for an infant school was granted. 'The Committee were very happy to do all they could in granting them at a very moderate rent, and a large and very interesting school is carried on under those very arches.'[23] During the commercial crisis of 1866 unemployment relief at 9s a week was given to upwards of 400 men in Bethnal Green 'in three vacant railway arches which have been kindly let for the purpose.'[24] They can be seen in the illustration on Plate 12, engaged in breaking granite for the roads. More casually, the arches were used as overnight shelter by the human derelicts of Victorian society; by spirit drinkers and unsuccessful criminals, by Gustav Doré's 'sleepers out'.[25] A railway arch was chosen as the symbol of ultimate degradation by the popular Victorian artist Augustus Egg, for his narrative paintings showing the fate of an unfaithful wife.[26]

Wherever the arches of railway viaducts appeared, the wretched flotsam of urban life followed. Complaints concerning their deteriorating effect were made against the London and South Western, the Eastern Counties, the Greenwich and the Blackwall railway companies in London: and repeated on similar occasions in the provinces. 'A viaduct,' wrote one resident in east London, 'would not be tolerated in a respectable neighbourhood and undoubtedly renders a bad one worse.'[27] Nor, as time passed, was any improvement apparent. The first bad impressions were only confirmed by further experience.

'I travel something from 25,000 to 28,000 miles a year by railway,' said an engineer in 1866, 'and have done so for the last 25 years. I have my eyes pretty well open generally and I know no railway passing through a town on arches . . . without it being to my mind a very

---

[22] HLRO, Min., (M.S. & L.), H.L., 1866, 16 July, pp. 8–12.
[23] H.C., 1846, XVII, QQ.413–4 (Tite).
[24] *Illustrated London News*, 15 February 1868, 156.
[25] Gustav Doré and Blanchard Jerrold, *London: a Pilgrimage* (1872).
[26] Graham Reynolds, *Painters of the Victorian Scene* (1953), Plate 49.
[27] H.C., 1846, XVII, App. 16, pp. 273–4.

serious detriment to the town property through which it passes.'[28]
'You see it in all towns,' the Town Clerk of Manchester concurred,
'if you go along a railway with a viaduct; the very character of the
property you look down upon shows that it is not the place where
improvements may be looked for—the viaduct puts a stop absolutely
to any improvement from the time it is constructed.'[29]

2. *The railways and the location of industry*

There was, however, another side to the coin. To residential property
owners and to industrial firms using road cartage the viaducts were a
nuisance and obstruction, but to the heavier industrial firms in the
suburbs the railway lines gave valuable linkages with suppliers and
markets. In each of the major Victorian cities the same tendency for
industry to disperse into the inner districts, to the river side, or to more
distant suburbs is apparent.

It is difficult to know how much to assign to the influence of rail
connections, in view of the other powerful influences working to
produce the same result. The growing scale of the business units engaged
in manufacture demanded acreages of floor space which could only be
acquired by moving out from the city centre. The large urban factory in
the central district was an anachronism by the 1860's, progressively
squeezed out of the city centre by rising land values; though the small
scale workshops specialising in the clothing, furniture, printing, precious
metals and jewellery, watchmaking, precision engineering and the light
metal trades, showed a surprising tenacity, particularly in Birmingham
and London, and continued to multiply in the inner districts, or even
in certain quarters of the city centre.

Again, it is difficult, in view of the supremacy of carting over short
distances, to assess the significance of railway linkages in the redistribution of industry. For every factory with railway sidings there were
a dozen without; but those which took advantage of direct rail connections tended to be the larger and more modern. Some, specially in
heavy engineering, formed groupings of firms large enough to dominate
employment in their district, as at Gorton, or Newton Heath, near
Manchester, or Springburn near Glasgow.

The connection between the large firms in the areas just mentioned
and the railways was unusually close because they were all suppliers
of engines and rolling stock. The Manchester firm of Beyer, Peacock
and Company, although at first it produced a variety of ironmongery
in a centrally located factory, soon became identified with locomotive

[28] HLRO, Min., (M.S. & L.), H.L., 1866, 16 July, p. 78 (Bateman).
[29] BTHR PYB 1/383, Q.2995.

manufacture and with Gorton.[30] 'What a change has come over the scene,' wrote John Higson in *The Gorton Historical Recorder*. 'The ancient trees are felled, the lanes are being superseded by roads and are assuming modernised appellations; pack horses are fled; their place is supplied by railway engines—In the course of time, the situations of our hedgerows and fields will become lost under the sites of streets and houses, and form a part of the vast city of Manchester.'[31] By the late 1860's over forty acres was covered by the works and sidings at Gorton, and a further forty five acres and thirteen miles of sidings covered part of Newton Heath.[32] Another Manchester firm, Sharp, Stewart and Company, which had originally made cotton machinery, and had also been located centrally (at the Atlas works, between Oxford Street and Great Bridgewater Road), performed a still more complex migration in 1885, not to the outskirts of Manchester, but to the specialised engineering suburb of Springburn in Glasgow.[33]

These engineering works form special cases, of course, because of their intimate business and sales connections with the railways, but they are important enough in themselves to be mentioned by name; and they produced the interesting phenomenon of extremely specialised areas in Glasgow, Manchester and east London which were virtually suburban versions of Crewe or Swindon.[34]

Evidence also exists of other large firms, not directly connected as suppliers and manufacturers to the railway companies, which built new premises adjacent to the railways or, if already established, sought rail linkages. Soho, near Birmingham, for example, one of the cradles of the Industrial Revolution, where Matthew Boulton's factory pre-dated the railways by seventy years, secured early connections with the main line to Wolverhampton.[35] Some other established Birmingham firms moved out of the central area in a similar manner to that seen in Manchester. Tangye's, for example, left the small factory at Clement Street, where they had made the hydraulic rams and pulley blocks upon which the firm's fortunes had been founded, and moved to an eleven acre site half-way between the G.W. railway Handsworth, and the

[30] *The Engineering and other Industries of Manchester and District* (1887), 47. 'Gorton Foundry', in the *Manchester Guardian*, 2 July 1925.

[31] *Op. cit.* (Droylsden, 1852), p. V.

[32] *Manchester of Today: an Epitome of Results* (Manchester, 1888), 149. 'Works visited etc.', MRL 620 94273 INI.

[33] *Manchester City News*, 28 March 1903. Great Central Railway, *Official Album* (1902). Old Glasgow Club, *Transactions* 8 January 1951.

[34] Stratford in east London occupied a position similar to that filled by Gorton in Manchester, or Springburn in Glasgow. *London: Aspects of Change* (ed. R. Glass et al, 1964), 64. 6,800 workmen were employed there at one time, compared with 17,000 at Gorton.

[35] D. C. Eversley, 'Industry and Trade, 1500–1880', *A History of the County of Warwick* (Victoria County History, 1964), VII, 132–40.

L. & N.W. railway Soho stations.[36] The entirely new factory of the B.S.A. company likewise set up its works and colony at Small Heath on the Oxford line.[37] All three of these were also engineering works, though not connected with locomotives or rolling stock; but at King's Norton other light manufacturers, from paper to india-rubber making, were established near the railway line.[38]

An assessment of the importance of rail connections to the suburban industrialist must await a more detailed study. It will not be an easy task, for although the relative costs of alternative modes of transport for supplies and finished goods must have been carefully considered by entrepreneurs, particularly at the height of the railway rates controversy in the 1880's, yet published business histories are disappointingly silent on this point.[39]

However, in lieu of contemporary information, a great deal can be sketched in *ex post*, from the geographical distribution of industrial works spreading outwards from the great towns, and this has been done, in convenient form and with great local knowledge, by the surveys carried out for the British Association, at Birmingham, Manchester, Glasgow and Liverpool.[40] At London, although a great deal of similar material has been gathered in original theses, only one, by P. G. Hall, has been published.[41] To avoid the repetition of much that is already familiar, and requires extremely detailed topography, the reader is referred to these well illustrated studies. From them and from other local sources, the emergence by the late nineteenth century of Manchester's 'industrial collar', of the wide belt of industrial building in the Midlands from Birmingham towards Wolverhampton, and of Liverpool's and Glasgow's changing districts of industrial specialisa-

[36] *Birmingham Mail*, 13 July 1880.

[37] D. C. Eversley, *loc. cit.* 132–3.

[38] G. C. Allen, *The Industrial Development of Birmingham and the Black Country* (1929), 291 *et. seq.* M. J. Wise and P. O'N. Thorpe, *loc. cit.* 222–4.

[39] Modern work, taking the form of questionnaires to industrial firms, suggests that whilst transport costs and facilities rank very high in most firms' calculations, other considerations receive only slightly less weight. Some of these—planning permission, the incidence of local taxes—have received new significance in the twentieth century; but one consideration often mentioned as critical, and which applied with undiminished force in the nineteenth century, is the availability of low priced units of land, located where future expansion would be practicable. T. E. McMillan Jnr., 'Why Manufacturers Choose Plant Locations', *Land Economics*, XLI (1965), 239–46.

[40] *Birmingham and its Regional Setting: a Scientific Survey* (British Association, Birmingham, 1950); *The Glasgow Region: a General Survey* (ed. R. Miller and J. Tivy, Glasgow, 1958); *A Scientific Survey of Merseyside* (ed. W. Smith, Liverpool, 1953); *Manchester and its Region* (ed. C. F. Carter, Manchester, 1962).

[41] P. G. Hall, *The Industries of London since 1861* (1962). See also J. E. Martin 'Three Elements in the Industrial Geography of Greater London', *Greater London* (ed. J. T. Coppock and H. C. Prince, 1964), 246–65.

tion, can be approximately traced on the ground. But the course of industrial history in each great town, its successes in certain fields of manufacture, and abandonment or failure in others, the extent of diversification in its manufacturing base; these are matters which cannot be linked by any simple causal chain to the coming of the railways. The railways are merely one element in the whole network of external economies which bound together the areas of regional specialisation associated with each great city.

As part of the growth of inter-dependent industries, physical proximity, or cheap and easy access to fellow-manufacturers engaged on other stages of the production process, was obviously of cardinal importance; but it could be achieved by means other than rail linkages, and the more closely concentrated the region, the less use were main line railways within it. This applied even to large-scale manufacturers, but for the small scale producers operating on short runs and small quantities from ready built factories or workshops in the Victorian cities' inner districts the linkages between them were of a complexity which made them quite unsuitable for short-haul by the railways. The small, miscellaneous loads of the Birmingham or London manufacturer, the frequent need for trans-shipment for further processing after a short journey, the heavy terminal charges, made the railways slow and uneconomic for the local movement of goods. In his study of London's industries in the later nineteenth century, Peter Hall has given a fascinating picture of the small trades, depending upon close connection with component suppliers and associated skills, and constituting 'incomparably the major industrial area of London.' 'With this type of productive organisation', he points out, 'the real assembly line runs through the streets; a journey around the Victorian manufacturing crescent (of inner north and east London) on any typical weekday reveal the extraordinary congestion of goods vehicles, hurrying in all directions about their business.'[42] Clearly railway goods trains were not suited to the maintenance of such local and rapid linkages.

If we are looking for what Colin Clark has dubbed 'micro-locational factors', it could be argued that we find them rather more in the case of the canals than the railways.[43] The industrial concentration around the Port Dundas canal basin, in the north of Glasgow, is far more striking than any rail-based concentration.[44] In Birmingham the two mile stretch of canal between Bordesley and Aston had already 124

[42] Greater London, 227–8.

[43] Colin Clark, 'The Location of Industries and Population', Town Planning Review, 35 (1964–5), 195, 211 et. seq.

[44] Peter Fleming, Map of the City of Glasgow (1807 and 1821). George Martin, Map of the City of Glasgow, (1842). S. G. Checkland, 'The British Industrial City as History: the Glasgow Case', Urban Studies, I (1964), 45.

works and wharves along its bank twenty five years before the railways were constructed; and the 'tongues of industrial development' out to Smethwick and towards Derby were also located along the Birmingham and Wolverhampton and Fazeley canals.[45] These routes were later reinforced by railways, which followed the canals closely, for reasons suggested earlier, but the prior locational impulse was that of the canals. In Manchester the Ashton and Rochdale canals, built at the turn of the eighteenth century, attracted over a hundred textile mills, breweries, chemical works and foundries; and other industrial users spread along the Bolton, Bury and Junction canals.[46] In Liverpool the industrial grouping along the canals was less marked. The Leeds and Liverpool canal, which entered from the north, accumulated a few mills, vitriol and gas works along its banks; but the other major canals all entered the Mersey upstream, and their effect was lost in the general port and river traffic; and in London the effect of urban canals was necessarily limited.[47] Where canals had been established, however, even in London, they continued—like the Regent's Canal and Hertford Union canals in East London—to attract industry to their sides throughout the nineteenth century. Eight-ninths of the traffic on these canals was simply for local transfer by the end of the century, and soap, varnish and tar works congregated along the banks.[48]

In the Midlands and North, where canals had always been more successful and widespread than the London area, they also continued to attract industry throughout the railway age. The effect of their established location was cumulative. 'The canals have been in existence a great many years, and a great many mills and industries of various kinds have been carried on upon the banks of the canals, brought there by the facilities which the canals afforded from time to time, and the traffic to all those places could not be carried so conveniently by rail as it could by canal.'[49] They were far better suited for local, factory to factory traffic of single loads than main line railways; and the water they supplied was invaluable to industrial users. In fact several canals

---

[45] A. E. Smailes, *The Geography of Towns* (1964), 94–5, and Fig. 12. *Conurbation: A Survey of Birmingham and the Black Country*, (Birmingham, 1948), 18, 'Remote from natural communications it owes its creation to its mineral resources, but its structure to canals and railways.'

[46] L. Wharfe, 'The Emergence of the Metropolis', *Rich Inheritance* (ed. N. J. Frangopulo, Manchester, 1962), 107–9.

[47] Wilfred Smith, 'The Location of Industry', *A Scientific Survey of Merseyside* (Liverpool, 1953), 179. Jonathan Bennison, *Plan of the Town and Port of Liverpool* (1835).

[48] Henry Rees, *The North Eastern Expansion of London since 1770* (London M.Sc. Econ. thesis, 1946), 52–63. See also J. E. Martin, 'Three Elements in the Industrial Geography of Greater London', *Greater London* (ed. J. T. Coppock and H. C. Prince, 1964), 258–61 and Fig. 53.

[49] H.C., 1872, XIII, Q.4182.

with urban stretches, such as the Regent's canal in London, found themselves earning an appreciable proportion of their revenues from selling their water rather than from carrying traffic; and in general urban canals continued to provide exceptions to the general picture of decline in waterborne transport.[50] Birmingham still imported over a million tons of coal by canal in the late 1860's; and a correspondence of great vehemence conducted with the canal company was one of the major preoccupations of the Chamber of Commerce in 1870.[51] It was to the idea of enlarged, or 'ship', canals that the Corporations of Manchester and Birmingham naturally turned early in the following decade.[52] If we are looking for locational factors for industry, within the area of the three conurbations, Manchester, Birmingham and Glasgow, the railways must obviously share their role with the canals.

Two points of particular relevance to urban history emerge from studies of railways, canals, and the regional location of industry. The first is that nearly all goods, except those manufactured near the point of export, or those marketed locally, spent part of their journey as railway freight. Coastal shipping and canals were competitive for minerals, building materials, for industrial goods on very short distances, and for some categories of agricultural produce, but otherwise long distance transport virtually *was* railway transport. To this extent the possession of private sidings, or the seeking of locations adjacent to the line, was not the distinguishing mark it might at first appear. Indeed there were cases of firms which had local access to a branch line still finding it worth their while to cart their goods to a more central terminus.[53] On the whole, however, it is clear that the direct rail transport of goods from suburban sites was not open to the same objections as the transport of passengers. Although similar inconveniences tended to build up at peak hours, time was not so critical a factor; and, for all the complaints, the freight rates for merchandise goods were well within the means of manufacturers and

[50] The Regent's Canal company sold 5,000,000 gallons of water per day, the greatest amount, in proportion to its length, of any canal. The Grand Junction company sold 4,000,000. For E. J. Lloyd's arguments on the subject of short distance competition by canals see H.C., 1872, XIII, QQ.5060–78.

[51] A differential urban rate was levied on canal traffic in Birmingham. Letter, 3 July 1870, BRL, Chamber of Commerce Reports, 1865–87.

[52] BRL, Council Proceedings, Committee appointed to investigate the possibility of enlarging the Birmingham and Worcester canal for 200 ton vessels, Report 20 March 1888. Charles Hadfield, *British Canals: an Illustrated History* (1959), 247–54.

[53] Glasgow City Archives, *Petitions, Briefs and Minutes of Proceedings*, Glasgow Corporation Tramways, Bill II, 425. Turton also reports, in a recent survey, that only 3 firms out of 18 situated in the 'railway towns' of Swindon, Crewe, Eastleigh and Ashford, received or distributed more than 50% of their freight by rail. B. J. Turton, *loc. cit.* 110.

their agents. Indeed the appeal was put forward, more than once, that 'Trains that would deal with men as you deal with the clothes they wear and the food they eat, passing them at the same rate of price (*i.e.* 14 workmen per ton) would enable you to give a greater amount of assistance to the labouring classes in London than by any other mode.'[54] Moreover the charge on goods, whether high or low, could be handed on ultimately to the consumer. The working man was not in an analogous position regarding his own transport costs. So although, when his works migrated from Bridge Street, Birmingham, to Bournville, Richard Cadbury regularly walked the distance, and his biographer describes him helping his workmen to clear the snow off the *tram lines* in the winter, at least the railway accommodation for his products and raw materials was far more adequate than that for his men.[55]

The second point, stemming from what has been said, is that to the extent to which the suburban dispersal of factories was associated with an increased supply of suburban workers' houses, the problem of urban congestion and overcrowding was being tackled in the most effective way possible. It was all very well to agitate for the provision of really cheap workmen's services as the means of enabling the working class to enjoy the low rents and low death rates of the suburbs, whilst working in the city, but the 'dormitory' ideal raised serious practical problems. A more logical solution was to disperse both industry and workers, and to do it in that sequence. 'At present it operates this way,' William Denton complained in 1884, 'the railway companies avoid the employers of labour, and they only remove the employed, and then you must have overcrowding; whereas if the employers of labour were removed—then their people would go with them.'[56] When the Metropolitan railway were building their extension from Aldersgate to Moorfields, for example, their route was selected so as to avoid Whitbread's Brewery. If they had not, the consequence, Denton claimed, would have been that Whitbreads would simply have moved to the outskirts, taking the workpeople's traffic they generated with them. 'At the present moment most of the large brewers are occupying ground which they only occupied in the first instance because it was at a distance from London at that time; but London has come up to them.'[57] He saw more hope in moving industries outwards, where there was building room, so that the workmen might be able to live near their work, than in cheap fares. Yet although, in his evidence, Denton strongly enjoined this policy upon the Royal Commission on the

---

[54] H.C., 1846, XVII, QQ.2829–31.
[55] H. C. Alexander, *Richard Cadbury of Birmingham* (1906), 232.
[56] H.C., 1884–5, XXX, Q.10688.
[57] *Ibid.* Q.10695–7.

Housing of the Working Classes, its implications were too drastic to gain acceptance. The railway companies would have had to be directed to pass, where possible, through expensive industrial property; a course which was impractical, belated, and certain to meet with the firmest resistance from the parties involved. Not merely were his views not taken up, but they were not even given passing mention in the Commissioners' Report. A glance at two cases where the compulsory purchase of factories was envisaged, is sufficient to show why the recommendation seemed hopelessly impracticable. At one stage of the M.S. & L.'s central station plans in Manchester, the scheduling of the Oxford St. works of Messrs. Sharp, Stewart & Co. fell under discussion. The Corporation of Manchester favoured the idea, but did they realise, Mr. Denison Q.C. asked, that the factory was valued at half-a-million?[58] Moreover, as the N.B. railway company's dealings with the Coatbridge Iron Works demonstrated, no factory premises could be partially taken. In view of the complex factors which might be involved in a change of layout, or the loss of part of their space, factory owners and their solicitors had the right to insist that the *whole* premises, or none at all, be scheduled. The subsequent legal discussions also led, on occasions, to troublesome concessions over future rates of carriage.[59]

Even without legislative encouragement, however, the migration of industry to sites on the outskirts or in the suburbs of the major cities gathered momentum in the last quarter of the century. But it must be recalled that the fastest growing employment sector in Britain's economy in the late nineteenth century was not in manufacture but in tertiary, white-collared services, and many of these were associated with the city's central districts.[60] So the problem of urban housing remained, and to many it still seemed at the end of the century that the only solution lay in 'improved locomotion'. If rail services were cheapened and extended, 'the relief of pressure would be immediate', Charles Booth wrote in 1901. 'The action would be something like that of land drainage on stagnant, water-logged land; whereas the attempt to meet the evils of overcrowding by piling up great blocks of model dwellings is like an attempt to obviate a marshy foundation by putting in concrete, digging a hole and pumping out the water.'[61]

[58] BTHR PYB 1/383, 18 May 1866, QQ.3302–5.
[59] G. U. Coll. Sol. Papers. Box 3, N.B. railway company, Coatbridge branch.
[60] The real problem was the transfer of the central business functions, as some observers realised by the end of the nineteenth century. 'Any transfer of work to the country will not do more than slightly reduce the rate at which the business population of London has been growing in recent years.' H.C., 1906, XLI, Q.4743.
[61] Charles Booth, *Improved Means of Locomotion as a first step towards the cure of the Housing Difficulties of London* (1901), 17.

3. *The railways and suburban growth*

a. *Glasgow, Liverpool, Manchester and Birmingham*
It has already been noted that in each of the great cities of Victorian Britain the increase in activity, and expansion of area of the central business districts antedated the coming of the railways by at least half a century. In a similar way, the development of suburbs also preceded the provision of railway services, by periods of at least a decade or two for each of the larger cities, with one exception.

Glasgow
The exception was Glasgow, where suburban life, in the English sense, was slow to develop, and throughout the century owed even less to rail connections than the other cities. The two main areas of prosperous middle-class residence, Langside/Pollokshields and Kelvinside, were both situated no more than two or three miles from the centre; too close for rail services to be attractive, even if they had been adequately provided. The most rapidly growing working class 'suburbs' such as Maryhill, Partick or Bridgeton likewise were very close to the centre, within easy walking distance for those with employment there.

Attempts to fit railway transport into this narrow compass were peculiarly unsuccessful and belated. The Cathcart circle line, intended to develop southern suburban traffic, by means of stations less than half a mile apart, was partially opened in 1887, too late to be said to have influenced the extent or direction of suburban building to more than a marginal extent. The maximum journey travelled upon it was three miles, and the inconvenience of going to fixed stations for the 20 to 30 minute service had to be taken into account.[62]

Attempts to run a suburban service from east to west were still more unsuccessful. A dozen stations were provided along the 6¼ miles of the Glasgow Central railway; but the line was not opened until 1896–7—within five years of the electrification of the trams. Since it included lengthy underground sections, the further burden of underpinning streets and diverting sewers added to the cost, and all the subsequent drawbacks of steam operation through tunnels were encountered.[63]

At a greater distance from the city there were, even from late 1840's, a few out-of-town residents with business to transact in Glasgow sufficiently frequently to make it worth buying a contract ticket; but these wealthy commuters were not numerous—all season tickets on the Caledonian line, including the Clyde coast, only came to £1,000 *per*

[62] G. H. Robin, *Railway World* (1963), 53–7, 102–8.
[63] GRL B76055–6 contains in two volumes the petitions, evidence and counsel's speeches on this line. It was to cost £1,231,458, GRL B76055. Manuscript estimates by Charles Forman.

annum in the early 1860's.[64] Attempts were made to encourage further building on the Dumbartonshire and Ayrshire coasts by offering free travel for eleven years to all those who had newly taken houses with a rental above a certain minimum figure, but this act of calculated generosity failed to encourage the growth of an outer ring of dormitory suburbs. Indeed Glasgow never developed symptoms of the suburban sprawl typical of many other cities until well into the twentieth century, and remains an extraordinarily compact and densely populated city.

In the nineteenth century Glasgow itself was the dormitory, the Singer Works at Clydebank, or the various steel works at Newton and Coatbridge, were the work destinations. The workmen's train services which were running in the late nineteenth century tended to assist this curious 'reverse', or outward flow of commuters, rather than to disperse the resident population. When Robert Millar, General Manager of the Caledonian, was giving evidence to the Select Committee on Workmen's Trains, 1903/5, he was questioned carefully, and almost incredulously, upon this point.

'It was the reverse of London? You took from your populous centre workmen to work away from the centre and you brought them back at night?—That is so; and that is the rule in Scotland. It is not absolutely the case, but it is the rule. A great many engineering works starting in Glasgow originally, the population settled down round about the engineering and shipbuilding works. As the city increased, the works were sent out into the country and the population remained.'[65]

Liverpool

All the other cities, however, showed early signs of suburban growth. Thomas Baines, historian of Liverpool in the mid-nineteenth century, marvelled at the 'effect of the great facilities for locomotion', changing both town and countryside around the Mersey. 'Comparatively few large and beautiful dwelling houses are now built in town, while thousands are scattered over the sea-shore, from Southport to Hoylake.' The wealthy had already begun by the 1820's to desert Abercromby Square and take villas in the 'pleasant villages from Bootle to Aigburth.'[66]

However, Baines makes it clear that he is using 'locomotion' in the more general sense which the Victorians attached to the word. The instruments of this 'locomotion' were the steamers, which began services in the 1820's, and the omnibuses, which started in 1831, and were running ten or twelve routes at the time Baines wrote.[67] There

[64] BTHR (Edinburgh) CAL 4/71, Traffic Statements 1850–65.
[65] H.C., 1905 (270) VIII, QQ.6, 238–40.
[66] T. Baines, *Liverpool in 1859* (1859), 8.
[67] *Idem, History of the Commerce and Town of Liverpool* (1852), 629.

were, in fact, no railway lines connecting Grassendale and Aigburth with the centre of Liverpool until the decade following Baines' *History of the Commerce and Town of Liverpool*. This early suburban traffic between the more prosperous southern suburbs and the central business district was carried mainly by omnibus and private carriage; and it was advanced by Ramsay Muir in 1910 as the main factor in the evolution of the extremely localised Bold Street/Church Street/Lord Street shopping avenue.[68] This shopping axis, with its extensions along Castle Street and North John Street, lay on the direct line between the office quarter and the wealthy southern suburbs, and the approaching or departing road traffic tended to be narrowly channelled down this single route.[69]

Liverpool's main suburban growth of mid century (1831–71) was likewise largely independent of railway development. The most substantial growth, from 7,000 to 122,500, took place in the districts immediately north east of the centre, Kirkdale, and Everton; both no more than two miles, or a half-hour's walk, from the central area, and rather less than that from the new northern docks. Toxteth Park, to the south, was increased in population by the processes of site-infilling and denser building from 24,000 to 80,000 over the same period, and West Derby, to the east, from 9,600 to 50,600; but both of these were within three or four miles of the city centre.[70] Further out, acting as middle class outriders of this suburban extension, villa settlements were to be found in clusters inland, spread evenly in an arc, Walton, Knowsley, Huyton, Wavertree, Childwall and Woolton, and along the coast to the north as far as Southport.[71]

At first, residents in these outer suburbs had to make do with little or no railway connection, but one of the objectives of the Cheshire Lines Committee's ring railway in the 1870's was, as James Allport explained, to cater for the profitable first and second class traffic which this building generated. 'Our line is not only an accommodation for our goods traffic to the North, it really gives a very good suburban railway . . . there are a great deal of villa sites and it would be a line very much used for that purpose as a suburban railway.'[72] George Underdown, General Manager of the Manchester, Sheffield and Lincolnshire railway, also spoke in support of the 'omnibus services' they had been

---

[68] Ramsay Muir, *loc. cit.* 237–40. Wilfred Smith, 'The Urban Structure of Liverpool', *Merseyside: A Scientific Survey* (British Association, 1953), 197.

[69] J. A. Picton, *op. cit.* (1875), I, 417.

[70] Sheila Marriner. 'History of Liverpool, 1700–1900', *Merseyside: a Scientific Survey* (Liverpool, 1953) 107–114.

[71] T. Baines, *op. cit.* (1859), 8–9.

[72] HLRO, Min., H.C., 1874, 28 April, pp. 28–9, S.C. on C.L.C. (North Liverpool Extension to Ranelagh Street).

asked to open to Hunt's Cross, Childwall, Much Woolton 'and other pretty areas'. 'Excuse me, who asked you?' a landowner's counsel interposed. 'A gentlemen who lives in the neighbourhood. One gentleman?—Yes. I thought it was one.'[73]

The traffic was deliberately limited at the outset to the type of passenger who could afford to pay full fares, or receive a concession for buying a contract ticket, and even with this restriction, its inception was greeted by landowners with mixed feelings.[74] The most successful bulk traffic was not developed until the last decades of the century, with the extension of more modest red brick houses for the lower middle class clerks northwards to Waterloo, Crosby and beyond. From these homes came the relatively heavy daily short-distance traffic which the Lancashire and Yorkshire railway carried into Exchange Station, conveniently located on the fringe of the office quarter.[75]

Manchester

In Manchester the extension of suburbs followed a similar course to that of Liverpool. The feature of the first quarter of the nineteenth century which excited comment was the movement of the fashionable residential district from the toll-gate-guarded inner areas of Victoria Park and Ardwick out to Alderley Edge and Wilmslow, or even further to Bowdon and Knutsford. This was at first a movement of a small, but wealthy and land-hungry, group of the new middle-class 'Cottentots' and relied upon private carriages; but by the early 1830's, when the horse-omnibuses began their services to Pendleton, Rusholme, Broughton, Cheetham Hill, Eccles, Harpurhey, Newton Heath, and Didsbury, the middle-class exodus increased in volume.[76]

Apart from the Altrincham branch of the Manchester South Junction railway, opened in the late 1840's, there was little attempt to develop 'dormitory' traffic by any of the main line companies serving Manchester. The bulk of their traffic consisted of inter-city travellers, arriving from Stockport, Oldham, Rochdale and Liverpool: the twice-weekly tradesman, the commercial traveller returning or setting out on medium or long-distance journeys.[77] The numbers of season ticket holders were small until the last decades of the century, and the number of regular commuters of the modern, daily, strap-hanging type, probably did not

---

[73] *Ibid.* 29 April, p. 21.

[74] Mr. Haywood was the principal objector, but Derby and Sefton also owned land on the route and petitioned against the bill. *Ibid.* Petitions. (These are mentioned in the first MS. pages before p. 1 of the first day's proceedings.)

[75] Ramsay Muir, *loc. cit.* 240.

[76] T. W. Freeman, *loc. cit.* 54–6, and Fig. 16.

[77] BTHR PYB 1/383, 29 May 1866, QQ.631–8.

amount, in the 1860's, to more than a few thousands per day.[78] The horse omnibus was competitive, even on the Stockport run; and a glance at the siting of intermediate stations is enough to show that the new middle class suburbs must have relied principally upon the omnibus.

In Manchester, as in other cities, rail journeys by the working class were reserved for holidays and the occasional excursion.[79] All that the suburban railway and horse omnibus services did for Manchester was to siphon off the well-to-do, and leave the main bulk of the working class in the centre, and in the inner ring of speculative terrace houses.

'A large portion of the middle-class, the clerks, warehousemen and others seize upon the new suburbs,' wrote a contemporary, referring to Manchester in the early 1870's, 'vacating their houses in town, which are most frequently absorbed for shop and business purposes, or subdivided and sublet, until the dwelling which has served for one household contains as many families as it did persons.'[80]

The exodus was confined to the middle class. The working class remained in the state Leon Faucher had described in 1845, 'struggling for a few feet of land in the midst of some filthy purlieu.'[81] Suggestions were made in Manchester, as in the other cities, that facilities for a wider social class to travel daily might circumvent the danger of central overcrowding to health; and the Health Officer pointed to the marked difference between central death rates and those outside the city boundary. In the 1880's a pressure group, similar to those campaigning for cheap trains in London, was formed to urge the reluctant railway companies 'to enable workmen to live among more healthy surroundings, and to allow them to work at greater distances from their houses than formerly.'[82]

[78] Nor would the number increase until there was a marked improvement in local services, wrote a contemporary in the 1880's. 'Rusholme will demand to be placed in better communication with Old Trafford and Pendleton and Broughton, and Cheetham will seek to be connected with Hulme and Chorlton by some means which will not consume a great part of the day in going and returning.' *Manchester City News* (1881–2), Notes and Queries, MRL 9427 M 9 A.

[79] By the end of the century an impressive amount of working class holiday traffic was handled for the longer journeys to the west coast seaside resorts during the 'Wakes' weeks, the fares being paid in advance through 'going off' clubs. *Railway Magazine*, XXVIII, (1911), 10.

[80] G. T. Robinson, 'On Town Dwellings for the Working Class', *Trans. Manch. Stat. Soc.* (1871–2), 68.

[81] Leon Faucher, *op. cit.* 93.

[82] Lancs. Federation of Trades and Labour, *Cheap Trains for Workmen* (1899), MRL 385–31. This pamphlet attacked both the Cheap Trains Sub-Committee of the Corporation, which only secured 'inadequate, and in some cases trivial, reductions', and the railway companies who (it alleged) were using the tax reliefs granted to them to give relief on the profitable middle class contract traffic whilst retaining 'oppressive' fares for workpeople.

Even in the closing decades of the nineteenth century, however, central conditions had not been noticeably eased by cheaper railway transport in Manchester. Indeed cheap railway transport had not been offered. In the Manchester district between 1884 and 1900 a half-fare, or a single fare for a return ticket, was called a 'workmen's fare'; on this basis the two most popular journeys, to Gorton 2½ miles and to Miles Platting 1½ miles, cost 2½d and 1½d respectively. The two or three workmen's trains which ran to Oldham charged 7d for 9½ miles; that is, three shillings and sixpence per week, a sum quite beyond the budget of most working men in the 1890's.[83] They would be satisfied, they said, with a weekly fare of 1s 6d for journeys of from six to ten miles.[84] Such a tariff might begin to bring daily rail travel within the reach of the working class, particularly if the irksome restrictions on hours, and on returning early from work if ill or paid off, were removed.

As late as 1904, a special sub-committee on the Housing of the Working Class, set up by Manchester Corporation, still clung to the belief that 'cheap and rapid transit is the only cure' for the working class housing problem. It was a formula which had, by now, been repeated for nearly sixty years; but by 1904 the corporation was looking to a different medium and to its own resources for the solution. 'The modern electric tramway,' the sub-committee concluded, 'will come to the rescue.'[85] All the northern cities relied greatly on the tram, but none more than Manchester, which by 1905 had four times as many trams per head of the population as London, and even twice as many as Glasgow.[86]

It is doubtful, in fact, whether the solution of the working class housing problem could be vested in any transport medium, since it sprang from deficiencies in demand which went far beyond the power of cheap rate fares, or relatively small differentials in rent, to redress. But the street tramway certainly seemed to have much to recommend it by comparison with railways. Not merely could a municipal corporation control the laying out of routes, but it could constantly supervise the frequency of services and the issue of cheap tickets, using a municipal rate if necessary to sponsor transport at fares below real costs.

[83] H.C., 1900 (187) LXVI pt. 1, 52.

[84] Lancs. Federation of Trades and Labour, *loc. cit.*

[85] Sanitary Committee, *Housing of the Working Class, History of the Schemes and Description etc.* (Manchester, 1904), 10.

[86]   *No. of inhabitants*
         per mile of tramway
         Manchester   8,937
         Liverpool   13,368
         Glasgow   14,216
         London   33,661
H.C., 1905, XXX, 587.

Even the ordinary horse tram produced a marked effect. 'Within a few years the old, despised horse tramway had created a new volume of traffic', argued H. H. Gordon, in a discussion at the Royal Statistical Society in 1918, 'which was larger than that aggregated in two generations before, by railways or omnibuses.'[87] H. H. Gordon was referring to the horse trams in the course of an argument to show that the building cycle in London, which reached a peak in the late 1870's, was associated with the introduction of horse trams; a view which J. Parry Lewis has discussed in a recent book.[88]

When the tramways were electrified, and average speeds rose to seven or eight miles per hour, not merely was the effective radius of operation increased, and building diffused along the routes, especially near the fare stages, but the capacity of the central areas to absorb traffic was also increased. C. R. Bellamy, the General Manager of Liverpool's tramways, even claimed that a fourfold increase in the street traffic-handling capacity of the central area was achieved by the electric tram, compared with the horse omnibus or cab.[89] John M. McElroy, the Manchester tramways manager, gave similar evidence.[90] Manchester, Liverpool and Glasgow were as busy as London, it was argued, but did not create the same sense of confusion in their central districts because the streets were not cluttered with omnibuses and cabs.[91]

All in all, the tramway deserves more thorough consideration than it can be given in this brief digression. In America the notion that something as prosaic as a horse-drawn tram could produce 'streetcar suburbs', or 'star-shaped cities' has been entertained for some time, but the idea has only been partially tested in Britain.[92]

Birmingham

In Birmingham the development of new suburbs depended at first upon the private carriage and omnibus. The Colmore and Calthorpe lands at New Hall and Edgbaston, formed the earliest inner suburbs; and they, like Islington (named and planned after its London counterpart) were intended at first to provide a more elegant and spacious

[87] J. Calvert Spensley, 'Urban Housing Problems', *Journal of the Royal Statistical Society*, LXXXI (1918), 162–228. Gordon's point is made on p. 226, and is discussed in J. Parry Lewis, *Building Cycles and Britain's Growth* (1965), 130–2.

[88] J. Parry Lewis, *op cit.* 131.

[89] H.C., 1906, XL, Q.25481–553.

[90] *Ibid.* Q.25762 *et. seq.*

[91] In London, of course, tramcars were banned from the central area. T. C. Barker and Michael Robbins, *op. cit.* 186 *et. seq.*

[92] Wilbur R. Thompson, *A Preface to Urban Economics* (Baltimore, 1965) 362. Sam B. Warner, *Street car suburbs: the progress of growth in Boston, 1870–1900* (Cambridge, Mass., 1962).

retreat for the new moneyed class of the early nineteenth century.[93] The New Hall estate, just west of Snow Hill, was too central to remain residential for long, but underwent a metamorphosis to business uses similar to that in Blythswood, Glasgow. Edgbaston, however, remained residential throughout the nineteenth century, and retained the reputation of being pre-eminently the 'carriage trade' area.

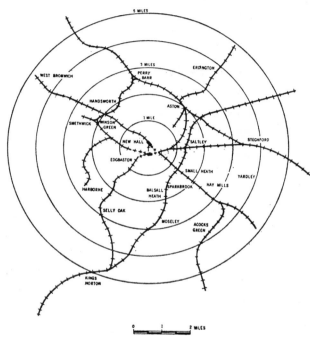

Location of Birmingham's suburbs.

Other new suburbs which were well established before the railway age were at Small Heath to the east, and Sparkbrook to the south. Though not as exclusive as Edgbaston, both suburbs contained houses laid out in generous style; a few could be found with grounds of ten to fifteen acres, and whole streets with average rents of £100 per house *per annum*.[94] All were connected, by the first omnibuses, to the central district in 1834 and 1835; though the fares charged by Messrs. Smith and Doughty, the first omnibus operators (e.g. 8d return to Small

---

[93] M. J. Wise and P.O'N. Thorpe, *loc. cit.* 214.
[94] *Birmingham Daily Mail*, 17 September 1903, house and 16 acres Small Heath. *The Property Advertiser* 2 May 1881, houses in Beechfield Rd. Sparkbrook, renting at £80–£110 *per annum*.

Heath), were almost as much out of reach of the ordinary artisan as the £100 rentals.[95]

By 1836 two omnibus companies, The Birmingham Omnibus Conveyance Company and the Midland Omnibus Company, had commenced operations on a larger scale; the latter-named company running railway feeder services from the High Street to the Vauxhall station, the former plying through West Bromwich and Wolverhampton to Dudley. The development of these services largely remained, for thirty years, a special field for the small operator to show his enterprise. William Sheppard, Joseph Brookes, William Mayer and Thomas Chapman were amongst the small entrepreneurs who operated the extending network of routes shown in Wrightson and Webb's Directories in the 1840's, to Nechells, Saltley, Handsworth, Smethwick, and Camp Hill.[96]

A resident of Handsworth, in his reminiscences, placed the decade of most rapid growth of services as the 1860's, 'when the need of some regular communication with the parent city of Birmingham had to be met . . . and it was met by a service of omnibuses. . . . At first, two rival proprietors monopolised the service, one named Tolley and one named Mayner (*sic*). From Villa Cross to town there was a half-hourly service, and the fare for the single journey was 6d—in snowy and difficult weather sometimes raised to eightpence or ninepence. As was inevitable, however, the steadily growing requirements of the locality brought competition in due time, first in the shape of rival omnibuses, and later in the form of the more modern tramway. This was just as the toll-gates were beginning to disappear.'[97] In 1872 the Birmingham and Staffordshire Tramway began operations through Handsworth and West Bromwich; and by 1900 tramcars were providing transport over the 3 miles for 1d, at two or three minute intervals during the busiest part of the day. The railways played virtually no part in this suburban extension. 'For a wide reaching parish like Handsworth its railway accommodation had always been miserably inadequate.'[98]

By the 1880's the suburbs just mentioned, together with Aston and Ashted, were already referred to as 'the old suburbs'.[99] Aston Manor, indeed, was the largest suburb bordering upon Birmingham at the time of the Boundary dispute of 1888, mustering a population of 66,000, as against the 22,500 of Balsall Heath, the 25,000 of Handsworth and the average of about 9,000 each for Harborne, Erdington, Yardley,

[95] Alec G. Jenson, *Early Omnibus Services in Birmingham*, 1834–1905 (1963), 2–3.
[96] *Ibid.* 4–5.
[97] F. W. Hackwood, *Handsworth, Old and New* (Handsworth, 1908), 70–1.
[98] *Ibid.* 72.
[99] Robert K. Dent, *Old and New Birmingham* (Birmingham, 1880), 618.

Moseley and Selly Oak.[100] But Aston was only 1½ to 2 miles north of the city centre, within easy omnibus or even walking distance; and the railway served only the north and east of the area by means of the Aston and Witton stations.[101]

Between 1880 and the end of the century the Taylor and Stechford estates, which had limited the extension of residential building to the south at Moseley, and to the east at Stechford, were broken up and laid out for building.[102] Yardley and Acock's Green also developed as residential areas in the last decades of the century to the east, Erdington and Perry Barr to the north east and north, Harborne to the south west. These outlying districts, three or four miles from the centre, were predominantly middle class, and the omnibus journey was uncomfortably long and expensive. Consequently the increase of railway facilities, on a limited scale, and avoiding cheap fares, played an important part in their early development. The Birmingham West Suburban railway, authorised in 1871, ran out through Selly Oak and Bournville to King's Norton and handled specifically suburban commuter traffic.[103] 'Naturally the opening of the West Suburban Railway played a not unimportant part in the development of the district', the *Birmingham Daily Mail* wrote, in an account of Selly Oak and Bournville in 1903, 'but it is to the trams that the influx of the present population is chiefly due.'[104]

The Harborne railway opened to traffic in 1874, and carried local passengers out to Harborne, and also, by a circular half-hour service, to Soho, Handsworth and Perry Barr, where property values quadrupled over the next twelve years.[105] Yet this traffic was, as the prospectuses had anticipated, a traffic of 'business people' with adequate means to rent or purchase, looking for 'favourite neighbourhoods'; and the numbers involved, though significant, were not as large as has sometimes been assumed. The British Association survey, for example, describes Acock's Green, three miles south-east of the centre, as growing to considerable size by 1880 'because of ease of railway communication', a view which is considerably over-simplified.[106] In fact Yardley parish

---

[100] C. Houghton, *A Short History of the Boundary Question* (Birmingham, 1888) 6.

[101] H. A. Botwood, *A History of Aston Manor* (Birmingham, 1889), 78. 1860–80 was the period of most rapid growth.

[102] *Birmingham Daily Mail*, 15 October and 3 December 1903. W. S. Brassington, *Notes on the History of King's Norton* (Birmingham, 1880), 41 *et. seq.*

[103] C. E. Stretton, *The Railways of Birmingham* (1897), BRL 173855. For a good map of suburban railways see C. R. Elrington, 'Communications', *A History of the County of Warwick* (Victoria County History, 1964), VII, 41.

[104] *Birmingham Daily Mail*, 12 November 1903.

[105] *Railway Magazine* (1900), 289 *et. seq.* (1915), 421 *et. seq.* C. Houghton, *op. cit.* 10.

[106] M. J. Wise and P. O'N. Thorpe, *loc. cit.* 224.

(which included not merely Acock's Green but also Stechford, Yardley, Sparkhill, Greet and Haymills) only increased in population from 3,000 to 17,000 between 1861 and 1891. 'They were able, so to speak, to keep themselves to themselves', a contemporary newspaper account of Acock's Green and Olton remarked in 1903. 'An unseen tide of bricks marched through Sparkbrook to Greet, and through Small Heath to Haymills,' until 'the village' itself was threatened, but for a long time 'a railway service suited to the few rather than the many, kept them select, and the absence of any other popular means of conveyance adapted to the needs of the multitude enabled both places to set at defiance the advancing tide from a great town.'[107]

This was not merely journalistic licence; as is demonstrated by the figures for the yearly issue of tickets at Acock's Green in 1903, which were specially collected for a Great Western railway traffic analysis. 221,000 tickets were issued in the year, and even assuming that every ticket was issued to a commuter, the number travelling up to Birmingham daily would only be about eight hundred. The Small Heath and Sparkbrook stations, on a similar basis of calculation, may have added a further twelve hundred in 1903.[108]

'The trams will wake up the railway company, which for years has been content to serve "the Green" with a monopolistic consideration based upon its own interests rather than those of the public', the *Birmingham Daily Mail* prophesied. 'Already, it can be seen, the Great Western has been brought to its senses. The issue of third class season tickets about a year ago was a sign of the times.'[109] Unfortunately the railway company had left its initiative too late, and between 1903 and 1914 the numbers of tickets and the money receipts at Acock's Green, Small Heath and Sparkbrook stations steadily declined.

It was the same story at the stations on the opposite side of Birmingham, to the west and north west. The Handsworth and Smethwick traffic, which reached a daily total of possibly seven hundred passengers by 1903, halved over the next ten years; the Soho and Winson Green issue of tickets fell from about four hundred to less than a hundred per day.[110] These stations were all in the Greater Birmingham area, within three miles of Snow Hill, and exposed to competition from trams and (after 1904) from motor omnibuses.

The most resilient traffic returns were from stations at a greater distance; over the thirteen miles to Wolverhampton, for example, the train service was able to retain its passengers.[111] Whether Wolverhamp-

[107] *Birmingham Daily Mail*, 26 November 1903.
[108] BTHR GW 4/281, p. 12.
[109] *Birmingham Daily Mail*, 26 November 1903.
[110] BTHR GW 4/281, p. 14–16.
[111] *Loc. cit.* p.20.

ton could be described as a suburb of Birmingham is another matter. It was certainly not one in the accepted dormitory sense, but a city in its own right.

This indeed is commonly the picture in the northern and Midland cities. The length of journey over which railways could begin to operate efficiently would take a traveller in the provinces from the centres of the great cities out to Wolverhampton, Paisley, St. Helens or Stockport —to cities with a clearly independent economic life of their own. Only in the London area, where the population reached six and a half millions by 1901, and residential development was most widely spread, would similar lengths of journey fail to clear the frontier of suburbia. Consequently it is to London that we must turn for the strongest case in favour of the precocious development of railway suburbs.

b. *London*
The work journey
In London, although the tradition of suburban travel was even older—William Cobbett had spoken in the 1820's of the stock-jobbers who worked on 'Change and travelled by coach as far as Brighton—the position was not basically dissimilar.[112] Outer suburban nuclei which had originated in the days of the short-stage coach were rapidly enlarged by the omnibus, and, further out, by railway services; the railway really came into its own operating over twenty mile distances, like that from Redhill or Reigate to London. Moreover, members of the middle-class with the inclination and the means to buy land and build in the outer suburbs, and with enough time and money to travel up to town, were sufficiently numerous in the Metropolis to cause the provision, within a few decades, of a wide-ranging suburban rail service, for a small social class, which was unparalleled in the other Victorian cities.

It must be emphasised, however, that even in the London area regular suburban travel was confined to a relatively small class until the 1860's. It was far larger than in any provincial city, but then London itself was eight times as large as any other British city. Viewed in this light its 27,000 commuters a day who arrived by rail in the mid-1850's does not seem disproportionate; and falls into perspective when placed alongside the 244,000 daily foot and omnibus passengers entering the City.[113] Evidence laid before the Select Committee on Metropolitan Turnpikes in 1856 claimed that the early development of many of the

---

[112] William Cobbett, *Rural Rides* (1825), I, 149.

[113] 27,000 is a deliberate overstatement. It includes all passengers using Fenchurch Street and London Bridge stations on the assumption that they were heads of households on daily work journeys. I agree with T. C. Barker and Michael Robbins, *op. cit.* 58, that the daily total was probably only 6–10,000, but have taken a higher figure to avoid any suggestion of understatement in the argument which follows.

suburbs four or five miles out, like Clapham or Hammersmith, and even some of the inner suburbs, like Islington or Holloway, was partly influenced by the horse omnibus services offered. 'Builders and parties in the district,' it was suggested, 'raised money to get the omnibuses up there.'[114]

As in the other cities, however, the numbers who could afford to travel daily by sixpenny omnibus were necessarily limited, and one must be careful not to assume that commuting to the City was, even in the inner suburbs, the only or even the commonest work journey.[115] Evidence suggests that only a small proportion of the working population, a quarter to a third at most, used any form of public transport at all; the rest either had local jobs, or if their work took them to the centre, they walked, sometimes using toll short-cuts, or 'halfpenny hatches' to shorten their journey.[116] Even in the suburb of Camberwell, with its high percentage of clerical workers, H. J. Dyos concluded, 'the development of adequate facilities for suburban travel was apparently irrelevant.'[117]

Reliance upon walking extended, in the 1850's, not merely to the street traders, the casual and manual labourers, but also the clerks who had to be at their desks at a fixed time. Dickens has left a picture of them quitting their houses in Somers Town and Camden Town and 'pouring into the City, or directing their steps towards Chancery Lane and the Inns of Court. Middle-aged men, whose salaries have by no means increased in the same proportion as their families, plod steadily along, apparently with no object in view but the counting-house.'[118]

One has only to look at contemporary opinion or at the fares structure to realise that, as in the provinces, the suburban railway passenger in the mid-1860's was still predominantly middle class. 'It is only within the last few years that persons of my condition of life,' said Charles Pearson in 1846, 'have been satisfied to live out of town; we were crammed and jammed together in the City, and believed that it was essential to our convenience and to our happiness. Now 6d takes us by an omnibus backwards and forwards; the poor man has not 6d to give.'[119]

[114] H.C., 1856, XIV, QQ.1391–3, and Harold Pollins, 'Transport Lines and Social Divisions', *London, Aspects of Change* (R. Glass et. al. 1964), 34.

[115] Commuting by omnibus at five or six shillings a week may be compared with the average mid-century money wage for operatives of twenty-one or twenty-two shillings. G. H. Wood, 'Real Wages and the Standard of Comfort since 1850', *Journal of the Royal Statistical Society* (1909), Table 2.

[116] H. J. Dyos, *Victorian Suburb: a Study of the Growth of Camberwell* (Leicester, 1961), 62–3. M. L. Moore, *A Century's Extension of London's Passenger Transport Facilities, 1830–1930.* (London Ph.D. thesis), 31.

[117] H. J. Dyos, *op. cit.* (1961), 63.

[118] Charles Dickens, *Sketches by Boz*, scene 1, quoted in H. C. Prince, *loc. cit.* 112.

[119] H.C., 1846, XVII, Q.2834.

Charles Pearson, who as City Solicitor qualified, one would have thought, as one of the more affluent members of the middle-class, was putting forward the plea, reiterated again and again over the next fifty years, in London and in the provinces, for a really cheap and convenient rail service, as a means of spreading the social, sanitary and even (in Pearson's view) the moral advantages of suburban life to a wider class. It is worth noting that he did not expect the extension of this privilege right down to the bottom of the social scale, but only to the better order of 'mechanics'. 'You have, amongst the superior order of the mechanical poor, 100,000 persons who come to their work into or close to the City every morning at six or seven o'clock; 100,000 mechanics who are earning 25/- to 35/- per week; you have 25,000 clerks, the superior order of warehouseman, and so on, earning their £80, £90, £100 or £120 a year who come in at nine o'clock in the morning.'[120] It was to this group, the lower middle and upper working classes, that he wished to see the advantages of suburban life extended by cheap rail travel. And so it was, over the period between 1850 and 1880, but only gradually, and only to this still limited class. Nor was this achieved entirely by the agency of the railways, which, even in London, were neither quite as revolutionary, nor revolutionary in quite the way that has sometimes been supposed.

If one takes as an example of prevailing fares in the mid-1860's the suburban contract tickets on the Great Northern line, the second-class season to Moorgate from Finchley, Mill Hill or Wood Green cost roughly £13 10s, say 5s per week; from a slightly more distant suburb like Barnet, the cost was roughly 10s per week.[121] Such fares were, after twenty years, still ten times as high as the fares which Pearson had thought would be necessary to give mobility to a wider class. Moreover, the Great Northern was one of the more enterprising railways in its suburban ticket policy.

Early suburban travel and the growth of the outer suburbs

It may seem, halting for a moment in the mid-1860's, that there is here a paradox concerning suburban growth. One cannot argue with the evidence for the growth and new prosperity by the 1860's, even of remoter suburbs out of range of the horse omnibus. How then can the railways' case possibly be overstated?

The marked growth of outer suburbs can be reconciled with the restricted high-fares policy, described in an earlier chapter, by taking two further factors into account. First of all, there has been, in some of the more enthusiastic writing on the subject, a general tendency to

[120] *Ibid.* Q.2829.
[121] BTHR RCH 1/115, Superintendent's Minutes, January 1866–December 1869.

overestimate the rôle of the commuter in suburban life. Even in the twentieth century, with motor buses and cars, deep tube extensions and electrified rail services, the vitality and extent of the economic activity which the suburbs generate on their own account is often under-estimated. If one examines the employment patterns in commuter suburbs in the extreme dormitory areas at the end of a century of change, the following picture emerges. In 1951, out of the 2,413,000 employed persons who were night-time residents of the inner and outer rings of suburbs fringing the administrative county of London, 496,000, or one person in five, travelled to the central area.[122] By comparison, nearly a million of the suburban resident population worked locally and a further four hundred thousand only made short journeys to adjoining local authority areas; and, of course, those who resided without 'working' in the official meaning of the word—the older people, children, housewives etc.—did not leave the area, except occasionally. Moreover, as John Westergaard observes, 'a considerable expansion of service trades was needed to cater for the rapidly growing population of the outer areas' and these areas themselves contained substantial 'wedges' or 'pockets' of secondary employment.[123] There was therefore a certain amount of cross movement, or inflow into the outer suburbs each day from adjacent areas, so that their net loss of working population was only 27 per hundred, or approximately 600,000. The total number of residents in the same areas (including the 'non-working' population) was approximately 6,000,000.

In other words, between seventy-five and ninety *per cent* of the population, even of a modern suburb, are genuine residents and require the necessary services and amenities provided locally for their day-to-day life. 'Certainly the daily journey into the Central Area provides the clearest index of the interdependence of the various parts of the conurbation', writes James H. Johnson, in a study of recent suburban growth, 'but the importance of this movement for residents in all the twentieth-century suburbs should not be exaggerated.'[124]

Unfortunately there are no figures by which we could arrive at a similar calculation of job-ratios for the suburbs of the 1860's or 1900's, interesting though such a study would be. It would surely be reasonable to assume, however, that more than ninety *per cent* of their growing

[122] John Westergaard, 'Journeys to Work in the London Region', *Town Planning Review*, XXVIII (1957–8), 41, 45. The 'central area' as defined in this study includes the City of London, Holborn, Finsbury, Westminster, St. Marylebone and St. Pancras.

[123] John Westergaard, *loc. cit.* 42–3. Westergaard also submitted written evidence to the Royal Commission on Local Government in Greater London, 1957 (1962), V, 656 *et seq.*

[124] James H. Johnson, 'The Suburban Expansion of Housing in London', *Greater London* (ed. J. T. Coppock and Hugh C. Prince, 1964), 152.

populations were resident. It is equally clear that it would be widely mistaken to assume that everyone residing in the suburbs earned their living in London; even more so to imagine that they travelled up by train.

The nearest that available evidence will stretch to such an analysis of job-ratios is the inadequate calculation carried out for the inner suburbs at the close of the nineteenth century by the L.C.C.[125] This enquiry was confined to 167 societies or branches of Trade Unions, mustering 160,000 members, in an area where the total number of workers totalled perhaps 330,000, and suggested that 25·3% or 82,500 people may have made daily journeys.[126]

The point worth underlining here is that approximately 250,000 of the working population in the area of South London covered by this investigation did *not* travel to work in 1890. The six or seven hundred thousand non-working members of the population in the area covered by the investigation also, by definition, did not travel to work. Indeed, only one person in twelve in the southern suburbs used public transport of any sort, railway, tram or omnibus, to get to his work in 1890; three other wage earners worked locally; and the remaining eight from each dozen were the members of the wage-earners' families who remained in the suburbs throughout the week.

Even in the inner suburbs, which might be supposed to be more completely dependent than those at a distance, substantial amounts of local employment were generated. Although it tended to be over-shadowed by the traffic and economic activity of the central business district, and the bustle of the growing entertainment and shopping areas in the centre of London, there were strong currents of suburban life which should not be ignored. The pronounced character and ties which attached to many of the suburbs at the turn of the century suggest that it would be a mistake to regard them as mere appendages of the central district, or creations of the railway service.

The same argument may be applied, with varying results, to the outer suburbs. Some of them, particularly those to the south of London, tended to cluster round pre-existing villages and small towns, where a nucleus of skills and services already existed. The railway suburb was very rarely planted arbitrarily in the middle of open fields, and on the occasions when it was—as at Linford Essex, where 'the farmland was left with an odd sprinkling of houses that looked as though they had strayed from Ilford High Street'—the results were

[125] 'Job-ratio' is the expression coined by Westergaard to describe the number of employed persons recorded in the day time census of a given area per hundred employed persons resident there at night. *Loc. cit.* 38–9.

[126] L.C.C. *Report on the Inadequacy of Workmen's Train Services on the South London Railways* (1897), quoted in H. J. Dyos, JTH, I (1953), 12.

sufficient to discourage further speculation of the same sort. More commonly the initial picture in the 1860's and 1870's was that of a 'village with a railway' rather than that of a railway suburb. When Edgar Harper, the L.C.C.'s Statistical Officer, who made a closer and earlier study of this subject than anyone, was asked how—since the services were not good and the fares were relatively high—he accounted for the growth of the southern outer London suburbs, he replied that 'a part of the growth must fairly be ascribed to the growth of old towns such as Croydon, Epsom, Kingston and Richmond, part of which is independent of the provision of railway facilities to central London.'[127]

The second point, stemming from what has just been said, is that the relatively exclusive first class daily travellers, who were the principal beneficiaries up to the 1860's, and the somewhat wider, but still predominantly middle-class commuters of the 1870's and 1880's, though relatively small in numbers, were able to release great potentialities for expansion in the undeveloped rural districts around London. The type of commuter in the 1860's, whose money was driving up land prices near railway stations within a thirty-mile radius of London, was characterised by Seymour Teulon (in 1866) as 'a gentleman who wants to buy 20 or 30 acres of land and build himself a good house.'[128] Even if he could not afford thirty acres he still tended to be what a writer to *The Builder* described as a 'pursy citizen'. 'We only build nowadays for the *gentry*. . . . One would think that there was no increase of population lower down than the classes which rejoice in £500 a year.'[129]

Although the gentleman in question might travel to his professional or commercial work in town, he left behind him not merely his numerous family—wife, unmarried daughters, younger children—but also a considerable retinue of local, or locally resident, servants. If he wished 'to keep a station in accordance with his income', as the Victorian books on domestic economy put it, he would, at £1000 per year, employ three female servants, a coachman, a footman, and keep stables with two horses and a coach, or at any rate, a phaeton. The middle-class scale rose at one end to twenty-two domestics, ten horses and four coaches at £5,000 a year, down to two maidservants, one horse and a groom at £400 a year—the retiring pension for an army officer of middle rank.[130] Keeping up such an establishment was not a matter of free choice, but *de rigueur* (to use the Victorians' own phrase).

Although visitors and the newspapers arrived by train, most of the

---

[127] H.C., 1906, XLI, Q.5058.
[128] H.C., 1867, XXXVIII, Q.16585. Teulon's evidence was given on 26 April 1866.
[129] *The Builder*, October 1848, quoted in Parry Lewis *op. cit.* 86.
[130] Quoted in C. S. Peel, 'Homes and Habits', *Early Victorian England* (ed. G. M. Young, 1934), 126.

products required by the family and servants in the mid-Victorian outer suburb were provided locally; even the shop goods tended to arrive by cart, unless they were brought back as parcels on the passenger train after a visit to town.[131] The money spent with local tradesmen supplying and maintaining the house in its turn stimulated the growth of local service industry, and drew in further labour from the surrounding countryside. Indeed, as their size increased beyond a certain point the outer suburbs tended to provide services for a rapidly extending local area of their own, and even attracted, according to their character, either small scale industry or retired people seeking out-of-town residence.[132]

A further point of note concerning the suburban commuter of the 1850's and 1860's, is that, since he asked no special fares reduction, he was free to choose his site within a wide arc around the whole of London. Some railway services and areas were more attractive than others, of course; and in this profitable and more limited range of suburban traffic there does seem to have been genuine desire, on the part of the companies, to compete over services and even, within limits, over fares. Although Seymour Teulon's 'gentleman' came from the southern outer suburbs, which were particularly well served, he could also be found to the west or north of London. Edwin Chadwick, for example, had bought a piece of land on the Richmond line, 'intending to build upon it, but was prevented from doing so. I was told, however, not to sell it again as it would "pay for keeping", and it has done so. I have sold a little more than half at the price I paid for the whole.'[133] Even in districts, the character of which has now markedly changed, such as Edmonton or Tottenham, to the north and north-east, the middle classes could be found. William Birt, manager of the Great Eastern, lived there himself and described it as 'a very nice district indeed', (in the 1860's) 'occupied by good families, with houses of £150 to £250 a year, with coach-houses and stables, and gardens, and a few acres of land.'[134] The £150 to £250 a year was the valuation at which such a house would rent, i.e. £5 a week, or four times the average working wage in London.

The expansion of daily suburban rail travel after 1860
Between the mid-1860's and the end of the century the social classes

[131] H.C., 1904, VII, QQ.1113–4.
[132] J. T. Coppock, 'Dormitory Settlements around London', *Greater London* (ed. J. T. Coppock and H. C. Prince, 1964), 266.
[133] H.C., 1867, XXXVIII, Q.984. Chadwick paid £350 per acre and estimated that it had risen in value of £800 to £1,000 per acre, 'an increase not entirely but *mainly* due to the formation of railways.'
[134] H.C., 1884–5, XXX, Q.10217.

to whom rail travel was the necessary link between job and home expanded to include less substantial members of the middle class, and even members of the class Pearson had described as 'superior mechanical poor', half a century earlier.

It cannot be said that this was the outcome of a strenuous and premeditated attempt to develop the traffic on the part of the railway companies. The Great Western, the L. & N.W. and the Midland refused point blank to make any concessions to suburban travellers or to workmen, in terms either of services or fares throughout the nineteenth century. The other newcomer from the north, the Great Central, cannily made arrangements that, since they ran their trains over another company's lines for part of the way, they would not pick up or carry any workmen passengers.[135] Between them these companies closed a great arc, of virtually ninety degrees, from west to north, to cheap suburban travel.

Even those companies which earned the reputation of a more active and generous policy do not stand up to close examination. The Great Northern railway, for instance, probably provides the best example of an enterprising suburban policy pursued by a trunk-route railway company, in the period from 1860 to 1900. Moreover, unlike the Great Eastern's, its policy was the product purely of market forces and not legislation. Since the Great Northern company fed most of its passengers for central London onto the Metropolitan railway it had not been put to the expense of clearing central residential areas, nor to the burdensome *quid pro quo* of providing Workmen's services for those members of the labouring classes it had dishoused.[136] Its growing traffic tended to be based upon the half-rate fare associated with the lower-middle class clerk—rather than with the quarter-rate workmen's fare; it also sold an unusually large number of season-tickets, and Grinling has suggested that the Great Northern's reluctance to abolish the distinction between second and third class sprang from the management's belief in the usefulness of the third class for specifically suburban traffic.[137]

In the last two decades of the century the Great Northern railway's passenger traffic increased from 12,900,000 to 30,000,000 passenger trips, or between 800,000 and 1,000,000 extra passenger trips per year.[138] If, for the sake of argument, all these extra journeys were made by clerks travelling to town from stations in the new suburbs, then about

---

[135] H.C., 1904, VII, Q.723.

[136] The 1883 Cheap Trains act only gave general powers, and no specific statutory obligations (by clauses inserted into the company's acts) were laid upon the G.N. *Copy of Statements furnished to the Board of Trade etc.* BTHR MT 2/57, 28.

[137] H. P. White, *op. cit.* III, 156–8; C. H. Grinling, *op. cit.* (1903), 300.

[138] *Ibid.* 354–6 T. C. Barker and Michael Robbins, *op. cit.* 214–16.

1,600 extra clerks would be accommodated each year on the G.N.'s suburban services. If one then turns to look at the growth of the three largest suburbs directly on the G.N. i.e. Hornsey, Wood Green and Southgate, their joint rate of growth was, in fact, about 4,000 extra inhabitants *per annum* in the 1880's, rising to 5,000 in the 1890's.[139] Not all the inhabitants were breadwinners, but dividing the 5,000 by a factor of three (to find the appropriate increase in the number of employed persons) also produces the same figure of 1,600 *per annum*. Of course, all that this shows is that there is a superficial correspondence between the rate of growth of the three northern suburbs chosen, and the theoretical power of the Great Northern to absorb the extra traffic generated. An impossible number of correction factors would have to be added to show a closer correlation than this. Wood Green, Hornsey and Southgate—although spectacular examples of rapid growth—were not the only growing suburbs within the G.N.'s catchment area; and obviously not all the increased traffic can be assumed to be that of daily clerks. Yet undoubtedly a great deal of the traffic was of the extremely heavy peak-hour variety associated with commuting; equally, the northern suburbs produced an unusual balance of occupations dependent for employment upon the central business district, and even a style of architecture associated with the commuting clerk.[140]

In a sense, however, the spread of housing northwards for this social group may be seen as nothing more than the logical extension of the occupational zoning already established. The parishes of Islington and Hackney were the traditional homes of the clerk, conveniently placed within two miles of the City, and mustered 40,000 clerks at the time of Charles Booth's *Life and Labour of the People of London*.[141] The wedge-shaped expansion of such housing to distances of seven or eight miles from the Bank of England gave the railway an opportunity to operate over distances at which it was technically efficient. The rise in real wages, and the growth of demand for the services of white-collared employees, provided it with traffic.

Yet the Great Northern railway company could not be said to have

---

[139]

	1881	1891	1901
Hornsey	22,486	44,523	72,056
Wood Green	9,882	25,831	34,233
Southgate	8,289	10,970	14,993

H.C., 1906, XLII, 728–38, and Merlyn Rees, *The Social and Economic Development of Extra-Metropolitan Middlesex, 1800–1914* (London M.Sc. Econ. thesis, 1954), 68–74.

[140] C. H. Grinling, *op. cit.* (1903) 349–56, 374–6. G. F. A. Wilmot, *The Railway in Finchley* (Finchley Public Libraries Committee, 1962), 29–31. The houses were yellow stock brick and slate roofed, and sold for c.£400 in the late 1890's. Edwin Course, *op. cit.* (1962), 202; H. P. White, *op. cit.* III, 161.

[141] Charles Booth, *op. cit.* (1896), VII, App. IV, 492.

gone out of its way to acquire these commuters. What at first appeared a welcome 'suburban increment' to add to the profitable longer distance traffic was soon referred to, in Grinling's phase, as the 'suburban incubus'.[142] Pressures to extend the really cheap, 2d return, fares to the G.N.'s area, were firmly resisted. The cheap train fares that were run were not even advertised, until representations and legal action by cheap travel committees or the London County Council secured it.[143] Typical cheap fares of the 1890's on the G.N. from Hornsey or Finchley were 5d to 7d per day return. This was on the popular half-price ticket used by clerical workers arriving before eight a.m.; workmen's tickets were available at quarter-price but the passengers on these trains arrived in London before six a.m.; the ordinary third-class return, after eight a.m., was a shilling to one and twopence.[144] Compared with the fares of thirty years earlier (5s per week contract ticket) the drop in fares could not be called revolutionary.

The attitude of the G.N.'s chairman, Henry Oakley, could not have been made clearer. To all representations from the L.C.C. and the Board of Trade concerning the unreasonable hours, the inadequacy, and the expensiveness of the Great Northern's service, he replied to the effect that, 'it is not practicable to lay down any general rule . . . either with reference to hours of running or the rate to be charged, . . . the accommodation already afforded . . . meets all the requirements that have yet been made.'[145] His main practical objections were to the heavy expenses which mass traffic incurred at and near the terminals, and to the extremely short time over which these facilities, and the extra rolling stock, were fully employed. The demand for cheap travel, he asserted, 'would be all right if they do it all day and all night, but unfortunately, it is only between such a short time that we have not the means of making a profit.'[146]

This 'peak-hour' problem—which Charles Pearson had not foreseen in his scheme—made Oakley all the more determined not to allow his more profitable trains to be squeezed out. To make a conession on workmen's tickets by allowing them to arrive later in the morning would mean that the profitable half-fare passengers would simply receive the difference in fare as a gift from the Great Northern; to allow later half-fare tickets would cut into the still more profitable

[142] C. H. Grinling, *op. cit.* 300–4, 354–6.
[143] H.C., 1903, VIII, 597 *et. seq.*
[144] T. C. Barker and Michael Robbins, *op. cit.* 216.
[145] H.C., 1894 (C7542) LXXXV, 4–5.
[146] *Ibid.* 20. He also objected to the difficulty in providing insurance for accidents at very low fares, as did the G.E., which suggested £100 limit to compensation. This, as Cheap Train committees pointed out indignantly, was the maximum value the railway companies were prepared to put on a workman's life. *Copy of Statements etc.*, BTHR MT 2/57, 4.

ordinary return tickets. When he was asked, in addition to making concessions over fares and times, to run services over distances and to areas where no clear and full-price demand had shown itself to his satisfaction, his refusal was categorical. Nor was Oakley unusual in this; his views were shared by directors and managers, even on the southern lines. The chairman of the South Eastern railway spoke in similar terms, as did the chairman of the London, Brighton and South Coast railway—even descending to particulars as to how much *per annum* the South Eastern and the L.B. & S.C. railways would lose if any further fare concessions were made.[147] Charles Scotter, General Manager of the London and South Western, also shared the same views. Indeed at one stage of a conference called at the Board of Trade to enable representatives of the L.C.C. to meet the railway companies, the exchange became so heated that the formal procedure of record broke down, and the railway managers and local government officers spoke in an antiphonal chorus.[148]

Henry Oakley: I should strongly object to come under any obligation to run workmen's trains beyond a distance of 10 miles. . . . There is a huge area there, of 15 to 20 miles, where the houses are scarcely to be seen.
Two officers of the L.C.C.:
They will soon come.
Run the trains and they will come.
Henry Oakley and Charles Scotter:
That, I say, is a dream.
Yes, a dream.

Yet the traffic did grow, if not by design, at least in response to demand pressure. The railways were not pressed any further upon the issue which had provoked the joint expostulation from Oakley and Scotter. Indeed when the London Reform Union and the National Association for the Extension of Workmen's Trains took a test case, concerning the G.N. and the North London railway, before the Railway Commissioners, Mr. Justice Wright in his summing up specifically stated, 'it is certainly not the duty of the Commission to lay upon the railway companies the onus of opening up neighbourhoods to create a demand for cheap trains.'[149] Partly, no doubt, this matter was avoided the more readily because by 1900 the prospects of electrified tramways promised more effective dispersal of urban population than local railways, partly because this was an issue upon which the railways could not be pushed any further without being asked to abandon the whole commercial principle upon which they operated. The trams, in

[147] H.C., 1894 (C7542) LXXXV, 16.
[148] *Ibid.* 29.
[149] *The London Echo*, 21 July 1899. The *Echo* conducted a crusade for cheap fares. *Railways and Canal Traffic Cases*, X, 293.

fact, lived up to their promise, and with their free way-leaves and inexpensive equipment were well suited to the running of pioneer routes in anticipation of demand; the horse omnibuses with their still greater flexibility of service, continued to be the most appropriate means of providing transport for areas of lighter density or more uncertain prospects.[150]

The development of traffic in anticipation of demand

Here was the crux of the whole matter; the question as to whether railways pursued a policy of cheap suburban fares in anticipation of demand. If this were so, and if it could be shown that this was, in fact, the systematic policy and regular practice of the railway companies serving London, then there would be some justification for describing the railways as an important *cause* of suburban growth in the period up to 1900.

The only area where a convincing case has been made out for sufficiently massive and early suburban growth, prompted and sustained by rail services, is in the north east; the area of Edmonton and Walthamstow. There a spectacular, tenfold, increase of population took place between 1861 and 1901.[151] By the end of the century not merely did the north-eastern suburbs house 50% more than any other outer section, but the housing densities and the rate of immigration into the area were 100% greater than those in other sections.[152]

There can be little doubt that this enormous growth of suburban population, out of all keeping with the general average, was assisted by the extremely cheap fares offered by the Great Eastern railway; though the tendency of new industry in the Lea valley to provide increased employment for non-commuters in the outer eastern zones must not be overlooked.[153] In contrast to the examples cited earlier, the proportion travelling from this area to work in central London may have come to one person in six of the total, one in two of the working population.

The stages by which the Great Eastern came to assume its role in the 1860's and 1870's do not suggest a consciously pursued and premeditated course of action. The company had already, to use the General Manager's own words, 'had the obligation put upon it' by the Act of 1864 to issue workmen's tickets. Since the company grossly over-reached itself in constructing the Liverpool Street terminal, and

[150] H.C., 1872, XII, QQ.368–71.
[151] W. Ashworth, 'Type of Economic and Social Development in Suburban Essex', *London, Aspects of Change* (ed. R. Glass et. al. 1964), 83.
[152] H.C., 1906, XL, Q.5057.
[153] *Ibid.* Q.5152. J. E. Martin, *loc. cit.* 258–62.

found itself in Chancery for a time in the mid-sixties, traffic had to be taken wherever it could be found: but the General Manager, William Birt, made it quite clear that, in his view, the social changes and speculative building set in motion by the Great Eastern's penny fares to Edmonton and Walthamstow had 'utterly destroyed the neighbourhood for ordinary passenger traffic. . . . Indirect loss (to the shareholders) arises from the fact of the district where workmen are located being spoilt, and the ordinary passenger traffic being pushed out. . . . Do you think that the ordinary traffic paid better than the workmen?— I am sure of it.'[154]

J. F. S. Gooday, William Birt's successor, felt the same grievances just as acutely. The better paying ordinary fare traffic was not two or three times as great in volume as the cheap tickets, as on all the other London lines. It was approximately equal in volume to the cheap fares. As for the first class seasons, this traffic was rapidly diminishing. 'They do not move further down the Great Eastern line,' Gooday asserted, 'they move over to the Brighton and other companies' lines, where the workman does not exist to such an extent. I was manager of the Brighton line, and can speak to that.'[155]

Apart from the Great Eastern railway company's operations from Liverpool Street, there is little in the other London railway companies' services to suggest more than a normal response to demand pressures; a reasonably lively response in south London, a distinctly tardy one to the north-west and west.[156]

A complete and detailed summary of the overall position was produced for the Royal Commission on London Traffic of 1906 by Edgar Harper, and appears in the form of a statistical appendix in Vol. III of their Report. From this the table overleaf has been constructed.[157] Impressive though Harper's achievement is for a traffic census conducted over sixty years ago, it leaves much to be desired. Even assuming that the figures' accuracy is beyond reproach a substantial allowance should be made in the total arrivals for journeys not made by the head of the household or not made by him for work purposes; for the substantial irregular business traffic of local tradesmen and market people, resident in the suburbs, but taking advantage of the cheap morning fares to arrange purchases and sales; for the seasonal and weekend excursion traffic; together with the growing number of journeys generated by rising incomes and increasing leisure, for the

---

[154] H.C., 1884–5, XXX, QQ.10218–21.
[155] H.C., 1906, XL, Q.18559.
[156] H. J. Dyos, *JTH*, I (1953), 15–16, refers to unequal provisions in south London. Even as late as 1912 workmen's tickets only accounted for 40% of the total in the 6–8 mile zone, falling off to 35% in the 8–10 and 20% in the 12–15 mile zones.
[157] H.C., 1906, XLI, App. 6, Tables Nos. 35, 47, 170–80.

SUBURBAN LONDON, 1901

		Population	Increase 1891–1901	No. of population increase /No. of immigrants	Average rent per room per week	Density per acre
Population of outer suburbs	West	420,041	45%	130,816/ 84,357	2/4d	4·3
	North	417,009	43·9%	128,304/ 75,062	2/0½d	5·9
	East	675,300	62·4%	259,566/167,036	2/0d	11·5
	South-East	295,819	30·3%	68,776/ 40,535	1/10¾d	4·5
	South-West	239,778	29·1%	53,941/ 32,698	1/11¼d	4·7
		2,047,947	45·5%	640,403/399,688	2/0d	5·9

		At workmen's 2d fare	Other workmen's fares, up to 11d	Cheap or half-price fare	Total by cheap	Ordinary fares	Total
Daily arrivals by rail from inner and outer suburbs	West	5,820	15,275	675	21,770	44,066	65,836
	North	1,820	8,377	2,954	13,131	57,778	70,929
	East	19,929	20,807	14,262	54,998	62,597	117,595
	South-East	—	18,917	—	18,917	69,510	88,427
	South-West	—	23,119	—	23,119	44,566	67,685
		27,569	86,495	17,891	131,955	278,517	410,472

purposes T. C. Barker enumerates—day trips up to town to visit the various exhibitions which were a feature of late Victorian London, journeys for shopping and for entertainment.[158] Exactly how many of the 410,000 total of daily arrivals would survive after these subtractions is a matter for pure guesswork, but 250,000 *bona fide* daily commuters would seem to be a generous estimate. Add to it the numbers arriving by tram and omnibus and the result is, even by 1906, a formidable movement of the working population, perhaps one man in four, from the inner and outer suburbs into the City and West End.[159]

Even though Harper's figures may be insufficiently informative in certain respects, however, they merit condensation into a table and discussion at some length because, for all their failings, they give an unusually detailed picture of urban rail traffic in London at the turn of the century. Two points, in particular, stand out from the evidence: the contrast between the geographical distribution of travel at different fares; and the relative volumes of travel at the different fare rates.

It is clear, for example, that, in spite of the attention attracted at the time, and since, to cheap fares, the proportion they formed of all London's daily rail traffic was small. The really cheap 2d fares formed only seven *per cent* of the total; other concession fares of all sorts only a third. Out of the one and a half million members of the lower clerical and manual working class who were eligible for cheap fares, Harper estimated, only twenty-seven thousand got the 2d fare, and only one hundred and thirty-two thousand got any type of cheap fare.[160] 'I find the cheap train has practically no effect on the distribution of population', Harper concluded. 'Strange to say, they do not have the effect of distributing the population. They are a boon, it seems to me, to an existing population in the locality; but where you get the *2d trains*, there you not only get those trains crowded, but you get an enormous growth of population.'[161]

The preponderance of cheap traffic from the eastern suburbs is outstanding. The Great Eastern had virtually a monopoly of the 2d return traffic, bringing nearly 20,000 daily at 2d return in forty-eight trains from the suburbs. A further 35,000 passengers followed at reduced rates in seventy-four more trains.

The numbers arriving from other compass points at workmen's fares (in column two) may seem at first sight to be large enough to bear comparison with the Great Eastern; nineteen thousand from the south-east, twenty-three thousand from the south-west, and fifteen thousand from the west. But these fares, though called 'workmen's'

[158] T. C. Barker and Michael Robbins, *op. cit.* 203–8.
[159] H.C., 1905 (Cd. 2597) XXX, 4–8.
[160] H.C., 1906, XL, Q.4756.
[161] *Ibid.* Q. 5180–2.

ranged in price up to 9d, 10d and 11d per day. They represented those clerical workers who were singled out for sympathetic reference by the Commissioners.[162]

'The vast majority of people who come to their business in the centre of London every day, and who do not actually perform manual labour, possess very limited incomes, and, by the nature of their employment, are compelled to preserve a respectable appearance. If they fail to do so they may lose their employment, and very seriously impair their prospect of advancement. To such persons the payment of a daily fare constitutes an appreciable pecuniary burden.'

These were the suburban dwellers who formed the middle range of travellers, one hundred and five thousand, as opposed to twenty-seven thousand benefiting from the really cheap 2d return fare. Both groups of travellers were dwarfed by the two hundred and eighty thousand who paid the full ordinary fare.

On the whole the picture is one of a traffic owing its expansion primarily to the widening of effective demand and the growth of a larger class who could afford to pay the railways' charges, rather than of the revolutionary expansion of popular suburban travel by active promotion and cost reductions.

There remains the notable exception, the Great Eastern railway company, which more than any other assumed, albeit involuntarily, the role of anticipating and creating demand. Moreover the company managed to carry workmen up to $10\frac{3}{4}$ miles for a penny without making a loss, even excluding the £1,750,000 remission of duty for which the Great Eastern's cheap services qualified it between 1883 and 1903.[163] And although the operational difficulties of peak-hour cheap travel may have been unwelcome, they did not prove insuperable. Indeed it was argued at the time that the Great Eastern's services proved that similar action was technically within the grasp of all the railway companies serving London.

There was also the further point suggested to the Select Committee on Workmen's Trains in 1904, that if other companies could see their way to adopting policies as generous as the Great Eastern, the pressure would be taken off that company as 'many of what are now sparsely populated districts would be rapidly built up.'[164] Perhaps more important still, from a social point of view, would be the effect this further relief would have upon the working class suburbs in the north-east. The L.C.C.'s statistical officer, Edgar Harper, laid great stress upon this point in his evidence to the Committee. 'It is essential, to prevent

[162] H.C., 1905 (Cd. 2597) XXX, 16. The average weekly fare for these travellers would be approximately 2s 6d.
[163] H.C., 1904, VII, Q.47.
[164] *Ibid.* Q.569.

the overcrowding of the working class towards the north-east, that similar facilities should be given all round London.'[165]

In other words, there was a danger that the poor living conditions and overcrowding of the dilapidated inner districts might simply be transplanted, if cheap fares were restricted to one enclave. 'There is abundant undeveloped land which could be used to provide healthy homes for the working class in other districts', argued George Dew, member of the L.C.C.'s Housing Committee, '. . . certain districts have been shut right away from the workpeople.'[166]

The report of the Select Committee, when it appeared in 1905, was visibly influenced by this evidence. 'Unless this spreading of the population is provided for by cheap locomotion for workmen,' it warned, 'the worst results to the welfare of the population must ensue, by the overcrowding of the workmen into the comparatively few districts to and from which such cheap locomotion is at present provided.'[167] The L.C.C. had brought home its anxieties to the government. The next logical step was for the L.C.C. to take into its own hands the provision of suburban passenger transport services.

One is left with the question as to what other reasons there may have been for the failure of railway companies in all the major cities to develop energetically cheap and widely distributed passenger traffic services, apart from the operational difficulties and finer profit margins; neither of which—as the Caledonian and the Great Eastern railway companies showed—rendered commercial operation completely impossible.

Of course it is possible—and this would be the easiest explanation of the wearisome, foot-dragging proceedings which followed the Cheap Trains Act of 1883—that the whole failure to develop cheap traffic can be assigned to indolence and inertia on the part of the railway companies: that it was flagging entrepreneurial drive which made the operational problems seem a good and sufficient reason for declining to take risks.

Yet there was sufficient energy, and a large enough supply of capital, for the completion of the Inner Circle line in the early 1880's, and for the expensive entry into London of the Great Central in the following decade. Where there seemed to be an opportunity to stake a claim to profitable new traffic, the railway companies did not hesitate to spend freely, even wastefully. One might have thought that the sheer scale of operation of the Great Eastern, the reasonable dividend returns (3%)

[165] *Ibid.* Q.48.
[166] *Ibid.* QQ.692, 781.
[167] H.C., 1905 (270), VIII, Report p. XIII.

which it maintained, when it had recovered from the expenditure on Liverpool Street station, and the loud public acclaim its policy commanded from Select Committees, local authorities and reforming pressure groups, would have weighed in the scale against the L. & N.W., G.W., and Midland railway companies' anxiety over their trunk main-line traffic. A larger accommodation, on more generous terms, for short-distance traffic could surely have been made if there had been, in the estimation of Partington, Grierson, and Arnold, the respective traffic managers of each company, a clear opportunity. There were other reasons, quite outside the railway companies' control, why the cheap ticket traveller was 'shut away from abundant undeveloped land', discussion of which raises the large general question of the railways and the land market.

XII

Railways and the land market

1. *Railway services and the social geography of the suburbs*

Up to the mid-1860's, it has been suggested, the extension of rail services over the whole area around London had taken place evenly, with no more difference between one compass point and another than might be accounted for by the vicissitudes of competition and the existing differences between counties. And if the railways with northern entrances to London seemed less interested in short distance traffic, this seemed natural enough for major trunk routes. To the south and south-east, the lack of industry and of large cities, and the relatively short distances involved, gave a strong incentive to the development of intensive local traffic, as E. A. Course and H. Pollins have already pointed out; and this tendency was augmented by the existence to the south and south east, of a large number of towns and villages of reasonable size to provide nuclei for further residential building.[1] Some were spas and watering places, or seaside resorts, some market towns or old established boroughs. In total they provided more pre-existing centres around which suburban development could cluster in the third quarter of the nineteenth century than other areas near the capital. To the north and north-west, by comparison, the countryside was less diverse and agriculturally less rich, and there were long-standing reasons why the detached villages were smaller and more widely spaced.[2] But, in general, the pattern of suburban train services, though still socially exclusive, did not appear at all inflexible. There seemed to be nothing, in 1865, to prevent the even-spread geographical extension of services as incomes and effective demand rose.

Whilst commuting was confined to the more prosperous ranges of

[1] E. Course, 'Transport and Communication in London', *The Geography of Greater London* (ed. R. Clayton, 1964), 74–111. H. Pollins, 'Transport Lines and Social Divisions', *London, Aspects of Change* (R. Glass *et. al.* 1964), 39.

[2] James H. Johnson, *loc. cit.* 144.

the middle class, marked social distinctions between the rail services offered by the different companies, or the residential accommodation offered by the outlying railway suburbs, were not apparent. Low density villa settlement at a discreet distance from the station was the rule. Occasionally there were complaints that the new middle class immigrants had let down the social tone: as at Brighton, where the race meetings and assembly rooms declined, aristocratic patronage was withdrawn, and the remaining older residents learned to accept reluctantly the new pattern, of middle class residents, and working class excursionists 'disgorged on the Steyne from the cancer-like arms of the railroad'.[3] But in general the middle classes were welcome both as residents and passengers. They asked no fares concessions and travelled by contract ticket. They could afford to pay well for land and to lay out their houses with 'drives' and shrubbery, in respectful imitation of the country houses owned by the class with whom they now shared the country's government.

Yet social distinctions, in area and service, were only concealed whilst suburban rail travel retained its limited character. By the turn of the century, those of the working class whose jobs enabled them to live at a distance, and who sought to leave the central and inner districts were all channelled out to the north-eastern, or to a lesser extent, to the south-eastern suburbs. The railway network, in 1899, to quote B. F. C. Costelloe, the chairman of the Local Government Committee of the L.C.C., had become 'an imperfect system of transit devised almost entirely for middle and upper class requirements.'[4]

It will already be clear from the historical evidence which has been put forward earlier that Costelloe's account of the basic features of suburban railway service fell within the limits of pardonable exaggeration. The historical evidence on this point may be substantiated by reference to the present day socio-economic zones in the London area. J. Westergaard's written evidence to the Royal Commission on Local Government, 1962, shows clearly that the pattern of residential zoning, by class and income, in central and suburban London still bears the imprint of the limited transport facilities which characterised the closing decades of the nineteenth century.[5] The Victorian working class zones spreading eastwards from the central district, were merely extended further eastwards; both to the north and south along the Thames, and to the north-east, along the Great Eastern railway route. The predominantly middle class outer areas of north-west and south London gave rise to mid-twentieth century outer suburbs of the same social

[3] H. C. Brookfield, *A Regional Study of Urban Development in Coastal Sussex since the Eighteenth Century* (London Ph.D. thesis, 1950), 149–56.
[4] B. F. C. Costelloe, *The Housing Problem* (1899), 56.
[5] *Loc. cit.* V, 656–98.

colouring. James H. Johnson, who has summarised Westergaard's information in the map reproduced below, comments upon the way in which 'those areas which are less socially desirable tend to have grown as an extension of similar areas around the fringes of Victorian London.'[6] In other words, where clear distinctions of social status existed between the different areas of Victorian London, they have tended simply to be perpetuated and extended further outwards into adjacent

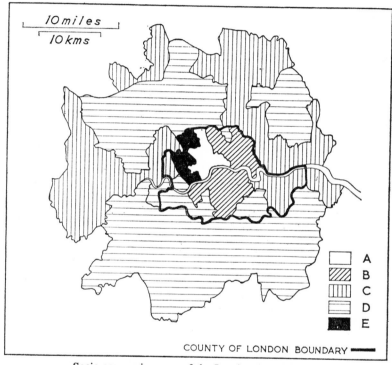

Socio-economic zones of the London conurbation

Key: A, central London zone; *B*, inner working-class zones; *C*: middle and outer zones of relatively low social status; *D*, middle and outer zones of relatively high social status; *E*, West End and Hampstead zones.

Based on a map by J. Westergaard, and reproduced from James H. Johnson, 'Suburban Expansion of Housing in London', *Greater London*, (ed. J. T. Coppock and Hugh C. Prince, Faber, 1964), 149.

[6] James H. Johnson, *loc. cit.* 149. It should be added that the western area of working class housing shown in the map, like the modern light industrial development associated with it, is largely a product of the 1919–39 period. For reasons already suggested the area was relatively lightly developed in Victorian times. Peter Hall, 'Industrial London: a General View', *Greater London* (ed. J. T. Coppock and Hugh C. Prince, 1964), 237–42.

O

suburbs, as if all social classes were castes and all travel were pedestrian; and there is little sign of the revolutionary breaking-down of the social homogeneity of areas which the more sanguine advocates of cheap travel anticipated in the late nineteenth century.

The questions still remain, however, as to whether the railway services of the late nineteenth century played a positive or merely neutral role in the evolving pattern of suburban social zoning, and whether the railway companies acted—as Costelloe suggested—by conscious design.

Certainly expressions of opinion by railway managers can be found which appear to substantiate Costelloe's interpretation. Edward Watkin, for instance, after speaking of the Metropolitan railway's showplace of model cottages and gardens, which had been built near the company's works at Neasden, seven miles north-east of London, went on to suggest that railway companies in general might 'with very great good indeed, be permitted to build little colonies in places contiguous to their railways.'

'All the questions about the arrangement of trains and so forth would be in their hands, and therefore it would be more easy than for independent people, would it not?' the Commissioners asked.

'Yes. It would be more easy,' Watkins replied, 'Of course, it is hardly the function of a railway company, but it is difficult to say where the function of a corporation does end.'[7]

Watkin was next asked whether railway companies shrank from providing services to encourage the formation of neighbourhoods with housing for people with low incomes, in case the effect of cheap housing were 'to drive out a richer class, who are more profitable customers.' He did not directly answer this question—and indeed it was fairly obvious that any railway company would prefer passengers who were prepared to pay higher fares and pay them in advance—but he did define a little more narrowly where the cheap housing should be located. 'I can imagine, for instance, that if we carried passengers, say to Hastings or Folkestone, at the same price we carry them to Ramsgate or Margate, and if we were to alter the character of these places from popular resorts of tolerably well-to-do people, to popular resorts of people who have very little money to spend, mischief might be done; and the point would be *to try to select proper places* for these colonies of working people.'[8]

The 'proper places' were already in course of selection in the 1870's, and the General Manager of the company which had earned the reputation of being the poor man's benefactor, William Birt of the Great Eastern, also expressed views on the subject to the Royal Com-

[7] H.C., 1884–5, XXX, Q.10479.
[8] *Ibid.* Q.10483. My italics.

mission on the Housing of the Working Classes which were similar to Watkin's, but even blunter. The selection of the workmen's escape routes to the suburbs should be strictly limited, he claimed, for two reasons. First, the spread of working class districts robbed the railway companies of remunerative traffic, 'That is our main objection; that it does seriously interfere with our revenue earning.' 'Do you consider,' a member of the Commission asked him, 'that a railway company can possibly put it forward, even as a moral claim, that they have an interest that shall be considered in excluding what you might call a low class of people from a certain district, so that they might have that district as a high class district from which to earn a good dividend?— I do indeed.'[9]

So far, though he was being unusually frank, one might say that Birt was simply speaking as a businessman concerning a matter which directly affected his company's fortunes. His second point, however, takes us onto rather different ground.[10]

'Allow me to say that from the Edmonton district, and from the Walthamstow and Stratford districts, we issue tickets to Liverpool Street, and that these districts are spoilt for ordinary residential purposes. What we would urge is this, that the working classes should be kept to these districts. We, the Great Eastern Railway Company, are prepared to provide any number of trains that may be wanted for their accommodation, but we shall have to urge, probably before the Board of Trade, that other districts which are not spoilt should not be thrown open to the working classes, otherwise these districts will become spoilt too. There is no hardship, I submit, in limiting the districts thrown open to the working classes.'

There could be no clearer expression of the company's wish to develop rail services for areas of less intensive, higher quality residential building; a desire which, as W. Ashworth and H. J. Pollins have recently pointed out, was translated into effective policy in the years just before and after the 1914–18 war.[11]

These views can also be found explicitly in the evidence of other railway managers, though not usually so openly expressed.[12] Weight is added to them by the fact that Watkin was Chairman of the Metropolitan and the South Eastern railways, both of which were considered progressive in their policy over suburban traffic, and Birt was General Manager of the only line to offer a chance of escape at a fare which was

[9] *Ibid.* QQ.10320, 10325. Mr. Lyulph Stanley put the second question to him.
[10] *Ibid.* Q. 10326.
[11] H. Pollins, *loc. cit.* (1964), 45, W. Ashworth, 67.
[12] The General Manager of the G.N. also put it 'We want to open up a district for something a little better than workmen.' H.C., (Cd 5052), 1910. See also W. R. Lawson, *British Railways—a Financial and Commercial Survey* (1913), 292–4, and H.C., 1906, VII, Q.1111.

less than the differential in rents between the suburbs and the central slums. Yet Birt speaks as if he regarded himself as the gatekeeper of a ghetto. Was Costelloe perhaps correct in suggesting that the suburban railway system was 'devised' almost entirely for middle and upper class requirements?

No doubt Birt and Watkin did not find it any easier than others to shed the class prejudices which went with their income and social position; but unless one subscribes to a very debased form of Marxism indeed, it would hardly seem likely that their whole policy, and that of the other railway managers, was simply a concerted attempt to keep the poor in their place. If an interpretation in terms of class is to be rejected as too flimsy, what other motives, apart from the operational considerations discussed earlier, could serve to explain their attitude?

2. *Underlying causes of railway policy*

Three further reasons for the railway companies' inaction may be discerned; two of them of lesser, the third of crucial importance. The first was that, apart from the passenger traffic, which was of dubious profitability for working class services, the railway companies stood to gain little else from the establishment of a suburb. 'When a new suburb, if I may put it so, "springs up",' Frederick Harrison, General Manager of the L. & N.W. was asked in 1905, 'do you say it does not benefit the railway to a very material extent?' 'There is,' he replied, 'something in all building materials at the outset; but when the population is there, their food and all the commodities they require generally go by road.'[13] The dependence of the suburbs upon the railway station, though real enough in one sense, was not as complete as a superficial glance might suggest. The bustle of activity in the new suburbs chiefly benefited the local tradesmen and carters who supplied most local needs. Miscellaneous goods, by rail to Walthamstow and Edmonton, for example, came to a mere 24 lb and 12 lb per head per year of their population of 156,000 compared with 1,603 lb per head per year for the 12,500 inhabitants of a town like Chelmsford, thirty miles from London. Even coal was carted: the railways taking 4,000 tons a year to Walthamstow and Edmonton, but 7,500 tons to Chelmsford.[14] Here was a strong disincentive to strenuous promotion of suburban services.

A second disincentive was the grievance, of long standing, relating to the system of rating, or local taxation, of the railways. Without going fully into the history of this issue, the main objection to the system was this: that when the parish rates for railways had been fixed in the 1840's—at the time when railway companies seemed to have the key to

[13] H.C., 1905, VIII, Q.622.
[14] H.C., 1904, VII, QQ.1113-4, and H.C., 1906, XLI, App. 56, 583.

unlock all the country's capital—an extremely onerous method of calculation had been introduced. Its effect was to burden the railways with an utterly disproportionate share of local taxation. For example, in Huyton, a suburb of Liverpool, out of 2,615 acres in the parish, the railway took 25; but its share of the £15,039 rates raised in the parish came to £5,267. Other examples could be, and were, multiplied endlessly by Samuel Laing and other angry directors, from all parts of the country. 'Why should a country village', it was asked, 'be allowed to tax the source from which those very advantages (of connection with London) were derived?'[15]

Several anomalies contributed to the heavy incidence of this tax burden. It had been laid down (in the London and South Western, Mitcheldever case) that the estimated rental of a railway should be the amount a tenant might give if he leased the railway from the company.[16] However, unlike other property in the countryside—residential, farm or factory buildings—the permanent way could not be considered to have any rental value in itself, or be convertible for any alternative uses. So the only way of assessing it was taken to be upon the receipts of the railway company: its trade was assumed to be attached to its realty.[17] This immediately put a railway company in a different category from mills, farms, or factories where the value of machinery and the quality and amount of output was ignored. Industrial assessment was regulated solely by the probable amount of rent which would be paid for the buildings, the profits earned on the premises being wholly exempt from taxation. As a result of this method of assessment the railways paid twenty times as much as industrial users per head of employees.[18]

The tax also placed them on a different footing from all other companies or individuals deriving a profit from carriage, none of whom paid more than formal license fees.[19] Nor did the payment of the lion's share give them a larger voice in vestry affairs; for no one was allowed more than six votes, however large their holding, or contribution to the rates. 'We seem to have been a sort of public plunder,' said Daniel Neilson of Liverpool.[20]

This was a burden the railway companies had become resigned to bearing; but the pressure to run workmen's services to suburban areas after 1883, revived the old grievances over rating. When it was suggested, for example, that any losses incurred in running cheap services

[15] LRL, *Public Meeting of Railway Shareholders* (1849), 4.
[16] H.L., 1844, XI, 475.
[17] C. de L. Nash, *Railway and Land Taxation* (1844), 9–10.
[18] MRL, *Rating of Railways, Public Meeting at Manchester* (1849).
[19] LRL, *Public Meeting of Railway Shareholders* (1849), 16.
[20] *Ibid.* 6–7.

should be met by a levy on the rates, the railway companies' immediate response was to point to the disproportionate share of the rates which they themselves already paid, and the fact that the rates might be used for such purposes as sponsoring rival tramway services. Such a contributory levy would merely be taking money out of one pocket to put it in the other: and on the three occasions when a rate was suggested as an 'equitable concession', to encourage the development of less profitable services on the urban frontier, in 1867, 1884 and 1906, the suggestion was rejected by the railway managers.[21]

Their second objection to rating was the very considerable increase in rates which accompanied the transformation of a rural area into a suburb: an increase which was all the greater if the public utilities necessary for a large concentration of workers' houses were to be provided. The low rated workers' houses, in fact, presented a serious problem to the new suburban authorities themselves in the working class areas. 'We want a fair sprinkling of the class that will take a house which is assessed at over £16 per year', stated the chairman of the Walthamstow Urban District Council.[22] As it stood, five-sixths of all houses in the Walthamstow U.D.C. area were rated at below £16 per annum in 1904, and the simple rule was followed that the greater the proportion of low rented houses the higher the rate in the £ must be. As a rural district became a suburb the rates went up, in other words; and if the suburb was working class, instead of middle class, they went up, on average, to 10s in the £ as opposed to 5s in the £.[23] In either case the railway companies had to pay more, but the amount was proportionately greater, and the *per capita* residential contribution to them peculiarly unfavourable from the railway companies' point of view, in a working class suburb. Not merely that, but as the rates steadily rose in an area, shopkeepers, tradesmen and the 'better class' of people tended to move out, both depriving the railways of more lucrative traffic and leaving them to shoulder the rates alone.[24] The Select Committee on Workmen's Trains of 1903–5 admitted, in their Report, the force of the complaints put to them on this score.

'It is quite apparent, as the railway companies urged,' ran the Chairman's Second Draft Report, 'that their action in giving travelling facilities will tend to increase the value of the land, and by consequence the rents and the rates (of which the companies always pay a large

[21] H.C., 1867, XXXVIII, Q.984 (Chadwick), H.C., 1884–5, XXX, QQ. 12933, 12950–5 (Shipton), H.C., 1906, XL, Q.5244 (Harper).
[22] Q.1964 in H. of C. S.C. evidence on City and North East Suburban Railway, quoted by J. F. Gooday, H.C., 1906, XLI, App. 56, 581–3.
[23] H.C., 1904, VII, Q.1113. Edmonton was 10s 5d and Walthamstow 9s 9d compared with 5s to 8s for other suburban areas.
[24] H.C., 1906, XL, Q.18568.

proportion) in the favoured locality. But this indirect, although it may be inevitable, consequence ought not, we think, to be allowed to outweigh the inestimable advantage of spreading the working population and so relieving congested centres. If in any case of exceptional hardship it should be thought advisable to rate the railway company's property in the developing district at *e.g.* agricultural value, we do not shrink from suggesting that this course be taken.'[25] The concession held out in the final sentence was too tenuous and too late to affect the railway managers.

The third and most important issue—which had also been mentioned in passing by the Select Committee chairman—was that of land ownership. Here again, it seemed, the railways got the worst of both worlds, both as purchasers and as vendors. They were, of course, considerable purchasers of land; ten acres per mile for a country line, plus large tracts for sidings and stations.

Their direct effects, as purchasers, upon the land market can be seen in the scale of awards for arbitration cases, given according to the procedures laid down in the Lands Clauses Consolidation Act and the Railways Clauses Consolidation Act of 1845. These procedures quickly established the principle that the sums to be paid for the land compulsorily acquired by a railway company should be based upon its value to the *vendor*, together with further amounts as compensation for interruption of business, loss of goodwill, damages for the intersection and severance of the property and for any deterioration which could successfully be argued.[26] To this sum was added a further 10% for compulsory purchase, raised to 50% in rural areas.[27]

The safeguarding of property could hardly have gone further, and indeed, from the records of independent valuations carried out by both parties at the time of sale, it appears likely that the railway companies commonly paid twice the current market value of land. The Lands Clauses procedure was an open invitation to any landowner on the outskirts of a town to produce a plan showing that his land, though open fields, or market gardens and summerhouses, was potentially valuable suburban building land; and examples of these non-existent estates, whose paper streets would be deranged by the railways, have been mentioned in the *Case Histories*.

More exasperating still for the railway companies were the verdicts sympathetic local juries returned even on land without development prospects, however shadowy.[28] 'It is altogether a Jury question,' one

[25] H.C., 1905 (270) VIII, Report p.XXI.
[26] See App. 3 *infra.*
[27] H.C., 1906, XL, Q.19894.
[28] The excessive awards by local juries and arbitrators also caused complaint from local authorities attempting to proceed under the Artisans' Dwellings Act. H.C., 1884–5, XXX, 12640–5 (Lefevre).

railway solicitor admitted in a confidential brief to a company's witnesses, 'when land is in the market, *whether compensation should be given for the gain the vendor might have had by retaining it for longer.*'[29] Payment, in other words, had to be made, on occasions, even for the loss of *possible future gain* on undeveloped land; and in this way future prices were anticipated and made real.

The railways' direct impact on the land market was enough to cause, in itself, a marked rise in local land prices; but as it was always the buyer, the railway company drew no benefit whatsoever from this rise in land values.

Nowhere was the rise in values more tantalising than in the suburbs. Although central land values as a whole in the Victorian cities may have risen by something of the order of 75% to 100% in the thirty years after 1840, and values in the more favoured streets by three to five fold, land prices in the outer suburban districts appreciated by ten to twentyfold over the same period. 'If the first railway engine,' Henry Davies wrote in 1861, 'had been laden and fed funnel-wise, with guineas, and if the wheels had been constructed with an apparatus for whirling the gold by centrifugal action over the land it traversed we should have an allegory in action which would correctly describe the working of the railway system.'[30] Evidence based upon prices asked in estate agents' offices, and upon Seymour Teulon's submissions to the Royal Commission of 1867, suggests the following table of mid-century suburban land values.[31]

	Per acre 1839	Per acre 1869
Redhill	£50	£700
Hastings (1849)	£300	£2,000—£10,000
Weybridge	£20	£4,000
Reigate n.d.	£35	(1867) £1,000
Caterham n.d.	£30	(1867) £400

35% increment was the immediate average increase in value which Teulon assigned directly to the influence of the railways, over areas situated within one mile of the line, on level roads, falling off to 25% in two miles, and, more gradually, to amounts which were still perceptible up to six miles from the line. These observations tally well with more recent work on land values and suburban railways. Charles Hayes' work on the Chicago, Burlington and Quincy railroad may seem too far removed in time and circumstance from mid-Victorian Surrey

[29] *Memorandum for Witnesses*, Yorkhill Jury Trial, Mrs. Graham Gilbert's case, Glasgow Univ. Coll. of Solicitor's Papers, Box 1. My italics.
[30] H. Davies, *The Way Out* (1861), 32.
[31] H.C., 1865, XXXVIII, QQ.16485-8, *The Builder*, XXVII (1869), 205.

for any useful analogy to be drawn, but the patterns he found, once stated, have an inevitable and commonsense quality about them which invites comparison. Residential values appreciated as the distance from the line was reduced, until a point between a quarter and half a mile from the tracks was reached, where values were depressed. The point-to-point values 'formed a jagged line, with peaks close to the stations and dips between the stations'; and around each he found a 'rough pyramid with its apex at or near the suburban station.'[32]

In this wealth which they were creating, the railways had no share. Indeed if they required to extend their works at any time they might well find themselves contributing involuntarily, by the jury and arbitration procedures, to give the upward spiral of land prices yet another turn, at their own expense.

The statutory powers under which they were empowered to buy land also compelled them to sell lands surplus to requirement on completion of their scheme. They were usually given ten years in which to dispose of the land 'in such manner as they deem most advantageous'; and it was possible to apply for an extension of the time period, providing it could be shown that the land, though still unused, was likely to be required for the purposes sanctioned by the original Act. At the end of the ten years the land had to be offered back for sale to the original owner or his heirs, in whom the absolute right of pre-emption was vested. If he refused to buy it back, or could not 'after diligent enquiry' be found, then the land could still not be put up for sale in the open market. It must be offered, as if under Enclosure Bill procedure, 'to the person or several persons whose lands shall immediately adjoin the lands so proposed to be sold.'[33] The lands superfluous to railway requirements could, whilst unused, be let, or put to any use the railway company chose, provided they did not offer it for sale. Only one exception to this is recorded by Hodges' *Law of Railways*; that allowed by the Metropolitan Inner Circle Completion Act, 1874, which allowed the company to grant building leases and sell ground rents.[34]

So even on the few occasions when the railway company found itself in the role of vendor, it did not enjoy the full increment in land value which the passage of time, and its own expenditure in the district, might seem to merit. 'The witnesses that are brought up, as a rule,

---

[32] Charles R. Hayes, 'Suburban Residential Land Values Along the C.B. and Q. Railroad', *Land Economics*, XXXLII (1957), 177–81. The original idea of such a pattern came from Homer Hoyt, *One Hundred Years of Land Values in Chicago* (Chicago, 1933).

[33] W. Hodges, *A Treatise on the Law of Railways* (7th ed. 1888), I, 332.

[34] 37 & 8 Vic., c. 199, sec. 64–5.

generally prove to their own satisfaction that the land has sunk away enormously, and that the construction of our railway has injured the whole thing,' complained one railway director. 'If you are compelled to sell,' he was asked, 'do you labour under any difficulty in getting the additional value?—Yes we do; and then the adjacent owner does nothing to encourage us. He knows that the time will come when he may pounce down upon it and claim it at agricultural value, while meanwhile we have been building up a track, and he gets the whole benefit of our expenditure, in addition to the great advantage he has got from the increment of his own property. I may point out that the Lands Clauses Act was passed at a time when landowners were absolutely supreme in Parliament, in 1845, and did just whatever they liked; and although we have to pay large sums for injuring the property that we go through, and pay large sums by way of severance, we do not get anything whatever for the increment in value we give to the balance of the land. We may turn a property from £100 an acre value into a value of £500 an acre; but the owner will come along and charge us with the whole cost of the severance of his property, and the depreciation of his property by the side of our railway, and we are not entitled to claim a shilling set off by reason of the additional value which we put upon the balance of the land.'[35]

Although the sale of surplus lands constituted a welcome rebate on many schemes amounting on occasions to a return of about 20% of the original capital laid out, the railway companies' powers of sale were only limited.[36] They certainly did not extend to the purchase and re-sale of lands at improved ground rents, the short term development of building land, or the laying out of estates—and it was in these ways that the richest harvests were being reaped. Whilst the railway companies invested large amounts of capital with no better prospect than a three to five *per cent* return, adroit country gentlemen, suburban landowners, speculative solicitors and builders doubled and trebled their capital in a decade.[37]

It was suggested from time to time that at any rate some of the railway companies should be given additional legislative powers to own and sell land. Charles Pearson proposed a scheme in which the railway company would be proprietor and landlord as well as carrier; and Henry Davies, in 1861, suggested an iron tramway for traction engines, with a belt of 200–400 feet of land on either side belonging to

[35] H.C., 1906, XL, QQ.19892–4.

[36] John R. Kellett, *JTH*, VI (1964), 236.

[37] D. A. Reeder, *op. cit.* 106–7 quotes examples in the Notting Hill area in west London of appreciations of value from £800 to £1,800 in four, and £2,400 in six years in the 1850's.

the company.[38] R. W. Perks, an M.P., and ex-chairman of the Metropolitan District railway also suggested in 1904 that railway companies should be allowed to buy land to obtain a portion of the additional value they were creating.

If this were allowed, 'for railway companies projecting lines out onto unbuilt upon areas', the whole interest of the railway companies in energetic suburban development might be reoriented. 'My suggestion is, not to ask for bounties or bonuses, or local authorities subsidising our railways,' said Perks, 'but to ask for permission to acquire, and if we choose, to hold and get the increment of any uncovered building land, without being subject to these conditions as to sale.'[39] If his own company, the Metropolitan, were allowed to take, in this way, two or three hundred acres for development and sale, and were further allowed to run co-ordinated road services of electric powered feeder cars, to extend the catchment area of their suburban stations, it would be possible to abolish the 'Workmen's' ticket, claimed Perks, and to institute a new low price uniform fare, bringing regular suburban travel within the range of a far wider social class.[40]

The prospect of railway companies adding to their already considerable powers by becoming speculative landlords might well have been expected to cause any Commission to reflect carefully before adopting Perks' recommendations; but the Royal Commission on London Traffic of 1905–6, 'perhaps the strongest commission ever appointed by any British government', came down in favour of the proposal, as a most likely means of promoting that rapid and even spread of suburban growth which all agreed was so desirable.[41]

'We think it right to point out,' wrote the Commissioners, 'that the provision of the means of transit is a costly business and that some "recoupment" might be obtained by the judicious acquisition beforehand, at a fair price, of the land intended to be opened out for building.' London's traffic problems, the Commission decided, were capable of technical solution: 'there is no physical obstacle which could not be overcome by engineering skill; the difficulty is simply one of money.'[42]

[38] H. Davies, *op. cit.* 46. The idea was taken up again by the Light Railways movement. Why could not very light railways be laid, at a cost of £4,000 per mile instead of £40,000, if the margins of existing roads were used? See Joseph Taylor's letter to *The Builder*, XXVII (1869), 1 May, 351.

[39] H.C., 1906, XL, Q.19896.

[40] As the American policy had been for some years, H.C., 1884–5, XXX, QQ. 14175–7 (Meyer). On the other hand the Metropolitan railway company itself had tried feeder and catchment road services from 1866–1901, and discontinued them. The farming-out of subordinate operations caused financial and technical difficulties. P. A. Keen, 'Metropolitan Railway Road Services', *JTH* I (1953), 216–37.

[41] *Parliamentary Debates*, CLXX (1907), 179.

[42] H.C., 1905 (Cd. 2597) XXX, Report pp. 16, 30, 71. The land was to be bought by agreement and not be part of the compulsory purchase schedule.

A share in some of the direct appreciation of land values created, in part, by expenditure on transport improvements, would unlock large enough funds to cover any necessary expenditure; and would still leave untouched increments of 'betterment' in adjacent lands which would be substantial enough to give landowners an interest in laying out their property to accommodate the new communities.

However, no action, either upon this count or upon any of the Royal Commission's other recommendations, was taken by the new Liberal government which came to office after the electoral landslide of 1906. 'Governments are always "very fully alive" to the importance of the subject and so on; but then they always appeal to the wisdom of *festina lente*', complained Lord Ribblesdale in 1907, in reply to the 'sparse and shadowy' answer he had received, like Sir John Dickson Poynder 'in another place'.[43] They, and many other busy and distinguished men had given generously of their time over two years to produce a massive eight volume report which *The Times* described as 'publicly accepted as the standard text-book in France, Germany and America on urban traffic.' 'That appears to be the whole unction which the Commissioners are ever likely to be able to lay to their bosoms', Lord Ribblesdale concluded.[44]

The report and its recommendations disappeared into the pigeonholes; the new government pleading 'the greater urgency of other matters with which we have to deal.'[45] Some suggested that the report had been sabotaged by the L.C.C., through the influence John Burns exercised over Lloyd George. Whatever the political causes, the recommendations were laid aside indefinitely; and in the different post-war atmosphere the licensing of railway companies as real-estate speculators was more remote than ever. Apart from which, the deep tube railway, the municipally sponsored electric tram route and the motor omnibus were beginning to lay the new patterns of twentieth century urban and suburban traffic.

It is difficult to say whether, if the concessions suggested by Perks and endorsed by the Royal Commission of 1905–6, had been granted earlier, the pattern of suburban development would have been substantially different; whether total growth would have been accelerated or more evenly spread, or the social composition of the suburbs affected. One cannot escape the feeling that the railway companies, as speculative proprietors, might well have found themselves influenced by the same factors which decided suburban landlords, for preference, to give over their estates to limited-density high rental settlement.

This, certainly, was the policy eventually pursued by the only railway

[43] *Parliamentary Debates*, CLXXXI (1907), 10.
[44] *Ibid*. CLXX, 187.
[45] *Ibid*. CLXX, 189.

company exempted from the statutory ban upon residential estate ownership—the Metropolitan.[46] Watkin felt uneasy, from the beginning, about the long-term existence of such a large amount of surplus land. 'Parliament might,' he warned, 'some day say that it was a dangerous thing for a small railway company to have a rent roll of £80,000 a year, with about 1,000 tenants, and they (the Metropolitan) might be unwillingly compelled to sell the property.'[47] Accordingly it was deemed discreet to divide the ordinary stock into two portions, one representing railway earnings, and the other the rentals and profits of the surplus estate, and later still (in 1919) to set up a subsidiary company, Metropolitan Railway Country Estates, to which the Surplus Lands Committee's work was transferred.[48] The policies pursued by this company in the Rayners Lane, Amersham and Rickmansworth areas of the Chilterns in the 1920's and 1930's may perhaps be a misleading guide; but 'Metroland' (as their advertisements described the area they served) was typified by modest middle-class semi-detached houses, and there was little to mark the unusual parentage of the estates.[49]

Apart from this, historical practice gives little indication of the policies which might have been pursued had the privilege of land-ownership been bestowed, at an early date, to a larger number of companies. There were, of course, the well-known railway-owned houses, at Crewe and other railway towns, and various Metropolitan lodging houses owned by railway companies, like the Polygon building at St. Pancras. But there is a great difference between buildings acquired and put up, with shareholders' assent, to accommodate the company's workpeople or meet its rehousing obligations, and the free purchase of land as part of a scheme of speculative building and estate development by railway companies. Railway companies had no corporate authority to make such speculative purchases, still less to undertake the development and re-sale of lands acquired under compulsory purchase schedules.

There was, on the other hand, nothing to stop the directors of railway companies, or their contractors and solicitors, from using their business knowledge to make private investments in land; and a great deal of such speculation went on in the course of railway building.[50]

[46] Under 37 and 8 Vic. c. 199, sec. 64–5, as already mentioned.
[47] *The Economist*, 25 July 1885, 912.
[48] Every £100 stockholder was given £50 Surplus Lands stock, H.C., 1906, XL, Q.19549.
[49] H. P. White, *op. cit.* III, 137, Edwin Course, *op. cit.* (1962), 217–8, J. T. Coppock, 'Dormitory Settlements around London', *Greater London* (ed. J. T. Coppock and H. C. Prince, 1964), 275–9.
[50] Yerkes at Golders Green, Peto at Southend, H. Pollins, *loc. cit.* (1964), 51, Edwin Course, *op. cit.* (1962), 216.

However, no one, even the most highly placed in the company's counsels, could be completely sure, until the bill had passed the committees of both Houses, that a projected line would not be modified, or rejected. So from the previous November, when bills had had to be deposited, everyone was as wise as the railway directors. As Francis Gilbert, engineer of the Acton and Hammersmith railway remarked, in 1874, 'The moment a line is deposited and there appears a chance of carrying on, the speculative builders of London all rush to the ground to cover it with houses. Many cases have arisen where the Act has not gone through one committee before the builders were on the spot and commencing to sell.'[51] Such specialised dealings were better left to the solicitors, valuers and builders, who knew where to buy, what to pay, and how to exploit a site; and one would expect to find the railway directors placing private investments through them, rather than acting directly in their own names.

One practice which was severely frowned upon if it came to light, of course, was to buy land privately and then sell it at greatly enhanced prices to one's own company. John Parson's resignation from the Metropolitan railway in 1863 followed the discovery that he, together with Major-General Boileau and Colonel St. Quintin, two landowners in Fulham and Kensington, had just sold small pieces of land for which they had paid £800 per acre to the Metropolitan at the rate of £20,000 per acre.[52]

Rewarding though private investments by the directorate of the railway companies may have been to individuals, the effect upon company policy was different from that which statutory permission for corporate investment and sale of land might be expected to have produced. It was, no doubt, possible on occasions for an interested party to bend the opinions of his fellow-directors, and of the full-time professional staff of a railway company, to favour execution of a plan which would enhance his own private property investments. But such a policy could not be pursued overtly, and there was more than a possibility that other members of the company might feel some alternative scheme was more to their own advantage. Moreover, the railway companies did not belong to their directorates to use indiscriminately to promote their own indirect gain. There was a duty to return a profit to the shareholders which ensured that schemes, by and large, would have to stand on their own merit. If there had been a corporate interest in land purchase many of the objections to outright speculation in the choice of combined routes and land purchases would have been re-

---

[51] D. A. Reeder, *op. cit.* 105. The actual provision of facilities was the signal for a further rush of speculative builders. H.C., 1904, VII, Q.138.
[52] D. A. Reeder, *op. cit.* 270. T. C. Barker and Michael Robbins, *op. cit.* 126.

moved, and the whole background to railway policy on suburban fares and services substantially changed.

Perhaps the best guide one can find to the possible results of an entry by the railways into the speculative land market, is to look at their operations at the so-called 'railway ports', Holyhead, Fleetwood and Grimsby, where the railways invested heavily in docks. Although there are, of course, certain fundamental differences, this is possibly the nearest parallel one can find to the railway companies becoming landowners. The result, from the railway companies' point of view was satisfactory in terms of the direct financial return; and the three ports grew at a far faster rate than the norm for Britain.[53] Admittedly the financial return was partly the result of technical economies in trans-shipment; but, leaving the results aside, a point germane to the present discussion is the violent reaction which the preferential railway rates, given to develop traffic at the new ports, caused amongst established interests. This sustained outcry would have been redoubled if railway companies had been given the power to set up their own cheap housing estates around London and other cities, and to run services at privileged fares, or charge rents which included a season ticket. Railway amalgamations had already raised the fear of monopoly, and railway rates had been the subject of detailed enquiry and complaint by the 1880's.[54] Whatever the Royal Commission of 1905–6 might feel, violent opposition could be expected, not merely from those who favoured public or municipal schemes to link transport and residential development, but also, on the other flank, from the landowners, builders and solicitors who had been the contingent beneficiaries of railway promotion.

So the railway companies continued to enter the land market only as buyers, for specialised uses, and under unfavourable terms. The sense of injustice to which this gave rise was referred to by Charles Booth, who admitted that 'divergence of opinion had arisen as to the increment of site values which would follow' the growth of suburban centres. Booth, who had become convinced by his close study of London's conditions, as had Charles Pearson fifty years earlier, that cheap travel was the only answer to central housing difficulties, argued, in 1901, that the 'plums of advantage' should, if necessary, be thrown to the speculator, if it helped to speed the exodus of the working class. 'Are we to allow a disgraceful state of things to continue . . . and per-

[53] *Railway Rates and Railway Administration as affecting the Trade of Liverpool* (Liverpool, 1881), 11–12. Holyhead's trade with Ireland had doubled within ten years, whilst Liverpool's had only increased by 7%.

[54] H.C., 1881 (374) XIII and XIV; H.C., 1882 (317) XIII. In the following decade no fewer than six reports on rates were laid before Parliament by the Board of Trade, and two reports by Select Committees.

haps grow worse', he asked, 'because of a dispute as to the apportionment of the profit which will come from its abatement?'[55]

His question was meant to be a rhetorical one, but the answer was by no means as certain as Booth assumed. The apportionment of the increments in land value was, in fact, highly material to the speed and extent of suburban growth, and those who stood to benefit most from it either stood outside the railway companies, or drew their benefits outside their corporate framework.

3. *Apportioning the increments inl and value*

Two compromise solutions to the problem of apportioning land values were possible. The landowners might at any rate *give* the land necessary for railway building, or cede it on generous terms, instead of wringing from the railway companies the last penny of that compensation which the law so generously allowed. Or the landowners might be induced to put up substantial amounts of the capital necessary for railway extensions. By either of these methods the landowners would be contributing something in return for the increments they were likely to receive.

Both methods were practised, to a certain extent, but both were subject to certain drawbacks. Although there were no instances of outright gifts of land to the railway companies, there were quite a large number of examples of sale on very favourable terms. 'The landowners along there were so anxious to get a line made,' said a director of the South Eastern railway company (referring to the Caterham branch) 'that I believe the company bought the land on very good terms.'[56] Sometimes the generosity of the terms of sale was offset by the insertion of clauses in the deed of sale giving the right to demand that a station be erected when a stated number of houses had been built on the remaining land. At others the value of the bargain was reduced by awkward accommodation works and other stipulations. But quite generous local inducements were offered in this way, particularly in the free-ranging period of middle class suburban commuting in the 1850's and 1860's.

Two important points arose concerning these concessions over the selling price of land. The first was that although it might seem no more than fair to offer in this way to share the land profits to be made, it was essentially a bargain struck between individual landowners and the company. And though some might give, all would benefit in a given area. It was for this reason that J. B. Denton, in a paper to the Institute

---

[55] C. Booth, *Improved Means of Locomotion as a First Step towards the Cure of the Housing Difficulties of London* (1901), 4.
[56] H.C., 1867, XXXVIII, Q.16488.

of Surveyors, in 1869, rejected this means of encouraging railway promotion. 'A better scheme must be devised than that of asking landowners to give their land for nothing.'[57] The second point, to which reference will be made later, is that the initiative in such a transaction came largely from the area concerned: it was a local offer, and if it was not forthcoming the railways either had to pay the full price or look elsewhere.

There were also a large number of examples, dating back to the earliest railways, of suburban and urban landowners offering support to railway schemes by means of direct capital investment. 'A large landowner will take shares, or will subscribe to the line,' Mr. Rodwell explained to the House of Lords' Committee on the Central London Railway bill in 1871, 'for the purpose of getting the indirect advantages of railway communication to the district. He subscribes in such a case, not expecting to get a return upon his investment but for the purpose of getting the communication and indirect advantages of the railway.'[58] Rodwell was counsel for Lord Southampton, 109 of whose houses in the Tottenham Court Road area were scheduled, and who was in the curious position of subscribing to a railway whilst opposing it in committee. It was possible, Rodwell's argument ran, to wish to encourage in principle the building of additional lines of communication, whilst wishing to stand up for one's right over details; and the correct procedure for this was to oppose the bill, even a bill for a company in which one might have bought shares, but to oppose it merely on clauses and not on the preamble.

Others were less exacting about their terms than Lord Southampton, and merely subscribed unequivocally, looking to the indirect benefits, like Captain Ross. Captain Thomas Ross may well stand as a typical example of the smaller urban landowner who turned to railway investment in this spirit. 'I have subscribed £1,000 to this railway, the first I ever subscribed to,' he told the South London railway bill Select Committee, in 1857, 'because I lose tenants repeatedly by not being able to say positively that there will be a railway.'[59] He owned 78 houses in Clapham, 'all full of clerks', earning from £100 up to £400 per year, and able to pay a decent rent of £30 to £50 a year. They were discouraged, however, by the sixpenny, three-quarters of an hour, omnibus ride, and lengthy walk to travel to and from their work. 'My property is going to the dogs for want of a railway.'[60]

Other landowners were prepared not merely to subscribe but even

[57] J. B. Denton, 'On the Future Extension of the Railway System', *Trans. Institut. of Surveyors*, I (1868–9), 128–38, and discussion subsequently in *The Builder*, XXVII (1869), 205, 229.

[58] BTHR PYB 1/534, 20 July 1871, p. 10.

[59] BTHR PYB 1/84, 15 June 1857, p. 19.

[60] *Loc. cit.* p. 17.

to build their own branch line. The building of the Bexleyheath line, south east of London, by local initiative in the 1890's provides an excellent illustration of the methods employed by local promoters. Several landowners (one also a barrister) and two retired railway contractors floated the scheme, chose the route to pass through their property to the greatest advantage, and allocated a station each to themselves. Barnehurst station was opened for Colonel Barne, one of the landowners—though it was thirty years before housing went up on the scale anticipated; the site of Bexleyheath station was altered by a quarter of a mile to bring it onto land which Mr. Kersey, one of the directors and shareholders, owned and wished to develop; Kidbroke station was the price which had to be paid to persuade the Earl of St. Germans to withdraw his opposition; Eltham Park station was opened, by agreement with Lord Rowallan, to accommodate passengers from his estate.[61] Once parliamentary powers had been secured, the Bexleyheath railway company was taken over by the South Eastern railway company, as had originally been intended by the local promoters; though an approach to the London, Chatham and Dover company was required to persuade the S.E. to absorb the speculators' branch.

Edwin Course, in his interesting study of this line, also refers to a major difficulty encountered at Bexleyheath which, in fact, tended to recur regularly wherever local landowners and developers had promoted a line. It was the reluctance or inability to meet subsequent calls upon shares.[62] To subscribe for a railway in the sense of putting down one's name and paying the first ten *per cent* on the shares was one thing; it was quite another to meet subsequent calls for the remaining ninety *per cent* at a time when capital might be urgently required for developing the land through which the railway was to pass.[63] D. A. Reeder reports similar reluctance to pay the full amount on railway shares in the west London suburbs. An initial rush by large landowners to invest, in Notting Hill, Hammersmith, and west Kensington, was followed by tardy payments of share calls. 'It may be,' he writes, 'that what capital the local promoters had was tied up in trade, buildings or house property, at the time when the railway they had brought into being needed further finance.'[64]

Another obstacle which intervened, even for landowners who were willing to invest in railways, was the state of common law regarding charges against entailed estates. By 1874, the time of the land survey

---

[61] Edwin Course, *The Bexleyheath Railway, 1883–1900* (Woolwich, 1954), *passim*; *idem, op. cit.* (1962), 207–15.

[62] *Ibid.* 211.

[63] The commonest way of avoiding further calls was to sell the shares, even at a loss. *The Economist*, 21 October 1848, 1186.

[64] D. A. Reeder, *op. cit.* 101.

usually known as 'The New Domesday Book', something of the order of one half to two-thirds of English and Welsh land was entailed: that is to say, excluded from the free market by being attached to the family name.[65] The settlement could be set aside, and the estate broken up and sold in whole or in part, but only by 'expensive, prolix and vexatious' legal procedures.[66]

In a similar way the lands held by corporate bodies, ranging from the Brewers' Company to the Ecclesiastical Commissioners, were inalienable.[67] So that, like the private owners of settled estates, these corporations were in the peculiar position of being able to dispose of their land to a railway company—whose compulsory purchase schedule overrode even entail—but not able to dispose of it, or part of it, to raise money to invest in the railway company, or even to invest in the development of the rest of their estate. Since the land could not freely be sold, the usual way to meet any expenditures that were required to improve the estate, therefore, was to charge terminable annuities against it. A Private Bill would be secured for corporate or entailed property, setting out the advantages of the estate, 'lying commodiously', or 'conveniently situate' for building, stating the present and the probable improved rents, and the sum to be borrowed.

As the law stood until 1863 an estate's rent roll could only be burdened with these annuities for such tangible improvements as drainage and building, but in April of that year a Lords' Select Committee met to consider whether power should be granted to charge entailed estates for the purchase of railway shares, as being an improvement of a similar order.[68] Evidence was heard from many witnesses, including John Clutton, Agent for the Crown Estates, and an experienced railway valuer, who expressed the view that railways formed much better security than drainage for those seeking to improve their estate; a view in which he was supported, though more grudgingly, by George Ridley, one of the Enclosure and Tithe Commissioners.[69]

The money for railway shares would have been lent, to the landowners willing to burden their estates with the charge, by Land Improvement

[65] F. M. L. Thompson, *English Landed Society in the Nineteenth Century* (1963), 66–70.

[66] Although in law strict settlement was theoretically distinct from entail, in practice settlement was the usual instrument by which primogeniture was enforced. G. C. Brodrick, 'The Law and Custom of Primogeniture', *Systems of Land Tenure in Various Countries* (Cobden Club Papers, ed. J. W. Probyn, 1876). This article was itself typical of the agitation for a free land market in the 1870's which led to the Settled Land Act of 1882. Thereafter life tenants were able to sell easily, but the building even of branch railways was virtually finished. F. M. L. Thompson, *op. cit.* 319–26.

[67] Vera Zoond, *Housing Legislation in England, 1851–67* (London M.A., 1932), 17.

[68] H.C., 1863 (209) VII.

[69] *Ibid.* 23 March 1863, QQ.418–41; QQ.357–92.

companies, which already advanced money for improvements of the traditional kind, but had no power to make advances for shares. 'We are,' said William Napier, the managing director of one of these companies, 'agents between the money market and the landed interest.'[70] 'Supposing that a General Act were passed,' Earl Hardwicke asked Napier, 'what do you think would be the effect of it on the speculative railway world; would it not be immediately to turn loose an immense number of speculative solicitors over the whole country talking to the farmer, and immediately suggesting that every atom of land must be railroaded?'[71]

Hardwicke's suspicious attitude must have been shared by his fellow peers on the committee, for its final report, though conceding that the evidence laid before them 'proved that both the letting and selling value of land is in general greatly increased by its having the advantage of easy access to a railway', and that landowners 'would probably have contributed much more largely to these undertakings but for the obstacles opposed by the present state of the law', cautiously recommended that the Enclosure Commissioners should be consulted in each case, and that no charges should be levied until the Enclosure Commissioners were shown the railway completed and opened for traffic.[72]

These recommendations were incorporated into the Improvement of Land Act, 1864, and, of course, rendered the Act quite useless from the railway promoters' point of view. If the annuity could not be charged until the line was complete the whole point was lost, as the builder and contractor Charles Fox complained.[73] What was needed was loan capital, or share purchase, in advance of construction. Moreover the attitude of the Enclosure Commissioners was one of considerable scepticism. How would they know what services would be run, even if the required stations were opened, or how long those services would be maintained? What would be their frequency, convenience and cost? 'Drainage is not a speculation,' said one of the Enclosure Commissioners, George Darby, 'As to drainage I can see my way; as to buildings I get into considerable difficulty; but when I come to what I consider still more speculative as to value, namely railways, of course my difficulty is infinitely increased.'[74]

It can readily be seen, without multiplying further examples, that

[71] *Ibid.* 18 March 1863, Q.289–97. They charged 6½% and collected the improved rent charges. However his company—formed in 1853—had no power to advance money on railways. Q.197.

[72] *Ibid.* Q.270.

[72] *Ibid.* 23 April 1863, Report.

[73] *The Builder*, XXVII (1869), 209.

[74] H.C., 1863 (209), VII, 23 March, Q.303.

both of the suggested compromises over apportioning the land profit had serious drawbacks. Gifts of land, or sale on terms which represented a sacrifice of potential value by particular owners, were bound to be limited in scale so long as the benefits of rail communication could be seen to be general and not particular in effect. Share subscriptions by landowners to defray the cost and to share the risk of extending the line were handicapped by the state of the law and, if advanced out of spare funds, tended to fall short as soon as the scheme got under way, at the very moment when they were most needed. This is what happened for a time to the Metropolitan District railway in the mid-1860's, which came to a halt when confronted by 'the cabbage and asparagus fields of Fulham'.[75]

In fact, to the extent to which they helped to finance a line, landowners were deliberately choosing a smaller return on part of their capital. Their real interest lay in withdrawing capital from the scheme as soon as it was clear that other investors with less ambitious expectations, or with less local knowledge and opportunity for property speculation, could be induced to take over. Very large returns were possible, after all, in property dealings which owed nothing whatsoever to the railways. It was possible, if the requisite amount of capital were on hand at the right moment, to bring off a *coup* like that of the Glasgow surveyor and valuer Thomas Smellie. Choosing the area of Pollokshields and Bella-houston, rapidly growing inner suburbs, he bought a plot of land for £12,000 (plus £20,000 for the mineral rights) in March of 1863, and sold it in October of the same year for £102,000, trebling his capital in six months. This piece of property, on the Paisley road, was in no way connected with the railway, or even with the steady appreciation of land values. 'I do not call the difference an increase of value at all,' he explained, 'I call it buying in a slump and selling in detail.'[76] Railway investment, however much it might in general march with property appreciation, would obviously have to take second place if competition for funds occurred; and incidents similar in kind, if not in scale, to the land deal just mentioned, occurred in all rapidly-growing areas of the Victorian city.

4. *Demand and supply factors in the urban land market*

The inability of railway companies to share in the profits to be made from appreciation of land values, and the failure of methods to bridge the divergence of interests between the companies and landowners has an important bearing upon the pattern of suburban growth, and the participation of different railway companies in that growth.

[75] D. A. Reeder, *op. cit.* 94.

[76] Glasgow Univ. Coll. Solicitors' Papers, *Respondent's Proof*, p. 15, N.B. railway company v. Blackie and Bain, 1866–7.

The outcome of the railways' incapacity to reap corporate benefit from anything except the traffic a line generated was to give them a neutral, passive role in the outward spread of the larger Victorian cities. They played the classic role of intermediary between the supply and demand forces in the land market. On the one hand, the supply of residential land was subject to many factors quite outside the control of railway companies; on the other hand, the development of effective demand for housing was a slow and massive process in which the railway companies' influence in the nineteenth century was important at the margin, rather than paramount.

Considered in this light the observations of the railway managers concerning rail services and social class begin to make sense, and cease to appear either priggish or conspiratorial. That this was the way in which they themselves viewed their role can be argued from a closer examination of their opinions. Henry Partington, for example, speaking for the L. & N.W.—which was one of the most reluctant to concede cheap fares—revealed the ground upon which his company ultimately stood, in a series of exchanges with the Select Committee on Workmen's Trains, in 1904. At first he maintained, rather aggressively, that the L. & N.W., unlike some other companies, had never had any specific statutory obligation put upon it.[77] Then, realising that such a legalistic approach made no impression upon the Committee, he shifted his ground, placing the responsibility for his company's diminutive traffic in workmen's tickets at the door of the landowners in his area, who 'often object to the character of their property being deteriorated by the introduction of the working class.'

This opinion was no mere piece of self-justification put out by Partington to fox the Select Committee. In their confidential internal memoranda the railway companies had already debated this subject, and Partington had expressed similar views even more frankly in April 1898. 'What is more to the point,' he said, 'the Cheap Trains Act presumes that certain districts where the landowners and others are notoriously averse to the introduction of the working class element would become reconciled to it. The L. & N.W.'s London and suburban district is generally not working class, and there is no probability that the adoption of facilities for that class would make it otherwise.'[78] Henry Oakley, who presided over this meeting of the railway companies, emphatically rejected the role of social reformers for which the Cheap Trains Act had cast the railway companies. 'After discussion the companies are of the opinion that it would not be practicable or desirable

---

[77] H.C., 1904, VII, QQ.1813–45. Significantly Partington, who had the supervision of workmen's fares, was only an Assistant Goods Manager. The members of the S.C. were openly ruffled at the L. & N.W.'s casual attitude in sending a junior offcial.

[78] BTHR LNW 4/150, 4 April 1898.

to alter the principle of their present arrangements which have been the growth of many years, and are found to adapt themselves well to the wants and necessities of the Districts of varying character through which the Suburban lines of the several companies pass.'[79]

If reform of a suburb's class structure, and of its prevailing rents and class of residential accommodation were required, it was of little use expecting railway companies, who were reluctant intermediaries expressly forbidden to take part in property development themselves, to reshape their districts by means of a time-table and fares schedule.

The study of the considerations influencing the supply of land, and of making effective the growing demand for it, in and around Britain's major cities, is an extremely large subject, which has only here and there received the detailed historical treatment it merits. Nevertheless, in the more limited context of railway building it is possible to suggest some of the factors which entered into the equation.

a. *Demand*

On the demand side, the main factors were rising real incomes, improved means of raising credit for house-owning, the rate at which new jobs were created—in the outskirts as well as the central district—and the pressure of immigration from the countryside. To these demographic, employment and income factors must be added, if lengthier work journeys were contemplated, the general decrease in the length of the working day. Indeed, one of the earlier commentators upon the rise of the suburbs, S. J. Low, writing in the *Contemporary Review*, 1891, placed this higher in importance than rising incomes. A man 'is able to live in the suburbs, not so much because he has more wages as because he has more time.'[80]

The interaction of these demand factors with those of supply produced a long rhythm of building cycles which, as far as residential building was concerned, shared a sturdy independence of the more general trends in the Victorian economy's trade cycle. Recent studies by economic historians have devoted much attention to the phasing, amplitude and local variations of these building cycles.[81]

Three points arise from the historical study of demand factors in housing which are relevant to the present enquiry. In the first place, it is clear that building cycles tend to be very closely associated with migration cycles; indeed that some building cycles are 'little more than

---

[79] *Ibid.* Report on meeting.

[80] *Contemporary Review*, IX (1891), 557.

[81] H. J. Habbakkuk, A. K. Cairncross, E. W. Cooney, D. J. Coppock, P. J. O'Leary, W. A. Lewis, J. P. Lewis, S. B. Saul, Brinley Thomas, B. Weber and others. For a recent discussion and bibliography see J. Parry Lewis, *Building Cycles and Britain's Growth* (1965).

a migration cycle in disguise.'[82] Although the quantitative processes of internal migration have only recently been investigated, and our knowledge of them is incomplete, studies which have been carried out suggest that the growth of suburban building activity does not require explanation, as is still occasionally assumed, solely in terms of an outward current of house-seekers from the city centre.

The suburbs themselves were distinguished by mortality rates which were extremely favourable, on occasion as little as a half to two thirds of those in the central districts; and, indeed, the health of suburban life constituted one of its positive attractions.[83] Over the second half of the nineteenth century, therefore, perhaps 30% of the suburbs' population increase might be assigned to their own internal surpluses of births over deaths. Then again it is clear that internal migration did not take place mainly over long distances, or exclusively by railway routes. The new recruits to the growing suburbs were primarily drawn in from the surplus population in the immediately surrounding countryside. Contrary to popular impression, it was to the suburbs rather than to the city centre that most immigrants tended to go. R. Lawton's study of the distribution of Liverpool's population in the mid-nineteenth century showed the largest proportions of the suburban population had either been born locally, or had immigrated from the adjacent countries of Lancashire and Cheshire.[84] Roughly 45% of the inhabitants of the nine outer areas fell into this category. A further 25% of residents in the outer districts were long-distance immigrants from all parts of England, Wales, Ireland and Scotland. The remaining 30% came from 'the Liverpool area', including cross migrants from other outer suburban areas.[85] In other words at least 70%, and perhaps 75% to 80%, of Liverpool's suburban growth in the mid-nineteenth century was due to the arrival of immigrants from immediately neighbouring counties or from further afield; only 20% to 30% of the increase was due to migration from the city centre. This was also the impression gained by H. J. Dyos in his detailed study of the area south of the Thames. 'The usual picture of central London,' he writes, 'as the reception area for immigrants, who moved to the outer suburbs later, is

[82] A. K. Cairncross, *Home and Foreign Investment, 1870–1913* (Cambridge, 1953), 25.

[83] Even at the end of the nineteenth century death rates in, for example, Manchester, varied from 15·21 for the sparsely populated suburbs, to 29·22 for the 30,000 still living in the Central district, or 28·32 for Ancoats. This disparity was, in fact, one of the arguments used by cheap fares reformers. T. R. Marr, *op. cit.* 17 *et. seq.* Birmingham showed the same contrasting figures for Edgbaston and the central parishes. D. E. C. Eversley, *loc. cit.* 135.

[84] R. Lawton, 'The Population of Liverpool in the mid-nineteenth century', *Trans. of Hist. Soc. Lancs & Chesh.* 107 (1955), 89–120.

[85] *Loc. cit.* 119, Table 2.

misleading. Immigrants into the suburbs were far more numerous than those into central London itself.'[86] There is no evidence to suggest that the process of internal migration should have operated in a radically different way north of the Thames, or in the suburbs of Manchester and Birmingham.

It follows that it is not essential to postulate improved and cheapened rail transport to explain the suburban growth of population in the late nineteenth century. Looking at a series of maps of the rapid growth of towns it is all too easy to regard the great cities as growing organisms, rapidly expanding outwards from a central point, and to look upon the railways as necessary arteries in this organic growth. In fact the great part of population growth appears to have taken place by accretion at the periphery, not as the result of outward expansion; and the employment and travel patterns of the majority of immigrants were dictated by the requirements of the suburban life into which they had moved.

The second observation concerning housing demand and the railways concerns the money incomes of those who were to be housed and transported. As is well known, both money incomes and real incomes rose in the last third of the nineteenth century by between a third and a half; and the proportion of individual budgets spent on accommodation also tended to increase as income levels rose.[87] But this still left the number of would-be owner occupiers who could afford to purchase sites and houses relatively small.[88] Even amongst the middle classes houses were frequently rented, not bought, and amongst the ranks of the new suburbanites in the 1870's and 1880's only in Birmingham and London did the numbers of owner-occupied houses excite comment.[89]

The Royal Commission on Friendly and Benefit Building Societies, 1872, commented upon the rapid spread of facilities for raising mortgages, and estimated that perhaps five-sixths of those raised were on houses of a lower value than £300.[90] Yet with advances of only sixty *per cent* not uncommon, this still required that the intending house purchaser would have to save capital equal, possibly, to a year's salary; a task no easier to perform then than it is now. There were, besides,

[86] H. J. Dyos, *The Suburban Development of Greater London, South of the Thames, 1836–1914* (London Ph.D., 1952), 424.

[87] Money wages 1860, 1880, 1900 moved 58 to 72 to 94, cost of living 113, to 105, to 86. Yet average rents (1880–1900) actually increased by $12\frac{1}{2}\%$. A. L. Bowley, *Wages and Income in the United Kingdom since 1860.* (Cambridge, 1937), 28–32, 119–20.

[88] Between 70% and 85% of residential property was rented in the last two decades of the nineteenth century. H. J. Dyos, *op. cit.* (1961), 90, D. J. Olsen, *op. cit.* 6.

[89] In Birmingham some 13,000 small houses were stated to be owner-occupied in the early 1870's. MRL, Report of M.O.H., 19 January 1872, 34 *et. seq.* In London, although leasehold was the rule, it was possible to obtain freehold possession in the less thickly populated areas. H.C., 1887, XIII, QQ.4894, 4975, 5119.

[90] H.C., 1872, XXVI, and H. Bellman, *The Thrifty Three Millions* (1935), 31–40.

legal obstacles to the extension of the successful Victorian principles of self-help and co-operation into the sphere of housing.[91]

As a result the situation was such in the 1880's that it was possible to advance, as a serious and plausible argument, the opinion that effective demand for freehold purchase was so inadequate, even amongst the tradesmen and better-paid artisans, that the rapid extension of towns would have been impossible if the whole capital for purchase and building had had to be advanced by the occupiers.[92] By and large, even at the end of the century, the tenant and the lodger were far more common than the owner occupier.

The bearing of this upon railway fares and policy is fairly clear. The residents of the new suburbs of Walthamstow and Edmonton, who formed the working class commuter traffic of the Great Eastern, could afford, in addition to the time for travel and the annual expenditure (in small daily sums) of £2 10s in workmen's tickets, a rent of approximately £25 *per annum*. Even if the train fare had been reduced to nothing their annual rent paying ability would only have increased to £27 10s *per annum*. Altering the rail services to make, for example, the fare for the seven miles from Waterloo station to Wimbledon equal the fare for the seven miles from Liverpool Street station to Tottenham would not have made the working man and his family any more welcome in Wimbledon, or enabled him to purchase accommodation there with £25 *per annum*. For him there were houses at the right rent in the marshy lands to the north-east or in the 'mud and water' district of Fulham.[93] If he could rise to £30 *per annum*, West Kensington Park or Queen's Park could provide a middling range of rented houses; and if he had assured, reasonably-paid and respectable employment, and approached a Building Society, he might raise the mortgage on £300 for a house at Tottenham or Lambeth.[94]

The third point, arising from the shortage of effective demand for housing, is that those well-to-do middle class proprietors who had, perhaps several decades earlier, purchased freeholds or long leases on villas, often with substantial grounds, tended to exercise, together with

[91] Vera Zoond, *op. cit.* 19. A charter to begin operating as an improved dwellings company could cost £1,000 in the 1860's.

[92] H.C., 1887, XIII, QQ. 2747–56.

[93] The average weekly expenditure on rents of Charles Booth's classes B, C and D came to 6s 10½d, to 8s 7½d, and that of his 'comfortable' class E to 11s 1½d. Charles Booth, *op. cit.* I, 133. The specific examples he gives for Walthamstow are mostly lower—3s 6d per half house per week, or 4s 6d per floor—but those in better employment rose to £20 or even £30 per year (*i.e.* 7s 9d to 11s 6d per week). *Ibid.* I, 312–3. For Fulham see D. A. Reeder, *op. cit.* 52. Some of the north-eastern suburbs were also described as 'marsh places, hardly fit to erect houses on'. H.C., 1904, VII, Q.722.

[94] *The Survey of London*, XXVI (1956), 12, 138. Edwin Course, *op. cit.* (1962), 202. D. A. Reeder, *op. cit.* 48, 54.

their neighbours and ground landlords, a conservative economic influence over the district in which they had settled.

In certain areas where the break up of estates and the invasion of cheap speculative housing had gone too far to be withstood, the older inhabitants, as Charles Booth observed, 'by selling their land or disposing of their leases in this way, have managed to turn to profitable account the influx which it has been rather fashionable to lament.'[95] In general, however, the middle class suburb was more than able to defend itself against encroachment in the later nineteenth century. Sometimes the sanctions were very rigorous. The building of houses below a value of £1,000 or £1,500 could be specifically forbidden in a bill of sale for land—as in parts of Wimbledon.[96] On some Croydon estates in the last two decades of the century the minimum prime cost for houses specified in covenants was £600.[97] At least one other area, Tunbridge Wells, sent a strongly worded petition *against* reductions in train fares, on the grounds that cheap access from London might lower the district's social tone.[98]

Normally such extreme pressures were unnecessary. 'Houses were built,' W. Ashworth concluded from his recent examinations of the north-eastern suburbs of London, 'with an eye to the tastes and means of people in a particular range of social and economic circumstances, and from the very beginning of rapid suburban development it was common for most of the houses in one locality to be fairly similar in quality and cost. If a family's social condition changed considerably it was quite likely to want a different type of house, which often did not exist in its present neighbourhood, and consequently it would have to move to another district altogether, with a different but not less homogeneous social character.'[99] To any reader familiar with the social topography of his district the point needs no further elaboration. In Britain the names of suburbs have precise, though changing, nuances of meaning; they are not simply place-names but carry distinct social undertones.

Given this tendency towards social homogeneity in suburban zoning, the railway's policy appears no more than an appropriate response to demand. For some areas the provision of a limited and not particularly cheap transport service was a positive asset, and part of these areas' attractiveness to the type of resident they sought. Captain Ross, the

[95] Charles Booth, *op. cit.* I (1892), 297–8.

[96] H. J. Dyos, *op. cit.* (1952), 394.

[97] R. C. W. Cox, *Some Aspects of the Urban Development of Croydon, 1870–1940* (Leicester M.A. thesis, 1966), 147.

[98] Edwin Course, *op. cit.* (1962), 205. The petition was sent in 1874 to the South Eastern railway company.

[99] W. A. Ashworth, 'Types of Social and Economic Development in Suburban Essex', *London, Aspects of Change* (ed. R. Glass *et al.* 1964), 80.

estate developer in Clapham mentioned earlier, who had been trying to attract the new clerical lower-middle class resident in 1857, had spoken of a meeting of proprietors at the Boyer Arms, Manor Street, Clapham, where 'several proprietors said they were afraid to interfere in favour of the railway; that some of the higher order of people in Clapham, who keep their carriages there, were against it.'[100] The movement of the carriage-folk out to remoter southern suburbs was referred to later by *The Times* (1874). 'The people who can afford to spend £60 a year in season tickets fly further off and carry Wandsworth and Clapham into the heart of Surrey.'[101] £60 was, of course, more than twice the combined rent and fare of a Walthamstow or Edmonton commuter; and the first class season ticket customer was received just as deferentially at his railway station as at the new West End stores for 'the carriage trade'.

The movement of fashion can, to a certain extent, be traced with the aid of suburban Court Directories, but the essential point to be noted here is that the London and South Western or the London Brighton and South Coast railway companies were no more responsible for the emergence of a particular category of housing in Surrey (the so-called 'stockbrokers' belt') than the Great Western was for the emergence of the villas at Ealing, Barnes, Richmond and Windsor. The areas were given their character primarily by freely operating market bids for residential uses, and they only required relatively restricted rail services.

b. *Supply*

The timing and extent of suburban expansion in late Victorian Britain was largely determined by the gradual development of effective demand, through the operation of the population movement, employment and income factors to which reference has been made above. Supply factors, however, were perhaps still more critical in determining the topography of suburban growth. The supply of investment capital, though important in the long term, played a less immediate part in the provision of housing than might be supposed. 'There is no evidence to show that a building boom was ever terminated because capital was attracted to other directions,' S. B. Saul concluded in 1962; and his conclusion concerning the behaviour of the economy as a whole would find local application in areas where soundly based schemes were in progress.[102] Indeed it might even be the case that schemes which were

---

[100] BTHR PYB 1/84, 15 June 1857, p. 8.

[101] *The Times*, 25 June 1874, 9.

[102] S. B. Saul, 'House Building in England, 1890–1914', *Ec.HR*, XV (1962), 134. J. Calvert Spensley, *loc. cit.* 185–97 gives a full account of the factors influencing supply, including the rate of interest on capital, with examples of the effect a change in interest rates might have.

not particularly sound might still be executed, if the local builders, solicitors and speculators were committed to them. Once an opportunity, or imagined opportunity, had been created, by a change in the local land market, the operations of the speculative builder and solicitor showed a sturdy indifference to the finer points of national finance. Only considerations such as these can explain the wide variations in the timing of building cycles between one area, or one town, and another. 'Building' as S. B. Saul puts it, 'was internally and positively determined for the most part, and was not a residual activity.'[103] The *Building Societies' Gazette*, reviewing the apparently irrational bursts of activity in the London area, came to the same conclusion: that houses were not 'built in accordance with the rules of supply and demand, but to develop, as it is called, estates and to create ground rents.'[104]

The creation of improved ground rents was the primary concern of the landowner, and—the argument will now be put forward—it was his influence, above all, which was stamped upon the character of neighbourhoods, and of the railway services which they would attract, and were able or willing to support. Time and again the local proprietors' control of land supply, and their attitude towards the course of development in the outlying areas they owned, together with the attitudes of the established residents and builders, determined the type of service the railway companies could offer. An interesting clash between James Allport, General Manager of the Midland railway company, and C. D. Sturge, a local resident who complained to the Royal Commission of 1867 concerning the Midland's apathetic suburban policy near Birmingham, serves to illustrate the strict limits within which railway policy was confined.

The Great Western railway company, Mr. Sturge pointed out, had opened stations for local traffic at Acock's Green, Solihull and Knowle, 4, 7, and 11 miles respectively from Birmingham, and land in those areas had undergone the profitable conversion from agricultural to building uses. By comparison, the Midland railway company, Sturge complained, had only opened one station, at King's Norton, 7 miles out, and ran only a lethargic service of five trains a day. There had therefore been no equivalent rise in the value of land near King's Norton.[105] Since the further cross questioning, and Allport's rejoinder, illustrate the uneasy balance of interests between resident landowner and railway company which had already emerged clearly by the 1860's, they are perhaps worth detailed recapitulation and comment.

'You do not think,' Sturge was asked, 'that it is part of the duty of a railway company to look after the interests of the owners of land and

[103] S. B. Saul, *loc. cit.* 135.
[104] *Building Societies' Gazette*, 1 January 1909, quoted in Saul *loc. cit.*
[105] H.C., 1867, XXXVIII, QQ.785–8.

to so regulate their traffic that they shall raise the value of their land?—No, but of course the railway takes land compulsorily; it is presumably on the understanding that the company shall do their best to develop the trade.'[106] The Commissioners put it to Mr. Sturge that the railways had, in fact, paid generously for any land they had acquired, including an element of compensation for the forced sale. 'Does it not follow that the landowner has no claim upon the company to cultivate traffic in his particular neighbourhood?—He has this claim I think that when a railway is once made no one else is allowed to make another in the same direction.'[107]

These were the typical arguments used against the railway company. Allport, in his reply, denied that land had failed to appreciate at all at King's Norton. Mr. Sturge had mentioned £60 to £80 an acre as the selling price of land; the Midland railway had paid £500 an acre, and Allport had cause to believe that general values had trebled since the railway was built. If this increase were not enough, Allport concluded, 'My answer to him is this, that we run five trains each way per day to King's Norton, which is not a large place; and in that neighbourhood until a recent period there has been a very considerable difficulty in obtaining land. The Baroness Windsor would not sell any land for building purposes. I admit that it is a very beautiful district, and if land could be readily obtained, it would be in the interest of the Midland company, and I am sure they would avail themselves of it, to encourage the building of suburban residences; but there has been a very considerable difficulty until recently in getting land at all. There are two or three landowners who have refused to part with their land, the Baroness Windsor especially, and she probably has the best for residences.'[108] Here was one instance where the supply of land for residential development was not forthcoming, and to look at the number of stations on the Midland line, or count the services and fares would be irrelevant.

It was a similar story at another Birmingham suburb, Solihull, where traffic up to the city centre still only amounted to three or four hundred passengers per day, and receipts at the ticket office averaged £220 per week, even in 1903.[109] 'The railway is only tolerated at a distance,' wrote a contributor to the *Birmingham Daily Mail* in that year.[110]

'Let a stranger seek the whereabouts of the village as he stands outside the station and his eye will search in vain, unless perchance it alights on the top

[106] *Ibid.* Q.789.
[107] *Ibid.* Q.798.
[108] *Ibid.* Q.12415.
[109] BTHR GW 4/281, 10–11.
[110] *Birmingham Daily Mail*, 19 November 1903.

of the grey church steeple, which a belt of shady trees only just fails to obliterate from view. It is good step to the High Street with its leafy avenue.'

'Where are the *small* houses?' asks the stranger, emphasising the adjective. And the answer comes that there are none—except the cottages. The real explanation is that the landowners do not want them and will not have them. They mean to keep the place select. So it follows that, save for the needs of those who live and labour in the village, there are no houses built in Solihull of what may be termed the common or garden variety. They must cost £500, at the very least, to put up. Only upon that condition can one obtain the necessary land.'

Similar attitudes towards the disposal of land, and to the types and cost of rail service required, can be seen in the Birmingham suburbs of Acock's Green or Moseley, the Manchester suburbs of Didsbury or Knutsford, the Liverpool suburbs of Allerton, Wavertree, Litherland or Grassendale, or in many of the outer London suburbs. Indeed the closer and more detailed the study, the more important become the attitudes and decisions of local landowners, builders, and established residents, and the less readily does the mere establishment of a rail linkage seem to provide the dramatic explanation of the course of suburban growth.

Perhaps the village of Radlett, near St. Albans, of which J. T. Coppock has made a close local study, may serve as an example of a London suburb far enough out to be totally dependent upon a railway link for daily communication with the City, but deriving part of its residential attraction from the fact that the service was restricted and expensive. In 1868, when Radlett station (on the Midland (St. Pancras) line) was opened, the whole adjacent area was owned in four blocks; three mansion houses—Newberries, Aldenham Lodge and Newlands, each set in extensive park or meadow land; and the large Kendall estate of farms and woodland, owned by Lord Phillimore. The village itself consisted merely of a few score cottages for local agricultural and domestic workers.[111] For thirty years, the village remained substantially unchanged, in spite of its rail connection; the principal addition by the time of the 1896 Ordnance Survey being a school. Between 1894 and 1914, however, the village grew rapidly, the most important reason being not so much the improvement or cheapening of train services, as the change in the attitude of local landowners. An estate office was opened on the Kendall estate, and the land was conveyed by Lord Phillimore to his son Robert, who was willing both to sell detached plots and to commission builders; Aldenham Lodge was sold to a developer from St. Albans, who laid it out in roads and building sites. Newberries and Newlands came onto the market later, in the inter-war period. The new houses which arose on the Kendall and Aldenham

---

[111] J. T. Coppock, *loc. cit.* 279–81.

Lodge estates at the turn of the century were substantial, and built to a density of four per acre. In marked contrast, a small working class quarter of crowded terrace houses, ten to the acre, was run up immediately to the west of the railway station for the growing numbers who found local employment, as domestic servants, tradesmen's assistants and in retail and service occupations. The village remained exclusive, and at least one newcomer mentioned the poor train service as the reason he had chosen Radlett for residence.[112]

Of course other late nineteenth century examples could be found, both in the inner and outer suburbs, in which the situation was the reverse of that at King's Norton, Solihull or Radlett, and local landowners pressed forward eagerly with land for development at the mere rumour of a railway linkage. Even so, there was a strong preference for middle class estate development; and the further out the suburb, the fewer alternative means of transport there were, and the more complete the dependence on the railway, the stronger this preference became.

In general the most important single factor in determining the release of estates of villas, parkland, and farms onto the market may well have been simply the fortuitous timing of the landowner's death. Added to this were the questions of possible debt burdens, or the financial circumstances and personal inclinations of the inheritors of the estate; and sometimes the original landowner's intentions might extend beyond his own lifetime, by means of clauses in a will, or by restrictive entails or settlements. A widow might wish to dispose of part of the estate but keep the house; an heir might wish to sell the whole property, or alternatively to develop it energetically himself—by selling freehold plots under covenant, by leasing to a developer, or by directly engaging a builder; trustees might wish to postpone any decision for the time being. R. C. W. Cox, one of the most recent researchers into the factors affecting the land market in a suburban area, confronted with these complicated personal and legal factors, has been tempted to conclude that, in Croydon at any rate, 'the timing of the process of sale for building is largely a matter of chance.'[113] One 82-acre estate in Croydon came onto the market because the East India Company's training college was closed down after the Indian Mutiny; another 87-acre estate, ripe for residential development, was bought from the Earl of Eldon by a paper-mill owner from Kent, who proceeded to ignore its development potential, and merely used the estate for private residence himself; confining his sales to the detachment of a few parcels of land (such as the Lodge) and making careful, but uncovenanted transfers of ownership. At his death the surplus land, surrounded on

112 *Ibid* 281–4.
113 R. C. W. Cox, *op. cit.* 144.

three sides by other buildings, was presented by his daughter to the public as open parkland.[114]

Apart from the marked personal influence of landowners, varying from the orthodox to the status-seeking, or occasionally the bizarre, the land market was also subjected to further inertia by the provisions of the legal code. For example, in the rapidly growing residential suburb of Hampstead the four hundred acre estate belonging to Sir Thomas Maryon Wilson was withheld from the market until his death, in 1869, because there was no heir-apparent to agree that the entail should be broken.[115] In this case, again, the critical factor was the original proprietor's death. It is impossible, at the moment, to say how common a cause for the break-up of estates the death of the owner was, compared with other factors—the collapse of banks, the miscarriage of investments, over-spending and mismanagement of the estate, foolish business ventures. But it seems reasonable to suggest that personally owned estates did not respond, within intervals of time which would constitute reasonable supply lags in other economic fields, to the opportunities presented from year to year. Even the land Companies and Building Societies, which purchased land with a view to long-term speculation, cannot always have found it easy to pursue consistent policies. Like personal owners, they sometimes suffered from vicissitudes in their internal finances, and did not generally control enough of the land supply to be free to choose, and adhere to, particular development policies. The placing of land on the market is not, after all, a matter which can be executed precipitately without loss; and so the business firms, and the corporate and the charitable bodies disposing of land had, in most areas, to take their cue from the decisions of private landowners.

Between the 1850's and 1890's, the supply of land was relatively plentiful in relation to the numbers of middle-class commuters with the funds and inclination to live at a distance from the city centre, and a blank wall was usually presented only by landowners who genuinely wished to stay in residence themselves, or by those wealthy enough not to be tempted to break up an asset as valuable and rapidly appreciating as a well situated estate. All this changed, however, as the numbers able to travel increased and began, under the cheap fares, to include those whose means precluded them from purchasing and properly maintaining property, who were looking for low-rented accommodation, and whose social tastes and behaviour were considered to depreciate the value of existing adjacent property in the district. Confronted with this relative alteration in the conditions of demand to supply, more landowners near the great cities came under pressure to accept housing

[114] *Ibid.*, 138–141.
[115] Hugh C. Prince, *loc. cit.* 130.

standards which might depreciate their own, or their neighbour's' holdings.[116] In this context it is easy to understand how exclusive train services might tacitly be welcomed as a means of socially filtering the growing inflow of residents.[117]

The attitude could not be carried to extremes, of course, by those who controlled the supply of land, for even the meanest accommodation could provide ground rents which showed a substantial improvement over agricultural rents; and there was a tendency, therefore, on inferior ground, to accept any residential development rather than none. If any more promising development were in view, however, the owner tended to wait for the further appreciation which might accrue to him if he held his land in reserve. The attitude was described by Edgar Harper, Statistical Officer to the L.C.C. in these words. 'It may be an advantage to a landowner to have a large block of small property of this kind' (the Walthamstow/Edmonton kind) 'put upon his land; he would get an immediate return; but then, on the other hand, if that small property did not come, years afterwards he might get a better class of property if he could wait; so that there is something on each side.'[118]

Apart from this preparedness to wait for better development prospects there were also a number of anxieties felt about railway schemes by landowners which added to their hesitation. What about the landowner who supported a scheme, had his land intersected and then found he was 'left remote from the station?', asked J. B. Denton.[119] This had been known to happen not infrequently. What about the scheme which a landowner originally supported but which went into suspended animation, tied up his land and made it difficult to get tenants, and was kept alive indefinitely by five yearly Extension of Powers bills?[120] What about the land schemes projected with a railway as an essential and integral part, like those of the Muswell Hill Estate and Alexandra Palace companies, which were let down by a railway abandonment bill?[121] These doubts frequently added to the considerations already mentioned, to curb still further the enterprise of estate owners, upon which alone the

[116] Examples given before the Town Holdings Select Committee included Hornsey, where it was 'impossible to get freehold in consequence of land being held by one proprietor', and Finsbury Park where 350 acres were held by three owners. H.C., 1887, XIII, QQ.9312, 4765.

[117] See William Birt's argument concerning Noel Park in App. 4.

[118] H.C., 1904, VII, Q.143.

[119] The Builder, XXVII, (1869), 205, 229.

[120] For this reason landowners' counsel sometimes asked the Committees to make sure that there was an adequate fund to pay their clients in full and without delay for land scheduled to be taken. BTHR PYB 1/534, 20 July 1871, 9–10.

[121] Putting an investment of £650,000 in jeopardy, counsel for the two companies claimed. BTHR PYB 1/483, 6 April 1869, p. 11 (Merewether).

railway companies, in the existing state of the law in 1900, could rely for suburban traffic.

5. Conclusion

The remarkable growth of Britain's major cities in the nineteenth century, and the internal processes by which each arranged its expanding use of land for commerce, industry and housing, is an extremely complex phenomenon, not likely to be explained by any search for single causes. The growth of the residential suburbs, for instance, was a process in which social aspirations and prejudices played a part as important as strictly economic factors; and even within the commercial world of the city centre movements of fashion took place which could not always be explained in simple terms of access, floor space and rentals.

The desire to reduce these confusing and intricate elements of urban growth to some sort of order has occasionally led writers to seek in the railways a prime cause which would provide a single major explanation of the expansion of the great cities and their suburbs by means, almost literally, of a *deus ex machina*.

Unfortunately the truth about the railways is by no means as simple as some would have it.[122] It would, indeed, be very convenient if the railways could provide such a key, and if the growth of a district could be explained merely by establishing the date of opening of its station. But, as already pointed out, the railways' contribution to growth was shared with other more modest forms of transport to an extent often overlooked, and loose generalisations about effects should not be made on the basis of mere physical rail linkage, without consideration of subsequent services, fares and traffic.

The direct effects of railway building are, after all, considerable enough in themselves to require no exaggeration. They profoundly influenced the internal flows of traffic, the choices of site and patterns of land use, the residential densities and development prospects of the central and inner districts of the Victorian city in the ways which have been discussed and illustrated. They manipulated local authorities, overloaded Parliament, wrecked or evaded attempts at bureaucratic control, monopolised for specialised uses large areas of urban land which are only partially being released again in the 1960's, cut great swathes through the cities as completely as a blitz. Admittedly the nature and timing of the outward expansion of residential housing

---

[122] As in Isard's classic statement of the extreme view. 'Transport and building construction, both vital economic activities, represent in a rough manner the beginning and end of the causal relation respectively.' W. Isard, 'A Neglected Cycle: the Transport-Building Cycle', *Review of Economic Statistics*, 24 (1942), 149.

depended partly upon the growth of demand factors in the economy; the location of that growth depended partly upon land ownership; but it was the railways which made feasible the widely spaced clusters of villa residences which provided a Victorian nucleus for the more intensive development of many a dormitory suburb in the twentieth century.

Behind these spectacular effects of Victorian railways upon urban landscapes and society several much older and larger processes can be perceived. Two to which attention is particularly drawn by the subject matter of the present enquiry are: the slowly-developing patterns of land ownership, together with the peculiarly complex superstructure of law and precedent attached to them in Britain; and the multifarious and persistent market activities generated within the city itself.

The Land, together with Capital and Labour, constitute the great factors of production in classical economic theory; and, in a sense, the whole of economic history can be viewed as no more than the unfolding of these prime elements. But although very full studies of the role of capital have exercised some of the most perceptive writers in economic history in the last two decades, and the study of the role of labour has traditionally been of great importance for even longer, there has been a tendency—perhaps because of the agricultural connotations of the word—to regard land as an element of decreasing importance in the increasingly urban and industrial economy of the late nineteenth century; although some writers have attempted to redirect attention to this most important topic.[123] In fact, dwelling house rents consistently grew faster than the National Income, increasing their share from 5% to 7½%.[124] Specifically urban site rents played a large part in this increase, and an idea of the order of magnitude of the share which fell to them may be seen from H. W. Singer's calculations. By 1913 'urban land rent exceeded the profits of railways, or the income from Home, Colonial and Foreign Government securities, or the total income-tax yield, all taken for the whole of the United Kingdom.'[125] The increase in the average price paid for housing increased by 85% between 1845 and 1913; an increase which is more remarkable than it may seem at first glance, since wholesale prices, and even building costs, were not significantly higher in 1913 than in 1845.[126] Part of this cost was

[123] F. M. L. Thompson, *op. cit. Idem* 'The Land Market in the Nineteenth Century', *Oxford Economic Papers*, IX (1957), 285–308. David Spring, 'The English Landed Estate in the Age of Coal and Iron: 1830–1880', *Journal of Economic History*, XI (1951), 3–24.

[124] B. R. Mitchell and Phyllis Deane, *op. cit.* 366. The figures are £12,200,000 (in 1801, when the Gross National Income was £232,000,000) to £134,200,000 (1901, Gross National Income £1,642,900,000) or from roughly 5% to 7½%.

[125] H. W. Singer, 'An Index of Urban Land Rents and House Rents in England and Wales, 1845–1913', *Econometrica*, 9 (1941), 228.

[126] J. Parry Lewis, *op. cit.* 156.

undoubtedly produced by the marked improvement in the average standard of house—its size, internal space, and amenities. But part was also produced by the general commercial pressures which gave added value to the urban sites themselves, and placed an unearned increment in the pockets of the great and small urban landlord. Whilst house rents rose by 85% between 1845 and 1914, the actual land, or site, rents rose by nearly 1200% upon the area built up in 1845.[127]

Indeed, as will have been implicit in much that has been said earlier, it is necessary, even in the shadow of one of the most revolutionary forces of the nineteenth century, to turn away from the technology and economics of transport to explain the patterns which emerged on the ground in the great Victorian cities. If cities were featureless checkerboards, a model for a rail transport could be, and indeed has been, sketched out; but cities, in August Lösch's phrase, 'are miniature copies of the economic landscape'.[128] At any given moment the precise ways in which each city absorbs or exploits innovation, and the specific alterations in the pattern of its land uses, are critically influenced by pre-existing factors; of which the most important single one, in the context of the present enquiry, has seemed to be the framework of land titles.

In many ways urban landowners were the most important single agents of change; more important than the railway managers, whose imagination and foresight could often be exercised only within very strict limits. The landowners profited at all stages of railway building, and probably exercised the greatest single influence upon the selection of central sites, upon the location and character of suburbs; and even exercised a lesser, though still considerable influence, upon the costs of the service offered.

The antique and cumbersome body of common law regarding property in England and Scotland served to magnify the influence which would naturally have attached to land title under any circumstances. However much the railways may have been free to frustrate or evade interference by local and central government in the nineteenth century, no one could for a moment entertain the thought that they were free of the trammels of common law. And, under the law regarding entail and settlement, the ideal was that the land should not change hands or change uses at all; such flexibility as the market might have shown was still further reduced, and the legally privileged position of the owner of settled land maintained, often against his will. Railway initiative was curbed, municipal enterprise reduced to impotence in the late nineteenth century because all projects were 'tainted and paralysed', as Joseph Chamberlain complained, 'by the incurable timidity with which

[127] H. W. Singer, *loc. cit.* 224, 230.
[128] August Lösch, *The Economics of Location* (Yale, 1954), 440.

Parliament is accustomed to deal with the sacred rights of property.'[129]

Chamberlain's strictures may partly have been the product of a moment's exasperation in a man of action, but they were also, it may be argued, not an inaccurate comment upon the conduct of Parliamentary business. It is still impossible to look through the Commons' and Lords' *Journals* or Committee Minutes, *Hansard*, or the *Private and Local Statutes*, without experiencing a sense of surprise at the distribution of Parliamentary attention. The greater part of Parliamentary time seems to be taken up by legislation not to decide how the country should be governed, but by whom it should be owned. A random sample of Parliamentary business is as likely to produce Enclosure Bills, in the eighteenth and early nineteenth centuries, as affairs of political or diplomatic moment; and in the mid-nineteenth century Railway Bills came to occupy a similar proportion of Parliamentary time. Though radically different in nature and content both Enclosure and Railway Bills shared one characteristic in common. They were both legislative acts to re-arrange existing property rights and relations; and, indeed, in some important particulars, such as the privileges bestowed upon adjacent property owners, they were drafted in an identical spirit.[130]

It may seem no more than a natural distortion of perspective that so great a proportion of Parliamentary time should be occupied by discussions concerning property in a body which, although it conducted debates upon Cabinet and executive decisions, was primarily concerned with making laws. But perhaps it is worth reminding ourselves that, in the view of most of the electorate until 1867, or even 1884, this was the prime function of Parliament: not to develop positive policies, even upon such matters of domestic concern as public sanitation, and certainly not on railway building, but simply to maintain the rule of common law and to safeguard property. In a country possessing no open frontier, fortunate enough not to be subjected to pressing military or strategic considerations, and with an ancient and complex system of property laws, railway building tended to be strongly influenced by land ownership titles.

Yet although land ownership exercised such a powerful influence upon the rapidly evolving cities of the nineteenth century there is, as yet, no full scale and concerted investigation of urban land ownership and land enterprise. The deposited solicitors' papers which could give a closer insight into the mechanism of urban growth are still largely unused, and indeed are being dispersed and destroyed at an alarming

---

[129] *Fortnightly Review*, new series XXXIV (1883), 767. The burden this excessive regard for property rights placed upon local authorities is described in detail in W. Ashworth, *The Genesis of Modern British Town Planning* (1965), 101–10.

[130] W. Hodges, *op. cit.* I, 332.

rate. The study of the solicitor as entrepreneur, and the treatment of surveyors' or Building Society records, though of absorbing interest, still await historical presentation.

The second of the larger and older processes upon which some side-light is thrown by the study of urban railways is that of the city's market activities. These activities, measured in modern terms by the incidence of land values, are in a sense as old as the city itself, and were both a function and a cause of the Victorian city's increase in size. The histories of London and the four great provincial cities diverge markedly in this respect; for London already manifested many of the typical features of the great city at the time the provincial centres were mere craft villages. The problems raised by the emigration of the upper classes to the suburbs, together with the closely associated problem of defining the boundaries of municipal jurisdiction and taxation—both of which one might think of as typically Victorian problems—occurred in London as early as the late seventeenth century. Indeed it was the tendency of the business classes to earn a living in the central district whilst shunning the duties of municipal office and the burdens and taxes of central residence, rather than the ravages of the Great Fire and Plague, which brought the Corporation of London to the point of declared bankruptcy in the 1690's.[131]

Although the other cities did not demonstrate such mature urban symptoms two hundred and fifty years before the coming of the railways, they all began to undergo some fragments of the same experience in the course of the next hundred years. The impact of the greatly increased maritime trade of the early and mid-eighteenth century; the shocks to the urban structure when manufacture lost its dependence on rural waterpower, and when each city became a reception centre for the rural population explosion in the late eighteenth century: each of Britain's five great cities found its own way of encountering and absorbing these experiences.

The major adjustments required to come to terms with the locomotive in the nineteenth century constituted just another episode. If the steam locomotive by some chance had not been invented, economic progress would not have halted—as economists on both sides of the Atlantic have been at pains to point out recently.[132] The process of capital formation would have continued, as would the processes of urban growth, and of the evolution of central business, credit and marketing functions in the five largest Victorian cities; though they

[131] John R. Kellett, *The Causes and Progress of the Financial Decline of the Corporation of London, 1660–94* (London Ph.D. thesis, 1952) 264–315.

[132] R. W. Fogel, *Railroads and American Economic Growth* (Baltimore, 1964). B. R. Mitchell, 'The Coming of the Railway and United Kingdom Economic Growth', *Journal of Economic History*, XXIV (1964), 315–336.

would have been directed into different moulds. If one bears in mind the large practical role in urban growth played by orthodox, horse-drawn transport, and the very broad limits within which growth was possible without steam locomotion—at least to the two million population total achieved by pre-railway London—the railways fall into a more modest perspective. To stress the subordination of railway building to these larger processes, and to underline the pre-eminent importance of property ownership and land value patterns, is not to diminish the importance of the railways, but rather to attempt to weave them into the more general texture of urban history.

Appendices

1. Land costs as an element in railway expenditure during the constructional phase, 1825–50.

2. Agreement between Brassey, Peto, Betts and others, and the Union railway company.

3. A note on nineteenth-century compulsory purchase and arbitration procedures.

4. Evidence by the general manager of the Great Eastern railway company to the Royal Commission on the Housing of the Working Classes, 1884–5.

Appendix I

Land costs as an element in railway expenditure during the constructional phase, 1825–50

The table below presents a revised estimate for the various elements of railway expenditure in the second quarter of the nineteenth century. Similar calculations have already been presented before, by Harold Pollins ('A Note on Railway Constructional Costs 1825–1850', *Economica*, 19 (1952), 395–406) in an article which, though it has served for many years as a valuable corrective to the wilder stories of 'blackmail' land prices, leans in the direction of understating the quantities of investment capital consumed in land purchase.

There are, to put it as briefly as possible, two grounds for objection to the table in *Economica*. First, although the 27 companies listed do include most of the major lines, the method of assessment Pollins has adopted—'using figures taken from the Accounts at a date within a short period after the completion of the individual lines'—leads to anomalous results. For example, the total expenditure of the Liverpool and Manchester, the Grand Junction, and the London and Birmingham railway companies taken from Accounts dated 31.5.30, 30.6.37 and 31.12.38 respectively, comes to £739,165, £1,496,037 and £4,751,135. At the other end of the scale the Accounts of the Chester and Holyhead, or the South Wales railway companies are examined for 31.12.50 and 30.6.54, and their total expenditures given as £3,223,062 and £3,546,143. The proportions spent upon land are stated in each case, and are no doubt individually accurate. But it makes no statistical or historical sense to add together these sets of monetary figures, gathered at intervals spanning twenty four years. At the time the Chester and Holyhead, and the South Wales companies had spent three to three and a half millions each, the three constituent companies of the L. & N.W. amalgamation had spent not seven millions—the weight attached to them in the *Economica* table—but twenty millions. In other words, the expenditure of the later, and usually smaller, companies is exaggerated by the wide time scale used for the selection of monetary statements.

This difficulty is represented in the text of the article as a necessary evil. 'The ideal of course would be to have figures giving the total constructional costs of the railways with the proportions spent on the different components under the headings of land, parliamentary expenses and permanent way expenditure. But such statistics are not directly available.' A table giving this information has come to light in the course of the present research, giving the constructional and the land costs separately, the Parliamentary expenses, and the cost of Railway Plant for a large number of companies, in return to an order of the House of Lords dated 3 May 1849; and the statistics concerning the main companies are reproduced below.

Although such a return from a wide range of companies at (as nearly as possible) the same moment of time escapes the statistical anomalies referred to above, it is still open to the objection that it depends upon figures supplied by the companies themselves, and which are, therefore, subjected to lags of information, or even deliberate distortion. But although all the items might be subjected to alteration, there is no reason to suppose that land prices were more likely to be inflated than other items; indeed quite the reverse, for although the engineering expenses were occasionally exceeded, with reason, the land estimates were often grossly exceeded without apparent reason. To deal with technical problems gave one range of error; but to try to estimate the land market gave quite another; and the later the project, the more expensive the compensation charges, and the more elaborate the accommodation works tended to become. The Lands Clauses and the Railways Clauses Consolidation Acts, which exercised an inflationary effect on railway land prices and compensation charges (as I have argued in *Journal of Transport History*, VI (1964), 222–240), did not go onto the statute books until 1845, and examples have been cited in the present work of the expenses incurred in subsequent decades under the procedures laid down in 8 Vic., c. 18, and 8 Vic., c. 20.

The second, less important objection concerns the conclusion, suggested by a footnote in the *Economica* article, that the proportion of land to total costs would gradually fall through time. No doubt, in its broadest sense, this is perfectly true. In 1900 the land and sites bought sixty years earlier would seem to be remarkable bargains, if they were written down at their original cost; and this would apply as much to railways as to any other long-term land purchasers. On the other hand, the most spectacular and expensive land purchases were not over until the late 1860's, and it is partly a measure of the high prices then paid that so many decades should elapse before the burden of land purchase could be said to lie lightly upon the companies concerned. It should also be remembered that even after the main purchases were over, enlargements, 'easements', cut-offs and link lines continued even up to the first decade of the twentieth century in the major cities and their environs. So the point of interpretation still open is that of the time at which land purchase began to fall significantly as a proportion of total railway expenditure. It may well have been in the late 1860's or 1870's; but there is certainly little evidence of it during the period 1825–1850. Indeed, as may be seen by comparing the percentage in the 'Land as % of total' column in the table below with their equivalent in the *Economica* table, the proportions spent upon land did not generally decline in the 1840's, but actually rose (in spite of their greatly increased capitalisation) for some of the companies operating from Britain's larger cities. On the one hand, the London and Brighton, or the Eastern Counties railway companies—both heavy spenders on their initial land purchases—dropped one *per cent* to 18·1%, and eleven *per cent*, to 16·6% respectively in the proportions of their expenditures devoted to land purchase during the course of the 1840's, whilst their overall expenditures doubled or trebled. The Midland and Great Western companies maintained a roughly constant proportion. On the other hand large companies could be cited, like the London and North Western, and London and South Western, in which land costs rose during the 1840's, from 14% to 16% and from 17% to 21·6% respectively upon capitals which had almost trebled.

It does not seem likely, therefore, that land costs fell much below the proportion of 16½% in the two decades after 1850, and even by the end of the century it would be surprising if they had fallen below 10 or 11%.

TABLE—APPENDIX I

in £000's

Railway Company*	Constructional Cost	Law Charges	Land and Property	Parliamentary Expenses	Engineers' Charges	Plant	Total Expenditure	Land as % of total	Land as % of constructional cost
1. Manchester, Sheffield and Lincolnshire (XVI, 414)	3,334	46	557	321	110	350	4,718	11·81	16·71
2. Glasgow, Paisley and Greenock (XVI, 312–3)	687	13	123	30	7	73	933	13·18	17·90
3. London and Blackwall (XVI, 315)	492	21	582	66	11	94	1,266	45·97	118·29
4. Birmingham, Wolverhampton and Dudley (XVI, 294)	None	—	184	36	11	None	Not Available	—	—
5. Birmingham, Wolverhampton and Stour Valley (XVI, 295–6)	291	Nil	310	33	20	None	654	47·40	106·53
6. Lancashire and Yorkshire (XVI, 237)	6,445	19	1,287	453	136	683	9,023	14·26	19·97
7. Glasgow, Paisley, Kilmarnock and Ayr (XVI, 80)	1,615	18	268	153	55	235	2,344	11·43	16·59
8. London and North Western (XVI, 374–5)	13,302	143	3,153	714	290	2,075	19,677	16·02	23·70
9. East and West India Docks and Birmingham Junction (XVI, 306)	100	16	295	11	6	None	428	68·93	295·00
10. Caledonian (XV, 22)	3,102	1	622	302	25	427	4,479	13·89	20·05
11. East Lancashire (XV, 35)	1,762	20	602	124	41	148	2,697	22·32	34·17
12. Great Western (XV, 106–7)	6,960	105	1,133	245	202	927	9,572	11·84	16·28

13. London and South Western (XV, 124–5)	2,883	167	1,003	†	64	529	4,646	21·59	34·79
14. Manchester South Junction (XV, 137)	313	14	200	3	11	34	575	34·78	63·90
15. North Staffordshire (XV, 142–3)	2,250	33	403	153	48	204	3,091	13·04	17·91
16. South Staffordshire (XV, 180–1)	341	5	152	69	8	60	635	23·94	44·57
17. East Anglian (XV, 235)	750	4	270	73	23	94	1,214	22·24	36·00
18. Eastern Union (XV, 243–4)	1,158	47	172	62	28	132	1,599	10·76	14·85
19. Edinburgh and Glasgow (XV, 247)	1,503	13	396	145	39	304	2,400	16·50	26·35
20. Great Northern (XV, 258)	2,292	122	985	†	85	222	3,706	26·58	42·98
21. Midland (XV, 288–9)	9,397	119	1,764	560	288	1,714	13,842	12·74	18·77
22. South Eastern (XV, 314–5)	5,375	138	1,459	420	116	525	8,033	18·16	27·14
23. Eastern Counties (XV, 357)	4,952	162	1,276	251	214	823	7,678	16·62	25·77
24. London, Brighton and South Coast (XV, 419)	4,002	297	1,097	†	118	552	6,066	18·08	27·41
25. York and North Midland (XV, 435)	1,998	21	547	72	93	400	3,131	17·47	27·38
26. York, Newcastle and Berwick (XV, 442–3)	2,505	7	400	93	39	667	3,711	10·78	15·97
GRAND TOTAL	77,809	1,551	19,240	4,389	2,088	11,272	116,349	16·54	24·73

* In brackets, the reference to H.L. Accounts and Papers, 1849, XVI and 1850 XV.
† Included under 'Law Charges'.

Appendix II

'Memorandum of Agreement between the Glasgow and South Western Railway Company of the first part the Edinburgh and Glasgow Railway Company of the second part the City of Glasgow Union Railway Company of the third part and Charles Waring Esquire of Victoria Street Westminster contractor taking burden on himself for Thomas Brassey messieurs Peto and Betts John Kelk and Messrs. Waring Brothers all of London Contractors of the fourth part.

'With reference to the Heads of Arrangement entered into between and among the parties hereto of the first, second and third parts dated 7th May 1864 of which all the parties hereto approve it is hereby agreed as follows viz;

'1. The fourth party agree to subscribe for and take so much of the capital of the City of Glasgow Union Railway Company as the Directors of that Company may be unable to issue to the public.

'2. The fourth party to have the contract for all the Works and stations excepting the Edinburgh and Glasgow Company's goods station at the College (which that Company are to form at their own cost) on terms to be hereafter settled by the Engineers of the Glasgow and South Western, the Edinburgh and Glasgow and the Union Companies. The prices to be fixed by the Engineers in conjunction with the said Charles Waring on the basis of yielding a profit to the Contractors of ten per cent. In the event of any difference of opinion among the Engineers and the said Charles Waring as to prices the same shall be referred to Thomas Harrison, C.E. of London.

'3. The City of Glasgow Union Harbour Tramways Bill to be withdrawn and in the event of the loss of the Union Railway Bill by its being rejected by Parliament the Glasgow and South Western and the Edinburgh and Glasgow Companies each to pay one third of the expenses including the expenses of the Tramways Bill not exceeding £1,500 to each Company.

'4. The fourth party shall bear one-third of the expense of the City of Glasgow Union Railway and the City of Glasgow Union Harbour Tramway Bills should the Union Railway Bill be lost but not exceeding £6,000 sterling.

'In witness whereof the several parties hereto have subscribed this Memorandum this 7th day of May 1864

(signed for)   Thomas Brassey
Peto and Betts
John Kelk and Waring Brothers
Charles Waring
Jas. B. Stewart
James King
Walter Macfarlane'

HLRO., Min., H.C., 1864, 13 May, p. 275, S.C. on Union Railway.

Appendix III

A note on nineteenth-century compulsory purchase and arbitration procedures

From the earliest railway projects it was necessary, to prevent any scheme authorised by Parliament from being indefinitely delayed by individual owners of plots along the projected route, for compulsory powers of acquisition to be simultaneously granted. This practice had already evolved under the Canal Bills, but was systematised in 1845 by the Lands Clauses Consolidation Act and the Railways Clauses Consolidation Act. Each individual proprietor was carefully listed in the Books of Reference and a description and topographical record of his property deposited with the Select Committee minutes, and a general procedure for purchasing the lands involved was also laid down. This is where the information from central sources ends. What the properties might be worth, how adjacent residences or businesses might be affected, has been left to indirect evidence or to conjecture.

In practice, of course, the story did not end but began with the sanctioning of each scheme. The next step was to send a formal printed notice to each owner informing him that his land would be required, and inviting him to tender an estimate of the value of the property affected both directly and by indirect loss, deterioration or inter-sectional damage (8 Vic., c. 19, clauses 17–19). If this claim was considered acceptable the deal was settled quickly between the property owner and the railway company, and the solicitors' records merely note the agreed sum and the conveyancing. If his claim was considered excessive then, under the Lands Clauses Consolidation Act, arbiters (usually local builders or valuators) would be appointed by each party and would submit their cases to a mutually-agreed 'oversman' who would finally decide the award. The oversman was empowered by the

Lands Clauses Act to petition the Sheriff Court for writs summoning necessary witnesses and his Decree Arbitral was legally binding. The procedures laid down in English and Scottish law by the statutes 8 Vic., c. 18, and 8 Vic., c. 19, respectively were virtually identical. The terminology is slightly different: the 'oversman' in Scotland is described as the 'umpire' in England. Clauses restraining municipal corporations from selling land without the approbation of the Treasury, and specifying how notice shall be served on them, are included in the English Lands Clauses Act. Slightly different arrangements are made for expenses. The basic procedures of arbitration or Jury Trial remain the same in each country.

To assist the oversman in reaching his valuation each arbiter adduced opinions and estimates by at least eight or ten builders, valuators, owners of comparable sites or businesses, etc. By the nature of the case these all tended to be men with local knowledge, some with railway claims of their own pending. The method of valuation they adopted is described by one as follows: 'After examining the property and measuring the buildings I made myself acquainted with the sales in the neighbourhood for the last 10 years. These sales, especially the voluntary ones, I consider the best test of the value of ground.' These sales of neighbouring property were used as a species of 'upset' or 'reserve' price, below which the value of the property in question should not be allowed to descend.

The alternative to arbitration, which the vendors could elect to use if they wished, was the Jury Trial; a lengthy and expensive procedure adopted only when the size of the property at issue justified it. On the other hand Jury Trials could be even more favourable to the vendor, for the Jurors had the power to decide an award quite arbitrarily, as if they were awarding damages in a civil case rather than determining property values (8 Vic., c. 19, clauses 35–54).

The preparation of material for these Jury Trials, or to put before the arbiters and oversman, was the task of firms of local solicitors; each firm being employed by the railway company to carry through all the negotiations for a particular line or section. Their papers therefore include 'precognitions' or briefings for witnesses, valuators' reports, sometimes with maps and tables of land prices in a neighbourhood over the previous decade or two, reports of mining engineers on the value of minerals under the site in question, together with other papers.

It may be helpful to those wishing to use solicitors' records to identify and place in sequence the documents likely to be found for each case. *Claim, Answer to Claim*, provide a definition of the area, and the type of business involved and state each party's point of view. *Reports, Valuations, Maps* are the next in sequence; documents by architects, mining engineers, valuators for which a fee was charged. *Notes of Evidence* and the more formal *Precognitions* briefed witnesses. Miscellaneous *Searches* for property titles, *Lists* of documents and witnesses to be summoned by writ, internal *Memoranda* or summaries of the case in progress with suggested compromises etc. follow, together with *Memorials for the Opinion of Counsel*, and *Counsel's Replies*, consulting qualified opinion on the finer points in the case. Printed Memoranda for the Use of Witnesses may follow, and sometimes *Proofs of the Hearing* summarising the course of the arbitration of trial. Finally, *Notes on the Proposed Award* give the outcome of each case.

Appendix IV

10,288. While we are on this point I should like to ask you this; when a new district is opened up, and filled with workmen's houses, what conditions do you require before putting on extra workmen's trains, or giving them the privilege of a lower payment; do you require that a certain number of them should avail themselves of it as a rule?—We object very strongly to the granting of these workmen's tickets from any other districts than those from whence they issue at the present time.

10,289. Do you know that a new district is being formed by the Artisans Dwellings' Company at Green Lanes at a place called Noel Park, close to the Green Lanes Station?—I know it very well.

10,290. You are aware that there is to be a population there eventually of something like from 18,000 to 20,000 people; will it be probable that the workmen's trains will be available from that part?—If the Great Eastern directors have the settlement of that question, there certainly will not be workmen's trains; but of course the Board of Trade, under the Act passed last session, have got powers to deal with a case of that kind. At the same time we recognise the importance of encouraging dwellings like those that have been and are now in course of erection at Noel Park, and we now issue at that station third-class monthly season tickets. You will find that a man with one of these third-class monthly season tickets can get to London at a reduction of about 25 per cent off the price of an ordinary return ticket.

10,291. Will you tell the Commission what the charge is for a monthly season ticket; I mean the workmen's season ticket from Green Lanes. I suppose it will probably be double the twopenny fare you charge?— More than double. I have got it here; it is 12s 6d; that is the price for a third-class monthly season ticket between Green Lanes, which is Noel Park, and London, and that is equal to a reduction of about 25 per cent off the ordinary return ticket.

10,292. If you were to give the same privilege from Green Lanes as you do from Edmonton and Enfield now it would no doubt attract workmen in greater numbers there; but would it not also by so doing increase your general traffic as well?—It would do us a very large amount of injury, and would cause the same public annoyance and inconvenience upon the Green Lanes line, as exists already upon the Stamford Hill and Walthamstow lines.

10,293. Do you imagine that by denying to the people in this Noel Park Estate the same privilege that they have at Edmonton you would tend to the securing of a better class of people at Noel Park; a higher class of people?—I have no doubt of that; I imagine that no one living in Noel Park could desire to possess the same class of neighbours as the residents of Stamford Hill have in the neighbourhood of St. Anne's Road. The reports current in the district of the men residing there are of a character that would deter anyone from wishing for neighbours of that kind in any part.

10,294. Do you think that a considerable number of those using your monthly season tickets from Noel Park would prefer to pay more, rather than have the rush of the penny train travellers?—I should think so, and I hope so.

Evidence of William Birt, General Manager of the Great Eastern railway company to the Royal Commission on the Housing of the Working Classes, H.C., 1884–5, XXX, QQ.10288–94.

Index

Index

Aagesen, Aage, 311
Abandonment, warrants of, 79
Accommodation works, 210, 277, 400, 402
Acock's Green, 363–4, 413, 415
Acton, 63
Acworth, W. M., 60*n.*, 64, 83*n.*, 84*n.*, 85, 95, 260*n.*, 271*n.*
Adam, Robert, 253
Adderley, James, 133*n.*
Adshead, Joseph, 150, 154*n.*, 155
Agar Town, 341–2
Agar, William, 342
Aigburth, 355–6
Aintree, 291
Airdrie, 93
Albert Buildings, Lambeth, 329
Alderley Edge, 357
Alexander, H. C., 352*n.*
Alexandra Palace Estate Company, 418
Allan, C. M., 69*n.*
Allen, Cecil J., 260*n.*, 263
Allen, G. C., 348*n.*
Allerton, 415
Altrincham, 156
Amalgamation, 6, 10, 64, 142, 161–3, 222, 228, 278–9, 399
Amersham, 397
Ancoats, 338, 341, 343–4, 408*n.*
Anderston, 293
Arbitration awards, 126, 132, 184–6, 214–15, 232, 391, 393, 435

Ardwick, 174, 357
Artizan's Dwelling Inquiry, 134
Ashford, 351*n.*
Ashley, W. J., 96*n.*
Ashted, 362
Ashton, 172
Ashworth, W., 67*n.*, 323*n.*, 376*n.*, 387, 411, 422*n.*
Aspinall, James, 175*n.*
Aston, 349, 362–3
Auden, G., 131*n.*
Avonmouth, 195

Bagwell, P. S., 67*n.*, 74*n.*
Bahnhofstrasse, 306
Baines, T., 120*n.*, 188*n.*, 190*n.*, 204, 319*n.*, 355, 356*n.*
Baker, H., 158*n.*, 323*n.*, 325*n.*, 338*n.*
Baker, J. C. Y., 263
Balsall Heath, 362
Bancroft, James, 107, 111, 114–15
Banfield, Frank, 247*n.*, 254*n.*
Bannatyne, A. & D. J., 212, 225, 231*n.*
Banning, C. B., 305
Barber, Robert, 114
Barker, T. C., 1*n.*, 46*n.*, 50*n.*, 51*n.*, 73*n.*, 75, 80, 116*n.*, 250*n.*, 255*n.*, 257*n.*, 261*n.*, 263, 265*n.*, 267*n.*, 275*n.*, 279*n.*, 281*n.*, 288*n.*, 292*n.*, 313*n.*, 317–18, 360*n.*, 365*n.*, 372*n.*, 374*n.*, 379, 398*n.*

Q 441